BASIL

II

LCL 215

BASIL

LETTERS 59–185

WITH AN ENGLISH TRANSLATION BY
ROY J. DEFERRARI

HARVARD UNIVERSITY PRESS
CAMBRIDGE, MASSACHUSETTS
LONDON, ENGLAND

First published 1928

LOEB CLASSICAL LIBRARY® is a registered trademark
of the President and Fellows of Harvard College

ISBN 978-0-674-99237-5

*Printed on acid-free paper and bound by
The Maple-Vail Book Manufacturing Group*

CONTENTS

CONTENTS

CONTENTS

CONTENTS

CONTENTS

PREFATORY NOTE

St. Basil's letters in the present volume include numbers LIX to CLXXXV, and in nearly every case are of great human interest. Highly technical letters, as, for example, on the Trinity or on the Canons, do not appear.

All of the letters included here, with the exception of numbers LXIV and CII, appear in the MS. known as Coislinianus 237 (sig. = E). No letter of this volume, however, appears in any of the other MSS. collated by the author, *i.e.* Parisinus 506 (A), Parisinus 763 S (B), Parisinus 967 (C), Parisinus 1021 S (D), and Parisinus 1020 S (F). The last-named MS. (F), noted in the Benedictine edition as Harlaeanus, has since the time of that edition been greatly curtailed, a large portion at the end having been destroyed. This accounts for the appearance of readings from that MS. as noted by the Benedictine editors, and not as my own collations. Other important or interesting readings from the edition of the Benedictines have also been included in the critical apparatus. One probably important fact has been noted in the process of this work : the Benedictine editors frequently quoted readings as found only in the earlier editions (*editi antiqui*), and apparently without any MS. authority, but our collation of E has shown most of these readings to exist also in that MS.

PREFATORY NOTE

I am greatly indebted to the members of my Greek seminar of the years 1925–26 and 1926–27, with whom many of these letters were made an object of special study, for much assistance in bringing this second volume to a completion. In a special manner, I wish to acknowledge my indebtedness also to Mr. Martin R. McGuire, Instructor in Greek and Latin of the Catholic University of America.

Roy J. Deferrari.

NOTE ON LETTER VIII

Although the question of the authenticity of Letter VIII had been raised at times, and Abbé Bessières had called attention to a rather weak manuscript tradition for it in the Basilian corpus, no one had given the matter any serious attention. It remained for Robert Melcher in an article entitled "Der 8 Brief des hl. Basilius, ein Werk des Evagrius Pontikus" (*Münsterische Beiträge zur Theologie*, Heft 1, 1923),[1] to treat the subject for the first time in a definitive manner. The Very Reverend Melcher not only demonstrates convincingly that the letter does not belong to St. Basil, but makes a strong case for assigning it to Evagrius and for dating it toward the end of the fourth century. He approaches his problem from the strictly philological and historical point of view, and especially from the view-point of theological content.

[1] I regret that this important monograph did not come to my attention until Vol. I was well through press.

COLLECTED LETTERS OF
SAINT BASIL

ΤΟΥ ΕΝ ΑΓΙΟΙΣ ΠΑΤΡΟΣ ΗΜΩΝ
ΒΑΣΙΛΕΙΟΥ ΕΠΙΣΤΟΛΑΙ

LIX

Γρηγορίῳ θείῳ

Ἐσιώπησα. μὴ καὶ ἀεὶ σιωπήσομαι, καὶ ἀνέξομαι ἐπὶ πλεῖον τὴν δυσφορωτάτην ζημίαν τῆς
σιωπῆς κυρῶσαι κατ' ἐμαυτοῦ[1] μήτε αὐτὸς ἐπιστέλλων, μήτε ἀκούων προσφθεγγομένου ; ἐγὼ
μὲν γὰρ μέχρι τοῦ παρόντος ἐγκαρτερήσας τῷ
σκυθρωπῷ τούτῳ δόγματι, ἡγοῦμαι πρέπειν
κἀμοὶ τὰ τοῦ προφήτου λέγειν· ὅτι Ἐκαρτέρησα
ὡς ἡ τίκτουσα, ἀεὶ μὲν ἐπιθυμῶν ἢ συντυχίας
ἢ λόγων,[2] ἀεὶ δὲ ἀποτυγχάνων διὰ τὰς ἁμαρτίας
τὰς ἐμαυτοῦ. οὐ γὰρ δὴ ἄλλην τινὰ αἰτίαν
ἔχω τοῖς γινομένοις ἐπινοεῖν,[3] πλήν γε δὴ τοῦ

[1] Paulo post Harl. τὰ αὐτὰ τῷ προφήτῃ.
[2] λόγου E.   [3] εἰπεῖν duo MSS.

---

[1] Written at about the same time as the preceding letter,
in 371. The subject matter is likewise the same as that of
Letter LVIII. Basil's uncle Gregory, bishop of an unknown
see, was in sympathy with the disaffected bishops of Basil's
province. Gregory of Nyssa, in an effort to bring about a
reconciliation between his uncle and brother, went so far
as to forge more than one letter in the name of the uncle.
This crude counterfeit, when discovered, naturally increased

COLLECTED LETTERS OF SAINT BASIL

LETTER LIX

To Gregory, his Uncle[1]

I HAVE kept silence. But shall I always keep silence, and shall I endure[2] still longer to impose upon myself the most unbearable punishment of silence, by neither writing myself nor hearing the greeting of another? For having up to the present time persevered in this sullen resolution, I believe that it is fitting to apply the words of the prophet[3] to myself also: "I have been patient as a woman in labour," always longing for an interview or a discussion with you, but always failing to obtain them on account of my sins. For I certainly cannot imagine any other reason for what is happening, except that, as I am convinced, I am paying the

the bitter feeling between the two, which was overcome later only with difficulties.

[2] Cf. Isa. 42. 14. The reading of the Septuagint according to Swete (Cambridge, 1912) is: ἐσιώπησα, μὴ καὶ ἀεὶ σιωπήσομαι καὶ ἀνέξομαι; ὡς ἡ τίκτουσα ἐκαρτέρησα, ἐκστήσω καὶ ξηρανῶ ἅμα The Douay Version, which is clearly based on a different text, reads: "I have always held my peace, I have kept silence, I have been patient, I will speak now as a woman in labour: I will destroy, and swallow up at once."

[3] Cf. note 2 above.

πεπεῖσθαι παλαιῶν ἁμαρτημάτων ἐκτιννύειν
δίκας, ἐν τῷ χωρισμῷ τῆς ἀγάπης σου· εἰ δὴ
καὶ ὀνομάζειν χωρισμὸν ὅσιον ἐπὶ σοῦ καὶ οὑτι-
νοσοῦν τῶν τυχόντων, μὴ ὅτι γε ἡμῶν, οἷς ἐξ
ἀρχῆς ἐν πατρὸς γέγονας χώρᾳ.

Ἀλλ' ἡ ἁμαρτία μου νῦν, οἷα νεφέλη βαθεῖά
τις ἐπισχοῦσα, πάντων ἐκείνων ἄγνοιαν ἐνεποίη-
σεν. ὅταν γὰρ ἀπίδω, πλὴν τοῦ ἐμοὶ λύπην
τὸ γινόμενον φέρειν, μηδὲν ἕτερον ἐξ αὐτοῦ
κατορθούμενον,[1] πῶς οὐχὶ εἰκότως ταῖς ἐμαυτοῦ
κακίαις ἀνατίθημι τὰ παρόντα; ἀλλ' εἴτε
ἁμαρτίαι τῶν συμβάντων αἰτίαι, τοῦτό μοι
πέρας ἔστω τῶν δυσχερῶν· εἴτε τι[2] οἰκονομούμενον ἦν, ἐξεπληρώθη πάντως τὸ σπουδαζόμενον.
οὐ γὰρ ὀλίγος ὁ τῆς ζημίας χρόνος. διὸ, μηκέτι
στέγων, πρῶτος ἔρρηξα φωνήν, παρακαλῶν ἡμῶν
τε αὐτῶν ἀναμνησθῆναι καὶ σεαυτοῦ, ὃς πλέον
ἢ κατὰ τὸ τῆς συγγενείας εἰκὸς παρὰ πάντα τὸν
βίον τὴν κηδεμονίαν ἡμῶν ἐπεδείξω, καὶ τὴν
πόλιν νῦν ἡμῶν ἕνεκεν ἀγαπᾶν, ἀλλὰ μὴ δι'
ἡμᾶς ἀλλοτριοῦν σαυτὸν τῆς πόλεως.

Εἴ τις οὖν παράκλησις ἐν Χριστῷ, εἴ τις
κοινωνία Πνεύματος, εἴ τινα[3] σπλάγχνα καὶ
οἰκτιρμοί, πλήρωσον ἡμῶν τὴν εὐχὴν ἐνταῦθα
στῆσον τὰ κατηφῆ, ἀρχήν τινα δὸς τοῖς φαιδρο-
τέροις πρὸς τὸ ἑξῆς, αὐτὸς τοῖς ἄλλοις καθη-
γούμενος ἐπὶ τὰ βέλτιστα, ἀλλ' οὐχὶ ἀκολουθῶν
ἑτέρῳ[4] ἐφ' ἃ μὴ δεῖ. καὶ γὰρ οὐδὲ σώματος

---

[1] κατορθούμενον, πῶς οὐχί] κατορθούμενος, πῶς οὐκ editi
antiqi.
[2] τό add. editi ; om. E.   [3] τινα] τις E.
[4] ἑτέροις Harl.

4

penalty for my old offences in this separation from
your love—if indeed it is not sacrilege to use the
word "separation" in connexion with you and anybody in the world, much less in connexion with
ourself, for whom, from the first, you have taken a
father's place.

But now my guilt, having spread over me like
a heavy cloud, has caused me to be ignorant of
all this. For when I consider that no other result
of what is happening, except its bringing sorrow
to me, is satisfactory, how can I in all reason help
ascribing the present state of affairs to my own
wickedness? But if sins are answerable for what
has taken place, let this be the end of my difficulties; or if some sort of discipline was intended,
the object has been completely fulfilled. For not
short is the time of my punishment. Therefore,
containing myself no longer, I have been the first
to speak out, exhorting you to be mindful both of
us and of yourself, who throughout our whole life
have shown greater solicitude for us than the nature
of our relationship requires, and also at this time to
cherish the city for our sake, instead of alienating
yourself from the city[1] on account of us.

If, then, there is any consolation in Christ, if
there is any communion of the Spirit, if there is
any compassion and pity, fulfil our prayer: Here and
now put an end to our dejection, grant some beginning to greater cheerfulness for the future, yourself guiding the rest of us to the best course, but
not following another to what is wrong. For indeed

---

[1] *i.e.* Caesarea. Basil, on being elevated to the metropolitan see of Caesarea, was very anxious to secure the
support of the various bishops, among them his uncle Gregory,
who was in sympathy with the bishops of the opposition.

5

χαρακτὴρ ἴδιος οὕτω τινὸς ἐνομίσθη, ὡς τῆς σῆς
ψυχῆς τὸ εἰρηνικόν τε καὶ ἥμερον. πρέποι[1] δ'
ἂν οὖν τῷ τοιούτῳ τοὺς ἄλλους ἕλκειν πρὸς
ἑαυτόν, καὶ παρέχειν πᾶσι τοῖς ἐγγίζουσί σοι,
ὥσπερ μύρου τινὸς εὐωδίας, τῆς τοῦ σοῦ τρόπου
χρηστότητος ἀναπίμπλασθαι. καὶ γὰρ εἴ τι
καὶ ἀντιτεῖνόν ἐστι νῦν, ἀλλὰ μικρὸν ὕστερον
καὶ αὐτὸ τὸ τῆς εἰρήνης ἀγαθὸν ἐπιγνώσεται.
ἕως δ' ἂν ἐκ τῆς διαστάσεως αἱ διαβολαὶ χώραν
ἔχωσιν, ἀνάγκη ἀεὶ τὰς ὑποψίας ἐπὶ τὸ χεῖρον
συναύξεσθαι. ἔστι μὲν οὖν οὐδὲ ἐκείνοις πρέπον
ἀμελεῖν ἡμῶν, πάντων δὲ πλέον τῇ τιμιότητί
σου. καὶ γὰρ εἰ μὲν ἁμαρτάνομέν τι, βελτίους
ἐσόμεθα νουθετούμενοι. τοῦτο δὲ ἄνευ συντυχίας
ἀμήχανον. εἰ δὲ οὐδὲν ἀδικοῦμεν, ἀντὶ τίνος
μισούμεθα; ταῦτα μὲν δὴ οὖν[2] τὰ τῆς ἰδίας
ἐμαυτοῦ δικαιολογίας[3] προΐσχομαι.

Ἃ δ' ἂν ὑπὲρ ἑαυτῶν αἱ ἐκκλησίαι εἴποιεν, οὐκ
εἰς καλὸν τῆς διαστάσεως ἡμῶν ἀπολαύουσαι,
βέλτιον μὲν[4] σιωπᾶν. οὐ γὰρ ἵνα λυπήσω τοῖς
λόγοις κέχρημαι τούτοις,[5] ἀλλ' ἵνα παύσω τὰ
λυπηρά. τὴν δὲ σὴν σύνεσιν πάντως οὐδὲν δια-
πέφευγεν· ἀλλὰ πολλῷ μείζω καὶ τελειότερα
ὧν ἡμεῖς νοοῦμεν αὐτὸς ἂν ἐξεύροις τῇ διανοίᾳ,
καὶ ἄλλοις εἴποις, ὅς γε[6] καὶ εἶδες πρὸ ἡμῶν
τὰς βλάβας τῶν ἐκκλησιῶν[7] καὶ λυπῇ μᾶλλον
ἡμῶν πάλαι δεδιδαγμένος[8] παρὰ τοῦ Κυρίου

---

[1] πρέπει E.
[2] δὴ οὖν om. E.
[3] διστολογίας editi antiqi.
[4] με E.
[5] τούτοις add. E; om. editi.
[6] ὅς γε] ὥστε E.
[7] τὰς βλάβας τῶν ἐκκλησιῶν] τῶν ἐκκλησιῶν τὴν ζημίαν
alii MSS.

6

no trait of any man's body has been considered so characteristic of him as peacefulness and gentleness are characteristic of your soul. It would be meet, therefore, for a man of your character to draw others to himself, and to afford to all who approach you an opportunity of being filled with the excellence of your character as with the fragrance of some perfume. For even if there is now a certain opposition, still, in a little while, the goodness of peace will of itself be recognized. But so long as, because of the present dissension, slanders are given room, suspicions will necessarily ever increase for the worse. It is accordingly not becoming even for the men I have in mind to ignore us, but still less for your Honour. For if we do anything sinful, we shall become better by being admonished. But this is impossible without an interview. And if we do no wrong, why are we hated? Such, then, are the statements which I submit in my own justification.

What the churches might say in their own defence for the advantage they are basely taking of our dissension, it is better to pass over in silence. For it is not to cause pain that I have employed these words, but to put an end to that which causes pain. Your sagacity is such that nothing has escaped it; but you might, by using your powers of discernment, discover for yourself and relate to others much greater and more serious instances than those which we know, seeing that you must have noticed, before we did, the harm being done to the churches, and by a distress greater than ours must long since have

---

ᵉ προδεδιδαγμένος editi antiqi.

μηδενὸς τῶν ἐλαχίστων καταφρονεῖν. νυνὶ δὲ
ἡ βλάβη οὐκ εἰς ἕνα ἢ δεύτερον περιορίζεται,
ἀλλὰ πόλεις ὅλαι καὶ δῆμοι τῶν ἡμετέρων
παραπολαύουσι συμφορῶν. τὴν γὰρ ἐπὶ τῆς
ὑπερορίας φήμην τί χρὴ καὶ λέγειν ὁποία τις
ἔσται περὶ ἡμῶν; πρέπει οὖν ἂν[1] τῇ σῇ μεγα-
λοψυχίᾳ τὸ μὲν φιλόνεικον ἑτέροις παραχωρεῖν·
μᾶλλον δὲ κἀκείνων ἐξελεῖν τῆς ψυχῆς, εἴπερ
οἷόν τε· αὐτὸν δὲ δι' ἀνεξικακίας νικῆσαι τὰ
λυπηρά. τὸ μὲν γὰρ ἀμύνεσθαι παντός ἐστι
τοῦ ὀργιζομένου, τὸ δὲ καὶ αὐτῆς τῆς ὀργῆς
ὑψηλότερον εἶναι, τοῦτο δὴ μόνου σοῦ, καὶ εἴ
τίς σοι τὴν ἀρετὴν παραπλήσιος. ἐκεῖνο δὲ οὐκ
ἐρῶ, ὅτι ὁ ἡμῖν χαλεπαίνων εἰς τοὺς μηδὲν
ἀδικήσαντας τὴν ὀργὴν ἐπαφίησιν.

Εἴτε οὖν παρουσίᾳ, εἴτε γράμματι, εἴτε κλήσει
τῇ πρὸς ἑαυτόν, εἴτε ὥπερ ἂν ἐθέλοις τρόπῳ,
παραμύθησαι ἡμῶν τὴν ψυχήν.[2] ἡμῖν μὲν γὰρ
εὐχὴ ἐπὶ τῆς Ἐκκλησίας φανῆναι τὴν θεοσέβειάν
σου, καὶ ἡμᾶς τε ὁμοῦ καὶ τὸν λαὸν θεραπεῦσαι
αὐτῇ τε τῇ ὄψει καὶ τοῖς λόγοις τῆς χάριτός
σου. ἐὰν μὲν οὖν τοῦτο ᾖ δυνατόν, τοῦτο κρά-
τιστον· ἐὰν δέ τι ἕτερον δόξῃ, κἀκεῖνο δεξόμεθα.
μόνον παγίως γνωρίσαι ἡμῖν τὸ παριστάμενον
τῇ φρονήσει σου παρακλήθητι.

been taught by the Lord to despise not even the least.[1] Now, however, the harm is not confined to one or two men, but whole cities and peoples get the benefit, indirectly, of our misfortunes. For as to what the talk concerning us will be beyond our borders, why need I speak of it? Therefore it would be becoming in your Magnanimity to leave contentiousness to others; nay rather, to pluck it even from their hearts if it is at all possible, and yourself through your forbearance to vanquish this painful state of affairs. For whereas the taking of revenge is appropriate to anyone who is aroused to anger, yet to rise superior to anger itself belongs in truth to you alone or to any man who may be like you in virtue. This, however, I shall forbear to say—that he who is wroth with us is letting his rage fall on those who have done nothing wrong.

Accordingly, either by your presence, or by a letter, or by an invitation to visit you, or by whatever way you may wish, pray comfort our soul. For our prayer is that your Reverence may be seen in our Church, and that you may heal at once both ourselves and the people by your very presence and by the words of your grace. If this, then, is possible, it will be best; but if something else may seem best to you, we shall accept it also. Only yield to our request to inform us exactly as to what your prudence decides.

[1] Cf. Matt. 18. 10. ὁρᾶτε μὴ καταφρονήσητε ἑνὸς τῶν μικρῶν τούτων. "See that you despise not one of these little ones."

---

[1] ἅν om. E.

[2] παραμύθησαι ἡμῶν τὴν ψυχήν] παραμυθῆσαι ἡμῶν τ᾿ν ψυχὴν καταξίωσον editi antiqi, Harl.

9

LX

Γρηγορίῳ θείῳ

Καὶ πρότερον ἡδέως εἶδον τὸν ἀδελφόν μου. τί γὰρ οὐκ ἔμελλον, ἀδελφόν τε ὄντα ἐμαυτοῦ, καὶ τοιοῦτον; καὶ νῦν[1] τῇ αὐτῇ διαθέσει προσεδεξάμην ἐπιδημήσαντα, μηδέν τι τῆς ἐμαυτοῦ στοργῆς παρατρέψας. μηδὲ γὰρ γένοιτό τι τοιοῦτο παθεῖν μηδέν, ὅ με τῆς φύσεως ἐπιλαθέσθαι καὶ ἐκπολεμωθῆναι πρὸς τοὺς οἰκείους ποιήσει. ἀλλὰ καὶ τῶν τοῦ σώματος ἀρρωστημάτων, καὶ τῶν ἄλλων ἀλγεινῶν τῆς ψυχῆς, παραμυθίαν ἡγησάμην[2] εἶναι τὴν τοῦ ἀνδρὸς παρουσίαν· τοῖς τε παρὰ τῆς τιμιότητός[3] σου δι' αὐτοῦ κομισθεῖσι γράμμασιν ὑπερήσθην· ἃ καὶ ἐκ πολλοῦ μοι ἐπεθύμουν ἐλθεῖν, οὐκ ἄλλου τινὸς ἕνεκεν ἢ τοῦ μὴ καὶ ἡμᾶς τι[4] σκυθρωπὸν διήγημα τῷ βίῳ προσθεῖναι, ὡς ἄρα τις εἴη τοῖς οἰκειοτάτοις πρὸς ἀλλήλους διάστασις, ἡδονὴν μὲν ἐχθροῖς παρασκευάζουσα, φίλοις δὲ συμφοράν, ἀπαρέσκουσα δὲ Θεῷ, τῷ ἐν τῇ τελείᾳ ἀγάπῃ τὸν χαρακτῆρα τῶν ἑαυτοῦ μαθητῶν θεμένῳ. διὸ καὶ ἀντιφθέγγομαι ἀναγκαίως εὔχεσθαί σε ὑπὲρ ἡμῶν παρακαλῶν, καὶ τὰ ἄλλα κήδεσθαι ἡμῶν ὡς οἰκείων.

Τὸν δὲ νοῦν τῶν γινομένων[5] ἐπειδὴ αὐτοὶ ὑπὸ ἀμαθείας συνιέναι[6] οὐκ ἔχομεν, ἐκεῖνον ἐ-

---

[1] δέ editi et MSS., om. E.
[2] αὐταρκεστάτην add. Med. et Harl.
[3] κοσμιότητος E.
[4] τι om. E.
[5] τῶν γεγραμμένων alii MSS.
[6] ἀμαθίας συνεῖναι E.

LETTER LX

To Gregory, his Uncle[1]

In times past I have always been glad to see my brother. Why should I not have been, since he is not only my brother but such a man! And at the present time I have welcomed him on his visit in the same mind, having in no wise altered my affection for him. May no such misfortune ever befall me as would cause me to forget the ties of nature, and be set at enmity with my own kindred. On the contrary, I have considered the man's presence to be a consolation both for the ills of the body and for the afflictions of the soul as well; and I was exceedingly pleased with the letter from your Honour which he delivered, a letter which I had long been eager to receive, for one sole reason—that we might not, as others have done, attach to our lives a melancholy story of a quarrel which divided the nearest and dearest from one another, a quarrel which would afford pleasure to our enemies and be a calamity to our friends, and would also be displeasing to God, who has defined the distinguishing mark of His disciples as perfect love. Therefore I feel myself constrained to repeat my request that you pray for us, and that you in general care for us as your kinsman.

As for the significance of what has happened,[2] since we ourselves through our ignorance cannot

---

[1] Of the same date and on the same general topic as the preceding letter.

[2] Cf. Letter LIX, note 1.

11

κρίναμεν ἀληθῆ εἶναι νομίζειν, ὃν ἂν αὐτὸς ἡμῖν
ἐξηγήσασθαι καταξιώσῃς. ἀνάγκη δὲ καὶ τὰ
λειπόμενα παρὰ τῆς σῆς μεγαλονοίας ὁρισθῆναι,
τὴν συντυχίαν ἡμῶν τὴν πρὸς ἀλλήλους, καὶ καιρὸν τὸν πρέποντα, καὶ τόπον ἐπιτήδειον. εἴπερ οὖν
ὅλως ἀνέχεται καταβῆναι πρὸς τὴν ταπείνωσιν
ἡμῶν ἡ σεμνότης σου, καὶ λόγου τινὸς μεταδοῦναι
ἡμῖν, εἴτε[1] μετ' ἄλλων, εἴτε κατὰ σεαυτὸν βούλει
γενέσθαι τὴν συντυχίαν, ὑπακουσόμεθα, τοῦτο
ἅπαξ ἑαυτοῖς συμβουλεύσαντες, δουλεύειν[2] σοι
ἐν ἀγάπῃ καὶ ποιεῖν ἐκ παντὸς τρόπου τὰ εἰς
δόξαν Θεοῦ παρὰ τῆς εὐλαβείας σου ἡμῖν ἐπι-
τασσόμενα.[3]

Τὸν δὲ αἰδεσιμώτατον ἀδελφὸν οὐδὲν ἠναγκάσα-
μεν ἀπὸ γλώττης εἰπεῖν ἡμῖν· διότι οὔτε[4] πρότερον
μεμαρτυρημένον εἶχε τὸν λόγον ὑπὸ τῶν ἔργων.

LXI

Ἀθανασίῳ, ἐπισκόπῳ Ἀλεξανδρείας[5]

Ἐνέτυχον τοῖς γράμμασι τῆς σῆς ὁσιότητος, δι'
ὧν τοῦ ἡγεμόνος τῆς Λιβύης, τοῦ δυσωνύμου
ἀνδρός, κατεστέναξας. καὶ ὠδυράμεθα μὲν τὴν
ἡμετέραν[6] πατρίδα, ὅτι τοιούτων κακῶν μήτηρ
ἐστὶ καὶ τροφός· ὠδυράμεθα δὲ καὶ τὴν γείτονα

---

[1] καί add. E. [2] δουλεύσειν editi antiqi.
[3] γραφόμενα E. [4] τό add. E.
[5] τῷ μεγάλῳ Ἀθανασίῳ editi antiqi.
[6] ἡμετέραν] ἑαυτοῦ editi antiqi.

---

[1] Written about the year 371. This is the first of six
extant letters written by St. Basil to the famous St.

comprehend it, we have decided to accept as true whatever explanation you have deigned to give us. But the matters which still remain must also be determined by your Magnanimity—our interview with each other, a suitable occasion, and a convenient place. So if your lofty dignity can at all endure to descend to our lowliness and to grant us some speech with you, then, whether you desire our interview to be private or in the presence of others, we shall answer the summons, inasmuch as we have decided once and for all upon this course for ourself— to serve you in love and in every way to do whatever, to the glory of God, your Reverence enjoins upon us.

As to our most venerable brother, we have not constrained him to tell us anything by word of mouth; the reason is that his words on a former occasion were not attested by the facts.

LETTER LXI

To Athanasius, Bishop of Alexandria [1]

I have read the letters of your Holiness, in which you have expressed your grief at the conduct of the governor of Libya, that man of evil name. We also have mourned for our country [2] because she is the mother and nurse of such evils; and we have

---

Athanasius. Basil is here answering a letter in which Athanasius announced that he had excommunicated a vicious governor of Libya, a native of Cappadocia. The remaining five letters from Basil to Athanasius (LXVI, LXVII, LXIX, LXXX, LXXXII) deal with the much more important matter of the union of the churches.

[2] Cf. Homer, *Od.* 13. 219: ὁ δ' ὀδύρετο πατρίδα γαῖαν.

τῆς ἡμετέρας[1] Λιβύην, τῶν ἡμετέρων κακῶν
ἀπολαύουσαν,[2] καὶ θηριώδει ἤθει παραδοθεῖσαν
ἀνδρὸς ὠμότητί τε ὁμοῦ καὶ ἀκολασίᾳ συζῶντος.
τοῦτο ἦν ἄρα τοῦ Ἐκκλησιαστοῦ τὸ σοφόν· Οὐαί
σοι, πόλις, ἧς ὁ βασιλεύς σου νεώτερος (ἐνταῦθα
δέ ἐστί τι καὶ χαλεπώτερον), καὶ οἱ ἄρχοντές σου
οὐκ[3] ἀπὸ νυκτὸς ἐσθίουσιν, ἀλλὰ μεσούσης τῆς
ἡμέρας ἀκολασταίνουσι, βοσκημάτων ἀλογώτεροι
ἀλλοτρίοις γάμοις ἐπιμαινόμενοι! ἐκεῖνον μὲν
οὖν αἱ μάστιγες μένουσι παρὰ τοῦ δικαίου κριτοῦ,
τῷ ἴσῳ μέτρῳ ἀντιμετρηθησόμεναι, ἃς αὐτὸς
προλαβὼν ἐπέθηκε τοῖς ἁγίοις αὐτοῦ.

Ἐγνωρίσθη δὲ καὶ τῇ ἐκκλησίᾳ ἡμῶν ἐκ τῶν
γραμμάτων τῆς σῆς θεοσεβείας, καὶ ἀποτρόπαιον
αὐτὸν πάντες ἡγήσονται,[4] μὴ πυρός, μὴ ὕδατος,
μὴ[5] σκέπης αὐτῷ κοινωνοῦντες, εἴπερ τι ὄφελος
τοῖς οὕτω κεκρατημένοις κοινῆς καὶ ὁμοψήφου
καταγνώσεως. ἀρκοῦσα δὲ αὐτῷ στήλη, καὶ
αὐτὰ τὰ γράμματα ἀναγινωσκόμενα πανταχοῦ.
οὐ γὰρ διαλείψομεν πᾶσιν αὐτοῦ καὶ οἰκείοις καὶ
φίλοις καὶ ξένοις ἐπιδεικνύντες· πάντως δέ, κἂν
μὴ ἅψωνται αὐτοῦ παραχρῆμα τὰ ἐπιτίμια, ὥσπερ
τοῦ Φαραώ, ἀλλ' εἰς ὕστερόν ποτε βαρεῖαν αὐτῷ
καὶ ἀλγεινὴν τὴν ἀνάδοσιν[6] οἴσει.

---

[1] ὑμετέρος E.
[2] ἀπολύσασαν E.
[3] οὐχί E.
[4] ἡγήσαντο E.
[5] δέ add. E (supra m 1ª).
[6] ἀντίδοσιν editi antiqi.

mourned, too, for our neighbouring land of Libya, which shares in these evils of ours, and has been delivered over to the brutal character of a man who spends his life equally in cruelty and licentiousness. This, then, it would seem, was the meaning of the wise saying of Ecclesiastes :[1] "Woe to thee, O land, when thy king is a child, and"—here is something even more severe—"when thy princes eat" not at night, but they revel licentiously at mid-day, being mad after the wives of others, more irrationally than cattle! Now as for him, the scourges of a just Judge await him, and they shall be meted out to him in an equal measure with those which he himself has already inflicted upon His saints.

He has become known to our Church also through the letter of your Reverence, and all men will account him abominable, sharing with him neither fire, nor water, nor shelter ; if in truth anything can be of avail to those who have thus won for themselves a common and unanimous condemnation. But sufficient for him is a published bulletin, and your letter itself read everywhere. For we shall not cease to show it to everyone who has to do with him, to relatives or family or strangers. At all events, even if the penalties imposed do not lay hold upon him immediately, even as upon the Pharaoh,[2] nevertheless at some later time they will bring upon him a heavy and grievous increment.

---

[1] Ecclesiastes 10. 16. Basil greatly expands the last part of this quotation. οὐαί σοι, πόλις, ἧς ὁ βασιλεύς σου νεώτερος, καὶ οἱ ἄρχοντές σου πρωὶ ἐσθίουσιν. "Woe to thee, O land, when thy king is a child, and when the princes eat in the morning."

[2] An allusion to the plagues and the final destruction of the Pharaoh as described in Exodus.

15

LXII

Τῇ Ἐκκλησίᾳ Παρνασσοῦ παραμυθητική

Καὶ ἔθει ἑπόμενοι παλαιῷ ἐκ μακρᾶς τῆς ἀκολουθίας κεκρατηκότι, καὶ τὸν καρπὸν τοῦ Πνεύματος, τὴν κατὰ Θεὸν ἀγάπην, ὑμῖν ἐπιδεικνύμενοι,
διὰ τοῦ γράμματος τὴν εὐλάβειαν ὑμῶν ἐπισκεπ-
τόμεθα, κοινωνοῦντες ὑμῖν τῆς τε ἐπὶ τῷ συμβάντι
λύπης, καὶ τῆς φροντίδος τῶν ἐν χερσίν. ὑπὲρ
μὲν οὖν τῶν λυπηρῶν τοσοῦτον λέγομεν, ὅτι καιρὸς
ἡμῖν ἀποβλέψαι πρὸς τὰ τοῦ Ἀποστόλου παραγ-
γέλματα, καὶ μὴ λυπεῖσθαι Ὡς καὶ οἱ λοιποί, οἱ
μὴ ἔχοντες ἐλπίδα· οὐ μὴν οὐδ᾽ ἀπαθῶς ἔχειν
πρὸς τὸ συμβάν, ἀλλὰ τῆς μὲν ζημίας αἰσθάνεσθαι,
ὑπὸ δὲ τῆς λύπης μὴ καταπίπτειν, τὸν μὲν ποιμένα τοῦ τέλους μακαρίζοντας, ὡς ἐν γήρᾳ πίονι
τὴν ζωὴν καταλύσαντα, καὶ ταῖς μεγίσταις παρὰ
τοῦ Κυρίου τιμαῖς ἐναναπαυσάμενον.

Περὶ δὲ τῶν λοιπῶν ἐκεῖνα παραινεῖν ἔχομεν,
ὅτι προσήκει, πᾶσαν ἀποθεμένους κατήφειαν,
ἑαυτῶν γενέσθαι, καὶ πρὸς τὴν ἀναγκαίαν πρό-
νοιαν τῆς Ἐκκλησίας διαναστῆναι, ὅπως ἂν ὁ
ἅγιος Θεὸς ἐπιμεληθείη τοῦ ἰδίου ποιμνίου, καὶ
παράσχοιτο ὑμῖν ποιμένα κατὰ τὸ αὐτοῦ θέλημα,
ποιμαίνοντα ὑμᾶς μετ᾽ ἐπιστήμης.

---

[1] This letter, written ostensibly to console the people of
Parnassus on the loss of their bishop, was composed, according to Maran (*Vita S. Basilii*, xvi), before the visit of
Valens in 372, which gave the Arians of this church such
power. Parnassus was a town in Northern Cappadocia, on
the right bank of the Halys, at a ford a few miles higher up
than modern Tchikin Aghyl. The real purpose of this letter
was to urge the Parnassenes to elect an orthodox bishop.

LETTER LXII

CONSOLATION TO THE CHURCH OF PARNASSUS [1]

FOLLOWING an old custom which has become prevalent through a long observance, and also making manifest to you the fruit of the Holy Ghost, which is the divine love, we visit your Piety by letter, sharing with you both your grief at what has befallen and your anxiety concerning the matters now at hand. In regard to these painful circumstances, then, we have only this to say—that it is seasonable for us to fix our gaze upon the exhortations of the Apostle,[2] and not to be sorrowful " even as others who have no hope "; we should not, however, be indifferent to what has occurred, but while being sensible of our loss, we should not be overcome by our grief, accounting our shepherd happy for his end, as having left this life at a ripe old age,[3] and as having gone to rest amid the highest honours the Lord can give.

As for the rest, we must admonish you that, after you have put away all sorrow, you should become your own masters, and should rise up and face your unavoidable duty of providing for the Church, to the end that the holy God may assume charge over His flock, and, in accordance with His will, may supply you with a shepherd who will tend you wisely.

This they did in the person of Hypsis (or Hypsinus), whom the Arians expelled in 375 in favour of a certain Ecdicius. Cf. Letter CCXXXVII.

[2] Thess. 4. 13.

[3] Cf. Homer, *Odysey*, 19. 367-8 : ἀρώμενος εἷος ἵκοιο | γῆράς τε λιπαρὸν θρέψαιό τε φαίδιμον υἱόν. " With prayer that thou mightest reach a sleek old age and rear thy glorious son."

17

LXIII

Ἡγεμόνι Νεοκαισαρείας

Τὸν σοφὸν ἄνδρα, κἂν ἑκὰς ναίῃ χθονός, κἂν μήποτ' αὐτὸν ὄσσοις προσίδω, κρίνω φίλον· Εὐριπίδου ἐστὶ τοῦ τραγικοῦ λόγος. ὥστε, εἰ, μήπω τῆς κατ' ὀφθαλμοὺς ἡμῖν συντυχίας τὴν γνῶσίν σου τῆς μεγαλοφυΐας χαρισαμένης, φαμὲν εἶναι φίλοι σου καὶ συνήθεις, μὴ κολακείαν εἶναι [1] τὸν λόγον κρίνῃς. ἔχομεν γὰρ φήμην πρόξενον τῆς φιλίας, μεγαλοφώνως τὰ σὰ πᾶσιν [2] ἀνθρώποις συμβοώσαν. ἀφ' οὗ μέντοι καὶ τῷ αἰδεσιμωτάτῳ Ἐλπιδίῳ [3] συνετύχομεν, τοσοῦτόν σε ἐγνωρίσαμεν, καὶ οὕτω κατ' ἄκρας ἑαλώκαμέν σου, ὡσανεὶ πολὺν χρόνον συγγεγονότες, καὶ διὰ μακρᾶς τῆς πείρας τῶν ἐν σοὶ καλῶν τὴν γνῶσιν ἔχοντες. οὐ γὰρ ἐπαύσατο ὁ ἀνὴρ ἕκαστα ἡμῖν τῶν περὶ σὲ διηγούμενος, τὸ μεγαλοπρεπὲς τῆς ψυχῆς, τοῦ φρονήματος τὸ ἀνάστημα, τῶν τρόπων τὴν ἡμερότητα, ἐμπειρίαν πραγμάτων, σύνεσιν γνώμης, σεμνότητα βίου φαιδρότητι [4] κεκραμένην, λόγου δύναμιν, τἆλλα ὅσα αὐτὸς μὲν διὰ πολλῆς τῆς πρὸς ἡμᾶς ὁμιλίας ἀπηριθμήσατο, ἡμῖν δὲ γράφειν οὐκ ἦν δυνατόν, ἵνα μὴ ἔξω τοῦ μέτρου τὴν

---

[1] εἶναι om. E.   [2] τὰ σὰ πᾶσιν] ἅπασιν E.
[3] Ἑλλαδίῳ E, Harl.   [4] φαιδρότητα E.

---

[1] Written about 371. Cf. Maran, *Vita S. Basilii*, xvi.
[2] From an unknown play of Euripides. Cf. Nauck. *Trag. Graec. Frag.*, No. 902: τὸν ἐσθλὸν ἄνδρα, κἂν ἑκὰς ναίῃ χθονός, κἂν μήποτ' ὄσσοις εἰσίδω, κρίνω φίλον. Note that Basil has σοφόν for ἐσθλόν. For similar expressions, cf. Iamblichus,

LETTER LXIII

To the Governor of Neocaesarea [1]

" The wise man, e'en though he dwell in a distant land, though I may never behold him with my eyes, I account my friend," is a saying of the tragic poet Euripides.[2] If, therefore, in spite of the fact that no face-to-face meeting has as yet given us the pleasure of acquaintance with your Magnanimity, we say that we are your friend and associate, do not consider this assertion to be flattery. For as the promoter of our friendship we have Fame, who with mighty voice proclaims your deeds to all mankind. Ever since the day, moreover, on which we met the most reverend Elpidius,[3] we have known you to be so great a man, and we have been so utterly captivated by you, as if we had been associated with you for a long time, and had knowledge of your noble qualities through long experience. For Elpidius did not cease recounting to us your every characteristic—your magnanimity, the loftiness of your spirit, the gentleness of your manners, experience in affairs,[4] sagacity of judgment, dignity of life mingled with affability, ability as an orator, and the many other qualities which he enumerated to us in the course of a long conversation, but which we cannot mention to you now without carrying the letter beyond its

de vita Pythag. 33. 237 ; Procop. Gaz., Epist., 154 ; and Cicero, de nat. deorum, 1. 44. 121.

[3] Note that some MSS. read Helladius. In the following letter, however, all MSS. agree on Elpidius.   Cf. also Letters LXXVII and LXXVIII. The Elpidii mentioned herein may or may not be the same man.

[4] For the same expression, cf. Antiphon 5. 1 : τὴν ἐμπειρίαν τῶν πραγμάτων.

ἐπιστολὴν προαγάγωμεν. πῶς οὖν οὐκ ἔμελλον
ἀγαπᾶν τὸν τοιοῦτον ; πῶς γοῦν ἠδυνάμην
ἐμαυτοῦ κρατῆσαι, πρὸς τὸ μὴ οὐχὶ καὶ ἐκβοῶν
τὸ τῆς ψυχῆς ἐμαυτοῦ πάθος διασημαίνειν ;

Δέχου τοίνυν τὴν προσηγορίαν, ὦ θαυμάσιε, ἐκ
φιλίας ἀληθινῆς καὶ ἀδόλου σοι προσαγομένην·
πόρρω γὰρ θωπείας δουλοπρεποῦς τὰ ἡμέτερα·
καὶ ἔχε ἡμᾶς τῷ καταλόγῳ τῶν σεαυτοῦ φίλων
ἐναριθμίους, γράμμασι συνεχέσι σαυτόν τε δεικνὺς
καὶ παραμυθούμενος τὴν ἀπόλειψιν.

LXIV

Ἡσυχίῳ

Ἐμὲ πολλὰ μὲν ἦν καὶ ἐξ ἀρχῆς τὰ συνάπτοντά
σου τῇ τιμιότητι, ὅ τε περὶ λόγους κοινὸς ἔρως,
πολλαχοῦ παρὰ τῶν πεπειραμένων περιφερόμενος,[1]
ἥ τε πρὸς τὸν θαυμάσιον ἄνδρα Τερέντιον[2] ἡμῖν
ἐκ παλαιοῦ φιλία. ἐπεὶ δὲ καὶ ὁ πάντα ἄριστος,
καὶ πάσης ἡμῖν οἰκειότητος ὄνομα ἐκπληρῶν, ὁ
αἰδεσιμώτατος ἀδελφὸς Ἐλπίδιος εἰς λόγους ἀφίκετο, καὶ ἕκαστα τῶν ἐν σοὶ καλῶν διηγήσατο
(δυνατώτατος δέ, εἴπερ τις ἄλλος, καὶ ἀρετὴν
ἀνθρώπου καταμαθεῖν, καὶ παραστῆσαι ταύτην

---

[1] συμπεριφερόμενος Codex Medicaens.
[2] Τερεντῖνον editi antiqi.

---

[1] *i.e.* of "friend."
[2] *i.e.* for the lack of the Governor's personal presence.
[3] Dated with the preceding letter. Nothing is known of
this Hesychius, except such information as may be gathered
from the present letter and Letter LXXII.

proper limits. How, then, could I help loving such a man? How, at any rate, could I so far control myself as not with loud voice to make known my soul's emotion?

Accept, therefore, admirable sir, the appellation,[1] which is applied to you out of a friendship that is true and genuine; for our character is far removed from servile adulation; and do you keep us numbered in the roll of your friends, by frequent letters, both showing yourself to us and consoling us for the lack.[2]

LETTER LXIV

To Hesychius[3]

Even from the beginning there have been many things which have bound me to your Honour—your love of letters, common to me also, which is everywhere bruited abroad by men who have had experience of it, and our long-time friendship for that admirable man Terentius.[4] But when, too, that most excellent man, who satisfies the title of every intimate relationship with us,[5] our most venerated brother Elpidius,[6] conversed with us and described each of your noble qualities (and he, if any man, has superlative ability both to discern a man's virtues

[4] Terentius: a general and count of the orthodox faith. Cf. Letters XCIX, CCXIV, CCXVI. For a letter from Basil to the daughters of Terentius, deaconesses at Samosata, cf. Letter CV.

[5] Cf. *Iliad*, 6. 429-30: Ἕκτορ, ἀτὰρ σύ μοί ἐσσι πατὴρ καὶ πότνια μήτηρ | ἠδὲ κασίγνητος, σὺ δέ μοι θαλερὸς παρακοίτης. "Hector, truly thou art to me father and revered mother, and brother, as thou art to me a goodly husband."

[6] Cf. Letter LXIII, note 3.

τῷ λόγῳ), τοσοῦτον ἡμῖν τὸν ἐπὶ σοὶ πόθον ἐξέ-
καυσεν, ὥστε εὔχεσθαι ἡμᾶς ἐπιστῆναί σέ ποτε
τῇ παλαιᾷ ἑστίᾳ ἡμῶν, ἵνα μὴ ἀκοῇ μόνον, ἀλλὰ
καὶ πείρᾳ τῶν ἐν σοὶ καλῶν ἀπολαύσωμεν.

LXV

Ἀταρβίῳ [1]

Καὶ τί πέρας ἔσται τῆς σιωπῆς, εἰ ἐγὼ μέν, τὰ ἐκ
τῆς ἡλικίας πρεσβεῖα ἀπαιτῶν, ἀναμένοιμι παρὰ
σοῦ γενέσθαι τὴν ἀρχὴν τῆς προσφωνήσεως, ἡ δὲ
σὴ ἀγάπη ἐπὶ πλεῖον βούλοιτο τῇ βλαβερᾷ κρίσει
τῆς ἡσυχίας [2] ἐγκαρτερεῖν; ἀλλ' ὅμως ἐγώ, τὴν
ἐν τοῖς φιλικοῖς ἧτταν νίκης ἔχειν δύναμιν ἡγησάμενος, ὁμολογῶ σοι μὲν παραχωρεῖν τῆς ἐπὶ τῷ
δοκεῖν περιγεγενῆσθαι τῆς οἰκείας κρίσεως φιλοτι-
μίας. αὐτὸς δὲ πρῶτος ἐπὶ τὸ γράφειν ἦλθον,
εἰδὼς ὅτι ἡ ἀγάπη πάντα στέγει, πάντα ὑπομένει,
οὐδαμοῦ ζητεῖ τὸ ἑαυτῆς· διόπερ οὔτε [3] ἐκπίπτει
ποτέ. ἀταπείνωτος γὰρ ὁ κατὰ ἀγάπην τῷ πλη-

---

[1] Αὐταρκίῳ cod. Claromontanus.
[2] συκοφαντίας quinque MSS.   [3] οὐδέ E.

---

[1] Of the year 371, or, according to Maran, some time
before 373, when the enmity between Atarbius and Basil
became manifest. Atarbius was a bishop of Neocaesarea,
and probably related to Basil. Cf. Letter CCX. Letters
LXI, CXXVI, CCIV, CCVII, and CCX contain information
on this break, and subsequent effort on the part of Basil to
mend the breach and to rescue Atarbius from the errors of
Sabellianism. Tillemont wrongly makes Atarbius an Armenian bishop, but he belongs clearly to Neocaesarea, since
(1) he is so designated in some MSS. of St. Basil's letters;

and to make them known by speech), he enkindled
in us such a longing for you, that we pray that you
may some day visit this old fireside of ours, so that
not only by report but by actual experience also we
may derive pleasure from the noble qualities which
reside in you.

LETTER LXV

To Atarbius[1]

WHAT end indeed would there be of our silence,
if I should claim the prerogative of my age, and
wait for you to take the initiative in salutation, but
your Affection should wish to persevere still longer
in its baneful resolution of keeping silent? However, since I consider that in matters of friendship
defeat has the force of victory, I acknowledge that
I am conceding to you what you make a point of—
the appearance of having seemingly prevailed over
my own judgment. But I myself have been the
first to begin writing because I know well that
"charity beareth all things, endureth all things,
seeketh not her own," and so "never falleth
away."[2] For he who subjects himself to his neigh-

(2) the character and circumstances of Atarbius, as depicted
in Letters LXI and CXXVI, entirely agree with those of
the unnamed bishop of Neocaesarea referred to in Letters
CCIV, CCVII, and CCX; (3) in the Acts of the Council of
Constantinople he represents the province of Pontus Pole-
moniacus, of which Neocaesarea was the Metropolis.

[2] A rather loose quotation of 1 Cor. 13. 5, 7, and 8: ἡ
ἀγάπη . . . οὐ ζητεῖ τὰ ἑαυτῆς . . . πάντα στέγει, πάντα
πιστεύει, πάντα ἐλπίζει, πάντα ὑπομένει. ἡ ἀγάπη οὐδέποτε
ἐκπίπτει. "Charity . . . seeketh not her own . . . beareth
all things, believeth all things, hopeth all things, endureth
all things. Charity never falleth away."

σίον ὑποτασσόμενος. ὅπως οὖν καὶ αὐτὸς πρὸς
γοῦν τὸ ἑξῆς τὸν[1] πρῶτον καὶ μέγιστον καρπὸν
τοῦ Πνεύματος ἐπιδεικνύμενος,[2] τὴν ἀγάπην, ἀπορ-
ρίψῃς μὲν τὸ τῶν ὀργιζομένων σκυθρωπόν, ὅπερ
ἡμῖν διὰ τῆς σιωπῆς[3] ὑποφαίνεις, ἀναλάβῃς δὲ
χαρὰν ἐν τῇ καρδίᾳ, εἰρήνην πρὸς τοὺς ὁμοψύχους
τῶν ἀδελφῶν, σπουδὴν καὶ μέριμναν ὑπὲρ τῆς τῶν
ἐκκλησιῶν[4] τοῦ Κυρίου διαμονῆς. γίνωσκε γάρ,
ὅτι, εἰ μὴ τὸν ἴσον ἡμεῖς ἀγῶνα ὑπὲρ τῶν ἐκκλησιῶν ἀναλάβοιμεν, ὁπόσον ἔχουσιν οἱ ἀντικείμενοι
τῇ ὑγιαινούσῃ διδασκαλίᾳ εἰς καθαίρεσιν αὐτῶν καὶ
παντελῆ ἀφανισμόν, οὐδὲν τὸ κωλῦον οἴχεσθαι
μὲν παρασυρεῖσαν ὑπὸ τῶν ἐχθρῶν τὴν ἀλήθειαν,
παραπολαῦσαι δέ τι καὶ ἡμᾶς τοῦ κρίματος, μὴ
πάσῃ σπουδῇ καὶ προθυμίᾳ ἐν ὁμονοίᾳ τῇ πρὸς
ἀλλήλους καὶ συμπνοίᾳ τῇ κατὰ τὸν Θεὸν τὴν
ἐνδεχομένην μέριμναν ὑπὲρ τῆς ἑνώσεως τῶν ἐκκλησιῶν ἐπιδειξαμένους.[5]

Παρακαλῶ οὖν, ἔκβαλε τῆς σεαυτοῦ ψυχῆς τὸ
οἴεσθαι μηδενὸς ἑτέρου εἰς κοινωνίαν προσδεῖσθαι.
οὐ γὰρ κατὰ ἀγάπην περιπατοῦντος οὐδὲ πληροῦν-
τός ἐστι τὴν ἐντολὴν[6] τοῦ Χριστοῦ τῆς πρὸς τοὺς
ἀδελφοὺς συναφείας ἑαυτὸν ἀποτέμνειν. ἅμα δὲ
κἀκεῖνο λογίζεσθαι τὴν ἀγαθήν σου προαίρεσιν
βούλομαι, ὅτι τὸ τοῦ πολέμου κακὸν κύκλῳ
περιιὸν καὶ πρὸς ἡμᾶς εἰσέλθοι ποτέ, κἂν μετὰ
τῶν ἄλλων καὶ ἡμεῖς τῆς ἐπηρείας παραπολαύ-

---

[1] τὸν om. E.   [2] ἐνδεικνύμενος E.
[3] ἀγάπης E.   [4] τοῦ Θεοῦ add. Harl.
[5] ἐπιδεξαμένους Med.   [6] τὸν νόμον editi antiqi.

---

[1] Cf. Gal. 5. 22 f.: ὁ δὲ καρπὸς τοῦ πνεύματός ἐστιν ἀγάπη,
χαρά, εἰρηνή, μακροθυμία, χρηστότης, ἀγαθωσύνη, πίστις, πραότης,

bour in a spirit of charity is not humbled. Therefore, for the future at any rate, see to it that
you too exhibit the first and greatest fruit of the
Spirit, charity,[1] and cast aside that sullen look of a
man in anger—which we can infer from the silence
you maintain—and once more take up joy into your
heart, peace toward brothers of kindred spirit, and
zeal and solicitude for the perpetuity of the churches
of the Lord. For be assured that, unless we assume
a labour in behalf of the churches equal to that
which the enemies of sound doctrine have taken
upon themselves for their ruin and total obliteration,
nothing will prevent truth from being swept away
to destruction by our enemies, and ourselves also
from sharing in the condemnation, unless with all
zeal and good will, in harmony with one another
and in unison with God, we show the greatest
possible solicitude for the unity of the churches.

I exhort you, therefore, to cast from your mind
the thought that you have no need of communion
with another. For it does not befit the character
of one who walks in charity, nor of one who fulfils
the command of Christ, to cut himself off from all
connexion with his brethren. At the same time
also I wish your good will to consider this—that
if the evil of the war [2] which now goes on all about
us should sometime come upon ourselves likewise,
and if we too along with the others shall receive

ἐγκράτεια· κατὰ τῶν τοιούτων οὐκ ἔστι νόμος. " But the fruit
of the Spirit is, charity, joy, peace, patience, benignity,
goodness [longanimity], mildness, faith, modesty, continency
[chastity]. Against such there is no law." The bracketed
words of the Douay version do not appear in the Greek.
The word order is also slightly changed.

[2] *i.e.* the persecutions of Valens.

σωμεν, οὐδὲ τοὺς συναλγοῦντας εὑρήσομεν, διὰ τὸ
ἐν καιρῷ τῆς εὐθυμίας[1] ἡμῶν μὴ προκαταβαλέσ-
θαι τοῖς ἠδικημένοις τὸν τῆς συμπαθείας ἔρανον.

LXVI

Ἀθανασίῳ, ἐπισκόπῳ Ἀλεξανδρείας

Οὐδένα τοσοῦτον ἡγοῦμαι λυπεῖν τὴν παροῦσαν
τῶν ἐκκλησιῶν κατάστασιν, μᾶλλον δὲ σύγχυσιν,
εἰπεῖν ἀληθέστερον, ὅσον τὴν σὴν τιμιότητα· συγ-
κρίνοντα μὲν τοῖς ἀρχαίοις τανῦν, καὶ παρὰ πόσον
ταῦτα ἐκείνων ἐξήλλακται λογιζόμενον, καὶ ὅτι εἰ
κατὰ τὴν αὐτὴν ὁρμὴν ὑπορρέοι ἐπὶ τὸ χεῖρον τὰ
πράγματα, οὐδὲν ἔσται[2] τὸ κωλῦον, εἴσω ὀλίγου
χρόνου πρὸς ἄλλο τι σχῆμα παντελῶς μεθαρμοσ-
θῆναι τὰς ἐκκλησίας. ταῦτα πολλάκις ἐπ᾽ ἐμαυτοῦ γενόμενος διενοήθην, ὅτι εἰ ἡμῖν οὕτως ἐλεεινὴ
τῶν ἐκκλησιῶν ἡ παρατροπὴ καταφαίνεται, ποίαν
τινὰ εἰκὸς ἐπὶ τούτοις ψυχὴν ἔχειν τὸν τῆς
ἀρχαίας εὐσταθείας καὶ ὁμονοίας περὶ τὴν πίστιν
τῶν ἐκκλησιῶν τοῦ Κυρίου[3] πεπειραμένον; ἀλλ᾽
ὥσπερ τὸ πολὺ τῆς λύπης τὴν σὴν τελειότητα περι-
ίσταται, οὕτως ἡγούμεθα προσήκειν καὶ τῆς ὑπὲρ
τῶν ἐκκλησιῶν μερίμνης τὸ πλέον τῇ σῇ διαφέρειν φρονήσει. πάλαι οἶδα καὶ αὐτός, κατὰ τὴν
ἐνυπάρχουσάν μοι μετρίως τῶν πραγμάτων κατά-
ληψιν, μίαν ἐπιγνοὺς ὁδὸν βοηθείας ταῖς καθ᾽

---

[1] εὐθηνίας editi antiqi.   [2] ἔστι E.
[3] Θεοῦ editi antiqi.

a share of its spitefulness, we shall find none to sympathize with us, because in the season of our tranquillity we failed to pay betimes our contribution of sympathy to the victims of injustice.

LETTER LXVI

To Athanasius, Bishop of Alexandria [1]

I consider that no one is so pained as your Honour at the present condition of the churches, or rather, to speak more truthfully, at their utter ruin ; for you can compare the present with the past, and reflect on the extent of the change that has taken place between them, and also on the thought that, if our affairs should continue to ebb for the worse at this same speed, there will be nothing to prevent the churches from being completely changed into some other form within a brief period of time. Many a time, while by myself, I have reflected upon this thought, wondering what, if to us the error of the churches appears so pitiable, the emotion must be in regard to the present state of affairs of a man who has experienced the pristine tranquillity and concord of the churches of the Lord touching the faith.[2] But just as greater sorrow devolves upon your Excellency, so we hold that it is proper for your prudence also to bear a greater solicitude for the churches. I also have long since been aware, from the moderate comprehension of events which I possess, that I recognize but one

---

[1] Written in 371. Cf. Letter LXI, note 1.

[2] Athanasius, born about 25 years before Basil, could well remember the peace of the Church preceding the outbreak of Arianism.

27

ἡμᾶς ἐκκλησίαις, τὴν παρὰ τῶν δυτικῶν ἐπισκόπων σύμπνοιαν. εἰ γὰρ βουληθεῖεν, ὃν ἀνέλαβον
ὑπὲρ ἑνὸς ἢ δύο τῶν κατὰ τὴν δύσιν ἐπὶ κακοδοξίᾳ
φωραθέντων ζῆλον, τοῦτον καὶ ὑπὲρ τῆς παροικίας
τῶν καθ᾽ ἡμᾶς μερῶν ἐπιδείξασθαι, τάχα ἄν τι
γένοιτο τοῖς κοινοῖς ὄφελος, τῶν τε κρατούντων τὸ
ἀξιόπιστον τοῦ πλήθους δυσωπουμένων, καὶ τῶν
ἑκασταχοῦ λαῶν ἀκολουθούντων αὐτοῖς ἀναντιρρήτως.

Τίς οὖν ταῦτα διαπράξασθαι τῆς σῆς συνέσεως
δυνατώτερος; τίς συνιδεῖν τὸ δέον ὀξύτερος; τίς ἐνερ-
γῆσαι τὰ χρήσιμα πρακτικώτερος; τίς πρὸς τὴν
καταπόνησιν τῶν ἀδελφῶν συμπαθέστερος; τίς τῆς
σεμνοτάτης σου πολιᾶς[1] πάσῃ τῇ δύσει αἰδεσι-
μώτερος;[2] κατάλιπέ τι μνημόσυνον τῷ βίῳ τῆς
σῆς ἐπαξίου πολιτείας, τιμιώτατε πάτερ. τοὺς
μυρίους ἐκείνους ὑπὲρ τῆς εὐσεβείας ἄθλους ἑνὶ
τούτῳ κατακόσμησον[3] ἔργῳ. ἔκπεμψόν τινας ἐκ
τῆς ἁγίας τῆς ὑπὸ σὲ ἐκκλησίας ἄνδρας δυνατοὺς
ἐν τῇ ὑγιαινούσῃ διδασκαλίᾳ πρὸς τοὺς κατὰ τὴν
δύσιν ἐπισκόπους· διήγησαι αὐτοῖς τὰς κατασχού-
σας ἡμᾶς συμφοράς· ὑπόθου τρόπον ἀντιλήψεως·
γενοῦ Σαμουὴλ ταῖς ἐκκλησίαις· πολεμουμένοις
τοῖς λαοῖς συγκακοπάθησον· ἀνένεγκε εἰρηνικὰς

---

[1] πολιτείας tres MSS. et Medicaeus sec. man.
[2] αἰδεσιμώτατος E.
[3] κατάστησον editi antiqi.

---

[1] παροικία: primarily "a sojourn in a foreign land"; then
applied, as here, to groups of Christians in general, since
Christians regarded themselves merely as sojourners in this
world. From this arose the meaning of "an ecclesiastical
district," "a diocese," and later "a parish."

avenue of assistance to the churches in our part of the world—agreement with the bishops of the West. For if they should be willing to exhibit in the case of the ecclesiastical districts [1] of our region that zeal which they have assumed in behalf of one or two persons [2] in the West who were discovered to be in heterodoxy, perhaps some benefit would result to our common interests, since our rulers are timid about the fidelity of the masses, and the peoples everywhere follow their bishops [3] unquestionably.

Who, then, is more capable of accomplishing this than a man of your wisdom? Who is keener to perceive what is needed? Who is more successful in working out useful projects? Who is more sympathetic towards the suffering of his fellow-men? What is more venerated in the entire West than the white hair of your majestic head? Most honoured father, bequeath to the living some memorial worthy of your polity. By this one work embellish those innumerable labours which you have performed for the sake of the true faith. Send forth from the holy church under your care to the bishops of the West a number of men who are mighty in the true doctrine. Describe to these bishops the misfortunes which afflict us. Suggest a method of assistance. Become a Samuel to the churches. Share in the sufferings of our people who are feeling the miseries of war. Offer prayers

[2] On the margin of the codex Regius Secundus is found this scholion: περὶ τῶν κατὰ Ῥώμην ἐπισκόπων Αὐξεντίου, καὶ τῶν περὶ αὐτόν. "Concerning the bishops at Rome, Auxentius, and those with him."

[3] According to the Benedictine editors, Valens is meant by τῶν κρατούντων, and the bishops, not the rulers, by αὐτοῖς. I have so interpreted the passage.

προσευχάς· αἴτησον χάριν παρὰ τοῦ Κυρίου,
εἰρήνης τι μνημόσυνον ἐναφεῖναι [1] ταῖς ἐκκλησίαις.
οἶδα ὅτι ἀσθενεῖς αἱ ἐπιστολαὶ πρὸς συμβουλὴν τοῦ
τοσούτου πράγματος. ἀλλ' οὔτε αὐτὸς τῆς παρ'
ἑτέρων παρακλήσεως χρήζεις, οὐ μᾶλλόν γε ἢ
τῶν ἀγωνιστῶν οἱ γενναιότατοι τῆς παρὰ τῶν
παίδων ὑποφωνήσεως· οὔτε ἡμεῖς ἀγνοοῦντα δι-
δάσκομεν, ἀλλ' ἐσπουδακότι τὴν ὁρμὴν ἐπιτείνο-
μεν.

Πρὸς μὲν οὖν τὰ λοιπὰ τῆς ἀνατολῆς ἴσως σοι
καὶ πλειόνων συνεργίας προσδεῖ, καὶ ἀνάγκη
ἀναμένειν τοὺς ἐκ τῆς δύσεως. ἡ μέντοι τῆς κατὰ τὴν
Ἀντιόχειαν ἐκκλησίας εὐταξία προδήλως τῆς σῆς
ἤρτηται θεοσεβείας· ὥστε τοὺς μὲν οἰκονομῆσαι,
τοὺς δὲ καθησυχάσαι, ἀποδοῦναι δὲ τὴν ἰσχὺν
τῇ ἐκκλησίᾳ διὰ τῆς συμφωνίας. καὶ γὰρ ὅτι
ὀφείλεις, κατὰ τοὺς σοφωτάτους τῶν ἰατρῶν, τῆς
ἐπιμελείας ἐκ τῶν καιριωτάτων ἄρχεσθαι, παντὸς
ἀκριβέστερον αὐτὸς ἐπίστασαι. τί δ' ἂν γένοιτο
ταῖς κατὰ τὴν οἰκουμένην ἐκκλησίαις τῆς Ἀντιοχείας ἐπικαιριώτερον ; [2] ἣν εἰ συνέβη πρὸς

---

[1] ἐναφεθῆναι editi antiqi.
[2] ἔτι καιριώτερον alii mss.   καιριώτερον editi antiqi.

---

[1] Combefisius observes the following scholion on the
margin of Codex Regius 25 : ὅτι τούτων τῶν εἰρηνικῶν προσευχῶν μέμνηται καὶ ἐν ταῖς μυστικαῖς εὐχαῖς τῆς θείας λειτουργίας ὁ
μέγας πατήρ. "The great father also recalls these prayers
for peace in the mystic prayers of the divine liturgy."
[2] Reference is made here to the schism caused by the
refusal of the Eustathian or Old Catholic party to recognize
Meletius as bishop of the whole orthodox party. After the
death of Eustathius himself, under whom the church of
Antioch had been a bulwark of orthodoxy, several bishops
entirely unequal to the task were elected to take his place,

for peace.[1] Ask as a grace from the Lord that He may send upon the churches some memories of peace. I know that letters are weak as regards giving advice in a matter of this character. Still, you yourself do not need exhortation from others any more than the best athletes require encouragement from boys, nor are we teaching one who is ignorant on these points, but, on the contrary, we are urging an additional effort on the part of one who is already earnestly at work.

Regarding the rest of the affairs of the East, you perhaps need the co-operation of a larger number also, and it is necessary to await those from the West. The good condition of the Church at Antioch, however, clearly depends upon your Piety, so that it is your duty to use forbearance toward some, to tranquillize others, and through concord to restore strength to the Church.[2] For you yourself understand more exactly than anyone else that, after the manner of the most learned physicians, you must give your first care to the most vital parts. Now what could be more vital to the churches of the world than the Church of Antioch? If it came to

and the church was rent with dissension. Finally, Meletius was elected as a compromise candidate. He seems to have been neither a thorough Nicene nor a decided Arian, although he was esteemed by such men as St. John Chrysostom, St. Gregory Nazianzen, St. Gregory of Nyssa, St. Basil, and even his adversary St. Epiphanius. The churches of the West and of Egypt for the most part supported Paulinus, who had been ordained by Lucifer of Cagliari, bishop of the Old Catholics. The East supported Meletius. The Benedictine editors suppose the word οἰκονομῆσαι, which is rendered "control," to refer to Paulinus, and Basil may here be urging the dismissal of Paulinus as bishop. Cf. St. Ambrose, Letter XIII, which deals with this same general topic.

ὁμόνοιαν ἐπανελθεῖν, οὐδὲν ἐκώλυεν, ὥσπερ[1]
κεφαλὴν ἐρρωμένην, παντὶ τῷ σώματι ἐπιχορη-
γεῖν τὴν ὑγίειαν. τῷ ὄντι δὲ τῆς σῆς δεῖται
σοφίας καὶ εὐαγγελικῆς συμπαθείας τὰ ἐκείνης
τῆς πόλεως ἀρρωστήματα· ἥ γε οὐχ ὑπὸ τῶν
αἱρετικῶν διατέτμηται μόνον, ἀλλὰ καὶ ὑπὸ τῶν
τὰ αὐτὰ φρονεῖν ἀλλήλοις λεγόντων διασπᾶται.
ταῦτα δὲ ἑνῶσαι καὶ εἰς ἑνὸς[2] σώματος συναγα-
γεῖν ἁρμονίαν ἐκείνου μόνου ἐστί, τοῦ καὶ τοῖς
ξηροῖς ὀστέοις τὴν εἰς νεῦρα καὶ σάρκα πάλιν
ἐπάνοδον τῇ ἀφάτῳ αὐτοῦ δυνάμει χαριζομένου.
πάντως δὲ τὰ μεγάλα ὁ[3] Κύριος διὰ τῶν ἀξίων
αὐτοῦ ἐνεργεῖ. πάλιν οὖν καὶ ἐνταῦθα τῇ σῇ
μεγαλοφυΐᾳ πρέπειν τὴν τῶν τηλικούτων διακονίαν ἐλπίζομεν, ὥστε καταστορέσαι μὲν τοῦ λαοῦ
τὸν τάραχον, παῦσαι δὲ τὰς μερικὰς προστασίας,
ὑποτάξαι δὲ πάντας ἀλλήλοις ἐν ἀγάπῃ, καὶ τὴν
ἀρχαίαν ἰσχὺν ἀποδοῦναι τῇ Ἐκκλησίᾳ.

LXVII

Ἀθανασίῳ, ἐπισκόπῳ Ἀλεξανδρείας

Ἐμοὶ μὲν ἐξαρκοῦν ἐφάνη ἐν τοῖς προτέροις
γράμμασι πρὸς τὴν σὴν τιμιότητα τοσοῦτον ἐνδείξασθαι, ὅτι πᾶν τὸ[4] κατὰ τὴν πίστιν ἐρρωμένον
τοῦ κατὰ τὴν ἁγίαν ἐκκλησίαν Ἀντιοχείας λαοῦ
εἰς μίαν συμφωνίαν καὶ ἕνωσιν χρὴ ἐναχθῆναι,
πρὸς τὸ δηλῶσαι, ὅτι τῷ θεοφιλεστάτῳ ἐπισκόπῳ

---

[1] ὥσπερεὶ E.   [2] μίαν E.
[3] ὁ om. E.   [4] ὅτιπερ τό editi antiqi.

pass that this church returned to a state of concord, nothing would prevent its affording health, in the manner of a sound head, to the whole body. And verily the ills of that city stand in need of your wisdom and evangelical sympathy; for it has not only been completely divided by heretics, but it is also being torn asunder by those who affirm that they hold identical opinions with one another. But to unite these parts and to bring them together into the harmony of a single body belongs to Him alone, who by his ineffable power grants even to dry bones a return once more to flesh and muscles. Certainly, however, the Lord performs His mighty deeds through those who are worthy of Him. Again, therefore, on this occasion also we express the hope that the conduct of such important matters may seem fitting to the nobility of your nature, so that you may calm the confusion of the people, put an end to factional usurpations of authority, subject all men to one another in charity, and restore to the Church her pristine strength.

LETTER LXVII

To Athanasius, Bishop of Alexandria [1]

It seemed to me sufficient in my former letter to point out so much to your Honour—that all that section of the people of the holy church of Antioch which is strong in its faith ought to be brought into a single harmony and union, my purpose being to show clearly that those who are now divided into

---

[1] Written at about the same time as the preceding, and on the same general topic.

Μελετίῳ δέοι τὰ εἰς μέρη πλείονα νῦν διηρημένα
συνάψαι. ἐπεὶ δὲ ὁ αὐτὸς οὗτος ὁ ἀγαπητὸς
συνδιάκονος ἡμῶν Δωρόθεος ἐναργεστέραν τὴν
περὶ τούτων ἐπεζήτησε μνήμην, ἀναγκαίως ἐπιση-
μαινόμεθα, ὅτι καὶ πάσῃ τῇ ἀνατολῇ δι᾽ εὐχῆς,
καὶ ἡμῖν τοῖς παντοίως αὐτῷ συνημμένοις ἐπιθυ-
μητόν, αὐτὸν ἰδεῖν τὴν ἐκκλησίαν διέποντα τοῦ[1]
Κυρίου, τῇ τε πίστει ἀνεπίληπτον ὄντα, καὶ τῷ
βίῳ οὐδεμίαν πρὸς τοὺς ἄλλους ἐπιδεχόμενον
σύγκρισιν, καὶ τῷ[2] τοῦ παντός, ὡς εἰπεῖν, σώματος τῆς ἐκκλησίας αὐτὸν προεστάναι, τὰ δὲ λοιπὰ
οἷον μερῶν ἀποτμήματα εἶναι.

Ὥστε πανταχόθεν ἀναγκαῖόν τε ὁμοῦ καὶ
σύμφερον τῷ ἀνδρὶ τούτῳ συναφθῆναι τοὺς ἄλλους,
ὥσπερ τοῖς μεγάλοις τῶν ποταμῶν τοὺς ἐλάττους·
περὶ δὲ τοὺς ἄλλους γενέσθαι τινὰ οἰκονομίαν,
τὴν κἀκείνοις πρέπουσαν, καὶ τὸν λαὸν εἰρη-
νεύουσαν, καὶ τῇ σῇ συνέσει καὶ περιβοήτῳ
ἐντρεχείᾳ καὶ σπουδῇ ἐπιβάλλουσαν. πάντως δὲ
οὐκ ἔλαθέ σου τὴν ἀνυπέρβλητον φρόνησιν, ὅτι
ἤδη καὶ τοῖς ὁμοψύχοις σου τοῖς κατὰ τὴν δύσιν
τὰ αὐτὰ ταῦτα συνήρεσεν,[3] ὡς δηλοῖ τὰ γράμματα τὰ διὰ τοῦ μακαρίου Σιλουανοῦ κομισθέντα
ἡμῖν.

---

[1] τοῦ om. E. [2] τό editi antiqi.
[3] συνήρεσκεν sex MSS. et editi antiqi.

several parties should unite with the bishop Meletius, dearly beloved of God. But since this same beloved deacon of ours, Dorotheus,[1] has requested that our memorial regarding these matters be made clearer, we perforce are now indicating to you that it is both the desire of the entire East in its prayers and our own also, who are completely in union with Meletius, to see the latter directing the Church of the Lord, since he is a man not open to censure as regards his faith, and in respect to his life admits no comparison with the rest, as also in this respect, that he stands at the head of the whole body of the Church, so to speak, while the residue are, as it were, segments of its limbs.

Accordingly it is for every reason necessary and at the same time expedient that all the rest should unite with this man, just as smaller streams unite with mighty rivers ; and respecting these others also, that some sort of an arrangement should be adopted which will be proper to them, will reconcile the people, and will be in accord with your own wisdom, your far-famed industry and zeal. Moreover, it surely has not escaped the notice of your unsurpassed wisdom that this same course of action has already been pleasing to your co-religionists in the West, as is evident from the letter which was brought to us by the blessed Silvanus.[2]

---

[1] Dorotheus, a deacon of the church of Antioch, attached to the communion of Meletius, and employed on several occasions by Basil to carry letters. Cf. Letters XLVIII, L, LII, LXI, LXII, CCLXXIII.

[2] Silvanus: his identity here cannot be determined exactly.

LXVIII

Μελετίῳ, ἐπισκόπῳ Ἀντιοχείας

Τέως μὲν ἐβουλήθημεν[1] κατασχεῖν παρ' ἑαυτοῖς τὸν εὐλαβέστατον ἀδελφὸν Δωρόθεον τὸν συνδιάκονον, ὥστε, ἐπὶ τῷ τέλει τῶν πραγμάτων ἀποπεμψάμενοι, γνωρίσαι δι' αὐτοῦ ἕκαστα τῶν πεπραγμένων τῇ τιμιότητί σου. ἐπεὶ δὲ ἡμέραν ἐξ ἡμέρας ὑπερτιθέμενοι εἰς πολὺ τοῦ χρόνου παρετάθημεν, καὶ ἅμα, ὡς ἐν ἀπόροις, βουλή τις ἡμῖν ἐνέπεσε περὶ τῶν πρακτέων,[2] ἀπεστείλαμεν τὸν προειρημένον ἄνδρα καταλαβεῖν ὑμῶν τὴν ὁσιότητα, καὶ δι' ἑαυτοῦ τε ἀνενεγκεῖν ἕκαστα, καὶ τὸ ὑπομνηστικὸν ἡμῶν ἐπιδεῖξαι, ἵνα, εἰ φανείη χρησίμως ἔχειν τὰ παρ' ἡμῶν ἐννοηθέντα, εἰς ἔργον ἐλθεῖν παρὰ τῆς ὑμετέρας τελειότητος σπουδασθείη.

Ὡς δὲ συντόμως εἰπεῖν, γνώμη ἐκράτησεν ἐπὶ τὴν Ῥώμην διαβῆναι τὸν αὐτὸν τοῦτον ἀδελφὸν ἡμῶν Δωρόθεον, διαναστῆσαί[3] τινας τῶν ἀπὸ[4] τῆς Ἰταλίας, πρὸς τὴν ἐπίσκεψιν ἡμῶν θαλάσσῃ χρησαμένους, ἵνα τοὺς ἐμποδίζοντας διαφύγωσι. τοὺς γὰρ παραδυναστεύοντας τοῖς κρατοῦσιν εἶδον μηδὲν βουλομένους μήτε δυναμένους ὑπομιμνήσκειν αὐτὸν[5] περὶ τῶν ἐκβεβλημένων, ἀλλὰ τὸ μή τι χεῖρον ἰδεῖν ἐν ταῖς ἐκκλησίαις γινόμενον κέρδος τιθεμένους. εἰ οὖν καὶ τῇ σῇ φρονήσει χρήσιμον εἶναι τὸ βούλευμα παρασταίη, καταξιώσεις καὶ ἐπιστολὰς τυπῶσαι, καὶ ὑπομνηστικὰ

---

[1] ἐβουλήθημεν E, ἠβουλήθημεν editi antiqi.
[2] προκειμένων tres MSS.   [3] διαστῆσαι E.
[4] ἐκ E.   [5] αὐτούς editi antiqi.

LETTER LXVIII

To Meletius, Bishop of Antioch [1]

For a time we wished to keep with us the most reverend brother Dorotheus,[2] our deacon, so that, sending him back at the conclusion of our business, we might use him to inform your Honour of our transactions in detail. But when we kept putting off this conclusion from day to day and found ourselves delayed for a considerable period of time, and when, too, in our perplexity a plan occurred to us regarding the course of action to be adopted, we despatched the aforementioned deacon to meet your Holiness, to report all the facts in person, and to present our memorandum, in order that, if our ideas should appear expedient, they might speedily be put into effect by your Perfection.

To put it briefly, this view prevailed: that this same brother of ours, Dorotheus, should cross over to Rome, and should urge that some of our brethren in Italy should visit us, travelling by sea, so as to avoid any who might seek to hinder them. For I have noticed that those who are very powerful at court are neither willing nor able to bring to the Emperor's attention the question of the exiles, but rather count it as gain that they see nothing worse happening to the churches. If, therefore, the plan should also seem expedient to your wisdom, you will deign to have letters written, and to dictate memo-

---

[1] Of the same date as the preceding. For the identity of Meletius, cf. Letter LXVI, note 4. For a description of his character by Basil, see the previous letter.

[2] Cf. letter above.

ὑπαγορεῦσαι περὶ ὧν χρὴ διαλεχθῆναι αὐτὸν καὶ
πρὸς τίνας.[1] ὥστε δὲ ἔχειν ἀξιοπιστίαν τινὰ τὰ
γράμματα, συμπαραλήψῃ πάντως τοὺς ὁμογνώ-
μονας, κἂν μὴ παρῶσι. τὰ δ' ἐνταῦθα ἔτι ἐστὶν
ἐν ἀδήλῳ, τοῦ Εὐϊππίου παραγενομένου μέν,
μηδὲν δὲ τέως ἐκφήναντος. ἀπειλοῦσι μέντοι καὶ
συνδρομήν τινα ὁμογνωμόνων αὐτοῖς ἔκ τε τῆς
Ἀρμενίας τῆς Τετραπόλεως, καὶ ἐκ τῆς Κιλι-
κίας.

LXIX

Ἀθανασίῳ, ἐπισκόπῳ Ἀλεξανδρείας

Ἦν ἐκ παλαιοῦ[2] περὶ τῆς σῆς τιμιότητος
ὑπόληψιν ἔσχομεν, ταύτην ὁ χρόνος προϊὼν ἀεὶ
βεβαιοῖ· μᾶλλον δὲ καὶ συναύξει ταῖς προσθήκαις τῶν κατὰ μέρος ἐπιγινομένων. ὅτι τῶν μὲν
ἄλλων τοῖς πλείστοις ἐξαρκεῖ τὸ καθ' ἑαυτὸν
ἕκαστον περισκοπεῖν, σοὶ δὲ οὐχ ἱκανὸν τοῦτο,
ἀλλ' ἡ μέριμνά σοι πασῶν τῶν ἐκκλησιῶν τοσαύτη, ὅση καὶ τῆς ἰδίως παρὰ τοῦ κοινοῦ
Δεσπότου ἡμῶν ἐμπιστευθείσης ἐπίκειται· ὅς γε
οὐδένα χρόνον διαλείπεις διαλεγόμενος, νουθετῶν,
ἐπιστέλλων, ἐκπέμπων τινὰς ἑκάστοτε τοὺς ὑπο-
τιθεμένους τὰ βέλτιστα. καὶ νῦν δὲ ἀπὸ τοῦ
ἱεροῦ πληρώματος τοῦ ὑπὸ σὲ κλήρου τὸν αἰδε-

---

[1] καὶ ὅτε ("and when") add editi antiqi.
[2] ἔκπαλαι tres MSS. recentiores.

---

[1] i.e., the deacon, Dorotheus.

randa regarding what matters he [1] must discuss and with what persons. In order, too, that your letters may possess a certain sanction, you will, of course, include the names of all those who are of like mind with yourself, even if they are not present. The state of affairs here is as yet not certain, for, although Euippius [2] is present, up to now he has made no disclosure. However, they are threatening to hold some sort of a meeting of those who are in sympathy with their views both from the Tetrapolis of Armenia and from Cilicia.

LETTER LXIX

To Athanasius, Bishop of Alexandria [3]

THE opinion of your Honour which we long ago conceived is being ever confirmed by the passage of time; or rather, it is even being enhanced by the new evidence of particular events. Athough most men deem it sufficient to look each to his own particular charge, this is not enough for you, but, on the contrary, you have as great solicitude for all the churches as for the one especially entrusted to you by our common Master; for at no time do you cease to discourse, to admonish, to write, and on each occasion to send out men who give the best advice. Even now we have received with great joy the most

[2] Euippius: a bishop with Arianizing tendencies, from whom in the cause of truth Basil felt obliged to separate. Cf. Letter CXXVIII. Eustathius of Sebaste, in 360, declaimed against Euippius as not worthy of the name of bishop, but in 376 he united with Euippius, and recognized the bishops and presbyters Euippius had ordained. Cf. Letters CCXXVI, CCXXXIX, CCXLIV, CCLI.

[3] Written at the same time as the preceding.

σιμώτατον ἀδελφὸν Πέτρον ἐκπεμφθέντα μετὰ
πολλῆς χαρᾶς ἐδεξάμεθα, καὶ τὸν ἀγαθὸν αὐτοῦ [1]
τῆς ἀποδημίας σκοπὸν [2] ἀπεδεξάμεθα, ὃν ἐπι-
δείκνυται κατ' ἐντολὰς τῆς σῆς τιμιότητος, τὰ
ἀντιτείνοντα προσαγόμενος, καὶ τὰ διεσπασμένα
συνάπτων. ὅθεν τι καὶ ἡμεῖς συμβαλέσθαι τῇ
περὶ τοῦτο σπουδῇ βουληθέντες, ἐνομίσαμεν
ἐπιτηδειοτάτην ἀρχὴν τοῖς πράγμασι δώσειν, εἰ,
ὥσπερ ἐπὶ κορυφὴν τῶν ὅλων, ἐπὶ [3] τὴν σὴν
ἀναδράμοιμεν τελειότητα, καὶ σοὶ συμβούλῳ τε
χρησαίμεθα καὶ ἡγεμόνι τῶν πράξεων. ὅθεν
καὶ τὸν ἀδελφὸν Δωρόθεον, τὸν διάκονον τῆς
ὑπὸ τὸν τιμιώτατον ἐπίσκοπον Μελέτιον
ἐκκλησίας, ἀγαθῷ κεχρημένον περὶ τὴν τῆς
πίστεως ὀρθότητα ζήλῳ, καὶ ἐπιθυμοῦντα καὶ
αὐτὸν τὴν εἰρήνην τῶν ἐκκλησιῶν ἐπιδεῖν, πρὸς
τὴν σὴν θεοσέβειαν ἀνεπέμψαμεν,[4] ὥστε, ταῖς
σαῖς ὑποθήκαις ἀκολουθοῦντα (ἃς καὶ τῷ χρόνῳ
καὶ τῇ τῶν πραγμάτων πείρᾳ, καὶ τῷ ὑπὲρ τοὺς
ἄλλους ἔχειν τὴν ἐκ τοῦ Πνεύματος συμβουλίαν,
ἀσφαλεστέρας ποιεῖσθαι δύνασαι), οὕτως ἐγχειρεῖν
τοῖς σπουδαζομένοις.

Ὃν καὶ ὑποδέξῃ δηλονότι, καὶ προσβλέψεις
εἰρηνικοῖς ὀφθαλμοῖς, στηρίξας τε αὐτὸν τῇ διὰ
τῶν προσευχῶν βοηθείᾳ, καὶ ἐφοδιάσας γράμμασι,
μᾶλλον δὲ καὶ παραζεύξας τινὰς [5] τῶν αὐτόθεν
σπουδαίων, ἐπὶ τὰ προκείμενα ὁδηγήσεις. ἐφάνη
δὲ ἡμῖν ἀκόλουθον ἐπιστεῖλαι τῷ ἐπισκόπῳ
Ῥώμης, ἐπισκέψασθαι τὰ ἐνταῦθα, καὶ δοῦναι
γνώμην, ἵν' ἐπειδὴ ἀπὸ κοινοῦ καὶ συνοδικοῦ

---

[1] αὐτοῦ om. E.   [2] κόπον E.   [3] ἐπί add. Capps.
[4] ἀνεπέμψαμεν Capps, ἀναπέμψαι MSS.   [5] τισί editi antiqi.

reverend brother Peter, sent from the holy company
of the clergy under your care, and we have approved
the noble object of his journey, which he explains
according to the commands of your Honour, winning
over the recalcitrant and uniting what has been torn
asunder.   Wherefore we also, wishing to make
some contribution to the general enthusiasm for
this matter, have thought we should be supplying a
most suitable initiative to our undertaking if we
should again have recourse to your Perfection, as to
the highest of all, and should make use of you as
both adviser and director of our actions.   Wherefore
we have again sent to your Piety our brother
Dorotheus, the deacon of the church under the
jurisdiction of the most honoured bishop Meletius,
he being a man of good zeal regarding orthodoxy in
faith, and like yourself eager to see peace in the
churches, to the end that he, following your counsels
(which you, by reason of your years and your
experience in affairs, and of your possessing beyond
the rest of us the guidance of the Spirit, are able
to make more nearly unerring), may with such
help from you take in hand the matters which are
the objects of our zeal.

You will no doubt give him welcome, and you will
regard him with the eyes of peace ; and when you
have buttressed him with the support of your prayers
and have furnished him with letters for his journey
—or better, have attached to him some competent
men from this region as companions—you will give
him directions for his mission.   It has seemed to us
advisable in the circumstances, moreover, to write
to the bishop of Rome, that he may examine into
the state of affairs here, and give us his opinion, so

δόγματος ἀποσταλῆναί τινας δύσκολον τῶν
ἐκεῖθεν, αὐτὸν αὐθεντῆσαι περὶ τὸ πρᾶγμα,
ἐκλεξάμενον ἄνδρας ἱκανοὺς μὲν ὁδοιπορίας πόνους
ὑπενεγκεῖν,[1] ἱκανοὺς δὲ πραότητι καὶ εὐτονίᾳ
ἤθους τοὺς ἐνδιαστρόφους τῶν παρ' ἡμῖν νουθε-
τῆσαι, ἐπιτηδείως δὲ καὶ οἰκονομικῶς κεχρημένους
τῷ λόγῳ, καὶ πάντα ἔχοντας μεθ' ἑαυτῶν τὰ
μετὰ Ἀρίμινον πεπραγμένα ἐπὶ λύσει τῶν κατ'
ἀνάγκην ἐκεῖ γενομένων· καὶ τοῦτο μηδενὸς
εἰδότος, ἀψοφητὶ διὰ θαλάσσης ἐπιστῆναι τοῖς
ὧδε, ὑπὲρ τοῦ φθάσαι τὴν αἴσθησιν τῶν ἐχθρῶν
τῆς εἰρήνης.

Ἐπιζητεῖται δὲ κἀκεῖνο παρά τινων τῶν ἐντεῦθεν, ἀναγκαίως, ὡς καὶ αὐτοῖς ἡμῖν κατα-

---

[1] διενεγκεῖν editi antiqi.

---

[1] On the Council of Ariminum or Rimini the Catholic
Encyclopaedia says : "The Council of Rimini was opened
early in July, 359, with over four hundred bishops. About
eighty Semi-Arians, including Ursacius, Germinius, and
Auxentius, withdrew from the orthodox bishops, the most
eminent of whom was Restitutus of Carthage ; Liberius,
Eusebius, Dionysius, and others were still in exile. The
two parties sent separate deputations to the Emperor, the
orthodox asserting clearly their firm attachment to the faith
of Nicaea, while the Arian minority adhered to the Imperial
formula. But the inexperienced representatives of the
orthodox majority allowed themselves to be deceived, and
not only entered into communion with the heretical delegates,
but even subscribed, at Nice in Thrace, a formula to the
effect merely that the Son is like the Father according to the
Scriptures (the words 'in all things' being omitted). On
their return to Rimini, they were met with the unanimous
protests of their colleagues. But the threats of the consul
Taurus, the remonstrances of the Semi-Arians against hinder-
ing peace between East and West for a word not contained

that, as it is difficult to send men from Rome by a
general synodical decree, he may himself exercise
full authority in this matter, selecting men capable
of enduring the hardships of a journey, and at the
same time capable, by the gentleness and vigour of
their character, of admonishing those among us who are
perverted, men who possess the power of appropriate
and effective speech and are fully cognizant of all
that has been done since the Council of Ariminum [1]
for the undoing of the actions taken there under
compulsion; and when all this has been done
without the knowledge of anyone, our thought is
that the bishop of Rome shall quietly, through a
mission sent by sea, assume charge of affairs here so
as to escape the notice of the enemies of peace.

It is also demanded by certain people here—quite
necessarily, as it seems to us as well—that they [2]

---

in Scripture, their privations and their home-sickness—all
combined to weaken the constancy of the orthodox bishops.
And the last twenty were induced to subscribe when
Ursacius had an addition made to the formula of Nice,
declaring that the Son is not a creature like other creatures.
Pope Liberius, having regained his liberty, rejected this
formula, which was thereupon repudiated by many who had
signed it. In view of the hasty manner of its adoption and
lack of approbation by the Holy See, it could have no
authority."

[2] *i.e.* the Romans, particularly the proposed commissioners.
Basil bore it ill that Marcellus, whom he regarded as a
trimmer, was in the words of St. Jerome "fortified by
communion with Julius and Athanasius, popes of Rome and
Alexandria." Cf. *De Vir. Illust.* 86: " se communione Julii
et Athanasii, Romanae et Alexandrinae urbis pontificum,
esse munitum." St. Athanasius, however, according to
Cardinal Newman, upheld him "to about A.D. 360," but
attacked his tenets pointedly, though without naming him,
in his fourth oration against the Arians.

φαίνεται, τὸν τὴν Μαρκέλλου αἵρεσιν αὐτοὺς [1]
ὡς χαλεπὴν καὶ βλαβερὰν καὶ τῆς ὑγιαινούσης
πίστεως [2] ἀλλοτρίως ἔχουσαν, ἐξορίσαι.[3] ἐπεὶ
μέχρι τοῦ νῦν ἐν πᾶσιν οἷς ἐπιστέλλουσι γράμμασι, τὸν μὲν δυσώνυμον Ἄρειον ἄνω καὶ κάτω
ἀναθεματίζοντες καὶ τῶν ἐκκλησιῶν ἐξορίζοντες
οὐ διαλείπουσι, Μαρκέλλῳ δέ, τῷ κατὰ διάμετρον
ἐκείνῳ τὴν ἀσέβειαν ἐπιδειξαμένῳ, καὶ εἰς αὐτὴν τὴν ὕπαρξιν τῆς τοῦ Μονογενοῦς θεότητος
ἀσεβήσαντι καὶ κακῶς τὴν τοῦ Λόγου προσηγορίαν ἐκδεξαμένῳ, οὐδεμίαν μέμψιν ἐπενεγκόντες
φαίνονται. ὃς Λόγον μὲν εἰρῆσθαι τὸν Μονογενῆ
δίδωσι, κατὰ χρείαν καὶ ἐπὶ καιροῦ προελθόντα,
πάλιν δὲ εἰς τὸν ὅθεν ἐξῆλθεν ἐπαναστρέψαντα,
οὔτε πρὸ τῆς ἐξόδου εἶναι, οὔτε μετὰ τὴν ἐπάνοδον
ὑφεστάναι. καὶ τούτου ἀπόδειξις [4] αἱ παρ᾽ ἡμῖν
ἀποκείμεναι βίβλοι τῆς ἀδίκου ἐκείνης συγγραφῆς
ὑπάρχουσιν. ἀλλ᾽ ὅμως τοῦτον οὐδαμοῦ διαβα-
λόντες [5] ἐφάνησαν, καὶ ταῦτα αἰτίαν ἔχοντες ὡς,
τὸ ἐξ ἀρχῆς κατ᾽ ἄγνοιαν τῆς ἀληθείας, καὶ εἰς
κοινωνίαν αὐτὸν ἐκκλησιαστικὴν παραδεξάμενοι.
ἐκείνου τε οὖν μνησθῆναι πρεπόντως ἀπαιτεῖ τὰ
παρόντα, ὥστε μὴ ἔχειν ἀφορμὴν τοὺς θέλοντας
ἀφορμήν, ἐκ τοῦ τῇ σῇ ὁσιότητι συνάπτειν τοὺς
ὑγιαίνοντας καὶ τοὺς πρὸς τὴν ἀληθῆ πίστιν

---

[1] αὐτοῖς E.   [2] διδασκαλίας ὡς E, Harl.
[3] ἐξορίζεσθαι editi antiqi.   [4] ἀποδείξεις E.
[5] οὐδαμοῦ διαβαλόντες] οὐδαμῶς διαβάλλοντες editi antiqi.

[1] On Basil's opinion of the heretical doctrines of Marcellus
of Ancyra, cf. Letters CXXV and CCLXIII. Marcellus had
upheld the cause of orthodoxy at Nicaea. Later, however,
while attacking the errors of Asterius, he was supposed to

should themselves exterminate the heresy of Marcellus[1] as being both dangerous and harmful, and
foreign to the true faith. For up to the present, in
all the letters which they send, while they do not
cease anathematizing the abominable Arius up and
down and banishing him from the churches, yet
against Marcellus, who has exhibited an impiety
diametrically opposed to that of Arius, who has in
fact been impious concerning the very existence of
the Only-begotten Godhead, and has accepted a
false signification of "the Word," they have
manifestly brought no censure whatever. He gives
it as his opinion that the Only-begotten was called
"the Word," that He made His appearance in time
of need and in due season, but returned again whence
He came, and that neither before His coming did
He exist nor after His return does He still subsist.[2]
And as proofs of this there exist the documents in
our possession containing that wicked essay of his.
But nevertheless, they have nowhere come out with
a repudiation of this man, and that too although
they are open to the charge of having (at the
beginning in ignorance of the truth) even received
him into ecclesiastical communion. Of this man,
therefore, the present circumstances demand that
appropriate mention be made, so that those who
seek an opportunity[3] may have no opportunity,
in consequence of our uniting with your Holiness
all who are sound in the faith, and of our reveal-

have taught that the Son had no real personality, but was
merely an external manifestation of the Father.

[2] ὑφεοτάναι, i.e. does not exist in essence.

[3] i.e. of following the heresy of Marcellus, as they could
safely do so long as he remained in good standing for
orthodoxy.

ὀκλάζοντας φανεροὺς πᾶσι ποιῆσαι· ὥστε τοῦ
λοιποῦ γνωρίζειν ἡμᾶς τοὺς ὁμόφρονας, καὶ μή,
ὡς ἐν νυκτομαχίᾳ, μηδεμίαν φίλων καὶ πολε-
μίων ἔχειν διάκρισιν. μόνον παρακαλοῦμεν
εὐθὺς ὑπὸ τὸν πρῶτον πλοῦν ἐκπεμφθῆναι τὸν
προειρημένον διάκονον, ἵνα δυνηθῇ κατὰ γοῦν τὸ
ἐφεξῆς ἔτος γενέσθαι τι, ὧν προσευχόμεθα.

Ἐκεῖνο δὲ καὶ πρὸ τῶν ἡμετέρων[1] λόγων
συνιεῖς τε αὐτὸς καὶ φροντιεῖς δηλονότι, ὅπως
ἐπιστάντες, ἐὰν ὁ Θεὸς θέλῃ, μὴ ἐναφῶσι ταῖς
ἐκκλησίαις[2] τὰ σχίσματα, ἀλλὰ τοὺς τὰ αὐτὰ
φρονοῦντας παντὶ τρόπῳ εἰς ἕνωσιν συνελάσωσι,
κἄν τινας ἰδίας τῶν πρὸς ἀλλήλους διαφορῶν
ἀφορμὰς εὕρωσιν[3] ἔχοντας, ὑπὲρ τοῦ μὴ τὸν
ὀρθοδοξοῦντα λαὸν εἰς πολλὰ κατατέμνεσθαι μέρη
τοῖς προεστῶσι συναφιστάμενον. πάντα γὰρ δεῖ
σπουδάσαι δεύτερα ἡγήσασθαι τῆς εἰρήνης, καὶ
πρὸ πάντων τῆς κατὰ Ἀντιόχειαν ἐκκλησίας
ἐπιμεληθῆναι, ὡς μὴ ἀσθενεῖν ἐν αὐτῇ τὴν ὀρθὴν
μερίδα περὶ τὰ πρόσωπα σχιζομένην. μᾶλλον
δέ, τούτων ἁπάντων καὶ αὐτὸς εἰς ὕστερον ἐπι-
μελήσῃ, ἐπειδάν, ὅπερ εὐχόμεθα, Θεοῦ συνεργοῦν-
τός σοι, πάντας λάβῃς τὰ τῆς καταστάσεως τῶν
ἐκκλησιῶν ἐπιτρέποντας.

---

[1] εἰρημένων editi antiqi.   [2] τὰς ἐκκλησίας E.
[3] τύχωσιν Vat. Cod. ac Reg. secund. et Coisl. sec.

ing to all men those who are slack in the true faith. The result will be that henceforth we shall be able to recognize those who are of one mind with us, instead of being like those who fight a battle at night—unable to distinguish between friends and foes. We only urge now that the deacon whom we have spoken of be sent away immediately, by the first boat, in order that some of the objects for which we pray may possibly be realized next year at least.

Our next observation you will both understand of yourself even before we make it, and will doubtless see to it that these men assuming charge, if God wills it, do not let schisms loose among the churches, but that they by every means urge into unity those who hold identical doctrines with us, even though they find some who have private reasons for differing with one another, in order that the orthodox laity be not cut up into many factions, by following their leaders into revolt. For they must zealously endeavour to count all things secondary to peace, and above all they must be solicitous for the Church at Antioch, lest the orthodox section of it be weakened by being divided on the question of the persons.[1] Or rather, you yourself will henceforth assume care of all these things, as soon as, according to our prayers, God being your helper, you shall have everyone entrusting into your care whatever pertains to the restoration of peace among the churches.

[1] *i.e.* of the Godhead.

LXX

Ἀνεπίγραφος περὶ συνόδου

Ἀρχαίας ἀγάπης θεσμοὺς ἀνανεοῦσθαι, καὶ πατέρων εἰρήνην τὸ οὐράνιον δῶρον Χριστοῦ καὶ σωτήριον, ἀπομαρανθὲν τῷ χρόνῳ, πάλιν πρὸς τὴν ἀκμὴν ἐπαναγαγεῖν, ἀναγκαῖον μὲν ἡμῖν καὶ ὠφέλιμον, τερπνὸν δὲ εὖ οἶδα ὅτι καὶ τῇ σῇ φιλοχρίστῳ διαθέσει καταφανήσεται. τί γὰρ ἂν γένοιτο χαριέστερον, ἢ τοὺς τοσούτῳ τῷ πλήθει τῶν τόπων διῃρημένους [1] τῇ διὰ τῆς ἀγάπης ἑνώσει καθορᾶν εἰς μίαν μελῶν ἁρμονίαν ἐν σώματι Χριστοῦ δεδέσθαι; ἡ ἀνατολὴ πᾶσα σχεδόν, τιμιώτατε πάτερ (λέγω δὲ ἀνατολὴν τὰ ἀπὸ τοῦ Ἰλλυρικοῦ μέχρις Αἰγύπτου), μεγάλῳ χειμῶνι καὶ κλύδωνι κατασείεται, τῆς πάλαι μὲν σπαρείσης αἱρέσεως ὑπὸ τοῦ ἐχθροῦ τῆς ἀληθείας Ἀρείου, νῦν δὲ πρὸς τὸ ἀναίσχυντον ἀναφανείσης καὶ οἰονεὶ ῥίζης πικρᾶς καρπὸν ὀλέθριον ἀναδιδούσης, κατακρατούσης λοιπὸν διὰ τὸ τοὺς μὲν καθ᾽ ἑκάστην παροικίαν προεστῶτας τοῦ ὀρθοῦ λόγου ἐκ συκοφαντίας καὶ ἐπηρείας τῶν ἐκκλησιῶν ἐκπεσεῖν, παραδοθῆναι δὲ τοῖς αἰχμαλωτίζουσι τὰς ψυχὰς τῶν ἀκεραιοτέρων τὴν τῶν πραγμάτων ἰσχύν. τούτων μίαν προσεδοκήσαμεν λύσιν τὴν τῆς ὑμετέρας εὐσπλαγχνίας ἐπίσκεψιν· καὶ ἐψυχαγώγησεν ἡμᾶς ἀεὶ τὸ παράδοξον τῆς ὑμετέρας ἀγάπης ἐν τῷ παρελθόντι χρόνῳ, καὶ φήμῃ

---

[1] διειργμένους editi antiqi.

---

[1] Written in the autumn of 371. All, including Tillemont

48

LETTER LXX

LETTER LXX

WITHOUT ADDRESS, CONCERNING A SYNOD [1]

To renew the ties of an old affection and to restore into full bloom the peace of the Fathers, that heavenly and salutary gift of Christ which has become withered by time, is for us both necessary and expedient, and I know well that it will seem delightful to your Christ-loving disposition also. For what could be more pleasant than to behold men who are separated from one another by so vast a diversity of places of residence, bound by the unity of love into a single harmony of members in the body of Christ? Almost the whole East, most honoured Father (by "East" I mean everything from Illyricum to Egypt),[2] is being shaken by a mighty storm and flood, since the heresy, sown long ago by Arius, the enemy of truth, and now already grown up into shamelessness, and, like a bitter root, producing a deadly fruit, at last prevails, because the champions of orthodox teaching in every diocese have been banished from their churches through slander and insult, and the administration of affairs has been surrendered to men who are making prisoners of the souls of those more pure in faith. As the one solution of these difficulties we have looked forward to the visitation [3] of your sympathetic heart; for in times gone by your marvellous affection has always refreshed us, and we were strengthened in our souls

and the Benedictine editors, are agreed that this letter is addressed to Pope Damasus.

[2] *i.e.* roughly, the two eastern prefectures of Diocletian and his successors.

[3] *i.e.* an official visit of a bishop.

φαιδροτέρα πρὸς βραχὺ τὰς ψυχὰς ἀνερρώσθημεν,
ὡς ἐσομένης ἡμῖν τινὸς ἐπισκέψεως παρ' ὑμῶν.
ὡς δὲ διημάρτομεν τῆς ἐλπίδος, μηκέτι στέγοντες
ἤλθομεν ἐπὶ τὴν διὰ τοῦ γράμματος [1] ἡμῶν
παράκλησιν, διαναστῆναι ὑμᾶς πρὸς τὴν ἀντίληψιν ἡμῶν, καὶ ἀποστεῖλαί τινας τῶν ὁμοψύχων,
ἢ τοὺς συμβιβάζοντας τοὺς διεστῶτας, ἢ εἰς
φιλίαν τὰς ἐκκλησίας τοῦ Θεοῦ ἐπανάγοντας, ἢ
τοὺς γοῦν αἰτίους τῆς ἀκαταστασίας φανερωτέρους[2]
ὑμῖν καθιστῶντας· ὥστε καὶ ὑμῖν φανερὸν εἶναι
τοῦ λοιποῦ, πρὸς τίνας ἔχειν τὴν κοινωνίαν
προσῆκε.

Πάντως δὲ οὐδὲν καινὸν [3] ἐπιζητοῦμεν, ἀλλὰ
τοῖς τε λοιποῖς τῶν πάλαι μακαρίων καὶ θεοφίλων
ἀνδρῶν σύνηθες, καὶ διαφερόντως ὑμῖν. οἴδαμεν
γὰρ μνήμης ἀκολουθίᾳ, παρὰ τῶν πατέρων ἡμῶν
αἰτηθέντων καὶ ἀπὸ γραμμάτων τῶν ἔτι καὶ νῦν
πεφυλαγμένων παρ' ἡμῖν, διδασκόμενοι, Διονύσιον
ἐκεῖνον, τὸν μακαριώτατον ἐπίσκοπον, παρ' ὑμῖν
ἐπί τε ὀρθότητι πίστεως καὶ τῇ λοιπῇ ἀρετῇ δια-
πρέψαντα, ἐπισκεπτόμενον διὰ γραμμάτων τὴν
ἡμετέραν ἐκκλησίαν τῶν Καισαρέων, καὶ παρα-
καλοῦντα τοὺς πατέρας ἡμῶν διὰ γραμμάτων,
καὶ πέμπειν τοὺς ἀπολυτρουμένους ἐκ τῆς αἰχ-
μαλωσίας τὴν ἀδελφότητα. ἐν χαλεπωτέρῳ

---

[1] τοῦ γράμματος] γραμμάτων editi antiqi.
[2] φανερώτερον editi antiqi.
[3] ἄκαιρον E, editi antiqi, δεινόν Clarom.

---

[1] i.e bishops of Rome. The Benedictine edition points out
that the kindness of the bishops of Rome, here mentioned
by Basil, is borne out by the evidence both of Dionysius,

for a brief space by the joyful report that we should receive a visitation from you. But since we have been cheated of our hope, unable to contain ourselves longer, we have had recourse to urging you by this letter to rouse yourself to our assistance, and to send us men of like mind with us, who will either reconcile the dissenters, or restore the churches of God to friendship, or will at least make more manifest to you those who are responsible for the confusion. It will thus be clear to you also for the future, with what men it is proper to have communion.

And the request we make is by no means a novel one, but, on the contrary, has been habitual not only with all the blessed and God-beloved men of the past, but also and especially with yourself.[1] For we know through a continuous tradition, by the teaching received from our Fathers in answer to our questions and from letters which even to this day are preserved among us, that Dionysius,[2] that most blessed bishop, who was pre-eminent among you both for the orthodoxy of his faith and for his virtue in general, was wont to visit our Church of Caesarea by letter, and to exhort our fathers by letter, and to send men to ransom the brethren from captivity. But our present state of affairs is

bishop of Corinth (cf. Eusebius, *Hist. Eccl.* 4, 23), of Dionysius of Alexandria (Dionysius to Sixtus II, in Euseb., *Hist. Eccl.* 7, 5), and of Eusebius himself in his history. The troubles referred to here took place in the time of Gallienus, when the Scythians plundered Cappadocia and the neighbouring countries (cf. Sozomen, *Eccl. Hist.* 2, 6).

[2] A Greek by birth, and consecrated July 22, A.D. 259, on the death of Sixtus II, during the persecution of Valerian. Nothing is recorded of him except his efforts against heresy.

δὲ νῦν καὶ σκυθρωποτέρῳ τὰ καθ' ἡμᾶς, καὶ
πλείονος δεόμενα τῆς ἐπιμελείας. οὐ γὰρ οἰκοδο-
μημάτων γηΐνων καταστροφήν, ἀλλ' ἐκκλησιῶν
ἅλωσιν ὀδυρόμεθα· οὐδὲ δουλείαν σωματικήν,
ἀλλ' αἰχμαλωσίαν ψυχῶν καθ' ἑκάστην ἡμέραν
ἐνεργουμένην παρὰ τῶν ὑπερμαχούντων τῆς
αἱρέσεως καθορῶμεν. ὥστε εἰ μὴ ἤδη διανα-
σταίητε πρὸς τὴν ἀντίληψιν, μικρὸν ὕστερον
οὐδὲ οἷς ὀρέξετε τὴν χεῖρα εὑρήσετε, πάντων
ὑπὸ τὴν ἐπικράτειαν τῆς αἱρέσεως γενομένων.

LXXI

Γρηγορίῳ Βασίλειος [1]

Ἐδεξάμην τὰ γράμματα τῆς σῆς εὐλαβείας [2]
διὰ τοῦ αἰδεσιμωτάτου ἀδελφοῦ Ἑλληνίου· καὶ
ὅσα ἐνέφηνας ἡμῖν, αὐτὸς ταῦτα γυμνῶς διηγήσατο. ἀκούσαντες δὲ ὅπως [3] διετέθημεν, οὐκ ἀμφι-
βάλλεις πάντως. πλὴν ἀλλ' ἐπειδὴ ἐκρίναμεν
πάσης λύπης ἀνωτέραν ποιεῖσθαι τὴν πρὸς σὲ
ἀγάπην ἐδεξάμεθα καὶ ταῦτα ὡς ἦν προσῆκον,

---

[1] Γρηγορίῳ ἑταίρῳ alii MSS.
[2] τῆς σῆς εὐλαβείας] τῆς εὐλαβείας σου editi antiqi.
[3] αὐτὸς ταῦτα . . . ὅπως] καὶ ταῦτα διηγησαμένου ἀκούσαντες
ὅπως editi antiqi.

---

[1] Written in the year 371. Gregory Nazianzene had
already refused to aid in effecting the election of Basil as
Archbishop of Caesarea. He later refused to support him
in his throne, by refusing to accept any high responsibilities
such as τήνδε τῆς καθέδρας τιμήν (cf. Greg. Naz., Or. XLIII),
possibly the coadjutor-bishopric at Caesarea. Gregory's

more difficult and more gloomy, and requires greater
solicitude.   Indeed, it is not the destruction of
earthly buildings that we mourn, but the seizure of
churches ; nor is it corporeal slavery that we behold,
but the captivity of souls which is being brought
about daily by the champions of the heresy.   Accordingly, unless you immediately rouse yourself to our
assistance, you will shortly not even find men to
whom to stretch forth your hand, since all will have
come under the dominion of the heresy.

LETTER LXXI

BASIL TO GREGORY[1]

I RECEIVED the letter of your Reverence through
our most reverend brother Hellenius,[2] who in person
related in plain language what you had intimated
to us.   How we were affected in hearing this, you
certainly can be in no doubt.   However, since we
have decided to put our love for you above any
grievance, we have received even these communications in a becoming manner, and we pray the holy

---

plea was that it was better for Basil's own sake that there be
no suspicion of favour to personal friends, and he begged to
be excused for staying at Nazianzus.   Cf. Greg. Naz , Letter
XLV.   The present letter is partly an answer to the letter
from Gregory which announced this stand, partly a plea that
Gregory pay no attention to certain Nazianzene scandal-
mongers who had charged Basil with heterodoxy.

[2] Hellenius: a surveyor of customs at Nazianzus, the
confidential friend both of Basil and Gregory Nazianzene.
Besides delivering to Basil the message here referred to, we
find him in 372 conveying a message from the bishops of
Lesser Armenia.   Cf. Letter XCVIII.

καὶ εὐχόμεθα τῷ ἁγίῳ Θεῷ, τὰς λειπομένας
ἡμέρας ἢ ὥρας[1] οὕτω[2] διαφυλαχθῆναι ἐν τῇ
περὶ σὲ διαθέσει, ὡς καὶ ἐν τῷ κατόπιν χρόνῳ,
ἐν ᾧ οὐδὲν ἡμῖν αὐτοῖς οὔτε μικρὸν οὔτε μεῖζον
ἐλλελοιπόσι συνέγνωμεν.

Εἰ δὲ ὁ δεῖνα ἄρτι, παρακύψαι φιλοτιμούμενος
πρὸς τὸν βίον τῶν Χριστιανῶν, εἶτα οἰόμενος
αὐτῷ σεμνότητά τινα φέρειν τὸ ἡμῖν συνανατρί-
βεσθαι, ἅ τε οὐκ ἤκουσε κατασκευάζει, καὶ ἃ
μὴ ἐνόησεν ἐξηγεῖται, θαυμαστὸν οὐδέν. ἀλλ᾽
ἐκεῖνο θαυμαστὸν καὶ παράδοξον, ὅτι τούτων
ἀκροατὰς ἔχει τοὺς γνησιωτάτους μοι τῶν παρ᾽
ὑμῖν ἀδελφῶν, καὶ οὐκ ἀκροατὰς μόνον, ἀλλὰ
καὶ μαθητάς, ὡς ἔοικεν. εἴ γε[3] καὶ ἄλλως ἦν
παράδοξον τοιοῦτον μὲν εἶναι τὸν διδάσκοντα,[4]
ἐμὲ δὲ τὸν διασυρόμενον, ἀλλ᾽ οὖν τῶν καιρῶν
ἡ καταστροφὴ ἐπαίδευσεν ἡμᾶς πρὸς μηδὲν
δυσκολαίνειν. πάλαι γὰρ τὰ τούτων ἀτιμότερα
συνήθη ἡμῖν γέγονε διὰ τὰς ἁμαρτίας ἡμῶν.
ἐγὼ τοίνυν, εἰ μὲν οὐδέπω τοῖς αὐτοῦ ἀδελφοῖς
δέδωκα πεῖραν τῆς ἐμαυτοῦ περὶ τὸν Θεὸν
αἱρέσεως,[5] οὐδὲ νῦν ἔχω τι ἀποκρίνασθαι· οὓς
γὰρ οὐκ ἔπεισεν ὁ μακρὸς χρόνος, πῶς συμπείσει
ἐπιστολὴ βραχεῖα; εἰ δὲ ἐκεῖνα αὐτάρκη, λῆροι
νομιζέσθωσαν τὰ παρὰ τῶν διαβαλλόντων. πλὴν
γε ὅτι, ἐὰν ἐπιτρέψωμεν στόμασιν ἀχαλινώτοις
καὶ καρδίαις ἀπαιδεύτοις λαλεῖν περὶ ὧν ἂν

---

[1] ἡμῶν add. Harl. [2] οὕτω om. E. [3] γάρ E.
[4] τοιούτους δὲ τοὺς ἀνεχομένους add. editi antiqi.
[5] προαιρέσεως Harl., Vat., et Clarom.

---

[1] Basil avoids mentioning the slanderer by name.

God that for the days or hours that are left to us
we may be preserved in the same disposition toward
you as in the past, during which we have been
conscious of having fallen short in nothing, be it
small or great.

But if the person we have in mind,[1] aspiring to
peer into the life of the Christians,[2] and also thinking
that his being associated with us may bring him a
certain degree of prestige, has recently proceeded
to trump up things which he has not heard and to
relate things of which he has gained no knowledge,
there is nothing surprising in that. But the surprising and indeed incredible thing is this— that he
finds as hearers of these slanders the truest to me of
the brethren among you, and not merely as hearers,
but even, it seems, as disciples. Even though, on
general grounds, it was incredible that such a man
as he should be the teacher and I the object of his
disparagement, yet the topsy-turvy condition of the
times has taught us to be vexed at nothing. For
charges more ignominious than these have for a
long time become familiar to us in punishment for
our sins. As for me, therefore, if I have never yet
given this fellow's brethren a proof of my opinions
regarding God, I certainly have no answer to give
now; for how will a brief letter persuade those
whom a long life has not convinced? But if that
life is in itself sufficient, let that which emanates
from the slanderers be considered mere nonsense.
Yet we must remember that if we suffer unbridled
mouths and uneducated minds to prattle about

[2] The intimation is that he cannot really enter into the
brotherhood of Christians, much as he would like to do so,
but can only peer at it.

55

ἐθέλωσιν,[1] καὶ ἕτοιμα ἔχωμεν πρὸς ὑποδοχὴν
τὰ ὦτα, οὐ μόνον ἡμεῖς τὰ τῶν ἄλλων παρα-
δεξόμεθα, ἀλλὰ καὶ ἕτεροι τὰ ἡμέτερα.

Τούτων δὲ αἴτιον ἐκεῖνο, ὃ πάλαι μὲν παρεκά-
λουν μὴ γίνεσθαι, νῦν δὲ ἀπαγορεύσας σιωπῶ,
τὸ μὴ συντυγχάνειν ἡμᾶς ἀλλήλοις. εἰ γὰρ κατὰ
τὰς ἀρχαίας συνθήκας, καὶ κατὰ τὴν ὀφειλομέ-
νην νῦν ταῖς ἐκκλησίαις παρ' ἡμῶν ἐπιμέλειαν,
τὰ πολλὰ τοῦ ἐνιαυτοῦ μετ' ἀλλήλων διή-
γομεν, οὐκ ἂν ἐδώκαμεν πάροδον τοῖς διαβάλ-
λουσι. σὺ [2] δέ, εἰ δοκεῖ, τούτους μὲν ἔα χαίρειν,
αὐτὸς δὲ παρακλήθητι συγκάμνειν ἡμῖν εἰς τὸν
προκείμενον ἀγῶνα καὶ συντυχεῖν μεθ' ἡμῶν τῷ
καθ' ἡμῶν στρατευομένῳ. εἰ γὰρ ὀφθῆς μόνον,
ἐφέξεις [3] αὐτοῦ τὴν ὁρμὴν καὶ τοὺς συγκροτου-
μένους ἐπὶ τῷ καταστρέψασθαι τὰ τῆς πατρίδος
πράγματα διαλύσεις, γνώριμον αὐτοῖς κατα-
στήσας, ὅτι αὐτὸς τῇ τοῦ Θεοῦ χάριτι τοῦ καθ'
ἡμᾶς συλλόγου κατάρχεις,[4] καὶ φράξεις πᾶν
ἄδικον στόμα τῶν λαλούντων κατὰ τοῦ Θεοῦ
ἀνομίαν. ἂν ταῦτα γένηται, αὐτὰ τὰ πράγματα
δείξει, τίς μὲν ὁ κατακολουθῶν σοι ἐπὶ τὰ καλά,
τίς δὲ ὁ μετοκλάζων καὶ προδιδοὺς δειλίᾳ τὸν
λόγον τῆς ἀληθείας. ἐὰν δὲ τὰ τῆς ἐκκλησίας
προδιδόμενα ᾖ, ὀλίγος [5] μοι λόγος διὰ ῥημάτων
πείθειν τοὺς τοσούτου με [6] τιθεμένους ἄξιον, ὅσον [7]
ἂν τιμήσωνται ἄνθρωποι οὔπω ἑαυτοὺς [8] μετρεῖν
δεδιδαγμένοι. μετ' οὐ πολὺ γάρ, τῇ τοῦ Θεοῦ

---

[1] θέλωσι Ε.   [2] σοι Ε, editi antiqi.
[3] ὑφέξεις Ε.   [4] κατάρξεις editi antiqi.
[5] οὐδείς Ε.   [6] σε editi antiqi.

whatever they please, and if we hold our ears ready
to receive, not only shall we receive a false idea of
the affairs of the others, but they will do the same
as to ours.

Now the cause of the present state of affairs is one
which I have long urged you not to permit to arise,
but which I now through very weariness of repe-
tition pass over in silence—the fact that we do not
meet one another. For if we, living up to our old
agreements and to the responsibility which we now
owe to the churches, were in the habit of spending
the greater part of the year together, we should
not have given access to these calumniators. But
do you, if you approve, disregard these men, and of
your own accord be pleased to co-operate with us in
the struggle now at hand and to meet, in company
with us, the enemy who is arrayed against us. For
if you are merely seen, you will stop his attack and
will utterly disperse those who are organizing themselves to overthrow their country, by making it
known to them that you yourself by the grace of
God are the leader of our forces, and that you will
close every wicked mouth of such as utter lawlessness
against God. If this is done, the facts themselves
will show who it is that follows you to the goal of
honour, and who it is that shifts hither and thither
and in his cowardice betrays the word of truth.
But if the interests of the Church are once be-
trayed, little need be said by me with the idea of
persuading by words those who estimate my worth
at what men may estimate it who have not yet
learned to measure their own selves. For in no

---

⁷ ὅσου E.   ⁸ ἑαυτοῖς E.

χάριτι, ἡ διὰ τῶν ἔργων ἀπόδειξις τὰς συκοφαντίας ἐλέγχει, διοτι[1] προσδοκῶμεν ὑπὲρ τοῦ λόγου
τῆς ἀληθείας τάχα μέν τι καὶ μεῖζον πείσεσθαι·
εἰ δὲ μή, πάντως γε τῶν ἐκκλησιῶν καὶ τῶν
πατρίδων ἀπελαθήσεσθαι. ἐὰν δὲ καὶ μηδὲν τῶν
ἐλπιζομένων γένηται, οὐ μακράν ἐστι τὸ τοῦ
Χριστοῦ δικαστήριον. ὥστε, εἰ μὲν τὴν συντυχίαν, διὰ τὰς ἐκκλησίας ἐπιζητεῖς ἕτοιμος συνδραμεῖν ὅπουπερ ἂν προκαλῇ·[2] εἰ δέ, ἵνα τὰς
συκοφαντίας διαλύσω, οὐ σχολή μοι νῦν ἀποκρίνασθαι περὶ τούτων.

LXXII

Ἡσυχίῳ

Οἶδά σου καὶ τὴν πρὸς[3] ἡμᾶς ἀγάπην, καὶ
τὴν περὶ τὰ καλὰ σπουδήν. διόπερ χρήζων
δυσωπῆσαι τὸν ποθεινότατον υἱὸν Καλλισθένην,
ἡγησάμην, εἰ κοινωνόν σε λάβοιμι τῆς φροντίδος,
ῥᾷον κατορθώσειν τὸ σπουδαζόμενον. λελύπηται
ὁ ἀνὴρ κατὰ τοῦ λογιωτάτου Εὐστοχίου, καὶ
λελύπηται δικαίαν λύπην. ἐγκαλεῖ αὐτοῦ τοῖς
οἰκέταις θράσος κατ᾽ αὐτοῦ καὶ ἀπόνοιαν. τοῦ-

---

[1] ὅτι E.   [2] προσκαλῇ editi antiqi.   [3] περί editi antiqi.

[1] Perhaps Basil is referring to martyrdom.
[2] Basil probably refers here both to Caesarea, the place of
his birth, and the Pontus, the region of his bringing-up.
Cf. Vol I, p. 48, note 1.
[3] Written at about the same time as the preceding. On
Hesychius, cf. Letter XLIV.

great while, by the grace of God, the evidence of
our deeds will refute their slanders, because we
expect to suffer very soon some even greater misfortune[1] for the sake of the doctrine of truth; or,
if not that, then at least certainly to be banished
from the churches and from our countries.[2] But even
if none of these things to which we confidently look
forward comes to pass, the judgment of Christ is not
far off. Therefore, if you ask for the conference it
is for the churches' sake that I am ready to meet
with you wherever you summon me; but if it is in
order that I may refute these calumnies, then at
present I have no leisure to make any reply about
them.

LETTER LXXII

To Hesychius[3]

I am fully conscious both of your love for us and
of your zeal for what is honourable. Therefore, since
I am anxious that our most beloved son Callisthenes[4]
be placated, I have thought that, if I were to take
you as an associate in my design, I should more
easily bring to pass what I so strongly desire. He
has conceived a grievance against the most eloquent
Eustochius, and he has just grounds for his grievance. He accuses the servants of Eustochius of
insolence toward him, aye, and of madness. We
think it proper that he should be exhorted, being

---

[4] Callisthenes and Eustochius, mentioned below, were
both laymen of Cappadocia. Nothing is known about them
except such information as may be obtained from the present
and the following letters.

τὸν ἀξιοῦμεν παρακληθῆναι, ἀρκεσθέντα[1] τῷ
φόβῳ, ὃν ἐφόβησεν αὐτούς τε[2] τοὺς θρασυνο-
μένους καὶ τοὺς τούτων δεσπότας, καταλῦσαι
τὴν φιλονεικίαν, δόντα τὴν χάριν. οὕτω γὰρ
ἀμφότερα ὑπάρξει[3] καὶ τὸ παρὰ ἀνθρώποις
σεμνόν, καὶ τὸ παρὰ Θεῷ εὐδόκιμον, ἐὰν τῷ φόβῳ
θελήσῃ τὸ μακρόθυμον ἀναμίξαι. αὐτός τε οὖν,
εἴ τις σοι[4] προϋπάρχει φιλία πρὸς τὸν ἄνδρα
καὶ συνήθεια, αἴτησον παρ' αὐτοῦ τὴν χάριν
ταύτην· καὶ οὓς ἐὰν γνῷς ἐν τῇ πόλει δυναμένους
αὐτὸν δυσωπῆσαι, κοινωνοὺς λάβε τῆς φροντίδος,
εἰπὼν αὐτοῖς, ὅτι τὸ γινόμενον ἐμοὶ μάλιστα
κεχαρισμένον ἔσται.

Καὶ ἀπόπεμψαι τὸν συνδιάκονον πράξαντα[5]
ὧν ἕνεκεν ἀπεστάλη. αἰσχύνομαι γάρ, κατα-
φυγόντων πρός με τῶν ἀνθρώπων, μὴ δυνηθῆναι
αὐτοῖς γενέσθαι τι χρήσιμον.

LXXIII

Καλλισθένει

Ηὐχαρίστησα τῷ Θεῷ[6] τοῖς γράμμασιν ἐντυχὼν τῆς εὐγενείας σου· πρῶτον μέν, ὅτι ἀνδρὸς
τιμᾶν ἡμᾶς προαιρουμένου ἀφίκετό μοι προση-
γορία· καὶ γὰρ πολλοῦ μὲν[7] ἀξίαν τιθέμεθα
τῶν ἀρίστων ἀνδρῶν τὴν συντυχίαν· δεύτερον
δὲ εἰς εὐφροσύνην, τὸ μνήμης ἀγαθῆς τυγχάνειν.
σύμβολον δὲ μνήμης γράμματα, ἅπερ ἐπειδὴ

---

[1] ἀρκεσθῆναι παρακληθέντα E, Med.   [2] τε om. E.
[3] ὑπάρχει Harl.   [4] σοι om. E.
[5] τι add. E, editi antiqi.   [6] τῷ ἁγίῳ add. editi antiqi.

content with the fear which he has instilled into the insolent servants themselves and into their masters, to grant them forgiveness and put an end to the quarrel. For in this way he will obtain two things—the respect of men and the approval of God—if he will consent to mingle forbearance with the fear which he inspires. Do you, then, if you have any well-established friendship or intimacy with the man, ask this favour of him; and if you happen to know those persons in the city who are able to appease his anger, receive them as associates in this design, telling them that the doing of this thing will give me the greatest pleasure.

Send back our deacon, also, but only after he has accomplished the purpose for which he was sent. For I am ashamed, when the men in question have taken refuge with me, that the rendering of some service to them should prove beyond my powers.

LETTER LXXIII

To Callisthenes [1]

When I had read the letter of your Nobility, I gave thanks to God: first, because greetings came to me from a man who desired to honour us (for we value highly association with the best men), and secondly, because of the pleasure I received from such kind remembrance. A letter, indeed, is a token of remembrance, and when I received yours

[1] Of the same date as the preceding and on the same subject. On Callisthenes, cf. the previous letter, note 2.

---

7 μέν om. E.

ἐδεξάμην καὶ κατέμαθον τὸν ἐν αὐτοῖς νοῦν,
ἐθαύμασα ὅπως τῷ ὄντι κατὰ τὴν πάντων ὑπόληψιν πατρικὴν[1] ἀπένειμε[2] τὴν αἰδῶ. τὸ γὰρ
φλεγμαίνοντα καὶ ὠργισμένον καὶ ὁρμήσαντα
πρὸς τὴν τῶν λελυπηκότων ἄμυναν, παραλῦσαι
μὲν τὸ πολὺ τῆς σφοδρότητος, ἡμᾶς δὲ τοῦ
πράγματος κυρίους ποιήσασθαι, ἔδωκεν ἡμῖν
εὐφρανθῆναι ὡς[3] ἐπὶ τέκνῳ πνευματικῷ. ἀντὶ
οὖν τούτων τί ἄλλο λειπόμενόν ἐστιν ἢ εὔχεσθαί
σοι τὰ ἀγαθά; φίλοις μέν σε ἥδιστον εἶναι,
ἐχθροῖς δὲ φοβερόν, πᾶσι δὲ ὁμοίως αἰδέσιμον,
ἵνα καὶ οἱ τῶν προσηκόντων τι ἐλλελοιπότες,
αἴσθησιν λαβόντες τῆς ἐν σοὶ πραότητος, ἑαυτῶν
καθάψωνται, ὅτι εἰς τοιοῦτόν[4] σε ὄντα ἐξή-
μαρτον.

Ἐπειδὴ οὖν[5] προσέταξας τοὺς οἰκέτας ἐπὶ τὸν
τόπον ἐν ᾧ τὴν ἀταξίαν ἐπεδείξαντο διαχθῆναι,[6]
ἀξιῶ τὸν σκοπὸν μαθεῖν, καθ᾽ ὃν ἐπιζητεῖ τοῦτο
ἡ χρηστότης σου. εἰ μὲν γὰρ αὐτὸς παρέσῃ καὶ
αὐτὸς εἰσπράξῃ[7] τῶν τετολμημένων τὴν δίκην,
παρέσονται μὲν οἱ παῖδες. τί γὰρ ἄλλο δεῖ
γενέσθαι, εἰ τοῦτό σοι κέκριται; πλὴν ἀλλ᾽
ἡμεῖς οὐκ οἴδαμεν ποίαν ἔτι χάριν εἰληφότες
ἐσόμεθα, ἐάν περ μὴ ἐξαρκέσωμεν[8] ἐξελέσθαι
τοὺς παῖδας τῆς τιμωρίας. εἰ δὲ αὐτόν σε ἡ
ἐπὶ τῆς λεωφόρου ἀσχολία καθέξει, τίς ὁ ὑποδεχόμενος ἐκεῖ τοὺς ἀνθρώπους; τίς δὲ ὁ μέλλων
αὐτοὺς ἀντὶ σοῦ ἀμύνεσθαι; ἀλλ᾽ εἰ δοκεῖ σοι

---

[1] ἡμῖν add. E, editi antiqi.   [2] ἀπένειμες editi antiqi.
[3] ὡς om. E.   [4] τοσοῦτόν editi antiqi.
[5] δέ editi antiqi.   [6] διαδεχθῆναι E.
[7] εἰσπράξεις editi antiqi.   [8] ἐξαρκέσομεν editi antiqi.

and learned its purport, I marvelled that the respect you accorded to me was in very truth, according to the conception which all men have, that of a son to a father. For the fact that a man who is blazing with indignation and eager to take vengeance on those who have injured him, should abandon for the most part the vehemence of his emotions, and give us full authority in the matter, afforded us such cause for rejoicing as though it were in a spiritual son. In return for this, therefore, what else is left than to invoke blessings upon you—that you may be most pleasing to your friends, formidable to your enemies, and respected by all alike—in order that those who have at all failed in their duties towards you, perceiving the forbearance of your character, may blame themselves for having wronged so admirable a man as yourself?

Since, therefore, you have given orders that the slaves be taken to the place in which they exhibited their rebellious attitude, I feel that I must learn the object for which your Excellency demands this. For if you are to be there in person and in person to exact the penalty for their audacious deeds, the slaves will indeed be there (for what other course is possible, if this is your decision?), yet as for ourselves, on the other hand, we do not perceive what extra favour we shall have received if our influence does not suffice to secure for the slaves a remission of their punishment. But if you yourself shall be detained by the demands upon your time during the journey, who is to receive the men at the designated place, and who is to punish them in your stead? But if it is your wish that they be brought into your presence and this is your absolute decision, then give

ἐλθεῖν αὐτοὺς εἰς ὄψιν καὶ τοῦτο πάντως κέκριται,
μέχρι Σασίμων κέλευσον γενέσθαι αὐτῶν τὴν
παράστασιν, καὶ αὐτοῦ δεῖξον σεαυτοῦ τὸ πρᾷον
τοῦ ἤθους καὶ μεγαλόθυμον. λαβὼν γὰρ ὑπο-
χειρίους τοὺς παροξύναντας, καὶ ἐν τούτῳ τὸ
εὐκαταφρόνητον[1] τῆς σεαυτοῦ[2] ἀξίας ἐπιδειξάμενος, ἄφες αὐτοὺς ἀβλαβεῖς, ὡς ἐν τοῖς προτέροις
γράμμασι παρεκαλέσαμεν, ἡμῖν μὲν διδοὺς τὴν
χάριν, παρὰ δὲ Θεοῦ τὴν ἐφ᾽ οἷς ποιεῖς ἀντίδοσιν
ἐκδεχόμενος.

Καὶ ταῦτα λέγω, οὐχ ὡς οὕτως ὀφείλοντος
τελεσθῆναι τοῦ πράγματος, ἀλλὰ συνενδιδοὺς τῇ
ὁρμῇ σου, καὶ φοβούμενος μή τι ὑπολείπηται[3]
ἄπεπτον τοῦ θυμοῦ, καὶ ὥσπερ ἐπὶ τῶν φλεγμαι-
νόντων ὀφθαλμῶν καὶ τὰ ἁπαλώτατα τῶν βοη-
θημάτων ὀδυνηρὰ φαίνεται, οὕτω καὶ νῦν ὁ
ἡμέτερος λόγος ἐξαγριάνῃ σε μᾶλλον ἢ κατα-
στείλῃ. ἐπεὶ τὸ εὐπρεπέστατον ἦν, καὶ σοὶ
μέγιστον κόσμον ἐνεγκεῖν δυνάμενον καὶ ἐμοὶ
ἀρκοῦν πρὸς τοὺς ἐμαυτοῦ φίλους καὶ ἡλικιώτας
εἰς σεμνολόγημα, τὸ ἡμῖν ἐπιτραπῆναι τὴν
ἐκδίκησιν. πάντως δὲ εἰ καὶ ὀμώμοσται σοὶ
δοῦναι αὐτοὺς[4] εἰς[5] τιμωρίαν κατὰ τοὺς νόμους,
οὔτε ἡ παρ᾽ ἡμῶν ἐπιτίμησις ἐλάττων ἐστὶν εἰς
ἐκδίκησιν, οὔτε ὁ θεῖος νόμος ἀτιμότερος τῶν
ἐμπολιτευομένων τῷ βίῳ νομίμων.

Ἀλλ᾽ ἦν δυνατὸν αὐτούς, ἐνταῦθα ἐπιστρα-
φέντας τοῖς ἡμετέροις νομίμοις, ἐν οἷς καὶ αὐτὸς
τὴν ἐλπίδα ἔχεις τῆς σωτηρίας, καὶ σὲ τῆς ἐπὶ
τῷ ὅρκῳ ἀνάγκης ἐλευθερῶσαι, καὶ αὐτοὺς

---

[1] ἀκαταφρόνητον E. [2] σῆς editi antiqi.
[3] ὑπολίπηται E. [4] αὐτοῖς E. [5] εἰς om. E.

orders that their appearance take place no farther away than Sasima, and there show the gentleness and magnanimity of your character. For having once taken into your power those who have angered you, and having by that act clearly indicated that your dignity is not to be made the object of contempt, send them away unharmed, as we besought you in our previous letter, to us granting that favour, but at God's hands awaiting the recompense for your deeds.

I say these things, moreover, not because I think the incident ought to be closed in this way, but by way of conceding something to your impetuous spirit, and because I am afraid that some part of your anger may remain undigested, and that just as, in the case of inflammation of the eyes, even the mildest remedies seem painful, so now our words may arouse your fury instead of calming it. For the fact is that the most befitting solution—the one which is capable of bringing you the greatest credit and is sufficient to enhance the dignity of my standing with my friends and contemporaries—would have been to entrust the punishment into our hands. And certainly, even if you have bound yourself by oath to give them over to the vengeance of the laws, a stern reprimand by us is no less effective in vindicating justice, nor is God's law held in slighter honour than the civil usages which play a part in the lives of men.

Nay, it would have been possible for them to be converted here in this place through the usages of our Church, in which you yourself have your hope of salvation, and thus to set you free from the obligation of your oath, and at the same time σύμμετρον τοῖς ἡμαρτημένοις ἐκπληρῶσαι τὴν δίκην.

᾽Αλλὰ πάλιν μακρὰν ποιῶ τὴν ἐπιστολήν. ὑπὸ γὰρ τοῦ σφόδρα σπουδάζειν πιθανός σοι γενέσθαι, οὐδὲν τῶν εἰς διάνοιαν ἐρχομένων ἀποσιωπῆσαι ἀνέχομαι, φοβούμενος μὴ παρὰ τοῦτο ἄπρακτός μοι ἡ αἴτησις γένηται, ἐλλιπῶς μου τὴν διδασκαλίαν ποιησαμένου. ἀλλ᾽, ὦ τιμιώτατον καὶ γνήσιον θρέμμα τῆς ᾽Εκκλησίας, βεβαίωσον καὶ ἐμοὶ τὰς ἐλπίδας, ἃς ἔχω νῦν ἐπὶ σοὶ καὶ τὰς πάντων συμφώνως περὶ τῆς σῆς ἐμμελείας καὶ πραότητος μαρτυρίας, καὶ ἐπίστειλον τῷ στρατιώτῃ ἀπαλλαγῆναι ἡμῶν ἐν τάχει, ὃς νῦν γε οὐδὲν ἐπαχθείας οὐδὲ ὕβρεως ἐλλέλοιπε, μᾶλλον αἱρούμενός σε μὴ λυπῆσαι ἢ πάντας ἡμᾶς οἰκείους ἔχειν καὶ φίλους.

LXXIV

Μαρτινιανῷ

᾽Εμὲ τί οἴει πόσου ποτ᾽ ἂν τιμήσασθαι τὸ εἰς ταὐτὸν ποθ᾽ ἡμᾶς ἀλλήλοις ἐλθεῖν καὶ ἐπὶ

---

[1] Of the year 371, and addressed to Martinianus, a personal friend of Basil but otherwise unknown. There seems no good reason for calling Martinianus an official of Cappadocia, as Mr. B. Jackson does. On the other hand, the profusion of literary allusions in the letter, and the compliments to the knowledge of history and of mankind that Martinianus possessed, suggest that he was a philosopher or man of letters. Cf. W. M. Ramsay, Basil of Caesarea, *Expositor*, 5 Series, Vol. III (1896), 54.

The policy of the Byzantine government had been uniformly directed to subdividing the great provinces with a view to diminishing the power of the provincial governors. Cappadocia was to be thus divided in 371 by the Emperor Valens, resolved on this step probably by his enmity towards the "orthodox" bishop. In any case, this subdivision would naturally have been made sooner or later by an "orthodox" themselves to pay the penalty commensurate with their crimes.

But again I am making my letter long. For since I am exceedingly anxious to convince you, I cannot allow myself to pass over in silence any of the ideas that come into my mind, fearing lest otherwise my request may prove unsuccessful,—if I fail to furnish an adequate presentation of the case. But, most honoured and true son of the Church, confirm both the hopes which I now have in you and the unanimous testimony of all to your moderation and gentleness, and command to depart from us at once the soldier, who up to now has omitted nothing in the way of annoyance and insolence, since he chooses rather to avoid offending you than to have us all as his devoted friends.

LETTER LXXIV

To Martinianus [1]

How highly, think you, would I for my part prize the privilege of our some day meeting one

bishop, solely as a political policy ; and as a matter of fact Cappadocia was later divided into three parts by Justinian. Valens' hatred for Basil, however, was exhibited by his leaving the smaller part of Cappadocia to the metropolis, Caesarea, and making the new province of Second Cappadocia decidedly larger. Caesarea was seriously affected by this change, and shrank to less than half its former size. Basil exerted himself to the utmost in its behalf, but the three letters (the present and two following) which he wrote entreating the intercession of certain influential persons with Valens in favour of Caesarea, are among the poorest in the collection. They are inflated and exaggerated in their description of the loss that would result to Caesarea, and show no appreciation of the causes that recommend the subdivision. The true greatness of Basil, however, appeared immediately afterwards, when Valens came to Caesarea.

πλεῖον σοὶ συγγενέσθαι, ὥστε πάντων ἀπολαῦσαι
τῶν ἐν σοὶ καλῶν; καὶ γὰρ εἰ μέγα πρὸς μαρτυρίαν παιδεύσεως τὸ πολλῶν ἀνθρώπων ἰδεῖν
ἄστεα, καὶ νόον γνῶναι, τοῦτο οἶμαι δι' ὀλίγου
χαρίζεσθαι τὴν σὴν ὁμιλίαν. τί γὰρ διαφέρει
πολλοὺς ἰδεῖν κατὰ μέρος, ἢ ἕνα τὸν[1] πάντων
ὁμοῦ τὴν πεῖραν ἀναδεξάμενον; μᾶλλον δὲ ἐγὼ
καὶ πλεῖστον ἂν ἔχειν εἴποιμι τὸ διάφορον, ὅσα
ἀταλαίπωρον τὴν γνῶσιν τῶν καλῶν προξενεῖ,
καὶ καθαρὰν τῆς πρὸς τὸ χεῖρον ἐπιμιξίας συνά-
γει τὴν ἱστορίαν τῆς ἀρετῆς. εἴτε γὰρ πρᾶξις
ἀρίστη, εἴτε λόγος μνήμης ἄξιος, εἴτε πολιτείαι[2]
ἀνδρῶν ὑπερπεφυκότων τοὺς ἄλλους, πάντα τῷ
σῷ ταμιείῳ τῆς ψυχῆς ἐναπόκειται. ὥστε οὐκ
εἰς ἐνιαυτὸν μόνον, ὡς ὁ Ἀλκίνοος[3] τοῦ Ὀδυσσέως, ἀλλ' εἰς πάντα μου τὸν βίον εὐξαίμην ἂν
σου ἀκούειν, καὶ μακρὸν ἄν μοι γενέσθαι τούτου
γε ἕνεκα τοῦτον, καὶ ταῦτα δυσκόλως πρὸς αὐτὸν
διακείμενος. τί δήποτ' οὖν ἐπιστέλλω νῦν,
παρεῖναι δέον; ὅτι με[4] κάμνουσα ἡ πατρὶς
ἐπείγει πρὸς ἑαυτήν. οἷα γὰρ πέπονθεν, οὐκ
ἀγνοεῖς, ὦ ἄριστε· ὅτι Πενθέως τρόπον Μαινάδες
ὄντες τινές, δαίμονες,[5] αὐτὴν διεσπάσαντο.
διαιροῦσι γὰρ αὐτὴν καὶ ἐπιδιαιροῦσιν· ὥσπερ

[1] τῶν editi antiqi.
[2] πολιτεῖα E.
[3] Ἀλκίνους E, editi antiqi.
[4] κἀμέ E, MSS. Med.
[5] Perhaps a marginal gloss.

[1] Cf. *Odyssey*, I. 3 ff.: πολλῶν δ' ἀνθρώπων ἴδεν ἄστεα καὶ νόον
ἔγνω, | πολλὰ δ' ὅ γ' ἐν πόντῳ πάθεν ἄλγεα ὃν κατὰ θυμόν, etc.
"Many were the men whose cities he saw and whose mind
he learned, aye, and many the woes he suffered in his heart
upon the sea, seeking to win his own life and the return of

another and of having for myself a longer association with you, so as to enjoy all the noble qualities that are yours? For if it is important as a proof of education "to have seen the cities of many men and to have learned their minds,"[1] this boon is, I think, conferred in a short time by converse with you. For what superiority is there in seeing many men one by one over seeing one single person who has taken to himself the experience of all mankind? Nay, rather should I say that there is the greatest superiority in whatever provides without hardship an acquaintance with what is noble, and brings together, unsullied by any admixture of evil, the entire record of virtue. For whether it be a noble deed, or a saying worthy of remembrance, or the polities of men who have surpassed all their fellows in natural endowments, all these things are stored away in the treasure-house of your soul. Therefore not merely for a year, like Alcinous listening to Odysseus,[2] but for my whole life I should pray that I might listen to you, and that my life might be prolonged on that account at least, even though I am discontented with it. Why in the world, for instance, am I now writing, when I ought to be with you? It is because my afflicted country urges me to hurry to succour her. For you are not unaware, my good friend, of what she has suffered—that like Pentheus she has been torn asunder by veritable Maenads, demons in fact. They are dividing her, and again dividing her, just as incompetent physicians

---

his comrades." Cf. also the imitation of Horace in *De Arte Poetica*, 142: Qui mores hominum multorum vidit et urbes.

[2] Cf. *Odyssey*, Bks. 7, 8, 9.

οἱ κακοὶ τῶν ἰατρῶν, χαλεπώτερα τὰ ἕλκη
ποιοῦντες τῇ παρ' ἑαυτῶν ἀπειρίᾳ. ἐπεὶ οὖν
κέκμηκε κατατεμνομένη, λείπεται αὐτὴν θερα-
πεύειν, ὡς ἀρρωστοῦσαν. ἐπέστειλαν οὖν[1]
ἐπείγοντες ἡμᾶς οἱ πολῖται· καὶ ἀνάγκη ἀπαντᾶν,
οὐχ ὥς τι ὄφελος ἐσομένους τοῖς πράγμασιν,
ἀλλὰ τὴν ἐκ τῆς ἀπολείψεως μέμψιν ἐκκλίνοντας.
οἶσθα γάρ, ὡς εὔκολοι μὲν ἐλπίσαι οἱ ἀμηχα-
νοῦντες, εὔκολοι δέ που καὶ καταμέμψασθαι,
ἐπὶ τὸ παρεθὲν ἀεὶ τρέποντες τὰς αἰτίας.

Καίτοι ἔγωγε καὶ αὐτοῦ τούτου ἕνεκεν ἐδεόμην
σοι συνελθεῖν καὶ δοῦναι γνώμην· μᾶλλον δὲ παρακαλέσαι ἐνθυμηθῆναί τι νεανικὸν καὶ πρέπον τῷ
σεαυτοῦ φρονήματι, καὶ εἰς γόνυ κλιθεῖσαν τὴν
πατρίδα ἡμῶν μὴ περιιδεῖν, ἀλλὰ καταλαβόντα
τὸ στρατόπεδον εἰπεῖν μετὰ παρρησίας τῆς σῆς
μήτοι νομίζειν αὐτοὺς δύο κεκτῆσθαι ἀντὶ μιᾶς
ἐπαρχίας. οὐ γὰρ ἐξ ἄλλης τινὸς οἰκουμένης
ἐπεισήγαγον τὴν ἑτέραν,[2] ἀλλὰ παραπλήσιόν τι
πεποιήκασιν, ὥσπερ ἂν εἴ τις ἵππον ἢ βοῦν
κεκτημένος, εἶτα διχῇ διελὼν δύο νομίζοι ἔχειν
ἑνὸς ἄντι·[3] οὔτε γὰρ δύο ἐποίησε, καὶ τὸν ἕνα
διέφθειρεν· εἰπεῖν δὲ καὶ τοῖς παραδυναστεύουσι,
μὴ τοῦτον αὔξειν τὸν τρόπον τὴν βασιλείαν, οὐ
γὰρ ἐν ἀριθμῷ εἶναι τὴν δύναμιν, ἀλλ' ἐν τοῖς
πράγμασιν· ἐπεὶ νῦν γε ἡγούμεθα τοὺς μὲν ἀγνοίᾳ
τῆς ἀληθείας ἴσως, τοὺς δὲ τῷ μὴ βούλεσθαι

---

[1] γ' οὖν Ε.   [2] ἡμέραν Ε.   [3] ἀντὶ ἑνός Ε.

who make wounds worse because of their own in-experience. Therefore, since she has become ill under such dissection, the task remains to heal her as a patient weakened by sickness. Accordingly our fellow-citizens have written urging us to hasten to them, and we must answer the summons, not with the thought that we shall be of any help to them in their difficulties, but in order to avoid the censure that would be occasioned by our failing them. For you know how prone to hope are those who are in distress, but prone, methinks, also to find fault, ever directing their charges against what has been left undone.

And yet for this very reason I wanted to meet you and express my mind to you; or rather to beg you to devise some vigorous measure, worthy of your wisdom, and not to ignore our country when she has fallen to her knees, but going to the court to bid them with your characteristic frankness to give up the notion that they possess two provinces instead of one. For not from some other portion of the earth have they brought in the second province, but what they have done is about the same as if a man, possessing a horse or an ox, should divide it into two parts, and then consider that he had two animals instead of one he had. For he has not created two and he has destroyed the one. I wanted to urge you also to tell those in authority not to try to increase their kingdom in this fashion, for power consists, not in numbers, but in actual things. And they should be told, since we are of the opinion that they now—some perhaps through ignorance of the truth, others through their unwillingness to give offence by their words, and others still through their un-

λυπεῖν τοῖς ῥήμασι, τοὺς [1] δὲ καὶ οὐ μέλον αὐτοῖς,
περιορᾶν τὰ γινόμενα. εἰ μὲν οὖν ἦν [2] δυνατὸν
αὐτὸν ἐλθεῖν πρὸς βασιλέα, τοῦτο κράτιστον μὲν
τοῖς πράγμασι, πρέπον δέ σου τῇ καλῇ [3] τοῦ βίου
προαιρέσει. εἰ δὲ βαρὺ ἄλλως καὶ διὰ τὴν ὥραν
τοῦ ἔτους καὶ διὰ τὴν ἡλικίαν, ὡς αὐτὸς ἔφης,
σύντροφον ἔχουσαν ἐν ἑαυτῇ τὸν ὄκνον, ἀλλὰ τό
γε [4] ἐπιστεῖλαι πόνος οὐδείς. ὥστε, τὴν ἀπὸ τῶν
γραμμάτων βοήθειαν χαριζόμενος [5] τῇ πατρίδι,
πρῶτον μὲν σαυτῷ συνειδήσεις μηδὲν τῶν εἰς
δύναμιν ἡκόντων ἐλλελοιπότι, ἔπειτα μέντοι καὶ
τοῖς κάμνουσιν, αὐτῷ τῷ φαίνεσθαι συναλγῶν,
ἀρκοῦσαν δώσεις παραμυθίαν. ἀλλ' εἴθε γὰρ ἦν [6]
οἷόν τε, αὐτὸν ἐπιστάντα τοῖς πράγμασιν, ὄψει
λαβεῖν αὐτὰ τὰ σκυθρωπά. οὕτω γὰρ ἂν ἴσως,
ἀπ' αὐτῆς τῆς ἐναργείας [7] τῶν ὁρωμένων συγκι-
νηθείς, ἀφῆκάς τινα φωνὴν πρέπουσαν καὶ τῇ σῇ
μεγαλονοίᾳ καὶ τῇ κατηφείᾳ τῆς πόλεως. σὺ δὲ
ἀλλ' ἡμῖν διηγουμένοις μὴ ἀπιστήσῃς. ἢ ὅτι Σι-
μωνίδου ὄντως ἤ τινος τοιούτου μελοποιοῦ ἐδεό-
μεθα, ἐναργῶς εἰδότος ἐπιστενάζειν τοῖς πάθεσι;
καίτοι τί λέγω Σιμωνίδην; δέον Αἰσχύλον εἰπεῖν,
ἢ εἰ δή τις ἕτερος, παραπλησίως ἐκείνῳ συμφορᾶς μέγεθος ἐναργῶς διαθέμενος, μεγαλοφώνως
ὠδύρατο.

---

[1] τοῖς E.   [2] ἦν om. E.   [3] ὅλη editi antiqi.
[4] τό γε] τότε editi antiqi.   [5] χαρισάμενος editi antiqi.
[6] ἦν om. E.   [7] ἐνεργείας E.

concern for such matters—are permitting these things to happen. Now if it were possible for you to go to the Emperor himself, this would be the best thing in the circumstances, and would be in keeping with your noble course of life. But if it is difficult on general grounds and because of the season of the year and your age, which, as you yourself have said, is subject to an indwelling slothfulness, still there is no labour in writing a letter at least. Accordingly, if you do your country the service of helping her by letter, you will, in the first place, have the consciousness of not having failed her in anything within your power, and, in the second place, you will be giving, by the very fact that you show sympathy, sufficient consolation to those who are afflicted. But would that it had been possible for you to be present on the scene in person, and to see with your own eyes the melancholy sight as it is. For thus, perhaps, stirred by the very vividness of what you had seen, you would have sent forth a cry of protest befitting both your magnanimity and the sorrow of the city. Nevertheless, when we tell you the facts, do not refuse to believe us. Or is it that we had need of a Simonides [1] in very truth, or a poet of his powers, with skill to bewail in impressive language great disasters? Yet why do I say Simonides? I should have said Aeschylus,[2] or someone else who, setting forth impressively as he did a mighty disaster, with mighty voice made lamentation.

[1] Basil is probably thinking of Simonides' lament on those who died at Thermopylae.
[2] Basil probably has in mind Aeschylus' "Seven Against Thebes" and the Orestean trilogy.

Σύλλογοι μὲν γὰρ ἐκεῖνοι, καὶ λόγοι, αἱ[1] κατ᾿
ἀγορὰν συντυχίαι τῶν ἐλλογίμων ἀνδρῶν, καὶ ὅσα
πρότερον ἐποίει τὴν ἡμετέραν ὀνομαστὴν πόλιν[2]
ἡμᾶς ἐπιλελοίπασιν· ὥστε τῶν περὶ παιδείαν καὶ
λόγους ἧττον ἂν φανείη νῦν τις ἐμβαλὼν τῇ
ἀγορᾷ ἢ Ἀθήνησι πρότερον οἱ ἀτιμίαν κατεγνωσ-
μένοι, ἢ[3] τὰς χεῖρας ὄντες μὴ[4] καθαροί. ἀντει-
σῆκται δὲ τούτοις Σκυθῶν τινῶν ἢ Μασσαγετῶν
ἀμουσία· μία δὲ φωνὴ ἀπαιτούντων καὶ ἀπαιτου-
μένων καὶ ξαινομένων ταῖς μάστιξι. στοαὶ δ᾿
ἑκατέρωθεν σκυθρωπὸν ἐπηχοῦσαι[5] οἷον οἰκείαν
δοκοῦσιν ἀφιέναι φωνὴν τοῖς γινομένοις ἐπιστε-
νάζουσαι. γυμνάσια δὲ κεκλεισμένα καὶ νύκτας[6]
ἀλαμπεῖς οὐκ ἐᾷ ἡμᾶς οὐδὲν λογίζεσθαι ἡ περὶ
τοῦ[7] ζῆν ἀγωνία. κίνδυνος γὰρ οὐχ ὁ τυχών, τῶν
κρατούντων ὑφαιρεθέντων, ὥσπερ ἐρείσμασι[8] πε-
σοῦσι συγκατενεχθῆναι τὰ πάντα. καὶ τίς ἂν
λόγος τῶν κακῶν τῶν ἡμετέρων ἐφίκοιτο; οἱ μὲν
οἴχονται φεύγοντες, μέρος τῆς βουλῆς ἡμῶν, οὐ
τὸ φαυλότατον, τὴν ἀειφυγίαν Ποδανδοῦ[9] προτι-
μήσαντες. ὅταν δὲ Ποδανδὸν εἴπω, τὸν Κεάδαν
με οἴου λέγειν τὸν Λακωνικόν, ἢ εἴ που[10] τῆς
οἰκουμένης εἶδες βάραθρον αὐτοφυές, ἃ δὴ καὶ
Χαρώνειά τισι προσαγορεύειν αὐτομάτως ἐπῆλθεν,
ἀέρα νοσοποιὸν[11] ἀναπνέοντα. τοιούτῳ τινὶ ἐοικὸς

---

[1] τε add. E. [2] πάλαι E, editi antiqi.
[3] ἢ] οἱ (καὶ ante οἱ in marg. m recen.) E. [4] οὐ E.
[5] ἀπηχοῦσαι Med. [6] νύκτες editi antiqi.
[7] τό editi antiqi. [8] ἐρείσματι E. [9] Προδανδοῦ E.
[10] εἴ που] ὅπου E. [11] φθοροποιόν editi antiqi.

---

[1] Modern Podando, in southern Cappadocia. Established
by Valens as the capital of the new division of the province.

For the gatherings of old, the orations, the conversations of learned men in the market-place, and all that formerly made our city famous, have left us; in consequence there is now less likelihood of a learned or eloquent man's entering our Forum than that in former days at Athens men would appear in public who had been convicted of dishonour or were impure of hand. Instead of such men the unrefinement of Scythians or Massagete tribes has come in; we hear but one sound—the voices of men dunning and being dunned, of men lacerated with whips. The porticoes resounding on either side with melancholy echoes seem, as it were, to give forth a voice of their own as they lament over what is being done. As for our closed gymnasia and lampless nights, we cannot take thought of them at all because of our struggle to keep alive. For the danger is not slight that, since those in authority have been removed, the whole edifice will collapse, as it were, together with the falling of its props. What words, indeed, could match our misfortunes? Some have gone into exile, a part of our Council, and that not the most ignoble, preferring exile for life to Podandus.[1] But when I say Podandus, imagine that I say Laconian Ceades,[2] or any other pit made by nature which you may have seen anywhere in the world, such places as men have been led to designate instinctively as Charonian, since they exhale a deadly vapour. Like some such place as these I would have you consider this accursed

---

[2] The name given by the Spartans to the pit into which condemned criminals were thrown; cf. Pausanias, 4, 18, 4; Thucydides, 1, 134; Strabo, 8, 367.

νόμισον καὶ τὸ Ποδανδοῦ κακόν· τριῶν τοίνυν μοι-
ρῶν, οἱ μὲν φεύγουσιν αὐταῖς γυναιξὶ καὶ ἑστίαις
ἀναστάντες· οἱ δὲ ἀπάγονται ὥσπερ αἰχμάλω-
τοι, οἱ πλεῖστοι τῶν ἐν τῇ πόλει ἄριστοι, ἐλεεινὸν
φίλοις θέαμα, ἐχθροῖς δὲ εὐχὴν ἐκπληροῦντες, εἰ
δή τις γέγονεν ὅλως τοσοῦτον ἡμῖν ἐπαρασάμενος.
τριτάτη δέ που μοῖρα λέλειπται· οὗτοι δέ, τήν τε
ἀπόλειψιν τῶν συνήθων[1] οὐ φέροντες, καὶ ἅμα
τῆς χρείας ἀτονώτεροι[2] ἀπελεγχόμενοι, πρὸς
αὐτὸ τὸ ζῆν ἀπειρήκασι.

Ταῦτά σε φανερὰ ποιῆσαι πᾶσι παρακαλοῦμεν
τῇ σεαυτοῦ φωνῇ καὶ τῇ σεαυτοῦ παρρησίᾳ τῇ
δικαίᾳ, ἣν ἔχεις ἀπὸ τοῦ βίου, ἐκεῖνο σαφῶς
προειπόντα, ὅτι, ἐὰν μὴ ταχὺ μεταβουλεύσωνται,
οὐδ᾽ ἕξουσιν εἰς οὓς τὴν φιλανθρωπίαν ἐνδείξονται.[3]
ἢ γὰρ γενήσῃ τι ὄφελος τοῖς κοινοῖς, ἢ τό γε τοῦ
Σόλωνος πεποιηκὼς ἔσῃ, ὃς τοῖς ἀπολειφθεῖσι τῶν
πολιτῶν ἀμύνειν[4] οὐκ ἔχων, τῆς ἀκροπόλεως ἤδη
κατεχομένης, τὰ ὅπλα ἐνδὺς πρὸ τῶν θυρῶν[5]
ἐκαθέζετο, εὔδηλος ὢν τῷ σχήματι τοῖς γινομένοις
οὐ συντιθέμενος. ἐκεῖνο δ᾽ ἀκριβῶς οἶδα, ὅτι, καὶ
εἴ τίς σου νῦν τὴν γνώμην μὴ ἀποδέχοιτο, μικρὸν
ὕστερόν σοι[6] εὐνοίας τε ὁμοῦ καὶ συνέσεως τὴν
μεγίστην[7] δόξαν προσθήσει ὅταν ἴδῃ τὰ πράγματα κατὰ τὴν πρόρρησιν ἀπαντήσαντα.

---

[1] συνοίκων Med. Harl.   [2] ἀπονώτερον E.
[3] ἐνδείξωνται editi antiqi.
[4] τῆς ἐλευθερίας add. editi antiqi.
[5] πυλῶν E.   [6] σοι om. E, editi antiqi.
[7] μεγάλην E.

Podandus. Well then, of the three sections of our city, some are going into exile, departing with their wives and hearths; some are being led away as captives, the majority of the best citizens of the state, a miserable spectacle to their friends, but thus fulfilling their enemies' prayers, if indeed any enemy that ever lived has called down so terrible a curse upon us. About a third part of the citizens is still left here ; and these, because they cannot endure the separation from their old acquaintances, and being at the same time too weak to cope with the necessities of their situation, despair of life itself.

We exhort you to make these circumstances known to all with that voice of yours and with that righteous boldness of speech which your condition of life confers upon you, proclaiming this fact clearly—that unless they quickly change their policies, they will not have any to whom they may show their benevolence. For you will either be of some assistance to the commonweal, or you will do as Solon[1] did, who, being unable, when the Acropolis already had been captured, to protect his fellow-citizens who were left behind, put on his armour and sat before the gates, making it clear by his attitude that he was not a party to the things being done. Moreover, I am absolutely certain of this, that, even though there may be one who will not now accept your decision in the matter, yet in a short time he will assign to you the greatest renown for both benevolence and wisdom, when he sees events turning out in accordance with your predictions.

---

[1] This story is related in Plutarch, *Solon*, 30, and Diogenes Laertius, 1, 49.

LXXV

Ἀβουργίῳ [1]

Πολλῶν ὄντων ἃ τὸ σὸν ἦθος ὑπὲρ τοὺς ἄλλους εἶναι πεποίηκεν, οὐδὲν οὕτως ἴδιόν ἐστι σὸν ὡς ἡ περὶ τὴν πατρίδα σπουδή, δικαίας αὐτῇ ἀποδιδόντος σου τὰς ἀμοιβάς, ἐξ ἧς ὁρμηθεὶς τοσοῦτος ἐγένου, ὥστε διὰ πάσης τῆς οἰκουμένης γνώριμον εἶναί σου τὴν περιφάνειαν. αὕτη τοίνυν ἡ πατρίς, ἡ σὲ ἐνεγκοῦσα καὶ θρεψαμένη, εἰς τὴν τῶν παλαιῶν διηγημάτων ἀπιστίαν περιελήλυθε· [2] καὶ οὐκ ἄν τις ἐπιστὰς ἡμῶν τῇ πόλει, οὐδὲ τῶν πάνυ συνήθων, αὐτὴν [3] γνωρίσειεν· οὕτως εἰς πᾶσαν ἐρημίαν ἀθρόως μετεσκεύασται, πολλῶν μὲν καὶ πρότερον αὐτῆς [4] ἀφαιρεθέντων τῶν [5] πολιτευομένων, νῦν δὲ σχεδὸν ἁπάντων εἰς τὴν Ποδανδὸν μετοικισθέντων. ὧν ἀκρωτηριασθέντες οἱ λειπόμενοι καὶ αὐτοὶ εἰς πᾶσαν ἀπόγνωσιν μεταπεπτώκασι, [6] καὶ πᾶσι τοσοῦτον ἐνεποίησαν [7] τῆς ἀθυμίας τὸν ὄγκον, ὥστε σπανίζειν λοιπὸν καὶ τῶν οἰκητόρων τὴν πόλιν, καὶ γεγενῆσθαι [8] τὰ τῇδε ἐρημίαν δεινήν, ἐλεεινὸν μὲν φίλοις θέαμα, πολλὴν δὲ χαρὰν καὶ εὐθυμίαν φέρον τοῖς πάλαι ἐφεδρεύουσιν ἡμῶν τῷ πτώματι. τίνος οὖν ἐστὶ χεῖρα ἡμῖν ὀρέξαι; ἢ τίνος συμπαθὲς [9] ἐφ' ἡμῖν ἀφεῖναι δάκρυον, ἀλλ' οὐχὶ τῆς σῆς ἡμερότητος,

---

[1] Ἀβουρτίῳ editi antiqi. [2] ἐλήλυθε tres MSS.
[3] αὐτῇ E, Med. [4] αὐτῆς om. E. [5] τῶν om. E.
[6] καταπεπτώκασι editi antiqi. [7] ἐνεποίησε E.
[8] γενέσθαι E. [9] συμπαθεῖς E, editi antiqi.

---

[1] Written at about the same time as the preceding letter;

LETTER LXXV

To Aburgius[1]

WHILE there are many qualities which have made your character superior to that of others, yet there is no trait so peculiarly your own as your zeal for your homeland, seeing that you render a just recompense to her from whom you were sprung and have reached so high an estate that your fame is known throughout the whole world. But now this very homeland herself, which bore and reared you, has reverted to the incredible condition of early legend; and no one of us, on revisiting the city, even one who had known her well, would recognize her, so completely has she been suddenly transformed into an utter solitude, since many of her citizens were even before this taken from her, and now almost all of them have emigrated to Podandus.[2] Mutilated by the loss of these, the remnants have themselves fallen into utter despair, and have produced in all the rest such an extreme measure of despondency, that the city now suffers a shortage even of inhabitants, and this district has become a terrible solitude, a spectacle inspiring pity in our friends, but affording great joy and satisfaction to those who have long waited for our fall. Whose privilege, therefore, is it to reach out a hand to us, whose is it to shed a tear of sympathy over us, if not your Clemency's, since you

---

another appeal to save Cappadocia from being divided into two provinces. Cf Letter LXXIV, note 1. Letters XXXIII, CXLVII, CLXXVIII. CXCVI, and CCCIV are also addressed to Aburgius, an important layman, friend and compatriot of Basil.

[2] See previous letter, note 3.

ὃς καὶ ἀλλοτρίᾳ συμπαθοῖς πόλει τοιαῦτα καμ-
νούσῃ, μὴ ὅτι γε τῇ σε παραγαγούσῃ εἰς τὸν βίον ;
εἴ τις οὖν δύναμις, ταύτην νῦν ἐπὶ τῆς παρούσης
χρείας ἡμῖν ἐπίδειξαι.[1] πάντως δὲ μεγάλην ἔχεις
τὴν παρὰ τοῦ Θεοῦ ῥοπήν, ὃς ἐπ' οὐδενὸς καιροῦ
καταλέλοιπέ σε, καὶ πολλὰς ἔδωκέ σοι τῆς παρ'
ἑαυτοῦ[2] εὐμενείας τὰς ἀποδείξεις· μόνον ἐὰν
θελήσῃς ὅλως διαναστῆναι πρὸς τὴν ἐπιμέλειαν
ἡμῶν, καὶ τῇ προσούσῃ σοι δυνάμει χρήσασθαι
εἰς τὴν ὑπὲρ τῶν πολιτῶν βοήθειαν.

LXXVI

Σωφρονίῳ μαγίστρῳ

Τὸ μὲν μέγεθος τῶν καταλαβουσῶν συμφορῶν
τὴν πατρίδα ἡμῶν αὐτὸν ἐμὲ ἠνάγκαζε,[3] καταλαβόντα τὸ στρατόπεδον, τῇ τε σῇ μεγαλοφυΐᾳ
διηγήσασθαι τὴν κατέχουσαν ἡμῶν τὴν πόλιν
κατήφειαν, καὶ τοῖς λοιποῖς ὅσοι ἐπὶ μεγίστης
ἐστὲ δυνάμεως τῶν πραγμάτων. ἐπειδὴ δὲ ἥ τε
τοῦ σώματος ἀρρωστία καὶ ἡ τῶν ἐκκλησιῶν
ἐπιμέλεια κατέχει με, τέως διὰ γράμματος ἀποδύρασθαι πρὸς τὴν σὴν μεγαλόνοιαν ἐπείχθην,
γνωρίζων, ὅτι οὔτε σκάφος ἐν πελάγει πνεύμασι
βιαίοις καταβαπτισθὲν οὕτως ἀθρόως ἠφανίσθη
ποτέ, οὐ σεισμοῖς ἐκτριβεῖσα πόλις, οὐχ ὕδασιν
ἐπικλυσθεῖσα, εἰς ἀθρόον[4] ἀφανισμὸν ἐχώρησεν
οὕτως, ὡς ἡ ἡμετέρα τῇ καινῇ ταύτῃ τῶν πραγ-

---

[1] ἐπίδειξε E.   [2] αὐτοῦ editi antiqi.
[3] ἄν add. editi antiqi.
[4] εἰς ἀθρόον . . . παντελῆ] εἰς ἀπώλειαν ἐχώρησε παντελῶς
οὕτως ὡς ἡ ἡμετέρα . . . εἰς ἀθρόον ἦλθεν ἀφανισμόν editi antiqi.

would sympathize even with a foreign city labouring under such misfortune, to say nothing of the city that brought you into life? If, therefore, you have any power to act, show it to us now in our present need. But assuredly you do possess great strength from God, who in no time of need has abandoned you, and who has given you many proofs of His goodwill—but only if you consent whole-heartedly to rise up and take us under your care, and to exercise the power which has come to you for the assistance of your fellow-citizens.

LETTER LXXVI

To Sophronius, the Master [1]

THE magnitude of the misfortunes which have fallen upon our country was constraining me to go to court and in person to describe the miseries which now afflict our city, not only to your noble self, but likewise to all others who, like you, are in positions of greatest influence in the state. But since both bodily ill-health and my solicitude for the churches detains me, I have been compelled meanwhile to pour out to your Magnanimity by letter my bitter lamentations, making known to you that no boat submerged on the high seas by violent winds has ever disappeared so quickly, no city destroyed by earthquakes or buried by floods of water has met with such sudden effacement from the earth, as our own, swallowed up by this new administration of our

---

[1] Of about the same date as the preceding, and on the same general topic. For Sophronius, *magister officiorum*, cf. Letter XXXII, note 1. Cf. also Letters XLVI, CLXXVII, CLXXX, CXCIII, CCLXXII.

μάτων οἰκονομίᾳ καταποθεῖσα εἰς ἀπώλειαν
ἐχώρησε παντελῆ. καὶ μῦθος γέγονε τὰ ἡμέτερα.
οἴχεται μὲν γὰρ τὸ πολίτευμα· πᾶν δὲ τὸ
πολιτικὸν [1] σύνταγμα, τῇ περὶ τοὺς κρατοῦντας
ἀθυμίᾳ καταλιπὸν [2] τὴν ἐν τῇ πόλει οἴκησιν, διὰ
τῆς ἀγροικίας πλανᾶται. ἐπιλέλοιπε δὲ λοιπὸν
καὶ ἡ τῶν ἀναγκαίων διάθεσις, καὶ ὅλως ἀωρότα-
τον θέαμα γεγένηται ἡ πρότερον ἀνδράσι τε
λογίοις ἐπαγαλλομένη καὶ τοῖς λοιποῖς, οἷς
εὐθηνοῦνται πόλεις ἀνενδεῶς διάγουσαι.

Μίαν δὲ ἐνομίσαμεν ὡς ἐν δεινοῖς παραμυθίαν
εἶναι, τὸ ἐπιστενάξαι τοῖς πάθεσιν ἡμῶν πρὸς τὴν
σὴν ἡμερότητα, καὶ παρακαλέσαι, εἴ τις δύναμις,
χεῖρα ὀρέξαι τῇ πόλει ἡμῶν εἰς γόνυ κλιθείσῃ.
τὸν δὲ τρόπον δι' οὗ ἂν γένοιο ἐν καιρῷ [3] τοῖς
πράγμασιν, αὐτὸς μὲν εἰσηγεῖσθαι οὐκ ἔχω, σοὶ
δὲ πάντως καὶ εὑρεῖν διὰ τὴν σύνεσιν ῥάδιον, καὶ
χρήσασθαι [4] τοῖς εὑρεθεῖσι, διὰ τὴν παρὰ Θεοῦ
σοι δεδομένην δύναμιν, οὐ χαλεπόν.

LXXVII

Ανεπίγραφος περὶ Θηρασίου

Ἒν καὶ τοῦτο τῆς ἀγαθῆς ἀρχῆς τοῦ μεγάλου
ἀπηλαύσαμεν Θηρασίου, τῆς σῆς λογιότητος τὴν

---

[1] πολιτῶν Vat.
[2] καταλιπόντες E, Harl., Reg. secundus, Clarom.
[3] σωτήρ add. editi antiqi.   [4] χρῆσθαι editi antiqi.

---

[1] Written at about the same time as the preceding, perhaps to the Elpidius mentioned in the following letter. The

affairs, has gone to utter destruction. And all that was ours has become no more than a legend. For gone is our government; and the whole body politic, having abandoned its domicile in the city through despondency over the fate of its magistrates, is wandering aimlessly through the countryside. Aye, even the marketing of the necessities of life has now ceased, and the city, which formerly was wont to glory both in its men of learning and in all else in which cities abound which enjoy freedom from fear, has become altogether a most unlovely spectacle.

Our sole consolation, considering the terrible plight we are in, has seemed to be to bewail our sufferings to your Clemency, and to urge you, if you have influence, to stretch a hand to our city now fallen to her knees. As to the means by which you may opportunely intervene in the situation, I cannot myself suggest them to you, but you by means of your sagacity can assuredly discover them readily and, once discovered, employ them without difficulty, through the influence which God has given you.

LETTER LXXVII

Without Address, about Therasius [1]

This one advantage we enjoyed from the good administration of the great Therasius—the visits

Therasius mentioned here appears to have been a governor of Cappadocia, who was removed from his office after a brief tenure of it, as the result of calumnious charges brought against him by certain corrupt persons to whom his excellent administration had caused annoyance. Therasius may be the governor in whose behalf Basil wrote to Sophronius, the prefect of Constantinople, in 372. Cf. Letter XCVI.

ἐπιδημίαν συνεχῶς ἡμῖν γινομένην. τὸ αὐτὸ δὲ
τοῦτο ἐζημιώθημεν στερηθέντες τοῦ ἄρχοντος.
ἀλλ᾽ ἐπειδὴ τὰ ἄπαξ ἡμῖν παρὰ τοῦ Θεοῦ
χαρισθέντα μένει βέβαια καὶ ταῖς ψυχαῖς
ἀλλήλων ἐνοικούμενα διὰ τῆς μνήμης, εἰ καὶ τοῖς
σώμασι διωρίσμεθα, γράφωμεν γοῦν συνεχῶς καὶ
φθεγγώμεθα [1] πρὸς ἀλλήλους τὰ ἀναγκαῖα, καὶ
μάλιστα νῦν, ὅτε ὁ χειμὼν τὴν ὀλιγοχρόνιον
ταύτην ἐκεχειρίαν ἐσπείσατο.

Ἐλπίζομεν δὲ μὴ ἀπολείψεσθαί σε τοῦ θαυμασιωτάτου ἀνδρὸς Θηρασίου, πρέπον εἶναι
κρίναντα κοινωνεῖν τῷ ἀνδρὶ τοιούτων φροντίδων,
ἤ γ᾽ οὐ μὲν οὖν [2] καὶ μάτην πρόφασιν ἀσμενίζοντα
παρέχουσάν σοι [3] ἰδεῖν τε τοὺς φίλους, καὶ παρ᾽
αὐτῶν θεαθῆναι. πολλὰ δὲ ἔχων εἰπεῖν καὶ περὶ
πολλῶν, εἰς τὴν συντυχίαν ὑπερεθέμην, οὐκ
ἀσφαλὲς εἶναι ἡγούμενος ἐπιστολαῖς τὰ τοιαῦτα
καταπιστεύειν.

LXXVIII

Ἀνεπίγραφος ὑπὲρ Ἐλπιδίου

Οὐκ ἔλαθεν ἡμᾶς ἡ ἀγαθή σου σπουδὴ περὶ τὸν
αἰδεσιμώτατον ἑταῖρον ἡμῶν Ἐλπίδιον, ὅπως τῇ
συνήθει σεαυτοῦ συνέσει ἔδωκας καιρὸν φιλανθρωπίας τῷ ἄρχοντι. ταύτην οὖν τὴν χάριν νῦν σε
τελειῶσαι παρακαλοῦμεν [4] διὰ τοῦ γράμματος,

---

[1] φθεγγόμεθα E.
[2] ἤ γ᾽ οὐ μὲν οὖν Capps, οὐ μὲν οὖν ed. Ben., ἡγούμενον omnes MSS. et editi.
[3] σε E, Reg. secundus, Clarom.
[4] παρακαλῶ μέν editi antiqi.

which your Excellence used continually to make to us. But we have been robbed of even this, now that we have been deprived of our governor. However, since favours we have once received from God abide steadfast and dwell through memory in the souls of both of us, even though we have been separated in body, let us at least write frequently and tell each other of our necessities, and particularly at this time when the storm has consented to this very brief period of truce.

We hope, however, that you will not forsake that most admirable man, Therasius, deeming it proper to share with him matters of such concern, or rather not without purpose availing yourself of an excuse which provides you an opportunity to see your friends and to be seen by them. However, though I have much to say on various topics, I have put them off until our meeting, not judging it safe to entrust such matters to letters.

LETTER LXXVIII

Without Address, in behalf of Elpidius[1]

We have not failed to notice your kind interest in our most venerable friend Elpidius, how in accordance with your usual sagacity you have given the prefect an occasion for exercising his benevolence. Therefore, we now urge you by this letter to complete this favour and to remind the Prefect to place over

---

[1] Of the same date as the preceding. It is difficult to identify this Elpidius. The cause of Basil's uneasiness seems to be the general situation spoken of in the several letters above.

καὶ ὑπομνῆσαι τὸν ἄρχοντα οἰκείῳ προστάγματι
ἐπὶ τῆς πατρίδος ἡμῶν καταστῆναι τὸν ἄνδρα
πᾶσαν σχεδὸν τὴν φροντίδα τῶν δημοσίων
ἐξηρτημένον. ὥστε πολλὰς ἕξεις καὶ εὐπροσώ-
πους ὑποβάλλειν προφάσεις τῷ ἄρχοντι, ἐξ ὧν
ἀναγκαίως ἐπιμένειν αὐτὸν τῇ πατρίδι ἡμῶν
προστάξει. οἷα δὲ τὰ ἐνταῦθα, καὶ ὅσου ἄξιος
τοῖς πράγμασιν ὁ ἀνήρ, πάντως οὐδὲν δεήσῃ παρ'
ἡμῶν διδαχθῆναι, αὐτὸς τῇ ἑαυτοῦ συνέσει
ἀκριβῶς ἐπιστάμενος.

LXXIX

Εὐσταθίῳ,[1] ἐπισκόπῳ Σεβαστείας

Καὶ πρὸ τοῦ δέχεσθαι τὰ γράμματα, ᾔδειν τὸν
πόνον ὃν ἔχεις ὑπὲρ πάσης ψυχῆς, ἐξαιρέτως δὲ
ὑπὲρ τῆς ἡμετέρας ταπεινώσεως, διὰ τὸ προβε-
βλῆσθαι ἐν τῷ ἀγῶνι τούτῳ· καὶ δεξάμενος[2]
παρὰ τοῦ αἰδεσιμωτάτου Ἐλευσινίου τὰ γράμ-

---

[1] Εὐσταθίῳ tantum habent E et Harl.
[2] δέ add. E, editi antiqi.

---

[1] Written in the year 371. Eustathius was bishop of
Sebaste or Sebasteia (modern Sivas), a town of the Pontus on
the northern bank of the Halys and capital of Armenia Minor
(c. A.D. 357–380). By his frequent changes of opinion,
Eustathius naturally lost the confidence of the rival schools
of theology, and was regarded with suspicion by all. However, he secured and for many years retained the affection
and respect of St. Basil.

On Basil's elevation to the episcopate in A.D. 370,
Eustathius showed the greatest joy, and expressed an
earnest desire to aid his friend in his new and responsible
office. The present letter exhibits the same kindly feeling
between the two bishops. On the plea that Basil would have

our country by an appropriate order the man who has dependent upon him nearly the whole care of its public affairs. Consequently you will be able to submit many fair-seeming reasons to the Prefect, which will of necessity induce him to order this man to remain in charge of our country. But what the situation is there, and how valuable the man is in the circumstances, you will certainly not need to be informed by us, since of your own sagacity you have accurate knowledge thereof.

LETTER LXXIX

To Eustathius, Bishop of Sebaste [1]

Even before receiving your letter, I was fully aware of the toil which you undergo for every soul, and especially for our own Humility,[2] because you must bear the brunt in this conflict; and when I received the letter from the most reverend Eleusinius,[3] and saw his very presence before me, I

need of fellow-helpers and counsellors, Eustathius recommended certain persons to his notice, who, as Basil later bitterly complained (Letter CCIII, 3), turned out to be spies of his actions and watchers of his words, interpreting all in a malevolent sense, and reporting his supposed heretical leanings to their chief. From the moment that Basil made this discovery until his death a bitter struggle was waged between the two. Basil was harassed continually until he died in A.D. 379, Eustathius himself dying soon after. Strangely enough, Peter, St. Basil's brother, succeeded Eustathius on the episcopal throne of Sebaste.

[2] A common title in Byzantine times.

[3] Known only from this letter. He was sent with the present letter, apparently to warn Basil of the approach of the Emperor Valens, and to express the apprehension he felt for the safety of Catholics, and especially for Basil himself.

ματα, καὶ αὐτὴν αὐτοῦ τὴν παρουσίαν θεασάμενος,
ἐδόξασα τὸ θεῖον¹ τὸ τοιοῦτον παραστάτην καὶ
συνασπιστὴν διὰ τῆς πνευματικῆς βοηθείας ἐν
τοῖς ὑπὲρ εὐσεβείας ἀγῶσι χαρισάμενον ἡμῖν.
γινωσκέτω δὲ ἡ ἀνυπέρβλητός σου θεοσέβεια
μέχρι νῦν προσβολὰς μέν τινας παρὰ τῶν
μεγάλων ἀρχόντων ἡμῖν γεγενῆσθαι, καὶ ταύτας
σφοδράς, τοῦ τε ἐπάρχου καὶ τοῦ περὶ τὸν κοιτῶνα
διαλεχθέντων ἰδιοπαθῶς² ὑπὲρ τῶν ἐναντίων·
τέως δὲ ἀτρέπτως ἡμᾶς πᾶσαν προσβολὴν ὑπο-
μεῖναι τῷ ἐλέει τοῦ Θεοῦ, τῷ χαριζομένῳ³ ἡμῖν
τὴν συνεργίαν τοῦ Πνεύματος καὶ ἐνδυναμώσαντι⁴
ἡμῶν δι' αὐτοῦ τὴν ἀσθένειαν.

LXXX

Ἀθανασίῳ, ἐπισκόπῳ Ἀλεξανδρείας

Ὅσον τῶν ἐκκλησιῶν τὰ ἀρρωστήματα ἐπὶ
τὸ μεῖζον πρόεισι, τοσοῦτον πάντες ἐπὶ τὴν σὴν
ἐπιστρεφόμεθα τελειότητα, μίαν ἑαυτοῖς ὑπολεί-
πεσθαι τῶν δεινῶν παραμυθίαν τὴν σὴν προστασίαν πεπιστευκότες· ὃς⁵ καὶ τῇ δυνάμει τῶν
προσευχῶν καὶ τῷ⁶ εἰδέναι τὰ βέλτιστα⁷ τοῖς
πράγμασιν ὑποτίθεσθαι, διασώσασθαι ἡμᾶς ἐκ

---

¹ τὸ θεῖον Capps (on account of the following τό), τὸν Θεόν
MSS. et editi.
² καί add. E.
³ τοῦ χαριζομένου Coisl. secundus, Reg. secundus.
⁴ ἐνδυναμώσαντος Coisl. secundus, Reg. secundus.
⁵ ὡς E, Med.   ⁶ τῷ] τό E.   ⁷ καὶ τό add. E.

---

¹ A title commonly applied to bishops in Byzantine
times.

glorified God, who, through His spiritual help, has blessed us with such an assistant and comrade-in-arms in our battles for the Faith. Let your unsurpassed Godliness[1] rest assured that up to the present time some attacks, and these violent ones, have been made upon us by high dignitaries, since both the Prefect[2] and the High Chamberlain[3] have spoken from peculiarly personal motives in favour of our enemies; but so far we have fearlessly sustained every attack through God's mercy, which is blessing us with the assistance of the Spirit, and through Him has strengthened our weakness.

LETTER LXXX

To Athanasius, Bishop of Alexandria[4]

The more serious the maladies of the churches become, the more we all turn to your Perfection, firmly convinced that the sole consolation left to us in our misfortunes is your patronage; for you, through the efficacy of your prayers and through your knowing how to offer the best suggestions in difficulties, are believed by all alike, who are even

---

[2] The *Praefectus Praetorio*. During the later Empire, *i.e.* after Diocletian, the *praefecti praetorio* lost their military power with the suppression of the Praetorian Guards by Constantine. Four prefects continued to be created, who governed the same provinces as before. Their sphere was essentially civil at this time, *i.e.* supreme administration of justice and the finances.

[3] In the charge of the private apartments of the Imperial palace was placed a favourite eunuch, who was styled *praepositus*, or *praepositus sacri cubiculi*, Prefect of the Sacred Bed-chamber.

[4] Written in 371. Cf. Letter LXI, note 1.

τοῦ φοβεροῦ τούτου χειμῶνος παρὰ πάντων
ὁμοίως τῶν καὶ κατὰ μικρὸν ἢ ἀκοῇ ἢ πείρᾳ
γνωριζόντων τὴν τελειότητα σοῦ πιστεύῃ.¹ διὸ
μὴ ἀνῇς καὶ προσευχόμενος ὑπὲρ τῶν ψυχῶν
ἡμῶν καὶ διεγείρων ἡμᾶς τοῖς γράμμασιν· ὧν εἰ
ᾔδεις ὁπόσον ἐστὶ τὸ ὠφέλιμον, οὐκ ἄν ποτε
παραπεσοῦσάν σοι γραμμάτων ἀφορμὴν πρὸς
ἡμᾶς ὑπερέβης. εἰ δὲ καταξιωθείημεν τῇ συνεργίᾳ
τῶν προσευχῶν τοῦ ἰδεῖν σε καὶ ἀπολαῦσαι τῶν
ἐν σοὶ ἀγαθῶν, καὶ προσθεῖναι τῇ ἱστορίᾳ τοῦ
ἡμετέρου βίου τὴν συντυχίαν τῆς μεγάλης σου
ὄντως καὶ ἀποστολικῆς ψυχῆς, πάντως ἂν ἑαυτοῖς²
ἐλογισάμεθα, ὧν ἐθλίβημεν³ ἐν πάσῃ τῇ ζωῇ
ἡμῶν, ἀντίρροπον παρὰ τῆς τοῦ Θεοῦ φιλανθρωπίας ἐσχηκέναι παραμυθίαν.

LXXXI

Ἰννοκεντίῳ ἐπισκόπῳ⁴

Ὅσον εὐθύμησα δεξάμενος γράμματα τῆς ἀγάπης σου, τοσοῦτον ἐλυπήθην, ὅτι βάρος ἐπέθηκας
ἡμῖν φροντίδος τῆς ὑπερβαινούσης ἡμᾶς. πῶς γὰρ
δυνηθῶμεν ἀπὸ τοσούτου διαστήματος τοσαύτης
ἡμεῖς οἰκονομίας περιγενέσθαι; ἕως μὲν γὰρ
ὑμᾶς ἔχει ἡ Ἐκκλησία, ὡς ἰδίοις στηρίγμασιν
ἐπαναπαύεται, ἐὰν δέ τι περὶ τῆς ὑμετέρας ζωῆς
ὁ Κύριος οἰκονομήσῃ, τίνας δύναμαι⁵ ὁμοτίμους

---

¹ πιστεύειν E.   ² αὐτοῖς editi antiqi.
³ ἐθλίβομαι editi antiqi.   ⁴ Ῥώμης add. absurde Clarom.
⁵ δύναται E.

---

¹ Of the year 372. According to the supposition of

90

slightly acquainted with your Perfection either by hearsay or by personal experience, to have saved us from the present fearful tempest. Therefore do not cease praying for our souls and arousing us by your letters; for if you had known how helpful these latter were, you would never have let pass any opportunity that was offered to you of writing to us. And if, through the co-operation of your prayers, we should be accounted worthy of seeing you, of enjoying the noble qualities that exist in you, and of adding to the experiences of our life a meeting with your truly great and apostolic soul, we should assuredly consider that we had received from the benevolence of God a consolation counter-balancing the afflictions which we have endured during our whole lifetime.

LETTER LXXXI

To Bishop Innocent [1]

Much as I rejoiced on receiving a letter from your Affection,[2] even so I was troubled, because you have put upon us a burden of care which surpasses our strength. For how shall we be able, at so great a distance, to prove equal to so important an administration? For although, so long as the Church has you, it rests, as it were, upon its own foundations, yet if the Lord make some dispensation regarding

Wittig, this letter belongs to St. John Chrysostom and is addressed to Pope Innocent I. Cf. his "Studien zur Geschichte des Papstes Innocenz I," in *Theologische Quartalschrift*, 84, 1902.

[2] " Your Affection " (ἀγάπη) was frequently used as a title at this time.

ἐντεῦθεν ὑμῖν εἰς τὴν ἐπιμέλειαν τῶν ἀδελφῶν
ἐκπέμπειν; ὅπερ σὺ ἐπεζήτησας διὰ τῶν γραμμάτων, καλῶς ποιῶν καὶ ἐμφρόνως, βουλόμενος ζῶν
ἰδεῖν τὸν μετὰ σὲ μέλλοντα κυβερνᾶν τὸ ἐκλεκτὸν
ποίμνιον τοῦ Κυρίου· ὃ καὶ ὁ μακάριος Μωϋσῆς
καὶ ἐπεθύμησε καὶ εἶδεν· ἐπεὶ οὖν καὶ ὁ τόπος
μέγας καὶ περιβόητος, καὶ τὸ σὸν ἔργον παρὰ
πολλοῖς ὀνομαστόν, καὶ οἱ καιροὶ χαλεποί, μεγάλου
χρείαν ἔχοντες κυβερνήτου διὰ τὰς συνεχεῖς ζάλας
καὶ τοὺς ἐπανισταμένους κλύδωνας τῇ Ἐκκλησίᾳ,
οὐκ ἐνόμισα ἀσφαλὲς εἶναι τῇ ἐμῇ ψυχῇ ἀφωσιω-
μένως τῷ πράγματι χρήσασθαι, μάλιστα μεμνημένος ὧν ἔγραψας, ὅτι μέλλεις ἐπὶ τοῦ Κυρίου
ἀντικαθίστασθαί μοι, δικαζόμενος πρός με ὑπὲρ
τῆς ἀμελείας τῶν ἐκκλησιῶν.

Ἵνα οὖν μὴ εἰσέλθω εἰς κρίσιν μετὰ σοῦ, ἀλλὰ
μᾶλλον κοινωνόν σε εὕρω[1] τῆς ἀπολογίας μου
τῆς ἐπὶ τοῦ Χριστοῦ, περιβλεψάμενος ἐν τῷ
συνεδρίῳ τοῦ πρεσβυτερίου τοῦ κατὰ τὴν πόλιν,
ἐξελεξάμην τὸ τιμιώτατον[2] σκεῦος, τὸν ἔκγονον
τοῦ μακαρίου Ἑρμογένους, τοῦ τὴν μεγάλην καὶ
ἄρρητον[3] πίστιν γράψαντος ἐν τῇ μεγάλῃ
συνόδῳ· πρεσβύτερον τῆς ἐκκλησίας ἐκ πολλῶν
ἤδη ἐτῶν, εὐσταθῆ τὸν τρόπον, ἔμπειρον κανόνων,
ἀκριβῆ τὴν πίστιν, ἐν ἐγκρατείᾳ καὶ ἀσκήσει
μέχρι νῦν διάγοντα· εἰ καὶ ὅτι τὸ εὔτονον αὐτοῦ

---

[1] ἔξω editi antiqi.   [2] τίμιον Harl., Med., et Clarom.
[3] ἄρρητον E, Harl., Clarom.

---

[1] He was the spiritual offspring of Hermogenes, having
been ordained by him. Hermogenes was bishop of Caesarea

your life, whom of like worth with yourself can I send hence to care for our brethren? As to what you have requested by your letter, acting rightly and wisely in your desire, while still living, to behold the one destined after you to guide the chosen flock of the Lord—even as the blessed Moses both desired and saw—since, now, your place is important and famous, and your achievements renowned among many, and the times are difficult, having need of a great helmsman because of the continual storms and the floods which rise against the Church, I have not thought it safe for my soul to treat the matter perfunctorily, especially when I remember what you have written, that you intend to oppose me before the Lord, and charge me with neglect of the churches.

In order, therefore, that I may not come into litigation with you, but rather may find in you an associate in my defence before Christ, having looked about in the assembly of the presbyters belonging to this city, I have chosen that most worthy vessel, the offspring[1] of the blessed Hermogenes—who, in the great Synod,[2] wrote the great and invincible creed. The man of whom I speak has been a presbyter of the Church already for many years, is firm of character, well learned in the canons, strict in the faith, and till now passing his life in continence and asceticism—though in truth the rigour of his

in Cappadocia and predecessor of Dianius. Cf. Letters CCXLIV, CCLXIII.

[2] *i.e.*, at Nicaea. Basil seems to forget that it was Leontius who was present at Nicaea as bishop of Caesarea, although Hermogenes may have been present in lower orders, and may have written the creed.

τῆς σκληραγωγίας λοιπὸν κατεδαπάνησε[1] τὴν
σάρκα· πτωχὸν καὶ μηδένα πορισμὸν[2] ἔχοντα
ἐν τῷ κόσμῳ τούτῳ, ὡς μηδὲ ἄρτου αὐτὸν εὐπορεῖν,
ἀλλὰ διὰ τῶν χειρῶν ἐκπλέκειν τὸν βίον μετὰ τῶν
ἀδελφῶν τῶν συνόντων αὐτῷ. τοῦτον ἐμοὶ βου-
λητόν ἐστιν ἀποστεῖλαι.

Εἰ οὖν καὶ αὐτὸς τοιούτου χρῄζεις ἀνδρός,
ἀλλὰ μὴ αὐτὸ τοῦτο νεωτέρου[3] τινὸς ἐπιτηδείου
μόνον πρὸς τὸ πέμπεσθαι καὶ τὰς βιωτικὰς
ἐξανύειν χρείας, ταχύ μοι διὰ πρώτης ἀφορμῆς
ἐπιστεῖλαι καταξίωσον, ἵνα πέμψω σοι τοῦτον
τὸν ἄνδρα, ἐκλεκτὸν ὄντα τοῦ[4] Θεοῦ, καὶ τῷ
πράγματι[5] ἐπιτήδειον, αἰδέσιμον τοῖς ἐντυγχά-
νουσι, καὶ ἐν πραότητι παιδεύοντα τοὺς ἀντι-
διατιθεμένους. ὃν ἠδυνάμην καὶ εὐθὺς ἐκπέμψαι·
ἀλλ' ἐπειδὴ αὐτὸς προλαβὼν ἐπεζήτησας ἄνθρωπον, τὰ μὲν ἄλλα καλὸν καὶ ἀγαπητὸν ἡμῖν, τοῦ
δὲ προειρημένου ἀνδρὸς παραπολὺ ἀποδέοντα,
ἠβουλήθην σοι φανερὰν γενέσθαι[6] τὴν ἐμαυτοῦ
γνώμην ἵν', εἰ χρῄζεις ἀνδρὸς τοιούτου,[7] ἢ
ἐκπέμψῃς τινὰ τῶν ἀδελφῶν τὸν συμπαραληψό-
μενον αὐτὸν περὶ τὰς νηστείας, ἢ ἐπιστείλῃς ἡμῖν,
ἐὰν μηδένα[8] ἔχῃς τὸν δυνάμενον τῆς μέχρις ἡμῶν
ὁδοιπορίας τὸν κάματον ὑποστῆναι.

[1] κατεδάμασε E, Harl., Clarom.
[2] παρισπασμόν Harl., Med., Clarom.
[3] τοῦτο νεωτέρου] αὐτονεωτέρου E.   [4] τοῦ om. E.

austere living has by now consumed his flesh—a mendicant and possessed of no means in this world, so that he cannot even provide himself with bread, but through the labour of his hands ekes out his existence in company with the brethren who are with him. This is the man I propose to send you.

If, then, you yourself feel the need of such a man, and not, in very truth, of some younger person, fit only for messenger service and to perform the common duties of life, be kind enough to write to me at the very earliest opportunity, that I may send you this man, who is the elect of God and fitted for this duty, inspiring the respect of those who meet him and schooling in gentleness his opponents. I might have sent him to you at once, but since you yourself anticipated me by asking for a certain person, a man who, though in general virtuous and beloved by us, yet falls far short of the one whom I have just mentioned, I wished to make my purpose clear to you, in order that, if you need a person of this character, you may either send one of the brethren at the time of the fast to escort him hence, or write to us, if you have no one able to undergo the labour of the journey all the way to us.

---

5 γράμματι E.

7 τηλικούτου E.

6 καταστῆσαι editi antiqi.

8 ἐὰν μηδένα] ἐάν τινα E.

LXXXII

Ἀθανασίῳ, ἐπισκόπῳ Ἀλεξανδρείας

Ὅταν μὲν πρὸς τὰ πράγματα ἀποβλέψωμεν καὶ τὰς δυσκολίας κατίδωμεν, ὑφ' ὧν πᾶσα ἀγαθὴ ἐνέργεια οἷον ὑπό τινος δεσμοῦ ἐμποδιζομένη κατέχεται, εἰς ἀπόγνωσιν ἑαυτῶν ἐρχόμεθα παντελῆ· ὅταν δὲ πάλιν πρὸς τὴν σὴν ἀπίδωμεν σεμνοπρέπειαν, καὶ λογισώμεθα, ὅτι σὲ ἰατρὸν τῶν ἐν ταῖς ἐκκλησίαις ἀρρωστημάτων ὁ Κύριος ἡμῶν ἐταμιεύσατο, ἀναλαμβάνομεν ἑαυτῶν τοὺς λογισμούς, καὶ ἐκ τοῦ κατὰ τὴν ἀπόγνωσιν πτώματος πρὸς τὴν ἐλπίδα[1] τῶν χρηστοτέρων διανιστάμεθα. λέλυται πᾶσα Ἐκκλησία, ὡς οὐδὲ ἡ σὴ φρόνησις ἀγνοεῖ. καὶ ὁρᾷς πάντως τὰ ἑκασταχοῦ, οἷον ἀφ' ὑψηλῆς τινος σκοπιᾶς τῆς τοῦ νοῦ θεωρίας· ὅπως, καθάπερ ἐν πελάγει, πολλῶν ὁμοῦ συμπλεόντων, ὑπὸ τῆς βίας τοῦ κλύδωνος πάντες ὁμοῦ ἀλλήλοις προσρήγνυνται· καὶ γίνεται τὸ ναυάγιον, πῆ μὲν ἐκ τῆς ἔξωθεν αἰτίας βιαίως κινούσης τὴν θάλατταν, πῆ δὲ ἐκ τῆς τῶν ἐμπλεόντων[2] ταραχῆς ἀντιβαινόντων ἀλλήλοις καὶ διωθουμένων. ἀρκεῖ

---

[1] πρὸς τὴν ἐλπίδα] τῇ ἐλπίδι Vat., Reg. uterque, Coisl. secundus.
[2] πλεόντων E, Harl.

---

[1] Written late in the year 371. Cf. Loofs. According to Tillemont (Note LX), the bishops referred to here by Basil, as not in communion with him, are in all probability the Macedonians.
[2] σεμνοπρέπεια, as frequently in Basil, is used here as a title.

LETTER LXXXII

To Athanasius, Bishop of Alexandria [1]

Whenever we regard our affairs and perceive the difficulties by which every virtuous activity is held in check, hindered as it were by fetters, we arrive at absolute despair of ourselves; but when, on the other hand, we look at your Holiness [2] and consider that our Lord has appointed you the physician to heal the maladies of the churches, we resume our reflections and from the depths of our despair we rise to the hope of better things. The whole Church has been disrupted, as your Wisdom [3] is also not unaware. Furthermore, you assuredly can see, from the lofty watch-tower, [4] so to speak, of your mental vision, what is happening on every hand—how, as on the deep when many ships are sailing together, all are dashed together the one against the other by the violence of the waves, and the shipwreck occurs, partly, it is true, by reason of the external cause which violently agitates the sea, but partly from the confusion that reigns among the sailors, who jostle against and oppose one another. It is enough to

---

[3] φρόνησις, also a title, found in both Athanasius and Basil.

[4] Note the fitness of this figure as applied to the Bishop of Alexandria, who could still see the marble lighthouse erected at the eastern extremity of the island of Pharos by Ptolemy II. Note also the sophistic manner in which Basil develops this figure. In general we may say that sophistic influence is seen more in the development of the metaphor by Basil than in his frequent use of it. Cf. Campbell, 108 ff. For a similar use of this nautical metaphor, cf. *De Spiritu Sancto*, 30.

ἐπὶ τῆς εἰκόνος ἐᾶσαι τὸν λόγον, οὔτε τῆς σῆς
σοφίας ἐπιτρεπούσης τι πλέον, οὔτε τῆς καταστάσεως ἐπιτρεπούσης ἡμῖν τὴν παρρησίαν. καὶ
πρὸς ταῦτα[1] τίς ἱκανὸς κυβερνήτης; τίς ἀξιό-
πιστος διαναστῆσαι τὸν Κύριον ἐπιτιμῆσαι τῷ
ἀνέμῳ καὶ τῇ θαλάσσῃ; τίς ἕτερος ἢ ὁ ἐκ παιδὸς
τοῖς ὑπὲρ τῆς εὐσεβείας ἐναθλήσας ἀγῶσιν;

Ἐπεὶ οὖν ὥρμηται νῦν γνησίως πᾶν τὸ περὶ
ἡμᾶς ὑγιαῖνον κατὰ τὴν πίστιν εἰς τὴν πρὸς
τοὺς ὁμοδόξους κοινωνίαν καὶ ἕνωσιν, θαρροῦντως[2]
ἤλθομεν εἰς τὴν παράκλησίν σου τῆς ἀνεξικακίας,
ἐπιστεῖλαι πᾶσιν ἡμῖν ἐπιστολὴν μίαν, παραίνεσιν ἔχουσαν τῶν πρακτέων. οὕτω γὰρ βού-
λονται παρὰ σοῦ τὴν ἀρχὴν ὑπάρξαι αὐτοῖς τῶν
κοινωνικῶν διαλέξεων. ἐπειδὴ δὲ ἴσως ὕποπτοι
καταφαίνονταί[3] σοι τῇ μνήμῃ τῶν παρελθόντων,
ἐκεῖνο ποίησον, θεοφιλέστατε πάτερ· ἐμοὶ τὰς
πρὸς τοὺς ἐπισκόπους ἐπιστολὰς διάπεμψαι ἢ
διά τινος τῶν αὐτόθεν[4] πιστῶν, ἢ καὶ διὰ τοῦ
ἀδελφοῦ Δωροθέου τοῦ συνδιακόνου ἡμῶν, ἃς
ὑποδεξάμενος οὐ ρότερον δώσω, μὴ[5] λαβὼν τὰς
παρ' αὐτῶν ἀποκρίσεις· ἐὰν δὲ μή, Ἡμαρτηκὼς
ἔσομαι εἰς σὲ πάσας τὰς ἡμέρας τῆς ζωῆς μου.
πάντως δὲ οὐ[6] πλείονος ἄξιον φόβου τοῦτο τῷ

---

[1] ταύτας E.
[2] θαρροῦντες editi antiqi, sed ed. Haganoenis θαρροῦντας.
[3] καταφανήσονται E, editi antiqi.   [4] αὐτόθι E.
[5] ἢ editi antiqi.   [6] οὐδέ editi antiqi.

---

[1] Cf. Luke 8. 24: ὁ δὲ ἐγερθεὶς ἐπετίμησε τῷ ἀνέμῳ καὶ τῷ
κλύδωνι τοῦ ὕδατος. "But he arising rebuked the wind and
the rage of the water."
[2] The story of St. Athanasius, as a "boy bishop," is
related by Socrates, *Ecc. Hist.* 1, 15, and Rufinus, *Ecc. Hist.*

dismiss the topic with this simile, since your wisdom permits nothing more and the situation permits us no freedom of speech. But who is the helmsman capable of meeting these dangers? Who can be trusted to arouse the Lord that He may rebuke the wind and the sea?[1] Who other than he who from childhood[2] has struggled in the contests in defence of the faith?

Since, therefore, all about us that is sound as regards the faith is already nobly moving toward communion and unity with those of like belief, with confidence have we resorted to this appeal to urge your Patience[3] to write to us all one general letter, containing advice on the course of action we should adopt. For in this manner they wish the initiative in their discussions regarding their communion to be provided by you. But since perhaps they seem to you suspicious because of your recollection of the past, most God-beloved father, act as follows: Send to me the letters intended for the bishops, either by one of your own faithful there, or even by our brother, the deacon Dorotheus,[4] and when I have received them I shall not give them out until I am in possession of the bishops' answers; for, otherwise, " I will be guilty of sin against thee all the days of my life."[5] Assuredly these words could not have

---

1, 14. While playing a game of baptism with his companions, Athanasius was noticed by Alexander, who thereupon had him educated at the episcopal palace.

[3] ἀνεξικακία, used as a title here; Patience or Forbearance.

[4] The deacon used so frequently by Basil in the service of a messenger.

[5] Cf. Gen. 43. 9 : ἡμαρτηκὼς ἔσομαι πρὸς σὲ πάσας τὰς ἡμέρας. " I will be guilty of sin against thee for ever." Judah is speaking to his father Jacob. Basil adds τῆς ζωῆς μου.

ἐξ ἀρχῆς εἰπόντι πρὸς τὸν πατέρα ἢ ἐμοὶ νῦν
πρὸς σὲ τὸν πνευματικὸν πατέρα λέγοντι. εἰ δὲ
τοῦτο παντὶ τρόπῳ ἀπηγόρευται παρὰ σοί, ἀλλ᾽
ἡμᾶς γε τῆς ἐπὶ τῇ διακονίᾳ αἰτίας ἄφες, ἀδόλως
καὶ ἀκατασκεύως, ἐπιθυμίᾳ τῆς εἰρήνης καὶ τῆς
πρὸς ἀλλήλους ἡμῶν συναφείας τῶν ὁμονοούντων
εἰς τὰ πρὸς τὸν¹ Κύριον, ἐπὶ τὴν πρεσβείαν ταύτην
καὶ μεσιτείαν² ἀφικομένους.

LXXXIII

Κηνσίτορι

Ἐμοὶ πρὸς τὴν σὴν εὐγένειαν συνήθεια μὲν καὶ
ἡ κατ᾽ ὀφθαλμοὺς συντυχία πάνυ βραχεῖα γέγονε,
γνῶσις δὲ ἡ ἐξ ἀκοῆς, δι᾽ ἧς πολλοῖς συναπτόμεθα
τῶν ἐπιφανῶν, οὐκ ὀλίγη τε οὐδὲ εὐκαταφρόνητος.
εἰ δὲ καὶ σοί τις ἐκ τῆς φήμης περὶ ἡμῶν ὑπάρχει
λόγος, αὐτὸς ἂν εἰδείης ἄμεινον. τὸ δ᾽ οὖν σὸν
παρ᾽ ἡμῖν τοιοῦτόν ἐστιν οἷον εἴπομεν.³ ἐπειδὴ
δὲ⁴ ἐκάλεσέ σε ὁ Θεὸς εἰς πρᾶγμα φιλανθρωπίας
ἐπίδειξιν ἔχον, δι᾽ οὗ δυνατόν ἐστι διορθωθῆναι
ἡμῶν τὴν πατρίδα παντελῶς ἐδαφισθεῖσαν, ἡγοῦμαι πρέπειν μοι ὑπομνῆσαί σου τὴν χρηστότητα,
ἵνα ἐπ᾽ ἐλπίδι τῆς παρὰ Θεοῦ ἀνταποδόσεως
τοιοῦτον σεαυτὸν καταξιώσῃς παρασχέσθαι, ὥστε

¹ τόν om. E.   ² καὶ μεσιτείαν om. E.
³ εἴποιμεν E, editi antiqi.   ⁴ δέ om. E.

---

¹ Written in 372. The valuation of property and levying of
taxes were based on the census books (*libri censuales*) prepared

inspired greater fear in the one who first addressed them to his father than they inspire now in me as I address them to my spiritual father. But if this idea of communion has been entirely rejected by you, still absolve us at least from all blame for our efforts, since honestly and frankly, through a desire for peace and mutual union among those who hold the same beliefs about the Lord, have we entered upon this embassy and mediation.

LETTER LXXXIII

To a Censitor [1]

My acquaintance and personal association with your Nobility [2] has been very brief, but my knowledge of you by report, through which we are brought in contact with many illustrious men, is neither slight nor inconsiderable. But whether we too have any reputation by report with you, you yourself would be the better judge. However, your reputation with us is what we have said. But since God has called you to an office which affords opportunities of displaying kindness, one through which it is possible to set upright again our country now completely levelled with the earth, I think it proper for me to bring a matter to your Excellency's [3] consideration, that in the hope of reward from God you may deign so to conduct yourself as to be held

under the supervision of the *censitores*. The latter were appointed by the Emperor, one for each province or smaller unit of territory. The method of procedure was that followed by the censor at Rome.
    [2] A Byzantine title.
    [3] Or " Goodness," also a Byzantine title.

ἀθανάτου μὲν τῆς μνήμης ἀξιοῦσθαι, γενέσθαι δὲ
αἰωνίων ἀναπαύσεων κληρονόμον, ἐκ τοῦ ἐλαφρο-
τέρας ποιῆσαι τοῖς καταπονουμένοις τὰς θλίψεις.

Ἐπειδὴ δὲ κἀμοί τίς ἐστι κτῆσις περὶ Χαμα-
νηνήν,[1] ἀξιῶ σε[2] προστῆναι αὐτῆς ὡς οἰκείας.
μὴ θαυμάζῃς[3] δέ, εἰ ἐμαυτοῦ λέγω τὰ τῶν φίλων,
μετὰ τῆς ἄλλης ἀρετῆς καὶ φιλίαν πεπαιδευμένος,
καὶ μεμνημένος τοῦ σοφῶς εἰπόντος, ἄλλον[4]
ἑαυτὸν εἶναι τὸν φίλον. τὴν τοίνυν κτῆσιν τὴν
διαφέρουσαν τῷδε, ταύτην ὡς ἐμαυτοῦ παρατί-
θεμαι τῇ τιμιότητί σου· καὶ παρακαλῶ, ἐπισκεψά-
μενον τὰ τῆς οἰκίας δυσχερῆ, δοῦναι αὐτοῖς καὶ
τῶν παρελθόντων χρόνων παραμυθίαν, καὶ πρὸς
τὸ μέλλον αἱρετὴν αὐτοῖς κατασκευάσαι τὴν
οἴκησιν, τὴν φευκτὴν καὶ ἀπηγορευμένην διὰ τὸ
πλῆθος τῆς ἐπικειμένης αὐτῇ συντελείας. σπου-
δάσω δὲ καὶ αὐτὸς περιτυχών σου τῇ κοσμιότητι
ἐντελέστερον περὶ ἑκάστου διαλεχθῆναι.

LXXXIV

Ἡγεμόνι

Σχεδὸν μὲν ἄπιστόν ἐστιν ὃ μέλλω γράφειν,
γεγράψεται δὲ τῆς ἀληθείας ἕνεκεν. ὅτι, πᾶσαν

---

[1] μηχανήν Med.   [2] ἀξιῶ σε] ἀξιῶσαι E.
[3] θαυμάσῃς E.   [4] ἄλλων E.

---

[1] Pythagoras is supposed to have been the first to utter
these words. They occur also in Aristotle, *Magna Moralia*,
II. 15 (ἕτερος ἐγώ), and in Cicero, *Laelius*, 21, 80 (*alter
idem*).

worthy of undying remembrance, and as to become an heir to eternal peace, for having lightened the burdens of such as are afflicted.

Since I too have a certain property in the vicinity of Chamanene, I request you to take care of it as you would of your own. But do not think it strange, if I call the property of my friends my own, since along with other virtues I have learned friendship, and have been mindful of the wise saying that a friend is another self.[1] This property, therefore, which belongs to him, I entrust to your Honour's[2] care just as if it were my own; and I urge you, after examining into the misfortunes of this household, to offer them both consolation for the past, and for the future to render desirable for them the residence which now is being shunned and abandoned on account of the multitude of taxes imposed upon it. I myself, moreover, shall be eager to meet your Decorum[3] and talk at greater length about each particular.

LETTER LXXXIV

To a Governor[4]

What I am about to write is almost incredible, but it shall be written for the sake of truth. It

---

[2] A Byzantine title.

[3] Also a Byzantine title.

[4] Written in 372. The person addressed is probably Elias, governor of Cappadocia. Basil here writes in behalf of an old man, whose four-year-old grandson has been placed on the senatorial roll, thus compelling his grandfather to serve again. Cf. also Letters XCIV and XCVI.

ἔχων ἐπιθυμίαν ὡς οἷόν τε ἦν πυκνότατα διαλέ-
γεσθαί σου τῇ καλοκἀγαθίᾳ, ἐπειδὴ εὗρον ταύτην [1]
γραμμάτων τὴν [2] ἀφορμήν, οὐκ ἐπέδραμον τῷ
ἑρμαίῳ, ἀλλ' ἀπώκνησα καὶ ἀνεδύην. τὸ οὖν
παράδοξον ἐν τούτῳ, ὅτι ἅπερ ηὐχόμην ὑπάρξαι,[3]
ταῦτα γενόμενα οὐκ ἐδεχόμην. αἴτιον δέ, ὅτι
αἰσχύνομαι δοκεῖν, μὴ φιλίας γε ἕνεκεν καθαρῶς,
ἀλλὰ χρείαν τινὰ θεραπεύων ἑκάστοτε, γράφειν.
ἀλλά με ἐκεῖνο εἰσῆλθεν (ὃ καὶ σὲ βούλομαι
διανοηθέντα, μήτοι νομίζειν ἡμᾶς ἐμπορικῶς μᾶλλον ἢ φιλικῶς ποιεῖσθαι τὰς διαλέξεις), ὅτι χρή
τι διάφορον ἔχειν τὰς τῶν ἀρχόντων προσρήσεις
παρὰ τοὺς ἰδιώτας. οὐ γὰρ ὁμοίως ἐντευκτέον
ἡμῖν ἰατρῷ τε ἀνδρὶ καὶ τῷ τυχόντι, οὔτε ἄρχοντι
δηλονότι καὶ ἰδιώτῃ· ἀλλὰ πειρατέον τοῦ μὲν ἐκ
τῆς τέχνης, τοῦ δὲ ἀπὸ τῆς ἐξουσίας ἀπολαύειν
εἰς τὰ ἡμέτερα. ὥσπερ οὖν τοῖς ἐν ἡλίῳ βαδί-
ζουσιν ἕπεται πάντως ἡ σκιά, κἂν αὐτοὶ μὴ
προέλωνται, οὕτω καὶ ταῖς πρὸς τοὺς ἄρχοντας
ὁμιλίαις ἀκολουθεῖ τι καὶ παρεμπόρευμα, ἡ τῶν
καμνόντων βοήθεια.

Τὴν μὲν οὖν πρώτην αἰτίαν τῆς ἐπιστολῆς
πληρούτω αὐτὸ τὸ προσειπεῖν σου τὴν μεγαλόνοιαν. ὅ, κἂν μηδεμία πρόφασις τῷ [4] γράφειν
προσῇ, ἀγαθὸν κεφάλαιον αὐτὸ χρὴ νομίζεσθαι.
προσείρησο [5] τοίνυν ἡμῖν, ὦ ἄριστε, καὶ φυλάττοιο

---

[1] τήν add. E.   [2] τήν om. E.   [3] ὑπάρξειν E, Med.
[4] τοῦ Harl., Med.   [5] προσείποιο editi antiqi.

---

[1] A Byzantine title, as also " your Magnanimity " below.

is this,—that although I had every desire to converse with your Nobility[1] as often as possible, when I found this present occasion for writing, I did not rush at my good fortune, but hesitated and drew back. Now the strange part of all this is that, when that very opportunity came for which I prayed, I was not inclined to take it. And the reason is that I am ashamed to seem to write, not disinterestedly out of friendship, but serving some advantage on every occasion. However, the thought occurred to me (I want you as well to reflect on this point, and thus refrain from considering that we carry on our discussions with you after the manner of merchants rather than of friends), that some distinction should be made between words addressed to officials and those addressed to private persons. For we ought not to converse in the same manner with a physician as with any ordinary person, nor, obviously, with a magistrate in the same way as with a person in private station, but from the skill of the one and from the authority of the other we should try to derive some benefit for ourselves. Therefore, just as a shadow always pursues those who walk in the sun, even though they themselves do not so wish, so too in intercourse with magistrates there is an attendant incident of trafficking—assistance for the afflicted.

Accordingly, let our very salutation of your Magnanimity fulfil the primary cause of our letter; this, even if no other pretext for writing were at hand, should be considered a good subject in itself. Receive, then, our salutation, most excellent Sir, and may you be protected in every act of your life, as you pass from office to office and as you confer

τῷ βίῳ παντί, ἀρχὰς ἐξ ἀρχῶν ἀμείβων καὶ
ἄλλοτε ἄλλους ταῖς ἐπιστασίαις εὐεργετῶν. τοῦτο
γὰρ ἐμοί τε ποιεῖν σύνηθες, καὶ σοὶ ὀφειλόμενον
παρὰ τῶν καὶ κατὰ μικρὸν πεπειραμένων τῆς
περὶ τὸ ἄρχειν σου ἀρετῆς.

Μετὰ δὲ τὴν εὐχήν, δέξαι καὶ τὴν ὑπὲρ τοῦ
ἀθλίου γέροντος ἱκεσίαν, ὃν ἀφῆκε μὲν τῶν δημοσίων γράμμα βασιλικόν· μᾶλλον δὲ καὶ πρὸ τοῦ
βασιλέως αὐτὸ τὸ γῆρας ἔδωκεν αὐτῷ τὴν ἀναγκαίαν ἀτέλειαν. ἐβεβαίωσας δὲ καὶ αὐτὸς τὴν
ἄνωθεν χάριν αἰδοῖ τῆς φύσεως, καὶ προμηθείᾳ
τῶν δημοσίων, ἐμοὶ δοκεῖν, ὡς ἂν μὴ ἀνθρώπῳ
παρανοοῦντι [1] διὰ τὸν χρόνον κινδυνεύοι [2] τι τῶν
κοινῶν.

Δι' ἑτέρας δὲ ὁδοῦ πάλιν πῶς αὐτὸν ἔλαθες, ὦ
θαυμάσιε, παραγαγὼν εἰς τὸ μέσον ; τὸν γὰρ
υἱιδοῦν [3] αὐτοῦ, οὔπω τέταρτον ἔτος ἀπὸ γενέσεως
ἄγοντα, κελεύσας τοῦ βουλευτηρίου μετέχειν, τί
ἄλλο καὶ οὐχὶ τὸν πρεσβύτην διὰ τοῦ ἐκγόνου
πάλιν ἐξ ἀρχῆς παράγεις εἰς τὰ δημόσια ; ἀλλὰ
νῦν ἱκετεύομεν ἀμφοτέρων σε λαβεῖν τῶν ἡλικιῶν
οἶκτον, καὶ ἀμφοτέρους ἀνεῖναι διὰ τὰ προσόντα
ἑκατέρῳ ἐλεεινά. ὁ μὲν γὰρ οὐκ εἶδε [4] γονέας,
οὐδ' ἐγνώρισε, ἀλλὰ δι' ἀλλοτρίων χειρῶν εἰς τὸν
βίον τοῦτον εἰσῆλθεν, εὐθὺς [5] ἐκ σπαργάνων [6]
ἀμφοτέρων ὀρφανισθείς· ὁ δὲ τοσοῦτον ἐταμιεύθη
τῷ βίῳ, ὡς μηδὲν αὐτὸν εἶδος συμφορᾶς παρελ-
θεῖν· ἐπείδε μὲν γὰρ υἱοῦ τελευτὴν ἄωρον· εἶδε δὲ
οἶκον ἔρημον διαδόχων· ὄψεται δὲ νῦν, ἐὰν μή τι

---

[1] παρανομοῦντι editi antiqi.   [2] κινδυνεύῃ editi antiqi.
[3] υἱὸν γοῦν editi antiqi.   [4] οἶδε editi antiqi.

benefits now on some and now on others by your government. For it is my custom to speak thus, and it is due to you from those who have experienced, even in small measure, the excellence of your administration.

After my prayer, receive also my petition in behalf of an unfortunate old man, whom an Imperial decree has exempted from public burdens; nay, rather, old age itself, even before the Emperor, had granted him the inevitable exemption. You yourself, also, have confirmed the Imperial favour by your respect for Nature, and by your prudent care of the public interests, as it seems to me, lest any public interest should be endangered by a man whose mind is becoming deranged through age.

But how, respected Sir, did you inadvertently drag him again into the midst of public affairs by another way? For when you commanded his grandson, not yet in his fourth year, to take his place in the municipal senate, what else are you doing than to drag the old man into public affairs afresh in the person of his grandchild? But now we beseech you to take pity upon the ages of both, and to exempt both on account of what is worthy of pity in each. For the one has not seen his parents, nor has he known them, but he entered this life through alien hands, having been bereft of both parents from his very swaddling clothes; and the other has been granted so long a period of life that he has escaped no form of calamity. For he saw a son's untimely death; he saw a house made destitute of its succession; and he will now see (unless you yourself hit upon

---

⁵ εὐθύς om. E.   ⁶ ἐπ' add. E.

107

αὐτὸς ἄξιον τῆς σεαυτοῦ φιλανθρωπίας διανοηθῇς,
τὴν παραμυθίαν τῆς ἀπαιδίας, ταύτην ἀφορμὴν
αὐτῷ μυρίων γενησομένην κακῶν. οὐ γὰρ δήπου
τὸ παιδίον εἰς βουλευτὰς συντελέσει, ἢ ἐκλέξει
τὰς εἰσφοράς, ἢ στρατιώταις χορηγήσει τὸ σιτη-
ρέσιον, ἀλλ' ἀνάγκη πάλιν τοῦ ἀθλίου γέροντος
τὴν πολιὰν καταισχύνεσθαι. δὸς οὖν χάριν καὶ
τοῖς νόμοις ἀκόλουθον καὶ τῇ φύσει συμβαί-
νουσαν, τῷ μὲν προστάξας μέχρι τῆς τῶν ἀνδρῶν
ἡλικίας συγχωρηθῆναι, τὸν δὲ ἐπὶ τῆς κλίνης
ἀναμένειν τὸν θάνατον. πραγμάτων δὲ συνέχειαν
καὶ τὸ τῆς ἀνάγκης ἀπαραίτητον ἄλλοι προβαλ-
λέσθωσαν. οὐ γὰρ δὴ τοῦ σοῦ τρόπου ἢ κακῶς
πράττοντας περιιδεῖν, ἢ νόμων ὀλιγωρῆσαι, ἢ
φίλοις μὴ εἶξαι καθικετεύουσι, κἂν τὰ ἐξ ἀνθρώπων σε περιεστήκει [1] πράγματα.

LXXXV

Περὶ τοῦ μὴ δεῖν ὀρκοῦν [2]

Οὐ παυόμεθα κατὰ πᾶσαν σύνοδον διαμαρτυ-
ρόμενοι καὶ ἰδίᾳ ἐν ταῖς συντυχίαις περὶ τῶν
αὐτῶν διαλεγόμενοι, ὥστε τοὺς ὅρκους ἐπὶ τοῖς
δημοσίοις τελέσμασι μὴ ἐπάγεσθαι παρὰ τῶν
ἀπαιτητῶν τοῖς ἀγροίκοις. λειπόμενον ἦν [3] καὶ

---

[1] περιέστηκε editi antiqi.

[2] ὥστε παύσασθαι τοὺς τῶν δημοσίων πράκτορας τοὺς ὅρκους
τοῖς ὑποτελέσιν ἐπάγοντας Harl., Reg. secundus, Coisl.
secundus.

[3] οὖν add. Reg. secundus.

some remedy worthy of your kindness) that this consolation of his childlessness is destined to become the cause of countless troubles. For of course the child will not be counted among the senators, or collect taxes, or furnish provision-money for soldiers, but it will be necessary for the white locks of the wretched old man again to be put to shame. Grant, therefore, a favour both consistent with the laws and in agreement with Nature, ordering that exemption be granted to the one until he reach man's estate, and that the other be allowed to await his death in his bed. Let others offer the excuse of pressing business and inexorable necessity! For indeed it is not in keeping with *your* character either to allow men to suffer hardships, or to belittle the laws, or to refuse to yield to the petitions of your friends, even if the personal affairs of your subjects crowd upon your attention.

LETTER LXXXV

About there Being No Necessity of Taking the Oath [1]

We do not cease protesting solemnly at every synod and arguing on the same matter in our private conversations, namely, that in regard to the public taxes oaths should not be required of the farmers by the collectors. It was left to us, also by letter on

---

[1] Written in the year 372. For the distress of the Cappadocians under the heavy burden of taxation, cf. Letter LXXIV and note 1. A very disagreeable feature of the system of taxation was the practice of putting the people of the country under oath as to their inability to pay. The Church condemned the taking of oaths.

διὰ τοῦ γράμματος περὶ τῶν αὐτῶν ἐνώπιον Θεοῦ
καὶ ἀνθρώπων διαμαρτύρασθαι, ὅτι προσήκει
παύσασθαι ὑμᾶς[1] τὸν θάνατον ταῖς ψυχαῖς τῶν
ἀνθρώπων ἐπάγοντας, καὶ ἄλλους ἐπινοῆσαί τινας
τρόπους τῶν ἀπαιτήσεων, τὰς δὲ ψυχὰς συγχω-
ρῆσαι τοῖς ἀνθρώποις ἀτρώτους ἔχειν. ταῦτα
πρὸς σὲ γράφομεν, οὐχ ὡς σοῦ δεομένου τῆς ἐκ
τῶν λόγων παρακλήσεως (οἴκοθεν γὰρ ἔχεις τὰς
περὶ τὸ φοβεῖσθαι τὸν Κύριον[2] ἀφορμάς), ἀλλ᾿
ἵνα διὰ σοῦ πάντες οἱ ἀνεχόμενοί σου διδαχθῶσι
μὴ παροργίζειν τὸν ἅγιον, μηδὲ ἀπηγορευμένον
πρᾶγμα τῇ πονηρᾷ συνηθείᾳ εἰς ἀδιαφορίαν
κατάγειν. καὶ γὰρ οὔτε ὄφελός τι αὐτοῖς πρὸς
τὰς ἀπαιτήσεις ἐκ τῶν ὅρκων ἐστί, καὶ ὁμολο-
γούμενον κακὸν τῇ ψυχῇ προσλαμβάνουσιν.
ἐπειδὰν γὰρ καταμελετήσωσι[3] τὰς[4] ἐπιορκίας οἱ
ἄνθρωποι, οὐκέτι ἑαυτοὺς[5] ἐπείγουσι πρὸς τὴν
ἔκτισιν, ἀλλὰ ἀπάτης ὅπλον καὶ ἀναβολῆς
ἀφορμὴν ἐξευρῆσθαι αὐτοῖς τὸν ὅρκον οἴονται.

Εἴτε οὖν ὀξεῖαν ἐπάγει τὴν ἀνταπόδοσιν τοῖς
ἐπιωρκηκόσιν ὁ Κύριος, οὐχ ἕξουσι τοὺς ὑπα-
κούοντας, τῶν ὑπευθύνων ὑπὸ τῆς τιμωρίας
ἀναλωθέντων· εἴτε διὰ μακροθυμίας ἀνέχεται ὁ
Δεσπότης (ὃ προλαβὼν εἶπον, ὅτι οἱ πεπειραμένοι τῆς ἀνοχῆς τοῦ Κυρίου καταφρονοῦσιν
αὐτοῦ τῆς χρηστότητος), μὴ ἀνομείτωσαν διακενῆς, μηδὲ παροξυνέτωσαν ἐφ᾿ ἑαυτοὺς τὸν Θεόν.

Εἴρηται ἡμῖν τὰ ἡμῖν ἐπιβάλλοντα· ὄψονται
οἱ ἀπειθοῦντες.

---

[1] ἡμᾶς E.   [2] τὸν Θεόν editi antiqi.
[3] καταμελήσωσι E, editi antiqi.

this same subject, to protest before God and men,
that you should cease bringing death upon men's
souls, but should think out some other methods of
tax-exaction, and permit men to keep their souls
uninjured. These things we are writing to you,
not with the thought that you are in need of our
written exhortation (for you have reasons at home
for fearing the Lord), but in order that through you
all who are subject to you may be taught not to
rouse the Holy One to anger, and not to render a
forbidden act a matter of indifference through evil
habit. For the people derive no help from the oaths
in combating the demand for taxes, but they do
receive into their soul an acknowledged evil. For
whenever men become fully practised in perjury,
they no longer exert themselves to make payment,
but think that the oath has been devised for them
as an instrument of deception and a pretext for
delay.

Now if the Lord brings swift retribution upon the
perjured, the collectors will have none to answer
their summons, for those will have been destroyed by
God's punishment who have committed the perjury;
and if the Master endures with patience (and as I
have said before, those who have experienced the
Lord's forbearance scorn His goodness), let them not
transgress the law for no benefit,[1] nor yet provoke
God against themselves.

We have spoken what is in keeping with our duty;
those who do not obey will see to it.

---

[1] *i.e.* they will not escape their taxes even if they swear to
their inability to pay them.

---

⁴ τὰς] τῆς E.   ⁵ αὐτούς E.

LXXXVI

Τῷ ἡγεμόνι

Οἶδα μεγίστην καὶ πρώτην σπουδὴν οὖσαν τῇ τιμιότητί σου πάντα[1] τρόπον χαρίζεσθαι τῷ δικαίῳ, δευτέραν δὲ τὸ καὶ τοὺς[2] φίλους εὖ ποιεῖν καὶ τῶν προσφευγόντων τῇ προστασίᾳ τῆς σῆς μεγαλονοίας ἀντιποιεῖσθαι. πάντα τοίνυν εἰς ταὐτὸν συνέδραμεν ἐπὶ τῆς παρούσης ὑποθέσεως. καὶ γὰρ δίκαιόν ἐστι τὸ πρᾶγμα, ὑπὲρ οὗ τὴν πρεσβείαν ποιούμεθα, καὶ ἡμῖν κεχαρισμένον, οὓς ἐν τοῖς φίλοις ἀριθμεῖν τοῖς σεαυτοῦ[3] κατηξίωσας, καὶ ὀφειλόμενον τοῖς τὴν στερρότητά σου εἰς τὴν ὑπὲρ ὧν πεπόνθασι βοήθειαν ἐπικαλουμένοις.

Σίτου γάρ, ὃν μόνον εἶχε πρὸς[4] τὴν ἀναγκαίαν τοῦ βίου διαγωγὴν ὁ ποθεινότατος ἀδελφὸς Δωρόθεος, διήρπασάν τινες ἐν Βηρίσοις[5] τῶν τὰ δημόσια διοικεῖν πεπιστευμένων, εἴτε ἀφ' ἑαυτῶν ἐλθόντες ἐπὶ τὴν βίαν, εἴτε καὶ ἑτέρων αὐτοῖς ὑποθεμένων. πλὴν οὐδαμόθεν αὐτοῖς τὸ πρᾶγμα ἀνέγκλητον, τί γὰρ ἧττον ἀδικεῖ ὁ οἴκοθεν πονηρὸς ἢ ὁ ἑτέρων κακίᾳ ὑπηρετούμενος; καὶ τοῖς πεπονθόσιν ἡ ζημία ὁμοία. τοῦτον ἀξιοῦμεν, δι' ὧν ἀφῃρέθη μὲν[6] ἀπολαβεῖν, καὶ μὴ ἐξεῖναι αὐτοῖς ἐπὶ ἑτέροις[7] τὴν αἰτίαν τῶν τετολμημένων ἀναφέρειν·[8] ὅσου δὲ[9] ἄξιον τὸ τὴν ἐκ τῆς σιτοδείας

---

[1] κατά E.   [2] τούς om. E.   [3] ἑαυτοῦ E, Med.
[4] πρός] εἰς E.   [5] Βηρίσσοις E.
[6] ἐξ αὐτῶν τὸ ἀφαιρεθέν add. editi Paris.
[7] ἑτέρους E.   [8] φέρειν E.
[9] ὅσου . . . τοσούτου] ὅσον . . . τοσοῦτον editi antiqi.

LETTER LXXXVI

To the Governor[1]

I know that the first and greatest object of your
Honour's zeal is to favour the cause of justice in
every way, and the second, to benefit your friends
and to take action in the interests of those who flee
to the protection of your Magnanimity. Hence we
are completely in accord in the present case. For
the thing for which we plead is just, and a favour to
us, whom you have deigned to number among your
friends, and an obligation due to those who implore
your Constancy for assistance in alleviating their
sufferings.

For the grain, which alone our very dear brother
Dorotheus possessed for meeting the necessities of
life, has been stolen by certain persons at Brisi of
those who are entrusted with the administration
of public affairs, whether they resorted to this act
of violence of their own accord, or were instigated
thereto by others. From no point of view, however,
is their action blameless. For in what respect does
he who is evil in himself commit less wrong than
he who serves the wickedness of others? To the
victims, moreover, the injury inflicted is the same.
We ask that Dorotheus shall get back the grain
from those by whom it was taken from him, and
that they should not be allowed to put the blame
for their audacity upon others. And as much as it

[1] Of the same year as the preceding. Some MSS. (Reg.
secundus and Bigot.) add to the present title: παραθετική
ὑπὲρ πρεσβυτέρων περὶ καθαρπαγῆς σίτου, "of recommendation
in behalf of presbyters on the stealing of grain."

διαφυγεῖν ἀνάγκην, τοσούτου τὴν χάριν τιμη
σόμεθα τὴν παρὰ τῆς σῆς μεγαλοφυΐας, ἐὰν ἄρα
δοῦναι καταξιώσῃς.

LXXXVII

Ἀνεπίγραφος ὑπὲρ τῶν αὐτῶν [1]

Ἐθαύμασα πῶς, σοῦ μεσιτεύοντος, τοσοῦτον
ἐτολμήθη κακὸν κατὰ τοῦ συμπρεσβυτέρου [2] ὥστε
ἦν μόνην εἶχεν ἀφορμὴν τοῦ βίου, ταύτην διαρπασ
θῆναι, καὶ τὸ δεινότατον, ὅτι οἱ τοῦτο τετολμη
κότες ἐπὶ σὲ [3] τὴν αἰτίαν ὧν πεποιήκασιν ἀνα
φέρουσιν· [4] ὃν οὐχ ὅπως ἐπιτρέπειν τὰ τοιαῦτα
γίνεσθαι, ἀλλὰ καὶ παντὶ σθένει διακωλύειν
ἀκόλουθον ἦν, μάλιστα μὲν κατὰ πάντων, εἰ δ᾽
ἄρα, κατὰ γοῦν τῶν πρεσβυτέρων, καὶ τούτων
ὅσοι ἡμῖν ὁμόψυχοι, καὶ τὴν αὐτὴν τῆς εὐσεβείας
ὁδὸν πορευόμενοι. εἴ τι οὖν φροντίζεις τοῦ
ἀναπαῦσαι ἡμᾶς, ταχέως διορθωθῆναι τὰ γενόμενα
ποίησον. δύνασαι γὰρ σὺν Θεῷ καὶ ταῦτα καὶ
ἔτι μείζω τούτων κατορθοῦν, οἷς ἂν ἐθέλῃς.
ἐπέστειλα δὲ καὶ τῷ ἄρχοντι τῆς πατρίδος, ἵνα,
ἐὰν ἀφ᾽ [5] ἑαυτῶν μὴ θελήσωσι ποιῆσαι τὰ δίκαια,
ἐκ [6] τῆς κινήσεως τῶν δικαστηρίων ἀναγκασθῶσι
ποιῆσαι.

---

[1] ἐπὶ κήσει E ; ἐπὶ ἐκδικήσει alii MSS. ; ἐπὶ οἰκήσει editi
antiqi.
[2] πρεσβυτέρου E, Med.   [3] ἐπὶ σέ om. E.
[4] εἰς add E, editi antiqi.
[5] ἐφ᾽ editi antiqi.   [6] διά E

is worth to escape the privations of a famine, at so much shall we value the favour bestowed by your Magnanimity, if you deign to grant it.

LETTER LXXXVII

WITHOUT ADDRESS, ON THE SAME SUBJECT [1]

I AM surprised that, with you acting as mediator, so great an outrage has been perpetrated against our presbyter [2]—that he has been plundered of the sole support of life which he possessed, and, worst of all, that the perpetrators of this deed lay the blame for the act which they have committed on you; for it was incumbent on you, not only not to allow such things to be done, but also, with all your power, to prevent their being done, if possible against any man, but if such things must be, against any presbyter at least, or, of presbyters, against such as are of like mind with us and are journeying along the same road of piety. If, therefore, you are at all concerned to put us at ease, see to it that what has been done be quickly rectified. For with God's help you can succeed in these and in still greater things for whomsoever you will. I have written also to the governor of my native land [3] in order that, if they do not wish to do what is right of themselves, they may be forced to do so under pressure of the courts.

[1] Of the same date and on the same subject as the preceding.
[2] *i.e.* Dorotheus. Cf. preceding letter.
[3] Cf. Letter VIII, Vol. I, p. 48, note 1.

LXXXVIII

Ἀνεπίγραφος, ἐπὶ ἀπαιτητῇ χρημάτων

Τὴν δυσκολίαν τῆς συγκομιδῆς τοῦ πραγ-
ματευτικοῦ χρυσίου πάντων μάλιστα ἡ σὴ
τιμιότης κατέμαθε· καὶ τῆς πενίας ἡμῶν οὐδένα
μάρτυρα τοιοῦτον ἔχομεν, οἷον σέ, ὃς ἐκ τῆς
μεγάλης φιλανθρωπίας καὶ συνέπαθες ἡμῖν καὶ
συμπεριηνέχθης μέχρι τοῦ παρόντος τὰ δυνατά,
οὐδαμοῦ τὸ πρᾷον τῆς ἑαυτοῦ τῶν τρόπων καταστάσεως ἐκ τῆς τῶν ἄνωθεν ἐπικειμένων ταραχῆς
παρακινήσας. ἐπεὶ οὖν ὑπολείπεται ἡμῖν ἐκ τοῦ
παντὸς σταθμοῦ ὀλίγον ἔτι χρυσίον, καὶ τοῦτο
ἀνάγκη ἐκ τοῦ ἐράνου, εἰς ὃν προετρεψάμεθα
πᾶσαν τὴν πόλιν, συγκομισθῆναι, παρακαλοῦμέν
σου τὴν ἡμερότητα μικρόν τι ἐκτεῖναι ἡμῖν τὴν
προθεσμίαν, πρὸς τὸ καὶ τοὺς ἔξω τῆς πόλεως
ὑπομνησθῆναι. ἐν ἀγροῖς γάρ ἐστι τὸ πολὺ τῶν
ἐν τέλει, ὡς οὐδὲ αὐτὸς ἀγνοεῖς. ἐὰν μὲν οὖν ᾖ
δυνατὸν παρὰ τοσάσδε λίτρας ἐκπεμφθῆναι,
τοσοῦτον γὰρ ἡμῖν ὑπολέλειπται, τοῦτο γενέσθαι
παρακαλοῦμέν σε· κἀκεῖνο ἐπαποσταλήσεται
ὕστερον· ἐὰν δὲ πᾶσα ᾖ ἀνάγκη ἀθρόον αὐτὸ
παραπεμφθῆναι τοῖς θησαυροῖς, ὅπερ ἐξ ἀρχῆς
ἠξιώσαμεν, πλατυτέραν ἡμῖν γενέσθαι τὴν προθεσμίαν.

---

[1] Of the same year as the preceding.

[2] The Benedictine editors remark on χρυσίον πραγμα-
τευτικόν (aurum comparatitium), that it was so called because
it was collected for the purpose of providing troops with
equipment, according to Gothofredus on *Cod. Theod.*, 7, 6, 3.
The provinces of the East, with the exception of Osroene
and Isauria, contributed gold instead of actual equipment.

LETTER LXXXVIII

LETTER LXXXVIII

WITHOUT ADDRESS, FOR A TAX-COLLECTOR [1]

THE difficulty of collecting gold furnished by contribution [2] your Honour has learned better than anyone else; moreover, we have no witness of our poverty better qualified than yourself, who out of your great kindness have both sympathized with us and, up to the present, have shown us indulgence as far as possible, never allowing the mildness of your disposition to be altered by the distraction occasioned by those in high authority who beset you. Since, therefore, a small amount of the whole sum we owe is still lacking, and this must be got together from the general contribution which we have urged the city as a whole to make, we beseech your Clemency to favour us by extending the period of grace a little in order that those who are absent from the city may be notified. For most of the magistrates are in the country, as you yourself are not unaware. Now, if it is possible that the money, less this particular number of pounds (for this is the sum we still lack), be sent, we ask you that this be done; and the above-named shortage will be dispatched later; but if it is absolutely necessary that the stated sum be forwarded to the treasury all at once, then grant us what we asked in the first place, namely, that the period of grace be extended for us.

A law by Valens on this subject and dated 368 reads: Omnem canonem vestium ex Kal. Sept. ad Kal. Aprilis largitionibus trade, proposita Rectori provinciae vel eius officio condemnationis poena; that is, the gold must be paid between Sept. 1 and April 1. Since Basil is here pleading for an extension of time, if not exemption, this letter may be dated shortly before April 1.

LXXXIX

Μελετίῳ, ἐπισκόπῳ Ἀντιοχείας

Ὁ ἀγαθὸς Θεός, παρασχόμενος ἡμῖν προφάσεις προσηγοριῶν πρὸς τὴν σὴν τιμιότητα, τὸ
σφοδρὸν τοῦ πόθου παραμυθεῖται. μάρτυς γὰρ
αὐτὸς τῆς ἐπιθυμίας ἡμῶν ἣν ἔχομεν εἰς τὸ
θεάσασθαί σου τὸ¹ πρόσωπον, καὶ ἀπολαῦσαι
τῆς ἀγαθῆς σου καὶ ψυχοφελοῦς διδασκαλίας.
καὶ νῦν δὲ διὰ τοῦ εὐλαβεστάτου καὶ σπουδαιο-
τάτου ἀδελφοῦ Δωροθέου τοῦ συνδιακόνου ἐρχο-
μένου παρακαλοῦμέν σε προηγουμένως προσεύχεσθαι ὑπὲρ ἡμῶν, ἵνα μὴ πρόσκομμα ὦμεν
τῷ λαῷ, μηδὲ ἐμπόδιον ταῖς ὑμετέραις εὐχαῖς
πρὸς τὸ δυσωπῆσαι τὸν Κύριον. ἔπειτα καὶ
ὑπομιμνήσκομεν καταξιῶσαί σε πάντα τυπῶσαι
διὰ τοῦ προειρημένου ἀδελφοῦ, καὶ εἴ τι δεῖ
ἐπισταλῆναι τοῖς κατὰ τὴν δύσιν, διὰ τὸ ὀφείλειν
ἀναγκαίως καὶ δι' ἡμετέρου αὐτοῖς ἀπενεχθῆναι
γράμματα, αὐτὸν ὑπαγορεῦσαι τὰς ἐπιστολάς.
ἡμεῖς γὰρ ἐπιτυχόντες Σαβίνου, τοῦ παρ' αὐτῶν
ἀποσταλέντος διακόνου, ἐπεστείλαμεν² πρός τε
τοὺς Ἰλλυριοὺς καὶ πρὸς τοὺς κατὰ τὴν Ἰταλίαν

---

¹ σου τὸ] τοῦτο editi antiqi.
² ἀπεστείλαμεν E, editi antiqi.

---

¹ Written before Easter 372   On Meletius, bishop of
Antioch, cf. Letters LVII and LXVIII.
² A deacon of the church of Antioch, and attached to the
communion of Meletius.   The year before (371) he had been
the bearer of two letters from Basil to Athanasius, entreating
him to use his influence with the Western Church to inter-

LETTER LXXXIX

To Meletius, Bishop of Antioch[1]

The good God, by affording us opportunities of addressing your Honour, assuages the intensity of our longing. For He Himself is a witness of the desire which we have to behold your countenance and to enjoy your good and soul-profiting instruction. And now through our most pious and zealous brother, the deacon Dorotheus,[2] who is setting out, we beseech you, primarily, to pray for us that we may not be a stumbling-block to the people, nor a hindrance to your own prayers for the placation of the Lord. And, secondly, we suggest that you deign to arrange all things through the brother just mentioned, and if there is any need of writing to those in the West, it being an urgent obligation that letters be sent to them from our side also, that you yourself dictate the letters. For we, on meeting the deacon Sabinus, who had been sent by them, have written to the Illyrians and to the

pose and heal the schism of the Church of Antioch, by inducing all the orthodox to join with Meletius and his party. Cf. Letters XLVIII, L, and LII. At the close of 371 Basil again sent Dorotheus to Athanasius, with letters to Pope Damasus and the Western bishops, asking for assistance in his efforts to unite the East. Cf. Letter LII. Dorotheus spent the winter in Italy negotiating to no purpose, and returned in 372 to Athanasius and Basil, bringing letters from Damasus which bore witness to the community of their faith, but offered no real assistance. Cf. Letters LXI, LXII, and CCLXXIII. Basil is now sending Dorotheus to Meletius requesting him to draw up more urgent letters to the bishops of the West. These letters, however, are to be sent to Rome, not by Dorotheus, but by the deacon Sabinus.

καὶ Γαλλίαν [1] ἐπισκόπους, καί τινας τῶν ἰδίως
πρὸς ἡμᾶς ἐπιστειλάντων. εὔλογον δὲ ὡς ἀπὸ
κοινοῦ [2] τῆς συνόδου ἀποσταλῆναί τινα τὸν
κομίζοντα δεύτερα γράμματα, ἅπερ αὐτὸς κέλευσον
τυπωθῆναι.

Καὶ περὶ τοῦ αἰδεσιμωτάτου ἐπισκόπου Ἀθανα-
σίου ἀκριβῶς γινώσκουσαν τὴν τελείαν σου
φρόνησιν ὑπομιμνήσκομεν, ὅτι ἀμήχανον τοῖς
παρ' ἐμοῦ γράμμασιν ἐπιδοῦναι ἢ [3] ποιῆσαί τι
τῶν ὀφειλομένων, ἐὰν μὴ καὶ παρ' ὑμῶν, τῶν τότε
τὴν κοινωνίαν αὐτοῦ ἀναβαλλομένων, δέξηταί
τινα τρόπον. αὐτὸς γὰρ λέγεται πάνυ ὡρμῆσθαι
πρὸς τὸ συναφθῆναι ἡμῖν, καὶ τὰ κατὰ δύναμιν συμβαλέσθαι, λυπεῖσθαι δέ, ὅτι καὶ τότε παρεπέμφθη
ἀκοινώνητος, καὶ ἔτι νῦν [4] ἀτελεῖς μένουσιν αἱ
ὑποσχέσεις.

Τὰ δὲ κατὰ τὴν ἀνατολὴν ὅπως διάκειται οὐκ
ἔλαθε πάντως τὰς ἀκοὰς τῆς θεοσεβείας σου, καὶ
δι' ἑαυτοῦ δὲ ἀκριβέστερον πάντα ὁ προειρημένος
ἀδελφὸς διηγήσεται. ὃν καταξίωσον εὐθὺς ἐκπέμ-
ψαι μετὰ τὸ Πάσχα, διὰ τὸ ἀναμένειν τὰς ἀπὸ
Σαμοσάτων ἀποκρίσεις· οὗ καὶ τὴν προθυμίαν
ἀπόδεξαι, καὶ εὐχαῖς αὐτὸν ἐνισχύσας, πρόπεμ-
ψον εἰς τὰ προκείμενα.

---

[1] καὶ Γαλλίαν om. Vat., Reg. secundus.
[2] κοινῆς editi antiqi.   [3] καί editi antiqi.   [4] νῦν om. E.

---

[1] Tillemont holds that this cannot apply to Athanasius
the Great, because it is unlikely that Meletius would refuse
him communion.   Maran (*Vita Basilii*, xxii), however,

bishops in Italy and Gaul, and to certain ones who had sent letters to us privately. It would be prudent that a messenger be sent carrying a second letter from the common synod, and do you yourself command this letter to be written.

Now regarding the most reverend bishop Athanasius, we must remind your perfect wisdom, which knows all accurately, that it is impossible to promote or accomplish any of those things which are necessary by means of letters from me, unless he receives his communion in some way from you also, who once deferred giving it. For he himself is said to have made every effort to unite with us, and, on his part, to have done all in his power; but he is now grieving, they say, because on the occasion in question he was sent away without communion, and because the promises which were made to him remain even yet unfulfilled.[1]

How conditions are in the East has assuredly not escaped the ears of your Holiness, and the brother whom we have mentioned above will in person relate everything more accurately. Be kind enough to send him away immediately after Easter, since he is awaiting the replies of the Samosatians; approve his zeal, and having fortified him with your prayers send him forth upon his present business.

---

shows not only that the circumstances fit in, but that the statement of Meletius' refusal is borne out by Letter CCLVIII, 3. It seems that Athanasius himself was so far committed to the other side in the Antiochene dispute that he could not recognize Meletius.

XC

Τοῖς ἁγιωτάτοις ἀδελφοῖς καὶ ἐπισκόποις τοῖς ἐν τῇ δύσει[1]

Ὁ ἀγαθὸς Θεός, ὁ ἀεὶ ταῖς θλίψεσι τὰς παρακλήσεις παραζευγνύς, ἔδωκεν ἡμῖν καὶ νῦν ἐπὶ[2] τῷ πλήθει τῶν ὀδυνῶν εὑρέσθαι τινὰ μετρίαν παράκλησιν ἐκ[3] τῶν γραμμάτων, ἃ παρὰ τῆς ὑμετέρας ὀρθότητος ὁ τιμιώτατος πατὴρ ἡμῶν Ἀθανάσιος[4] ὁ ἐπίσκοπος δεξάμενος διεπέμψατο ἡμῖν, ὑγιοῦς πίστεως μαρτυρίαν, καὶ τῆς ἀνεπηρεάστου ὑμῶν ὁμονοίας καὶ συμπνοίας ἀπόδειξιν ἔχοντα, ὥστε καὶ ποιμένας ἀναδεικνύναι[5] τοῖς ἴχνεσι τῶν πατέρων ἀκολουθοῦντας καὶ τὸν λαὸν τοῦ Κυρίου μετ' ἐπιστήμης ποιμαίνοντας. ταῦτα πάντα ηὔφρανεν[6] ἡμᾶς τοσοῦτον, ὥστε λῦσαι ἡμῶν τὴν κατήφειαν, καὶ μειδίαμά τι βραχὺ ταῖς ψυχαῖς ἡμῶν ἐμποιῆσαι ἀπὸ τῆς σκυθρωπῆς ταύτης τῶν πραγμάτων καταστάσεως,[7] ἐν ᾗ νῦν καθεστήκαμεν.

Ἐπέτεινε δὲ ἡμῖν τὴν παράκλησιν ὁ Κύριος διὰ τοῦ υἱοῦ ἡμῶν τοῦ εὐλαβεστάτου συνδιακόνου Σαβίνου, ὃς καὶ τὰ παρ' ὑμῖν καλὰ διηγησάμενος ἀκριβῶς ἔθρεψεν ἡμῶν τὰς ψυχάς· καὶ τὰ ἡμέτερα δέ,[8] τῇ πείρᾳ μαθών, ἐναργῶς ὑμῖν ἀναγγελεῖ, ἵνα προηγουμένως μὲν διὰ τῆς ἐκτενοῦς καὶ φιλοπόνου δεήσεως τῆς πρὸς τὸν Κύριον συνα-

---

[1] ἐπισκόποις δυτικοῖς συνοδική, "A synodical letter to the bishops of the West," E.
[2] ἐν E.   [3] τε add. E.   [4] Ἀθανάσιος om. Regii duo.
[5] ἀποδειχθῆναι Reg. secundus, Coisl. secundus. τούς add. E, editi antiqi.

122

LETTER XC

LETTER XC

To the Most Holy Brethren and Bishops of the West [1]

THE good God, who always yokes consolations with afflictions, has granted us even now amid the present multitude of woes that we should find a certain measure of consolation in the letters which our most honoured father, Bishop Athanasius, received from your orthodox selves and forwarded to us, being as they are a testimony to your sound faith, giving proof of your unalterable unanimity and concord, so that they show clearly that the shepherds are following the footsteps of the fathers and with knowledge are feeding the people of the Lord. All this has delighted us to such a degree as to dissolve our dejection and to engender in our souls a faint smile, as it were, after the gloom of the state of affairs in which we at present find ourselves.

And the Lord has increased our consolation through our son, the most reverend deacon Sabinus, who by his accurate account of the goodly situation among you has nourished our souls; and our condition in turn he will report to you plainly when he becomes familiar with it through experience, in order that, in the first place, you may unite with us in our struggle by your earnest and untiring prayer to the

---

[1] Written before Easter of 372. Newman takes this letter and also Letter XCII in close connexion with Letter LXX, which appears to be addressed to Pope Damasus.

---

⁶ εὔφρανεν E.   ⁷ κινήσεως quattuor MSS.   ⁸ δέ om. E.

γωνίζησθε ἡμῖν, ἔπειτα δὲ καὶ τὴν ἐνδεχομένην
ὑμῖν[1] παραμυθίαν ταῖς καταπονουμέναις ἐκκλησίαις εἰσενέγκασθαι μὴ παραιτήσησθε. κέκμηκε
γὰρ τὰ ἐνταῦθα, ἀδελφοὶ τιμιώτατοι, καὶ ἀπείρη-
κε πρὸς τὰς συνεχεῖς προσβολὰς τῶν ἐναντίων
ἡ Ἐκκλησία, ὥσπερ τι πλοῖον ἐν πελάγει μέσῳ
ταῖς ἐπαλλήλοις πληγαῖς τῶν κυμάτων βασα-
νιζόμενον, εἰ μή τις γένοιτο ταχεῖα ἐπισκοπὴ
τῆς ἀγαθότητος τοῦ Κυρίου. ὥσπερ οὖν ἡμεῖς
ἴδιον ἑαυτῶν ἀγαθὸν ποιούμεθα τὴν ὑμετέραν[2]
πρὸς ἀλλήλους σύμπνοιάν τε καὶ ἑνότητα, οὕτω
καὶ ὑμᾶς παρακαλοῦμεν συμπαθῆσαι ἡμῶν ταῖς
διαιρέσεσι, καὶ μή, ὅτι τῇ θέσει τῶν τόπων
διεστήκαμεν, χωρίζειν ἡμᾶς ἀφ' ἑαυτῶν, ἀλλ' ὅτι
ἑνούμεθα τῇ κατὰ τὸ Πνεῦμα κοινωνίᾳ, εἰς τὴν
ἑνὸς σώματος ἡμᾶς συμφωνίαν ἀναλαμβάνειν.

Γνώριμα δὲ τὰ θλίβοντα ἡμᾶς, κἂν ἡμεῖς μὴ
λέγωμεν· εἰς πᾶσαν γὰρ τὴν οἰκουμένην λοιπὸν
ἐξήχηται. καταπεφρόνηται τὰ τῶν πατέρων
δόγματα· ἀποστολικαὶ παραδόσεις ἐξουδένωνται·
νεωτεροποιῶν[3] ἀνθρώπων ἐφευρέματα ταῖς ἐκκλησίαις ἐμπολιτεύεται· τεχνολογοῦσι λοιπόν,
οὐ[4] θεολογοῦσιν, οἱ ἄνθρωποι· ἡ τοῦ κόσμου
σοφία τὰ πρωτεῖα φέρεται, παρωσαμένη τὸ
καύχημα τοῦ σταυροῦ. ποιμένες ἀπελαύνονται,
ἀντεισάγονται δὲ λύκοι βαρεῖς, διασπῶντες τὸ
ποίμνιον τοῦ Χριστοῦ. οἶκοι εὐκτήριοι ἔρημοι
τῶν ἐκκλησιαζόντων· αἱ ἐρημίαι πλήρεις τῶν
ὀδυρομένων. οἱ πρεσβύτεροι ὀδύρονται, τὰ παλαιὰ

---

[1] ἡμῖν E.   [2] ἡμετέραν E.
[3] ἐξουδένωνται· νεωτεροποιῶν] ἐξουθένηνται, νεωτέρων tres
Regii, Coisl. secundus.

Lord, and secondly, that you may not refuse to
bring all the consolation in your power to our suffering churches. For here all things are sick, most
reverend brethren, and in the face of the continuous
attacks of her enemies the church has given up the
struggle—like a ship in mid-sea when it is buffeted
by the successive blows of the waves—unless it
receive some speedy visitation of the goodness of
the Lord. Therefore, just as we consider your
agreement and unity with one another as a special
blessing for us, so too we beg you to sympathize
with our dissensions and not,[4] because we are
separated by our respective geographical positions,
to sever us from yourselves, but, inasmuch as we are
united in the communion of the Spirit, to take us
into the harmony of one single body.

The evils which afflict us are well known, even
if we do not now mention them, for long since have
they been re-echoed through the whole world. The
teachings of the Fathers are scorned; the apostolic
traditions are set at naught; the fabrications of
innovators are in force in the churches; these men,
moreover, train themselves in rhetorical quibbling
and not in theology; the wisdom of the world
takes first place to itself, having thrust aside the
glory of the Cross. The shepherds are driven away,
and in their places are introduced troublesome
wolves who tear asunder the flock of Christ. The
houses of prayer are bereft of those wont to assemble
therein; the solitudes are filled with those who
weep. The elders weep, comparing the past with

---

⁴ οὐ] καὶ οὐχί E.

συγκρίνοντες τοῖς παροῦσιν· οἱ νέοι ἐλεεινότεροι,
μὴ εἰδότες οἵων ἐστέρηνται.

Ταῦτα ἱκανὰ μὲν κινῆσαι πρὸς[1] συμπάθειαν
τοὺς τὴν Χριστοῦ ἀγάπην πεπαιδευμένους·
συγκρινόμενος δὲ τῇ ἀληθείᾳ τῶν πραγμάτων
ὁ λόγος παρὰ πολὺ τῆς ἀξίας αὐτῶν ἀπολείπεται.
εἴ τι οὖν παραμύθιον ἀγάπης, εἴ τις κοινωνία
Πνεύματος, εἴ τινα[2] σπλάγχνα οἰκτιρμῶν,[3]
κινήθητε πρὸς τὴν ἀντίληψιν ἡμῶν. λάβετε
ζῆλον εὐσεβείας, ἐξέλεσθε ἡμᾶς τοῦ χειμῶνος
τούτου. λαλείσθω καὶ παρ' ἡμῖν μετὰ παρρησίας
τὸ ἀγαθὸν ἐκεῖνο κήρυγμα τῶν πατέρων, τὸ
καταστρέφον μὲν τὴν δυσώνυμον αἵρεσιν τὴν[4]
Ἀρείου, οἰκοδομοῦν[5] δὲ τὰς ἐκκλησίας ἐν τῇ
ὑγιαινούσῃ διδασκαλίᾳ ἐν ᾗ ὁ Υἱὸς ὁμοούσιος
ὁμολογεῖται τῷ Πατρί, καὶ τὸ Πνεῦμα τὸ ἅγιον
ὁμοτίμως συναριθμεῖταί τε καὶ συλλατρεύεται·
ἵνα ἣν ὑμῖν[6] ἔδωκεν ὁ Κύριος ὑπὲρ τῆς ἀληθείας
παρρησίαν, καὶ τὸ ἐπὶ τῇ ὁμολογίᾳ τῆς θείας[7]
καὶ σωτηρίου Τριάδος καύχημα, τοῦτο καὶ ἡμῖν
διὰ τῶν ὑμετέρων εὐχῶν καὶ τῆς συνεργίας ὑμῶν
χαρίσηται. τὸ δὲ καθέκαστον αὐτὸς ὁ προειρημένος συνδιάκονος ἀναγγελεῖ ὑμῶν τῇ ἀγάπῃ.
καὶ πᾶσι δὲ τοῖς γενομένοις κανονικῶς παρὰ τῆς
ὑμετέρας τιμιότητος συνεθέμεθα, τὸν ἀποστολικὸν
ὑμῶν ζῆλον ὑπὲρ τῆς ὀρθοδοξίας ἀποδεξάμενοι.

---

[1] εἰς editi antiqi.   [2] τινα] τι E.
[3] καὶ οἰκτιρμοί E.   [4] τοῦ E.
[5] στερεοῦν editi antiqi, οἰκονομοῦν Harl., Regius.

the present; the young are more to be pitied, since they know not of what they have been deprived.

These facts are sufficient to move to sympathy those who have been taught the love of Christ; yet my speech in comparison with the true state of things falls far short of a worthy presentation of them. If, then, there is any consolation of love, if there is any communion of the Spirit, if there are any bowels of mercy, be moved to our assistance. Take up the zeal of piety, and rescue us from this storm. And let us also pronounce with boldness that good dogma[1] of the Fathers, which overwhelms the accursed heresy of Arius, and builds the churches on the sound doctrine, wherein the Son is confessed to be consubstantial with the Father, and the Holy Spirit is numbered with them in like honour and so adored; in order that the Lord through your prayers and your co-operation may also bestow upon us that fearlessness in the cause of truth, and that glory in the confession of the divine and saving Trinity, which He has given to you. The deacon whom we have mentioned will himself announce everything in detail to your Affection. Moreover, with all that has been done canonically by your Honours we are in agreement, having welcomed your apostolic zeal for orthodoxy.

---

[1] Basil in general seems to use δόγματα in the sense of doctrines and practices privately and tacitly sanctioned in the Church, and he reserves κηρύγματα for what is now usually understood as δόγματα.

---

⁶ ἡμῖν E.   ⁷ ἀληθείας editi antiqi.

XCI

Οὐαλεριανῷ, ἐπισκόπῳ Ἰλλυριῶν [1]

Χάρις τῷ Κυρίῳ,[2] τῷ δόντι ἡμῖν ἀρχαίας
ἀγάπης καρπὸν ἰδεῖν ἐν τῇ σῇ καθαρότητι, ὅς
γε τοσοῦτον διεστὼς τῷ σώματι, συνῆψας ἡμῖν
σεαυτὸν[3] διὰ γράμματος, καὶ τῷ πνευματικῷ
σου καὶ ἁγίῳ πόθῳ περιπτυξάμενος ἡμᾶς, ἀμύθητόν τι[4] φίλτρον ταῖς ψυχαῖς ἡμῶν ἐνεποίησας.
ἔργῳ γὰρ ἐμάθομεν τῆς παροιμίας τὴν δύναμιν,
ὅτι "Ὥσπερ ψυχῇ διψώσῃ ψυχρὸν ὕδωρ, οὕτως
ἀγγελία ἀγαθὴ ἐκ γῆς[5] μακρόθεν.

Δεινὸς γάρ ἐστι παρ᾽ ἡμῖν λιμὸς ἀγάπης,
ἀδελφὲ τιμιώτατε. καὶ ἡ αἰτία πρόδηλος, ὅτι
διὰ τὸ πληθυνθῆναι τὴν ἀνομίαν ἐψύγη[6] τῶν
πολλῶν ἡ ἀγάπη. διὰ τοῦτο καὶ πολλοῦ ἄξιον
ἡμῖν ἐφάνη τὸ γράμμα, καὶ ἀμειβόμεθά σε διὰ
τοῦ αὐτοῦ ἀνδρὸς τοῦ εὐλαβεστάτου συνδιακόνου
ἡμῶν καὶ ἀδελφοῦ Σαβίνου· δι᾽ οὗ καὶ γνωρί-
ζομέν σοι ἑαυτοὺς καὶ παρακαλοῦμέν σε ἐπα-

---

[1] Ἰλλυρικοῦ Harl., Reg. secundus, Coisl. secundus.
[2] Θεῷ nonnulli MSS.   [3] ἑαυτόν E.   [4] τό E, Med.
[5] γῆς] sic E, Med., Harl.   τῆς alii MSS. et editi.
[6] ψυγήσεται E.

---

[1] Before Easter of 372. St. Valerianus, bishop of Aquileia,
is first mentioned as being present at the council of Rome
in 371. Cf. Theodoret, *H.E.* 2, 17. He presided at the
council held in 381 at Aquileia against the Arian bishops
Palladius and Secundinus, although he took small part in
the discussion, St. Ambrose being the leader of the Catholics.
He was also at the council at Rome in 382. Cf. Theodoret,

LETTER XCI

To Valerian, Bishop of the Illyrians[1]

Thanks be unto the Lord, who has permitted us to see in your Purity the fruit of pristine love;[2] for you, though so far separated in body, have united yourself to us by letter, and embracing us with your spiritual and holy yearning you have engendered in our souls an ineffable affection. For by experience we have learned the force of the proverb that : "As cold water to a thirsty soul, so is good tidings from a far country."[3]

For terrible among us is the famine of love, most honoured brother. And the cause is manifest : "because iniquity has abounded, the charity of many has grown cold."[4] For this reason, indeed, your letter has seemed of great worth to us, and we are answering you through the same person, our most reverend deacon and brother, Sabinus; and through him, moreover, we both make our own con-

---

H.E. 5, 9. The date of his death is uncertain. He is commemorated on Nov. 27. Under his rule there grew up at Aquileia that group of people of whom Jerome was the most famous, and which he calls in his chronicle (A.D. 378) "a company of the blessed." Dorotheus or Sabinus had brought letters from Athanasius, and Sabinus one from Valerianus, and Basil is here taking the opportunity to reply.

[2] *i.e.* an exemplification of Christian love as taught in the early Church.

[3] Cf. Prov. 25. 25: ὥσπερ ὕδωρ ψυχρὸν ψυχῇ διψώσῃ προσηνές, οὕτως ἀγγελία ἀγαθὴ ἐκ γῆς μακρόθεν.

[4] Cf. Matt. 24. 12: καὶ διὰ τὸ πληθυνθῆναι τὴν ἀνομίαν, ψυγήσεται ἡ ἀγάπη τῶν πολλῶν.

"And because iniquity hath abounded, the charity of many shall grow cold."

γρυπνεῖν ταῖς ὑπὲρ ἡμῶν προσευχαῖς, ἵνα δῷ
ποτὲ ὁ ἅγιος Θεὸς καὶ τοῖς ἐνταῦθα πράγμασι
γαλήνην καὶ ἡσυχίαν, καὶ ἐπιτιμήσῃ τῷ ἀνέμῳ
τούτῳ καὶ τῇ θαλάσσῃ, ὥστε παύσασθαι ἡμᾶς
τοῦ σάλου καὶ τῆς ἀνατροπῆς, ἐν ᾗ νῦν καθεστήκαμεν, ἀεὶ καταποντισθήσεσθαι[1] παντελῶς
ἀναμένοντες.

Ἀλλὰ τοῦτο μεγάλως[2] ἐν τοῖς παροῦσιν ὁ
Κύριος ἡμῖν ἐχαρίσατο, τὸ ὑμᾶς ἀκούειν ἐν
ἀκριβεῖ συμφωνίᾳ καὶ ἑνότητι εἶναι πρὸς ἀλλήλους, καὶ ἀκωλύτως παρ' ὑμῖν τὸ κήρυγμα τῆς
εὐσεβείας περιαγγέλλεσθαι. ὁτεδήποτε γὰρ
(εἴπερ μὴ συγκέκλεισται λοιπὸν ὁ χρόνος τοῦ
κόσμου τούτου, ἀλλ' ἔτι ἡμέραι τῆς ἀνθρωπίνης
ζωῆς ὑπολείπονται) ἀνάγκη παρ' ὑμῶν ἀνανεω-
θῆναι τὴν πίστιν τῇ ἀνατολῇ, καὶ ὧν ἐλάβετε
παρ' αὐτῆς ἀγαθῶν, τούτων ἐν καιρῷ παρασχέσθαι αὐτῇ τὴν ἀντίδοσιν. τὸ γὰρ ὑγιαῖνον
ἐνταῦθα μέρος καὶ τὴν τῶν πατέρων εὐσέβειαν
ἐκδικοῦν ἱκανῶς κέκμηκε, πολλαῖς καὶ ποικίλαις
μηχανημάτων προσβολαῖς ἐν τῇ ἑαυτοῦ μεθοδείᾳ
τοῦ διαβόλου αὐτὸ κατασείσαντος. ἀλλ' εὐχαῖς
ὑμετέραις τῶν ἀγαπώντων τὸν Κύριον σβεσθείη
μὲν ἡ πονηρὰ καὶ λαοπλάνος αἵρεσις τῆς Ἀρείου
κακοδοξίας· ἀναλάμψειε δὲ ἡ ἀγαθὴ τῶν πατέρων
ἡμῶν διδασκαλία τῶν συνελθόντων κατὰ τὴν
Νίκαιαν, ὥστε σύμφωνον τῷ σωτηρίῳ βαπτίσματι τὴν δοξολογίαν ἀποπληροῦσθαι[3] τῇ μακαρίᾳ
Τριάδι.

dition known to you and beseech you to be vigilant in your prayers for us, in order that the holy God may some day grant calm and repose to our concerns here, and may rebuke this wind and sea, so that we can find rest from the tempest-tossing and confusion in which we now find ourselves, ever waiting to be plunged utterly into the deep.

But this great blessing the Lord has bestowed upon us in our present situation—that we hear that you are in strict harmony and unity with one another, and that without hindrance the proclamation of the true faith is being made among you. For at some time (unless the period of this world is now closed, but if days of human existence alone still remain) there must come from you a renewal of the faith for the East, and in due time you must render her a recompense for the blessings which you have received from her. For that portion of us here that is sound and that guards the true doctrine of our fathers has become quite weary, since the devil in his craftiness has struck it down by the many and cunning assaults of his machinations. But by the prayers of you who love the Lord may that wicked and deceiving heresy, the false doctrine of Arius, be extinguished ; may the good teaching of our fathers who met at Nicaea shine forth again, so that the doxology in harmony with saving baptism may be duly rendered to the Blessed Trinity.

---

[1] καταποντίζεσθαι editi antiqi.   [2] μέγας editi antiqi.
[3] ἀναπληροῦσθαι E.

XCII

Πρὸς Ἰταλοὺς καὶ Γάλλους

Τοῖς θεοφιλεστάτοις καὶ ὁσιωτάτοις ἀδελφοῖς[1] συλλειτουργοῖς[2] κατὰ τὴν Ἰταλίαν καὶ Γαλλίαν ὁμοψύχοις ἐπισκόποις Μελέτιος, Εὐσέβειος, Βασίλειος, Βάσσος, Γρηγόριος, Πελάγιος, Παῦλος, Ἄνθιμος, Θεόδοτος, Βίθος, Ἀβραάμιος, Ἰοβῖνος,[3] Ζήνων, Θεοδώρητος, Μαρκιανός, Βάραχος, Ἀβραάμιος, Λιβάνιος, Θαλάσσιος, Ἰωσήφ, Βοηθός, Ἰάτριος,[4] Θεόδοτος, Εὐστάθιος, Βαρσούμας, Ἰωάννης, Χοσρόης,[5] Ἰωσάκης,[6] Νάρσης, Μάρις, Γρηγόριος, Δαφνός,[7] ἐν Κυρίῳ χαίρειν.

Φέρει μέν τινα παραμυθίαν ταῖς ὀδυνωμέναις ψυχαῖς καὶ στεναγμὸς πολλάκις ἐκ βάθους τῆς καρδίας ἀναπεμπόμενος, καί που καὶ δάκρυον ἀποστάξαν τὸ πολὺ τῆς θλίψεως διεφόρησεν. ἡμῖν δὲ οὐχ, ὅσον[8] στεναγμὸς καὶ δάκρυον, παραμυθίαν ἔχει τὸ ἐξειπεῖν ἡμῶν τὰ πάθη πρὸς τὴν ἀγάπην ὑμῶν· ἀλλά τις ἡμᾶς καὶ ἐλπὶς χρηστοτέρα θάλπει, ὡς τάχα ἄν, εἰ ἐξαγγείλαιμεν ὑμῖν τὰ λυποῦντα ἡμᾶς, διαναστήσαιμεν[9] ὑμᾶς πρὸς

---

[1] ἀδελφοῖς om. E. [2] τοῖς add. E.
[3] Ἰουβῖνος Vat. ; Σαβῖνος editi antiqi.
[4] Ἀτρεῖος Vat., Coisl secundus, Reg. secundus.
[5] Χρυσορόης Coisl. secundus, Reg. secundus.
[6] Ἰσάκης Reg. secundus ; Ἰσάκις Coisl. secundus ; Ἰώσακις Harl.
[7] καὶ οἱ λοιποί add. ed. antiqi ; καὶ οἱ σὺν αὐτοῖς ἀδελφοί add. Med.
[8] ὅσην Regii duo, Coisl. secundus.
[9] διαναπτήσωμεν duo MSS. ; διαναστήσαντες Harl. ; διαναστήσομεν editi antiqi.

LETTER XCII

To the Italians and Gauls[1]

To our most God-beloved and holy brethren, co-workers in Italy and Gaul, bishops of like mind with us, we, Meletius,[2] Eusebius,[3] Basil,[4] Bassus,[5] Gregory,[6] Pelagius,[7] Paul, Anthimus,[8] Theodotus,[9] Vitus,[10] Abraham,[11] Jobinus,[12] Zeno,[13] Theodoretus, Marcianus, Barachus, Abraham,[14] Libanius, Thalassius, Joseph, Boethus, Iatrius,[15] Theodotus, Eustathius,[16] Barsumas, John, Chosroes, Iosaces,[17] Narses, Maris, Gregory,[18] Daphnus, send you greetings in the Lord.

Even a groan repeatedly uttered from the depths of the heart brings some degree of consolation to souls in affliction, and doubtless, too, a falling tear has swept away the greater portion of our anguish. But the telling of our woes to your Charity means for us, not consolation such as groans and tears may bring; nay, there is also hope for better things that warms us, a hope that perhaps, if we should announce to you the causes of our affliction, we might rouse you to take those measures for our

---

[1] Written in 372.   [2] Of Antioch.
[3] Of Samosata.   [4] Of Caesarea.
[5] Tillemont (*Basil*, Note LII) suggests Barses of Edessa.
[6] The elder, of Nazianzus.   [7] Of Laodicea.
[8] Of Tyana.   [9] Of Nicopolis.   [10] Of Carrhae.
[11] Of Batnae.   [12] Of Perrha.   [13] Of Tyre.
[14] Of Urimi in Syria.
[15] Maran would read Otreius of Melitine for Iatrius.
[16] Of Sebasteia.
[17] Maran would read Isaaces, identifying him with the Isacoces of Armenia Major.
[18] Probably Gregory of Nyssa, lately consecrated.

τὴν ἀντίληψιν ἡμῶν, ἣν πάλαι μὲν [1] προσεδοκήσαμεν παρ' ὑμῶν ταῖς κατὰ τὴν ἀνατολὴν
ἐκκλησίαις γενήσεσθαι, οὐδέπω [2] δὲ τετυχήκαμεν,
πάντως τοῦ [3] ἐν σοφίᾳ τὰ ἡμέτερα διοικοῦντος
Θεοῦ, κατὰ τὰ ἀθεώρητα αὐτοῦ τῆς δικαιοσύνης
κρίματα, πλείονι χρόνῳ παραταθῆναι ἡμᾶς [4] ἐν
τοῖς πειρασμοῖς τούτοις οἰκονομήσαντος. οὐ γὰρ
δήπου ἠγνοήσατε τὰ καθ' ἡμᾶς, ἀδελφοὶ τιμιώτατοι, ὧν ἡ ἀκοὴ καὶ ἐπὶ [5] τὰ ἔσχατα τῆς οἰκουμένης ἐξέδραμεν· [6] οὐδὲ ἀσυμπαθεῖς που ὑμεῖς
πρὸς τοὺς ὁμοψύχους τῶν ἀδελφῶν, μαθηταὶ
ὑπάρχοντες τοῦ Ἀποστόλου, τοῦ πλήρωμα εἶναι
τοῦ νόμου τὴν πρὸς τὸν πλησίον ἀγάπην διδά-
σκοντος. ἀλλ' ὅπερ εἴπαμεν, ἐπέσχεν ὑμῶν τὴν
ὁρμὴν ἡ δικαία τοῦ Θεοῦ κρίσις, ἐκπληρωθῆναι
ἡμῖν τὴν διατεταγμένην ἐπὶ ταῖς ἁμαρτίαις ἡμῶν
θλίψιν ἐπιμετροῦσα. [7] ἀλλὰ νῦν γοῦν, καὶ πρὸς
τὸν ὑπὲρ τῆς ἀληθείας ζῆλον καὶ τὴν ἡμετέραν
συμπάθειαν, διαναστῆναι ὑμᾶς παρακαλοῦμεν,
πάντα μαθόντας, καὶ ὅσα πρὸ τούτου τὰς ἀκοὰς
ὑμῶν διέφυγε, παρὰ τοῦ εὐλαβεστάτου ἀδελφοῦ
ἡμῶν τοῦ συνδιακόνου Σαβίνου, ὃς δυνήσεται
ὑμῖν καὶ ὅσα τὴν ἐπιστολὴν διαφεύγει παρ'
ἑαυτοῦ διηγήσασθαι· δι' οὗ παρακαλοῦμεν ὑμᾶς
ἐνδύσασθαι σπλάγχνα οἰκτιρμοῦ, καὶ ἀποθέσθαι
μὲν πάντα ὄκνον, ἀναλαβεῖν δὲ τὸν κόπον τῆς
ἀγάπης· καὶ μήτε ὁδοῦ μῆκος, μήτε τὰς κατ'
οἶκον ἀσχολίας, μήτ' ἄλλο τι τῶν ἀνθρωπίνων
ὑπολογίσασθαι.

---

[1] μέν om. E. [2] οὐδέποτε editi antiqi.
[3] τὰ πάντα add. E, editi antiqi. [4] ὑμᾶς E.
[5] εἰς editi antiqi. [6] διέδραμεν editi antiqi.

relief which we have long been expecting would
come from you to the churches in the East, but
which we have not yet received—surely for the
reason that God, who in His wisdom disposes our
affairs, has ordained according to the inscrutable
judgments of His justice that we should be racked
in these trials for a still longer period. For you
surely have not remained ignorant how affairs are
amongst us, most honoured brethren, whereof the
rumour has gone forth to the uttermost parts of the
world ; nor are you, methinks, without sympathy
for brethren of like mind with yourselves, being
disciples of the Apostle,[1] who teaches that the love
of neighbour is the fulfilling of the law. But, as
we have said, it is the righteous judgment of God,
meting out to us for fulfilment the suffering appointed for our offences, that has restrained your
interest in our behalf. But now at least, by your
zeal for the truth and by the sympathy you have for
us, we implore you to rouse yourselves, when you
have learned the whole story, even what has hitherto
escaped your ears, from our most revered brother,
the deacon Sabinus, who will be able to relate to you
by word of mouth whatever is not contained in our
letter. Through him we beseech you to put on the
bowels of mercy, to cast aside all hesitation, and to
take up the labour of love ; and to take into consideration neither length of journey, nor the business you
may have at home, nor any other concern of man.

---

[1] Cf. Rom. 13, 10 : ἡ ἀγάπη τῷ πλησίον κακὸν οὐκ ἐργάζεται·
πλήρωμα οὖν νόμου ἡ ἀγάπη.
"The love of our neighbour worketh no evil. Love
therefore is the fulfilling of the law."

---

⁷ ἐπιμετρήσασα editi antiqi.

Οὐ γὰρ περὶ μιᾶς ἐκκλησίας ὁ κίνδυνος, οὐδὲ δύο ἢ τρεῖς αἱ τῷ χαλεπῷ τούτῳ χειμῶνι παραπεσοῦσαι.[1] σχεδὸν γὰρ ἀπὸ τῶν ὅρων τοῦ Ἰλλυρικοῦ μέχρι Θηβαΐδος τὸ τῆς αἱρέσεως κακὸν ἐπινέμεται. ἧς τὰ πονηρὰ σπέρματα πρότερον μὲν ὁ δυσώνυμος Ἄρειος κατεβάλετο, ῥιζωθέντα δὲ διὰ βάθους ὑπὸ πολλῶν τῶν ἐν μέσῳ φιλοπόνως τὴν ἀσέβειαν γεωργησάντων, νῦν τοὺς φθοροποιοὺς καρποὺς ἐξεβλάστησεν.[2] ἀνατέτραπται μὲν γὰρ τὰ τῆς εὐσεβείας δόγματα, συγκέχυνται δὲ ἐκκλησίας θεσμοί. φιλαρχίαι δὲ τῶν μὴ φοβουμένων τὸν Κύριον ταῖς προστασίαις ἐπιπηδῶσι· καὶ ἐκ τοῦ προφανοῦς λοιπὸν ἆθλον δυσσεβείας ἡ προεδρία πρόκειται· ὥστε ὁ τὰ χαλεπώτερα βλασφημήσας εἰς ἐπισκοπὴν[3] λαοῦ προτιμότερος. οἴχεται σεμνότης ἱερατική· ἐπιλελοίπασιν οἱ ποιμαίνοντες μετ' ἐπιστήμης[4] ποίμνιον τοῦ Κυρίου, οἰκονομίας πτωχῶν εἰς ἰδίας ἀπολαύσεις καὶ δώρων διανομὰς παραναλισκόντων ἀεὶ[5] τῶν φιλαρχούντων. ἠμαύρωται κανόνων ἀκρίβεια. ἐξουσία τοῦ ἁμαρτάνειν πολλή· οἱ γὰρ διὰ σπουδῆς ἀνθρωπίνης[6] παρελθόντες ἐπὶ τὸ ἄρχειν ἐν αὐτῷ τούτῳ τῆς σπουδῆς τὴν χάριν ἀνταναπληροῦσι, τῷ πάντα πρὸς ἡδονὴν ἐνδιδόναι[7] τοῖς ἁμαρτάνουσιν. ἀπόλωλε κρίμα δίκαιον· πᾶς τις τῷ θελήματι τῆς καρδίας αὐτοῦ πορεύεται. ἡ πονηρία ἄμετρος, οἱ λαοὶ

---

[1] περιπεσοῦσαι editi antiqi.
[2] ἐξεβλάστησαν E, editi antiqi.
[3] ἐπίσκοπον alii MSS.   [4] τό add. E.
[5] ἀεὶ] πάντα Med , Harl.
[6] διὰ σπουδῆς ἀνθρωπίνης] σπουδαῖς ἀνθρωπίναις editi antiqi.

For the danger is not confined to a single church, nor are there two or three only which have been overthrown by this fierce tempest. For we can almost say that the curse of this heresy is spreading out from the borders of Illyricum to the Thebaid; its baneful seeds were formerly scattered by the infamous Arius, and, taking deep root through the efforts of many who have cultivated them assiduously in the meantime, they have now produced their death-dealing fruits. For the teachings of the true faith have been overthrown and the ordinances of the Church have been set at naught. The lust for office on the part of men who do not fear the Lord leaps upon the positions of high authority, and quite openly now the foremost place is offered as a prize for impiety; and consequently that man who has uttered the more horrible blasphemies is accounted the more worthy of the episcopal direction of the people. Gone is the dignity of the priesthood. None are left to tend the flock of the Lord with knowledge, while ambitious men ever squander the sums collected for the poor on their own pleasures and for the distribution of gifts. The strict observance of the canons has been weakened. Licence to commit sin has become widespread; for those who have come into office through the favour of men take this very means of returning thanks for the favour—conceding to sinners whatever will conduce to their pleasure. Just judgment is dead; each and every one proceeds according to the whim of his own heart. Wickedness goes beyond all

---

[7] διδόναι E, editi antiqi.

ἀνουθέτητοι, οἱ προεστῶτες ἀπαρρησίαστοι·
δοῦλοι γὰρ τῶν δεδωκότων τὴν χάριν, οἱ δι'
ἀνθρώπων ἑαυτοῖς τὴν δυναστείαν κατακτη-
σάμενοι. ἤδη δὲ καὶ ὅπλον τισὶ τοῦ πρὸς ἀλλήλους πολέμου ἡ ἐκδίκησις δῆθεν τῆς ὀρθοδοξίας
ἐπινενόηται, καὶ τὰς ἰδίας ἔχθρας ἐπικρυψάμενοι·
ὑπὲρ τῆς εὐσεβείας ἐχθραίνειν κατασχηματί-
ζονται. ἄλλοι δέ, τὸν ἐπὶ τοῖς αἰσχίστοις ἐκ-
κλίνοντες ἔλεγχον, τοὺς λαοὺς εἰς τὴν κατ'
ἀλλήλων φιλονεικίαν ἐκμαίνουσιν, ἵνα τοῖς κοινοῖς
κακοῖς τὸ καθ' ἑαυτοὺς συσκιάσωσι.

Διὸ καὶ ἄσπονδός ἐστιν ὁ πόλεμος οὗτος, τῶν
τὰ πονηρὰ εἰργασμένων τὴν κοινὴν εἰρήνην, ὡς
ἀποκαλύπτουσαν αὐτῶν τὰ κρυπτὰ τῆς αἰσχύνης,
ὑφορωμένων. ἐπὶ τούτοις γελῶσιν οἱ ἄπιστοι,
σαλεύονται οἱ ὀλιγόπιστοι· ἀμφίβολος ἡ πίστις,
ἄγνοια κατακέχυται τῶν ψυχῶν, διὰ τὸ μιμεῖσθαι[1]
τὴν ἀλήθειαν τοὺς δολοῦντας τὸν λόγον ἐν κα-
κουργίᾳ. σιγᾷ μὲν γὰρ τὰ τῶν εὐσεβούντων
στόματα, ἀνεῖται δὲ πᾶσα βλάσφημος γλῶσσα.
ἐβεβηλώθη τὰ ἅγια, φεύγουσι τοὺς εὐκτηρίους
οἴκους οἱ ὑγιαίνοντες τῶν λαῶν ὡς ἀσεβείας
διδασκαλεῖα, κατὰ δὲ τὰς ἐρημίας πρὸς τὸν ἐν
οὐρανοῖς Δεσπότην μετὰ στεναγμῶν καὶ δακρύων
τὰς χεῖρας αἴρουσιν. ἔφθασε γὰρ[2] πάντως καὶ
μέχρις ὑμῶν τὰ γινόμενα[3] ἐν ταῖς πλείσταις τῶν
πόλεων, ὅτι οἱ λαοὶ σὺν γυναιξὶ καὶ παιδίοις[4]
καὶ αὐτοῖς τοῖς πρεσβύταις,[5] πρὸ τῶν τειχῶν
ἐκχυθέντες, ἐν τῷ ὑπαίθρῳ τελοῦσι τὰς προσευχάς, φέροντες πάσας τὰς ἐκ τοῦ ἀέρος κακο-

[1] μισεῖσθαι Med. [2] δέ editi antiqi.

138

bounds, the laity are deaf to admonition, their leaders are without freedom of speech ; for those who have obtained power for themselves through the favour of men are the slaves of those who have conferred the favour. And already, to serve them as a weapon in their warfare with one another, "the vindication of orthodoxy," forsooth, has been devised by some, and they, concealing their private enmities, pretend that they hate one another for religion's sake ! Still others, to avoid exposure for their shameful deeds, inflame the laity to mutual strife in order that they may use the public ills to screen their own conduct.

Hence this is a truceless war, for the perpetrators of these evil deeds dread a general peace on the ground that it will lay bare their hidden acts of shame. At this state of affairs unbelievers laugh, those of little faith waver ; the true faith is ambiguous ; ignorance is poured down upon souls by reason of the fact that those who maliciously falsify doctrine imitate the truth. For the lips of the pious are silent, yet every blasphemous tongue is let loose. Holy things have been profaned, those of the laity who are sound in faith flee the houses of prayer as schools of impiety, and in the solitudes they raise their hands with groans and tears to the Master in heaven. For surely what is happening in most of our cities has already reached even you— that the laity with their wives, their children, and even their aged, having poured forth in front of the walls, offer up their prayers under the open sky, enduring all the discomforts of the weather

---

³ γενόμενα editi antiqi.   ⁴ παισί editi antiqi.
⁵ πρεσβυτέροις E.

παθείας σὺν πολλῇ τῇ μακροθυμίᾳ, τὴν παρὰ
τοῦ Κυρίου ἀντίληψιν ἀναμένοντες.

Τίς θρῆνος τῶν συμφορῶν τούτων ἄξιος ; ποῖαι
πηγαὶ δακρύων κακοῖς τοσούτοις ἀρκέσουσιν ;[1]
ἕως οὖν ἔτι δοκοῦσιν ἑστάναι τινές, ἕως ἔτι ἴχνος
τῆς παλαιᾶς καταστάσεως διασώζεται,[2] πρὶν
τέλεον ταῖς ἐκκλησίαις ἐπέλθῃ[3] τὸ ναυάγιον,
ἐπείχθητε πρὸς ἡμᾶς, ἐπείχθητε ἤδη, ναὶ δεόμεθα,
ἀδελφοὶ γνησιώτατοι· δότε χεῖρα τοῖς εἰς γόνυ
κλιθεῖσι. συγκινηθήτω ἐφ᾽ ἡμῖν τὰ ἀδελφικὰ
ὑμῶν σπλάγχνα, προχυθήτω δάκρυα συμπαθείας.
μὴ περιίδητε τὸ ἥμισυ τῆς οἰκουμένης ὑπὸ τῆς
πλάνης καταποθέν· μὴ ἀνάσχησθε ἀποσβεσθῆναι
τὴν πίστιν, παρ᾽ οἷς πρῶτον ἐξέλαμψε.

Τί οὖν ποιήσαντες ἀντιλήψεσθε τῶν πραγμάτων, καὶ πῶς τὸ πρὸς τοὺς θλιβομένους συμπαθὲς
ἐπιδείξεσθε,[4] οὐ παρ᾽ ἡμῶν πάντως δεήσει μαθεῖν[5]
ὑμᾶς, ἀλλ᾽ αὐτὸ τὸ Πνεῦμα τὸ ἅγιον ὑμῖν ὑπο-
θήσεται. πλήν γε ὅτι τάχους χρεία πρὸς τὸ
περισώσασθαι τοὺς περιλειφθέντας, καὶ παρουσίας ἀδελφῶν πλειόνων, ὥστε πλήρωμα εἶναι
συνόδου τοὺς ἐπιδημοῦντας, ἵνα μὴ μόνον ἐκ τῆς
τῶν ἀποστειλάντων σεμνότητος, ἀλλὰ καὶ ἐκ τοῦ
οἰκείου ἀριθμοῦ τὸ ἀξιόπιστον εἰς διόρθωσιν ᾖ,[6]
καὶ τὴν ἐν Νικαίᾳ γραφεῖσαν παρὰ τῶν πατέρων
ἡμῶν πίστιν ἀνανεώσωνται,[7] καὶ τὴν αἵρεσιν ἐκ-
κηρύξωσι,[8] καὶ ταῖς ἐκκλησίαις τὰ εἰρηνικὰ
διαλέξονται, τοὺς τὰ αὐτὰ φρονοῦντας συνά-
γοντες[9] εἰς ὁμόνοιαν. τοῦτο γὰρ δήπου τὸ

---

[1] ἐπαρκέσουσι editi antiqi.   [2] διασώζηται E.
[3] ἐπελθεῖν Reg. duo.   [4] ἐπιδείξησθε E, Harl.
[5] μανθάνειν editi antiqi.   [6] ᾖ Capps, οἵ MSS. et editi.
[7] ἀνανεώσωνται Capps : ἀνανεώσονται MSS. et editi.

with great patience, while they await assistance from the Lord.

What song of lamentation can do justice to such calamities as these? What fountains of tears will be adequate for such misfortunes? Therefore, while some still seem to keep their feet, while a trace of the old order of things is still preserved, before complete shipwreck comes upon our churches, hasten to us, yes, hasten to us at once, we implore you, most true and dear brethren; stretch forth your hands to us who have fallen to our knees. Let your fraternal hearts be moved in our behalf, let your tears of sympathy be poured forth. Do not suffer half the world to be swallowed up by error; do not allow the faith to be extinguished in those lands where it first flashed forth.

What action you must take, then, to assist us, and how you are to show sympathy to those in affliction, surely you will not need to learn from us, but the Holy Spirit himself will direct you. But remember that there is need of haste, if those who are still left are to be saved, and of the presence of several brethren, that they in visiting us may complete the number of the synod, so that by reason not only of the high standing of those who have sent them, but also of the number of the delegates they themselves constitute, they may have the prestige to effect a reform; and may restore the creed which was written by our fathers at Nicaea, may banish the heresy, and may speak to the churches a message of peace by bringing those of like convictions into unity. For this, clearly, is the most pitiful

---

8 ἐκκηρύξουσι tres MSS. ; ἐκριζώσουσι editi antiqi.
9 συναγαγόντες E, Harl.

141

πάντων ἐλεεινότατον ὅτι καὶ τὸ δοκοῦν ὑγιαίνειν
ἐφ' ἑαυτὸ ἐμερίσθη· καὶ περιέστηκεν ἡμᾶς, ὡς
ἔοικε, παραπλήσια πάθη τοῖς ποτὲ κατὰ τὴν
Οὐεσπασιανοῦ πολιορκίαν τὰ Ἱεροσόλυμα περι-
σχοῦσιν. ἐκεῖνοί τε γὰρ ὁμοῦ μὲν τῷ [1] ἔξωθεν
συνείχοντο πολέμῳ, ὁμοῦ δὲ καὶ τῇ ἔνδοθεν
στάσει τῶν ὁμοφύλων κατανηλίσκοντο. ἡμῖν δὲ
πρὸς τῷ φανερῷ πολέμῳ τῶν αἱρετικῶν ἔτι καὶ
ὁ [2] παρὰ τῶν δοκούντων ὀρθοδοξεῖν [3] ἐπαναστὰς
πρὸς ἔσχατον ἀσθενείας τὰς [4] ἐκκλησίας κατή-
γαγεν. ἐφ' ἅπερ καὶ μάλιστα τῆς παρ' ὑμῶν
χρήζομεν βοηθείας, ὥστε τοὺς τὴν ἀποστολικὴν
ὁμολογοῦντας πίστιν, ἃ παρεπενόησαν [5] σχίσματα
διαλύσαντας, ὑποταγῆναι τοῦ λοιποῦ τῇ αὐθεντίᾳ
τῆς Ἐκκλησίας, ἵνα ἄρτιον γένηται τὸ σῶμα τοῦ
Χριστοῦ, πᾶσι τοῖς μέλεσιν εἰς ὁλοκληρίαν
ἐπανελθόν, καὶ μὴ μόνον τὰ παρ' ἑτέροις μακαρί-
ζωμεν ἀγαθά, ὅπερ νῦν ποιοῦμεν, ἀλλὰ καὶ τὰς
ἡμετέρας αὐτῶν ἐπίδωμεν ἐκκλησίας τὸ ἀρχαῖον
καύχημα τῆς ὀρθοδοξίας ἀπολαβούσας. τῷ ὄντι
γὰρ τοῦ ἀνωτάτου μακαρισμοῦ ἄξιον τὸ τῇ
ὑμετέρᾳ θεοσεβείᾳ χαρισθὲν παρὰ τοῦ Κυρίου τὸ
μὲν κίβδηλον ἀπὸ τοῦ δοκίμου καὶ καθαροῦ δια-
κρίνειν, τὴν δὲ τῶν πατέρων πίστιν ἄνευ τινὸς
ὑποστολῆς κηρύσσειν· ἣν καὶ ἡμεῖς ἐδεξάμεθα,
καὶ ἐπέγνωμεν ἐκ τῶν ἀποστολικῶν χαρακτήρων
μεμορφωμένην, συνθέμενοι καὶ αὐτῇ καὶ πᾶσι

condition of all—that even that group of us which is apparently sound has become divided against itself; and we are encircled, as it seems, by like calamities to those which once fell on Jerusalem during the siege of Vespasian. For the inhabitants of that city were at one and the same time being hemmed in by the war waged from outside and wasted by the dissension of their own people inside. And so it is with us: in addition to the open war waged by heretics, the other war that has come upon us from those who are supposed to be orthodox has reduced the churches to the last degree of weakness. It is against this that we are especially in need of your assistance, that those who confess the apostolic faith, having put an end to the schisms of their own devising, may henceforth become subject to the authority of the Church, that the body of Christ, having returned to unity in all its parts, may be made perfect, and that we may not only felicitate the good fortunes of others, as we now do, but may also see our own churches recover their ancient glory of orthodoxy. For truly it is a thing that calls for the highest felicitation, that it has been granted by the Lord to your piety to distinguish the spurious from the approved and the pure, and to proclaim the faith of the fathers without any evasion. This faith we too have received, and we recognized it from the apostolic traits with which it was characterized, having submitted ourselves both to it and

---

τοῖς ἐν τῷ συνοδικῷ γράμματι κανονικῶς καὶ
ἐνθέσμως δεδογματισμένοις.

XCIII

Πρὸς Καισαρίαν [1] πατρικίαν, περὶ κοινωνίας

Καὶ τὸ κοινωνεῖν δὲ καθ' ἑκάστην ἡμέραν, καὶ
μεταλαμβάνειν τοῦ ἁγίου σώματος καὶ αἵματος
τοῦ Χριστοῦ, καλὸν καὶ ἐπωφελές, αὐτοῦ σαφῶς
λέγοντος· ὁ τρώγων μου τὴν σάρκα, καὶ πίνων
μου τὸ αἷμα, ἔχει ζωὴν αἰώνιον. τίς γὰρ ἀμφι-
βάλλει, ὅτι τὸ μετέχειν συνεχῶς τῆς ζωῆς οὐδὲν
ἄλλο [2] ἐστὶν ἢ ζῆν πολλαχῶς; ἡμεῖς μέντοιγε
τέταρτον καθ' ἑκάστην ἑβδομάδα κοινωνοῦμεν, ἐν
τῇ Κυριακῇ, ἐν τῇ τετράδι, καὶ ἐν τῇ παρασκευῇ,
καὶ τῷ Σαββάτῳ, καὶ ἐν ταῖς ἄλλαις ἡμέραις ἐὰν
ᾖ μνήμη ἁγίου [3] τινός.

Τὸ δὲ ἐν τοῖς τοῦ διωγμοῦ καιροῖς ἀναγκάζεσθαί

---

[1] πρὸς Καισάριον πατρίκιον περὶ κοινωνίας Colbertinus MS. ;
in quodam codice Regio occurrit fragmentum huius epistolae
sic inscriptum : ἐκ τῆς πρὸς Καισάριον ἐπιστολῆς.
[2] τι add. quidam MSS.   [3] μάρτυρος editi antiqi.

---

[1] For this synodical letter, cf. Theodoret 1, 8 and Socrates
1, 9. The Benedictine editors are surprised that Basil shows
agreement with this synodical letter, since it defines the Son
as τῆς αὐτῆς ὑποστάσεως καὶ οὐσίας (of the same essence and
substance). It is, however, not in the synodical letter, but
in the anathemas originally appended to the creed, that it is
denied that He is of a different substance or essence. Even
here it is not said positively that He is of the same substance
or essence. For a discussion of these theological terms, cf.
Letters VIII and XXXVIII with notes.

to all the doctrines which have been canonically and legally promulgated in the synodical letter.[1]

LETTER XCIII

To The Patrician, Caesaria,[2] on Communion

And also to take communion every day, that is to say, to partake of the holy body and blood of Christ, is good and beneficial, since He himself clearly says: "He that eateth My flesh, and drinketh My blood, hath everlasting life."[3] For who can doubt that sharing continually in the life is nothing else than living in many ways? We for our part, however, take communion four times each week—on Sunday, on Wednesday, on Friday, and on Saturday[4]—and on the other days only when there is a commemoration of a saint.[5]

On the question of a person being compelled, in

---

[2] Written in 372. Note that some MSS. read Caesarius. Tillemont (*Basil*, Note XXXIV) says that Arnaud does not consider this letter as Basil's, but that he gives no reason for denying its authenticity. Tillemont himself thinks that it is a fragment of a letter, and indeed the first words appear to be a continuation. Although it is lacking in many manuscripts, there appears no worthy reason for doubting its authorship.

[3] John 6. 54.

[4] The Greek meanings are literally: Lord's Day, the Fourth, Preparation, and Sabbath.

[5] Note the variant reading μάρτυρος, "of a martyr." Basil in a letter to Saint Ambrose (CXCVII) says the same honour was accorded to Saint Dionysius of Milan at his place of burial as to a martyr. Gregory Thaumaturgus at Neocaesarea, Athanasius, and Basil, all received like honour soon after death.

τινα, μὴ παρόντος ἱερέως ἢ λειτουργοῦ, τὴν κοινωνίαν λαμβάνειν τῇ ἰδίᾳ χειρί, μηδαμῶς εἶναι βαρὺ
περιττόν ἐστιν ἀποδεικνύναι, διὰ τὸ καὶ[1] τὴν
μακρὰν συνήθειαν τοῦτο δι᾽ αὐτῶν τῶν πραγμάτων
πιστώσασθαι. πάντες γὰρ οἱ κατὰ τὰς ἐρήμους[2]
μονάζοντες, ἔνθα μὴ ἔστιν ἱερεύς, κοινωνίαν οἴκοι
κατέχοντες ἀφ᾽ ἑαυτῶν μεταλαμβάνουσιν. ἐν
Ἀλεξανδρείᾳ δὲ καὶ ἐν Αἰγύπτῳ ἕκαστος καὶ
τῶν ἐν λαῷ τελούντων ὡς ἐπὶ τὸ πλεῖστον ἔχει
κοινωνίαν ἐν τῷ οἴκῳ αὐτοῦ, καὶ ὅτε βούλεται[3]
μεταλαμβάνει δι᾽ ἑαυτοῦ. ἅπαξ γὰρ τὴν θυσίαν
τοῦ ἱερέως τελειώσαντος καὶ δεδωκότος, ὁ λαβὼν
αὐτὴν ὡς ὅλην ὁμοῦ, καθ᾽ ἑκάστην μεταλαμβάνων,
παρὰ τοῦ δεδωκότος εἰκότως μεταλαμβάνειν[4] καὶ
ὑποδέχεσθαι πιστεύειν ὀφείλει. καὶ γὰρ καὶ ἐν
τῇ ἐκκλησίᾳ ὁ ἱερεὺς ἐπιδίδωσι τὴν μερίδα καὶ
κατέχει αὐτὴν ὁ ὑποδεχόμενος μετ᾽ ἐξουσίας
ἁπάσης, καὶ οὕτω προσάγει τῷ στόματι τῇ ἰδίᾳ
χειρί. ταὐτὸν τοίνυν ἐστὶ τῇ δυνάμει, εἴτε μίαν
μερίδα δέξεταί τις παρὰ τοῦ ἱερέως, εἴτε πολλὰς
μερίδας ὁμοῦ.

[1] καί om. E.   [2] ἐρημίας multi MSS.
[3] καὶ ὅτε . . . ἑαυτοῦ om. E, editi antiqi.
[4] μεταλαμβάνει E, alii MSS.

---

[1] Cf. Catholic Encyclopaedia, under "Eucharist." In
general it is by Divine and ecclesiastical right that the laity
should as a rule receive communion only from the consecrated
hand of the priest. Cf. *Trent Sess*. XIII, cap. VIII. The

times of persecution when no priest or ministrant is present, to take communion with his own hand, it is superfluous to point out that this is in no wise sinful, since long custom has sanctioned this practice from the very force of circumstances. For all who live the monastic life in the solitudes, where there is no priest, keep the communion at home and partake of it from their own hands. At Alexandria also and in Egypt, each person, even those belonging to the laity, as a rule keeps the communion in his own home, and partakes of it with his own hands when he so wishes. For when the priest has once consummated the offering and has given it, he who has received it ought confidently to believe that he is partaking of it, even as he has received it, all at once, even when he partakes of it daily. So it is when the rite is performed in the church also—the priest hands over the portion, and the recipient in receiving it has complete right of possession, and by such right raises it to his mouth with his own hand. It is, therefore, in respect of authority, one and the same thing, whether a communicant receives a single portion from the priest or many portions at once.[1]

---

practice of the laity giving themselves Holy Communion was formerly, and is to-day, allowed only in case of necessity. In early Christian times it was customary for the faithful to take the Blessed Sacrament to their homes and communicate privately, a custom to which Basil refers above. Cf. also Justin Martyr, *Apol.* I, 85 ; Tertullian, *De Orat.* XIX, and *Ad Uxor.* II, 5 ; Cyprian, *De Lapis,* CXXXII ; and Jerome, *Letter* CXXV. Up to the ninth century it was usual for the priest to place the Sacred Host in the right hand of the recipient, who kissed it and then placed it in his own mouth. Women, from the fourth to the ninth centuries, were required to have a cloth wrapped about their right hand in this ceremony.

XCIV

Ἠλίᾳ ἄρχοντι τῆς ἐπαρχίας [1]

Ὥρμησα μὲν καὶ αὐτὸς καταλαβεῖν σου τὴν
τιμιότητα, ὡς ἂν μὴ τῇ ἀπολείψει ἔλαττόν τι
ἔχοιμι τῶν διαβαλλόντων· ἀλλ᾽ ἐπειδὴ ἡ ἀρρωστία
τοῦ σώματος διεκώλυσε, σφοδρότερον πολλῷ τῆς
συνηθείας ἐπιθεμένη, ἀναγκαίως ἦλθον ἐπὶ τὸ
γράμμα. ἐγὼ τοίνυν, ὦ θαυμάσιε, συντυχὼν
πρώην τῇ τιμιότητί σου, ὥρμησα μὲν καὶ περὶ
πάντων τῶν κατὰ τὸν βίον μου πραγμάτων
ἀνακοινώσασθαί σου τῇ φρονήσει,[2] ὥρμησα δὲ
καὶ τῶν ἐκκλησιῶν ἕνεκα[3] ποιήσασθαί τινα λόγον,
ὡς ἂν μὴ ταῖς μετὰ ταῦτα διαβολαῖς χώρα τις
ὑπολείποιτο.[4] ἀλλ᾽ ἐπέσχον ἐμαυτόν, λογιζόμενος
περίεργον εἶναι παντελῶς, καὶ πέρα τοῦ μέτρου
φιλότιμον, ἀνδρὶ τοσοῦτον[5] πλῆθος πραγμάτων
ἐξηρτημένῳ ἔτι καὶ τὰς ἔξω τῶν ἀναγκαίων
ἐπιβάλλειν φροντίδας. ὁμοῦ τε,[6] εἰρήσεται γὰρ
τἀληθές, καὶ ἄλλως ὤκνησα μήποτε εἰς ἀνάγκην
ἔλθωμεν ταῖς κατ᾽ ἀλλήλων ἀντιλογίαις τρῶσαι
τὴν ψυχήν σου, ὀφείλουσαν ἐν τῇ καθαρᾷ περὶ
τὸν Θεὸν εὐλαβείᾳ τέλειον τὸν μισθὸν τῆς θεοσεβείας[7] καρποῦσθαι. τῷ ὄντι γάρ, ἐάν σε πρὸς
ἑαυτοὺς ἐπιστρέψωμεν[8] ἡμεῖς, ὀλίγην σοι σχολὴν
πρὸς τὰ δημόσια καταλείψομεν, καὶ παραπλήσιον
ποιήσομεν, ὥσπερ ἂν εἴ τις κυβερνήτην, νεοπαγῆ

---

[1] τῷ ἄρχοντι τῆς ἐπαρχίας E, Med.　　[2] φροντίσει E.
[3] τοῦ add. editi antiqi.　　　　　　　[4] ὑπολίποιτο E.
[5] τοσούτῳ E.　　　　　　　　　　　[6] τε] δέ E.
[7] θεότητος E.　　　　　　[8] ἐπιστρέψωμεν editi antiqi.

LETTER XCIV

To Elias, Governor of the Province [1]

I MYSELF have been eager to visit your Honour, lest through failure to do so I should fare worse than my calumniators; but since the ill-health of my body has prevented it, besetting me much more violently than usual, of necessity I have had recourse to writing. When, therefore, respected Sir, I recently met your Honour, I strongly desired to communicate with your wisdom concerning all my temporal affairs, and I desired, too, to hold converse with you in behalf of the churches, so that no room should be left for slanders hereafter. But I checked myself, deeming it altogether officious and unduly zealous to load additional and unnecessary cares on a man already weighed down with such a multitude of duties. At the same time—for the truth must be told—I hesitated especially through fear of being forced, by any controversy we might have with one another, to wound your soul, which in its pure piety toward God is entitled to reap the perfect reward of religion. For truly, if we turn your attention to ourselves, we shall leave you scant leisure for your public duties, and we shall be acting like a man who would burden with an additional cargo a pilot who guides a newly-built ship in the midst of a great

---

[1] Written in 372, at the departure of Valens. On Elias, governor of Cappadocia, cf. also Letters LXXXIV, XCVI. In the present letter, Basil defends himself from the calumnies brought against him by his enemies regarding the church and the hospital he had recently established in the suburbs of Caesarea. Cf. Greg. Naz., *Oratio* XX; Theodoret, *Ecc. Hist.* IV, 19; and Sozomen, VI, 34.

ναῦν ἐν μεγάλῳ κλύδωνι διευθύνοντα, τῇ προσ-
θήκῃ τοῦ φόρτου καταβαρύνοι, δέον ἀφαιρεῖν τι
τῶν ἀγωγίμων καὶ συνεπικουφίζειν ὡς δυνατόν.
ὅθεν μοι δοκεῖ καὶ βασιλεὺς ὁ μέγας, τὴν πολυ-
πραγμοσύνην ἡμῶν ταύτην καταμαθών, ἐᾶσαι
ἡμᾶς ἐφ' ἑαυτῶν τὰς ἐκκλησίας οἰκονομεῖν.

Τοὺς μέντοι ταῖς ἀδόλοις ἀκοαῖς σου παρε-
νοχλοῦντας ἐρωτηθῆναι βούλομαι, τί χεῖρον ἔχει
τὰ δημόσια παρ' ἡμᾶς; ἢ τί μικρὸν ἢ μεῖζον τῶν
κοινῶν ἐκ τῆς ἡμετέρας περὶ τὰς ἐκκλησίας
οἰκονομίας ἠλάττωται; πλὴν εἰ μή τις λέγοι
βλάβην τοῖς πράγμασι φέρειν, οἶκον εὐκτήριον
μεγαλοπρεπῶς[1] κατεσκευασμένον[2] ἀναστῆσαι τῷ
(*)εῷ ἡμῶν, καὶ περὶ αὐτὸν οἴκησιν, τὴν μὲν ἐλευ-
θέριον ἐξῃρημένην[3] τῷ κορυφαίῳ, τὰς δὲ ὑποβε-
βηκυίας τοῖς θεραπευταῖς τοῦ θείου διανενεμη-
μένας ἐν τάξει,[4] ὧν ἡ χρῆσις κοινὴ πρός τε ὑμᾶς
τοὺς ἄρχοντας καὶ τοὺς παρεπομένους ὑμῖν. τίνα
δὲ ἀδικοῦμεν, καταγώγια τοῖς ξένοις οἰκοδομοῦντες,
τοῖς τε[5] κατὰ πάροδον ἐπιφοιτῶσι καὶ τοῖς θεραπείας τινὸς διὰ τὴν ἀσθένειαν δεομένοις, καὶ τὴν
ἀναγκαίαν τούτοις παραμυθίαν ἐγκαθιστῶντες,
τοὺς νοσοκομοῦντας, τοὺς ἰατρεύοντας, τὰ νωτο-
φόρα, τοὺς παραπέμποντας; τούτοις ἀνάγκη καὶ
τέχνας ἕπεσθαι, τάς τε πρὸς τὸ ζῆν ἀναγκαίας, καὶ
ὅσαι πρὸς εὐσχήμονα βίου διαγωγὴν ἐφευρέθησαν·
οἴκους πάλιν ἑτέρους ταῖς ἐργασίαις ἐπιτηδείους,
ἅπερ πάντα τῷ μὲν τόπῳ κόσμος, τῷ δὲ ἄρχοντι
ἡμῶν σεμνολόγημα, ἐπ' αὐτὸν τῆς εὐφημίας ἐπα-

---

[1] μεγλλοπρεπές editi antiqi.   [2] κατασκευασμένον E.
[3] ἐξηρτημένην alii MSS.   [4] ἐν τάξει] ἐντάξαι editi antiqi.
[5] τε om. E.

150

storm, when he ought rather to relieve him of a portion of his freight and lighten the vessel as far as possible. It is for this reason, it seems to me, that the great Emperor, on his part, having learned about this officious tendency of ours, has allowed us to govern the churches ourselves.

I wish, however, that those who keep annoying your honest ears be asked what harm the state receives at our hands; or what, either small or great, of the public interests has suffered injury through our government of the churches; unless, indeed, someone may say that it inflicts injury upon the state to raise in honour of our God a house of prayer built in magnificent fashion, and, grouped about it, a residence, one portion being a generous home reserved for the bishop, and the rest subordinate quarters for the servants of God's worship arranged in order—access to all of which is alike free to you magistrates yourselves and to your retinue. And whom do we wrong when we build hospices for strangers, for those who visit us while on a journey, for those who require some care because of sickness, and when we extend to the latter the necessary comforts, such as nurses, physicians, beasts for travelling and attendants? [1] There must also be occupations to go with these men, both those that are necessary for gaining a livelihood, and also such as have been discovered for a decorous manner of living. And, again, they need still other buildings equipped for their pursuits, all of which are an ornament to the locality, and a source of pride to our governor, since their fame redounds to your

---

[1] One of the duties of the clergy at this time was to act as guides and escort. Cf. Letters XCVIII and CCXLIII.

νιούσης. ὅς γε οὐδὲ τούτου ἕνεκεν πρὸς τὴν
ἐπιστασίαν ἡμῶν ἐξεβιάσθης, ὡς μόνος ἐξαρκῶν
τῷ μεγέθει τῆς γνώμης τά τε κατερρυηκότα τῶν
ἔργων[1] ἀναλαβεῖν, καὶ οἰκίσαι τὰς ἀοικήτους,
καὶ ὅλως εἰς πόλεις τὰς ἐρημίας μετασκευάσαι.
τὸν οὖν εἰς ταῦτα συνεργοῦντα ἐλαύνειν καὶ
ὑβρίζειν, ἢ τιμᾶν καὶ περιέπειν, ἀκολουθότερον
ἦν ; καὶ μὴ οἰηθῇς, ὦ ἄριστε, λόγον μόνον εἶναι
τὰ παρ' ἡμῶν· ἤδη γάρ ἐσμεν ἐν τῷ ἔργῳ, τὰς
ὕλας τέως συμποριζόμενοι.

Τὰ μὲν οὖν πρὸς τὴν τοῦ ἄρχοντος ἀπολογίαν
τοιαῦτα. ἃ δὲ δεῖ πρὸς τὰς τῶν φιλαιτίων μέμψεις,
ὡς Χριστιανῷ καὶ φίλῳ πεφροντικότι ἡμῶν τῆς
ὑπολήψεως ἀποκρίνασθαι, ἀναγκαῖον νῦν ἀποσιωπῆσαι, ὡς καὶ μακρότερα τοῦ μέτρου τῆς ἐπιστολῆς, καὶ ἄλλως οὐκ ἀσφαλῆ[2] γράμμασιν
ἀψύχοις καταπιστεύεσθαι. ἵνα δὲ μὴ τὸν πρὸ
τῆς συντυχίας χρόνον ταῖς διαβολαῖς τινῶν ὑπαχ-
θείς, ὑφεῖναί τι τῆς περὶ ἡμᾶς εὐνοίας ἀναγκασθῇς,
τὸ τοῦ Ἀλεξάνδρου ποίησον. καὶ γὰρ ἐκεῖνόν
φασι, διαβαλλομένου τινὸς τῶν συνήθων, τὴν
μὲν ἑτέραν τῶν ἀκοῶν ἀνεῖναι τῷ διαβάλλοντι,
τὴν δὲ ἑτέραν ἐπιμελῶς ἐπιφράξασθαι τῇ χειρί,
ἐνδεικνύμενον ὅτι δέοι τὸν ὀρθῶς κρίνειν μέλλοντα
μὴ ὅλον εὐθὺς τοῖς προλαβοῦσιν ἀπάγεσθαι, ἀλλὰ
τὸ ἥμισυ τῆς ἀκροάσεως ἀκέραιον διασώζειν πρὸς
ἀπολογίαν τῷ μὴ παρόντι.

[1] τῶν ἔργων] τῷ χρόνῳ sex alii MSS. ; τῷ χρόνῳ add. editi
antiqi.
[2] ἀσφαλές E.

[1] Of this story about Alexander cf. Letter XXIV.

credit. Nor was it, indeed, on this account that you have been forced to give attention to our affairs —that, namely, you, by reason of the magnitude of your wisdom, are competent single-handed to restore the works which have fallen into ruin, to people the uninhabited areas, and in general to transform the solitudes into cities! Was it, therefore, the more consistent course to harass and insult the man who co-operates with you in these works, or rather to honour him and show him every consideration? And do not think, most excellent Sir, that our protest consists of words alone; for we are already in action, being engaged meanwhile in getting our materials together.

So much, then, for our defence to you as the governor. But as to the answer which we ought to make to you as a Christian and as a friend solicitous of our reputation, in reply to the criticisms of the censorious, this we must pass over in silence at this time as being not only too long for the compass of this letter, but also unsafe to be trusted to soulless written characters. But in order that during the time before our meeting you may not, being gradually influenced by the slanders of certain persons, be forced to relinquish to some extent your goodwill toward us, do what Alexander did. For they say that when a friend of his was being slandered he gave the slanderer free access to one ear, but carefully obstructed the other with his hand, showing that he who intends to judge justly ought not to be at once wholly carried away by those who get at him first, but should keep half his hearing uncontaminated for the plea of the absent party.[1]

XCV

Εὐσεβίῳ, ἐπισκόπῳ Σαμοσάτωι

Πάλαι ἐπιστείλας τῇ θεοσεβείᾳ σου ἄλλων τέ
τινων ἕνεκεν καὶ τοῦ συντυχεῖν ἡμᾶς ἀλλήλοις,
διήμαρτον τῆς ἐλπίδος, οὐκ ἀφικομένων τῶν γραμμάτων εἰς τὰς χεῖρας τῆς σῆς τιμιότητος, τοῦ
μακαρίου διακόνου Θεοφράστου δεξαμένου μὲν τὰ
γράμματα ἡμῶν ἐπί τινα περιοδείαν ἀναγκαίως
ἀποδημούντων,[1] μὴ διαπεμψαμένου δὲ τῇ θεοσεβείᾳ σου, τῷ προκαταληφθῆναι τῇ ἀρρωστίᾳ ὑφ'
ἧς ἐτελεύτησεν. ὅθεν τοσοῦτον ὕστερος ἦλθον
τοῦ καιροῦ πρὸς τὸ γράφειν, ὥστε μηδὲ ὄφελός
τι ἐλπίζειν ἐκ τῆς ἐπιστολῆς ἔσεσθαι ταύτης, εἰς
στενὸν παντελῶς κατακλεισθέντος τοῦ χρόνου.
ὁ γάρ τοι θεοφιλέστατος ἐπίσκοπος Μελέτιος καὶ
Θεόδοτος ἐπέταξαν ἡμῖν πρὸς αὐτοὺς διαβῆναι,
ἀγάπης τε ἐπίδειγμα τὴν[2] συντυχίαν ποιούμενοι,
καί τινα καὶ διόρθωσιν γενέσθαι τῶν νῦν παρα-
λυπούντων βουλόμενοι. ἀπέδειξάν τε ἡμῖν χρόνον
μὲν τῆς συντυχίας τὰ μέσα τοῦ προσιόντος μηνὸς
Ἰουνίου, τόπον δὲ Φαργαμοῦν[3] τὸ χωρίον, ἐπίση-
μον μαρτύρων περιφανείᾳ[4] καὶ πολυανθρωπίᾳ
συνόδου τῆς κατὰ ἔτος ἕκαστον παρ' αὐτοῖς τελου-

---

[1] ἀποδημοῦντος editi antiqi. [2] σήν add. E.
[3] Φαρμαγοῦν E. [4] ἐπιφανεία E.

---

[1] Placed by Loofs in May of 372. For Eusebius cf. earlier
letters.
[2] Probably the bearer of a letter from Basil to Meletius in

LETTER XCV

To Eusebius, Bishop of Samosata [1]

ALTHOUGH I long ago wrote to your Piety in regard both to other matters and especially our meeting each other, I was disappointed in my hope, since my letters did not reach the hands of your Honour; for the blessed deacon Theophrastus [2] received the letters from us as we were setting out upon an unavoidable journey abroad, [3] but did not deliver them to your Piety on account of his being seized beforehand by the illness whereof he died. For this reason I have set about writing to you so tardily in comparison with the proper moment that I do not even hope that any benefit will come from this letter, since the time has been reduced to absolutely the scantiest margin. For the most God-beloved bishops, Meletius and Theodotus, [4] bade us go over to them, making such a visit a proof of my love, and also desiring that some amendment might be formed of the things which now trouble them. Moreover, they set as the time of our meeting the middle of the approaching month of June, and as the place, Phargamos, made illustrious by the glory of martyrs and by the largely attended synod held

---

371. Cf. Letter LVII. μακάριος, "blessed," as usual in Christian Greek, here means "deceased."

[3] περιοδεία may here mean the regular tour of a bishop to the parishes of his diocese.

[4] Theodotus of Nicopolis was disturbed about Basil's being in communion with Eustathius. On Meletius, bishop of Antioch, cf. Letters LVII, LXVIII, LXXXIX, CXX, CXXIX, CCXVI and notes.

μένης. ἐπεὶ δὲ ἔδει με, μετὰ τὴν ἐπάνοδον μαθόντα
τὴν κοίμησιν τοῦ μακαρίου διακόνου, καὶ τὰς
ἐπιστολὰς ἀργὰς παρ' ἡμῖν κειμένας, μὴ ἡσυ-
χάσαι, διὰ τὸ ἔτι ἡμέρας ἡμῖν τριάκοντα καὶ τρεῖς
ἐπὶ τὴν προθεσμίαν ὑπολελεῖφθαι, ἀπέστειλα κατὰ
σπουδὴν τῷ αἰδεσιμωτάτῳ ἀδελφῷ Εὐσταθίῳ τῷ
συλλειτουργῷ ἡμῶν τὰ γράμματα ταῦτα, ὥστε δι'
αὐτοῦ παραπεμφθῆναί σου τῇ σεμνότητι,[1] καὶ
πάλιν ἐν τάχει ἀνακομισθῆναι ἡμῖν τὰς ἀποκρίσεις. εἰ μὲν γὰρ δυνατὸν ἢ ἄλλως ἄρεσκοι
σοι παραγενέσθαι, καὶ αὐτοὶ παρεσόμεθα· εἰ δὲ
μή, αὐτοὶ μέν, ἂν ὁ Θεὸς θέλῃ, τὸ περυσινὸν
ἀποτίσομεν χρέος τῆς συντυχίας, ἐὰν μή τι πάλιν
ἐπιγένηται ἡμῖν ἐξ ἁμαρτιῶν κώλυμα· τὴν δὲ τῶν
ἐπισκόπων ἔντευξιν εἰς ἕτερον χρόνον ὑπερθησόμεθα.

XCVI

Σωφρονίῳ μαγίστρῳ

Καὶ τίς οὕτω φιλόπολις, ὃς τὴν ἐνεγκοῦσαν καὶ
θρεψαμένην πατρίδα ἴσα γονεῦσι τιμῶν, ὡς αὐτὸς
σύ, κοινῇ τε πάσῃ τῇ πόλει καὶ ἰδίᾳ ἑκάστῳ τὰ
ἀγαθὰ συνευχόμενος, καὶ οὐκ εὐχόμενος μόνον,
ἀλλὰ καὶ βεβαιῶν τὰς εὐχὰς διὰ σαυτοῦ;[2]
δύνασαι γάρ που σὺν Θεῷ τὰ τοιαῦτα, καὶ δύναιό
γε ἐπὶ μήκιστον, οὕτω χρηστὸς ὤν.

Ἀλλ' ὅμως ἐπὶ σοῦ ὄναρ ἐπλούτησεν ἡ πατρὶς

---

[1] τιμιότητι editi antiqi.   [2] διὰ σαυτοῦ] δι' ἑαυτοῦ Ε.

---

[1] Written in 372, on the removal of Elias as governor of

there every year. And since it was imperative for
me, after learning on my return home that the now
blessed deacon had fallen asleep, and that the letters
were still lying here untouched, not to be idle,
seeing that only thirty-three days are still left before
the appointed time, I have sent this letter in all haste
to our most reverend brother and fellow-worker,
Eustathius, that through him it may be forwarded
to your Majesty and that your reply may be
speedily returned to us. For if it is possible or,
in general, pleasing to you to come, we ourselves
also shall be there; but if not we shall, God willing,
ourselves discharge last year's debt and meet you,
unless some obstacle again arise, on account of our
sins, to prevent it; and we shall defer the meeting
of the bishops to another time.

LETTER XCVI

To Sophronius, Master [1]

WHAT man is so patriotic, honouring equally with
his parents the fatherland which gave him birth
and reared him, as are you yourself, who invoke
blessings for the whole city in common and for each
individual citizen, and not praying only, but also
confirming your prayers by your personal efforts?
For it is doubtless by God's aid that you are able to
do such things, and may you for the longest time
continue to be able, excellent man that you are.

But nevertheless it was under you that our city

Cappadocia. Cf. Letters LXXXIV and XCIV, which Basil
addresses to Elias.

ἡμῶν, ἄνδρα μὲν ἔχουσα τὸν τὴν ἐπιμέλειαν
αὐτῆς ἐπιτραπέντα, οἷον οὔ φασιν ἄλλον οἱ τὰ
παλαιότατα τῶν παρ' ἡμῖν ἐπιστάμενοι ἐπὶ τῶν
ἀρχικῶν[1] θρόνων πρότερον ἀναβῆναι, ἐπηρείᾳ δέ
τινων ἀφαιρεθεῖσα ταχέως, οἳ τὸ ἐλεύθερον τοῦ
ἀνδρὸς καὶ ἀθώπευτον τοῦ πρὸς αὐτὸν πολέμου
ἀφορμὴν ἐποιήσαντο, καὶ διαβολὰς αὐτῷ κατε-
σκεύασαν, λαθόντες τὰς ἀκοὰς τῆς σῆς τελειότητος. διὸ πανδημεὶ πάντες σκυθρωπάζομεν,
ζημιωθέντες ἄρχοντα μόνον δυνάμενον εἰς γόνυ
κλιθεῖσαν ἤδη τὴν πόλιν ἡμῶν ἀνορθῶσαι, ἀληθῆ[2]
φύλακα τοῦ δικαίου, εὐπρόσιτον τοῖς ἀδικουμένοις,
φοβερὸν τοῖς παρανομοῦσιν, ἴσον καὶ πένησι καὶ
πλουσίοις, καὶ τὸ μέγιστον, τὰ τῶν Χριστιανῶν
πράγματα πρὸς τὴν ἀρχαίαν ἐπανάγοντα τιμήν.
τὸ γάρ, ὅτι ἀδωρότατος ὢν ἴσμεν ἀνθρώπων, καὶ
οὐδενὶ[3] παρὰ τὸ δίκαιον χαριζόμενος, ὡς μικρότερα
τῆς λοιπῆς ἀρετῆς τοῦ ἀνδρὸς παρελίπομεν.

Ταῦτα ὀψὲ μὲν[4] τοῦ καιροῦ μαρτυρούμεν,
ὥσπερ οἱ μονῳδοῦντες ἑαυτοὺς[5] παραμυθούμενοι,
οὐχὶ τοῖς πράγμασί τι ποιοῦντες χρήσιμον.
πλὴν οὐδὲ τοῦτο ἄχρηστον, ἐν τῇ μεγάλῃ σου
ψυχῇ τὴν μνήμην τοῦ ἀνδρὸς ἀποκεῖσθαι,[6] χάριν
τε εἰδέναι ὡς εὐεργέτῃ[7] τῆς ἐνεγκούσης, καὶ εἴ τις
ἐπιφύοιτο αὐτῷ τῶν διὰ τὸ μὴ προτιμηθῆναι τοῦ
δικαίου χαλεπαινόντων, ὑπερμαχεῖν καὶ προΐ-
στασθαι, πᾶσι ποιήσαντα φανερόν, ὅτι οἰκεῖον
σεαυτῷ τὸν ἄνδρα τίθεσαι, ἀρκοῦσαν ἀφορμὴν εἰς

---

[1] τῶν ἀρχικῶν θρόνων] τὸν ἀρχικὸν θρόνον editi antiqi.
[2] ἀκριβῆ editi antiqi.   [3] οὐδέν multi MSS.
[4] μέν om. E.   [5] ἑαυτοῖς E, editi antiqi.
            [6] καί add. E.

became rich as in a dream, because it had in charge of its administration a man whose like never before ascended the governor's seat, as those declare who are familiar with our ancient history, and then, through the malicious spite of a certain man, was speedily deprived of him—men who made the generosity of the man and his immunity from flattery an excuse for their war upon him, and trumped up against him calumnies, deceiving the ears of your Perfection. Therefore we are one and all, the entire people, dejected at having been deprived of a governor who alone is able to raise again our city, which had already been brought to its knees, who is a true guardian of justice, easy of access for the victims of injustice, terrible to law-breakers, fair to both poor and rich, and, greatest of all, who was restoring Christianity to its ancient honour. For the fact that he was the most incorruptible man we know, and that he never granted a favour in violation of justice, we have passed over as of less significance than the man's other virtues.

But to these things we are bearing witness too late, when the proper season is past, just like those who console themselves by singing dirges but do nothing useful to better their condition. Yet this is not useless—that the recollection of the man should be stored up in your great soul, and that you should feel grateful to him as the benefactor of the land that bore you ; and, if any of those who are angry at not having been preferred to this just man should attack him, that you should fight for him and defend him, making it clear to all that you hold this man as one closely bound to you, considering

---

7 εὐεργέτην E.

οἰκειότητα τὴν ἀγαθὴν περὶ αὐτοῦ μαρτυρίαν
τιθέμενος καὶ τὴν τῶν πραγμάτων πεῖραν, οὐ
κατὰ τὴν τῶν χρόνων ἀναλογίαν ὑπάρχουσαν.
ἃ γὰρ οὐδ᾽ ἂν ἐν πολλοῖς ἔτεσι παρ᾽ ἄλλου
γένοιτο, ταῦτα ἐν ὀλίγῳ παρ᾽ αὐτοῦ κατώρθωται.
ἀρκοῦσα δ᾽ ἡμῖν¹ χάρις καὶ τῶν συμβάντων παραμυθία, ἐὰν καὶ βασιλεῖ συστήσῃς αὐτόν, καὶ τὰς
ἐπενεχθείσας αὐτῷ διαβολὰς ἀποσκευάσῃ. ταῦτά
σοι πᾶσαν² οἴου τὴν πατρίδα διὰ μιᾶς τῆς ἡμε-
τέρας³ φωνῆς διαλέγεσθαι, καὶ κοινὴν εἶναι πάντων εὐχήν, γενέσθαι τι τῷ ἀνδρὶ διὰ τῆς σῆς
τελειότητος δεξιόν.

XCVII

Τῇ βουλῇ Τυάνων

Ὁ ἀνακαλύπτων βαθέα καὶ φανερῶν βουλὰς
καρδιῶν Κύριος ἔδωκε καὶ τοῖς ταπεινοῖς σύνεσιν
τῶν δυσθεωρήτων, ὥς τινες οἴονται, τεχνασμάτων.
οὐδὲν οὖν ἡμᾶς ἔλαθεν, οὔτε τῶν πεπραγμένων τι
κεκρυμμένον. ἀλλ᾽ ὅμως ἡμεῖς οὔτε ὁρῶμεν οὔτε
ἀκούομεν ἄλλο τι ἢ τὴν εἰρήνην τοῦ Θεοῦ καὶ ὅσα ⁴
πρὸς αὐτὴν φέρει. εἰ γὰρ καὶ ἕτεροι δυνατοί, καὶ
μεγάλοι, καὶ ἑαυτοῖς πεποιθότες, ἀλλ᾽ ἡμεῖς οἱ μη-

---

¹ ἡ add. E.   ² πᾶσαν om. E.
³ ἡμέρας E.   ⁴ τοιαῖτα E, editio Paris.

---

¹ Written in 372. Valens was ever hostile to Cappadocia.
Partly to vent his wrath upon it, and partly to obtain a
greater amount of revenue, he had in 370 determined to
divide it into two provinces. Podandus, an insignificant

as sufficient grounds for the attachment the excellent
testimony you receive concerning him and also your
experience of his deeds—an experience which is not
in accordance with the example of the times. For
that which could not have been brought about by
another in many years has been accomplished in a
short time by him. It will be a sufficient favour to
us, and a consolation for our afflictions, if you will
recommend him to the Emperor, and will do away
with the slanders that have been brought against
him. Consider that your whole country is addressing these words to you through our single voice, and
that it is the common prayer of all that something
favourable may come to the man through your
Perfection.

LETTER XCVII

To the Senate of Tyana[1]

He who reveals hidden things and makes manifest
the counsels of the heart, even the Lord, has
bestowed upon the lowly a knowledge of artifices
which some think are difficult to understand.
Therefore nothing has escaped our notice, nor has
anything that has been done remained concealed
from us. Yet we ourselves, nevertheless, neither see
nor hear anything but the peace of God and whatsoever leads to it. For even if others are powerful,
and great, and confident in themselves, we, on the

town at the foot of Mt. Taurus, was to be the chief seat of
the new province, and half of the executive was transferred
there. The resulting dismay and dejection of Caesarea are
depicted vividly by Basil in Letters LXXIV, LXXV, and
LXXVI.

δέν, καὶ τοῦ μηδενὸς ἄξιοι· ὥστε οὐκ ἄν ποτε[1] τοσοῦτον ἑαυτοῖς λάβοιμεν, ὡς ἐν τῇ μονώσει
δύνασθαι νομίσαι περιέσεσθαι τῶν πραγμάτων,
ἀκριβῶς εἰδότες, ὅτι πλέον ἡμεῖς τῆς ἑνὸς ἑκάστου
τῶν ἀδελφῶν ἐπικουρίας δεόμεθα ἢ ὅσον ἡ ἑτέρα
τῶν χειρῶν τῆς ἑτέρας. ἐπεὶ καὶ ἐξ αὐτῆς τῆς
τοῦ σώματος ἡμῶν κατασκευῆς τὸ ἀναγκαῖον τῆς
κοινωνίας ὁ Κύριος ἡμᾶς ἐδίδαξεν. ὅταν γὰρ
πρὸς αὐτὰ ταῦτα ἀπίδω[2] τὰ μέλη ἡμῶν, ὅτι ἐν
οὐδὲν ἑαυτῷ πρὸς ἐνέργειαν αὔταρκες, πῶς ἐμαυτὸν
λογίσομαι ἐξαρκεῖν ἑαυτῷ πρὸς τὰ τοῦ βίου
πράγματα; οὔτε γὰρ ἂν ποὺς ἀσφαλῶς βαδίσειε,
μὴ συνυποστηρίζοντος τοῦ ἑτέρου, οὔτε ὀφθαλμὸς
ὑγιῶς ἴδοι, μὴ κοινωνὸν ἔχων τὸν ἕτερον καὶ μετ᾽
αὐτοῦ συμφώνως προσβάλλων τοῖς ὁρατοῖς. ἡ
ἀκοὴ ἀκριβεστέρα ἢ δι᾽ ἀμφοῖν τοῖν πόροιν τὴν
φωνὴν δεχομένη, καὶ ἀντίληψις κραταιοτέρα τῇ
κοινωνίᾳ τῶν δακτύλων. καὶ ἀπαξαπλῶς οὐδὲν
οὔτε τῶν ἐκ φύσεως οὔτε τῶν ἐκ προαιρέσεως
κατορθουμένων ὁρῶ ἄνευ τῆς τῶν ὁμοφύλων
συμπνοίας ἐπιτελούμενον· ὅπου γε καὶ αὐτὴ ἡ
προσευχὴ μὴ ἔχουσα τοὺς συμφωνοῦντας ἀδρανεσ-
τέρα ἐστὶ πολλῷ ἑαυτῆς, καὶ ὁ Κύριος ἐπηγγείλατο μέσος γενήσεσθαι μεταξὺ δύο ἢ τριῶν
ἐπικαλουμένων αὐτὸν ἐν ὁμονοίᾳ. καὶ αὐτὴν δὲ
τὴν οἰκονομίαν ὁ Κύριος κατεδέξατο, ἵνα εἰρηνο-

---

[1] ὥστε οὐκ ἄν . . . ὡς] μηδενὸς οὐκ ἄν ποτε τοσοῦτον ἑαυτοὺς
ὑπολάβοιμεν, ὥστε editi antiqi.

contrary, are nothing, and worth nothing; consequently we would never attribute so much to ourselves as to consider that single-handed we could surmount our difficulties, for we know very clearly that we need the help of each and every brother more than one hand needs the other. Indeed, from the very constitution of our bodies the Lord has taught us the necessity of the community. For whenever I look upon these very limbs of ours, and see that no one of them is sufficient in itself to produce action, how can I reason that I of myself suffice to cope with the difficulties of life? For one foot could not make a stride safely unless the other supported it, nor could the eye see accurately unless it had the other as its partner and, working in harmony with it, cast its glance upon the objects of sight. The hearing is more exact when it receives sound through both its channels; and the grasp of the hand is stronger through the combined efforts of the fingers. And to sum up, I see that none of those things which are accomplished either by nature or by deliberate choice is completed without the union of the related forces; since, in truth, even prayer itself, if it be not voiced by many together, is much less efficacious than it might be, and the Lord has promised that He would be in the midst of two or three who should invoke Him together.[1] And indeed the reason why the Lord took up his very stewardship was that He might

---

[1] Cf. Matt. 18, 20 : οὗ γάρ εἰσι δύο ἢ τρεῖς συνηγμένοι εἰς τὸ ἐμὸν ὄνομα, ἐκεῖ εἰμὶ ἐν μέσῳ αὐτῶν. "For where there are two or three gathered together in My name, there am I in the midst of them."

---

[2] ἀπίδωμεν editi antiqi.

ποιήσῃ διὰ τοῦ αἵματος τοῦ σταυροῦ αὐτοῦ εἴτε
τὰ ἐπὶ τῆς γῆς εἴτε τὰ ἐν τοῖς οὐρανοῖς.

Ὥστε, διὰ ταῦτα πάντα, ἐν εἰρήνῃ μένειν τὰς
λειπομένας ἡμῶν ἡμέρας εὐχόμεθα, ἐν εἰρήνῃ δὲ
γενέσθαι τὴν κοίμησιν ἡμῶν αἰτοῦμεν. ὑπὲρ
ταύτης οὐδὲ πόνον ἐλλείπειν[1] ὅντινα οὖν ἔγνωκα,
οὐ ταπεινόν τι φθέγξασθαι ἢ ποιῆσαι, οὐχ ὁδοιπορίας μῆκος ὑπολογίσασθαι, οὐκ ἄλλο τι τῶν
ὀχληρῶν[2] ὑποστείλασθαι, ὥστε τῶν μισθῶν τῆς
εἰρηνοποιίας ἐπιτυχεῖν. κἂν μὲν ἔπηταί[3] τις
ταῦτα καθηγουμένοις ἡμῖν, τοῦτο ἄριστον, καὶ
εὐχὴ[4] τυγχάνει πέρας· ἐὰν δὲ πρὸς τὴν ἐναντίαν
ἀφέλκῃ,[5] ἐγὼ μὲν οὐδὲ οὕτω τῆς ἐμαυτοῦ κρίσεως
ἀποστήσομαι. αὐτὸς δὲ ἕκαστος τῆς οἰκείας
ἐργασίας ἐν ἡμέρᾳ τῆς ἀνταποδόσεως τοὺς καρποὺς ἐπιγνώσεται.

XCVIII

Εὐσεβίῳ, ἐπισκόπῳ Σαμοσάτων

Πάνυ ὡρμημένος καταλαβεῖν τὴν Νικόπολιν,
μετὰ τὸ δέξασθαι τὰ παρὰ τῆς ὁσιότητός[6] σου
γράμματα ἄρνησιν ἔχοντα τῆς ἀφίξεως, παρείθην
ἀπὸ[7] τῆς ἐπιθυμίας[8] καὶ πάσης ὁμοῦ τῆς ἀσθενείας ἀνεμνήσθην. ἦλθε δέ μοι εἰς ἔννοιαν καὶ ἡ
τῶν κεκληκότων ἀφοσίωσις, ὅτι, παροδικὴν πρὸς

---

[1] λείπειν E.   [2] μοχθηρῶν E, Harl., Vat.
[3] ἔποιτο editi antiqi.
[4] εὐχὴ Capps ; εὐχῆς MSS. et editi.
[5] ἐφέλκοι τῆς αὐτῆς editi antiqi.
[6] κοσμιότητος vulgata.   [7] ὑπό E, editi antiqi.

through the blood of His cross establish peace both on earth and in heaven.[1]

Therefore, on account of all this, we pray that we may abide in peace for the rest of our days, and in peace we ask that our last sleep may come upon us. For the sake of this peace, therefore, I have determined to neglect no effort whatever, not to omit anything as too humble to say or do, not to take into account the length of any journey, and not to shrink before any irksome thing, if so I may obtain the rewards of peace-making. And if anyone follows us who are leading the way in this matter, that is excellent, and my prayer is fulfilled; but if anyone pulls in an opposite direction, I will not be moved thereby to renounce my decision. But each one himself on the day of retribution will acknowledge the fruits of his own works.

LETTER XCVIII

To Eusebius, Bishop of Samosata [2]

Although I had been exceedingly eager to visit Nicopolis, yet, after receiving the letter of your Holiness containing the statement that you were not going there, I relinquished my desire, and at the same time remembered all my infirmities of health. Moreover, the perfunctory manner of those who had invited me came to my mind—that after extending

---

[1] *i.e.*, by His Incarnation, the community of Man and God.
[2] According to Loofs (p. 25), this letter was written at Sebaste in the middle of June 372.

---

[3] αθυμίας E, Harl., editi antiqi.

ἡμᾶς ποιησάμενοι τὴν κλῆσιν διὰ τοῦ αἰδεσιμωτάτου ἀδελφοῦ Ἑλληνίου τοῦ ἐξισοῦντος Να-
ζιανζόν, δεύτερον περὶ τῶν αὐτῶν ὑπομιμνήσκοντα[1]
ἢ ὁδηγοῦντα ἡμᾶς οὐ κατηξίωσαν[2] ἀποστεῖλαι.
ἐπεὶ οὖν ὕποπτοι αὐτοῖς ἐσμὲν διὰ τὰς[3] ἁμαρτίας
ἡμῶν, ἐφοβήθημεν μή που τὸ φαιδρὸν αὐτοῖς τῆς
πανηγύρεως τῇ παρουσίᾳ ἡμῶν ἐπιθολώσωμεν.
μετὰ μὲν γὰρ τῆς σῆς μεγαλοφυΐας καὶ πρὸς τοὺς
μεγάλους ἀποδύσασθαι πειρασμοὺς οὐκ ὀκνοῦμεν,
ἄνευ δὲ σοῦ οὐδὲ ταῖς τυχούσαις θλίψεσιν
ἀντιβλέψαι αὐτάρκως ἔχομεν. ἐπεὶ οὖν ἐκκλησιαστικῶν ἕνεκεν γίνεσθαι ἡμῶν ἡ πρὸς αὐτοὺς
ἔντευξις ἔμελλε, τὸν μὲν τῆς πανηγύρεως καιρὸν
παρελίπομεν, εἰς ἡσυχίαν δὲ καὶ ἀτάραχον διαγωγὴν τὴν συντυχίαν ὑπερεθέμεθα, καὶ προῃρή-
μεθα καταλαβόντες τὴν Νικόπολιν διαλεχθῆναι
περὶ τῶν ταῖς ἐκκλησίαις ἀναγκαίων τῷ θεοφιλεστάτῳ ἐπισκόπῳ Μελετίῳ, εἰ μέλλοι παραι-
τεῖσθαι τὴν ἐπὶ Σαμόσατα[4] ὁδόν· εἰ δὲ μή, αὐτῷ[5]
συνδραμούμεθα, ἐὰν παρ' ἀμφοτέρων τοῦτο ἡμῖν
κατάδηλον γένηται, παρά τε αὐτοῦ ἐκείνου
ἀντιγράψαντος ἡμῖν περὶ τούτων (ἐπεστείλαμεν
γάρ), καὶ παρὰ τῆς σῆς θεοσεβείας.

Ἐπισκόποις δὲ τοῖς ἐκ τῆς δευτέρας Καππα-
δοκίας συντυγχάνειν ἐμέλλομεν· οἵ, ἐπειδὴ ἑτέρας

---

[1] ὑπομνήσκοντα Harl. [2] οὐ κατηξίωσαν] οὐκ ἠξίωσαν E.
[3] τὰς] τῆς E. [4] Σαμοσάτων Harl.
[5] αὐτοῦ E, editi antiqi.

---

[1] A surveyor of Customs at Nazianzus, and confidential
friend of both Basil and Gregory Nazianzene. He was an
Armenian by race, was married, and the father of a family.

to us a passing invitation through our most reverend brother, Hellenius,[1] regulator of taxes at Nazianzus, they did not think it worth while to send a messenger to remind us of this same matter again or to act as our escort. Since, then, because of our sins we are suspected by them, we feared lest perchance by our presence we might disturb their joy of the festival. For in company with your Magnanimity we do not shrink from stripping ourselves for even great trials, but without you we are not self-reliant enough to face even ordinary afflictions. Hence, inasmuch as our meeting with them was to be concerned with ecclesiastical matters, we have let pass the occasion of the festival, we have postponed our meeting to a period of peace and tranquillity, and we have determined to visit Nicopolis and to take up the question of the needs of the churches with the most God-beloved bishop Meletius,[2] in case he should decline to make the journey to Samosata. But if he should not decline, we shall travel thither with him, provided this be made clear to us by you both—by him through a letter written to me in reply regarding this matter (for we have written to him), and by your Piety.

It was also our intention to meet the bishops of Cappadocia Secunda; but they, when they had been

---

He had a brother who, like himself, had acquired reputation by his eloquence. Both were employed in the administration of justice. In 371 Hellenius conveyed a letter from Gregory to Basil; cf. Basil, Letter LXXI. Hellenius' official title was ἐξισωτής (*peraecquator*), whose chief duty was to conduct extraordinary local revisions of taxes. Such officials were directly responsible to the praetorian prefects.

[2] For this Meletius, cf. Letters LVII, LXVIII, LXXXIX, CXX, CXXIX, and CCXVI.

ὠνομάσθησαν ἐπαρχίας, ἐνόμισαν ἀθρίως καὶ
ἀλλοεθνεῖς καὶ ἀλλόφυλοι πρὸς ἡμᾶς γεγενῆσθαι
οἳ τοσοῦτον ἡμᾶς ἠγνόησαν, ὅσον οἱ μηδὲ τὴν
ἀρχὴν πεπειραμένοι,[1] μηδὲ εἰς λόγους ποτὲ
ἀφικόμενοι.[2] προσεδοκᾶτο δὲ καὶ ἑτέρα συντυχία
τοῦ αἰδεσιμωτάτου ἐπισκόπου Εὐσταθίου, ἡ καὶ
γενομένη ἡμῖν. διὰ γὰρ τὸ παρὰ πολλῶν κατα-
βοᾶσθαι αὐτὸν ὡς περὶ τὴν πίστιν παραχα-
ράσσοντά τι, ἀφικόμεθα αὐτῷ εἰς λόγους, καὶ
εὕρομεν σὺν Θεῷ πρὸς πᾶσαν ὀρθότητα εὐγνωμόνως
ἀκολουθοῦντα. τὰ δὲ τῶν ἐπισκόπων γράμματα
παρὰ τὴν αἰτίαν αὐτῶν ἐκείνων οὐκ ἐκομίσθη τῇ
τιμιότητί σου, οὓς ἐχρῆν τὰ παρ' ἡμῶν δια-
πέμψασθαι· ἀλλὰ καὶ ἐμὲ παρῆλθε, τῇ συνεχείᾳ
τῶν φροντίδων ἐκκρουσθέντα τῆς μνήμης.

Τὸν δ' ἀδελφὸν[3] Γρηγόριον κἀγὼ ἠβουλόμην[4]
οἰκονομεῖν ἐκκλησίαν τῇ αὐτοῦ φύσει σύμμετρον.
αὕτη δὲ ἦν πᾶσα εἰς ἓν συναχθεῖσα ἡ ὑφ' ἡλίῳ.[5]
ἐπειδὴ[6] δὲ τοῦτο ἀδύνατον, ἔστω ἐπίσκοπος, μὴ
ἐκ τοῦ τόπου σεμνυνόμενος, ἀλλὰ τὸν τόπον
σεμνύνων ἀφ' ἑαυτοῦ. ὄντως γὰρ μεγάλου ἐστὶν
οὐ τοῖς μεγάλοις μόνον ἀρκεῖν, ἀλλὰ καὶ τὰ μικρὰ
μεγάλα ποιεῖν τῇ ἑαυτοῦ δυνάμει.

---

[1] πεπειρασμένοι editi antiqi.   [2] ἀφικνούμενοι editi antiqi.
[3] ἐμόν, τόν, add. editi antiqi.   [4] ἐβουλόμην E.
[5] ὑφ' ἡλίῳ] ὑφήλιος Med. ; ὑφ' ἥλιον Bigot., Reg. secundus,
Coisl. secundus.
[6] ἐπεί editi antiqi.

---

[1] Cf. previous letter and note.
[2] According to Tillemont, this reference is to Basil's own
brother, Gregory of Nyssa. Maran, however (*Vita Basilii*,
xxiv), thinks this false, due partly to the introduction into
the text of the word ἐμόν, which he eliminates. He points

named as of another province,[1] immediately thought
that they had become of a different race and stock
from us, and they ignored us as thoroughly as would
those who have never had acquaintance with us at
all and have never come into converse with us.
Another meeting, too, with the most reverend bishop
Eustathius was expected by us, and this actually
took place. For since he was being denounced by
many on the ground that he was falsifying the faith
in some way, we entered into conference with him,
and we found him, by God's grace, candidly in
harmony with all orthodoxy. The letter of the
bishop was not delivered to your Honour through
the fault of those same persons who should have
forwarded the letter from us; but the matter
escaped my attention, having been driven from my
memory by continual cares.

I also had wished that my brother Gregory[2] were
governing a church commensurate with his talents.
But such a church would be the whole church under
the sun merged into one! But since this is impossible,
let him be a bishop, not receiving dignity from his
see, but himself conferring dignity upon the see.
For it is the part of a truly great man not merely to
be equal to great things, but also to make little
things great by his own power.

out also that Gregory of Nyssa, although unwilling to accept
consecration, never objected after it took place, and was
even sent to Nazianzus to console the younger Gregory, who
was in distress under like circumstances. Furthermore,
Gregory of Nyssa was consecrated in the regular manner, on
the demand of the people and clergy with the assent of the
bishops of the province. Cf. Letter CCXXV. On the other
hand, Gregory the younger was consecrated to Sasima without
these formalities. Hence it is probably the latter who is
here referred to.

COLLECTED LETTERS OF SAINT BASIL

Τί δὲ δεῖ¹ ποιῆσαι τῷ Παλματίῳ, μετὰ
τοσαύτας παρακλήσεις τῶν ἀδελφῶν ἔτι ὑπηρε-
τοῦντι τῷ Μαξίμῳ πρὸς τοὺς διωγμούς ; ἀλλ'
ὅμως οὐδὲ νῦν ὀκνοῦσιν ἐπιστεῖλαι· παραγενέσθαι
γὰρ καὶ ὑπὸ ἀσθενείας² σώματος καὶ ὑπὸ ἀσχολιῶν οἰκειακῶν οὐκ ἐπιτρέπονται.

Γίνωσκε μέντοι, θεοφιλέστατε πάτερ, ὅτι πάνυ³
χρῄζει τῆς παρουσίας σου τὰ ἡμέτερα, καὶ
ἀνάγκη σε τὸ τίμιον γῆρας ἔτι ἅπαξ κινῆσαι,
ὑπὲρ τοῦ στῆσαι περιφερομένην λοιπὸν καὶ ἐγγὺς
πτώματος οὖσαν τὴν Καππαδοκίαν.

XCIX

Τερεντίῳ Κόμητι

Πάνυ πολλὴν σπουδὴν ἐνστησάμενος πειθαρ-
χῆσαι μερικῶς γοῦν καὶ τῷ βασιλικῷ προστάγματι

¹ ποιῆσαι Med. ² τοῦ add. E.
³ πᾶν editi antiqi.

---

¹ Otherwise unknown.
² Governor of Cappadocia, successor of Elias, and himself
succeeded by Antipater. Cf. Tillemont, note 58. Although,
as here indicated, he persecuted the orthodox, in the next
year, when he was removed from office and accused of
embezzlement of public funds, he had no warmer advocate
than Basil. There are three letters of Basil in his behalf to
influential laymen, begging them to befriend him in his
extremity ; to Aburgius (Letter CXLVII) ; to Trajan (Letter
CXLVIII), and another inscribed, probably falsely, to Trajan
(Letter CXLIX). The persecutions here mentioned may
not be persecutions in the ecclesiastical sense, but severe
exactions of tribute.

But what is to be done in the case of Palmatius,[1] who after so many admonitions from his brethren still supports Maximus[2] in his persecutions? Yet even now they do not hesitate to write to him; for they are not permitted to visit him on account of bodily ill-health[3] and their pressing duties at home.

Now be assured, most God-beloved father, that our situation needs your presence exceedingly, and you must bestir your venerable age once again, that you may give support to Cappadocia, which is even now tottering and near its fall.

LETTER XCIX

To Count Terentius[4]

Although at the outset I felt very great eagerness to obey, in part at least, both the Imperial

---

[3] Probably of Palmatius himself.

[4] Written from Satala in July or August 372. Cf. Loofs, 27. Terentius was general and count under Valens, and, though orthodox, held the Arian emperor's favour. Ammianus Marcellinus (27, 12; and 30, 1) belittles him because of his Christianity. Basil addresses the present letter to Terentius, who is in Iberia, in command of twelve legions, and details the difficulties, caused chiefly by Theodotus, in the way of carrying out the Emperor's order to supply Armenia with bishops. The Emperor's order had been enforced by a private letter from Terentius himself.

A still longer letter from Basil to Terentius, written during the Antiochene schism, A.D. 375, seeking to divert him from the side of Paulinus to that of Meletius, is Letter CCXIV.

Another letter of Basil's (CV) is addressed to the daughters of Terentius, who were deaconesses at Samosata.

καὶ τῷ φιλικῷ τῆς σῆς τιμιότητος γράμματι, οὗ
ἐγὼ πάντα λόγον καὶ πᾶσαν γνώμην γέμειν ὀρθῆς
προαιρέσεως καὶ ἀγαθῆς διανοίας πεπίστευκα, εἰς
ἔργον ἀγαγεῖν τὴν προθυμίαν οὐκ ἐπετράπην.[1]
αἴτιον δὲ τὸ μὲν πρῶτον καὶ ἀληθέστατον αἱ ἐμαὶ
ἁμαρτίαι, πανταχοῦ μοι προαπαντῶσαι καὶ
ὑποσκελίζουσαί μου τὰ διαβήματα· ἔπειτα καὶ ἡ
τοῦ δοθέντος ἡμῖν εἰς συνεργίαν ἐπισκόπου πρὸς
ἡμᾶς ἀλλοτρίωσις. οὐκ οἶδα γὰρ ὅ τι παθὼν ὁ
αἰδεσιμώτατος ἀδελφὸς ἡμῶν Θεόδοτος, ὁ ἐπαγ-
γειλάμενος ἡμῖν ἐξ ἀρχῆς πάντα συμπράξειν, καὶ
προθύμως ἡμᾶς ἀπὸ Γητασῶν ἐπὶ Νικόπολιν
καταγαγών,[2] ἐπειδὴ εἶδεν ἡμᾶς ἐπὶ τῆς πόλεως,
οὕτως ἡμᾶς ἐβδελύξατο, καὶ οὕτως ἐφοβήθη τὰς
ἁμαρτίας ἡμῶν, ὡς μήτε εἰς ἑωθινὴν εὐχὴν μήτε
εἰς ἑσπερινὴν ἀνασχέσθαι ἡμᾶς παραλαβεῖν·
δίκαια μὲν ποιῶν, ὡς πρὸς ἡμᾶς, καὶ πρέποντα
τῷ ἐμῷ βίῳ, οὐ λυσιτελοῦντα δὲ τῇ κοινῇ καταστάσει τῶν ἐκκλησιῶν βουλευόμενος. τὴν δὲ
αἰτίαν τούτων προέφερεν ἡμῖν, ὅτι ἠνεσχόμεθα εἰς
κοινωνίαν τὸν αἰδεσιμώτατον ἐπίσκοπον Εὐστάθιον
παραδέξασθαι. τὸ μέντοι γενόμενον παρ᾽ ἡμῶν
τοιοῦτόν ἐστιν.

Ἡμεῖς, κληθέντες εἰς σύνοδον παρὰ τοῦ
ἀδελφοῦ Θεοδότου τελουμένην[3] καὶ ὁρμήσαντες
δι᾽ ἀγάπην ὑπακοῦσαι τῇ κλήσει, ἵνα μὴ δόξωμεν
ἄπρακτον καὶ ἀργὴν ποιεῖσθαι τὴν συντυχίαν,

[1] ἐτράπην editi antiqi.   [2] καταγαγεῖν editi antiqi.
[3] τελειουμένην editi antiqi.

---

[1] Bishop of Nicopolis in Lesser Armenia, an aged prelate
of high character and unquestioned orthodoxy. Theodotus
was greatly respected by St. Basil, but he was extremely

ordinance and the friendly letter of your Honour, whose every word and every thought I am convinced is filled with right purpose and good intentions, I was not permitted to turn my desire into action. And the reason, the primary and the truest one, is my sins, which come forth to meet me on every side and trip my steps; and, secondly, our alienation from the bishop assigned to co-operate with us. For I do not know what has happened to our most reverend brother Theodotus,[1] that after promising us in the beginning to help in every way, and eagerly bringing us down from Getasa to Nicopolis, yet when he saw us in the city he so loathed us, and so feared our sins, that he could not bring himself to take us with him to either morning or evening prayers; what he did was just, so far as we are concerned, and befitting my life, but was not working for the best interests of the common organization of the churches. But he alleged to us as the cause of this treatment the fact that we had received the most reverend bishop Eustathius into communion. What we have done, however, is this.

When we were summoned to a synod which was being held by our brother Theodotus, and for charity's sake were eager to obey the summons, in order that we should not seem to render the meeting futile and of no effect, we made a special effort to

annoyed at Basil's reluctance to sever connexions with Eustathius of Sebaste. On this very account he refused to co-operate with Basil in giving bishops to Lesser Armenia, and he virtually excommunicated Basil on the latter's arrival, by invitation, at Nicopolis. Brotherly relations between the two, however, were later re-established. Two of Basil's extant letters are addressed to Theodotus: Letters CXXI and CXXX.

ἐσπουδάσαμεν εἰς λόγους ἐλθεῖν τῷ προειρημένῳ
ἀδελφῷ Εὐσταθίῳ. καὶ προετείναμεν αὐτῷ τὰ
περὶ τῆς πίστεως ἐγκλήματα, ὅσα προφέρουσιν
αὐτῷ οἱ περὶ τὸν ἀδελφὸν Θεόδοτον, καὶ ἠξιώσαμεν, εἰ μὲν ἔπεται τῇ ὀρθῇ πίστει, φανερὸν ἡμῖν
καταστῆσαι, ὥστε ἡμᾶς εἶναι κοινωνικούς· εἰ δὲ
ἀλλοτρίως ἔχει, ἀκριβῶς εἰδέναι, ὅτι καὶ ἡμεῖς
ἕξομεν πρὸς αὐτὸν ἀλλοτρίως. πολλῶν τοίνυν
γενομένων λόγων πρὸς ἀλλήλους, καὶ πάσης
ἐκείνης τῆς ἡμέρας ἐν τῇ περὶ τούτων σκέψει
δαπανηθείσης, καταλαβούσης λοιπὸν τῆς ἑσπέ-
ρας, διεκρίθημεν ἀπ᾽ ἀλλήλων, εἰς οὐδὲν ὁμο-
λογούμενον πέρας τὸν λόγον [1] προαγαγόντες. τῇ
δὲ ἑξῆς πάλιν, ἕωθεν συγκαθεσθέντες, περὶ τῶν
αὐτῶν διελεγόμεθα, ἐπελθόντος ἤδη καὶ τοῦ
ἀδελφοῦ Ποιμενίου, τοῦ πρεσβυτέρου τῆς Σεβαστείας, καὶ σφοδρῶς ἡμῖν τὸν ἐναντίον γυμνάζοντος
λόγον. κατὰ μικρὸν οὖν ἡμεῖς τε, ὑπὲρ ὧν ἔδοξεν
ἡμῖν ἐγκαλεῖν, ἀπελυόμεθα, κἀκείνους εἰς τὴν [2]
τῶν ἐπιζητουμένων ὑφ᾽ ἡμῶν συγκατάθεσιν
προηγάγομεν,[3] ὥστε χάριτι τοῦ Κυρίου εὑρεθῆναι
ἡμᾶς μηδὲ εἰς τὸ σμικρότατον πρὸς ἀλλήλους
διαφερομένους. οὕτω τοίνυν περὶ ἐννάτην που
ὥραν ἀνέστημεν ἐπὶ τὰς προσευχάς, εὐχαριστή-
σαντες τῷ Κυρίῳ τῷ δόντι ἡμῖν τὸ αὐτὸ φρονεῖν
καὶ τὸ αὐτὸ λέγειν. ἐπὶ τούτοις ἔδει με καὶ
ἔγραφόν τινα παρὰ τοῦ ἀνδρὸς ὁμολογίαν λαβεῖν,
ὥστε καὶ τοῖς ἐναντιουμένοις αὐτῷ φανερὰν

---

[1] τῶν λόγων E, τὸν λόγον in marg. manu recente.
[2] ὑπέρ add. E.   [3] προσηγάγομεν editi antiqi.

---

[1] Otherwise unknown.

enter into conference with our brother Eustathius just mentioned. And we presented to him the charges regarding his faith, such as our brother Theodotus and his followers bring against him, and we asked him, in case he followed the orthodox Faith, to make this fact manifest to us so that we might be in communion with him; but if he was otherwise disposed, we asked him to know clearly that we too should be otherwise disposed toward him. Thereupon, after we had conversed much with each other, and after the whole of that day had been consumed in the examination of these matters, evening having now fallen, we parted from each other without having brought our discussion to any conclusion to which we could both agree. But after we had again assembled on the morning of the following day, we were entering upon a discussion of the same subject, when our brother, Poimenius,[1] presbyter of Sebasteia, entered our conference also, and began vigorously to press the opposing doctrine against us.[2] Little by little we for our part, according-ingly, kept clearing away the charges upon the strength of which they seemed to accuse us, and we brought them to such an assent regarding the subjects of our investigation that by the grace of the Lord we found ourselves to be differing from one another not even in the smallest point. Thus, therefore, somewhere about the ninth hour we arose for prayer, thanking the Lord who had given us to think and speak the same things. In confirmation of this I ought to have obtained also a written confession from the man, so that his assent might

---

[2] "Us" and "we" here mean the writer, St. Basil, and not Basil and Eustathius.

γενέσθαι τὴν συγκατάθεσιν, καὶ τοῖς λοιποῖς
ἱκανὴν εἶναι τοῦ ἀνδρὸς τῆς προαιρέσεως τὴν
ἀπόδειξιν. ἀλλ' ἐβουλήθην αὐτὸς ὑπὲρ[1] πολλῆς
ἀκριβείας, τοῖς ἀδελφοῖς συντυχὼν τοῖς περὶ
Θεόδοτον, παρ' αὐτῶν λαβεῖν γραμματεῖον
πίστεως, καὶ αὐτὸ[2] προτεῖναι τῷ προειρημένῳ·
ἵνα ἀμφότερα γένηται, ἥ τε ὀρθὴ πίστις παρ'
αὐτοῦ ὁμολογηθῇ,[3] καὶ αὐτοὶ πληροφορηθῶσι,
μηδεμίαν ἔχοντες ἀντιλογίας ὑπόθεσιν ἐκ τοῦ τὰς
παρ' αὐτῶν προτάσεις παραδεχθῆναι. ἀλλὰ
πρὶν μαθεῖν τίνος ἕνεκεν συνετύχομεν, καὶ τί
ἡμῖν ἐκ τῆς ὁμιλίας κατώρθωται, οἱ περὶ τὸν
ἐπίσκοπον Θεόδοτον οὐκέτι ἡμᾶς εἰς τὴν σύνοδον
προτρέψασθαι κατηξίωσαν. ἀλλ' ἀπὸ μέσης
ἀνεζεύξαμεν[4] τῆς ὁδοῦ, ἀθυμήσαντες, ὅτι ἀτελεῖς
ἡμῖν ποιοῦσι τοὺς ὑπὲρ τῆς εἰρήνης τῶν ἐκκλησιῶν
καμάτους.

Μετὰ ταῦτα τοίνυν, ἐπειδὴ κατέλαβεν ἡμᾶς ἡ
ἀνάγκη τῆς ἐπὶ τὴν Ἀρμενίαν ὁδοῦ, εἰδὼς τοῦ
ἀνδρὸς τὸ ἰδιότροπον καὶ βουλόμενος ὑπὸ[5] μάρτυρι ἀξιοπίστῳ αὐτός τε ὑπὲρ τῶν πεπραγμένων
ἀπολογήσασθαι κἀκεῖνον πληροφορῆσαι, ἦλθον
ἐπὶ τὰ Γήτασα τὸν ἀγρὸν τοῦ θεοφιλεστάτου
ἐπισκόπου Μελετίου, συμπαρόντος μοι[6] καὶ
αὐτοῦ τοῦ προειρημένου Θεοδότου· καὶ οὕτως
ἐκεῖ, ἐπειδὴ ἐνεκλήθημεν παρ' αὐτοῦ ἐπὶ τῇ[7]
πρὸς Εὐστάθιον συναφείᾳ, εἶπον τὸ[8] ἐκ τῆς συν-

---

[1] ὑπέρ R.J.D., ὑπό MSS. et editi.   [2] οὗτοι E.
[3] ὁμολογῆται tres MSS. recen.   [4] ἀνέζευξαν editi antiqi.
[5] ἐπί nonnulli MSS.   [6] μου E.
[7] ἐπὶ τῇ . . . συναφείᾳ] περὶ τῆς . . . συναφείας nonnulli
MSS.

be made clear also to those who oppose him and might be for the rest a sufficient demonstration of the man's convictions. But I desired on my own account, for the sake of complete accuracy, to meet our brothers, the followers of Theodotus, receive from them a written testimonial of faith, and present this to the afore-mentioned Theodotus; my purpose was that two things might be accomplished, namely, that the orthodox Faith should be confessed by him, and that his followers should themselves be fully informed, they having thus no ground for controversy by reason of the fact that the propositions had been accepted by themselves. But before learning for what reason Eustathius and I had met, and what success had been achieved by us as a result of our conference, the followers of the bishop Theodotus no longer deemed it proper to invite us to the synod. But in the middle of our journey we turned back, disheartened that they were rendering of no avail our labours in behalf of the peace of the churches.

After this, therefore, when the necessity of a journey to Armenia fell upon us, being well acquainted with the peculiar character of the man and desirous of having the support of a most trustworthy witness in defending myself for my actions and of giving him full information, I came to Getasa, the field of the most God-beloved bishop Meletius, the afore-mentioned Theodotus being also present at the time; and thus in that place, when we were accused by him on the ground of our connexion with Eustathius, I told him of the happy outcome of our

---

8 τὸ . . . κατόρθωμα] τὰ . . . κατορθώματα E.

τυχίας κατόρθωμα, ὅτι ἔλαβον αὐτὸν εἰς πάντα
ἡμῖν ὁμοδοξοῦντα. ὡς δὲ διεβεβαιοῦτο ἔξαρνον
γεγενῆσθαι μετὰ τὴν ἀφ' ἡμῶν ἀναχώρησιν, καὶ
διαβεβαιοῦσθαι αὐτὸν τοῖς ἰδίοις αὐτοῦ [1] μαθηταῖς, ἢ μὲν εἰς μηδὲν ἡμῖν περὶ τῆς πίστεως
συντεθεῖσθαι, ἀπήντων ἐγὼ πρὸς ταῦτα (καὶ
σκόπει, θαυμασιώτατε, εἰ μὴ δικαιοτάτας [2] καὶ
ἀναντιρρήτους ἐποιούμην πρὸς τοῦτο τὰς ἀποκρίσεις), ὅτι ἐγὼ μὲν πέπεισμαι, εἰκάζων ἐκ τῆς
λοιπῆς εὐσταθείας τοῦ ἀνδρός, μὴ οὕτως αὐτὸν
κούφως περιτρέπεσθαι πρὸς τὰ ἐναντία, μηδὲ νῦν
μὲν ὁμολογεῖν νῦν δὲ ὑπὲρ ὧν εἶπεν ἀρνεῖσθαι,
ἄνδρα καὶ τὸ ὑπὲρ τῶν τυχόντων ψεῦδος ὡς
φοβερὸν ἀποφεύγοντα, μὴ ὅτι γε περὶ τῶν
τηλικούτων πραγμάτων καὶ οὕτω παρὰ πᾶσι
βεβοημένων,[3] ἑλέσθαι ἄν ποτε ἐναντιωθῆναι τῇ
ἀληθείᾳ. εἰ δὲ ἄρα καὶ ἀληθῆ εἶναι συμβῇ τὰ
θρυλλούμενα παρ' ὑμῶν, προτεῖναι αὐτῷ γραμματεῖον πᾶσαν ἔχον τῆς ὀρθῆς πίστεως τὴν ἀπόδειξιν χρή. ἐὰν μὲν οὖν εὕρω αὐτὸν συντιθέμενον
ἐγγράφως, ἐπιμενῶ τῇ κοινωνίᾳ· ἐὰν δὲ λάβω
ἀναδυόμενον, ἀποστήσομαι αὐτοῦ τῆς συναφείας.
ἀποδεξαμένου τὸν λόγον τοῦ ἐπισκόπου Μελετίου
καὶ τοῦ ἀδελφοῦ Διοδώρου τοῦ συμπρεσβυτέρου
(παρῆν γὰρ τοῖς γινομένοις), συνθέμενος ὁ αἰδεσιμώτατος ἀδελφὸς Θεόδοτος ἐκεῖ, καὶ παρακα-
λέσας ἡμᾶς κατελθεῖν ἐπὶ Νικόπολιν, ἵνα καὶ
τὴν ἐκκλησίαν αὐτοῦ ἐπισκεψώμεθα, καὶ αὐτὸν
λάβωμεν τῆς μέχρι Σατάλων ὁδοιπορίας συνέμπορον, καταλιπὼν [4] ἡμᾶς ἐν Γητάσοις, ἐπειδὴ

---

[1] ἑαυτοῦ E.
[2] δικαιοτάτως καὶ ἀναντιρρήτως Reg. primus et Bigot.

meeting, that I found him agreeing with us in
every belief. But as he kept maintaining that
Eustathius had denied all this after taking his departure from us, and had personally declared to his
own disciples that in truth he had not come into
any agreement whatever on the question of faith,
I met these charges (and observe, most respected
Sir, whether I did not make the most just and
irrefutable replies thereto) by saying that I was
convinced, basing my judgment on the general
stability of the man's character, that he would not
be so lightly turned to opposite views, that he would
not now agree and now deny what he had just
said, and that a man who shuns falsehood even in
trivial affairs as a fearful thing, to say nothing of
matters of such importance and so talked of by all,
would never choose to gainsay the truth. But if he
did do this, and if what is common talk among you
should turn out to be true, we ought to propose
to him a written statement containing a complete
proof of his orthodox faith. If, then, I find that
he affirms his agreement in writing, I shall remain
in communion with him; but if I catch him drawing
back, I shall sever all connexions with him. Although the bishop Meletius and our brother Diodorus,
the presbyter (for he was present while all this was
going on), accepted this decision, and although our
most reverend brother Theodotus agreed on that
occasion, and urged us to go down to Nicopolis in
order that we should not only visit his church but
also take him as a fellow-traveller on our journey
as far as Satala, yet he left us at Getasa, and when

---

³ βεβοημένον E ; δ αβεβοημένων editi antiqi.

⁴ συνέμπορον, καταλιπών] συνέκπορον καταλιπόντα editi antiqi.

κατελάβομεν τὴν Νικόπολιν, ἐπιλαθόμενος ὧν τε παρ' ἐμοῦ[1] ἤκουσεν.[2] ὧν τε συνέθετο ἡμῖν, ἐκείναις ταῖς ὕβρεσι καὶ ταῖς ἀτιμίαις, ἃς μικρῷ πρόσθεν διηγησάμην, καταισχύνας ἡμᾶς ἀπέπεμψε.

Πῶς οὖν ἦν δυνατόν μοι, τιμιωτάτη κεφαλή,[3] ποιῆσαί τι τῶν προστεταγμένων, καὶ δοῦναι ἐπισκόπους τῇ Ἀρμενίᾳ, οὕτω πρός με τοῦ κοινωνοῦ τῆς φροντίδος διατεθέντος, παρ' οὗ ἐγὼ προσεδόκων τοὺς ἐπιτηδείους ἄνδρας εὑρήσειν; διὰ τὸ εἶναι ἐν τῇ παροικίᾳ αὐτοῦ καὶ εὐλαβεῖς καὶ συνετοὺς καὶ τῆς γλώττης ἐμπείρους καὶ τὰ λοιπὰ ἰδιώματα τοῦ ἔθνους ἐπισταμένους· ὧν εἰδὼς τὰ ὀνόματα, ἑκὼν[4] σιωπήσομαι, ἵνα μή τι ἐμπόδιον γένηται πρὸς τὸ ἐν ἑτέρῳ γοῦν χρόνῳ χρησιμευθῆναι τὴν Ἀρμενίαν.

Καὶ νῦν γενόμενος μέχρι Σατάλων ἐν τοιούτῳ σώματι, τὰ μὲν λοιπὰ ἔδοξα τῇ τοῦ Θεοῦ χάριτι καθιστᾶν, εἰρηνεύσας τοὺς τῆς Ἀρμενίας ἐπισκόπους, καὶ διαλεχθεὶς αὐτοῖς τὰ πρέποντα, ὥστε ἀποθέσθαι τὴν συνήθη ἀδιαφορίαν[5] καὶ ἀναλαβεῖν τὴν γνησίαν τοῦ Κυρίου ὑπὲρ τῶν ἐκκλησιῶν σπουδήν, δοὺς αὐτοῖς καὶ τύπους περὶ τῶν ἀδιαφόρως κατὰ τὴν Ἀρμενίαν παρανομουμένων, ὅπως αὐτοῖς προσῆκεν ἐπιμελεῖσθαι. ἐδεξάμην δὲ καὶ ψηφίσματα παρὰ τῆς ἐκκλησίας Σατάλων, παράκλησιν ἔχοντα δοθῆναι αὐτοῖς παρ' ἡμῶν ἐπίσκοπον. ἐπιμελὲς δέ μοι τοῦτο ἐγένετο, καὶ τὴν περιχυθεῖσαν βλασφημίαν τῷ ἀδελφῷ ἡμῶν

---

[1] τε παρ' ἐμοῦ] παρ' ἡμῶν E.   [2] ἤκουσαν editi antiqi.
[3] κεφαλῇ E.   [4] ἑκουσίως editi antiqi.

we arrived at Nicopolis, forgetful alike of what he
had heard from me and what he had agreed to with
us, he put us to shame with those acts of insolence
and indignity which I mentioned a little while ago,
and sent us away.

How then was it possible for me, most honoured
Sir, to perform any of the commands laid upon me,
and to furnish bishops to Armenia, when my associate
in the business was thus disposed towards me, the
man through whom I expected to discover the
suitable men? The reason is that in his parish
there are pious and sagacious persons, who are
skilled in the language and are well versed in the
other peculiarities of that nation. Although I know
their names, I shall willingly remain silent, lest
anything should arise to prevent their being of
service to Armenia at another time.

And now having come to Satala in such a state of
body, I seem, by the grace of God, to have settled
all other questions; for I have established peace
among the bishops of Armenia, and have argued
with them in befitting terms to put aside their
customary indifference, and to take up again the
true zeal of the Lord in behalf of the churches;
I have also given them rules regarding those acts,
due to indifference, which are committed throughout
Armenia in violation of the law, to show them how
it is fitting that they should take heed of those
things. I have received, too, a voted decision from
the church of Satala, with the request that a bishop
be given them by us. This matter has concerned
me, and also to investigate the slander which has

---

⁵ διαφοράν Bigot., Reg. secundus, Coisl. secundus.

Κυρίλλῳ τῷ ἐπισκόπῳ Ἀρμενίας ἀνερευνῆσαι·
καὶ διὰ τῆς χάριτος τοῦ Θεοῦ εὕρομεν αὐτὴν
ψευδῶς κινηθεῖσαν ἐκ διαβολῆς τῶν μισούντων
αὐτόν· ἣν καὶ φανερῶς ὡμολόγησαν ἐφ᾿ ἡμῶν.
καὶ ἐδόξαμεν μετρίως ἡμεροῦν πρὸς αὐτὸν τὸν ἐν
Σατάλοις λαόν, ὥστε μηκέτι αὐτοῦ τὴν κοινωνίαν
φεύγειν. εἰ δὲ μικρὰ ταῦτα καὶ οὐδενὸς ἄξια,
ἀλλὰ παρ᾿ ἡμῶν οὐδὲν ἦν πλέον δυνατὸν γενέσθαι,
διὰ τὴν ἐκ τῆς τοῦ διαβόλου περιεργίας ἡμῶν
αὐτῶν πρὸς ἀλλήλους ἀσυμφωνίαν. ταῦτά με
ἔδει[1] σιωπᾶν, ἵνα μὴ δόξω δημοσιεύειν ἐμαυτοῦ
τὰ ὀνείδη· ἀλλ᾿ ἐπειδὴ οὐκ ἦν ἄλλως ἀπολογή-
σασθαί σου τῇ μεγαλοφυΐᾳ, εἰς ἀνάγκην ἦλθον
πᾶσαν τῶν γεγονότων τὴν ἀλήθειαν διηγήσασθαι.

O

Εὐσεβίῳ, ἐπισκόπῳ Σαμοσάτων

Οὕτως εἶδον τὰ γράμματα τῆς ἀγάπης σου ἐν
τῇ γείτονι χώρᾳ τῆς Ἀρμενίας,[2] ὡς ἂν ἴδοιεν οἱ
θαλαττεύοντες πυρσὸν ἐν πελάγει πόρρωθεν
φρυκτωρούμενον, ἄλλως τε κἂν ἀγριαίνουσά πως
τύχοι[3] ἡ θάλασσα ὑπ᾿ ἀνέμων. καὶ γὰρ φύσει
μὲν ἡδὺ καὶ παρηγορίαν ἔχον πολλὴν τὸ τῆς σῆς
σεμνότητος γράμμα, τότε δὲ μάλιστα τὴν ἀπ᾿
αὐτοῦ[4] χάριν ὁ καιρὸς συνηύξησεν,[5] ὃν ὁποῖος

---

[1] ταῦτά με ἔδει] ταῦτα ἔδει μέν editi antiqi.
[2] τῶν Ἀρμενίων editi antiqi.   [3] τύχῃ editi antiqi.
[4] ἀπ᾿ αὐτοῦ] ἐπ᾿ αὐτῷ E, Harl.
[5] προσηύξησεν editi antiqi.

been heaped upon our brother, Cyril, the bishop of Armenia; and through the grace of God we have found that it was falsely fomented by the calumny of his enemies, and this the latter have openly confessed before us. And it seems that in a measure we have reconciled the laity in Satala to him, so that they no longer avoid his communion. Now if these things are trivial and of no importance, on the other hand there was nothing further which we could do, owing to our discord between one and another, caused by the busy activity of the devil. I ought to have kept silent on these matters, that I may not appear to be spreading abroad the reproaches against myself; but since I could make my defence to your Magnanimity in no other way, I have found it necessary to relate the whole truth of what has taken place.

LETTER C

To Eusebius, Bishop of Samosata [1]

I BEHELD the letter of your Charity in this neighbouring country of Armenia, with the same feelings with which men at sea would behold a beacon fire shining from afar upon the deep, especially if the sea should chance to be in an angry state by reason of the winds. For the letter of your August Reverence, though naturally possessing sweetness and great consolation, then especially had its charm enhanced by the occasion of its arrival. What the occasion

[1] According to Loofs (30), written from Armenia in July or August 372. Previous letters addressed by Basil to Eusebius of Samosata are XXVII, XXX, XXXI, XXXIV, XLVII, XLVIII, XCV, XCVIII.

ἦν, καὶ ὅπως ἡμᾶς λυπήσας, ἐγὼ μὲν οὐκ ἂν
εἴποιμι, κρίνας ἅπαξ ἐπιλαθέσθαι[1] τῶν λυπηρῶν·
ὁ μέντοι συνδιάκονος ἡμῶν διηγήσεταί σου τῇ
θεοσεβείᾳ.

Ἐμὲ δὲ ἐπέλιπε παντελῶς τὸ σῶμα, ὥστε μηδὲ
τὰς σμικροτάτας κινήσεις δύνασθαι ἀλύπως
φέρειν. πλὴν ἀλλ' εὔχομαι δυνηθῆναί μοι τὴν
παλαιὰν ἐπιθυμίαν νῦν γοῦν διὰ τῆς βοηθείας
τῶν σῶν προσευχῶν ἐκπληρωθῆναι· εἰ καὶ ὅτι
πολλήν μοι πεποίηκε τὴν δυσκολίαν ἡ ἀποδημία
αὕτη, τοσούτῳ χρόνῳ ἀμεληθέντων τῶν κατὰ τὴν
ἡμετέραν ἐκκλησίαν πραγμάτων. ἐὰν δὲ ὁ Θεός,
ἕως ἐσμὲν ὑπὲρ γῆς, καταξιώσῃ ἡμᾶς ἰδεῖν ἐπὶ
τῆς ἐκκλησίας ἡμῶν τὴν σὴν θεοσέβειαν, ὄντως
ἀγαθὰς ἐλπίδας καὶ ἐπὶ τοῖς μέλλουσιν ἕξομεν,
ὡς οὐ πάντη ἐσμὲν[2] ἀπόβλητοι τῶν δωρεῶν τοῦ
Θεοῦ. τοῦτο γοῦν, ἐὰν ᾖ δυνατόν, παρακαλοῦμεν
ἐπὶ τῆς συνόδου γενέσθαι, ἣν δι' ἔτους ἄγομεν ἐπὶ
τῇ μνήμῃ τοῦ μακαρίου[3] μάρτυρος Εὐψυχίου
προσεγγιζούσῃ λοιπὸν κατὰ τὴν ἑβδόμην ἡμέραν
τοῦ Σεπτεμβρίου μηνός. καὶ γὰρ καὶ φροντίδος
ἄξια ἡμῖν περίκειται[4] πράγματα τῆς παρὰ σοῦ
δεόμενα συνεργίας, εἴς τε κατάστασιν ἐπισκόπων
καὶ εἰς βουλὴν καὶ σκέψιν τῶν μελετωμένων καθ'
ἡμῶν παρὰ τῆς χρηστότητος Γρηγορίου τοῦ

---

[1] ἐκλαθέσθαι E.   [2] γενησόμεθα editi antiqi.
[3] μακαριωτάτου editi antiqi.   [4] πρόκειται E.

was, and how it pained us, I should not myself
speak, having determined once and for all to forget
my grievances. Our deacon, however, will relate
everything to your Piety.

My body has failed me so completely that I am
unable to make even the slightest movement without
pain. However, I pray that now, at any rate, my
old desire can be fulfilled through the assistance of
your prayers; although it is true that this absence
abroad has caused me great difficulties, since the
affairs of our own church have been neglected for so
long a time. Yet if God, while we are still on
earth, will deem us worthy to see your Piety in our
church, we shall have truly bright hopes for the
future also, that we shall not be wholly excluded
from the gifts of God. This, then, if it be possible,
we beg you to have take place at the synod which
we convene every year on the seventh of September
in memory of the blessed Eupsychius,[1] an event
which is now approaching. Moreover, we are encompassed by matters worthy of serious attention
which stand in need of your assistance, namely, the
question of establishing bishops, and the matter of
investigating and deliberating about the actions
meditated against us by Gregory of Nyssa in his

---

[1] Eupsychius appears in the Roman calendar, and his
martyrdom is celebrated on April 9 (*Boll. Acta. SS.* April 9).
He suffered in the reign of Julian for the part he took in
the demolition of a temple to Fortune. Cf. Sozomen, *Ecc.
Hist.* V, 11. Julian gave orders that the temple should be
rebuilt. This order was never fulfilled, but a church was
erected on the spot, dedicated to the memory of Eupsychius.
Basil here entreats Eusebius of Samosata to be present at
the festival of Eupsychius, and in Letter CCLII he summons
the bishops of Pontus to the festival of the dedication of this
church.

Νυσσαέως ὃς συνόδους συγκροτεῖ κατὰ τὴν
Ἀγκύραν καὶ οὐδένα τρόπον ἐπιβουλεύων ἡμῖν
ἀφίησιν.

CI

Παραμυθητική [1]

Εὐχῆς ἄξιον ἦν, πρώτην διαπεμπομένους
ἐπιστολήν, εὐθυμοτέραν ἔχειν [2] τὴν τῶν γραμμάτων ὑπόθεσιν. οὕτω γὰρ ἂν ἡμῖν τὰ κατὰ
γνώμην ὑπῆρξε, διότι πᾶσι βουλόμεθα τοῖς ἐν
εὐσεβείᾳ ζῆν προαιρουμένοις πάντα τὸν βίον εἰς
ἀγαθὸν εὐοδοῦσθαι. ἀλλ' ἐπειδὴ ὁ διοικῶν τὴν
ζωὴν ἡμῶν Κύριος, κατὰ τὴν ἄρρητον αὐτοῦ
σοφίαν πάντως πρὸς τὸ σύμφερον τῶν ψυχῶν
τῶν ἡμετέρων ταῦτα ᾠκονόμησε γενέσθαι, δι' ὧν
σοι μὲν ὀδυνηρὰν κατέστησε τὴν ζωήν, ἡμᾶς δέ,
τοὺς τῇ κατὰ Θεὸν ἀγάπῃ συνημμένους, εἰς
συμπάθειαν ἤγαγε, μαθόντας παρὰ τῶν ἀδελφῶν
ἡμῶν ἐν οἷς γέγονας, ἀναγκαῖον ἡμῖν ἐφάνη τὴν
ἐνδεχομένην παράκλησιν προσαγαγεῖν σοι. εἰ
μὲν οὖν ἦν δυνατὸν καὶ διαβῆναι μέχρι τοῦ τόπου
ἐν ᾧ συμβαίνει διάγειν σου τὴν εὐγένειαν, περὶ
παντὸς ἂν τοῦτο ἐποιησάμην. ἐπεὶ δὲ καὶ ἡ τοῦ
σώματος ἀρρωστία καὶ τῶν συνεχόντων ἡμᾶς
πραγμάτων τὸ πλῆθος καὶ αὐτὴν ταύτην ἣν
ὑπέστημεν ὁδὸν ἐπὶ πολλῇ τῶν καθ' ἡμᾶς
ἐκκλησιῶν ζημίᾳ παρεσκεύασε, διὰ γραμμάτων

---

[1] τῇ ὁμοζύγῳ Ἀρινθαίου add. editi antiqi ; πρὸς τινὰ θλίψεσιν
ἀδικήτοις περιπεσόντα Regius secundus ; τινὶ θλίψεσιν ἀδικήτοις
περιπεσόντι Bigot.

[2] σχεῖν E.

simplicity,[1] who convenes synods at Ancyra, and in no way ceases to plot against us.

LETTER CI

CONSOLATORY [2]

IT were worthy of prayer that in sending our first letter to you we might have had a more cheerful subject about which to write. If that had been so, everything would have been as we wished, for we desire that the whole life of all who choose to live in true religion should prosper well. But since the Lord who dispenses our lives has surely arranged these things according to His ineffable wisdom for the good of our souls, and so has made your life a life of sorrow, and has brought us, who are joined to you by the love of God, to feel sympathy for your plight, on hearing from our brothers in what troubles you were, it seemed that we must send you all possible consolation. Now if it had been possible to cross over to where your Nobility happens to live, I should have considered it of the greatest importance to do so. But since our bodily weakness and the manifold duties which occupy us caused even this journey which we had in mind to involve great harm to the churches under our care, we were eager to

---

[1] As the Benedictine edition points out, this opposition was due not to want of affection but to want of tact. For a similar display of lack of tact on the part of Gregory of Nyssa, cf. Letter LVIII.

[2] Written in 372. Editions anterior to the Benedictine add to the title τῇ ὁμοζύγῳ Ἀρινθαίου, "to the wife of Arinthacus," but no manuscript known to us contains it.

ἐπισκέψασθαί σου τὴν σεμνότητα προεθυμήθημεν,
ὑπομιμνήσκοντες, ὅτι αἱ θλίψεις αὗται οὐκ ἀργῶς
τοῖς δούλοις τοῦ Θεοῦ παρὰ τοῦ ἐπισκοποῦντος
ἡμᾶς Κυρίου γίνονται, ἀλλὰ ἐπὶ δοκιμασίᾳ τῆς
ἀληθινῆς πρὸς τὸν κτίσαντα ἡμᾶς Θεὸν ἀγάπης.
ὡς γὰρ τοὺς ἀθλητὰς οἱ τῶν ἀγώνων κάματοι τοῖς
στεφάνοις προσάγουσιν, οὕτω καὶ τοὺς Χριστια-
νοὺς ἡ ἐν τοῖς[1] πειρασμοῖς δοκιμασία πρὸς τὴν
τελείωσιν ἄγει, ἐὰν μετὰ τῆς πρεπούσης ὑπομονῆς
ἐν εὐχαριστίᾳ πάσῃ τὰ οἰκονομούμενα παρὰ τοῦ
Κυρίου καταδεξώμεθα.

Ἀγαθότητι Δεσπότου διοικεῖται τὰ πάντα.
οὐδὲν τῶν συμβαινόντων ἡμῖν ὡς λυπηρὸν ὑποδέχεσθαι χρή, κἂν πρὸς τὸ παρὸν ἅπτηται τῆς
ἀσθενείας ἡμῶν. εἰ γὰρ καὶ τοὺς λόγους ἀγνοοῦ-
μεν, καθ᾿ οὓς ἕκαστον τῶν γινομένων[2] ὡς καλὸν
παρὰ τοῦ Δεσπότου ἡμῖν ἐπάγεται, ἀλλ᾿ ἐκεῖνο
πεπεῖσθαι ὀφείλομεν, ὅτι πάντως συμφέρει τὸ
γινόμενον ἢ ἡμῖν διὰ τὸν τῆς ὑπομονῆς μισθὸν ἢ
τῇ παραληφθείσῃ ψυχῇ, ἵνα μή, ἐπὶ πλέον τῇ
ζωῇ ταύτῃ ἐπιβραδύνασα τῆς ἐμπολιτευομένης
τῷ βίῳ κακία ἀναπλησθῇ. εἰ μὲν γὰρ ἐν τῇ
ζωῇ ταύτῃ ἡ τῶν Χριστιανῶν ἐλπὶς περιώριστο,
εἰκότως χαλεπὸν ἂν ἐνομίσθη τὸ θᾶττον δια-
ζευχθῆναι τοῦ σώματος· εἰ δὲ ἀρχὴ τοῦ ἀληθινοῦ
βίου τοῖς κατὰ Θεὸν ζῶσίν ἐστι τὸ τῶν δεσμῶν
τούτων τῶν σωματικῶν τὴν ψυχὴν ἐκλυθῆναι, τί
λυπούμεθα, ὡς καὶ[3] οἱ μὴ ἔχοντες ἐλπίδα ; παρακλήθητι οὖν μὴ ὑποπεσεῖν τοῖς πάθεσιν, ἀλλὰ
δεῖξαι ὅτι ὑπέρκεισαι καὶ ὑπερῆρας.

---

[1] αὐτοῖς add. editi antiqi.   [2] γιγνομένων E.
[3] καί om. E.

visit your August Reverence by letter, and to remind
you that these afflictions do not come in vain to
God's servants from the Lord who watches over us,
but as a test of their genuine love for the God who
created us. For as the toils of their contests bring
athletes their crowns, so the test which comes to
Christians through their tribulations leads them
on to perfection, if with fitting patience in all
thanksgiving we accept the Lord's dispensations.

By the goodness of God are all things disposed.
Nothing that happens to us should be accepted as
grievous, even if for the present it touches our
weakness. For even if we are ignorant of the words
according to which everything that happens is
brought to us as a blessing from God, yet we should
at least be convinced of this—that assuredly whatever happens is good, either for us through the reward
won by our patience or for the soul which we have
received, lest by tarrying longer in this world the
soul be contaminated by the wickedness which in-
heres in human life. For if the hope of Christians
were limited to this life, the early separation from
the body would reasonably be thought hard ; but if
for those who live according to God the beginning
of the true life is the release of the soul from
these bodily bonds, why then are we sorrowful even
as those who have no hope ?[1] Therefore, I beg of
you, do not succumb to your woes, but show that
you stand above them and have transcended them.

---

[1] Cf. 1 Thess. 4, 12: οὐ θέλω δὲ ὑμᾶς ἀγνοεῖν, ἀδελφοί, περὶ τῶν
κεκοιμημένων, ἵνα μὴ λυπῆσθε, καθὼς καὶ οἱ λοιποὶ οἱ μὴ ἔχοντες
ἐλπίδα "And we will not have you ignorant, brethren,
concerning them that are asleep, that you be not sorrowful,
even as others who have no hope."

CII

Σαταλεῦσι πολίταις

Ἐγὼ τάς τε ἰδίας ὑμῶν παρακλήσεις καὶ τὰς τοῦ λαοῦ παντὸς δυσωπηθείς, καὶ ἐδεξάμην[1] τὴν φροντίδα τῆς καθ᾽ ὑμᾶς ἐκκλησίας, καὶ ὑπεσχόμην ὑμῖν ἐνώπιον Κυρίου μηδὲν ἐλλείψειν τῶν εἰς δύναμιν ἐμὴν ἡκόντων. διὸ ἠναγκάσθην, κατὰ τὸ γεγραμμένον,[2] οἷον τῆς κόρης τοῦ ἐμοῦ ὀφθαλμοῦ ἅψασθαι. οὕτως τὸ ὑπερβάλλον τῆς καθ᾽ ὑμᾶς τιμῆς οὐδενός μοι συνεχώρησεν εἰς μνήμην ἐλθεῖν, οὐ συγγενείας, οὐ τῆς ἐκ παιδὸς συνηθείας τῆς ὑπαρχούσης μοι πρὸς τὸν ἄνδρα, πρὸ τῶν παρ᾽ ὑμῶν αἰτηθέντων· ἀλλὰ πάντων μὲν τῶν ἰδίᾳ μοι ὑπαρχόντων πρὸς αὐτὸν εἰς οἰκειότητος λόγον ἐπιλαθόμενος, μὴ ὑπολογισάμενος δὲ μηδὲ τοῦ στεναγμοῦ τὸ πλῆθος, ὃ καταστενάξει μου ὁ λαὸς ὁ τὴν προστασίαν αὐτοῦ ζημιωθείς, μὴ πάσης αὐτοῦ τῆς συγγενείας τὸ δάκρυον, μὴ μητρὸς αὐτοῦ γηραιᾶς καὶ ἐπὶ μόνῃ τῇ παρ᾽ αὐτοῦ θεραπείᾳ σαλευούσης τὴν θλίψιν εἰς καρδίαν λαβών· πάντων ὁμοῦ τοιούτων ὄντων[3] καὶ τοσούτων ἀλογήσας, ἑνὸς ἐγενόμην, τοῦ τὴν ὑμετέραν ἐκκλησίαν κατακοσμῆσαι μὲν τῇ τοῦ τηλικούτου ἀνδρὸς προστασίᾳ, βοηθῆσαι δὲ αὐτῇ ἐκ τῆς χρονίας ἀπροστασίας εἰς γόνυ λοιπὸν κλιθείσῃ,

---

[1] κατεδεξάμην Harl.   [2] εἰρημένον Harl., Med.
[3] ἀλγεινῶν Med.

---

[1] Placed by the Benedictine edition in 372, but by Loofs (20 f.) in 373. This letter concerns the appointment of a

LETTER CII

To the Citizens of Satala [1]

STIRRED to shame by your own pleadings as well as by those of all the laity, I have taken over the care of your church, and have promised you before the Lord to leave nothing undone which is within my power. Therefore, as it is written, I was forced to touch, as it were, the apple of my eye.[2] Thus my overwhelming respect for you has not permitted me to call to mind either ties of relationship or my intimacy with the man which dates from childhood, before what has been requested by you; but, forgetting all that passed privately between him and me in the nature of friendship, paying no heed to the multitude of lamentations which the people uttered against me when deprived of his rule, or to the tears of all his relatives, not taking to heart the affliction of his aged mother whose only anchor is his care of her; disregarding one and all the many and serious considerations of this sort, I became engrossed with but one concern—to adorn your church with the leadership of such a man, and to succour it, bowed to its knees as it was from the long lack of leadership, and standing in need

---

bishop for the see of Satala in the north-east of Armenia Minor.

[2] Cf. Zech. 2, 8 : διότι τάδε λέγει Κύριος Παντοκράτωρ 'Οπίσω δόξης ἀπέσταλκέν με ἐπὶ τὰ ἔθνη τὰ σκυλεύσαντα ὑμᾶς, διότι ὁ ἁπτόμενος ὑμῶν ὡς ἁπτόμενος τῆς κόρης τοῦ ὀφθαλμοῦ αὐτοῦ. "For thus saith the Lord of hosts: After the glory he hath sent me to the nations that have robbed you: for he that toucheth you, toucheth the apple of my eye."

καὶ πολλῆς καὶ δυνατῆς χειραγωγίας εἰς τὸ
διαναστῆναι δεομένη.[1]

Τὰ μὲν οὖν ἡμέτερα τοιαῦτα. τὰ δὲ παρ' ὑμῶς
ἀπαιτοῦμεν λοιπὸν μὴ ἐλάττονα φανῆναι τὴν
ἡμετέρας ἐλπίδος καὶ τῶν ὑποσχέσεων ἃς πε-
ποιήμεθα τῷ ἀνδρί, ὅτι πρὸς οἰκείους καὶ φίλους
αὐτὸν ἐξεπέμψαμεν, ἑκάστου ὑμῶν ὑπερβαλέσθαι
τὸν ἕτερον ἐν τῇ περὶ τὸν ἄνδρα σπουδῇ καὶ
ἀγάπῃ προθυμουμένου. ὅπως οὖν ἐπιδείξησθε[2]
τὴν καλὴν ταύτην φιλοτιμίαν, καὶ τῷ ὑπερβάλ-
λοντι τῆς θεραπείας παρακαλέσητε αὐτοῦ τὴν
καρδίαν, ὥστε λήθην μὲν αὐτῷ ἐγγενέσθαι πατρίδος, λήθην δὲ συγγενῶν,[3] λήθην δὲ λαοῦ
τοσοῦτον ἐξηρτημένου τῆς προστασίας αὐτοῦ
ὅσον παιδίον νεαρὸν τῆς μητρῴας θηλῆς.

Προαπεστείλαμεν δὲ Νικίαν, ὥστε τὰ γενόμενα
φανερὰ καταστῆσαι τῇ τιμιότητι ὑμῶν, καὶ
προλαβόντας ὑμᾶς ἑορτάζειν καὶ εὐχαριστεῖν τῷ
Κυρίῳ τῷ δι' ἡμῶν[4] καταξιώσαντι τὴν εὐχὴν
ὑμῶν ἐκπληρωθῆναι.

CIII

Σαταλεῦσιν[5]

Ἤγαγεν εἰς ἔργον ὁ Κύριος τοῦ λαοῦ αὐτοῦ[6]
τὰ αἰτήματα, καὶ ἔδωκεν αὐτῷ διὰ τῆς ἡμετέρας
ταπεινώσεως ποιμένα ἄξιον μὲν τοῦ ὀνόματος,
καὶ οὐ κατὰ τοὺς πολλοὺς καπηλεύοντα τὸν

---

[1] δεομένης editi antiqi.   [2] ἐπιδείξεσθε editi antiqi.
[3] συγγενείας editi antiqi.   [4] ἡμᾶς editi antiqi.
[5] ἀνεπίγραφος ἐπὶ ἐκκλησίᾳ E.   [6] αὐτοῦ om. E.

of some great and powerful guidance to enable it to rise again.[1]

So much regarding ourselves. And now we beg you, on your part, not to fall short of our hopes, or of the assurances which we made the man, that you to whom we sent him are devoted friends, each one of you being eager to surpass the other in zeal for him and in love. Therefore see that you display that noble rivalry, and cheer his heart by the overwhelming force of your solicitude, that he may come to forget his fatherland, his relatives, and his people, who have been as dependent on his protection as is a young child on its mother's breast.

We have sent Nicias[2] on ahead to tell your honourable selves what has happened, and that you on receiving the news may hold festival and give thanks to the Lord who has seen fit through us to fulfil your prayer.

LETTER CIII

To the People of Satala[3]

THE Lord has brought the prayers of His people to a fulfilment, and through our humble instrumentality has given them a shepherd worthy of the name, one who does not, like most men,

---

[1] The person Basil has in mind is Poemenius. Cf. Letter CXXII.

[2] Otherwise unknown.

[3] Of the same date as the preceding, and on the same general topic.

λόγον, δυνάμενον δὲ καὶ ὑμῖν[1] τοῖς τὴν ὀρθότητα
τοῦ κηρύγματος ἀγαπῶσι καὶ τὴν κατ᾽ ἐντολὰς[2]
τοῦ Κυρίου ζωὴν καταδεξαμένοις ἀρέσκειν καθ᾽
ὑπερβολὴν ἐν τῷ ὀνόματι[3] τοῦ Κυρίου τοῦ
πληρώσαντος αὐτὸν τῶν πνευματικῶν αὐτοῦ
χαρισμάτων.

CIV

Μοδέστῳ ὑπάρχῳ

Αὐτὸ τὸ γράφειν πρὸς ἄνδρα τοσοῦτον, κἂν
μηδεμία πρόφασις ἑτέρα προσῇ, μέγιστόν ἐστι
τῶν εἰς τιμὴν φερόντων τοῖς αἰσθανομένοις· διότι
αἱ πρὸς τοὺς παμπληθὲς[4] τῶν λοιπῶν ὑπερέ-
χοντας ὁμιλίαι μεγίστην τοῖς ἀξιουμένοις[5] περιφάνειαν προξενοῦσιν. ἐμοὶ δ᾽ ὑπὲρ πατρίδος
πάσης ἀγωνιῶντι ἀναγκαία πρὸς τὴν σὴν μεγαλόνοιαν ἡ ἔντευξις, ἧς ἱκετεύω πράως καὶ κατὰ τὸν
σεαυτοῦ τρόπον ἀνασχέσθαι, καὶ χεῖρα ὀρέξαι
τῇ πατρίδι ἡμῶν εἰς γόνυ ἤδη[6] κλιθείσῃ.[7] ἔστι
δὲ ὑπὲρ οὗ ἱκετεύομέν[8] σε τὸ πρᾶγμα τοιοῦτον.
Τοὺς τῷ Θεῷ ἡμῶν ἱερωμένους, πρεσβυτέρους

---

[1] ἡμῖν editi antiqi.   [2] ἐντολὴν E.
[3] ῥήματι editi antiqi.   [4] παμπληθεῖς editi antiqi.
[5] τήν add. E.   [6] ἤδη om. E.
[7] ἐλθούσῃ editi antiqi.   [8] ἱκετεύωμεν E.

---

[1] Written in 372; on the taxation of the clergy. Modestus
was Prefect of the Praetorium, and a persecutor of Catholics
under Valens. At the command of Valens, he offered Basil
the choice between deposition and communion with the
Arians. Shortly after this, Modestus fell seriously ill, which

make traffic of the title, but who is capable in the extreme of satisfying you who love the orthodox doctrine and have accepted the life that is in accordance with the Lord's commands, in the name of the Lord who has filled him with His spiritual blessings.

LETTER CIV

To the Prefect Modestus[1]

THE very act of writing to so great a man, even if there be no other excuse, is most conducive to honour in the eyes of the discerning; for intercourse with men who are overwhelmingly superior to the rest of mankind affords the greatest distinction to such as are deemed worthy of it. As for me, as I strive earnestly for my country as a whole, I must needs address to your Magnanimity this petition (which I entreat you to suffer calmly even according to your character), that you stretch forth a helping hand to our fatherland now bowed to its knees. And the matter regarding which we seek your help is this.

Those who are consecrated to our God, that is

he regarded as divine judgment for his insolence towards Basil. Modestus at once summoned the holy man to his sick bed, and, humbly begging pardon for his behaviour, commended himself to his prayers. Modestus soon recovered, which he attributed to Basil's intercessions, and he accordingly regarded him with the greatest reverence. Henceforth Basil's influence with Modestus was so great that he was constantly importuned for letters of favour to the Prefect. Six of these letters of St. Basil are extant: the present one, CX, CXI, CCLXXIX, CCLXXX, and CCLXXXI.

καὶ διακόνους, ὁ παλαιὸς κῆνσος ἀτελεῖς ἀφῆκεν.¹
οἱ δὲ νῦν ἀπογραψάμενοι, ὡς οὐ λαβόντες παρὰ
τῆς ὑπερφυοῦς σου ἐξουσίας πρόσταγμα,² ἀπε-
γράψαντο, πλὴν εἰ μὴ πού τινες ἄλλως εἶχον
ὑπὸ τῆς ἡλικίας τὴν ἄφεσιν. δεόμεθα οὖν
μνημόσυνον τῆς σῆς εὐεργεσίας τοῦτο ἡμῖν ἀφεθῆναι,³ παντὶ τῷ ἐπιόντι χρόνῳ ἀγαθὴν περὶ
σοῦ μνήμην διαφυλάττον, καὶ συγχωρηθῆναι κατὰ
τὸν παλαιὸν νόμον τῆς συντελείας τοὺς ἱερα-
τεύοντας·⁴ καὶ μὴ εἰς πρόσωπον τῶν νῦν κατα-
λαμβανομένων γενέσθαι τὴν ἄφεσιν (οὕτω γὰρ
εἰς τοὺς διαδόχους ἡ χάρις μεταβήσεται, οὓς οὐ
πάντως συμβαίνει τοῦ ἱερατεύειν ἀξίους εἶναι),
ἀλλὰ κατὰ τὸν ἐν τῇ ἐλευθέρᾳ ἀπογραφῇ τύπον
κοινήν τινα συγχώρησιν κληρικῶν γενέσθαι, ὥστε
ὑπὸ τῶν οἰκονομούντων τὰς ἐκκλησίας τοῖς ἑκάστοτε λειτουργοῦσι τὴν ἀτέλειαν δίδοσθαι.

Ταῦτα καὶ τῇ σῇ μεγαλοφυΐᾳ ἀθάνατον τὴν
ἐπὶ τοῖς ἀγαθοῖς δόξαν διαφυλάξει, καὶ τῷ
βασιλικῷ οἴκῳ πολλοὺς τοὺς ὑπερευχομένους
παρασκευάσει, καὶ αὐτοῖς τοῖς δημοσίοις μέγα
παρέξει ὄφελος, ἡμῶν οὐ πάντως τοῖς κληρικοῖς,
ἀλλὰ τοῖς ἀεὶ καταπονουμένοις τὴν ἀπὸ τῆς ἀτε-
λείας παραμυθίαν παρεχομένων· ὅπερ⁵ οὖν καὶ
ἐπὶ τῆς ἐλευθερίας⁶ ποιοῦμεν, ὡς ἔξεστι γνῶναι
τῷ βουλομένῳ.

¹ ἀφῆκαν editi antiqi.   ² προστάματα E, Harl.
³ ἐναφεθῆναι editi antiqi.
⁴ τῆς . . . ἱερατεύοντας] τὴν συντελείαν τοῖς ἱερατεύουσι E.
⁵ ὥσπερ editi antiqi.   ⁶ ἐλευθέρας E.

---

¹ The Benedictine edition notes that the words "presbyters
and deacons" are probably a marginal gloss, which crept

presbyters and deacons,[1] the earlier census left immune from taxation. But the present registrars, alleging that they had received no authorization from your high Lordship, have enrolled them, with the exception perhaps of some who are otherwise exempt because of old age. Therefore we ask that this exemption be granted us as a memorial of your beneficence, which will protect your good name for all future time, and that according to the old law those who act as priests be exempt from contribution, and that the exemption be not granted to the persons of those who now receive it (for in that case the favour would pass to their heirs, who might not be at all worthy of priestly duties), but that a general concession be granted the clergy according to the draft of the open register,[2] so that exemption may be given by those who regulate the affairs of the churches to such as on each occasion are in the service.

This will not only keep the glory of the good deeds of your great Lordship immortal, but it will also increase the number of those who pray for the Imperial house, and will confer a great benefit even upon the public revenues, since we give the relief which is derived from our immunity from taxation, not altogether to the clergy, but to those who are at any time in distress; indeed, this is just what we do when we are free to do so, as anyone who wishes may find out.

into the text early in the MSS. tradition, since all the MSS. seem to have it. Moreover, by ἱερωμένους and all cognate words Basil always means the whole clergy. Cf. Letter IV and note.

[2] Probably the public census list.

CV

Διακόνοις θυγατράσι Τερεντίου Κόμητος [1]

Ἐγὼ καὶ Σαμοσάτοις ἐπιστὰς προσεδόκησα συντεύξαθαι τῇ κοσμιότητι ὑμῶν· καὶ ἐπειδὴ διήμαρτον τῆς συντυχίας, οὐ μετρίως ἤνεγκα τὴν ζημίαν, λογιζόμενος πότε εἴη ἢ ἐμοὶ δυνατὸν πάλιν πλησιάσαι τοῖς καθ᾽ ὑμᾶς χωρίοις ἢ [2] ὑμῖν [3] αἱρετὸν τὴν ἡμετέραν καταλαβεῖν. ἀλλ᾽ ἐκεῖνα μὲν κείσθω ἐν τῷ θελήματι τοῦ Κυρίου.

Τὸ δὲ νῦν ἔχον, ἐπειδὴ εὗρον τὸν υἱὸν Σωφρόνιον πρὸς ὑμᾶς ἐξορμῶντα, ἡδέως αὐτῷ τὴν ἐπιστολὴν ἐπέθηκα [4] ταύτην, προσηγορίαν ὑμῖν κωμίζουσαν καὶ τὴν ἡμετέραν γνώμην δηλοῦσαν, ὅτι οὐ διαλιμπάνομεν τῇ τοῦ Θεοῦ χάριτι μεμνημένοι ὑμῶν, καὶ εὐχαριστοῦντες ὑπὲρ ὑμῶν τῷ Κυρίῳ ὅτι ἀγαθῆς ῥίζης ἀγαθὰ βλαστήματά ἐστε, ἔγκαρπα τοῖς ἀγαθοῖς ἔργοις, καὶ τῷ ὄντι ὡς κρίνα ἐν μέσῳ ἀκανθῶν. τὸ γὰρ ὑπὸ τοσαύτης διαστροφῆς τῶν παραφθειρόντων τὸν λόγον τῆς ἀληθείας περικυκλουμένας μὴ ἐνδοῦναι πρὸς τὰς ἀπάτας, μηδὲ τὸ ἀποστολικὸν τῆς πίστεως κήρυγμα καταλιπούσας πρὸς τὴν νῦν ἐπιπολάζουσαν καινοτομίαν [5] μετατεθῆναι, πῶς οὐχὶ μεγάλης μὲν πρὸς τὸν Θεὸν εὐχαριστίας ἄξιον, μεγάλους δὲ ὑμῖν ἐπαίνους δικαιότατα προξενεῖ;

---

[1] Φερεντίου κόμητος editi antiqi.   περὶ πίστεως add. quidam MSS.
[2] εἰ add. E.   [3] ἢ ὑμῖν] ἢ εἰ ὑμῖν editi antiqi.
[4] ἐπέδωκα editi antiqi.   [5] κενοφωνίαν E.

LETTER CV

LETTER CV

To the Deaconesses, Daughters of Count
Terentius [1]

WHEN I visited Samosata I expected to meet your
Modesties; and when I missed this meeting, I did
not bear the disappointment lightly, wondering
when it might either be possible for me to visit your
country again or convenient for you to visit ours.
However, let all this rest with the will of the
Lord.

As to the present, when I found that my son
Sophronius [2] was setting out in your direction, I
gladly entrusted him with this letter, which conveys
to you our greetings, and makes known our mind—
that by God's grace we never cease to be mindful of
you, and to thank the Lord for you that you are goodly
scions of a goodly stock, fruitful in good works, and
in very truth like lilies among thorns. [3] For that you
have not given way to deceptions, surrounded as you
are by the gross perversity of men who destroy the
word of truth, and that you have not abandoned the
apostolic proclamation of faith and gone over to the
popular novelty of the day—does this not call for
great thanksgiving to God, and does it not most
justly bring you great commendation ? You have

[1] Written in the autumn of 372. Cf. Loofs 33. For
Count Terentius, cf. Letter XCIX and note.
[2] Perhaps the disciple of Eustathius, noted in Letter
CXIX.
[3] Cf. Cant. 2, 2: Ὡς κρίνον ἐν μέσῳ ἀκανθῶν, οὕτως ἡ πλησίν
μου ἀνὰ μέσον τῶν θυγατέρων. " As the lily among thorns, so is
my love among the daughters."

εἰς Πατέρα καὶ Υἱὸν καὶ ἅγιον Πνεῦμα πεπιστεύ
κατε· μὴ προδῶτε ταύτην τὴν παρακαταθήκην·
πατέρα τὴν πάντων ἀρχήν· Υἱὸν μονογενῆ, ἐξ
αὐτοῦ γεννηθέντα, ἀληθινὸν Θεόν, τέλειον ἐκ τε
λείου, εἰκόνα ζῶσαν, ὅλον δεικνύντα ἐν ἑαυτῷ τὸν
Πατέρα· Πνεῦμα ἅγιον, ἐκ Θεοῦ τὴν ὕπαρξιν ἔχον,[1]
τὴν πηγὴν τῆς ἁγιότητος, δύναμιν ζωῆς παρεκτι
κήν, χάριν τελειοποιόν, δι' οὗ υἱοθετεῖται ἄνθρωπος,
καὶ ἀπαθανατίζεται[2] τὸ θνητόν, συνημμένον Πατρὶ
καὶ Υἱῷ κατὰ πάντα ἐν δόξῃ καὶ[3] ἀϊδιότητι, ἐν
δυνάμει καὶ βασιλείᾳ, ἐν δεσποτείᾳ καὶ θεότητι,
ὡς καὶ ἡ τοῦ σωτηρίου βαπτίσματος παράδοσις
μαρτυρεῖ.

Οἱ δὲ κτίσμα λέγοντες ἢ τὸν Υἱὸν ἢ τὸ Πνεῦμα,
ἢ ὅλως αὐτὸ[4] εἰς τὴν λειτουργικὴν καὶ δουλικὴν
κατάγοντες τάξιν, μακράν εἰσι τῆς ἀληθείας, ὧν
φεύγειν προσήκει τὰς κοινωνίας καὶ ἐκτρέπεσθαι
τοὺς λόγους ὡς δηλητήρια ὄντα[5] ψυχῶν· ἐὰν δέ
ποτε δῷ[6] ἡμῖν ὁ Κύριος γενέσθαι κατὰ ταὐτόν,
πλατύτερον ὑμῖν τοὺς περὶ τῆς πίστεως ἐκθησό
μεθα λόγους, ὥστε μετ' ἀποδείξεων γραφικῶν καὶ
τὸ τῆς ἀληθείας ἰσχυρὸν καὶ τὸ σαθρὸν τῆς
αἱρέσεως ὑμᾶς ἐπιγνῶναι.

CVI

Στρατιώτῃ

Ὑπὲρ πολλῶν ἔχοντες εὐχαριστεῖν τῷ Κυρίῳ,
ὧν καὶ ἠξιώθημεν παρ' αὐτοῦ ἐπὶ τῆς ἐπιδημίας

---

[1] ὕπαρξιν ἔχον] ὕπαρχον quidam MSS.
[2] ἐπαθανατίζεται editi antiqi.   [3] ἐν add. E.

believed in Father, Son, and Holy Ghost; do not prove false to this sacred trust: Father, the beginning of all things; only begotten Son, born from Him, true God, Perfect from Perfect, living image, displaying the Father entirely in Himself; Holy Spirit, with His subsistence from God, fount of Holiness, power that gives life, grace that gives perfection, whereby man is adopted, and the mortal made immortal, joined to the Father and the Son in every phase of glory and eternity, of power and royalty, of sovereignty and divinity, as even the tradition of the baptism of salvation doth testify.

Those who speak of the Son or the Spirit as a creature, or who in general place the Spirit in the category of servile and slavish things, are far from the truth, and we should avoid communion with these and turn away their words as being snares for the soul. But if ever the Lord grants that we be together again, we shall so set forth to you at greater length the doctrine of the Faith, that by proofs taken from Scripture you may recognize the strength of the truth and the rottenness of the heresy.

LETTER CVI

To a Soldier[1]

ALTHOUGH we can thank the Lord for many things of which in our travels we have been considered

[1] Written in 372.

COLLECTED LETTERS OF SAINT BASIL

ἡμῶν,[1] μέγιστον ἀγαθὸν ἐκρίναμεν τὴν γνῶσιν
τῆς σῆς τιμιότητος, τὴν παρὰ τοῦ ἀγαθοῦ Δεσπότου παρασχεθεῖσαν ἡμῖν. ἔγνωμεν γὰρ ἄνδρα
δεικνύντα, ὅτι καὶ ἐν τῷ στρατιωτικῷ βίῳ δυνατὸν
τῆς πρὸς Θεὸν ἀγάπης τὸ τέλειον διασῶσαι, καὶ
ὅτι οὐκ ἐν τῇ περιβολῇ τῆς ἐσθῆτος, ἀλλ' ἐν τῇ
διαθέσει τῆς ψυχῆς ὁ Χριστιανὸς ὀφείλει χαρακ-
τηρίζεσθαι.

Καὶ τότε οὖν μετὰ πάσης ἐπιθυμίας συνετύ-
χομέν σοι, καὶ νῦν, ὁσάκις ἂν εἰς μνήμην ἔλθωμεν,
μεγίστης ἀπολαύομεν εὐφροσύνης. ἀνδρίζου
τοίνυν, καὶ ἴσχυε, καὶ τὴν πρὸς Θεὸν ἀγάπην
τρέφειν καὶ πολυπλασιάζειν ἀεὶ σπούδαζε, ἵνα
σοι καὶ ἡ τῶν ἀγαθῶν παρ' αὐτοῦ χορηγία ἐπὶ
μεῖζον προΐῃ. ὅτι δὲ καὶ ἡμῶν μέμνησαι, οὐδεμιᾶς ἑτέρας ἀποδείξεως προσδεόμεθα, τὴν ἐκ τῶν
πραγμάτων ἔχοντες μαρτυρίαν.

CVII

Ἰουλίττῃ ἐλευθέρᾳ

Πάνυ ἠθύμησα τοῖς γράμμασιν ἐντυχὼν τῆς
εὐγενείας σου, ὅτι σε πάλιν αἱ αὐταὶ περιέχουσιν
ἀνάγκαι. καὶ τί δεῖ ποιεῖν πρὸς ἀνθρώπους οὕτω
παλίμβολον [2] ἐπιδεικνυμένους τὸ ἦθος, καὶ ἄλλοτε
ἄλλα λέγοντας, καὶ ταῖς ἰδίαις ὁμολογίαις μὴ
ἐμμένοντας; εἰ γὰρ μετὰ τὰς ἐπ'[3] ἐμοῦ καὶ τοῦ

---

[1] ὑμῶν E.   [2] παλίμβουλον E.
[3] ἀπ' editi antiqi.

---

[1] Written in 372. Julitta, a widow lady of Cappadocia, is
being harassed by the guardian of her heirs. Basil writes

worthy by Him, yet we have counted as the greatest blessing that acquaintance with your Honour which was granted us by the good Master. For we have come to know a man who proves that even in military life one may preserve the perfection of love for God, and that a Christian should be marked, not by the fashion of his clothing, but by the disposition of his soul.

Now at the time we were quite eager to meet you, and now, as often as we call you to memory, we experience the greatest pleasure. Therefore play the man, and be strong, and always strive to foster and increase your love of God, that the supply of the blessings He bestows upon you may grow greater and greater. Moreover, that you on your part are mindful of us we need no further proof, for we have the witness of your deeds.

LETTER CVII

To the Widow Julitta [1]

I was very angry when I read in the letter of your Nobility that the same difficulties again beset you. And how should we deal with men who display such perverse natures, and say one thing on one occasion and another on another, and never abide by their agreements? For if, after making such promises in the presence of myself and the ex-

this and the next two letters in an effort to relieve her of these troubles. Tillemont, though on insufficient grounds, is inclined to identify her with other widows ($\grave{\epsilon}\lambda\epsilon\upsilon\theta\acute{\epsilon}\rho\alpha\iota$), to whom Basil addressed letters.

ἀπὸ ὑπάρχων ὑποσχέσεις, νῦν, ὡς μηδενὸς εἰρη
μένου, οὕτω στενοχωρεῖ τὴν προθεσμίαν, ἔοικε
παντελῶς ἀπηρυθριακέναι πρὸς ἡμᾶς ὁ ἀνήρ.

Πλὴν ἀλλ' ἐπέστειλα αὐτῷ, ἐντρέπων αὐτὸν
καὶ ὑπομιμνήσκων τῶν αὐτοῦ ὑποσχέσεων. ἐπέ
στειλα δὲ καὶ Ἑλλαδίῳ, τῷ οἰκείῳ τοῦ ὑπάρχου,
ἵνα δι' αὐτοῦ διδαχθῇ τὰ κατὰ σὲ ὁ ὕπαρχος.[1]
αὐτὸς γὰρ μέχρι τοσούτου θαρρῆσαι δικαστῇ
τοσούτῳ οὐκ ἐνόμισα ἐπίβαλλον[2] εἶναί μοι, διὰ
τὸ μηδέ πω περὶ ἰδιωτικοῦ πράγματος αὐτῷ
ἐπεσταλκέναι, καὶ ὑφορᾶσθαι κατάγνωσίν τινα,
ὡς οἶδας, εὐκόλως τῶν μεγάλων ἀνδρῶν ἀγριαι
νόντων πρὸς τὰ τοιαῦτα· εἰ μέντοι τι ἔσται
ὄφελος, ἔσται τοῦτο διὰ Ἑλλαδίου, ἀνθρώπου
καὶ χρηστοῦ καὶ περὶ ἡμᾶς διακειμένου, καὶ Θεὸν
φοβουμένου, καὶ παρρησίαν ἀμύθητον ἔχοντος
πρὸς τὸν ἄρχοντα. δυνατὸς δὲ ὁ ἅγιος διαγαγεῖν[3]
σε πάσης θλίψεως, μόνον ἐὰν ἀληθινῇ καὶ γνησίᾳ
καρδίᾳ ἐπελπίσωμεν ἐπ' αὐτόν.

CVIII

Τῷ κηδεμόνι τῶν κληρονόμων Ἰουλίττης

Ἐθαύμασα ἀκούσας ὅτι, τῶν χρηστῶν ἐκείνων
καὶ πρεπόντων τῇ σῇ ἐλευθερίᾳ ὑποσχέσεων ἐπι
λαθόμενος, νῦν σφοδροτάτην καὶ ἀπαραίτητον
ἐπάγεις τὴν ἀπαίτησιν τῇ ἀδελφῇ τῇδε· καὶ τί
εἰκάσω ἐκ τῶν λεγομένων οὐκ ἔχω. σοί τε γὰρ

---

[1] ἔπαρχος E. [2] ἐπιβάλλειν E.
[3] διάγειν editio Paris.

prefects, the man now, as if nothing had been said, shortens the time of grace as you report, he seems to have utterly lost all sense of shame before us.

However, I did write to him, rebuking him and reminding him of his promises. And I wrote also to Helladius,[1] one of the Prefect's household, that the Prefect might be informed of your affairs through him. For I did not think that it was incumbent upon me to make bold to such an extent myself with so important an officer, because I had never written to him about a matter of private business, and I feared some censure—for, as you know, men of high station are easily incensed over such matters. If, however, there is to be any assistance forthcoming, it will be through Helladius, a good man, well disposed towards us, God-fearing, and enjoying untold freedom of speech with the Prefect. But the Holy One can guide you through every affliction, if only with a true and sincere heart we place our hopes in Him.

LETTER CVIII

To the Guardian of the Heirs of Julitta[2]

I have been surprised to hear that you, forgetting those excellent promises which were so becoming to your generosity, now place a very harsh and rigorous demand on this sister of ours; and I do not know what to think of these reports. For I am not only

---

[1] This Helladius, except for the present letter and Letter CIX, is unknown.

[2] Of the same date as the preceding and on the same general topic.

πολλὴν παρὰ τῶν πεπειραμένων σου μαρτυρου-
μένην ἐλευθερίαν σύνοιδα, καὶ τῶν ὑποσχέσεών
σου μέμνημαι ὧν ἐποίησας ἐπ' ἐμοῦ καὶ τοῦδε,[1]
λέγων ἐλάττονα μὲν γράφειν χρόνον, πλείονα δὲ
συγχωρήσειν διὰ τὸ[2] βούλεσθαι συμπεριφέρεσθαι
τῇ ἀνάγκῃ τοῦ πράγματος, καὶ συγγνώμην παρέχειν τῇ ἐλευθέρᾳ ἀναγκαζομένῃ τοσοῦτον ἀθρόως
ἐκ τῆς οἰκίας προΐεσθαι χρῆμα.

Τίς οὖν ἡ αἰτία δι' ἣν ἡ τοσαύτη μεταβολὴ
γέγονεν ἐγὼ νοεῖν οὐκ ἔχω. πλὴν ὅπερ ἂν ᾖ,
παρακαλῶ σε, μεμνημένον τῆς σεαυτοῦ ἐλευ-
θεριότητος καὶ πρὸς τὸν Κύριον ἀπιδόντα τὸν
ἀμειβόμενον τὰς χρηστὰς προαιρέσεις, δοῦναι τὸν
καιρὸν ὃν ἐξ ἀρχῆς ὑπέσχου τῆς ἀνέσεως, ἵνα
δυνηθῶσι συμπωλήσαντες τὰ ἑαυτῶν διαλῦσαι
τὸ χρέος. δῆλον δὲ ὅτι κἀκείνων μέμνημαι, ὅτι
ὑπέσχου, εἰ λάβοις τὸ ὁμολογηθὲν χρυσίον, πάντα
τὰ ὁμολογηθέντα χαρτία, καὶ τὰ ἐπὶ τῶν ἀρχόντων πραχθέντα καὶ τὰ ἰδιωτικῶς γενόμενα,[3] παρα-
δώσειν τῇ προειρημένῃ.

Παρακαλῶ οὖν, καὶ ἡμᾶς τίμησον καὶ κτῆσαι
παρὰ τῷ Κυρίῳ μεγάλην ἑαυτῷ εὐλογίαν, ἀνα-
μνησθεὶς τῶν σεαυτοῦ ὑποσχέσεων, γινώσκων ὅτι
ἄνθρωπος εἶ καὶ αὐτὸς[4] ἀναμένειν ὀφείλεις τοὺς
καιροὺς ἐν οἷς δεηθήσῃ τῆς παρὰ τοῦ Θεοῦ ἀντι-
λήψεως· ἣν μὴ ἀποκλείσῃς σεαυτῷ διὰ τῆς
παρούσης σκληρότητος, ἀλλ' εὐτρέπισον τοὺς
οἰκτιρμοὺς τοῦ Θεοῦ ἐπὶ σαυτόν, πᾶσαν χρηστότητα
καὶ ἐπιείκειαν τοῖς καταπονουμένοις ἐπιδειξάμενος.

---

[1] καὶ τοῦδε] τοῦ δὲ λόγου conj. Combefisius.
[2] διὰ τὸ] δεῖ τῷ E, editi antiqi.
[3] γινόμενα editi antiqi.   [4] καί add. E.

acquainted with your great liberality, to which those who have experienced it bear witness, but I also remember the promises made by you in the presence of myself and this man ;[1] for you said that, though you were naming a shorter time in writing, you would grant a longer term because you wished to meet the necessities of the case, and that you were showing indulgence to the widow in view of her being under the necessity of paying out so great a sum of money from her substance all at once.

Now what the cause is of this great change that has taken place in you I cannot understand. But whatever it is, I beg you, remembering your own generosity, and gazing upon the Lord who requites good resolutions, to grant the term of grace which you promised in the beginning, that they may be able to sell their property and discharge the debt. And it is evident that I remember this also very well—that you promised, if you should receive the sum agreed upon, to give back to the aforesaid widow all the stipulated documents, both those that were done in the presence of the magistrates and those that were executed privately.

Do you, accordingly, I pray, both honour us and obtain great praise for yourself with the Lord by being mindful of your promises, realizing that you are a man and must expect occasions when you will yourself need help from God ; and do not exclude yourself from this help by persisting in your present severity, but make ready God's mercies for yourself by showing every kindness and clemency to those who are in distress.

---

[1] *i.e.* the ex-prefect.

CIX

Ἑλλαδίῳ Κόμητι

Πάνυ παραιτούμενος δι' ὄχλου εἶναι τῇ χρηστό-
τητί σου διὰ τὸ μέγεθος τῆς περὶ ὑμᾶς ἀρχῆς, ἵνα
μὴ δόξω ἀμέτρως ἐμφορεῖσθαι τῆς φιλίας ὑμῶν,
ὅμως ὑπὸ τῶν ἀναγκῶν ἡσυχάζειν οὐκ ἐπιτρέ-
πομαι. τὴν γοῦν ἀδελφὴν τήνδε, καὶ πρὸς γένος
ἡμῖν οὖσαν καὶ διὰ χηρείαν καταπονουμένην καὶ
παιδὸς ὀρφανοῦ πράγματος [1] φροντίζουσαν, ἐπεὶ
εἶδον λοιπὸν ὑπὲρ δύναμιν ἀφορήτοις ἀνάγκαις
συνεχομένην, κατελεήσας καὶ παθὼν τὴν ψυχὴν
ἔσπευσα παρακαλέσαι σε, ἵνα, εἴ τις δύναμις, τῷ
ἀποσταλέντι παρ' αὐτῆς ἀνθρώπῳ καταξιώσῃς
συμπρᾶξαι, πρὸς τὸ ὅπερ αὐτὴ παριοῦσα [2] ὑπέσχετο ὑφ' ἡμῶν, ἤδη τοῦτο αὐτὴν ἀποδοῦσαν τῆς
εἰς τὸ πλέον ἐπηρείας ἀπαλλαγῆναι. ὑπέσχετο
γὰρ τὸ κεφάλαιον δοῦσα συγχωρεῖσθαι τοὺς
τόκους.

Νῦν τοίνυν οἱ φροντίζοντες αὐτῆς τῶν κληρο-
νόμων μετὰ τὸ κεφάλαιον καὶ τὴν τῶν τόκων
εἴσπραξιν ἐπιχειροῦσι ποιήσασθαι. ὡς οὖν εἰδὼς
ὅτι Κύριός ἐστιν ὁ τὰ τῶν χηρῶν καὶ ὀρφανῶν
ἰδιοποιούμενος, οὕτω σπούδασον χρήσασθαι ἑαυτὸν τῇ σπουδῇ τῇ ὑπὲρ τοῦ πράγματος ἐπ' ἐλπίδι
τῆς παρ' αὐτοῦ τοῦ Θεοῦ ἡμῶν μισθαποδοσίας.
οἶμαι γὰρ καὶ τὴν ἡμερότητα τοῦ θαυμασιωτάτου
ἐπάρχου [3] μαθοῦσαν ὅτι τὸ κεφάλαιον ἐκτέτισται,

---

[1] πραγμάτων E.
[2] παριοῦσα Bigot. alter secunda manu, περιοῦσα alii MSS. et
editi.　　　　[3] ὑπάρχου conj. ed. Ben.

LETTER CIX

To Count Helladius [1]

Although I must earnestly beg pardon for troubling your Excellency in view of the magnitude of the office you hold, lest I shall seem to be making an immoderate use of your friendship, yet I am not permitted by my necessities to hold my peace. At any rate, when I beheld this sister (a relative of ours, suffering the affliction of widowhood, and anxious about the substance of her fatherless son)—when, I say, I beheld her beset beyond her strength with intolerable hardships, being filled with pity for her and sick at heart, I have hastened to urge you, if it is in any way possible, to deign to co-operate to this end with the messenger whom she has sent, that, namely, since this woman has already paid the amount she promised in person and in our presence, she may be freed from all further spiteful annoyance. For she promised to pay the principal on condition of being relieved of the interest.

Now, then, those who act as guardians of her heirs, the principal having been paid, are trying to exact payment of the interest also. Therefore, do you, as one who knows that the Lord makes the affairs of widows and orphans His own, yourself strive to employ all your zeal in this matter in the hope of the reward which our God Himself will give. For I think that our kind and most admirable Prefect, on learning that the principal has been paid, will

[1] On the same subject as the two preceding letters, and of the same time. Except for the present letter and Letter CVII, this Helladius is unknown.

συμπαθήσειν τῷ ἐλεεινῷ λοιπὸν καὶ ἀθλίῳ οἴκῳ
εἰς γόνυ κλιθέντι καὶ οὐκέτι ἀρκοῦντι ταῖς ἔξωθεν
αὐτῷ ἐπαγομέναις ἐπηρείαις. παρακαλῶ οὖν, καὶ
τῇ ἀνάγκῃ σύγγνωθι δι᾽ ἣν ὤχλησά[1] σοι, καὶ τῷ
πράγματι σύμπραξον κατὰ τὴν δύναμιν, ἣν ἔδωκέ
σοι ὁ Χριστὸς χρηστῷ καὶ ἀγαθῷ τὸν τρόπον
ὄντι, καὶ εἰς ἀγαθὸν οἷς ἔλαβες κεχρημένῳ.

CX

Μοδέστῳ ὑπάρχῳ

Ὅσης ἡμῖν τιμῆς καὶ παρρησίας μεταδίδως, τῇ
ἡμερότητι τοῦ τρόπου καταβαίνειν πρὸς ἡμᾶς ἀνε-
χόμενος, τοσαύτην σοι καὶ ἔτι πλείω ἐν παντὶ
τῷ βίῳ παρὰ τοῦ ἀγαθοῦ ἡμῶν Δεσπότου τὴν
αὔξησιν γενέσθαι[2] τῆς περιφανείας εὐχόμεθα.
ἐμὲ δὲ καὶ πάλαι ἐπιθυμοῦντα γράφειν καὶ ἀπολαύειν τῆς παρὰ σοῦ τιμῆς, κατεῖχεν ἡ πρὸς τὸ
ὑπερέχον αἰδώς, εὐλαβούμενον μήποτε νομισθῶ
ἀμέτρως ἐμφορεῖσθαι τῆς παρρησίας.

Νῦν δὲ ὁμοῦ μὲν καὶ τὸ λαβεῖν τὴν ἐξουσίαν[3]
τοῦ ἐπιστέλλειν παρὰ τῆς ἀπαραβλήτου σου
μεγαλοφυΐας, ὁμοῦ δὲ καὶ χρεία τῶν καταπονουμένων ἐξεβιάσατό με πρὸς τὸ θαρσεῖν. εἴ τις οὖν
καὶ παρὰ τῶν μικρῶν ἐπὶ τοῖς μεγίστοις[4] ἱκετηρίας
ἰσχύς, παρακλήθητι, θαυμασιώτατε, φιλανθρώπῳ
νεύματι ἐλεεινῇ ἀγροικίᾳ τὴν σωτηρίαν χαρίσασ-

---

[1] ἠνόχλησα conj. ed. Ben.
[2] γεγενέσθαι E.
[3] Νῦν . . . ἐξουσίαν om. E.
[4] μεγάλοις E.

sympathize with this pitiful and wretched household, which is now bowed to its knee and is no longer able to cope with the spitefulness which is visited upon it from the outside. Therefore, I entreat you (and pardon the necessity which forces me to trouble you), lend your assistance to this matter also according to the power which Christ has given to you, who are noble and of good character and have always employed for a good end what you have received.

LETTER CX

To the Prefect Modestus [1]

What measure of honour and of frankness in speech you bestow upon us, when in the kindness of your heart you consent to condescend to us, may that same measure and still more of enhancement of your fame be given to you throughout your life by our good Master, we pray. Although I have long wished to write and to take advantage of the honour you show me, yet respect for your higher station restrained me, careful as I was lest I be thought to avail myself unduly of the freedom you accord me.

But now two things—my having received permission from your incomparable Magnanimity to write, and likewise the need of those who are in distress—have constrained me to be bold. So if the prayers of the small are of any avail with the great, be pleased, most admirable Sir, by your benign assent to bestow salvation upon a pitiful rustic people, and give orders that the tax on iron be made tolerable

[1] Written in 372, on the tribute of iron paid at Mount Taurus. On Modestus, cf. Letter CIV and note.

θαι, καὶ τοῖς τὸν Ταῦρον οἰκοῦσι τὸν σιδηροφόρον
φορητὴν προστάξαι γενέσθαι τὴν τοῦ σιδήρου
συντέλειαν, ὡς μὴ εἰς ἅπαξ αὐτοὺς ἐκτριβῆναι,
ἀλλὰ διαρκῆ αὐτῶν εἶναι τὴν ὑπηρεσίαν τοῖς
δημοσίοις· οὗ μάλιστα πάντων μέλειν τῇ ἀξια-
γάστῳ σου φιλανθρωπίᾳ πεπείσμεθα.

CXI

Μοδέστῳ ὑπάρχῳ

Ἄλλως μὲν οὐκ ἂν ἐθάρρησα δι' ὄχλου γενέσθαι
τῇ μεγαλοφυΐᾳ σου, εἰδὼς καὶ ἐμαυτὸν μετρεῖν
καὶ τὰς ἐξουσίας γνωρίζειν. ἐπειδὴ δὲ εἶδον
ἄνδρα φίλον ἐναγωνίως διακείμενον ἐπὶ τῷ μετα-
κληθῆναι, ἀπετόλμησα αὐτῷ δοῦναι τὴν ἐπιστολὴν
ταύτην, ἵνα ἀνθ' ἱκετηρίας[1] αὐτὴν προβαλλόμενος
τύχῃ τινὸς φιλανθρωπίας. πάντως δέ, εἰ καὶ
ἡμεῖς οὐδενὸς λόγου ἄξιοι, ἀλλ' αὐτὸ τὸ μέτριον[2]
ἱκανὸν δυσωπῆσαι τὸν φιλανθρωπότατον τῶν
ὑπάρχων[3] καὶ ἡμῖν δοῦναι συγγνώμην, ἵνα, εἰ
μὲν μηδὲν πεπλημμέληται τῷ ἀνδρί, σωθῆναι
αὐτὸν δι' αὐτὴν τὴν ἀλήθειαν, εἰ δὲ καὶ ἥμαρτεν,
ἀφεθῆναι αὐτῷ δι' ἡμᾶς τοὺς ἱκετεύσαντας.

Οἷα δὲ τὰ ἐνταῦθα τῶν πραγμάτων ἐστί, τίς
μᾶλλον ἐπίσταται σοῦ, τοῦ καὶ ἐπιβλέποντος τὰ
παρ' ἑκάστῳ[4] σαθρὰ καὶ τῇ θαυμασίᾳ προμηθείᾳ
τὰ πάντα διακρατοῦντος ;

---

[1] ἱκεσίας Reg. uterque, Coisl. secundus.
[2] μέτρον editi antiqi.
[3] ἐπάρχων E, Med.
[4] ἑκάστου editi antiqi.

for the inhabitants of the iron-bearing Taurus, so
that they may not be ruined once for all, but that
their service to the treasury of the state may continue to be rendered—an object in which beyond
all others we are convinced that your admirable
Benevolence is concerned.

LETTER CXI

To the Prefect Modestus [1]

In other circumstances I should not have made
bold to trouble your Excellency, knowing both
how to measure my own importance and how to
estimate the powers of others. But when I saw a
friend in great distress of mind by reason of a
summons, I ventured to give him this letter, that by
casting it before you in lieu of the suppliant's token [2]
he might obtain a measure of kindness. But in any
case, even if we are of no account, yet our very
restraint will suffice to placate the most kind-hearted
of prefects and to secure us forgiveness, to the end
that, if the man has done no wrong, he may be
saved through the influence of the truth itself, but
if he has indeed sinned, that his sin may be forgiven
him through us who make supplication.

But as to our own situation here, who is better
informed than you, who both observe what is corrupt
in every man and by your wonderful forethought
keep all things under your control?

[1] Of the same date as the preceding. For Modestus, cf.
Letter CIV and note.
[2] An olive-branch held in the hands of a suppliant, as a
symbol of his condition and claim.

CXII

Ἀνδρονίκῳ ἡγεμόνι [1]

Εἰ μὲν οὕτως εἶχον σώματος, ὥστε ῥᾳδίως ὑπομένειν ὁδοιπορίας δύνασθαι καὶ τὰ τοῦ χειμῶνος
δυσχερῆ φέρειν, οὐκ ἂν ἐπέστελλον, ἀλλ' αὐτὸς
παρὰ [2] τὴν σὴν μεγαλοψυχίαν ἐβάδιζον δυοῖν [3]
ἕνεκεν· τοῦ τε παλαιὸν [4] ὑποσχέσεως ἐκτῖσαι
χρέος (οἶδα γὰρ ὁμολογήσας παρέσεσθαι τῇ
Σεβαστείᾳ καὶ ἀπολαῦσαί [5] σου τῆς τελειότητος·
ὅπερ ἐποίησα μέν, διήμαρτον δὲ τῆς συντυχίας,
μικρὸν κατόπιν τῆς σῆς καλοκἀγαθίας παραγενό-
μενος), ἑτέρου δέ, τοῦ τὴν πρεσβείαν δι' ἐμαυτοῦ
πληρῶσαι, ἣν ἀποστεῖλαι [6] τέως ἀπώκνουν, μικρότερον ἐμαυτὸν κρίνων ἢ ὥστε τοιαύτης τυγχάνειν
χάριτος, καὶ ἅμα λογιζόμενος, ὅτι οὔτε ἄρχοντα [7]
οὔτε ἰδιώτην ὑπὲρ οὐδενὸς ἄν τις λέγων διὰ γραμμάτων πείσειεν οὕτως, ὡς αὐτὸς παρών, καὶ τὰ
μὲν ἀπολυόμενος [8] τῶν ἐγκλημάτων, τὰ δὲ ἱκε-
τεύων, τοῖς δὲ συγγνώμην παραιτούμενος ἔχειν·
ὧν οὐδὲν ἂν [9] ῥᾳδίως δι' ἐπιστολῆς γένοιτο. πᾶσιν
οὖν τούτοις ἐν ἀντιθείς, σὲ τὴν θείαν κεφαλήν,
καὶ ὅτι ἐξαρκέσει τὴν γνώμην ἐνδείξασθαί σοι,
ἣν περὶ τοῦ πράγματος ἔχομεν, τὰ δὲ λοιπὰ
προσθήσεις παρὰ σεαυτοῦ,[10] πρὸς τὴν ἐγχείρησιν
οὐκ ἀπώκνησα.

---

[1] ὑπὲρ τοῦ πρεσβυτέρου add. E.   πρὸ πρεσβυτέρου add. Vat.,
Med.
[2] πρός editi antiqi.   [3] δυαῖν E.   [4] παλαιάς E.
[5] ἀπολαύσειν editi antiqi.   [6] ὑποστῆναι E. editi antiqi.
[7] ἄρχονται E.   [8] ἀποδυόμενος E.   [9] ἄν om. E.

LETTER CXII

To Andronicus, General[1]

If I were strong enough in body to be able easily to endure travelling and to bear the hardships of winter, I should not now be writing to you, but should be proceeding to your Magnanimity in person with two purposes in view—to discharge the long-standing debt of a promise (for I know that I agreed to visit Sebasteia and enjoy the company of your Perfection; and I did go there, but missed meeting you, since I arrived a little too late for your noble self), and, secondly, to perform in person the mission which I have thus far hesitated to fulfil by a communication, since I judged myself too insignificant a person to obtain such a favour, and at the same time considered that no one in pleading another's cause could win over an official or a private citizen so well by stating his case in writing as by being present in person, orally disposing of some of his client's charges, pleading excuse for others, and asking pardon for the rest—none of which things could easily be done by letter. So, weighing against these disadvantages one single advantage—yourself, a god-like man—and considering that it will suffice to indicate to you the judgment we have concerning the affair, to which you will add out of your own knowledge what is lacking, I have not shrunk from making this attempt.

[1] Written in 372. Andronicus, to whom this letter is addressed, and Domitian, an offender, in whose behalf the letter is written, are otherwise unknown.

---

¹⁰ παρὰ σεαυτοῦ] παρ' ἑαυτοῦ E.

Ἀλλ' ὁρᾷς ὅπως κύκλῳ περίειμι ὀκνῶν καὶ
ἀναδυόμενος τὴν αἰτίαν ἐκφαίνειν ὑπὲρ ὧν ποιοῦμαι
τοὺς λόγους. Δομετιανὸς οὗτος ἐπιτήδειος ἡμῖν
ἐστιν¹ ἐκ τῶν γονέων ἄνωθεν, ὥστε ἀδελφοῦ μηδ'
ὁτιοῦν διαφέρειν. τί γὰρ ἄν τις μὴ τἀληθῆ λέγοι·
εἶτα τὴν αἰτίαν μαθόντες ἀφ' ἧς ταῦτα πέποιθε',
ἄξιον εἶναι τοῦ παθεῖν οὕτως ἔφαμεν. μηδὲ² γὰρ
ἔστω μηδείς, ὃς μικρὸν ἢ μεῖζον εἰς τὴν σὴν
ἀρετὴν ἀμελήσας³ τὴν τιμωρίαν ἐκφύγοι. ἀλλ'
ὁρῶντες τοῦτον περιδεῶς καὶ ἀδόξως ζῶντα, καὶ
ἐπὶ τῇ σῇ ψήφῳ κειμένην αὐτοῦ τὴν σωτηρίαν,
ἀρκοῦσαν αὐτὸν ἔχειν τὴν δίκην ἐκρίναμεν.
μεγαλόψυχόν τε ὁμοῦ καὶ φιλάνθρωπον διανοη-
θῆναί σε περὶ αὐτοῦ ἱκετεύομεν. τὸ μὲν γὰρ τοὺς
ἀντιτείνοντας ὑπὸ χεῖρα λαμβάνειν ἀνδρείου τε
καὶ ἄρχοντος ὡς ἀληθῶς, τὸ δὲ τοῖς ὑποπεπτωκόσι
χρηστὸν εἶναι καὶ πρᾷον μεγαλοφροσύνῃ πάντων
καὶ ἡμερότητι διαφέροντος. ὥστε ὑπάρξει σοι
βουληθέντι ἐν τῷ αὐτῷ τήν τε πρὸς τὸ ἀμύνασθαι
καὶ τὴν εἰς τὸ σῴζειν, ὡς ἂν ἐθέλοις,⁴ ἐπιδείξασθαι
μεγαλοψυχίαν. τοῦτο μέτρον ἀρκοῦν Δομετιανῷ
τῆς κολάσεως, τῶν προσδοκωμένων ὁ φόβος καὶ
ὧν ἄξιον οἶδεν ἑαυτὸν παθεῖν ὄντα. τούτοις
μηδὲν εἰς τιμωρίαν προσθεῖναι αὐτῷ ἱκετεύομεν.
καὶ γὰρ ἐκεῖνο σκόπει, ὅτι κύριοι μὲν τῶν ἠδικη-
κότων πολλοὶ τῶν πρότερον⁵ ἤδη γεγόνασιν, ὧν
οὐδεὶς πρὸς τοὺς ὕστερον διεπέμφθη λόγος·
ἀφῆκαν δὲ τὴν ὀργὴν οἱ φιλοσοφίᾳ τοὺς πολλοὺς
ὑπεράραντες, ὧν ἀθάνατος ἡ μνήμη τῷ χρόνῳ⁶

---

¹ ἐστίν om. E. ² μή E.
³ ἁμαρτήσας editi antiqi. ⁴ ἐθέλῃς editi antiqi.
⁵ προτέρων E.

But you see how I go about in a circle, hesitating and shrinking from making known the reason why I am writing this letter. This man Domitian is a friend of ours, as our parents were friends long before, so that he differs not at all from a brother. For why should one not tell the truth? Then on learning the reason why he is in his present plight, we declared that he deserved to suffer so. For let there be no man who, after slighting your Virtuous Self in any matter small or great, shall escape the penalty. But when we saw that this man lived in fear and ignominy, and that his salvation rested with your decision, we judged that he had received sufficient punishment; and we now beg you to consider his case with both magnanimity and kindness. For to keep the rebellious under one's hand is truly the part of a strong man and a ruler, but to be kind and gentle to the fallen is the mark of one who surpasses all men in magnanimity and kindness. And thus it will be within your power, if you so wish, to exhibit with the same person magnanimity both in exacting punishment and, as you would prefer, in granting succour. This is a sufficient measure of chastisement for Domitian—his fear of what lies in store for him, and of the punishment which he well knows he deserves to suffer. To all this we beg you to add nothing by way of vengeance. And consider this also, that there have been many among those who have gone before us who have exercised power over wrong-doers, of these no record has been passed on to posterity; but of those who, transcending the many through philosophy, have abated their wrath, an immortal remembrance has been handed down to

---

⁶ δίφ Vat., Reg. secundus, Coisl. secundus.

παντὶ παραδέδοται. προσκείσθω δὲ καὶ τοῦτο
τοῖς περὶ σοῦ διηγήμασι. δὸς ἡμῖν, τοῖς ὑμνεῖν
προαιρουμένοις τὰ σά, τὰς[1] ἐν τοῖς ἄνω χρόνοις
ἀδομένας[2] φιλανθρωπίας ὑπερβαλέσθαι. οὕτω
καὶ Κροῖσος τῷ παιδοφόνῳ τὴν ὀργὴν ἀφεῖναι
λέγεται, ἑαυτὸν παραδόντι εἰς τιμωρίαν· καὶ
Κῦρος ὁ μέγας αὐτῷ τούτῳ τῷ Κροίσῳ φίλος
γενέσθαι μετὰ τὴν νίκην. τούτοις σε συναριθ-
μήσομεν, καί, ὅση δύναμις ἡμετέρα, ταῦτα
ἀναγορεύσομεν, εἴπερ μὴ μικροί τινες εἶναι
παντάπασιν ἀνδρὸς τοσούτου κήρυκες νομισ-
θείημεν.

Ἐκεῖνο δὲ ἐπὶ πᾶσιν εἰπεῖν ἀναγκαῖον, ὅτι τοὺς
ὁτιοῦν ἀδικοῦντας οὐχ ὑπὲρ τῶν ἤδη γεγενημένων
κολάζομεν (τίς[3] γὰρ ἂν γένοιτο μηχανὴ μὴ γεγενῆσθαι τὰ πεπραγμένα ;), ἀλλ᾽ ὅπως ἂν ἢ αὐτοὶ
πρὸς τὸ λοιπὸν ἀμείνους γένοιντο, ἢ ἑτέροις
ὑπάρξειαν τοῦ σωφρονεῖν παράδειγμα.[4] τούτων
τοίνυν οὐθέτερον ἐνδεῖν[5] ἄν τις ἐν τῷ παρόντι
φήσειεν· αὐτός τε γὰρ καὶ μετὰ τὸν θάνατον
τούτων μεμνήσεται, τούς τε λοιποὺς τεθνάναι τῷ
δέει πρὸς τοῦτον ἀφορῶντας οἴομαι. ὥσθ᾽ ὅπερ
ἂν προσθῶμεν τῇ τιμωρίᾳ, τὴν ὀργὴν ἡμῶν αὐτῶν
ἀποπιμπλάναι δόξομεν· ὃ πολλοῦ δεῖν ἐπὶ σοῦ
ἀληθὲς εἶναι φαίην ἂν ἔγωγε, καὶ οὐδὲν ἂν τούτων
τῶν λόγων προήχθην εἰπεῖν, εἰ μὴ μείζονα τῷ
διδόντι τὴν χάριν ἐνεώρων ἢ τοῖς λαμβάνουσιν.
οὐδὲ γὰρ ὀλίγοις ἔσται καταφανὴς ἡ μεγαλοψυχία
τοῦ τρόπου. Καππαδόκαι γὰρ ἅπαντες ἀποσκο-
ποῦσι τὸ μέλλον, οἷς εὐξαίμην ἂν μετὰ τῶν

---

[1] τά Ε.   [2] ἀδόμενα Ε.   [3] τί Ε.
[4] παραδείγματα Reg. uterque et Coisl. secundus.

all time. And let this also be added to the reports
about you. Grant to us, who would fain hymn your
praises, to surpass the songs of good deeds sung in
previous ages. Thus even Croesus[1] is said to have
abated his wrath against the slayer of his son who
had given himself up for punishment; and Cyrus
the Great is said to have become friendly to this
very Croesus[2] after his victory over him. With
these shall we number you, and with all our power
shall we proclaim these deeds, unless we be considered as an altogether too insignificant herald of
so great a man.

And this plea we must always utter on every
occasion, that we punish those who do any wrong,
not for what has already taken place (for what means
can there be of undoing what has been done?), but
that they may either become better themselves in
future, or may be an example to teach wisdom to
others. So one might say that neither of these
conditions is lacking in the present case; for Domitian
himself will remember these things even after his
death, and I imagine that his fellows are frightened
to death through looking at him. Thus if we add
anything to his punishment, we shall seem to be
glutting our own anger, which I would say is far
from being the truth in your case, and I could not
have induced myself to say any of these things, did
I not see that the reward is greater for him who
gives than for those who receive. For not to a
mere few will the magnanimity of your character
be known. For all the Cappadocians are regarding
the future, and it would be my prayer that they

---

[1] Cf. Herodotus 1, 45.   [2] Cf. Herodotus 1, 88.

λοιπῶν ἀγαθῶν τῶν προσόντων σοι καὶ ταύτην [1]
ἀπαριθμήσασθαι.

Ὀκνῶ δὲ τοῦ γράφειν παύσασθαι, ἡγούμενός
μοι ζημίαν οἴσειν τὸ παρεθέν. τοσοῦτόν γε μὴν
προσθήσω, ὅτι πολλῶν ἐπιστολὰς [2] ἔχων ἐξαιτου-
μένων αὐτὸν πασῶν ἡγήσατο προτιμοτέραν εἶναι
τὴν παρ' ἡμῶν, οὐκ οἶδά που [3] μαθὼν εἶναί τινα
ἡμῶν λόγον παρὰ τῇ σῇ τελειότητι. ὅπως οὖν
μήτε αὐτὸς ψευσθῇ τῶν ἐλπίδων, ἃς ἐφ' ἡμῖν
ἔσχε, καὶ ἡμῖν ὑπάρξῃ πρὸς τοὺς ἐνταῦθα σεμνο-
λογεῖσθαι, παρακέκλησο, δέσποτα ἀνυπέρβλητε,
ἐπινεῦσαι πρὸς τὴν αἴτησιν. πάντως δὲ οὐδενὸς
χεῖρον τῶν πώποτε φιλοσοφησάντων ἐπέσκεψαι
τὰ ἀνθρώπινα, καὶ οἶδας ὡς καλὸς θησαυρὸς πᾶσι
τοῖς δεομένοις ὑπουργεῖν προαποκείμενος. [4]

CXIII

Τοῖς ἐν Ταρσῷ πρεσβυτέροις

Συντυχὼν τῷδε, πολλὴν ἔσχον τῷ ἁγίῳ Θεῷ
τὴν χάριν, ὅτι με καὶ διὰ τῆς αὐτοῦ παρουσίας
ἀπὸ πολλῶν θλίψεων παρεμυθήσατο, καὶ τὴν
ὑμετέραν ἀγάπην ἐναργῶς ἔδειξε δι' αὐτοῦ.
σχεδὸν γὰρ τὸν πάντων ὑμῶν περὶ τὴν ἀλήθειαν
ζῆλον ἐν τῇ τοῦ ἑνὸς ἀνδρὸς προαιρέσει κατέμαθον.
ἃ μὲν οὖν ἰδίᾳ διελέχθημεν πρὸς ἀλλήλους αὐτὸς
ὑμῖν ἀπαγγελεῖ· [5] ἃ δὲ παρ' ἐμοῦ γνωρισθῆναι
ὑμῶν προσῆκε τῇ ἀγάπῃ, ταῦτά ἐστιν.

[1] τοῦτο editi antiqi.   [2] ἐπιστολῶν E.
[3] οἶδά που] οἶδ' ὅπως editi antiqi.
[4] προαποκείμενός ἐστι editi antiqi.

might number this also with the rest of the virtues which you possess.

Yet I hesitate to cease writing, thinking that what has been omitted will cause me harm. So much at any rate I shall add, that although he had letters from many who were interceding for him, he considered the one from us to be more valuable than them all, having learned, I know not where, that a word from us was of weight with your Perfection. Therefore that he on his part may not be deceived in the hopes which he has placed in us, and that there may be for us some occasion for glorification before our people, be pleased, most illustrious master, to assent to our request. And assuredly you, no less than any of the philosophers of the past, have studied human life, and you know how goodly a treasure is laid up for all who help the needy.

LETTER CXIII

To the Presbyters at Tarsus[1]

On meeting this man, I was very grateful to the Holy God, because by sending him to me after many afflictions He comforted me, and through him gave clear proof of your love. For I can almost say that in the purpose of this one man I learned the zeal for the truth which all of you possess. Now, what we discussed privately with one another he himself will report to you ; but what your charity may fittingly learn from me is the following.

[1] Written in 372, and maintaining that the Nicene Creed alone should be required of the brethren.

---

5 ἐπαγγελεῖ editi antiqi.

Ὁ καιρὸς πολλὴν ἔχει ῥοπὴν πρὸς καταστροφὴν
τῶν ἐκκλησιῶν, καὶ τοῦτο πολὺν ἔχομεν ἤδη
χρόνον ἐξ οὗ καταμανθάνομεν. οἰκοδομὴ δὲ Ἐκκλησίας, καὶ σφαλμάτων διόρθωσις, καὶ συμ-
πάθεια μὲν πρὸς τοὺς ἀσθενοῦντας ὑπερασπισμὸς
δὲ πρὸς τοὺς ὑγιαίνοντας τῶν ἀδελφῶν οὐδὲ εἷς.
ἀλλ' οὔτε βοήθημα ἢ θεραπευτικὸν[1] τῆς προ-
κατασχούσης νόσου, ἢ προφυλακτικὸν τῆς προσδοκωμένης οὐδέν. καὶ ὅλως ἔοικε λοιπὸν ἡ τῆς
Ἐκκλησίας κατάστασις (ἵνα ἐναργεῖ χρήσωμαι
τῷ ὑποδείγματι, κἂν εὐτελέστερον εἶναι δοκῇ)
ἱματίῳ παλαιῷ, ὑπὸ τῆς τυχούσης προφάσεως
ῥᾳδίως καταρρηγνυμένῳ, ὃ πρὸς τὴν ἐξ ἀρχῆς
ἰσχὺν ἐπανελθεῖν πάλιν ἀδυνατεῖ. ὡς οὖν ἐν
καιρῷ τοιούτῳ, μεγάλης χρεία τῆς σπουδῆς καὶ
πολλῆς τῆς ἐπιμελείας εὐεργετηθῆναί τι τὰς ἐκκλησίας. εὐεργεσία δέ ἐστιν ἑνωθῆναι τὰ τέως
διεσπασμένα.[2] ἕνωσις δ' ἂν γένοιτο, εἰ βουλη-
θείημεν, ἐν οἷς μηδὲν βλάπτομεν τὰς ψυχάς,
συμπεριενεχθῆναι τοῖς ἀσθενεστέροις.

Ἐπεὶ οὖν πολλὰ στόματα ἤνοικται κατὰ τοῦ
Πνεύματος τοῦ ἁγίου καὶ πολλαὶ γλῶσσαι
ἠκόνηνται εἰς τὴν κατ' αὐτοῦ βλασφημίαν,
ἀξιοῦμεν ὑμᾶς, ὅσον ἐστὶν ἐφ' ὑμῖν,[3] εἰς ὀλίγον
ἀριθμὸν περιστῆσαι τοὺς βλασφημοῦντας· καὶ
τοὺς μὴ λέγοντας κτίσμα τὸ Πνεῦμα τὸ ἅγιον
δέχεσθαι εἰς κοινωνίαν, ἵνα μόνοι καταλειφθῶσιν
οἱ βλάσφημοι, καὶ ἢ καταισχυνθέντες ἐπανέλθωσι
πρὸς τὴν ἀλήθειαν, ἢ ἐπιμένοντες τῇ ἁμαρτίᾳ
ἀναξιόπιστοι ὦσι διὰ τὴν ὀλιγότητα. μηδὲν

---

[1] προθεραπευτικόν Med.   [2] διεσπυρμένα duo MSS.

The spirit of the times is much inclined to the destruction of the churches, and it is now a long time since we have learned this. As for the establishment of the Church, the correction of errors, sympathy for the brethren who are weak and protection of those who are sound—of these things not one! Nay, there is neither remedy nor cure for the disease which is already upon us, nor means of precaution against that which we await. And, in short, the condition of the Church now (to use a vivid example, even if it seems to be rather mean) is like that of an old cloak, which, being easily torn by an ordinary strain, cannot be again restored to its original strength. In such times, therefore, as these there is need of great diligence and much care that the churches may be in some way benefited. And a benefit it is that the parts which have hitherto been broken apart be united again. And a union might be effected if we should be willing to show indulgence to the weaker, whenever we can do so without causing harm to souls.

Since, therefore, the mouths of many have been opened against the Spirit, and many tongues have been whetted to utter blasphemy against Him, we believe that you ought, in so far as it is in your power, to reduce the number of blasphemers to a small number; those who do not call the Holy Spirit a creature should be received in communion with you, that the blasphemers may be left alone, and either, being put to shame, may return to the truth, or, abiding in their error, may be considered unworthy of belief by reason of the smallness of their

---

* ἡμῖν editi antiqi.

τοίνυν πλέον ἐπιζητῶμεν, ἀλλὰ προτεινώμεθα
τοῖς βουλομένοις ἡμῖν συνάπτεσθαι ἀδελφοῖς
τὴν ἐν Νικαίᾳ πίστιν· κἂν ἐκείνῃ συνθῶνται,
ἐπερωτῶμεν καὶ τὸ μὴ δεῖν λέγεσθαι κτίσμα τὸ
Πνεῦμα τὸ ἅγιον, μηδὲ κοινωνικοὺς αὐτῶν εἶναι
τοὺς λέγοντας. πέρα δὲ τούτων [1] ἀξιῶ μηδὲν
ἐπιζητεῖσθαι παρ' ἡμῶν. πέπεισμαι γάρ, ὅτι τῇ
χρονιωτέρᾳ συνδιαγωγῇ καὶ τῇ ἀφιλονείκῳ συγ-
γυμνασίᾳ, καὶ εἴ τι δέοι πλέον προστεθῆναι εἰς
τράνωσιν, δώσει ὁ Κύριος ὁ πάντα συνεργῶν εἰς
ἀγαθὸν τοῖς ἀγαπῶσιν αὐτόν.

CXIV

Τοῖς ἐν Ταρσῷ περὶ Κυριακόν [2]

Ὅσον ἐστὶ τὸ τῆς εἰρήνης ἀγαθόν, τί χρὴ
λέγειν πρὸς ἄνδρας υἱοὺς τῆς εἰρήνης; ἐπεὶ οὖν
τὸ μέγα τοῦτο καὶ θαυμαστὸν καὶ πᾶσι περι-
σπούδαστον τοῖς ἀγαπῶσι τὸν Κύριον κινδυνεύει
λοιπὸν εἰς ὄνομα ψιλὸν περιστῆναι διὰ τὸ
πληθυνθῆναι τὴν ἀνομίαν, ψυγείσης λοιπὸν ἐν
τοῖς πολλοῖς τῆς ἀγάπης, οἶμαι προσήκειν μίαν
ταύτην εἶναι σπουδὴν τοῖς γνησίως καὶ ἀληθινῶς
δουλεύουσι τῷ Κυρίῳ, τὸ ἐπαναγαγεῖν πρὸς
ἕνωσιν τὰς ἐκκλησίας τὰς πολυμερῶς καὶ πολυ-

[1] πέρα δὲ τούτων . . . παρ' ἡμῶν] παρὰ δὲ τούτων . . . παρ'
ὑμῶν editi antiqi.

[2] τοῖς αὐτοῖς περὶ Κυριακὸν παραπλήσια editi antiqi.

[1] Cf. Rom. 8. 28 : οἴδαμεν δὲ ὅτι τοῖς ἀγαπῶσι τὸν θεὸν πάντα
συνεργεῖ εἰς ἀγαθὸν τοῖς κατὰ πρόθεσιν κλητοῖς οὖσιν. "And
we know that to them that love God, all things work

number. Let us then seek nothing more, but merely propose the Creed of Nicaea to the brethren who wish to join us ; and if they agree to this, let us demand also that the Holy Spirit shall not be called a creature, and that those who do so call Him shall not be communicants with them. But beyond these things I think nothing should be insisted upon by us. For I am convinced that by longer association together and by mutual experience without strife, even if there should be need of some addition being made for clarification, the Lord who worketh all things together unto good to such as love Him [1] will concede this.

LETTER CXIV

To Cyriacus and his Followers at Tarsus [2]

Why need I tell men who are the sons of peace how great is the blessing of peace ? So, since this boon, great and wonderful and eagerly sought by all who love the Lord, is now in danger of being reduced to a mere name, " because iniquity hath abounded, the charity in many having now grown cold," [3] I think that those who really and truly labour for the Lord should have this one aim—to bring back into union the churches that have been severed from one another " at sundry times and in

together unto good, to such as, according to His purpose, are called to be saints."

[2] Written in 372, and, like the preceding letter, on the sufficiency of the Nicene Creed. The Cyriacus to whom this letter is addressed has not been identified.

[3] Cf. Matt. 24, 12: καὶ διὰ τὸ πληθυνθῆναι τὴν ἀνομίαν, ψυγήσεται ἡ ἀγάπη τῶν πολλῶν. " And because iniquity hath abounded, the charity of many shall grow cold."

τρόπως ἀπ' ἀλλήλων διατμηθείσας. ὃ δὴ καὶ
αὐτὸς ἐπιχειρῶν ποιεῖν οὐκ ἂν δικαίως πολυ-
πράγμονος αἰτίαν λάβοιμι. οὐδὲν γὰρ οὕτως
ἴδιόν ἐστι Χριστιανοῦ ὡς τὸ εἰρηνοποιεῖν· διὸ καὶ
τὸν ἐπ' αὐτῷ μισθὸν μέγιστον ἡμῖν ὁ Κύριος
ἐπηγγείλατο. συντυχὼν τοίνυν τοῖς ἀδελφοῖς
καὶ θεασάμενος αὐτῶν πολὺ μὲν τὸ φιλάδελφον
καὶ τὸ περὶ ὑμᾶς ἀγαπητικόν, πολλῷ δὲ ἔτι πλέον
τὸ φιλόχριστον¹ καὶ τὸ περὶ τὴν πίστιν ἀκριβές
τε καὶ εὔτονον, καὶ ὅτι πολλὴν ἀμφοτέρων ποιοῦν-
ται σπουδήν, τῆς τε ὑμετέρας ἀγάπης μὴ χω-
ρίζεσθαι καὶ τὴν ὑγιαίνουσαν πίστιν μὴ κατα-
προδοῦναι, ἀποδεξάμενος αὐτῶν τὴν ἀγαθὴν
προαίρεσιν ἐπιστέλλω τῇ σεμνότητι ὑμῶν, παρακαλῶν πάσῃ ἀγάπῃ ἔχειν αὐτοὺς ἡνωμένους
γνησίως καὶ πάσης ἐκκλησιαστικῆς φροντίδος
κοινωνούς· ἐγγυησάμενος καὶ αὐτοῖς τὴν ὑμετέραν
ὀρθότητα, ὅτι καὶ αὐτοὶ τῇ τοῦ Θεοῦ χάριτι τῷ
ὑπὲρ τῆς ἀληθείας ζήλῳ πρὸς πάντα ἐστὲ παρα-
τεταγμένοι, ὅσαπερ ἂν δέῃ² παθεῖν ὑπὲρ τοῦ
λόγου τῆς ἀληθείας.

Ἔστι δέ, ὡς ἐμαυτὸν πείθω, τὰ οὔτε ὑμῖν
ὑπεναντία, καὶ τοῖς προειρημένοις τῶν ἀδελφῶν
αὐτάρκη πρὸς πληροφορίαν, ταῦτα, ὁμολογεῖν
ὑμᾶς τὴν ὑπὸ τῶν πατέρων ἡμῶν ἐκτεθεῖσαν
πίστιν τῶν ἐν Νικαίᾳ ποτὲ συνελθόντων, καὶ
μηδεμίαν τῶν ἐκεῖ λέξεων ἀθετεῖν, ἀλλ' εἰδέναι
ὅτι τριακόσιοι δέκα καὶ ὀκτώ, ἀφιλονείκως συνιόν-
τες, οὐκ ἄνευ τῆς τοῦ ἁγίου Πνεύματος ἐνεργείας

---

¹ φιλόχρηστον E. ² δέοι editi antiqi.

¹ Cf. Heb. 1, 1 : πολυμερῶς καὶ πολυτρόπως πάλαι ὁ Θεὸς

divers manners." [1]   When I myself also attempt to accomplish this result I could not justly be accused of officiousness.   For no activity is so peculiarly Christian as making peace; wherefore the reward for this which the Lord has promised us is the highest.   So, after meeting the brethren, and observing how great is their brotherly love,[2] and their affection towards you, and how much greater still is their love for Christ and their strictness and vigour in the faith, and seeing that they were very zealous for two things—not to be separated from your charity and not to betray the sound faith—accepting their good purpose I am writing to your August Reverence, urging with all charity that you hold them truly united and sharing in all the solicitude of the Church; I have vouched to them also for your orthodoxy, saying that you likewise, by the grace of God, have in your zeal for the truth made yourselves ready to suffer whatever may be needful in behalf of the doctrine of truth.

The following conditions, I am convinced, are not contrary to your own feelings, and are satisfactory to the above-mentioned brothers by way of information—that you profess the faith as set forth by the Fathers who once assembled at Nicaea, and deny no one of the statements made there, but realize that three hundred and eighteen, coming together without strife, spoke not without the agency of the Holy

---

[1] λαλήσας τοῖς πατράσιν ἐν τοῖς προφήταις. "God, who at sundry times and in divers manners spoke in times past to the fathers by the prophets."

[2] Cf. Matt. 5, 9 : μακάριοι οἱ εἰρηνοποιοὶ ὅτι αὐτοὶ υἱοὶ Θεοῦ κληθήσονται. "Blessed are the peace-makers : for they shall be called the children of God."

ἐφθέγξαντο· προσθεῖναι δὲ τῇ πίστει ἐκείνῃ καὶ
τὸ μὴ χρῆναι λέγειν κτίσμα τὸ Πνεῦμα τὸ ἅγιον,
μὴ μέντοι μηδὲ τοῖς λέγουσι κοινωνεῖν, ἵνα καθαρὰ
ᾖ τοῦ Θεοῦ ἡ Ἐκκλησία, μηδὲν ζιζάνιον ἑαυτῇ
παραμεμιγμένον ἔχουσα. ταύτης αὐτοῖς τῆς
πληροφορίας παρὰ τῆς εὐσπλαγχνίας ὑμῶν
προτεθείσης, καὶ αὐτοὶ πρέπουσαν ὑμῖν ὑποταγὴν
ἕτοιμοί εἰσι παρασχέσθαι. αὐτὸς γὰρ ἐγγυῶμαι
τὸ μέρος τῶν ἀδελφῶν, ὡς εἰς οὐδὲν ἀντεροῦσιν,
ἀλλὰ πᾶσαν ὑμῖν ἐπιδείξονται εὐταξίας ὑπερ-
βολήν, ἑνὸς τούτου αὐτοῖς τοῦ ἐπιζητουμένου παρ'
αὐτῶν ὑπὸ τῆς ὑμετέρας τελειότητος ἑτοίμως
παρασχεθέντος.

CXV

Σιμπλικίᾳ αἱρετικῇ [1]

Ἀβούλως οἱ ἄνθρωποι καὶ μισοῦσι τοὺς κρείτ-
τονας καὶ φιλοῦσι τοὺς χείρονας. διὸ δὴ καὶ

---

[1] Βασίλειος add. E.

---

[1] Written in 372 or 373. The tone of this letter is wholly
unworthy of St. Basil, and not at all like that of the other
letters. There is, however, no other reason for doubting its
authenticity. The circumstances which led to the writing of
this letter may be learned from Gregory Nazianzenus, Letter
XXXVIII. It seems that a certain church in Cappadocia,
long without a bishop, had elected a slave of a certain
Simplicia, a wealthy and generous lady but of suspected
orthodoxy. Basil and Gregory unwisely ordained the man
without the consent of her owner, who threatened Basil
with the vengeance of her slaves and eunuchs. In the
present letter, Basil replies to her threats. After Basil died,
she harassed Gregory in an effort to get the ordination annulled.
Cf. Maran, *Vita Basilii*, XXV. The Migne edition states
that the codex Caesareus LXVII contains the following
prefatory note for this letter :

Spirit; and that you add to the aforesaid Creed that
one must not speak of the Holy Spirit as a creature,
nor have communion with those who so speak of
Him, in order that the Church of God may be pure,
having no darnel mixed with it. When this
assurance has been given them from the goodness of
your heart, they in turn are ready to offer you fitting
obedience. For I myself vouch to you in behalf of
the brethren that they will offer no opposition, but
will show you a full abundance of good discipline,
provided that this one thing which is demanded by
them be readily granted by your Perfection.

LETTER CXV

To the Heretic Simplicia [1]

Foolish it is for men both to hate their superiors
and to love their inferiors. Wherefore I myself now

τοῦ αὐτοῦ ἐπιστολὴ πρὸς Σιμπλικίαν περὶ εὐνούχων αὐτῆς.
αἱρετικὴ ἦν αὕτη. ἀρρωστήσαντος δὲ τοῦ μακαρίου Βασιλείου,
καὶ εἰσιόντος ἔν τινι λουτρῷ λυύσασθαι, ἡ αὐτὴ Σιμπλικία προσ-
τάττει εὐνούχοις καὶ κορασίοις ῥιφῆναι τὰ σάβανα αὐτοῦ ἔξω· καὶ
παρευθὺς ἡ δικαία κρίσις τοῦ θεοῦ ἀνεῖλέ τινας ἐξ αὐτῶν· καὶ ἡ
αὐτὴ Σιμπλικία ἔπεμψε χρήματα τῷ αὐτῷ μακαρίῳ Βασιλείῳ ἐξι-
λεουμένη τὸ πταῖσμα· ὁ δέ, μὴ δεξάμενος, ἔγραψεν αὐτῇ ταῦτα.

"Letter of the same to Simplicia, about her eunuchs. She
was a heretic. Now when Basil was ill, and was entering a
bath to wash, the same Simplicia ordered her eunuchs and
maids to throw his towels outside; and straightway the just
judgment of God destroyed some of them; and the same
Simplicia sent money to the same blessed Basil to make
amends for her insult; but he would not receive them and
wrote this to her." The writer of this comment was evidently
unacquainted with the letter of Gregory of Nazianzus quoted
above.

αὐτὸς κατέχω τὴν γλῶτταν, σιωπῇ τῶν ἐμῶν
ὕβρεων πνίγων τὸν ὄνειδον. ἐγὼ δὲ μενῶ τὸν
ἄνωθεν δικαστήν, ὃς οἶδε πᾶσαν κακίαν ἐν τέλει
ἀμύνεσθαι. κἂν γὰρ ὑπὲρ ψάμμον ἐκχέῃ[1] τις
χρήματα, βλάπτει ψυχήν, πατήσας τὸ δίκαιον.
ἀεὶ γὰρ θυσίαν Θεός, οὐχ ὡς χρῄζων, οἶμαι, ζητεῖ,
ἀλλὰ θυσίαν πολυτελῆ τὴν εὐσεβῆ καὶ δικαίαν
γνώμην δεχόμενος. ὅταν δέ τις ἑαυτὸν παρα-
βαίνων πατῇ, κοινὰς λογίζεται τὰς εὐχάς.

Σαυτὴν οὖν τῆς ἐσχάτης ἡμέρας ὑπόμνησον,
καὶ ἡμᾶς, εἰ βούλει, μὴ δίδασκε. ἴσμεν σου
πλείονα, καὶ[2] ταῖς ἔνδοθεν ἀκάνθαις οὐ τοσοῦτον
συμπνιγόμεθα· οὔτε ἐν ὀλίγοις καλοῖς δεκα-
πλασίονα κακίαν ἐπιμίγνυμεν. ἐπήγειρας ἡμῖν
σαύρας τε καὶ φρύνους, ἐαρινὰ δῆθεν θηρία, πλὴν
ὅμως ἀκάθαρτα. ἀλλ᾽ ἥξει πτερὸν[3] ἄνωθεν τὸ
ταῦτα νεμόμενον. ἐμοὶ γὰρ λόγος, οὐχ ὡς σὺ
νομίζεις, ἀλλ᾽ ὡς οἶδε κρίνειν Θεός. εἰ δὲ καὶ
μαρτύρων χρεία, οὐ δοῦλοι στήσονται, οὐδὲ
εὐνούχων γένος ἄτιμον καὶ πανώλεθρον· τοῦτο δὴ
τοῦτο, ἄθηλυ, ἄνανδρον, γυναικομανές, ἐπίζηλον,
κακόμισθον, ὀξύθυμον, θηλυδριῶδες,[4] γαστρίδου-
λον, χρυσομανές, ἀπηνές, κλαυσίδειπνον, εὐμετά-
βλητον, ἀμετάδοτον, πάνδοχον, ἀπροσκορές, μανι-
κὸν καὶ ζηλότυπον· καὶ τί γὰρ ἔτι εἰπεῖν ; σὺν
αὐτῇ τῇ γενέσει σιδηροκατάδικον. πῶς οὖν
τούτων[5] γνώμη ὀρθή, ὧν καὶ οἱ πόδες στρεβλοί ;
οὗτοι σωφρονοῦσι μὲν ἄμισθα διὰ σιδήρου·
μαίνονται δὲ ἄκαρπα δι᾽ οἰκείαν αἰσχρότητα.
οὐχ οὗτοι στήσονται τῆς κρίσεως μάρτυρες, ἀλλ᾽

---

[1] ἐκχέει editi antiqi. [2] ἐν add. E.
[3] πτηνόν Regius secundus et Coisl. secundus.
[4] θηλυδρῶδες E. [5] τούτῳ E.

check my tongue, by silence smothering the indignity of the insults offered me. But I shall await the Judge above, who knows how in the end to avenge all evil. For even if anyone pour out money like sand, he but harms his soul, having trampled on justice. For God always demands a sacrifice, not, I think, because He needs it, but because He accepts the pious and just mind as a costly sacrifice. But when anyone by transgression tramples upon himself, He considers his prayers profane.

Therefore be mindful of the last day, and, if you please, do not try to teach us. We know more than you, and are not so choked up within by thorns, nor do we mingle a tenfold evil with a few virtues. You have roused against us lizards and toads,[1] beasts of spring forsooth, but nevertheless unclean. But there will come a bird from above to feed on these. For it matters to me, not how you think, but how God knows how to judge. And if there be need also of witnesses, slaves will not stand forth, nor any disreputable and utterly accursed race of eunuchs,— yes, I mean just that—a race, neither feminine nor masculine, woman-mad, envious, of evil wage, quick to anger, effeminate, slaves to the belly, money-mad, coarse, grumbling about their dinner, fickle, stingy, ready to accept anything, disgusting, crazed, jealous —and yet why say more?—at their very birth doomed to the knife! How then can these possess true judgment, whose very feet are twisted? They are chaste without reward—thanks to the knife; and they rave with passion without fruition—thanks to their own lewdness. These will not stand as witnesses at the judgment, but the eyes of just

---

[1] Apparently the slaves and eunuchs.

ὀφθαλμοὶ δικαίων, καὶ ὄψεις ἀνδρῶν τελείων· ὅσοι
τότε ὁρῶσι, πρὸς ἃ βλέποντες νῦν εἰσὶ συνέσει.

CXVI

Φιρμίνῳ

Καὶ σπάνιά σου τὰ γράμματα, καὶ μικρὰ
ταῦτα, ἢ ὄκνῳ τοῦ γράφειν, ἢ ἄλλως, τὸν ἐκ
τοῦ πλήθους κόρον διαφεύγειν οἰκονομοῦντος,
ἤπου καὶ πρὸς βραχυλογίαν ἑαυτὸν συνεθίζοντος.
ἡμῖν μέντοι οὐδὲν ἐξαρκεῖ, ἀλλὰ κἂν ὑπερβάλλῃ
τῷ πλήθει, τῆς ἐπιθυμίας ἐστὶν ἐλάττω διὰ τὸ
βούλεσθαι¹ ἕκαστα περὶ σοῦ μανθάνειν, πῶς μέν
σοι τὸ σῶμα ἔχει, ὅπως δέ σοι τὰ τῆς ἀσκήσεως,
καὶ πότερον ἐπιμένεις τοῖς ἐξ ἀρχῆς ἐγνωσμένοις
ἤ τι καὶ μετεβουλεύσω, πρὸς τὰ συμπίπτοντα
τὴν γνώμην μετατιθέμενος.²

Εἰ μὲν οὖν ὁ αὐτὸς διέμεινας³ σεαυτῷ, οὐκ ἂν
πλῆθος γραμμάτων ἐπεζητοῦμεν, ἀλλ᾽ ἐξήρκει
ἡμῖν τοσοῦτον· ὁ δεῖνα τῷ δεῖνι· ὑγιαίνειν ἡμᾶς
ἴσθι, καὶ ἔρρωσο. ἐπεὶ δὲ ἀκούομεν ἃ⁴ καὶ
λέγειν αἰσχυνόμεθα, καταλιπόντα σε τὴν τῶν
μακαρίων προγόνων τάξιν, ἐπὶ τὸν πρὸς πατρὸς
πάππον αὐτομολεῖν καὶ Βρεττάνιον σπουδάζειν
γενέσθαι ἀντὶ Φιρμίνου, ἐπιζητοῦμεν αὐτὰ ταῦτα

---

¹ πάνθ᾽ add. editi antiqi.   ² μεταθέμενος editi antiqi.
³ διέμενες Med.   ⁴ ἀκούομεν ἃ] τὰ ἀκουόμενα E.

---

¹ Written about 372. Firminus, his father of like name,
and his grandfather, Bretannius, are known only from this
letter. It seems that Firminus had at one time resolved to

men and the countenances of whole men—all who then see with their eyes that which they now gaze upon with their understanding.

LETTER CXVI

To Firminus [1]

Your letters are rare, and these brief, either through reluctance to write, or for some other reason—because you plan to avoid the satiety that comes from numbers, or perhaps are even accustoming yourself to brevity of speech. We, however, are not at all satisfied, but even if there is an exceedingly great number, it falls short of our desire because we wish to know everything about you—how your health is, how it is with your practice of asceticism, and whether you abide by your original determination, or have made some change, altering your purpose to suit the circumstances.

Now if you had remained consistent with yourself, we should not be asking for a great number of letters, but so much would be enough for us: "So-and-so to So-and-so; rest assured that we are well, and good health to you." But since we hear what we are ashamed even to mention,—that you, forsaking the ranks of your blessed forefathers, have deserted to your paternal grandfather and are ambitious to become a Bretannius rather than a Firminus, these

become an ascetic. Later, however, he abandoned asceticism and joined the army, intent upon a military career. Basil, on hearing this, wrote the present letter. He exhorts him to abandon army life and imitate his father, who distinguished himself in civic duties, rather than his grandfather, Bretannius, who won military fame.

ἀκοῦσαι,[1] καὶ τοὺς λογισμοὺς μαθεῖν καθ᾽ οὓς
ἐπὶ ταύτην ἐλθεῖν τοῦ βίου τὴν ὁδὸν ὑπήχθης.
ἀλλ᾽ ἐπειδὴ αὐτὸς ἀπεσιώπησας αἰδοῖ τοῦ βου-
λεύματος, ἡμεῖς σε παρακαλοῦμεν μήτε[2] βου-
λεύεσθαι αἰσχύνης ἄξια, καὶ εἴ τι[3] ὑπέδραμέ
σου τὸν νοῦν, ἀπελάσαντα τοῦτο τῆς διανοίας
σεαυτοῦ γενέσθαι πάλιν, καὶ μακρὰ χαίρειν
εἰπόντα στρατείᾳ καὶ ὅπλοις καὶ ταῖς ἐπὶ[4] στρατοπέδου ταλαιπωρίαις, καταλαβεῖν τὴν πατρίδα, ἀρκοῦν πρὸς ἀσφάλειαν βίου καὶ πρὸς
πᾶσαν περιφάνειαν τὸ ἐξίσου τοῖς προγόνοις
κρατῆσαι τῆς πόλεως ἡγησάμενον· ὅπερ ἀπόνως
σοι παραγενήσεσθαι πεπιστεύκαμεν, πρός τε τὴν
ἐκ φύσεως ἐπιτηδειότητα ἀφορῶντες καὶ πρὸς τὴν
ἐρημίαν τῶν ἐνισταμένων. εἴτε οὖν μὴ γέγονεν
ἐξ ἀρχῆς ἡ γνώμη, εἴτε γενομένη πάλιν ἐκβέ-
βληται, γνώρισον[5] ἡμῖν ἐν τάχει· εἰ δέ, ὃ μὴ
γένοιτο, τὰ αὐτὰ μένει βουλεύματα, αὐτάγγελτος
ἡμῖν ἡκέτω ἡ συμφορά· γραμμάτων δὲ οὐ
δεόμεθα.

CXVII

Ἀνεπίγραφος, ἐπὶ ἀσκήσει

Ἐγὼ καὶ ἄλλως ὀφείλεσθαι τῇ ὑμετέρᾳ τιμιότητι ἐμαυτὸν νομίζω, καὶ τὸ νῦν δὲ τοῦτο φρόν-

---

[1] παρὰ σοῦ add. editio Paris.   [2] μήποτε E.
[3] καί add. E.   [4] τοῦ add. E.
[5] δήλωσον editi antiqi.

---

[1] Written about 372. This is clearly the answer of

very things we want to hear from you, and to learn
the considerations that have influenced you to enter
upon this manner of life. But because you yourself
have been silent through shame of your plan, we
exhort you never to plan things which call for shame,
and if any such thing has entered your mind, to
expel it from your thoughts and regain the mastery
over yourself, and, bidding a long farewell to military
life and to arms and to the toils of the camp, to
return to your native country, since as regards
security of life and all glory it is enough to be the
ruler, like your forefathers, of your own city through
your leadership; and in this we are confident that
you can succeed without difficulty, as we observe,
not only the fitness for rule which nature has given
you but also the absence of opponents. Whether,
therefore, this has not been your intention from the
beginning, or, having once been in your mind, has
been rejected again, inform us at once; but if, on
the other hand (and may it not come to pass), your
plans remain the same, let the misfortune come to
us self-announced, and we need no letters.

LETTER CXVII

Without Inscription, on Asceticism [1]

For other reasons I consider myself indebted to
your Honour, and now the present anxiety in which

Firminus to the preceding letter, and there appears no
reason for doubting its authenticity. This and all the other
unaddressed letters do not appear in MSS. of the Aa family,
but this is probably due to their having been unknown. Cf.
Bessières 156, 159, 160.

τισμα, ἐν ᾧ ἐσμέν, ἀναγκαίως ἡμᾶς ὑπευθύνους
ταῖς τῶν τοιούτων πραγμάτων ὑπηρεσίαις καθί-
στησι, κἂν οἱ τυχόντες ὦσιν[1] οἱ ἐπιτάττοντες,
μὴ ὅτι ὑμεῖς οἱ πολλοῖς δικαίοις καὶ ἄλλοις πρὸς
ἡμᾶς συναπτόμενοι. τὰ μὲν οὖν παρελθόντα εἰς
ἐξέτασιν ἀγαγεῖν οὐκ ἀναγκαῖον· ἐπεὶ ἐνῆν εἰπεῖν,
ὅτι ἡμεῖς ἐγενόμεθα ἑαυτοῖς τῶν[2] ταράχων αἴτιοι,
τῆς ἀγαθῆς ἐκείνης ἀσκήσεως καὶ μόνης ἀγούσης
πρὸς σωτηρίαν φιλονεικήσαντες ἀποστῆναι· διὸ
τάχα καὶ τῷ ταράχῳ τούτῳ εἰς πειρασμὸν
παρεδόθημεν.

Ἀλλ' ἐκεῖνα μὲν γέγονε καὶ ὑπομνήσεως ἠξιώθη,
ὥστε μὴ δεύτερον ἡμᾶς τοῖς ὁμοίοις περιπεσεῖν.
τὰ δὲ ἐφεξῆς, πάνυ βούλομαι πληροφορεῖσθαί
σου τὴν εὐλάβειαν, ὅτι τοῦ Θεοῦ συγχωροῦντος
ῥᾷστα ἡμῖν προσχωρήσει, τοῦ πράγματος καὶ
ἐννόμου ὄντος καὶ οὐδὲν ἔχοντος βαρύ, καὶ τῶν
φίλων ἡμῶν πολλῶν[3] ἑτοίμως χαριζομένων, ὄντων
ἐν τῷ στρατοπέδῳ. τυπωθήσεται οὖν παρ' ἡμῶν
δέησις, κατὰ τὴν ὁμοιότητα τοῦ προσδοθέντος
λιβέλλου τῷ βικαρίῳ, ἐν ᾗ ἐὰν μή τις γένηται
παρολκή, εὐθέως ἀποπεμψόμεθα τὴν ἐκ τοῦ
γράμματος[4] ἄδειαν παρεχόμενοι. πέπεισμαι δὲ

---

[1] εἰσίν E, editi antiqi.   [2] τῶν om. E.
[3] πολλῶν om. Vat., Med.   [4] πράγματος E.

---

[1] The civil government of the Empire was distributed into
thirteen dioceses. The first of these was subject to the
jurisdiction of the *court* of the East. The place of the
Augustal praefect of Egypt was no longer filled by a Roman

we find ourselves also of necessity places us under obligation for services in troubles of this kind, even if those who lay their commands upon us are ordinary persons and not, like yourself, men who are joined to us by many other just claims. Now it is not necessary to bring the past into review; for I might say that we were the cause of our own disturbances, since we strove to abandon that goodly practice of asceticism which alone leads to salvation; and so perhaps we were given over to this disturbance also by way of temptation.

But those matters are past, and have been considered worthy of mention only that we may not a second time fall into the same difficulties. As to the next step, however, I am quite anxious that your Reverence be informed that, God granting, it will easily turn out as we wish, the matter being lawful and involving no difficulty, and our friends at court, who are many, are glad to do us a favour. So a petition will be drawn up by us, modelled on the document that has been handed to the Vicar,[1] according to which, if there is no delay, we shall be quickly sent home by merely producing the permit based upon the writ.[2] And I am convinced that in

---

knight; but the name was retained. The eleven remaining dioceses—Asiana, Pontica, Thrace, Macedonia, Dacia, Pannonia or Western Illyricum, Italy, Africa, Gaul, Spain, and Britain—were governed by twelve *vicars* or *vice-prefects*.

[2] That a written discharge was necessary is plainly seen from Letter CXXIII of Gregory Nazianzenus, who thus addressed a certain Ellelichus: "Mamanta, the slave Reader, whose father was a soldier, was consecrated to God on account of his noble character. Give him to God and to us, but do not let him be numbered among vagabond soldiers. Give him his freedom in writing, so that he may not be threatened by others." Cf. Migne, Vol. 32, 534, note 99.

ἐν τοιούτοις μεῖζον τῶν βασιλικῶν προσταγμά-
των τὴν προαίρεσιν ἡμῶν ἰσχύειν, ἣν ἐὰν ἄτρεπτον
καὶ ἀκλινῆ ἐκ τοῦ κατὰ τὴν ἀκμὴν βίου ἐπιδει-
ξώμεθα, ἀνεπιχείρητος ἡμῖν καὶ ἄσυλος διὰ τῆς
τοῦ Θεοῦ βοηθείας τῆς παρθενίας ἡ φυλακὴ εἴη.

Τὸν δὲ ἐγχειρισθέντα ἡμῖν παρὰ σοῦ ἀδελφὸν
καὶ ἐθεασάμεθα ἡδέως, καὶ ἔχομεν ἐν τοῖς γνω-
ρίμοις, εὐχόμενοι ἄξιον εἶναι τοῦ Θεοῦ καὶ τῆς
σῆς μαρτυρίας.

CXVIII

Ἰοβίνῳ, ἐπισκόπῳ Πέρρης

Ἔχω σε χρεώστην ὀφλήματος ἀγαθοῦ. ἐδά-
νεισα γάρ σοι χρέος ἀγάπης, ὃ χρή με ἀπολαβεῖν
σὺν τόκῳ, ἐπειδὴ καὶ ὁ Κύριος ἡμῶν τὸ τοιοῦτον
εἶδος τῶν τόκων οὐ παραιτεῖται. ἀπόδος τοίνυν,
ὦ φίλη κεφαλή, ἐπιστὰς ἡμῶν τῇ πατρίδι. τοῦτο
μὲν οὖν ἐστιν αὐτὸ τὸ κεφάλαιον. τίς δὲ ἡ
προσθήκη; τὸ σὲ εἶναι τὸν παραγινόμενον, ἄνδρα
τοσοῦτον ἡμῶν διαφέροντα ὅσῳ[1] πατέρες εἰσὶ
βελτίους παίδων.

[1] ὅσον Ε.

such matters our principles are more powerful than the royal mandates, and that if we show them to be unswerving and without deviation from the very highest life, with the help of God the keeping of our celibacy would be unassailable and inviolate.

We were not only glad to see the brother whom you entrusted to us, but we also count him among our friends, praying that he may be worthy of God and of your testimony.

LETTER CXVIII

To Jovinus, Bishop of Perrha [1]

I CONSIDER you a debtor for a goodly debt. For I made you a loan, an obligation of love, which I ought to get back with interest, since even our Lord does not deprecate usury of this kind. Therefore, pay it back, my dear friend, by a visit to our land. That would be, to be sure, only the principal itself. But what would be the increase? The fact that it is you who pay the visit, a man so far superior to us as parents are better than their children.

[1] Written at the end of 372, or at the beginning of 373. This letter is an excellent example of the spirit of the Second Sophistic period of Greek rhetoric. The entire letter is a rather far-fetched metaphor. Basil has already visited Jovinus, and his visit is compared to a loan out at interest. That Jovinus repaid the visit we learn from Letter CXXVII. The MSS. vary between Jovinus and Jobinus. Furthermore, all do not agree in qualifying Jovinus as Bishop of Perrha. Some MSS. read Κέρρης, and others Πέργης. Tillemont and Maran, however, prefer the reading Πέρρης of six MSS. (4 Vat. Reg., 2nd Coisl., and Paris). Perrha was in Syria and not far from the seat of Eusebius of Samosata.

CXIX

Εὐσταθίῳ, ἐπισκόπῳ Σεβαστείας

Καὶ διὰ τοῦ αἰδεσιμωτάτου καὶ εὐλαβεστάτου
ἀδελφοῦ μου[1] Πέτρου προσφθέγγομαί σου τὴν
ἀγάπην,[2] παρακαλῶν σε ὡς διὰ πάσης προφάσεως
καὶ νῦν προσεύχεσθαι ὑπὲρ ἐμοῦ, ἵνα, μεταβαλ-
λόμενος[3] ἀπὸ τοῦ φευκτοῦ[4] τούτου καὶ βλαβεροῦ
τρόπου, γένωμαί ποτε ἄξιος τοῦ ὀνόματος τοῦ
Χριστοῦ. πάντως δέ, κἂν ἐγὼ μὴ λέγω, διαλεχ-
θήσεσθε πρὸς ἀλλήλους περὶ τῶν καθ' ἡμᾶς, καὶ
γνωρίσει σοι τὴν ἀκρίβειαν τῶν πεπραγμένων,
ὥστε μὴ παραδεχθῆναι ἀβασανίστως τὰς πονηρὰς
καθ' ἡμῶν ὑπονοίας, ἃς εἰκὸς κατασκευάζειν τοὺς
καὶ παρὰ τὸν τοῦ Θεοῦ φόβον καὶ παρὰ τὴν τῶν
ἀνθρώπων ὑπόληψιν εἰς ἡμᾶς ἐξυβρίσαντας. οἷα
γὰρ ἡμῖν ἐνεδείξατο ὁ γενναῖος Βασίλειος, ὃν
ἀντὶ φυλακτηρίου τῆς ἐμῆς ζωῆς παρὰ τῆς σῆς
εὐλαβείας ὑπεδεξάμην, ἐγὼ μὲν καὶ εἰπεῖν αἰσ-
χύνομαι· εἴσῃ δὲ τὰ καθ' ἕκαστα παρὰ τοῦ
ἀδελφοῦ ἡμῶν διδαχθείς. καὶ τοῦτο λέγω οὐκ
ἐκεῖνον ἀμυνόμενος (εὔχομαι γὰρ αὐτῷ μὴ λογισ-

---

[1] μου om. E.   [2] καί editi antiqi.
[3] μεταβαλόμενος E, Reg. secundus, Bigot. alter.
[4] ἀπευκτοῦ editi antiqi.

---

[1] Written at the end of 372 or beginning of 373. It deals
with the untrustworthiness of a certain Basil and Sophronius,
two henchmen of Eustathius, by whom they had been recommended to Basil. Eustathius was ruined by his love of
power and self-aggrandizement, which was probably the
source of his hypocrisy. Basil was loath to break with
Eustathius because of their mutual interest in asceticism,

LETTER CXIX

To Eustathius, Bishop of Sebaste[1]

I ADDRESS you, my dear friend, through my most reverend and pious brother Peter,[2] urging you on every occasion and especially now to pray for me, that, being transformed from this present abhorrent and harmful nature, I may one day become worthy of the name of Christ. But assuredly, even if I do not speak, you and he will converse with one another about our affairs, and he will make known to you every detail of what has happened, so that you may not admit without investigation the base suspicions against us, which these men are likely to trump up, who, regardless of the fear of God or of our reputation among men, have heaped insults upon us. For what sort of charges the noble [3] Basil has brought against us, the man whom I received from your Reverence as a guard of my life, I am indeed ashamed to say; but you will know every detail on being informed by our brother. And this I say, not to avenge myself upon this Basil (for I pray that it

and for a long time was blind to Eustathius' duplicity and Arian proclivities. As subsequent letters show, the present letter records the first of a series of events that eventually brought about a break between the two. Cf. Letter LXXXIX (and note), which is also addressed to Eustathius. For Eustathius' persistent heresy, cf. Letters CXXX, CCXXIII and CCXLIV.

[2] The present letter and Letter CCIII, written to the bishops of the Pontus, were carried by one named Peter, whom St. Basil designates as brother. It is uncertain whether this Peter is Basil's own brother or a spiritual brother.

[3] Ironical. For this Basil, cf. note 1.

θῆναι παρὰ τοῦ Κυρίου), ἀλλὰ βεβαίαν μοι τὴν
παρὰ σοῦ ἀγάπην μεῖναι ἡμῖν διοικούμενος, ἣν
φοβοῦμαι μὴ διασαλεύσωσι ταῖς ὑπερβολαῖς τῶν
διαβόλων, ἃς εἰκὸς αὐτοὺς κατασκευάσαι εἰς
ἀπολογίαν τοῦ πταίσματος. ὅπερ[1] δ' ἂν κατη-
γορήσωσιν ἡμῶν, ἐκεῖνο παρὰ τῆς σῆς ἀγχινοίας
ἐξεταζέσθωσαν, εἰ ἐνεκάλεσαν ἡμῖν, εἰ τὴν[2] διόρθωσιν τοῦ ἁμαρτήματος οὗ νῦν ἡμῖν ἐπάγουσιν
ἐπεζήτησαν, εἰ ὅλως φανερὰν ἑαυτῶν τὴν πρὸς
ἡμᾶς λύπην κατέστησαν. νῦν δέ, ἐν φαιδρῷ τῷ
προσώπῳ καὶ πεπλασμένοις[3] ἀγάπης ῥήμασιν
ἀμύθητόν τινα δόλου καὶ πικρίας βυθὸν τῇ ψυχῇ
συγκαλύπτοντες, διὰ τῆς ἀνελευθέρου φυγῆς[4]
ἐφανέρωσαν. ἐφ' ᾧ ὅσον μὲν ἡμῖν[5] ἐποιήσαντο
πένθος, ὅσον δὲ τὸν γέλωτα τοῖς ἀεὶ τὸν εὐλαβῆ
βίον ἐν τῇ ἀθλίᾳ ταύτῃ πόλει βδελυσσομένοις καὶ
τέχνην πρὸς τὸ πιστευθῆναι καὶ σχηματισμὸν
εἰς ἀπάτην τὸ πλάσμα τῆς σωφροσύνης[6] διαβε-
βαιουμένοις ἐπιτηδεύεσθαι, πάντως, κἂν ἡμεῖς
μὴ διηγησώμεθα, γνώριμον τῇ συνέσει σου. ὡς
μηδὲν ἐπιτήδευμα οὕτως ὕποπτον εἶναι πρὸς
κακίαν λοιπὸν τοῖς ἐνταῦθα, ὡς τὸ ἐπάγγελμα
τοῦ ἀσκητικοῦ βίου.

Ἃ πῶς χρὴ[7] θεραπευθῆναι, τῆς σῆς ἂν εἴη
συνέσεως φροντίσαι.[8] τὰ γὰρ παρὰ Σωφρονίου
συρραπτόμενα[9] ἐγκλήματα ἡμῖν οὐκ ἀγαθῶν
ἐστὶ προοίμια, ἀλλ' ἀρχὴ διαιρέσεως καὶ χωρισ-

---

[1] οὕπερ Medicaeus, Regius primus, Bigot. alter.
[2] εἰ τὴν . . . εἰ ὅλως] τὴν . . . ἢ ὅλως editi antiqi.
[3] τετιμημένοις tres MSS.   [4] σιωπῆς E, editi antiqi.
[5] ἡμῖν . . . δὲ] προξενοῦμεν E.
[6] ταπεινοφροσύνης E, Harl., Reg. secundus.
[7] ἃ πῶς] ὅπως οὖν E, editi antiqi.

may not be laid to his account by our Lord), but to make sure that your love for me shall abide steadfast, since I fear that these men may shake it by the exaggerated slanders which they have probably trumped up in defence of their error. But whatever accusation these persons may bring against us, let them be examined by you with all your acumen as to this—first, whether they have brought a formal complaint against us, secondly, whether they have sought the rectification of the error for which they now attack us, and, finally, whether they have made their grievance against us entirely clear. But as the case now stands, though they conceal within their souls, under their beaming countenances and their counterfeit expressions of affection, a depth of treachery and bitterness that defies description, yet through their ignoble flight they have made their grievance manifest. How much sorrow they have brought upon us in this matter, and how much occasion for ridicule they have furnished to those in this unhappy city who constantly express their contempt for the pious life and assert that our pretended practice of chastity is but a trick to get ourselves trusted and a pose intended to deceive, assuredly all this, even if we refrain from stating it, is well known to your sagacity; and the result is that no mode of life is so suspected as vicious by the people here as is the profession of asceticism.

How these things should be remedied would be the proper concern of your sagacity to devise. For the charges concocted against us by Sophronius are not a prelude of good things, but a beginning of

---

[8] φροντίς Vat.; καὶ φροντίδος tres alii MSS.

[9] συνερραμμένα editi antiqi.

μοῦ καὶ σπουδῇ τοῦ καὶ τὴν ἐν ἡμῖν ἀγάπην
ἀποψυγῆναι. ὃν ὑπὸ τῆς σῆς εὐσπλαγχνίας
παρακαλοῦμεν κατασχεθῆναι ἀπὸ τῆς βλαβερᾶς
ταύτης ὁρμῆς, καὶ πειραθῆναι τῇ παρ' ἑαυτοῦ
ἀγάπῃ κατασφίγγειν μᾶλλον τὰ διιστάμενα καὶ
μὴ[1] τοῖς πρὸς διάστασιν[2] ὡρμημένοις συνεπι-
τείνειν τὸν χωρισμόν.

CXX

Μελετίῳ, ἐπισκόπῳ Ἀντιοχείας

Γράμματα ἐδεξάμην παρὰ τοῦ θεοφιλεστάτου
ἐπισκόπου Εὐσεβίου, προστάσσοντα πάλιν γρα-
φῆναι τοῖς δυτικοῖς περί τινων ἐκκλησιαστικῶν.
καὶ ἐβουλήθη παρ' ἡμῶν τυπωθῆναι τὴν ἐπιστολὴν ὑπογραφῆναι δὲ παρὰ πάντων τῶν[3]
κοινωνικῶν. ἐπεὶ οὖν οὐχ εὗρον ὅπως ἐπιστείλω
περὶ ὧν ἐπέταξε, παρέπεμψα τὸ ὑπομνηστικὸν
τῇ θεοσεβείᾳ σου, ἵνα καὶ αὐτῷ ἐντυχὼν καὶ
τοῖς ἀναφερομένοις παρὰ τοῦ ποθεινοτάτου ἀδελ-

---

[1] καὶ μὴ] ἤ E.   [2] τὸ διαστασιάζειν editi antiqi.
[3] τῶν om. E.

---

[1] Probably written in A.D. 372. Letters CXX, CXXI,
CXXII, CXXIX, and CXXX are all related in the matter
of chronology. Tillemont and the Benedictine editors agree
in the actual dating, although they differ in the identity of
certain persons. Loofs (p. 29), in treating of these letters,

division and separation and an incentive to the cool-
ing even of the charity within us. We urge that
this man be restrained by your kindness of heart
from this hurtful impulse of his, and that your
affection rather strive to tighten that which is falling
apart and not to increase the tendency to schism in
those who are eager for disagreement.

LETTER CXX

To Meletius, Bishop of Antioch [1]

I HAVE received a letter from the most God-
beloved bishop Eusebius, enjoining that we write
again to the Westerners concerning certain ecclesi
astical affairs. He wished, furthermore, that the
letter be drawn up by us but signed by all those
in communion. Since, therefore, I have not discovered how to write about those things which he
has enjoined, I am sending his memorandum to your
Godliness in order that when you have read it and
given heed to the matters reported by our most

raises questions which he does not himself answer satis-
factorily. Indeed in several places his arrangement seems to
be contradicted by certain facts contained in the letters
themselves. I have retained the chronology of Tillemont and
the Benedictines.

For the identity of Meletius, cf. Letter LXVI, note 4.
Previous letters addressed to Meletius are LVII, LXVIII,
and LXXXIX. In this letter Basil continues his support of
the claims of Meletius, now exiled in Armenia, as the regular
Catholic bishop of Antioch, and he complains of the irregular
ordination of Faustus as bishop of an Armenian see by
Anthimus of Tyana, one of his opponents.

φοῦ Σαγκτισσίμου τοῦ συμπρεσβυτέρου προσέ-
χων,[1] αὐτὸς καταξιώσῃς ὡς παρίσταταί σοι[2]
περὶ τούτων τυπῶσαι, ἡμῶν ἑτοίμως ἐχόντων
καὶ[3] αὐτῷ συνθέσθαι καὶ ταχέως ποιῆσαι περι-
κομισθῆναι[4] τοῖς κοινωνικοῖς, ὥστε τὰς πάντων
ὑπογραφὰς ἔχοντα ἀπελθεῖν τὸν μέλλοντα ὁρμᾶν
πρὸς τοὺς κατὰ τὴν δύσιν ἐπισκόπους. ταχέως[5]
ἡμῖν τὸ παριστάμενον τῇ ὁσιότητί σου γνωρισθῆναι κέλευσον, ἵνα μὴ ἀγνοῶμεν τὰ δόξαντά
σοι.

Περὶ δὲ τῶν τυρευομένων[6] ἢ καὶ ἤδη ἐσκευωρη-
μένων καθ' ἡμῶν ἐν τῇ Ἀντιοχείᾳ ἀνοίσει[7] ὁ
αὐτὸς ἀδελφὸς τῇ τιμιότητί σου, ἐάν περ μὴ
προλαβοῦσα ἡ φήμη τῶν γενομένων φανερὰ
ποιήσῃ τὰ πεπραγμένα. καὶ γὰρ ἐγγύς ἐστιν
ἡ ἐλπὶς τῆς ἐκβάσεως τῶν ἀπειλουμένων.
γινώσκειν δὲ βούλομαι τὴν εὐλάβειάν σου, ὅτι
ὁ ἀδελφὸς Ἄνθιμος Φαῦστον, τὸν συνόντα τῷ

[1] προσχών E.
[2] παρίσταταί σοι] καταξιώσαις editi antiqi.
[3] σοι add. editi antiqi.　　[4] παρακομισθῆναι E.
[5] οὖν add. editi antiqi.　　[6] πορευομένων alii editi.
[7] ἀνύσει E, Med., Reg. secundus.

---

[1] Tillemont argues that Sanctissimus because of his Latin
name was a priest from the West. The Benedictine editor,
however, prefers to consider him a presbyter of Antioch,
since Roman names were at this time quite commonly given

beloved brother Sanctissimus,[1] our presbyter, you
may yourself deign to write as seems best to you
about these affairs ; for we are ready both to agree to
this and to cause it to be sent quickly around to
those in communion with us, so that the messenger
who is about to set out to visit the bishops of the
West may have the signatures of all when he departs.
Order whatever seems best to your Holiness to be
quickly made known to me, in order that we may not
be ignorant of your decisions.

And as regards what is being devised or even
what has already been fabricated against us at
Antioch, the same brother will inform your Honour,
unless previously the report of what has happened
shall have made clear what has been done. For in
truth hope is at hand that these threats will pass
away. But I wish your Reverence to know that our
brother Anthimus [2] has ordained and made a bishop

to Greeks. The latter seems correct, because Sanctissimus
displays unusual interest in Eastern affairs, and Basil calls
him his " most beloved," and " fellow-presbyter," and sends
him on several important missions. The following is a
chronology of his known journeys :

374. The Easterners send Sanctissimus and Dorotheus to
the West in the early spring.

375. Sanctissimus and Dorotheus return to the East through
Thrace. They probably visit Eusebius of Samosata, who was
exiled to Thrace in 374.

376. Sanctissimus makes an extensive tour of the East.

377. The Easterners communicate with the Westerners
through Sanctissimus to procure the condemnation of
Apollinarius and Eustathius.

[2] In 371 Anthimus, a contentious and ambitious prelate,
claimed to be metropolitan of Cappadocia Secunda with his
diocese Tyana as a metropolitan see. He was joined by
those prelates who opposed Basil's election to the see of
Caesarea.

πάπᾳ,[1] ἐπίσκοπον ἐχειροτόνησε, μηδὲ ψήφους
δεξάμενος, καὶ τῷ τόπῳ χειροτονήσας[2] τοῦ αἰδεσιμωτάτου ἀδελφοῦ Κυρίλλου· ὥστε στάσεων
ἐμπλῆσαι τὴν Ἀρμενίαν. ἵνα[3] τοίνυν μὴ καταψεύσωνται ἡμῶν,[4] μηδὲ αὐτοὶ τὴν αἰτίαν σχῶμεν
τῆς ἀταξίας τῶν γενομένων, ἐγνώρισα ταῦτα τῇ
σεμνότητί σου. δῆλον δέ, ὡς καὶ αὐτὸς καταξιώσεις γνώριμα ποιῆσαι τοῖς λοιποῖς. ἡγοῦμαι
γὰρ πολλοὺς λυπήσειν τὴν ἀταξίαν ταύτην.

CXXI

Θεοδότῳ, ἐπισκόπῳ Νικοπόλεως[5]

Πολὺς ὁ χειμὼν καὶ ἐπὶ τὸ μακρότατον παρα-
ταθείς, ὡς μηδὲ τὰς διὰ γραμμάτων παραμυθίας
ῥᾳδίως ἡμῖν ὑπάρχειν. ὅθεν ὀλιγάκις οἶδα καὶ
ἐπιστείλας τῇ εὐλαβείᾳ σου καὶ δεξάμενος γράμματα. ἀλλ᾽ ἐπειδὴ ὁ ποθεινότατος ἀδελφὸς ἡμῶν

---

[1] πάππῳ Coisl. secundus, Reg. secundus.
[2] τῷ τόπῳ χειροτονήσας . . . ἐμπλῆσαι] καταχειροτονήσας
. . . ἐμπληρῶσαι editi antiqi.
[3] ὥρα editi antiqi.   [4] ὑμῶν E.
[5] Ἀρμενίας add. Harl. Ἀρμενίας μικρᾶς add. editi antiqi,
nonnulli MSS.

---

[1] All information about Faustus is procured from Letters
CXX, CXXI, and CXXII of St. Basil. Smith and Wace
infer that he was Bishop of Satala, but Tillemont and the
Benedictine editors prove this to be untenable.

[2] The title pope (papa) was originally employed with great
latitude. In the East it has always been used to designate
simple priests. In the West, however, it seems from the
beginning to have been restricted to bishops. It was probably
in the fourth century that it became a distinctive title of the

of Faustus,[1] him who associates with the pope,[2] without having received votes, and having appointed him in the place of our most reverend brother Cyril; and in consequence Armenia has become filled with schisms. Therefore, that they may not lie against us, and that we ourselves may not be held responsible for the confusion produced by what has happened, I have made these things known to your August Reverence. And obviously you yourself will deign to make this known to the rest. For I think that the present confusion will distress many.

LETTER CXXI

To Theodotus, Bishop of Nicopolis [3]

THE winter is severe and very long drawn out, so that it is not easily within our power to have the consolation of even a letter. It is for this reason, I realize, that I have seldom either written to your Reverence or received a letter from you. But since

Roman Pontiff. Gregory VII finally prescribed that it be confined to the successors of Peter. To whom Basil here refers is an enigma.

[3] On the same subject, and of the same date as the preceding; one of the two (cf. CXXX) extant letters of St. Basil to Theodotus. Theodotus, Bishop of Nicopolis and Metropolitan of Lesser Armenia, was an aged prelate of noble character and unquestioned soundness of faith, and was highly esteemed by Basil. Theodotus, however, suspected Eustathius of Sebaste of unsound doctrine, and when Basil, who at first felt a warm friendship for Eustathius, was reluctant to give credence to these suspicions and even endeavoured to clear them away, he turned his suspicions upon Basil himself. Theodotus then became openly cold and discourteous, and refused to co-operate with Basil in the appointing of bishops to Lesser Armenia.

Σαγκτίσσιμος[1] ὁ συμπρεσβύτερος τὴν μέχρις ὑμῶν ὁδοιπορίαν ὑπέστη, δι' αὐτοῦ καὶ προσφθέγγομαί[2] σου τὴν κοσμιότητα,[3] καὶ παρακαλῶ προσεύχεσθαι ὑπὲρ ἐμοῦ καὶ χρῆσαι τὴν ἀκοὴν τῷ προειρημένῳ,[4] ὥστε παρ' αὐτοῦ διδαχθῆναι τὰ τῶν ἐκκλησιῶν ἐν οἵοις[5] ἐστὶ καὶ τὴν δυνατὴν σπουδὴν εἰσενέγκασθαι εἰς τὰ προκείμενα.

Γίνωσκε δὲ ὅτι Φαῦστος γράμματα ἔχων ἧκε πρὸς ἡμᾶς παρὰ[6] πάπα, ἀξιοῦντα αὐτὸν γενέσθαι ἐπίσκοπον. ἐπειδὴ δὲ ᾐτήσαμεν ἡμεῖς,[7] μαρτυρίαν τῆς σῆς εὐλαβείας καὶ τῶν λοιπῶν ἐπισκόπων, καταφρονήσας ἡμῶν πρὸς Ἄνθιμον ᾤχετο, καὶ παρ' αὐτοῦ λαβὼν τὴν χειροτονίαν χωρὶς ἡμετέρας ὑπομνήσεως ἐπανῆκε.

CXXII

Ποιμενίῳ, ἐπισκόπῳ Σατάλων

Πάντως ἐπεζήτησας[8] γράμματα παρὰ τῶν Ἀρμενίων, ὅτε ἐπανῆκαν διὰ σοῦ, καὶ τὴν αἰτίαν ἔμαθες, δι' ἣν οὐκ ἔδωκα αὐτοῖς τὴν ἐπιστολήν. εἰ μὲν οὖν εἶπον φιλαλήθως, ἔδωκας ἡμῖν αὐτόθεν

---

[1] Σαγκτήσιμος E, editi antiqi.
[2] προσφθεγγόμεθα E, Med.
[3] τιμιότητα E.   [4] εἰρημένῳ E.   [5] οἷς E.
[6] τοῦ add. E.   [7] ᾐτησάμην ἡμεῖς om. E, Med.
[8] ἐπιζητήσας editi antiqi.

---

[1] Cf. note 1, p. 246.
[2] Cf. note 1, p. 248.
[3] Cf. note 2, p. 248.
[4] Cf. note 2, p. 247.

our most beloved brother Sanctissimus,[1] the presbyter, has undertaken the journey to you, through him I salute your Decorum, and beseech you to pray for me and to lend audience to the aforesaid, that you may be informed by him in what condition the affairs of the churches are and bring all possible zeal to bear upon the matters aforementioned.

But be informed that Faustus[2] came to us with a letter from a pope,[3] asking that he be made bishop. But when we asked for a testimonial from your Reverence and from the rest of the bishops, showing contempt for us, he went to Anthimus,[4] and after receiving the election from him without any mention being made of us, he returned.

LETTER CXXII

To Poemenius, Bishop of Satala [5]

You must certainly have asked the Armenians for a letter as they returned through your country, and must have learned the reason why I had not given them the letter. Now if they spoke with regard for the truth, you granted us forgiveness on the spot;

[5] Written at the end of 372 or beginning of 373. Poemenius, Bishop of Satala in Armenia, was a near relation of Basil, and had been brought up with him in close intimacy. In 372 Valens commissioned Basil to appoint bishops to the vacant sees in Armenia, among which was Satala. In compliance with Imperial orders and the earnest petitions of both magistrates and people, St. Basil appointed Poemenius to the see in Satala. Cf. Letter CII, where Basil earnestly commends his friend to the good offices of his new flock. In the present letter reference is also made to the uncanonical appointment of Faustus by Anthimus, on which cf. the letters immediately preceding.

COLLECTED LETTERS OF SAINT BASIL

τὴν συγγνώμην· εἰ δὲ ἀπεκρύψαντο ἐκεῖνοι, ὅπερ
οὐκ¹ εἰκάζω—ἀλλὰ παρ' ἡμῶν ἄκουε.
Ὁ τὰ πάντα γενναῖος Ἄνθιμος, ὁ διὰ μακροῦ
χρόνου τὴν πρὸς ἡμᾶς εἰρήνην σπεισάμενος,
ἐπειδὴ εὗρε καιρὸν ἑαυτοῦ τε² κενοδοξίαν ἐκπληρῶσαι καὶ ἡμῖν λύπην τινὰ προξενῆσαι,
ἐχειροτόνησε τὸν Φαῦστον ἰδίᾳ αὐθεντίᾳ καὶ
ἰδίᾳ χειρί, οὐδενὸς ὑμῶν ἀναμείνας ψῆφον καὶ
ἡμῶν καταγελάσας ἀκριβολογουμένων περὶ τὰ
τοιαῦτα. ἐπεὶ οὖν συνέχεε μὲν παλαιὰν εὐταξίαν, κατεφρόνησε δὲ καὶ ὑμῶν, παρ' ὧν ἀνέμενον
ἐγὼ τὴν μαρτυρίαν δέξασθαι, ἐποίησε δὲ πρᾶγμα
οὐκ οἶδα εἰ εὐάρεστον τῷ Θεῷ, τούτου ἕνεκεν³
λυπηθεὶς πρὸς αὐτούς, οὐδεμίαν ἔδωκα ἐπιστολὴν
πρὸς οὐδένα τῶν Ἀρμενίων, οὐδὲ πρὸς τὴν σὴν
εὐλάβειαν. ἀλλ' οὐδὲ εἰς κοινωνίαν ἐδεξάμην
τὸν Φαῦστον, φανερῶς διαμαρτυρόμενος, ὅτι εἰ
μὴ ὑμέτερά μοι κομίσειε γράμματα, πάντα τὸν
χρόνον ἔσομαι καὶ αὐτὸς ἠλλοτριωμένος καὶ τοὺς
ὁμοψύχους μοι⁴ οὕτω διαθήσω πρὸς αὐτὸν
ἔχειν.
Εἰ μὲν οὖν ἰάσιμα τὰ γενόμενα, σπούδασον
αὐτός τε ἐπιστεῖλαι μαρτυρῶν αὐτῷ, εἰ ὁρᾷς
ἀγαθὴν τοῦ ἀνδρὸς τὴν ζωήν, καὶ τοὺς ἄλλους
προτρέψασθαι· εἰ δὲ ἀνίατα, καὶ τοῦτό μοι
φανερὸν ποίησον, ὥστε μηκέτι με αὐτοῖς καθόλου
προσέχειν, εἰ καὶ ὅτι, ὡς ἔδειξαν, ὥρμηνται
λοιπὸν πρὸς τὸν Ἄνθιμον ἑαυτῶν⁵ μεταθεῖναι
τὴν κοινωνίαν, ἡμῶν καὶ τῆς ἐκκλησίας ταύτης,
ὡς ἑώλων εἰς φιλίαν, καταφρονήσαντες.

¹ οὖν E.   ² τήν add. E.   ³ ἕνεκα E.

252

but if they concealed the facts, which I do not suppose—well, hear our story :

The in all respects noble Authimus, he who long ago made his peace with us, when he found an opportunity of satisfying his own conceit and of causing some vexation to us, consecrated Faustus by his own authority and with his own hand, waiting for the vote of no one of you and ridiculing us for being scrupulous about such matters. Since, then, he was violating an ancient orderly practice and had showed contempt even for you, from whom I was waiting to receive the testimonial, and had committed an act which I am inclined to consider displeasing to God, I, feeling aggrieved at the Armenians on this account, gave them no letter to anyone in Armenia, not even to your Reverence. Moreover, I did not even receive Faustus into communion, plainly giving witness that unless he should bring me a letter from you, I myself would be permanently estranged and would dispose those of like mind with me also to be so disposed toward him.

Now, if what has happened admits of a remedy, do you yourself hasten to write, bearing witness for him, if you see that the life of the man is good, and to urge the rest to do likewise. But if the situation is incurable, make this also clear to me, that I may no longer pay any attention to them at all —even if you must say that they have undertaken, as they have indicated, to transfer their communion to Authimus, in contempt of us and this church, having grown stale as regards friendship.

---

⁴ μου E.   ⁵ ἑαυτόν E

CXXIII

Οὐρβικίῳ μονάζοντι

Ἔμελλες ἡμῖν παρέσεσθαι (καὶ τὸ ἀγαθὸν ἐγγὺς) ἄκρῳ γοῦν δακτύλῳ καταψύξαι[1] ἡμᾶς ἐν τοῖς πειρασμοῖς φλεγομένους. εἶτα τί; αἱ ἁμαρτίαι ἡμῶν ἀντέβησαν καὶ διεκώλυσαν τὴν ὁρμήν, ἵν᾽ ἀθεράπευτα κάμνωμεν. ὥσπερ γὰρ ἐν τοῖς κύμασι τὸ μὲν λήγει, τὸ δὲ ἀνίσταται, τὸ δὲ ἤδη φρίκῃ μελαίνεται, οὕτω καὶ τῶν ἡμετέρων κακῶν τὰ μὲν πέπαυται, τὰ δὲ πάρεστι, τὰ δὲ προσδοκᾶται· καὶ μία τῶν κακῶν ἡμῖν, ὡς ἐπὶ τὸ πλεῖστον, ἀπαλλαγή, εἶξαι τῷ καιρῷ καὶ ὑπεξελθεῖν τοῖς διώκουσιν.

Ἀλλὰ καὶ πάρεσο ἡμῖν,[2] ἢ παραμυθούμενος, ἢ καὶ γνώμην δώσων, ἢ καὶ προπέμψων,[3] πάντως δὲ αὐτῷ τῷ ὀφθῆναι ῥᾴους ποιήσων. καὶ τὸ μέγιστον, εὔχου, καὶ ὑπερεύχου, μὴ καὶ τοὺς λογισμοὺς ἡμῶν βαπτισθῆναι ὑπὸ τοῦ κακοῦ καὶ τοῦ[4] κλύδωνος, ἀλλ᾽ ἐν πᾶσι διαφυλάσσειν τῷ Θεῷ τὸ εὐχάριστον, ἵνα μὴ ἐν τοῖς κακοῖς δούλοις ἀριθμηθῶμεν, ἀγαθύνοντι μὲν ἐξομολογούμενοι, παιδεύοντι δὲ διὰ τῶν ἐναντίων μὴ

---

[1] καταψύξων editi antiqi.
[2] πάρεσο ἡμῖν] ἡμῖν ἧκε μόλις editi antiqi.
[3] προσπέμψων editi antiqi.
[4] καὶ τοῦ om. quinque MSS.

---

[1] Written in 373, to Urbicius, a monk, about whom nothing is known, except for the present letter and Letter CCLXII. Basil here writes for consolation and advice. The period 372–374 was one of intense personal suffering for

LETTER CXXIII

To Urbicius, a Monk [1]

You were on the point of visiting us (and the blessing was near), to cool us with but the tip of your finger as we burned in the midst of temptations. Then what? Our sins stood in the way and prevented your setting out, that in our sickness we might find no healing. For just as among the waves one sinks, another rises, and a third is already turning black with rippling, so too with our troubles—some have ceased, others are at hand, and others are being awaited; and the one relief from our evils is, for the most part, to yield to the occasion and to withdraw from before our pursuers.

But pray do visit us, either to console us, or to give advice, or to send us on our way, but in any case by the very sight of you to make us easier at heart. And—most important of all—pray, and pray again, that our reason be not submerged by the flood of evil, but that in all things we may keep ourselves pleasing to God, in order that we may not be numbered among the wicked servants who thank Him when He grants blessings, but when He chastises through the opposite means do

St. Basil. He and his lifelong friend Gregory of Nazianzus had become estranged; Theodotus, Bishop of Nicopolis, for whom Basil had great esteem, had suspected him of heresy, and refused to co-operate with him in appointing bishops in Lesser Armenia; he had at last been forced to see the treachery and ingratitude of his former friend, Eustathius of Sebaste; and, finally, Eusebius of Samosata, his intimate and confidential counsellor, had been exiled to Thrace by the Emperor Valens.

προστιθέμενοι· ἀλλὰ καὶ δι' αὐτῶν τῶν δυσχερῶν
ὠφελώμεθα, μᾶλλον αὐτῷ πιστεύοντες, ὅτε καὶ
μᾶλλον χρήζομεν.

CXXIV

Θεοδώρῳ [1]

Λέγουσί τινες τοὺς ἑαλωκότας τῷ πάθει τοῦ
ἔρωτος, ὅταν κατά τινα βιαιοτέραν ἀνάγκην τῶν
ποθουμένων ἀπάγωνται, εἰ πρὸς τὴν εἰκόνα τῆς
ἀγαπηθείσης μορφῆς ἀποβλέψειαν, τὸ σφοδρὸν
ἀναπαύειν τοῦ πάθους διὰ τῆς ἐν ὀφθαλμοῖς
ἀπολαύσεως. εἰ μὲν οὖν ἀληθῆ ταῦτα ἢ [2] μὴ
λέγειν οὐκ ἔχω· ὃ δέ μοι πρὸς τὴν σὴν συμβέ-
βηκεν ἀγαθότητα οὐ πόρρω τῶν εἰρημένων ἐστίν.
ἐπειδὴ γὰρ γέγονέ τις διάθεσις ἐμοὶ πρὸς τὴν
ἱερὰν καὶ ἄδολόν σου ψυχήν, ἵν' οὕτως εἴπω,
ἐρωτική, τὸ δὲ ἀπολαύειν τῶν ποθουμένων, ὡς
οὐδὲ ἄλλο τι τῶν ἀγαθῶν, οὐκ ἐν εὐκολίᾳ ἡμῖν
ἐστι διὰ τὴν ἐκ τῶν ἁμαρτιῶν ἐναντίωσιν, ἐνόμισα
εἰκόνα τῆς ἀγαθότητός σου ἐναργεστάτην ἐν τῇ
τῶν εὐλαβεστάτων ἡμῶν ἀδελφῶν παρουσίᾳ
ἑωρακέναι. καὶ εἰ δίχα τούτων συνέβη τῇ σῇ
με περιτυχεῖν γνησιότητι, ἐλογισάμην ἂν ἐν σοὶ
κἀκείνους ἑωρακέναι· διότι τῆς ἀγάπης, λέγω,
τοσοῦτον ἐν ἑκάστῳ ὑμῶν τὸ μέτρον ἐστίν, ὡς
ἐπίσης τὴν περὶ τοῦ πλείονος ἑκάστῳ φιλονεικίαν
ἐμφαίνεσθαι. ἐπὶ τούτοις ηὐχαρίστησα τῷ ἁγίῳ
Θεῷ, καὶ εὔχομαι, εἴπερ ἔτι ὑπολείπεταί τις

---

[1] ἀσπαστική add. Reg. secundus, Coisl. secundus, editi
antiqi.

I cannot say; but that which has happened to me regarding your Goodness is not far from what I have described. For since I had conceived with respect to your holy and guileless soul what I may call an amatory disposition, but the enjoyment of the object of our desire, like all other blessings, is made difficult for us by the opposition of our sins, I thought that I saw a very distinct image of your Goodness in the presence of our very reverend brothers. And if, in their absence, I had fallen in with your Nobility, I should have considered that in you I had seen them also; for the measure of my love, I mean, is so great in the case of each of you that there appears in me an eager desire for the advantage of each in equal degree. For this I have thanked the holy God, and I pray, if any period of

---

[1] Written in A.D. 373. The identity of this Theodorus is quite unknown.

---

[2] $\bar{\eta}$ editi antiqi.

the home of Meletius, and there, in the presence of reliable
between himself . . . went first to Getasa,

LETTER CXXIV

not submit. Nay, let us derive benefit even from our very difficulties, trusting in Him the more when we stand the more in need.

LETTER CXXIV

To Theodorus[1]

Some say that those who are seized with the passion of love, whenever through some unusually urgent necessity they are parted from the object of their desire, if they can look upon the semblance of the beloved form in a picture, can check the violence of their passion through the pleasure they derive from the sight. Now whether this is true or not

life be yet left to me, that my life be made sweet
through you, since for the present, at least, I consider life a wretched thing and to be avoided,
separated as it is from association with those most
dear. For, in my opinion, there is nothing for
which a man may be joyful if he be separated from
those who truly love him.

LETTER CXXV

A Transcript of Faith Dictated by the most
Holy Basil, to Which Eustathius, the Bishop
of Sebaste, Subscribed [1]

Those who have formerly been committed to an
unorthodox confession of Faith and wish to pass

witnesses, he justified his conduct with Eustathius and
refuted the accusations of Theodotus. The latter, who was
present, maintained that Eustathius had denied any agreement with Basil's propositions. Accordingly, to satisfy
Theodotus, Basil offered to make Eustathius sign a profession of faith containing all the articles of the Nicene
Creed. Theodotus accepted the plan, and promised to assist
Basil in appointing bishops in Armenia. However, upon his
arrival in Nicopolis, Theodotus forgot all that had passed
and virtually excommunicated Basil. Under these circumstances, Basil was prevented from making the appointments.
Fatigued, disappointed, and grieved over the turn of affairs,
he returned home only to find sadly neglected conditions in
his own diocese.

St. Basil made a third visit to Armenia in the year 373,
probably on account of the ordination of Faustus. It was
on this trip that the people of Armenia demanded an assurance of the orthodoxy of Eustathius. St. Basil willingly
offered to go in person to Eustathius and have him sign
a profession of faith. The present letter was accordingly
drafted. Some think it is written by St. Basil together
with Theodotus, while others believe that it has the tone of a

βουλομένους, ἢ καὶ νῦν πρῶτον ἐν τῇ κατηχήσει
τοῦ λόγου τῆς ἀληθείας ἐπιθυμοῦντας γενέσθαι,
χρὴ τὴν ὑπὸ τῶν μακαρίων πατέρων ἐν τῇ κατὰ
Νίκαιάν ποτε συγκροτηθείσῃ συνόδῳ γραφεῖσαν
πίστιν. τὸ δὲ αὐτὸ τοῦτο χρήσιμον ἂν εἴη καὶ
πρὸς τοὺς ὑπονοουμένους ἐναντίως ἔχειν τῇ
ὑγιαινούσῃ διδασκαλίᾳ καὶ συσκιάζοντας ἑαυτῶν
ἀποφυγαῖς εὐπροσώποις τὸ τῆς κακοδοξίας
φρόνημα. καὶ γὰρ καὶ τούτοις αὐτάρκης ἡ
ἐγκειμένη πίστις. ἢ γὰρ διορθώσαιντο ἑαυτῶν
τὴν ἐν τῷ κρυπτῷ νόσον, ἢ συγκαλύπτοντες
αὐτὴν[1] ἐν τῷ βάθει, αὐτοὶ μὲν τὸ κρῖμα τῆς
ἀπάτης βαστάσουσιν, ἡμῖν δὲ τὴν ἀπολογίαν
κούφην ἐν τῇ ἡμέρᾳ τῆς κρίσεως παρασκευά-
σουσιν, ὅτε ἀποκαλύψει ὁ Κύριος τὰ κρυπτὰ
τοῦ σκότους, καὶ φανερώσει τὰς βουλὰς τῶν
καρδιῶν. λαμβάνειν τοίνυν αὐτοὺς ὁμολογοῦντας
προσήκει, ὅτι πιστεύουσι κατὰ τὰ ῥήματα τὰ
ὑπὸ τῶν Πατέρων ἡμῶν ἐκτεθέντα ἐν τῇ Νικαίᾳ
καὶ κατὰ τὴν ὑγιῶς ὑπὸ τῶν ῥημάτων τούτων
ἐμφαινομένην διάνοιαν.

Εἰσὶ γάρ τινες οἳ καὶ ἐν ταύτῃ τῇ πίστει

---

[1] ἑαυτήν E.

---

synodical decree. At any rate, a meeting was arranged and
the transcript signed in the presence of witnesses. For Basil's
own account of the signing, cf. Letter CCXLIV, sec. 2. But
Basil's suspicions, once aroused, were not easily allayed. He
accordingly proposed another meeting so that the prelates of
Caesarea and Sebaste might be united with one another and
their communion for the future be sincere. Both the place
and the date were decided upon, but Eustathius and his
colleagues failed to keep the appointment.

In spite of all efforts on the part of Eusebius of Samosata
to effect a reconciliation and finally to win Eustathius to the

over into unity with the orthodox, or those who now
for the first time wish to be instructed in the doctrine
of truth, must be taught in the articles of Faith as
drawn up by the blessed Fathers in the synod once
convened at Nicaea. And this same thing would
also be useful for those who are suspected of being
opposed to the sound doctrine and who seek to
cloak with specious subterfuges their unorthodox
views. For even for these the creed embodied
therein suffices. For either they may correct their
hidden malady, or, if they still conceal it in the
depth of their hearts, they will themselves bear the
responsibility for their deception, but for us they will
make easy our defence on the Day of Judgment,
when the Lord "will reveal the hidden things of
darkness and will make manifest the counsels of the
heart." [1] It is therefore fitting to receive them
when they confess that they believe according to
the words set forth by our Fathers at Nicaea and
according to the meaning disclosed by those words
when soundly interpreted.

For there are some who even in this creed pervert

Nicene faith, Eustathius, shortly after signing the present
letter, renounced communion with Basil and openly attacked
him on the ground of Apollinarism. Although pained at the
duplicity of his former friend, and distressed over his false
charges, Basil for about three years maintained a discreet
silence. He then for the first time openly defended himself
against the slanders of Eustathius. Cf. Letter CCXXIII.

[1] 1 Cor. 4, 5: ὥστε μὴ πρὸ καιροῦ τι κρίνετε, ἕως ἂν ἔλθῃ ὁ
Κύριος, ὃς καὶ φωτίσει τὰ κρυπτὰ τοῦ σκότους, καὶ φανερώσει τὰς
βουλὰς τῶν καρδιῶν· καὶ τότε ὁ ἔπαινος γενήσεται ἑκάστῳ ἀπὸ τοῦ
Θεοῦ. "Therefore judge not before the time ; until the Lord
come, who both will bring to light the hidden things of darkness, and will make manifest the counsels of the heart ;
and then shall every man have praise from God."

δολοῦντες τὸν λόγον τῆς ἀληθείας καὶ πρὸς τὸ
ἑαυτῶν βούλημα τὸν νοῦν τῶν ἐν αὐτῇ ῥημάτων
ἕλκοντες. ὅπου γε καὶ Μάρκελλος ἐτόλμησεν, ἀσε-
βῶν εἰς τὴν ὑπόστασιν τοῦ Κυρίου ἡμῶν Ἰησοῦ
Χριστοῦ καὶ ψιλὸν αὐτὸν ἐξηγούμενος λόγον,
ἐκεῖθεν προφασίσασθαι¹ τὰς ἀρχὰς εἰληφέναι,
τοῦ ὁμοουσίου τὴν διάνοιαν κακῶς ἐξηγούμενος.²
καί τινες τῶν ἀπὸ τῆς δυσσεβείας τοῦ Λίβυος
Σαβελλίου, ὑπόστασιν καὶ οὐσίαν ταὐτὸν εἶναι
ὑπολαμβάνοντες, ἐκεῖθεν ἕλκουσι τὰς ἀφορμὰς
πρὸς τὴν κατασκευὴν τῆς ἑαυτῶν βλασφημίας, ἐκ
τοῦ ἐγγεγράφθαι τῇ πίστει, ὅτι Ἐὰν δέ τις λέγῃ³
ἐξ ἑτέρας οὐσίας ἢ ὑποστάσεως τὸν Υἱόν, ἀναθεματίζει ἡ καθολικὴ καὶ ἀποστολικὴ ἐκκλησία.
οὐ γὰρ ταὐτὸν εἶπον ἐκεῖ⁴ οὐσίαν καὶ ὑπόστασιν.
εἰ γὰρ μίαν καὶ τὴν αὐτὴν ἐδήλουν ἔννοιαν αἱ
φωναί, τίς χρεία ἦν ἑκατέρων; ἀλλὰ δῆλον ὅτι,
ὡς τῶν μὲν ἀρνουμένων τὸ ἐκ τῆς οὐσίας εἶναι
τοῦ Πατρός, τῶν δὲ λεγόντων οὔτε ἐκ τῆς οὐσίας
ἀλλ' ἐξ ἄλλης τινὸς ὑποστάσεως, οὕτως ἀμφότερα,
ὡς ἀλλότρια τοῦ ἐκκλησιαστικοῦ φρονήματος,
ἀπηγόρευσαν. ἐπεὶ ὅπου γε τὸ ἑαυτῶν ἐδήλουν

---

¹ προφασίζεσθαι Coisl. secundus, Reg. secundus.
² ἐξηγούμενος om. E.
³ λέγει Harl.; λέξῃ editi antiqi.
⁴ ἐκεῖνοι editi antiqi.

---

¹ Marcellus of Ancyra was one of the bishops present at
the Councils of Ancyra and Nicaea. He was a strong
opponent of Arianism, but in his zeal to combat Arius
adopted the opposite extreme of modified Sabellianism. He
was several times condemned, dying deprived of his see in
374. Marcellus confused the Personality of God, declaring
that God was originally only one Personality, but at the

the doctrine of truth and stretch the sense of the words in it to suit their own purpose. For instance, even Marcellus,[1] acting impiously toward the person[2] of our Lord Jesus Christ and explaining Him as mere " Word," had the effrontery to profess that he had taken his principles from that creed, perversely explaining the meaning of " consubstantial." And some of those from the impious sect of the Libyan Sabellius,[3] understanding person and substance to be the same, draw from that creed the beginnings they use for the establishment of their own blasphemy, from the fact of its having been written in the creed that " if anyone says the Son is of a different substance or person, the Catholic and Apostolic Church anathematizes him." For it is not said therein that the substance and the person are the same. For if the words revealed one and the same meaning, what was the need of each separately? But it is evident that, since some denied that the Son is of the substance of the Father, and others said that He was not of the substance but of some other person, thus they condemned both positions as foreign to the opinion of the Church. For, when they came

---

creation of the universe the Word or Logos went out from the Father and was God's activity in the world. This Logos became incarnate in Christ and was thus constituted Son of God. The Holy Ghost likewise went forth as the third Divine Personality from the Father and from Christ according to St. John 20, 22. At the consummation of all things, however, Christ and the Holy Ghost will return to the Father, and the Godhead will be again an absolute Unity. Cf. Cath. Eucycl. under Marcellus of Ancyra. Cf. also Jerome, *De Vir. Ill.* 86.

[2] For a definition of the theological terms used in this letter, cf. Letter VIII and note.

[3] For Sabellius, cf. Introduction, Vol. I.

φρόνημα, εἶπον ἐκ τῆς οὐσίας τοῦ Πατρὸς τὸν
Υἱόν, οὐκέτι προσθέντες καὶ τὸ ἐκ τῆς ὑποστάσεως. ὥστε ἐκεῖνο μὲν ἐπ᾽ ἀθετήσει κεῖται τοῦ
πονηροῦ φρονήματος, τοῦτο δὲ φανέρωσιν ἔχει τοῦ
σωτηρίου δόγματος. δεῖ τοίνυν ὁμολογεῖν ὁμοούσιον
τὸν Υἱὸν τῷ Πατρί, καθὼς γέγραπται, ὁμολογεῖν
δὲ ἐν ἰδίᾳ μὲν ὑποστάσει τὸν Πατέρα, ἐν ἰδίᾳ δὲ
τὸν Υἱόν, καὶ ἐν ἰδίᾳ τὸ Πνεῦμα τὸ ἅγιον, καθὰ
καὶ αὐτοὶ σαφῶς ¹ ἐκδεδώκασιν. αὐτάρκως γὰρ
καὶ σαφῶς ² ἐνεδείξαντο εἰπόντες, φῶς ἐκ φωτός,
ὅτι ἕτερον μὲν τὸ γεννῆσαν φῶς, ἕτερον δὲ τὸ
γεννηθέν, φῶς μέντοι καὶ φῶς· ὥστε ἕνα καὶ
τὸν αὐτὸν εἶναι τὸν τῆς οὐσίας λόγον. ἐγκείσθω
δὴ ἡμῖν καὶ αὐτὴ ἡ πίστις ἡ κατὰ Νίκαιαν
συγγραφεῖσα.

Πιστεύομεν εἰς ἕνα Θεὸν Πατέρα ³ παντοκράτορα, πάντων ὁρατῶν τε καὶ ἀοράτων ποιητήν.
καὶ εἰς ἕνα Κύριον ⁴ Ἰησοῦν Χριστὸν τὸν Υἱὸν
τοῦ ⁵ Θεοῦ, γεννηθέντα ἐκ τοῦ Πατρὸς Μονογενῆ,
τουτέστιν, ἐκ τῆς οὐσίας τοῦ Πατρός· Θεὸν ἐκ
Θεοῦ, φῶς ἐκ φωτός, Θεὸν ἀληθινὸν ἐκ Θεοῦ
ἀληθινοῦ· γεννηθέντα, οὐ ποιηθέντα· ὁμοούσιον
τῷ Πατρί, δι᾽ οὗ τὰ πάντα ἐγένετο, τά τε ἐν τῷ
οὐρανῷ καὶ τὰ ⁶ ἐν τῇ γῇ· τὸν δι᾽ ἡμᾶς τοὺς ἀνθρώπους καὶ διὰ τὴν ἡμετέραν σωτηρίαν κατελθόντα,⁷
καὶ σαρκωθέντα, ἐνανθρωπήσαντα, παθόντα, καὶ
ἀναστάντα τῇ τρίτῃ ἡμέρᾳ, ἀνελθόντα εἰς τοὺς ⁸
οὐρανούς, ἐρχόμενον κρῖναι ζῶντας καὶ νεκρούς.
καὶ εἰς τὸ ἅγιον Πνεῦμα. τοὺς δὲ λέγοντας· Ἦν

---

¹ εὐσεβῶς Harl., Regius.
² σοφῶς Harl. secunda manu, editi antiqi.
³ Πατέρα om. E.   ⁴ ἡμῶν add. editi antiqi.

to revealing their opinion, they said that the Son
was of the substance of the Father, not going on
to add "of the person." Thus the former statement
is laid down as a rejection of faulty opinion, while
the latter contains the declaration of the doctrine
of salvation. It is necessary, therefore, to confess
the Son as of the same substance as the Father, as it
is written, and to confess the Father in His own
proper person, and the Son in His own, and the
Holy Ghost in His own, according as the Fathers
themselves have clearly set forth. For sufficiently
and clearly have they shown this when they said,
"Light of Light, the One which begot Light and
the Other which was begotten, and yet Light and
Light," so that the definition of the substance is
one and the same. Now let the creed itself, composed at Nicaea, be added by us.

We believe in one God the Father Almighty,
maker of all things, visible and invisible, and in
one Lord Jesus Christ, the Son of God, born of the
Father, the only Begotten, that is, of the substance
of the Father; God of God, Light of Light, true God
of true God; begotten not made; consubstantial
with the Father, by whom all things were made,
both in heaven and on earth; who for us men and
for our salvation came down and was incarnate, and
was made Man. He suffered and arose on the third
day, and He ascended into heaven and shall come
to judge the living and the dead. And in the Holy
Ghost. And as for such who say " There was a time

---

⁵ τοῦ om. E.   ⁶ καὶ τὰ] τά τε E.
⁷ ἐκ τῶν οὐρανῶν add. editiones Paris. et secunda Basil.
⁸ τούς om. E.

ποτέ, ὅτε οὐκ ἦν, καὶ πρὶν γεννηθῆναι οὐκ ἦν,
καὶ ὅτι ἐξ οὐκ ὄντων ἐγένετο, ἢ ἐξ ἑτέρας
ὑποστάσεως ἢ οὐσίας φάσκοντας εἶναι ἢ τρεπτὸν
ἢ ἀλλοιωτὸν τὸν Υἱὸν τοῦ Θεοῦ, τοὺς τοιούτους
ἀναθεματίζει ἡ καθολικὴ καὶ ἀποστολικὴ Ἐκκλησία.

Ἐπεὶ οὖν ἐνταῦθα τὰ μὲν ἄλλα ἀρκούντως
καὶ ἀκριβῶς διώρισται, τὰ μὲν ἐπὶ διορθώσει
τῶν βλαβέντων, τὰ δὲ εἰς προφυλακὴν τῶν
προσδοκωμένων ὑποφυήσεσθαι· ὁ δὲ περὶ τοῦ
Πνεύματος λόγος ἐν παραδρομῇ κεῖται οὐδεμιᾶς
ἐξεργασίας ἀξιωθεὶς διὰ τὸ μηδέπω τότε τοῦτο
κεκινῆσθαι τὸ ζήτημα, ἀλλ' ἀνεπιβούλευτον
ἐνυπάρχειν¹ ταῖς τῶν πιστευόντων ψυχαῖς τὴν
περὶ αὐτοῦ διάνοιαν· κατὰ μικρὸν δὲ προϊόντα
τὰ πονηρὰ τῆς ἀσεβείας σπέρματα, ἃ πρότερον
μὲν ὑπὸ Ἀρείου τοῦ προστάτου τῆς αἱρέσεως
κατεβλήθη, ὕστερον δὲ ὑπὸ τῶν τὰ ἐκείνου κακῶς
διαδεξαμένων, ἐπὶ λύμῃ τῶν ἐκκλησιῶν ἐξετράφη,
καὶ ἡ ἀκολουθία τῆς ἀσεβείας εἰς τὴν κατὰ τοῦ
Πνεύματος βλασφημίαν ἀπέσκηψεν·² ἀναγκαῖον
πρὸς τοὺς μὴ φειδομένους ἑαυτῶν, μηδὲ προορω-
μένους τὴν ἄφυκτον ἀπειλήν, ἣν τοῖς βλασφη-
μοῦσιν εἰς τὸ Πνεῦμα τὸ ἅγιον ὁ Κύριος ἡμῶν
ἐπανετείνατο,³ ἐκεῖνο προτείνειν, ὅτι χρὴ αὐτοὺς
ἀναθεματίζειν τοὺς λέγοντας κτίσμα τὸ Πνεῦμα
τὸ ἅγιον, καὶ τοὺς νοοῦντας οὕτω, καὶ τοὺς μὴ
ὁμολογοῦντας αὐτὸ φύσει ἅγιον εἶναι, ὡς ἔστι
φύσει ἅγιος ὁ Πατήρ, καὶ φύσει ἅγιος ὁ Υἱός,
ἀλλ' ἀποξενοῦντας⁴ αὐτὸ τῆς θείας καὶ μακαρίας
φύσεως. ἀπόδειξις δὲ τοῦ ὀρθοῦ φρονήματος τὸ

---

¹ ὑπάρχειν E.   ² ἐπέσκηψεν E, Regius.

when He was not," and "Before He was begotten He was not," or that "He came into existence from what was not," or who profess that the Son of God is of a different person or substance, or that He changeth, or is variable, such as these the Catholic and Apostolic Church anathematizes.

Since, therefore, all points with but one exception have been sufficiently and accurately defined herein, some as an emendation for what had been perverted, and others as a precaution against what was expected to arise—for the doctrine of the Holy Ghost was laid down cursorily, not being considered as necessary of elaboration, because at that time this question had not yet been agitated, but the sense of it was unassailably inherent in the souls of the faithful—but since, coming forth little by little, the baneful seeds of impiety, which had been sown before by Arius, the author of the heresy, and later by those who wickedly succeeded to his opinions, have been nurtured to the harm of the churches, and the succession of impiety has broken forth into blasphemy against the Spirit, in view of these things it is necessary to hold before those who have no pity for themselves nor foresee the inevitable threat which our Lord held over those who blaspheme the Holy Ghost, this conclusion—that we must anathematize those who call the Holy Spirit a creature, both those who think so, and those who will not confess that He is holy by nature, even as the Father is holy by nature, and as the Son is holy by nature, but deprive Him of His divine and blessed nature. And the proof of orthodox opinion

---

³ ἐπανετείνετο E.   ¹ ξενοῦντας E.

μὴ χωρίζειν αὐτὸ Πατρὸς καὶ Υἱοῦ (δεῖ γὰρ
ἡμᾶς βαπτίζεσθαι μέν, ὡς παρελάβομεν· πιστεύειν δέ, ὡς βαπτιζόμεθα· δοξάζειν δέ, ὡς
πεπιστεύκαμεν, Πατέρα καὶ Υἱὸν καὶ ἅγιον
Πνεῦμα), ἀφίστασθαι δὲ τῆς κοινωνίας τῶν
κτίσμα λεγόντων, ὡς φανερῶς βλασφημούντων·
ἐκείνου διωμολογημένου (ἀναγκαία γὰρ ἡ ἐπιση-
μείωσις διὰ τοὺς συκοφάντας), ὅτι οὔτε ἀγέννητον
λέγομεν τὸ Πνεῦμα τὸ ἅγιον· ἕνα γὰρ οἴδαμεν
ἀγέννητον καὶ μίαν τῶν ὄντων ἀρχήν, τὸν
Πατέρα τοῦ Κυρίου ἡμῶν Ἰησοῦ Χριστοῦ· οὔτε
γεννητόν· ἕνα γὰρ μονογενῆ ἐν τῇ παραδόσει τῆς
πίστεως δεδιδάγμεθα· τὸ δὲ Πνεῦμα τῆς ἀληθείας
ἐκ τοῦ Πατρὸς ἐκπορεύεσθαι διδαχθέντες, ἐκ τοῦ
Θεοῦ εἶναι ὁμολογοῦμεν ἀκτίστως. ἀναθεματίζειν δὲ καὶ τοὺς λειτουργικὸν λέγοντας τὸ
Πνεῦμα τὸ ἅγιον, ὡς διὰ τῆς φωνῆς ταύτης εἰς
τὴν τοῦ κτίσματος κατάγοντας τάξιν. τὰ γὰρ
λειτουργικὰ πνεύματα κτίσματα ἡμῖν ἡ Γραφὴ
παρέδωκεν, εἰποῦσα, ὅτι Πάντες εἰσὶ λειτουργικὰ
πνεύματα εἰς διακονίαν ἀποστελλόμενα. διὰ δὲ
τοὺς πάντα φύροντας καὶ μὴ φυλάσσοντας τὴν ἐν
τοῖς εὐαγγελίοις διδασκαλίαν, ἀναγκαῖόν ἐστι καὶ
τοῦτο προσδιαστείλασθαι[1] ὅτι φεύγειν δεῖ καὶ
τοὺς τὴν ἀκολουθίαν ἣν παρέδωκεν ἡμῖν ὁ Κύριος
ἐναμείβοντας, ὡς φανερῶς μαχομένους τῇ εὐσεβείᾳ,[2] καὶ Υἱὸν μὲν προτάσσοντας[3] τοῦ Πατρός,
Υἱοῦ δὲ τὸ Πνεῦμα τὸ ἅγιον προτιθέντας.
ἀκίνητον γὰρ καὶ ἀπαρεγχείρητον φυλάσσειν

---

[1] προδιαστείλασθαι E.   [2] ἀληθείᾳ editi antiqi.
[3] προστάσσοντας E.

is not to separate Him from the Father and the Son
(for we must be baptized as we have received the
words of baptism, and we must believe as we are
baptized, and we must give glory as we have believed,
to the Father, the Son, and the Holy Ghost), but to
abstain from communion with those, as open blasphemers, who call Him a creature; since this point
is agreed upon (for comment is necessary because of
the slanders), that we neither speak of the Holy
Spirit as unbegotten—for we recognize One unbegotten and One Beginning of all existing things,
the Father of our Lord Jesus Christ—nor speak of
Him as begotten—for we have been taught One
only begotten in the tradition of our Faith; and
having been taught that the Spirit of Truth proceeds from the Father, we confess it to be from
God without any act of creation. And we must
anathematize also those who speak of the Holy
Ghost as ministering, on the ground that by this
expression they lower Him to the order of creatures.
For Scripture has handed down to us the ministering
spirits as creatures, saying, "All are ministering
spirits sent to minister." [1]   And on account of those
who confuse everything and do not preserve the
teaching of the Gospel, it is necessary to lay down
this principle also—that we must avoid those who
change the order which our Lord had left us, as
being clearly enemies of religion, and place the Son
before the Father and put the Holy Spirit before
the Son.   For it is meet that we keep unaltered

---

[1] Cf. Heb. 1, 14: οὐχὶ πάντες εἰσὶ λειτουργικὰ πνεύματα, εἰς
διακονίαν ἀποστελλόμενα διὰ τοὺς μέλλοντας κληρονομεῖν σωτηρίαν;
"Are they not all ministering spirits, sent to minister for
them who shall receive the inheritance of salvation?"

προσήκει τὴν ἀκολουθίαν, ἣν ἐξ αὐτῆς τοῦ Κυρίου
τῆς φωνῆς παρελάβομεν, εἰπόντος· Πορευθέντες,
μαθητεύσατε πάντα τὰ ἔθνη, βαπτίζοντες αὐτοὺς
εἰς τὸ ὄνομα τοῦ Πατρὸς καὶ τοῦ Υἱοῦ καὶ τοῦ
ἁγίου Πνεύματος.

Ὑπογραφὴ Εὐσταθίου ἐπισκόπου.[1]

Εὐστάθιος ἐπίσκοπος σοὶ Βασιλείῳ ἀναγνοὺς
ἐγνώρισα, καὶ συνήνεσα τοῖς προγεγραμμένοις.
ὑπέγραψα δὲ συμπαρόντων μοι τῶν ἀδελφῶν, τοῦ
ἡμετέρου Φρόντωνος, καὶ τοῦ χωρεπισκόπου
Σεβήρου, καὶ ἄλλων τινῶν κληρικῶν.

CXXVI

Ἀταρβίῳ[2]

Παραγενόμενοι μέχρι τῆς Νικοπόλεως ἐπ'
ἐλπίδι τοῦ καὶ τὰς κινηθείσας ταραχὰς ἐπανορ-
θώσασθαι καὶ τὴν ἐνδεχομένην ἐπαγαγεῖν παραμυθίαν τοῖς ἀτάκτως καὶ παρὰ τὸν ἐκκλησια-
στικὸν θεσμὸν γενομένοις,[3] σφόδρα ἠθυμήσαμεν
μὴ καταλαβόντες σου τὴν χρηστότητα, ἀλλὰ
μαθόντες ἐξεληλακέναι σε πρὸς πᾶσαν ἔπειξιν,[4]
καὶ ταῦτα μεσούσης σχεδὸν τῆς συνόδου τῆς παρ'
ὑμῶν τελουμένης. διὸ ἀναγκαίως ἐπὶ τὸ γράμμα
ἤλθομεν, δι' οὗ ὑπομιμνήσκομεν ἀπαντῆσαι πρὸς

---

[1] Ὑπογραφὴ Εὐσταθίου ἐπισκόπου] καὶ ὑπέγραψεν Εὐστάθιος ὁ
Σεβαστείας ἐπίσκοπος Harl., Regius.
[2] Νικοπόλεως add. Clar. Νεοκαισαρείας add. E, Med.
[3] γεγενημένοις E, Med.   [4] ἐπίδειξιν E.

---

[1] Matt. 28, 19.
[2] Fronto was a priest under the jurisdiction of Theodotus,
Bishop of Nicopolis, to whose see he was elevated after the

and untampered with that order which we received from the very words of Our Lord, when He said, "Going teach ye all nations, baptizing them in the name of the Father, and of the Son, and of the Holy Ghost." [1]

Signature of Eustathius, Bishop.

I, Eustathius, bishop, after reading to you, Basil, have understood, and have approved what has been written above. And I have signed in the presence of my brothers, our Fronto,[2] the suffragan-bishop Severus,[3] and certain other members of the clergy.

LETTER CXXVI

To Atarbius [4]

Arriving at Nicopolis in the hope of setting right the troubles which had been stirred up and of providing all possible relief for what had happened irregularly and contrary to ecclesiastical law, we were greatly disappointed when we did not meet your Goodness, but learned that you had departed in all haste and indeed almost in the middle of the synod which was being held by you. Therefore we must have recourse to writing, through which we bid you

---

latter's death. However, he did not possess Theodotus' firmness of character, for he fell into heresy.

[3] Known only from this passage.

[4] Of the year 373. For Atarbius, Bishop of Neocaesarea, cf. Letter LXV. He was a relative of Basil, and the leader of the Neocaesareans in their revolt against Basil. Cf. Letter CCVII. The present letter is an excellent example of the firm and tactful way in which Basil dealt with such as wandered from the orthodox faith and as even had wronged himself.

ἡμᾶς, ἵνα αὐτὸς διὰ σαυτοῦ παραμυθήσῃ ἡμῶν
τὴν λύπην, ἣν μέχρι θανάτου λελυπήμεθα,
ἀκούσαντες ἐπὶ μέσης τῆς ἐκκλησίας τετολμῆσθαι
πράγματα οὔπω μέχρι τῆς ἡμέρας ταύτης εἰς
ἀκοὴν ἡμετέραν ἐλθόντα. καὶ ταῦτα μὲν εἰ καὶ
λυπηρὰ καὶ βαρέα, ἀλλ᾽ ἔτι φορ· ά, διὰ τὸ εἰς
ἄνθρωπον γεγενῆσθαι, ὃς τὴν ὑπὲρ ὧν πέπονθεν
ἐκδίκησιν τῷ Θεῷ ἐπιτρέψας, ὅλος ἐστὶ τῆς
εἰρήνης καὶ τοῦ μηδὲν παρὰ τὴν αὐτοῦ[1] αἰτίαν
βλαβερὸν γίνεσθαι[2] τῷ λαῷ τοῦ Θεοῦ.

Ἐπειδὴ δέ τινες τῶν τιμίων καὶ πάσης πίστεως
ἀξίων ἀδελφῶν ἀπήγγειλαν ἡμῖν, ὡς περὶ τὴν
πίστιν καινοτομουμένων τινῶν καὶ λαλουμένων
παρὰ σοῦ ὑπεναντίως τῇ ὑγιαινούσῃ διδασκαλίᾳ,
ἐπὶ τούτοις[3] πλέον συγκινηθέντες, καὶ πολὺν
ἀγῶνα ἀγωνιάσαντες τοῦ[4] μὴ πού τι[5] πρὸς τοῖς
μυρίοις τραύμασιν, οἷς πέπονθεν ἡ Ἐκκλησία
παρὰ τῶν εἰς τὴν ἀλήθειαν τοῦ Εὐαγγελίου
ἐξαμαρτόντων,[6] ἔτι καὶ ἄλλο ἀναφυῇ κακόν, ἀνα-
νεωθείσης τῆς παλαιᾶς τοῦ ἐχθροῦ τῆς Ἐκκλησίας Σαβελλίου αἱρέσεως (τούτοις γὰρ οἱ ἀδελφοὶ
ἀπήγγειλαν[7] ἡμῖν συγγενῆ εἶναι τὰ εἰρημένα),
τούτου ἕνεκεν ἐπεστείλαμεν, ἵνα μὴ ὀκνήσῃς
μικρὸν διάστημα κινηθεὶς καταλαβεῖν[8] ἡμᾶς, καὶ
τὴν ἐπὶ τούτοις πληροφορίαν παρασχόμενος, ἡμῶν
τε τὴν ὀδύνην καταπραῦναι, καὶ τὰς[9] τοῦ Θεοῦ
ἐκκλησίας παραμυθήσασθαι, τὰς νῦν ἀφορήτως
καὶ βαρέως ἐπί τε τοῖς πεπραγμένοις καὶ ἐπὶ τοῖς
θρυλλουμένοις εἰρῆσθαι παρὰ σοῦ λυπουμένας.

---

[1] ἑαυτοῦ E.   [2] γενέσθαι E, editi antiqi.
[3] τούτῳ E.   [4] τοῦ om E.
[5] τε editi antiqi.   [6] ἐξαμαρτανόντων Med. et Bigot.

to meet us, that you yourself in person may console
our grief, which has distressed us unto death, for
we heard that in the midst of the Church you dared
a thing which has never before this day come to our
hearing. But even these things, even if they are
painful and severe, are yet endurable, because they
have happened to a man who has entrusted to God
the requital of his sufferings and is wholly desirous
of peace and of having nothing harmful happen,
through any fault of his, to the people of God.

But since some of our honoured brothers who are
worthy of every trust have announced to us that
certain innovations in regard to the faith are being
made by you, and that things are being said by you
contrary to sound teaching, being aroused the more
on this account, and being in great distress lest perchance, in addition to the countless wounds which the
Church has suffered at the hands of those who have
erred against the truth of the Gospel, still another
evil may spring up, if there be a renewal of the
ancient heresy of Sabellius,[1] the enemy of the
Church (for our brothers announced that the words
spoken by you were akin to his), on this account we
have written, that you may not hesitate to rouse
yourself and undertake a short journey to us, and,
by furnishing us full information on these points, to
assuage our grief and to solace the churches of God,
which are now unbearably and seriously grieved at
what has been done and at what is generally
reported to have been said by you.

[1] Vol. I, Introduction.

---

[7] ἀπήγγελον editi antiqi.   [8] παραλαβεῖν E.
        [9] τοῦ add. E.

CXXVII

Εὐσεβίῳ, ἐπισκόπῳ Σαμοσάτων

Ὁ φιλάνθρωπος Θεὸς ὁ συμμέτρους ταῖς
θλίψεσι τὰς παρακλήσεις συνάπτων καὶ παρακαλῶν τοὺς ταπεινούς, ἵνα μὴ λάθωσιν ὑπὸ τῆς
περισσοτέρας λύπης καταποθέντες, ἴσην ταῖς
ἐπιγενομέναις ἡμῖν κατὰ τὴν Νικόπολιν ταραχαῖς
τὴν παραμυθίαν ἐπήγαγε, τὸν θεοφιλέστατον
ἐπίσκοπον Ἰοβῖνον ἐν καιρῷ ἐπιστήσας· ὃς ὅπως
εὐκαίρως ἡμῖν ἐπεφάνη, αὐτὸς διηγησάσθω.
ἡμεῖς γὰρ φειδόμενοι τοῦ μήκους τῆς ἐπιστολῆς
σιωπήσομεν, καὶ ἵνα μὴ δόξωμεν τοὺς ἐκ μετα-
βολῆς ἀγαπητοὺς ἡμῖν γενομένους¹ οἱονεὶ τῇ
ὑπομνήσει τοῦ σφάλματος στηλιτεύειν.

Ἀλλὰ παράσχοι ὁ ἅγιος Θεὸς ἐπιστῆναί σε
τοῖς ἡμετέροις τόποις, ὥστε περιπτύξασθαι μὲν
τὴν σὴν σεμνοπρέπειαν, διηγήσασθαι δὲ τὰ καθ᾽
ἕκαστον. πέφυκε γάρ πως τὰ κατὰ τὴν πεῖραν
λυπήσαντα ψυχαγωγίαν τινὰ² ἔχειν ἐν διηγή-
μασι.³ πλὴν ἀλλ᾽ ὑπὲρ ὧν τελείως μὲν ὡς πρὸς
τὴν εἰς ἡμᾶς ἀγάπην, προηγουμένως δὲ καὶ

---

¹ γινομένοι s E, Med.   ² τινά om. E.
³ πολλήν add. editi antiqi.

---

¹ Written about June 373. All that is definitely known
of Eusebius of Samosata is learned from the letters of St.
Basil the Great and St. Gregory of Nazianzus. He was
instrumental in the consecration of Meletius as Bishop of
Antioch, and was his staunch supporter during the long

LETTER CXXVII

To Eusebius, Bishop of Samosata [1]

Our merciful God, who applies consolations commensurate with our afflictions and consoles the downhearted, lest unaware they be overwhelmed by excessive grief, has brought to us a solace equal to the troubles that befel! us at Nicopolis, having caused the most God-beloved bishop, Jovinus, to come opportunely; and how very opportunely he appeared to us, let him himself tell. For we, to spare a long letter, shall say nothing ourselves, and also that we may not seem to denounce as it were publicly by the mention of their error those who by a change of heart have become dear to us.

But may the holy God grant that you may come to our region, so that I may embrace your August Reverence, and recount to you every particular. For it is natural somehow that matters which have grieved us when we experienced them can afford a certain gratification when we recount them. However, as regards those matters in which our most God-beloved bishop has been active—with complete

years of schism and exile. It was likewise through his efforts that Basil was elevated to the see of Caesarea. This was the beginning of a mutual and unbroken friendship. After Easter in 374, Eusebius was exiled to Thrace. He was recalled in 378, and on his return to Samosata was martyred. Previous letters addressed to him are XXVII, XXX, XXXI, XXXIV, XLVII, XLVIII, XCV, XCVIII, and C.

Shortly after Basil's return from Nicopolis, whither he had gone to investigate the trouble caused by the uncanonical consecration of Faustus, Jovinus paid him a visit and rallied to his support. Jovinus himself is apparently the bearer of this letter, telling the good news to Eusebius.

στιβαρῶς ὡς πρὸς τὴν τῶν κανόνων ἀκρίβειαν ὁ
θεοφιλέστατος ἐπίσκοπος ἐκινήθη, ἐπαίνεσον
αὐτόν, καὶ εὐχαρίστησον τῷ Κυρίῳ, ὅτι τὰ σὰ
θρέμματα πανταχοῦ τὸν χαρακτῆρα τῆς σῆς
σεμνότητος δείκνυσιν.

CXXVIII

Εὐσεβίῳ, ἐπισκόπῳ Σαμοσάτων

Ἐγὼ τὴν περὶ τὸ εἰρηνεύεσθαι τὰς ἐκκλησίας
τοῦ Κυρίου [1] σπουδὴν ἔργῳ μὲν ἐνδείξασθαι ἀξίως
οὔπω δεδύνημαι, ἐν δὲ τῇ καρδίᾳ μου τοσαύτην
ἔχειν ἐπιθυμίαν φημί, ὥστε ἡδέως ἂν καὶ τὴν
ζωὴν τὴν ἐμαυτοῦ προέσθαι ὑπὲρ τοῦ τὴν ὑπὸ
τοῦ πονηροῦ ἐξαφθεῖσαν φλόγα τοῦ μίσους κατα-
σβεσθῆναι. καὶ εἰ μὴ τῆς ἐπιθυμίας ἕνεκεν τῆς
κατὰ τὴν εἰρήνην ἠνεσχόμην ἐγγίσαι τοῖς κατὰ
Κολώνειαν τόποις, μὴ εἰρηνευθείη μοι [2] ἡ ζωή.
εἰρήνην μέντοι τὴν ἀληθινὴν τὴν ὑπ' αὐτοῦ τοῦ
Κυρίου καταλειφθεῖσαν ἡμῖν ἐπιζητῶ· καὶ ὃ
παρεκάλεσά [3] μοι εἰς πληροφορίαν ὑπάρξαι, οὐκ
ἄλλο τι ἐπιθυμοῦντός ἐστιν ἢ τῆς ἀληθινῆς
εἰρήνης, κἂν ἄλλως τινὲς διαστρέφοντες τὴν
ἀλήθειαν ἐξηγῶνται. ἐκεῖνοι μὲν οὖν κεχρήσθω-

---

[1] Θεοῦ quattuor MSS.   [2] μοῦ E.
[3] ὃ παρεκάλεσα] ὅπερ ἐκάλεσα editi antiqi.

---

[1] Written in 373. For Eusebius, see preceding letters.
This letter is Basil's reply to a letter from Eusebius, in
which Eusebius attempted to effect a reconciliation between
Basil and Eustathius of Sebaste. On Eustathius of Sebaste,
see preceding letters.

success as far as his love towards us is concerned, and especially and with great vigour so far as the exact observance of the canons is concerned—give him praise, and thank the Lord, that your disciples everywhere display the character of your Holiness.

LETTER CXXVIII

To Eusebius, Bishop of Samosata [1]

I HAVE not yet been able in a worthy manner to give practical proof of my zeal for establishing peace among the churches of the Lord, but in my heart I cherish, I affirm, so great a desire that I would gladly even lay down my life to extinguish this flame of hatred that has been stirred up by the evil one. And if it was not on account of this desire of peace that I consented to visit the region of Colonia,[2] may my life enjoy no peace. But it is the true peace left us by the Lord Himself that I am seeking ; and what I demanded should be put into my hands as a guarantee,[3] is the act of one who desires nothing other than the true peace, even though certain persons[4] distort the truth and

[2] Letters CCXXVII and CCXXVIII are addressed to the clergy and magistrates of Colonia in Armenia. This was probably the place at which, in the presence of Basil and others, Eustathius was to subscribe to the Creed as defined in Letter CXXV.

[3] *i.e.* of the orthodoxy of Eustathius of Sebaste.

[4] Probably the two monks, Basil and Euphronius, who had been recommended to St. Basil's service by Eustathius, and who had busied themselves spreading calumnies about St. Basil. Cf. Letter CXIX.

σαν ταῖς γλώσσαις αὐτῶν ἐφ' ἃ βούλονται·
πάντως γὰρ αὐτοῖς ποτὲ τῶν ῥημάτων τούτων
μεταμελήσει.

Τὴν δὲ σὴν ὁσιότητα παρακαλῶ μεμνῆσθαι τῶν
ἐξ ἀρχῆς προτάσεων, καὶ μὴ παράγεσθαι ἄλλας
ἀποκρίσεις ἀντ' ἄλλων ἐρωτημάτων δεχόμενον,[1]
μηδὲ ποιεῖν ἐνεργὰ τὰ σοφίσματα τῶν ἄνευ τῆς
περὶ τὸ λέγειν δυνάμεως ἀπ' αὐτῆς μόνης τῆς
γνώμης δεινότατα πάντων τὴν ἀλήθειαν κακουρ-
γούντων. προέτεινα γὰρ ἁπλᾶ καὶ σαφῆ καὶ
εὐμνημόνευτα ῥήματα· εἰ τοὺς μὴ δεχομένους τὴν
ἐν Νικαίᾳ πίστιν παραιτούμεθα εἰς κοινωνίαν,
καὶ εἰ μετὰ τῶν κτίσμα λέγειν τὸ Πνεῦμα τὸ
ἅγιον ἀποτολμώντων τὸ μέρος ἔχειν οὐκ ἀνεχόμεθα. ὁ δέ,[2] ἀντὶ τοῦ πρὸς ἔπος ταῖς ἐρωτήσε-
σιν ἀποκρίνασθαι, ἐκεῖνα ἡμῖν ἐρραψῴδησεν
ἅπερ ἀπέστειλας· καὶ τοῦτο οὐκ ἀφελείᾳ[3] γνώμης,
ὡς ἄν τῳ δόξαι,[4] οὐδὲ τῷ μὴ δύνασθαι συνορᾶν τὸ
ἀκόλουθον. ἀλλ' ἐκεῖνο λογίζεται, ὅτι ἀρνούμενος
μὲν ἡμῶν τὴν πρότασιν, τοῖς λαοῖς ἑαυτὸν κατάδηλον ποιήσει, συντιθέμενος δὲ ἡμῖν, τῆς μεσότητος
ἀποστήσεται, ἧς οὐδὲν αὐτῷ μέχρι τοῦ νῦν γέγονε
προτιμότερον. μὴ τοίνυν ἡμᾶς κατασοφιζέσθω,
μηδὲ μετὰ τῶν ἄλλων καὶ τὴν σὴν παρακρουέσθω
φρόνησιν· ἀλλὰ σύντομον ἡμῖν λόγον ἀποστει-
λάτω πρὸς τὸ ἐρώτημα, ἢ ὁμολογῶν τὴν κοινωνίαν
πρὸς τοὺς ἐχθροὺς τῆς πίστεως, ἢ ἀρνούμενος.
ἐὰν ταῦτα συμπείσῃς αὐτὸν καὶ πέμψῃς μοι
ὀρθὰς καὶ οἵας εὔχομαι τὰς ἀποκρίσεις, ἐγώ εἰμι

[1] δεχομένην editi antiqi. [2] ὁ δέ] οὐδέ E.
[3] ἀφελείᾳ E.
[4] ἄν τῳ δόξαι] αὐτῷ δόξαι E, editi antiqi.

278

interpret it otherwise. So let them employ their tongues as they will, for assuredly they will some day regret such words.

But I urge your Holiness [1] to be mindful of the primary propositions, and not to be led astray by accepting answers which do not correspond to the questions, and not to render effective the quibbles of men who, lacking all ability to speak on the strength of their mere opinions, corrupt the truth most dreadfully of all men. For I set forth propositions in terms which were simple, clear, and easily remembered : — whether we shall forbid the admission to our communion of those who do not accept the Nicaean Creed, and whether we shall refuse to have any participation with those who dare to call the Holy Spirit a creature. But he, instead of answering my questions word for word, recited the very same statements that you have written us ; and this he did with no simplicity of mind, as one might think, nor through any inability to realize the outcome. On the contrary, he has this in mind,—that if he denies our proposition, he will make his true self clear to the people, but that if he agrees with us, he will be withdrawing from the middle course, which has thus far been decidedly preferable to him. So do not let him outwit us. and do not let him deceive your wisdom as he has done with the rest ; but let him send us a succinct answer to the question, either confessing communion with the enemies of the faith or denying it. If you win him over to this and the answers you send me are direct and such as I pray for, I am the one who

---

[1] A title given in Byzantine times to bishops and monks, and sometimes to emperors.

ὁ τὰ κατόπιν πάντα ἡμαρτηκώς· ἐγὼ δέχομα
πᾶσαν τὴν αἰτίαν ἐκείνην ἐπ' ἐμαυτόν· τότε με
ἀπαίτει ταπεινοφροσύνης ἐπίδειξιν. ἕως δ' ἂν
μηδὲν γένηται τούτων, σύγγνωθι, θεοφιλέστατε
πάτερ, μὴ δυναμένῳ μετὰ ὑποκρίσεως θυσια-
στηρίῳ Θεοῦ παρεστάναι.[1] εἰ γὰρ μὴ τοῦτο
ἐφοβούμην, τίνος ἕνεκεν ἐμαυτὸν ἐχώριζον Εὐϊππίου, τοιούτου μὲν τὰ περὶ λόγους, τοσοῦτον δὲ
χρόνῳ[2] προήκοντος, τοσαῦτα δὲ τῆς πρὸς ἡμᾶς
φιλίας δίκαια κεκτημένου ; εἰ δὲ ἐκεῖνα καλῶς καὶ
προσηκόντως ὑπὲρ τῆς ἀληθείας ἐπράξαμεν, γελοῖον δή που τοῖς τὰ αὐτὰ ἐκείνῳ λέγουσι διὰ
τῆς τῶν εὐφυῶν τούτων καὶ χαριέντων μεσότητος
συναπτόμενον φαίνεσθαι.

Οὐ μὴν οὐδὲ παντελῶς μοι δοκεῖ τῶν μὴ δεχο-
μένων τὴν πίστιν ἀλλοτριοῦν ἑαυτούς, ἀλλὰ
ποιήσασθαί τινα τῶν ἀνδρῶν ἐπιμέλειαν κατὰ
τοὺς παλαιοὺς θεσμοὺς τῆς ἀγάπης, καὶ ἐπιστεῖλαι αὐτοῖς ἀπὸ μιᾶς γνώμης, πᾶσαν παράκλησιν μετ' εὐσπλαγχνίας προσάγοντας, καὶ τὴν
τῶν πατέρων πίστιν προτεινομένους προκαλεῖσθαι
αὐτοὺς εἰς συνάφειαν· κἂν μὲν πείσωμεν, κοινῶς
αὐτοῖς ἑνωθῆναι· ἐὰν δὲ ἀποτύχωμεν, ἀρκεῖσθαι
ἡμᾶς ἀλλήλοις, τὸν δὲ ἐπαμφοτερισμὸν τοῦτον
ἐξορίσαι τοῦ ἤθους, ἀναλαβόντας τὴν εὐαγγε-
λικὴν καὶ ἄδολον πολιτείαν, ᾗ συνέζων οἱ ἐξ

----

[1] παριστάναι editi antiqi.   [2] χρόνον editi antiqi.

----

[1] The superlative form of this adjective was used in
Christian times as a title applied to bishops, monks,
deacons, and emperors.

have been utterly at fault in the past; I take all
the blame upon myself; then you may demand of
me a proof of humility. But as long as none of
these things comes to pass, forgive me, most god-
beloved [1] father, if I cannot as a hypocrite stand at
God's altar. For if it were not for my fear of
hypocrisy, why did I separate myself from Euippius,[2]
so eminent in letters, so advanced in years, possessing so many claims to friendship with us? And if
on that occasion we acted nobly and properly in
support of the truth, surely it would be ridiculous
for me to appear to be united with those who,
through the mediation of these clever and charming
persons, make the same assertions as he made.

And yet it does not seem best to me to estrange
ourselves entirely from those who do not accept the
faith, but we should show some concern for these
men according to the old laws of charity and should
with one accord write letters to them, offering every
exhortation with kindliness, and proffering to them
the faith of the Fathers we should invite them to
join us; and if we convince them, we should be
united with them in communion; but if we fail, we
should ourselves be content with one another, and
should remove this present uncertainty from our
way of life, taking up again that evangelical and
guileless polity in which they lived who from the

---

[2] Euippius: a bishop of Arianizing doctrines, from whom
Basil felt it necessary for the cause of truth to separate
altogether. Cf. Letter LVI. Eustathius of Sebaste, in
A.D. 360, violently declaimed against Euippius as not deserving the name of bishop, but in A.D. 376, Eustathius
united with him and recognized the bishops and presbyters
he had ordained. Cf. Letters CCXXVI, CCXXXIX,
CCXLIV, CCLI.

ἀρχῆς προσελθόντες τῷ λόγῳ. ἦν γάρ, φησί,
τῶν πιστευσάντων καρδία καὶ ψυχὴ μία. ἐὰν
μὲν οὖν πεισθῶσί σοι, ταῦτα ἄριστα. εἰ δὲ μή,
γνωρίσατε τοὺς πολεμοποιούς, καὶ παύσασθε
ἡμῖν τοῦ λοιποῦ περὶ διαλλαγῶν ἐπιστέλλοντες.

CXXIX

Μελετίῳ, ἐπισκόπῳ Ἀντιοχείας

Ἤιδειν ὅτι ξενίσει τὴν ἀκοὴν τῆς τελειότητός
σου τὸ νῦν ἐπιφυὲν ἔγκλημα τῷ πάντα εἰπεῖν
εὐκόλῳ Ἀπολιναρίῳ. καὶ γὰρ οὐδὲ αὐτὸς τὸν
πρὸ τούτου χρόνον ἤμην ἐπιστάμενος ἔχειν·
ἀλλὰ νῦν οἱ Σεβαστηνοὶ διερευνησάμενοί ποθεν
αὐτὰ εἰς τὸ μέσον ἤνεγκαν, καὶ περιφέρουσι
σύνταγμα, ἐξ οὗ μάλιστα καὶ ἡμᾶς καταδικά-
ζουσιν, ὡς τὰ αὐτὰ φρονοῦντας, ἔχον ῥήσεις

---

[1] Cf. Acts, 4, 32: τοῦ δὲ πλήθους τῶν πιστευσάντων ἦν ἡ
καρδία καὶ ἡ ψυχὴ μία. "And the multitude of believers had
but one heart and one soul."

[2] The Benedictine edition has assigned the composition of
this letter to A.D. 373. Loofs presents rather unconvincing
arguments for both this letter and the following (CXXX)
being written in the summer of 375.

The addressee of this letter, St. Meletius, Bishop of
Antioch, was born in Melitene, Lesser Armenia, and died at
Antioch in 381. He apparently believed that truth lay in
delicate distinctions, but his formula was so indefinite that it
is difficult even to-day to grasp it clearly. He was neither a
thorough Nicene nor a decided Arian, and he passed alter-
nately as an Anomean, a Homoiousian, a Homoian, or a
Neo-Nicene, seeking always to remain outside any inflexible
classification. After his death his name long remained for the

beginning adhered to the Word.[1] "For," he says, "the believers had but one heart and one soul." If, then, they obey you, that will be best. But if not, recognize the instigators of the trouble, and henceforth cease writing to me about a reconciliation.

LETTER CXXIX

To Meletius, Bishop of Antioch [2]

I KNEW that the charge which has now sprung up against Apollinaris,[3] that man who is so ready to say anything, would surprise the ears of your Perfection.[4] For in fact not even I myself was aware until the present time that the situation was as it is ; but now the Sebastenes, having sought out these matters from some source, have brought them before the public, and they are circulating a document from which they bring accusations chiefly against us as well, on the ground that we hold the same views as those expressed in the document. It contains such

---

Eastern faithful a rallying sign and a synonym of orthodoxy.

Basil here writes to refute the charges made against him of teaching heresy, and he names Apollinaris as the real author of the heretical document used as evidence. He considers other matters also, including the action taken upon his case at the court.

[3] Apollinaris ('Απολινάριος) the Younger, Bishop of Laodicea, flourished during the first half of the fourth century. He was highly esteemed by Basil, it seems, until the year 376. He taught that Christ had a human body and a human sensitive soul, but no rational mind, the Divine Logos taking the place of this last.

[4] Byzantine title.

τοιαύτας· ὥστε πανταχῇ συνεζευγμένως, μᾶλλον
δὲ ἡνωμένως τῇ ἑτερότητι νοεῖν ἀναγκαῖον τὴν
πρώτην ταυτότητα, καὶ δευτέραν καὶ τρίτην
λέγοντας τὴν αὐτήν. ὅπερ γάρ ἐστι πρώτως ὁ
Πατήρ, τοῦτό ἐστι δευτέρως ὁ Υἱός, καὶ τρίτως
τὸ Πνεῦμα. αὖθις δὲ ὅπερ ἐστὶ πρώτως τὸ
Πνεῦμα τοῦτο δευτέρως τὸν Υἱόν, καθὸ δὴ καὶ ὁ
Κύριός ἐστι τὸ Πνεῦμα· καὶ τρίτως τὸν Πατέρα
καθὸ δὴ Πνεῦμα ὁ Θεός. καὶ ὡς βιαιότερον
σημᾶναι[1] τὸ ἄρρητον, τὸν Πατέρα πατρικῶς Υἱὸν
εἶναι, τὸν δὲ Υἱὸν υἱικῶς Πατέρα. καὶ ὡσαύτως
ἐπὶ τοῦ Πνεύματος, καθὸ δὴ εἷς Θεὸς ἡ Τριάς.

Ταῦτά ἐστι τὰ θρυλλούμενα, ἃ οὐδέποτε
δύναμαι πιστεῦσαι πλάσματα εἶναι τῶν περι-
φερόντων,[2] εἰ καὶ ὅτι ἐκ τῆς καθ᾽ ἡμῶν[3] συκοφαντίας οὐδὲν λογίζομαι αὐτοῖς ἀτόλμητον εἶναι.
γράφοντες γάρ τισι τῶν καθ᾽ ἑαυτούς, καὶ προσθέντες[4] τὴν καθ᾽ ἡμῶν διαβολήν, ἐπήγαγον
ταῦτα, ῥήματα μὲν αἱρετικῶν ὀνομάσαντες,[5] τὸν
δὲ πατέρα τῆς συγγραφῆς ἀποκρυψάμενοι, ἵνα
τοῖς πολλοῖς ἡμεῖς νομισθῶμεν εἶναι οἱ λογο-
γράφοι.[6] πλὴν ἀλλ᾽ οὐκ ἂν μέχρι τοῦ καὶ[7]
ῥήματα συνθεῖναι προῆλθεν αὐτῶν ἡ ἐπίνοια, ὥς
γε ἐμαυτὸν πείθω. ὅθεν, ὑπὲρ τοῦ καὶ τὴν καθ᾽
ἡμῶν κρατοῦσαν βλασφημίαν ἀπώσασθαι, καὶ
δεῖξαι πᾶσιν, ὡς οὐδὲν ἡμῖν ἐστὶ[8] κοινὸν πρὸς
τοὺς ἐκεῖνο λέγοντας, ἠναγκάσθημεν μνησθῆναι

---

[1] σημαίνει E.
[2] προφερόντων editi antiqi.
[3] ἡμᾶς E, Regius primus.
[4] προθέντες Coisl. secundus, Reg. secundus.
[5] ὀνομάζοντες editi antiqi.

statements as these : " Consequently it is necessary to conceive of the first identity in every case conjointly, or rather unitedly with the dissimilarity, saying that the second and the third are the same. For what the Father is first, the Son is secondly, and the Spirit thirdly. And again, what is first the Spirit, this is secondly the Son—inasmuch as the Lord is the Spirit—and thirdly the Father—inasmuch as the Spirit is God." And in order to express this unspeakable thought more forcefully : " That the Father is paternally the Son, and the Son is filially the Father. And in like manner with the Holy Ghost, inasmuch as the Trinity is one God."

These are the things that are being noised about, but I can never believe that these are fabrications of those who are spreading them abroad, although, on account of their slanderous charges against us, I consider that nothing is beyond the limits of their effrontery. For when writing to some of their own adherents, and after making this false accusation against us, they added the words mentioned above, calling them the expressions of heretics, but concealing the name of the father of the document, in order that to people at large we might be considered the author. However, their intelligence could not have carried them to the point of actually composing these statements, as I am convinced. Hence, for the sake of repudiating the charge of blasphemy that is prevalent against us, and of showing to all that we have nothing in common with those who say such things, we have been forced to mention this

---

[6] ὀλιγογράφοι E.   [7] μέχρι τοῦ καὶ] τοῦ μέχρι E.
[8] ἐστί om. E.

τοῦ ἀνδρός, ὡς προσεγγίζοντος τῇ ἀσεβείᾳ τοῦ
Σαβελλίου. καὶ ταῦτα μὲν εἰς τοσοῦτον.

Ἀπὸ δὲ τοῦ στρατοπέδου ἧκέ τις ἀγγέλλων,
ἐπὶ τῇ πρώτῃ κινήσει τοῦ κρατοῦντος, ἣν ἐκίνη-
σαν αὐτὸν οἱ τὰς διαβολὰς ἡμῶν¹ καταχέοντες,
γεγενῆσθαί τινα καὶ δευτέραν γνώμην, ὥστε μὴ
δοθῆναι ἡμᾶς ἐκδότους τοῖς κατηγόροις, μήτε
παραδοθῆναι ἡμᾶς τῷ ἐκείνων θελήματι, ὅπερ ἦν
ἐξ ἀρχῆς ὁρισθέν· ἀλλά τινα γενέσθαι τέως
ἀναβολήν. ἐὰν οὖν ἢ ταῦτα μένῃ, ἢ τούτων
τι δόξῃ φιλανθρωπότερον, σημανοῦμέν σου τῇ
θεοσεβείᾳ. ἐὰν δὲ κρατῇ τὰ πρότερα, οὐδὲ τοῦτό
σε λήσεται.

Ὁ μέντοι ἀδελφὸς Σαγκτίσσιμος πάντως ἐστὶ
παρ' ὑμῖν πάλαι, καὶ ἃ ἐπιζητεῖ δῆλα γέγονε τῇ
τελειότητί σου. εἰ οὖν φαίνεται ἀναγκαῖόν τι
ἔχειν ἡ πρὸς τοὺς δυτικοὺς ἐπιστολή, καταξίωσον
τυπώσας αὐτὴν διαπέμψασθαι² ἡμῖν, ὥστε
ποιῆσαι ὑπογραφῆναι παρὰ τῶν ὁμοψύχων καὶ
ἑτοίμην ἔχειν τὴν ὑπογραφήν, ἐν χάρτῃ κεχωρισ-
μένῳ ἐντετυπωμένην,³ ὃν δυνάμεθα συνάψαι τῷ
παρὰ τοῦ ἀδελφοῦ ἡμῶν τοῦ συμπρεσβυτέρου

---

¹ ἡμῖν editi antiqi.
² καταξίωσον . . . διαπέμψασθαι] καταξίαν . . . διαπέμψαι
editi antiqi.
³ ἐντετυπωμένην om. E.

---

¹ i.e. Apollinaris.
² Sabellius affirmed that there exists in God only a single
person, and that this unity or monad (μονάς) constitutes the
absolute being of God. When the divine essence departed
from its quiet and inactivity, manifesting itself and acting,

man's name [1] as one who is approaching the impiety of Sabellius.[2] But let so much suffice on this matter.

But a messenger has come from the court, saying that after the first excitement of the Emperor, to which he was impelled by those who were pouring out their slanders against us, a second resolution was determined upon—that we should not be surrendered to our accusers, nor should we be placed at the mercy of their will, as was decreed in the first place ; but that up to the present there has been delay. Therefore, if these matters remain as they are, or if some more kindly action is decided on, we shall inform your Godliness.[3] And if the former course prevail, this also will not be concealed from you.

But our brother Sanctissimus, at all events, has been with you for a long time, and your Perfection has become fully aware of what he has in mind. So, if the letter to the people of the West appears to contain anything that is important for us, be pleased to draft it and send it to us, in order that we may get it subscribed to by those of the same mind as ourselves, and that we may have the subscription ready, written upon a separate sheet of paper, which we can fasten to the sheet which is being carried around to us by our brother the pres-

---

it was called the Word (λόγος). It is the Word which created the world ; and again it is the Word which undertook the salvation of humanity. For this work it took three successive modes of existence : three aspects (πρόσωπα), three denominations (ὀνόματα), corresponding to the three economies which succeed each other in the order of salvation : Father, Son, and Holy Ghost. But these three modes of existence are transitory and accidental. Each of them is to cease at the same time as the object which necessitates each.

[3] A title usually given to the bishops in Byzantine times.

περικομιζομένῳ.[1] ἐγὼ μὲν γὰρ οὐδὲν εὑρὼν[2] συνεκτικὸν ἐν τῷ ὑπομνηστικῷ, οὐκ ἔσχον ὑπὲρ οὗ ἐπιστείλω τοῖς ἐν τῇ δύσει. τὰ μὲν γὰρ ἀναγκαῖα προείληπται· τὰ δὲ περιττὰ γράφειν παντελῶς μάταιον. περὶ δὲ τῶν αὐτῶν ἐνοχλεῖν μὴ καὶ γελοῖον εἴη ;

Ἐκείνη δέ μοι ἔδοξεν ὥσπερ ἀγύμναστος εἶναι ἡ ὑπόθεσις καὶ χώραν παρέχειν γράμμασι,[3] τὸ παρακαλέσαι αὐτοὺς μὴ ἀκρίτως δέχεσθαι τὰς κοινωνίας τῶν ἐκ τῆς ἀνατολῆς ἀφικνουμένων, ἀλλ᾽ ἅπαξ μίαν μερίδα ἐκλεξαμένους, τοὺς λοιποὺς ἐκ τῆς μαρτυρίας τῶν κοινωνικῶν προσλαμβάνεσθαι· καὶ μὴ παντὶ τῷ πίστιν γράφοντι ἐπὶ προφάσει δὴ τῆς ὀρθοδοξίας προστίθεσθαι. οὕτω γὰρ εὑρεθήσονται τοῖς μαχομένοις κοινωνοῦντες, οἳ τὰ μὲν ῥήματα πολλάκις τὰ αὐτὰ προβάλλονται, μάχονται δὲ ἀλλήλοις ὅσον οἱ πλεῖστον διεστηκότες. ἵν᾽ οὖν μὴ ἐπὶ πλεῖον ἡ αἵρεσις ἐξάπτηται[4] τῶν πρὸς ἀλλήλους διαστασιαζόντων ἀντιπροβαλλομένων τὰ παρ᾽ αὐτῶν γράμματα, παρακληθῆναι αὐτοὺς ἔδει κεκριμένας ποιεῖσθαι καὶ τὰς τῶν ἐντυγχανόντων αὐτοῖς κοινωνίας καὶ τὰς ἐγγράφως γινομένας κατὰ τὸν τύπον τῆς Ἐκκλησίας.

---

[1] κομιζομένου E.
[2] οὐδὲν εὑρὼν] οὐδὲν εὗρον Harl. ; οὐχ εὑρών editi antiqi.
[3] γράμματι editi antiqi.

byter. For since I found in the memorandum nothing especially important, I had no grounds for writing to those in the West. For those things which were necessary have been anticipated; and to write what is superfluous is wholly vain. And would it not even be ridiculous to trouble them about the same matters?

But the following subject seemed to me to be as it were undeveloped and to offer grounds for writing —the matter of urging them not to receive indiscriminately the communion of those coming from the East, but after once choosing a single portion of them, to accept the rest on the testimony of these already in communion; and of urging them not to take into communion everyone who writes down the Creed as a supposed proof of orthodoxy. For thus they will find themselves to be in communion with men prone to fight, who often put forward statements of doctrine which are identical, but then proceed to fight with one another as violently as the men who are of diametrically opposite opinions. In order, then, that heresy may not flame out still more on the part of those who in their conflict with one another bring forward their opposing formulae, the people of the West ought to be urged to exercise discrimination as regards both communion with those who come to them by chance and communion based upon a written document according to the law of the Church.[1]

[1] From this passage and from Letter CCXXIV the Benedictine editors perceive two kinds of communion: (1) personal, in the Eucharist and prayer, and (2) by letter.

---

[4] ἐξαπατῆται editi antiqi.

CXXX

Θεοδότῳ, ἐπισκόπῳ Νικοπόλεως

Καλῶς καὶ προσηκόντως ἡμῶν καθήψω, τιμιώτατε ὡς ἀληθῶς καὶ ποθεινότατε ἀδελφέ, ὅτι ἐξ
οὗ ἀνεχωρήσαμεν τότε τῆς σῆς εὐλαβείας τὰς
περὶ τῆς πίστεως ἐκείνας προτάσεις τῷ Εὐσταθίῳ
φέροντες, οὐδέν σοι οὔτε μικρὸν οὔτε μεῖζον τῶν
κατ᾿ αὐτὸν ἐδηλώσαμεν. ἐγὼ δὲ οὐχ ὡς εὐκατα-
φρονήτων¹ τῶν παρ᾿ αὐτοῦ γενομένων εἰς ἡμᾶς
ὑπερεῖδον, ἀλλ᾿ ὡς εἰς πάντας λοιπὸν τοὺς ἀνθρώπους διαβοηθείσης τῆς φήμης, καὶ οὐδενὸς τῆς
παρ᾿ ἡμῶν διδασκαλίας εἰς τὸ τὴν προαίρεσιν τοῦ
ἀνδρὸς διδαχθῆναι προσδεομένου. τοῦτο γὰρ καὶ
αὐτὸς ἐπενόησεν, ὥσπερ φοβούμενος μὴ ὀλίγους
σχῇ τῆς ἑαυτοῦ γνώμης μάρτυρας, εἰς πᾶσαν
ἐσχατιὰν τὰς ἐπιστολὰς ἃς καθ᾿ ἡμῶν συνέγραψε
διαπεμψάμενος. τῆς μὲν οὖν κοινωνίας ἡμῶν
αὐτὸς ἀπέρρηξεν ἑαυτόν, μήτε κατὰ τὸν ὡρισ-
μένον τόπον συνδραμεῖν ἡμῖν ἀνασχόμενος, μήτε
τοὺς μαθητὰς ἑαυτοῦ παραγαγών, ὅπερ ὑπέσχετο·
ἀλλὰ καὶ ἡμᾶς στηλιτεύων ἐν πανδήμοις συνό-

¹ καταφρονήτων editi antiqi.

---

¹ For the date of this letter, see note 1 of the preceding
letter. Theodotus, Bishop of Nicopolis, a staunch friend of
Basil, died in A.D. 375. He is mentioned in Letters XCII,
XCV, XCIX, CXXI, CCXXIX, and CCXXXVII.

LETTER CXXX

To Theodotus, Bishop of Nicopolis[1]

Nobly and fittingly have you upbraided us, most honoured in very truth and beloved brother, because, since the time when we departed from your Reverence, bringing those propositions concerning the Faith to Eustathius,[2] we have informed you of nothing either small or great in regard to his affairs. But as for me, it was not because I regarded as contemptible the charges which have been instigated by him against us that I have overlooked the matter, but because the report has now been noised abroad to the whole world, and because nobody needs any instruction from us as regards the purposes of this man. For he contrived this result himself—as if he were afraid that he would have but a few witnesses of his opinion—by sending to most distant parts the letters which he wrote against us. He of his own accord has thus severed himself from communion with us, for he did not fulfil his intention of meeting us at the appointed place, nor did he bring his disciples as he had promised; but he denounced us in the general synods,

---

[2] Eustathius of Sebaste, 300–377. He was bishop of Sebaste in 356, and was one of the founders of monasticism. He had studied under Arius, and wavered between semi-Arianism throughout his life. He was a close friend of Basil until the latter recognized his true character in 372 or 373. He had once signed the Nicene Creed, for he together with Theophilus and Silvanus went on a mission to Rome in 365–6, and acknowledged their adherence to the Nicene Creed before Pope Liberius. Cf. Letter CCXLV. He seems to have been a vacillating character, and it is said that he signed practically all the creeds of his age.

δοις, μετὰ τοῦ Κίλικος Θεοφίλου, γυμνῇ καὶ
ἀπαρακαλύπτῳ τῇ βλασφημίᾳ ὡς ἀλλότρια τῆς
ἑαυτοῦ[1] διδασκαλίας ταῖς ψυχαῖς τοῦ λαοῦ
ἐνσπείραντας δόγματα. ἱκανὰ μὲν οὖν ἦν καὶ
ταῦτα πᾶσαν ἡμῶν τὴν πρὸς αὐτὸν συνάφειαν
διαλῦσαι. ἐπειδὴ δὲ καὶ εἰς Κιλικίαν ἐλθών, καὶ
συντυχὼν Γελασίῳ τινί, πίστιν αὐτῷ ἐξέθετο, ἣν
μόνου[2] ἦν Ἀρείου συγγράψαι καὶ εἴ τις αὐτοῦ
γνήσιος μαθητής, τότε δὴ καὶ πλέον πρὸς τὸν
χωρισμὸν ἐβεβαιώθημεν, λογισάμενοι, ὅτι οὔτε
Αἰθίοψ ἀλλάξει ποτὲ τὸ δέρμα αὐτοῦ, οὔτε
πάρδαλις τὰ ποικίλματα αὐτῆς, οὔτε ὁ ἐν διαστρό-
φοις δόγμασι συντραφεὶς ἀποτρίψασθαι δύναται
τὸ κακὸν τῆς αἱρέσεως.

Ἐπενεανιεύσατο δὲ τούτοις καὶ γράψας καθ᾽
ἡμῶν, μᾶλλον δὲ συγγράψας λόγους μακροὺς
πάσης λοιδορίας καὶ συκοφαντίας γέμοντας· ὑπὲρ
ὧν οὐδὲν ἀπεκρινάμεθα τέως, διὰ τὸ διδαχθῆναι
παρὰ τοῦ ἀποστόλου, μὴ ἑαυτοὺς ἐκδικεῖν, ἀλλὰ
διδόναι τόπον τῇ ὀργῇ· καὶ ἅμα ἐννοήσαντες τὸ
βάθος τῆς ὑποκρίσεως, μεθ᾽ ἧς πάντα τὸν χρόνον
ἡμῖν προσηνέχθη, ἀφασίᾳ τινὶ ὑπ᾽ ἐκπλήξεως
κατεσχέθημεν.

Εἰ δὲ καὶ μηδὲν ἦν ἐκείνων, τὸ ὑπόγυον τοῦτο,
τὸ τολμηθὲν αὐτῷ, τίνι οὐκ ἂν φρίκην καὶ

---

[1] αὐτοῦ editi antiqi.   [2] μόνον editi antiqi.

---

[1] Theophilus was bishop of Castabala (also called Hiero-
polis) on the river Pyramis in Cilicia, whither he was trans-
lated from Eleutheropolis. Cf. Letters CCXLIV. and
CCXLV. He was on friendly terms with St. Basil at one
time, and was sent to Rome on an embassy. See note
above.

he along with the Cilician Theophilus,[1] saying
with bare and undisguised slander that we were
sowing a different doctrine from his in the souls
of the people. Accordingly, these circumstances
sufficed for our severing all connexions with him.
And when, having come into Cilicia and having met
there a certain Gelasius,[2] he set forth his creed to
him, a creed to which only an Arius could subscribe
or a real disciple of Arius, then in truth were we
more strongly confirmed in our separation from him,
considering that neither will an Ethiopian ever
change his skin, nor a leopard her spots,[3] nor is a
man who has been nourished on perverted doctrines
able to rid himself of the evil of heresy.

He has added to these acts of effrontery by
writing against us, or rather by composing long
tracts filled with every abuse and calumny; regarding which we have hitherto made no reply, because
we have been taught by the apostle not to avenge
ourselves, but to give place unto wrath;[4] and,
moreover, having considered the depth of the
hypocrisy which has characterized his dealings with
us at all times, we have been seized with a sort of
speechlessness through astonishment.

But even if none of these things had been, in whom
would not this last piece of audacity on his part

[2] This Gelasius is otherwise unknown.
[3] Cf. Jer. 13, 23: εἰ ἀλλάξεται Αἰθίοψ τὸ δέρμα αὐτοῦ καὶ
πάρδαλις τὰ ποικίλματα αὐτῆς; καὶ ὑμεῖς δυνήσεσθε εὖ ποιῆσαι
μεμαθηκότες τὰ κακά. "If the Ethiopian can change his skin,
or the leopard his spots : you also may do well, when you
have learned evil."
[4] Cf. Rom. 12, 19: μὴ ἑαυτοὺς ἐκδικοῦντες, ἀγαπητοί, ἀλλὰ
δότε τόπον τῇ ὀργῇ. "Revenge not yourselves, my dearly
beloved ; but give place unto wrath."

ἀποστροφὴν παντελῆ τοῦ ἀνδρὸς ἐνεποίησεν·
ὅς γε, ὡς ἀκούω (εἴ γε ἀληθὴς ὁ λόγος καὶ μὴ
πλάσμα ἐστὶν ἐπὶ διαβολῇ συντεθέν), ὅτι καὶ
ἀναχειροτονῆσαί τινας ἐτόλμησεν, ὃ μέχρι σήμερον
οὐδεὶς τῶν αἱρετικῶν ποιήσας φαίνεται. πῶς
οὖν δυνατὸν πράως φέρειν ἡμᾶς τὰ τοιαῦτα καὶ
ἰάσιμα εἶναι νομίζειν τοῦ ἀνδρὸς τὰ ἁμαρτήματα;
μὴ τοίνυν ψευδέσι λόγοις παράγεσθε, μηδὲ
ὑπονοίαις ἀνδρῶν πάντα εὐκόλως πρὸς τὸ κακὸν
ἐκλαμβανόντων πείθεσθε, ὡς ἄρα ἡμεῖς ἀδιάφορα [1] τιθέμεθα τὰ τοιαῦτα. γίνωσκε γάρ,
ποθεινότατε ἡμῖν καὶ τιμιώτατε, ὅτι οὔπω οἶδα
τοσοῦτον πένθος ἄλλοτε τῇ ψυχῇ μου παραδεξά-
μενος, ὅσον νῦν, ὅτε ἤκουσα τῶν ἐκκλησιαστικῶν
θεσμῶν τὴν σύγχυσιν. ἀλλὰ μόνον εὔχου, ἵνα
δώῃ ἡμῖν ὁ Κύριος μηδὲν κατὰ θυμὸν ἐνεργεῖν,
ἀλλ' ἔχειν τὴν ἀγάπην, ἥτις οὐκ ἀσχημονεῖ, οὐ
φυσιοῦται. ὅρα γὰρ ὅπως [2] οἱ μὴ ἔχοντες ταύτην ἐπήρθησαν μὲν ὑπὲρ τὰ μέτρα τὰ ἀνθρώπινα, ἐνασχημονοῦσι δὲ τῷ βίῳ, κατατολμῶντες
πράξεων, ὧν ὁ παρελθὼν χρόνος οὐκ ἔχει τὰ
ὑποδείγματα.

---

[1] ἀδιάφορα Coisl. secundus, Reg. secundus.
[2] πῶς editi antiqi.

---

[1] Cf. 1 Cor. 13, 4 and 5: ἡ ἀγάπη μακροθυμεῖ, χρηστεύεται·
οὐ φυσιοῦται, οὐκ ἀσχημονεῖ, οὐ ζητεῖ τὰ ἑαυτῆς. ἡ ἀγάπη οὐ

have produced a chill of horror and a complete
aversion for the man? For he, as I hear (if the
report be true and not a figment made up for the
purpose of calumny), has presumed also to re-ordain
certain men, a thing which up to the present no one
of the heretics appears to have done. How, then, is
it possible for us to endure such things mildly and to
consider that the errors of the man are curable?
Therefore, do not be led astray by his false words;
nor give credence to the suspicions of men who are
easily inclined to understand everything in a bad
sense, who assume, for instance, that we regard such
matters as of indifferent importance. For we wish
you to know, most beloved and honoured friend,
that I do not recall having ever received such deep
grief in my soul as at this moment, when I have
heard of the confusion in the ecclesiastical laws. But
only pray that the Lord may grant us to do nothing
in anger, but to have charity, which does not act
unseemly, and is not puffed up.[1] For, behold how
those who do not have this charity have been raised
above the bounds proper to men, and are now living
a most unseemly life, daring to commit deeds of
which the past possesses no examples.[2]

ζηλοῖ· ἡ ἀγάπη οὐ περπερεύεται, οὐ παροξύνεται, οὐ λογίζεται
τὸ κακόν. "Charity is patient, is kind: charity envieth not,
dealeth not perversely; is not puffed up; is not ambitious,
seeketh not her own, is not provoked to anger, thinketh no
evil."

[2] The Benedictine editors remark that Basil is not correct
in maintaining that there was no heretical precedent for such
actions. The Arians are charged with it in the Book of the
Prayers of Faustus and Marcellinus, *Bib. Patr.* V, 655. Cf.
also Constantius' letter to the Ethiopians against Fru-
mentius; Athan., *Apol. ad Const.* 31.

CXXXI

Ὀλυμπίῳ

Ὄντως ἡ τῶν ἀπροσδοκήτων ἀκοὴ ἱκανή ἐστι ποιῆσαι ἀνθρώπου[1] ἠχῆσαι ἀμφότερα τὰ ὦτα. ὃ καὶ ἐμοὶ νῦν συνέβη. εἰ γὰρ[2] καὶ τὰ μάλιστα γεγυμνασμέναις μου λοιπὸν ταῖς ἀκοαῖς προσέπεσε[3] τὰ περιφερόμενα καθ' ἡμῶν ταῦτα συντάγματα, διὰ τὸ καὶ πρότερον αὐτὸν ἐμὲ δεδέχθαι τὴν ἐπιστολήν, πρέπουσαν μὲν ταῖς ἐμαῖς ἁμαρτίαις, οὐ μὴν προσδοκηθεῖσάν ποτε γραφήσεσθαι παρὰ τῶν ἐπιστειλάντων· ἀλλ' ὅμως τὰ δεύτερα τοσαύτην ὑπερβολὴν ἐφάνη ἡμῖν ἔχειν ἐν ἑαυτοῖς τῆς πικρίας, ὥστε ἐπισκοτῆσαι τοῖς προλαβοῦσι. πῶς γὰρ οὐ μικροῦ τῶν φρενῶν ἔξω ἐγενόμην τῶν ἐμαυτοῦ, ἐντυχὼν τῇ πρὸς τὸν εὐλαβέστατον ἀδελφὸν Δαζίναν[4] ἐπιστολῇ, μυρίων μὲν ὕβρεων καὶ κατηγοριῶν ἀφορήτων γεμούσῃ καθ' ἡμῶν καὶ ἐπαναστάσεων, ὡς ἐν τοῖς χαλεπωτάτοις ἡμῶν κατὰ τῆς Ἐκκλησίας βουλεύμασιν εὑρεθέντων; εὐθὺς δὲ καὶ ἀποδείξεις τοῦ ἀληθεῖς εἶναι τὰς καθ' ἡμῶν βλασφημίας ἐπήχθησαν ἀπὸ συγγράμματος οὐκ οἶδα ὑπὸ τίνος γραφέντος. μέρη μὲν γὰρ ἐπέγνων, ὁμολογῶ, παρὰ[5] τοῦ Λαοδικέως Ἀπολιναρίου

---

[1] ἄνθρωπον Reg. secundus, Bigot., Coisl. secundus.
[2] γάρ om. E.   [3] προσέπεσον editi antiqi.
[4] Δεζίναν Med., Clarom.   [5] περί editi antiqi.

---

[1] Written in about 373, to Olympius, a wealthy layman of Neocaesarea and intimate friend of Basil. The subject of the letter is the same as that of the several preceding.

LETTER CXXXI

To Olympius[1]

TRULY the hearing of unexpected news is enough to make both ears of a man ring. This has now happened to me also. For although the reports of those writings which are being circulated against us have reached my ears, already exceedingly well practised in such matters (for even before that I myself had received the letter, which indeed befitted my sins, but which I never thought would be written by those who sent it), nevertheless the later reports have proven to have in them so great an excess of bitterness as to obscure all that has gone before. For how could I help becoming almost out of my senses when I read the letter addressed to our very reverend brother Dazinas,[2] a letter teeming with countless insults, with intolerable accusations against us and assaults, as though I had been detected in the most shameful plans against the Church? For example, proofs of the truth of the slanders against me were drawn from a work written by someone, I know not whom. For I did indeed recognize, I confess, that parts had been written by Apollinarius[3]

Other letters addressed to this Olympius are IV, XII, XIII, and CCXI.

[2] In this letter Eustathius accused Basil of bad faith and of Apollinarian errors.

[3] Apollinarius the Younger flourished in the latter half of the fourth century, and was at first highly esteemed by Athanasius and Basil, for his classical culture, piety, and steadfastness to the Nicene Creed during the Arian controversy. Later he became the author of the Christological heresy which bears his name.

γεγράφθαι, καὶ αὐτὰ οὐδὲ ἀναγνοὺς ἐξ ἔργου
ποτέ, ἀλλ᾽ ἀκούσας ἑτέρων ἀπαγγειλάντων· ἄλλα
δέ τινα εὗρον ἐγγεγραμμένα,[1] ἃ μήτε ἀνέγνων
ποτέ, μήτε[2] ἑτέρου λέγοντος ἤκουσα· καὶ τούτων
ὁ μάρτυς ἐν οὐρανῷ πιστός. πῶς οὖν οἱ τὸ
ψεῦδος ἀποστρεφόμενοι, οἱ τὴν ἀγάπην πλήρωμα
εἶναι τοῦ νόμου δεδιδαγμένοι, οἱ τὰ ἀσθενήματα
τῶν ἀδυνάτων βαστάζειν ἐπαγγελλόμενοι, ταύτας
ἡμῖν κατεδέξαντο τὰς συκοφαντίας ἐπενεγκεῖν
καὶ ἀπ᾽[3] ἀλλοτρίων συγγραμμάτων ἡμᾶς κατα-
κρῖναι,[4] πολλὰ λογισάμενος κατ᾽ ἐμαυτόν, ἐπινοεῖν
τὴν αἰτίαν οὐκ ἔχω, εἰ μή, ὅπερ ἐξ ἀρχῆς εἶπον,
μέρος ἔκρινα εἶναι τῶν ὀφειλομένων μοι διὰ τὰς
ἁμαρτίας κολάσεων καὶ τὴν ἐπὶ τούτοις λύπην.

Πρῶτον μὲν γὰρ κατεπένθησα τῇ ψυχῇ, ὅτι
ὠλιγώθησαν αἱ ἀλήθειαι ἀπὸ τῶν υἱῶν τῶν
ἀνθρώπων· ἔπειτα δὲ καὶ ἐφοβήθην αὐτὸς περὶ
ἐμαυτοῦ, μή ποτε πρὸς ταῖς ἄλλαις ἁμαρτίαις
καὶ τὴν μισανθρωπίαν πάθω, οὐδὲν πιστὸν ἐν
οὐδενὶ λογιζόμενος εἶναι, εἴπερ οἱ εἰς τὰ μέγιστα
παρ᾽ ἐμοῦ πιστευθέντες τοιοῦτοι μὲν περὶ ἐμέ,
τοιοῦτοι δὲ περὶ αὐτὴν ἐφάνησαν τὴν ἀλήθειαν.
γίνωσκε τοίνυν, ἀδελφέ, καὶ πᾶς ὅστις τῆς
ἀληθείας φίλος, μήτε ἐμὰ εἶναι τὰ συντάγματα,
οὔτε ἀρέσκεσθαι[5] αὐτοῖς, ἐπεὶ μὴ τῇ ἐμῇ γνώμῃ
συγγεγράφθαι. εἰ δὲ ἐπέστειλά ποτε πρὸ
πολλῶν ἐνιαυτῶν[6] Ἀπολιναρίῳ ἢ ἄλλῳ τινί,
ἐγκαλεῖσθαι οὐκ ὀφείλω, οὔτε γὰρ αὐτὸς[7] ἐγκαλῶ,
εἴ τις ἐκ τῆς ἑταιρίας τινὸς εἰς αἵρεσιν ἀπεσχίσθη

---

[1] γεγραμμένα E.   [2] ἢ E.   [3] ἐπ᾽ E.
[4] κατακρίνειν E, Harl., Reg. primus, Clarom.

of Laodicea, although I had never read them in his book but had merely heard others relate them; but I found certain other things written therein which I have never read nor heard anybody else state, and of these the faithful Witness is in heaven. How, therefore, those who scorn falsehood, who have been taught that charity is the fulfilment of the law, who profess to bear the infirmities of the weak, could have brought themselves to assail us with these calumnies and to condemn us from the writings of other men, this is a thing for which, though I have pondered deeply, I cannot discover the reason, unless, as I said in the beginning, I must conclude that the sorrow caused me by these things is a part of the punishments due me on account of my sins.

For, in the first place, I grieved in my soul, that truths had been made of little account by the sons of men; and, in the second place, I was also afraid for myself, lest some time, in addition to my other sins, I should also experience a hatred of mankind, reflecting that no trust is to be placed in any man, inasmuch as those who were most freely trusted by me have shown themselves so false to me and so false to truth itself. Know then, brother, and everyone who is a lover of truth, that these writings are not mine, nor are they pleasing to me, for they have not been composed according to my convictions. And if I ever wrote, many years ago, to Apollinarius or to any other person, I ought not to be blamed. For I, on my part, do not find fault, if any member of anybody's group has detached himself to go into heresy

---

⁶ ἀρκεῖσθαι editi antiqi.   ⁶ ἐτῶν editi antiqi.
⁷ ἐγώ add. editi antiqi.

(οἴδατε δὲ πάντως τοὺς ἄνδρας, κἂν ὀνομαστὶ μὴ
λέγω), διότι ἕκαστος τῇ ἰδίᾳ ἁμαρτίᾳ ἀποθανεῖται.
Ταῦτα νῦν μὲν ἀπεκρινάμην πρὸς τὸν ἀπο-
σταλέντα τόμον,[1] ἵνα αὐτός τε εἰδείης τὴν ἀλήθειαν
καὶ τοῖς βουλομένοις μὴ κατέχειν ὡς ἐν ἀδικίᾳ
τὴν ἀλήθειαν φανερὰν καταστήσῃς. ἐὰν δὲ δέῃ
καὶ πλατύτερον ὑπὲρ ἑκάστου τῶν ἐπενεχθέντων
ἡμῖν ἀπολογήσασθαι, καὶ τοῦτο ποιήσομεν, τοῦ
Θεοῦ συνεργοῦντος. ἡμεῖς, ἀδελφὲ Ὀλύμπιε,
οὔτε τρεῖς θεοὺς λέγομεν, οὔτε Ἀπολιναρίῳ
κοινωνοῦμεν.

CXXXII

Ἀβραμίῳ, ἐπισκόπῳ Βατνῶν

Πάντα τὸν ἀπὸ τοῦ μετοπώρου χρόνον ἠγνόησα
περὶ τῆς εὐλαβείας σου, ὅπου[2] διάγεις. καὶ γὰρ
πεπλανημένας τὰς φήμας εὕρισκον, τῶν μὲν
ἀπαγγελλόντων ἐν Σαμοσάτοις διατρίβειν σου
τὴν εὐλάβειαν, τῶν δὲ ἐν τῇ χώρᾳ, ἄλλων δὲ περὶ
τὰς βάτνας αὐτὰς διαβεβαιουμένων ἑωρακέναι·
διὸ οὐδὲ συνεχῶς ἐπέστειλα. νῦν δὲ μαθὼν ἐν
Ἀντιοχείᾳ διάγειν, ἐν τῇ οἰκίᾳ τοῦ αἰδεσιμωτάτου
Σατορνίνου τοῦ κόμητος, ἔδωκα τὴν ἐπιστολὴν
προθύμως τῷ ποθεινοτάτῳ καὶ εὐλαβεστάτῳ

---

[1] ἀλλά add. editi antiqi.   [2] ὅπως E.

---

[1] Cf. Letter CXXV ; also Greg. Naz. *Orat.* I and XXIX.
[2] Placed by the Benedictines in 373. Loofs prefers the
spring of 375 as the date of composition ; cf. pp. 28 ff. and
46 ff. Abramius or Abraham was bishop of Batnae in

(and you certainly know the men, even if I do not call them by name), for each one will perish by his own sin.

These answers I have made at the present time regarding the book that was sent, in order that you yourself may know the truth and may make it clear to such as do not wish to restrain the truth as guilty of an injustice. But if it is necessary to defend myself even more extensively regarding each of the charges brought against us, this also shall we do, God being our helper. As for us, Brother Olympius, we neither say that there are three Gods, nor do we keep communion with Apollinarius.[1]

LETTER CXXXII

To Abramius, Bishop of Batnae[2]

During the whole time since late autumn I have been ignorant of the whereabouts of your Reverence. For I kept receiving misleading rumours, some saying that your Reverence was sojourning in Samosata, others that you were in the country, while others maintained that they had seen you near Batnae itself. On this account I did not write regularly. But having just learned that you are staying in Antioch at the house of the most venerable Count Saturninus,[3] I have eagerly entrusted this letter to our most beloved and revered brother,

Osrhoene near the Euphrates. His name appears with those of Meletius, Eusebius, Basil, and others in the letter written by the bishops of the East to those of Italy and Gaul. Cf. Letter XCII. He also was present at the Council of Constantinople in 381.

[3] This Saturninus is not otherwise known.

301

ἀδελφῷ Σαγκτισσίμῳ τῷ συμπρεσβυτέρῳ,[1] δι' οὗ
προσφθέγγομαί σου τὴν ἀγάπην, παρακαλῶν
ὅπουπερ ἂν ᾖς μεμνῆσθαι μάλιστα μὲν τοῦ Θεοῦ,
εἶτα καὶ ἡμῶν, οὓς ἀγαπᾷν ἐξ ἀρχῆς προείλου, καὶ
ἔχειν ἐν τοῖς οἰκειοτάτοις ἀριθμουμένους.

CXXXIII

Πέτρῳ, ἐπισκόπῳ Ἀλεξανδρείας

Τῆς μὲν σωματικῆς φιλίας ὀφθαλμοὶ πρόξενοι
γίνονται, καὶ ἡ διὰ μακροῦ χρόνου ἐγγινομένη
συνήθεια βεβαιοῖ· τὴν δὲ ἀληθινὴν ἀγάπην ἡ τοῦ
Πνεύματος δωρεὰ συνίστησι, συνάπτουσα μὲν τὰ
μακρῷ διεστῶτα τόπῳ, γνωρίζουσα δὲ ἀλλήλοις
τοὺς ἀγαπητούς, οὐ διὰ σωματικῶν χαρακτήρων,
ἀλλὰ διὰ τῶν τῆς ψυχῆς [2] ἰδιωμάτων. ὃ δὴ καὶ
ἐφ' ἡμῶν ἡ τοῦ Κυρίου χάρις ἐποίησε, παρασχο-
μένη ἡμᾶς ἰδεῖν σε τοῖς τῆς ψυχῆς ὀφθαλμοῖς,
καὶ περιπτύξασθαί σε τῇ ἀγάπῃ τῇ ἀληθινῇ, καὶ
οἰονεὶ συμφυῆναί σοι καὶ πρὸς μίαν ἐλθεῖν ἕνωσιν
ἐκ τῆς κατὰ τὴν πίστιν κοινωνίας. πεπείσμεθα
γάρ σε ἀνδρὸς τοσούτου θρέμμα ὑπάρχοντα, καὶ
τὴν ἐκ παλαιοῦ διατριβὴν μετ' αὐτοῦ λαχόντα,
τῷ αὐτῷ πορεύεσθαι πνεύματι, καὶ τοῖς αὐτοῖς
στοιχεῖν τῆς εὐσεβείας δόγμασι.

Διὸ καὶ προσφθεγγόμεθά σου τὴν τιμιότητα,
καὶ παρακαλοῦμεν μετὰ τῶν ἄλλων καὶ τὴν περὶ

---

[1] ἡμῶν add. editi antiqi.　　　[2] ἀρετῆς editi antiqi.

---

[1] Cf. Letters CXX and CXXI.

LETTER CXXXIII

Sanctissimus,[1] our presbyter, through whom I salute
your Charity, begging that wherever you are you
will be mindful especially of God, then also of us,
whom from the beginning you chose to cherish and
to number among your most intimate friends.

LETTER CXXXIII

To Peter, Bishop of Alexandria [2]

Eyes are promoters of bodily friendship, and the
intimacy engendered through long association
strengthens such friendship. But true love is
formed by the gift of the Spirit, which brings together objects separated by a wide space, and
causes loved ones to know each other, not through
the features of the body, but through the peculiarities
of the soul. This indeed the favour of the Lord has
wrought in our case also, making it possible for us to
see you with the eyes of the soul, to embrace you with
the true love, and to grow one with you, as it were,
and to enter into a single union with you through
communion according to faith. For we are convinced that you, having been the spiritual nursling
of so great a man, and having been favoured with
long association with him, walk in the same spirit as
he and are guided by the same dictates of piety.

Therefore we salute your Honour, and entreat
you to take over from him, among other things, the

---

[2] Written in 373, to Peter, Bishop of Alexandria. This
Peter had succeeded Athanasius in May 373, by the latter's
request, who died on May 2 of that year. Basil begs him to
follow in the footsteps of Athanasius : in love for God, for
the brotherhood, and for Basil himself.

ἡμᾶς διάθεσιν τοῦ μεγάλου ἀνδρὸς διαδέξασθαι·
ἐπιστέλλειν τε ἡμῖν συνήθως τὰ κατὰ σαυτόν,
καὶ ἐπιμελεῖσθαι τῆς πανταχοῦ ἀδελφότητος τοῖς
αὐτοῖς σπλάγχνοις καὶ τῇ αὐτῇ προθυμίᾳ, ᾗ καὶ
ὁ μακαριώτατος [1] ἐκεῖνος περὶ πάντας ἐχρῆτο
τοὺς ἀγαπῶντας τὸν Θεὸν ἐν ἀληθείᾳ.

CXXXIV

Παιονίῳ πρεσβυτέρῳ

Ὅσον ηὔφρανας ἡμᾶς τοῖς γράμμασιν εἰκάζεις
που πάντως αὐτοῖς οἷς ἐπέστειλας· οὕτω τὸ καθα-
ρὸν τῆς καρδίας, ἀφ' ἧς προῆλθεν ἐκεῖνα τὰ
ῥήματα, ἀκριβῶς ἐκ τῶν γραμμάτων κατεμηνύετο.
καὶ γὰρ [2] ὁλκὸς μὲν ὕδατος δείκνυσι τὴν οἰκείαν
πηγήν, λόγου δὲ φύσις τὴν προενεγκοῦσαν αὐτὸν
καρδίαν χαρακτηρίζει. ὥστε ἄτοπόν τε καὶ πολὺ
τοῦ εἰκότος παρηλλαγμένον πεπονθέναι ὁμολογῶ.
σπουδάζων γὰρ ἀεὶ γράμμασιν ἐντυγχάνειν τῆς
τελειότητός σου, ἐπειδὴ ἔλαβον εἰς χεῖρας τὴν
ἐπιστολὴν καὶ ἀνέγνων αὐτήν, οὐχ ἥσθην μᾶλλον
τοῖς ἐπεσταλμένοις, ἢ ἠνιάθην τὴν ζημίαν, ὁπόση
γέγονεν ἡμῖν κατὰ τὸν τῆς σιωπῆς χρόνον,
διαλογιζόμενος.

Ἀλλ' ἐπειδὴ ἤρξω γράφειν, μὴ διαλίπῃς [3]

[1] μακάριος E.   [2] καί add. editi antiqi.
[3] διαλίποις multi MSS. non vetustissimi.

---

[1] Written in 373. Paeonius is otherwise unknown.
Letters CXXXIV, CXXXV, CCXXIII, CCCXXXIII
and CCCXXXIV have been quoted in certain studies of the
history of stenography. A. Schramm (*Korrespondenzblatt,*

great man's disposition toward us, to send me word of your affairs regularly, and to take care of the brotherhood everywhere with the same kindliness and the same zeal which that most blessed one employed toward all those who in truth love God.

LETTER CXXXIV

To the Presbyter Paeonius [1]

How much pleasure you gave us by your letter you no doubt fully surmise from the very tones you used in writing it; so accurately was the purity of heart whence those words proceeded revealed by what you wrote. For as a rill of water reveals its own true source, so the nature of one's speech shows the character of the heart that brought it forth. So I confess that I have experienced a strange and very unusual thing. For though always eager to read a letter from your Perfection, [2] when I had taken the letter in my hands and read it, I was not so much delighted by the message you had sent as I was vexed at the thought of how great a loss I had sustained during your period of silence.

But since you have begun to write, do not cease

Amtliche Zeitschr. des k. Stenographischen Instituts zu Dresden, 1903 (XLVIII), 221 and 241 ff.) would conclude from the present letter that Basil himself was a master of tachygraphy, and did not scorn to give instruction in it. F. Maier (*idem*, 1904 (XLIX) 42 ff.) rightly objects to this conclusion. In any case Basil employed tachygraphy, and had his difficulties with it. Cf. the present letter, and Letter CXXX.

[2] A Byzantine title, used usually of priests.

τοῦτο ποιῶν. εὐφρανεῖς γὰρ πλέον ἢ οἱ τὰ
πολλὰ χρήματα τοῖς φιλοπλούτοις διαπεμπό-
μενοι· τῶν δὲ γραφέων οὐδείς μοι παρῆν, οὔτε
τῶν καλλιγραφούντων οὔτε τῶν ταχυγράφων.
οὓς γὰρ[1] ἔτυχον ἐξασκήσας, οἱ μὲν ἀνέδραμον
ἐπὶ τὴν πρώτην τοῦ βίου συνήθειαν, οἱ δὲ ἀπειρήκασι πρὸς τοὺς πόνους, χρονίαις ἀρρωστίαις
κεκακωμένοι.

CXXXV

Διοδώρῳ,[2] πρεσβυτέρῳ Ἀντιοχείας

Ἐνέτυχον τοῖς ἀποσταλεῖσι βιβλίοις παρὰ τῆς
τιμιότητός σου. καὶ τῷ μὲν δευτέρῳ ὑπερήσθην,
οὐ διὰ τὴν βραχύτητα μόνον, ὡς εἰκὸς ἦν τὸν
ἀργῶς πρὸς πάντα καὶ ἀσθενῶς λοιπὸν διακείμενον, ἀλλ' ὅτι πυκνόν τε ἅμα ἐστὶ ταῖς ἐννοίαις,
καὶ εὐκρινῶς ἐν αὐτῷ ἔχουσιν αἵ τε ἀντιθέσεις
τῶν ὑπεναντίων καὶ αἱ πρὸς αὐτὰς ἀπαντήσεις·
καὶ τὸ τῆς λέξεως ἁπλοῦν τε καὶ ἀκατάσκευον
πρέπον ἔδοξέ μοι εἶναι προθέσει Χριστιανοῦ, οὐ
πρὸς ἐπίδειξιν μᾶλλον ἢ κοινὴν ὠφέλειαν συγ-
γράφοντος.[3] τὸ δὲ πρότερον, τὴν μὲν δύναμιν
ἔχον τὴν αὐτὴν ἐν τοῖς πράγμασι, λέξει δὲ πολυ-

---

[1] καί add. E.   [2] Θεοδώρῳ E, Med.
[3] γράφοντος editi antiqi.

---

[1] Written in 373. Cf. previous letter and note. This is
an exceedingly interesting letter, especially for the student
of the history of literary criticism. It contains Basil's ideas
on the rhetoric of his day, which were exactly such as a
person of good taste would hold to-day, although in all
probability a unique position in Basil's time. And we must

doing so. For you give more pleasure than do those who distribute large sums of money to the avaricious. But no one of my scribes has been at hand, either calligraphist or shorthand writer. For of those whom I have trained, some have gone back to their former manner of life, and the others have abandoned their labours, having been afflicted with chronic maladies.

LETTER CXXXV

To Diodorus, Presbyter of Antioch [1]

I HAVE read the books sent me by your Honour. And with the second I was exceedingly pleased, not only because of its brevity, which was likely to please a man who is inactive in all matters and in poor health besides, but because it is at once close-packed with ideas, and both the objections of our opponents and our answers to them are set forth in the work with the utmost clarity; and its simple and unlaboured style seemed to me to befit the purpose of a Christian, who writes not so much for display as for general edification. But the former work, which is of the same importance as to subject-matter, but is adorned with richer diction, with

say that St. Basil in his own works was consistent with this theory. He also characterizes at some length Plato's style and that of Aristotle and Theophrastus.

This Diodorus was a pupil of Silvanus, bishop of Tarsus. Cf. Theodoret, *Hist. Eccl.* 4, 24. In Letter XVI Theodoret speaks of his obligations to him as a teacher. In 378, Diodorus became bishop of Tarsus. Only a few fragments of his works are extant, for the major portion, it is said, was destroyed by the Arians. Cf. also Basil's Letter CLX.

τελεστέρᾳ καὶ σχήμασι ποικίλοις καὶ διαλογικαῖς
χάρισι κεκομψευμένον, πολλοῦ μοι ἐφάνη καὶ
χρόνου πρὸς τὸ ἐπελθεῖν[1] καὶ πόνου διανοίας
πρὸς τὸ καὶ συλλέξαι τὰς ἐννοίας καὶ παρα-
κατασχεῖν αὐτὰς τῇ μνήμῃ δεόμενον. αἱ γὰρ
ἐν τῷ μεταξὺ παρεμβαλλόμεναι διαβολαὶ τῶν
ὑπεναντίων καὶ συστάσεις τῶν ἡμετέρων, εἰ
καὶ γλυκύτητάς τινας ἐπεισάγειν δοκοῦσι διαλεκ-
τικὰς[2] τῷ συγγράμματι, ἀλλ' οὖν τῷ[3] σχολὴν
καὶ διατριβὴν ἐμποιεῖν διασπῶσι μὲν τὸ συνεχὲς
τῆς ἐννοίας καὶ τοῦ ἐναγωνίου λόγου τὸν τόνον
ὑποχαυνοῦσιν.

Ἐκεῖνο γὰρ πάντως συνεῖδέ[4] σου ἡ ἀγχίνοια,
ὅτι καὶ τῶν ἔξωθεν φιλοσόφων οἱ τοὺς διαλόγους
συγγράψαντες, Ἀριστοτέλης μὲν καὶ Θεόφραστος,
εὐθὺς αὐτῶν ἥψαντο τῶν πραγμάτων, διὰ τὸ
συνειδέναι ἑαυτοῖς τῶν Πλατωνικῶν χαρίτων τὴν
ἔνδειαν. Πλάτων δὲ τῇ ἐξουσίᾳ τοῦ λόγου ὁμοῦ
μὲν τοῖς δόγμασι μάχεται, ὁμοῦ δὲ καὶ παρα-
κωμῳδεῖ τὰ πρόσωπα, Θρασυμάχου μὲν τὸ θρασὺ
καὶ ἰταμὸν διαβάλλων, Ἱππίου δὲ τὸ κοῦφον
τῆς διανοίας καὶ χαῦνον, καὶ[5] Πρωταγόρου τὸ
ἀλαζονικὸν καὶ ὑπέρογκον. ὅπου δὲ ἀόριστα
πρόσωπα ἐπεισάγει τοῖς διαλόγοις, τῆς μὲν
εὐκρινείας ἕνεκεν τῶν πραγμάτων κέχρηται τοῖς
προσδιαλεγομένοις,[6] οὐδὲν δὲ ἕτερον ἐκ τῶν
προσώπων ἐπεισκυκλεῖ ταῖς ὑποθέσεσιν· ὅπερ
ἐποίησεν ἐν τοῖς Νόμοις.

Δεῖ οὖν καὶ ἡμᾶς τοὺς οὐ κατὰ φιλοτιμίαν

---

[1] ἐξελθεῖν editi antiqi.
[2] γλυκύτητας ... διαλεκτικάς] γλυκύτάτας ... διαλέξεις
Med., Harl.

figures of divers kinds, and with charms peculiar to
the dialogue, seemed to me to require a great deal
of time to peruse and much mental labour to grasp
its ideas and to retain them in the memory. For
the accusations of our opponents and the arguments
in defence of our own side which have been worked
into the context, even though they do seem to add
some dialectic attractions to the work, yet by causing
delay and waste of time disrupt the continuity of the
thought and loosen the tension of the argumentative
attack.

For assuredly your quick wit realizes this—that
those philosophers outside the faith who wrote
dialogues, Aristotle and Theophrastus for instance,
at once grappled with the facts themselves, because
they realized their own lack of the literary graces of
Plato. But Plato with the power of his eloquence at
one and the same time both attacks opinions and
ridicules the persons who represent them, attacking
the rashness and recklessness of Thrasymachus, the
levity and conceit of Hippias, and the boastfulness
and pompousness of Protagoras.[1] But whenever he
introduces indefinite characters into his dialogues, he
uses his interlocutors merely for the sake of giving
clarity to his subject matter, and brings nothing else
from the characters into the arguments; just as he
did in the *Laws*.

So it is necessary also for us, who do not set out

---

[1] *i.e.*, in the *Republic*, the *Hippias*, and the *Protagoras*
respectively.

---

³ τό E.   ⁴ συνοῖδε Harl., secunda manu.
⁵ καὶ] τοῦ δέ E.   ⁶ προδιαλεγομένοις tres MSS.

ἐρχομένους ἐπὶ τὸ γράφειν, ἀλλ' ὑποθήκας καταλιμπάνειν ὠφελίμων λόγων τῇ ἀδελφότητι προε-
λομένους, ἐὰν μέν τι πᾶσι προκεκηρυγμένον ἐπὶ
αὐθαδείᾳ τρόπου πρόσωπον ὑποβαλλώμεθα,[1]
τινὰ καὶ ἀπὸ[2] προσώπου ποιότητος παραπλέκειν
τῷ λόγῳ, εἴπερ ὅλως ἐπιβάλλει ἡμῖν διαβάλλειν
ἀνθρώπους, τῶν πραγμάτων ἀφεμένους.[3] ἐὰν δὲ
ἀόριστον ᾖ τὸ διαλεγόμενον, αἱ πρὸς τὰ πρόσωπα
διαστάσεις[4] τὴν μὲν συνάφειαν διακόπτουσι,
πρὸς οὐδὲν δὲ πέρας χρήσιμον ἀπαντῶσι.[5]

Ταῦτα εἶπον ἵνα δειχθῇ, ὅτι οὐκ εἰς κόλακος
χεῖρας ἀπέστειλάς σου τοὺς πόνους, ἀλλὰ ἀδελφῷ
τῷ γνησιωτάτῳ ἐκοινώνησας τῶν καμάτων.
εἶπον δὲ οὐ πρὸς ἐπανόρθωσιν τῶν γεγραμμένων,
ἀλλὰ πρὸς φυλακὴν τῶν μελλόντων. πάντως
γὰρ ὁ τοσαύτῃ περὶ τὸ γράφειν ἕξει καὶ σπουδῇ
κεχρημένος οὐκ ἀποκνήσει γράφων ἐπειδὴ οὐδὲ
οἱ τὰς ὑποθέσεις παρέχοντες ἀπολήγουσιν. ἡμῖν
δὲ ἀρκέσει μὲν ἀναγινώσκειν τὰ ὑμέτερα· τοῦ δὲ
δύνασθαι γράφειν τι τοσοῦτον ἀποδέομεν, ὅσον
μικροῦ δέω λέγειν, καὶ τοῦ ὑγιαίνειν, ἢ καὶ τοῦ
μετρίαν σχολὴν ἄγειν ἀπὸ τῶν πραγμάτων.

Ἀπέστειλα δὲ νῦν διὰ τοῦ ἀναγνώστου τὸ
μεῖζον καὶ πρότερον, ἐπελθὼν αὐτὸ ὡς ἐμοὶ
δυνατόν. τὸ δὲ δεύτερον[6] παρακατέσχον, βουλόμενος αὐτὸ μεταγράψαι, καὶ μὴ εὐπορῶν τέως[7]
τινὸς τῶν εἰς τάχος γραφόντων. μέχρι γὰρ
τοσαύτης ἦλθε πενίας τὰ ἐπίφθονα Καππαδοκῶν.

---

[1] χρή add. E. [2] τῆς τοῦ add. E.
[3] ἀφεμένοις editi antiqi. [4] διατάσεις editi antiqi.
[5] τοῦ λόγου add. editi antiqi.

to write for worldly honour, but propose to bequeath
to the brethren admonitions on edifying subjects, if
we introduce a character already well known to the
world for rashness of conduct, to weave something
derived from the quality of the character into the
treatise, if it is at all incumbent upon us to
censure men who neglect their duties. But if the
material brought into the dialogue be indefinite,
digressions against persons break its unity and tend
to no useful end.

All this I have said that it might be shown that
you have not sent your work into the hands of a
flatterer, but that you have given to a most sincere
brother a share in your toils. And I have spoken,
not to correct what has been written, but as a
warning for future writings. For assuredly a man
who has employed such aptitude and enthusiasm for
writing will not refrain from writing; since there
is no shortage of persons to supply you with subjects.
For us it will suffice to read what you write; but we
fall as far short of being able to write anything ourselves, as, I may almost say, of enjoying good health,
or of having even a modicum of leisure from active
affairs.

I have now sent back to you through the lector the
first and larger of your works, after reading it to the
best of my ability. The second, however, I have
kept, wishing to copy it, although as yet I am not
provided with any fast copyist. For to such a state
of poverty has the once envied condition of the
Cappadocians come!

---

⁶ καὶ μικρότερον add. editi Paris.   ⁷ τέος E.

CXXXVI

Εὐσεβίῳ, ἐπισκόπῳ Σαμοσάτων

Ἐν οἷος ἡμᾶς ὄντας κατέλαβεν ὁ χρηστὸς Ἰσαάκης[1] αὐτός σοι ἄμεινον διηγήσεται, εἰ καὶ μὴ ἀρκοῦσαν ἔχει τὴν γλῶσσαν, ὥστε τραγικῶς ἐξαγγεῖλαι τὸ ὑπεραῖρον τῶν παθῶν, τοσοῦτον ἦν τῆς ἀρρωστίας τὸ μέγεθος. καὶ τὸ εἰκὸς δὲ παντὶ γνώριμον τῷ ἐμὲ καὶ κατὰ βραχὺ ἐπισταμένῳ. εἰ γὰρ ἐν τῇ δοκούσῃ εὐεξίᾳ τῶν ἀπεγνωσμένων πρὸς τὸ ζῆν ἀσθενέστερον διεκείμην, γινώσκειν ἔξεστι τίς ἂν ἤμην ἐπὶ τῆς ἀρρωστίας. καίτοιγε ἐχρῆν (δὸς γὰρ τῷ πυρετῷ συγγνώμην ἐρεσχελοῦντι), ἐπειδή μοι κατὰ φύσιν ἦν τὸ νοσεῖν, ἐν τῇ μεταβολῇ ταύτῃ[2] τῆς ἕξεως ὑγείας[3] μοι νῦν τὸ κράτιστον περιεῖναι. ἀλλ' ἐπειδὴ μάστιξ τοῦ Κυρίου ἐστὶ προσθήκαις ταῖς κατὰ τὴν ἡμετέραν ἀξίαν τὸ ἀλγεινὸν ἐπιτείνουσα, ἀσθένειαν ἐπὶ τῇ ἀσθενείᾳ προσεκτησάμην, ὥστε τὸ ἀπὸ τούτου καὶ παιδὶ φανερὸν εἶναι, ὅτι πᾶσα ἀνάγκη οἰχήσεσθαι[4] ἡμῖν τὸ ἔλυτρον τοῦτο,[5] πλὴν εἰ μή που ἄρα ἡ τοῦ Θεοῦ φιλανθρωπία ἡμῖν ἐν τῇ μακροθυμίᾳ αὐτοῦ[6] χρόνους εἰς μετάνοιαν χαριζομένη,[7] ποιήσειε καὶ νῦν, ὡς καὶ πολλάκις πρότερον, λύσιν τινὰ καὶ πόρον[8] ἐκ τῶν ἀμηχάνων δεινῶν.[9] ταῦτα μὲν οὖν ἕξει ὡς αὐτῷ φίλον καὶ ἡμῖν συμφέρον.

---

[1] Ἰσαάκιος editi antiqi.   [2] ταύτης quattuor MSS.
[3] ὑγιείας E.   [4] οἰχήσεται E, Harl., Med.
[5] τούτου editi antiqi.   [6] καί add. E.
[7] χαριζομένου E.   [8] καί add. E.   [9] κακῶν E.

LETTER CXXXVI

To Eusebius, Bishop of Samosata [1]

In what condition the excellent Isaac [2] has found us he himself will relate to you better, even though his tongue is inadequate to proclaim in tragic fashion the transcendence of my sufferings, such was the seriousness of my illness. But probably this was known to everyone who was never so slightly acquainted with me. For if when in apparent good health I was really weaker than those of whose lives we despair, one may understand what I must have been during that illness. And yet I really ought (for you must grant indulgence to the fever that harasses me), since sickness used to be my natural state, in my present change of condition to be enjoying the best of health. But since it is the scourge of the Lord that goes on extending our bad health by new additions according to our deserts, I have acquired one infirmity after another, so that the result is plain to a child—that this shell of ours must quite certainly depart, unless perchance the mercy of God, in His magnanimity granting us the grace of a period of time for repentance, should now also, as on so many former occasions, bring about some release and some means of escape from our desperate straits. These things, however, shall be according to His pleasure and our own profit.

[1] Written in 373. This Eusebius was Bishop of Samosata on the Euphrates from 360 to 373. He was orthodox of faith, and a friend of Basil, Gregory Nazianzene, and Meletius, Bishop of Antioch. Cf. Letters XXVII, XXX, XXXI, XXXIV, etc.

[2] Otherwise unknown.

Τὰ δὲ τῶν ἐκκλησιῶν ὅπως οἴχεται καὶ προπέ-
ποται, ἡμῶν τῆς οἰκείας ἀσφαλείας ἕνεκεν τὰ τῶν
πλησίον περιορώντων καὶ οὐδὲ τοῦτο συνορᾶν
δυναμένων, ὅτι τῇ τοῦ κοινοῦ κακοπραγίᾳ [1] καὶ
τὸ καθ᾽ ἕκαστον συναπόλλυται, τί χρὴ καὶ
λέγειν; ἄλλως τε καὶ πρὸς ἄνδρα, ὃς πόρρωθεν
ἕκαστα προειδώς, καὶ προδιεμαρτύρω καὶ προε-
κήρυξας, καὶ αὐτός τε προεξανέστης, καὶ τοὺς
λοιποὺς συνεπήγειρας, ἐπιστέλλων, αὐτὸς παρα-
γινόμενος, τί οὐ ποιῶν, τίνα φωνὴν οὐκ ἀφιείς!
ὧν μεμνήμεθα μὲν [2] ἐφ᾽ ἑκάστῳ τῶν ἐκβαινόν-
των, ὠφελούμεθα δὲ ἀπ᾽ αὐτῶν οὐκέτι. καὶ νῦν
εἰ μὴ αἱ ἁμαρτίαι ἀντέστησάν μοι, καὶ τὸ μὲν
πρῶτον ὁ εὐλαβέστατος καὶ ἀγαπητὸς ἀδελφὸς
ἡμῶν Εὐστάθιος ὁ συνδιάκονος, εἰς νόσον χαλεπὴν
καταπεσών, εἰς ὅλους με δύο παρέτεινε μῆνας,
ἡμέραν ἐξ ἡμέρας τὴν σωτηρίαν αὐτοῦ περι-
μένοντα· ἔπειτα δὲ οἱ σὺν ἐμοὶ πάντες ἠσθένησαν,
ὧν τὰ μὲν καταλείμματα [3] ἐξαριθμήσεται [4] ὁ
ἀδελφὸς Ἰσαάκης· τὸ δὲ τελευταῖον αὐτὸς ἐγὼ
τῇ νόσῳ κατεσχέθην ταύτῃ· ἐπεὶ πάλαι ἂν ἤμην
παρὰ [5] τὴν σὴν τιμιότητα, οὐκ ὄφελός τι τοῖς
κοινοῖς παρεχόμενος, ἀλλ᾽ ἐμαυτῷ μέγα κέρδος
ἐκ τῆς συντυχίας σου [6] κτώμενος. καὶ γὰρ
ἐγνώκειν ἔξω τῶν ἐκκλησιαστικῶν γενέσθαι
βελῶν διὰ τὸ ἀφύλακτον ἡμῶν πρὸς τὰ σκευω-
ρούμενα [7] παρὰ τῶν ἐναντίων. σώζοι σε τῷ βίῳ

---

[1] δυσπραγίᾳ Reg. secundus, Coisl. secundus.
[2] μέν om. E.   [3] ἐγκαταλείμματα E.
[4] ἐξαριθμηθήσεται E.   [5] πρός E.
[6] σου om. E.   [7] σκαιωρούμενα Harl., Paris., Clarom.

---

[1] Cf. Dem. *Olynth.* 3, 22, 34: προπέτοται τῆς αὐτίκα χάριτος

As for the interests of the churches—how they
have gone to ruin and have been lightly sacrificed,[1]
while we, consulting our own personal safety, neglect
the good of our neighbours and are unable to see
even this, that the ruin of each of us is involved in
the common disaster—why need I say a word?
And especially so to a man like you who, foreseeing
everything long in advance, made protest and issued
proclamation beforehand, and not only was the first
to rise up yourself, but also helped to rouse the rest,
writing them letters, visiting them in person,
omitting what act, leaving what word unspoken!
These things we do indeed remember after each event
happens, but we no longer derive profit from them.
And now if my sins had not stood in my way,—that
is, first of all, our most reverend and beloved brother
and deacon, Eustathius,[2] falling grievously ill, caused
me no great anxiety for two whole months as I
waited day after day for his return to health; and
next, all my associates fell ill (of which things our
brother Isaac will enumerate all that I omit); and,
last of all, I myself was seized by this present
illness—but for these things I should long ago have
been by the side of your Honour, not lending you
any aid in the common cause, but deriving great
gain for myself from your company. For I had
decided to get out of the way of the missiles of the
ecclesiastics because I had no means of protecting
myself against the contrivances of my adversaries.
May the mighty hand of God preserve you unto

---

[1] τὰ τῆς πόλεως πράγματα. "The interests of the state have
been lightly sacrificed for mere present pleasure."

[2] This deacon enjoyed Basil's confidence, and once conveyed another letter for him to Eusebius of Samosata. Cf.
Letter XLVII.

παντὶ ἡ μεγάλη τοῦ Θεοῦ χείρ, τὸν γενναῖον
φύλακα τῆς πίστεως καὶ νήφοντα τῶν ἐκκλησιῶν
προστάτην· καὶ καταξιώσειεν ἡμᾶς πρὸ τῆς
ἐξόδου τῆς συντυχίας σου ἐπ' ὠφελείᾳ τῶν
ψυχῶν ἡμῶν.

CXXXVII

Ἀντιπάτρῳ

Νῦν μοι δοκῶ μάλιστα ἐπαισθάνεσθαι τῆς
ζημίας, ἣν ὑπομένω διὰ τὸ ἀρρωστεῖν, ὁπότε,
ἀνδρὸς τοιούτου τὴν πατρίδα ἡμῶν ἐφέποντος,
αὐτὸς ἀπεῖναι διὰ τὴν ἐπιμέλειαν τοῦ σώματος
ἀναγκάζομαι. μῆνα γὰρ ὅλον ἤδη προσκαθέζομαι [1] τῇ ἐκ τῶν αὐτοφυῶς θερμῶν [2] ὑδάτων θεραπείᾳ ὡς δή τι ὄφελος ἐντεῦθεν ἕξων. ἔοικα δὲ
διακενῆς πονεῖν ἐπὶ τῆς ἐρημίας, ἢ καὶ γέλωτος
τοῖς πολλοῖς ἄξιος εἶναι φαίνεσθαι, μηδὲ τῆς
παροιμίας ἀκούων τῆς οὐδὲν ἀπὸ θερμῶν ὄφελος
εἶναι τοῖς τεθνηκόσι λεγούσης.

Διόπερ καὶ οὕτως ἔχων βούλομαι πάντα παρεὶς
καταλαβεῖν σου τὴν σεμνοπρέπειαν, ὥστε τῶν ἐν
σοὶ καλῶν ἀπολαύειν καὶ τὰ κατὰ τὸν οἶκον τὸν
ἐμαυτοῦ πράγματα διὰ τῆς σῆς ὀρθότητος εὐπρε-
πῶς διαθέσθαι. ἐμὸς γάρ ἐστιν ἴδιος ὁ τῆς σεμνοτάτης μητρὸς ἡμῶν Παλλαδίας οἶκος, ἣν οὐ μόνον ἡ
τοῦ γένους οἰκειότης ἡμῖν συνάπτει, ἀλλὰ καὶ τὸ τοῦ

---

[1] μῆνα . . . προσκαθέζομαι om. E; ἤδη om. Harl. Med.
editi antiqi. προσκαθέσομαι editi antiqi.
[2] αὐτοφυῶς θερμῶν om. E.

---

[1] Written in 373. Antipater, governor of Cappadocia,

all mankind, you who are the noble guardian of the
faith and the vigilant champion of the churches;
and before our departure from this life may He
deem us worthy of an interview with you for the
good of our soul.

LETTER CXXXVII

To Antipater [1]

At this time I seem to be most sensible of the
loss which I suffer in being sick, when, on the
occasion of a man like you succeeding to the
governorship of our country, I am myself compelled
to be absent because of the care I must take of my
body. For during a whole month already have I
been assiduously undergoing the treatment of the
naturally hot waters, expecting to receive some
benefit therefrom. But it seems that I toil quite
uselessly in this solitary place, or that I even show
myself deserving of ridicule in the eyes of the many
for not heeding the proverb which says, "Warm
baths are of no use to the dead."

Wherefore, in spite of my present condition, I
desire, putting aside everything else, to go to your
gracious self, that I may have the benefit of your
excellent qualities and through your uprightness
may fittingly arrange the affairs of my own house.
For my very own is the house of our most revered
mother Palladia, whom not only the kinship of
family binds to us, but also the goodness of her

to whom Basil recommends the protection of Palladia, his
old friend and relative. Cf. Letters CLXXXVI and
CLXXXVII. Palladia is otherwise unknown.

τρόπου δεξιὸν ἀντὶ μητρὸς ἡμῖν εἶναι πεποίηκεν.
ἐπεὶ οὖν κεκίνηταί τις ταραχὴ περὶ τὸν οἶκον αὐτῆς,
ἀξιοῦμέν σου τὴν μεγαλόνοιαν μικρὸν ὑπερθέσθαι
τὴν ἐξέτασιν καὶ ἀναμεῖναι ἡμῶν τὴν παρουσίαν,
οὐχ ὥστε διαφθαρῆναί τὸ δίκαιον (μυριάκις γὰρ
ἂν ἀποθανεῖν ἑλοίμην ἢ τοιαύτην αἰτῆσαι χάριν
παρὰ δικαστοῦ φίλου τοῖς νόμοις καὶ τῷ δικαίῳ),
ἀλλ' ὥστε ἃ οὐκ εὐπρεπὲς ἐμοὶ γράφειν, ταῦτα
ἀπὸ στόματος ἀπαγγέλλοντός μου μαθεῖν. οὕτω
γὰρ οὔτε αὐτὸς τῆς ἀληθείας διαμαρτήσῃ, οὔτε
ἡμεῖς πεισόμεθά τι τῶν ἀβουλήτων. δέομαι οὖν,
τοῦ προσώπου ἐν ἀσφαλείᾳ ὄντος καὶ κατεχο-
μένου παρὰ τῆς τάξεως, ἀνεπαχθῆ ταύτην χάριν
καὶ ἀνεπίφθονον ἡμῖν καταθέσθαι.

CXXXVIII

Εὐσεβίῳ, ἐπισκόπῳ Σαμοσάτων

Τίνα με οἴει ψυχὴν ἐσχηκέναι, ὅτε τὴν ἐπιστολὴν ἐδεξάμην τῆς θεοσεβείας σου; εἰ μὲν γὰρ
πρὸς τὴν ἐν τῷ γράμματι ἀπεῖδον διάθεσιν, εὐθὺς
ὥρμων πέτεσθαι τὴν εὐθὺς[1] Σύρων, εἰ δὲ πρὸς τὴν
ἀρρωστίαν τοῦ σώματος, ὑφ' ἧς πεπεδημένος
ἐκείνην, ᾐσθανόμην οὐχὶ τοῦ πέτεσθαι μόνον
ἀλλὰ καὶ τοῦ ἐπὶ τῆς κλίνης στρέφεσθαι
ἐνδεῶς ἔχων. πεντηκοστὴν γὰρ ταύτην ἡμέραν
ἦγον ἐν τῇ ἀρρωστίᾳ, καθ' ἣν ἐπέστη ἡμῖν
ὁ ἀγαπητὸς καὶ σπουδαιότατος ἀδελφὸς ἡμῶν
συνδιάκονος Ἐλπίδιος· πολλὰ μὲν τῷ πυρετῷ

[1] εὐθὺ E.

character has caused to be a second mother to us. So, since some trouble has been stirred up concerning her house, we ask your Magnanimity to postpone your inquiry a little while, and to await our presence, not that justice may be foiled (for I should prefer to die ten thousand times than to ask such a favour of a judge who is a lover of the laws and of justice), but that you may learn from me by word of mouth those things which it does not become me to write. For thus you yourself will neither fail of the truth nor shall we suffer anything we would fain avoid. I therefore ask you, since the person in question is in safe custody and is held by the soldiers, to grant us this favour as one that can give no offence or cause any odium.

LETTER CXXXVIII

To Eusebius, Bishop of Samosata [1]

Into what state of mind, think you, did I come when I received the letter of your Holiness? [2] For if I looked at the spirit of your letter, I was straightway eager to fly straight to Syria, but if at the weakness of my body, because of which I lay fettered, I realized that I was incapable not only of flying but even of turning over on my bed. For that day on which Elpidius,[3] our beloved and most excellent brother and deacon, arrived was the fiftieth

---

[1] Written in 373. On Eusebius, Bishop of Samosata, cf. Letters XXVII, XXX, XXXI, XXXIV, XLVII, etc.

[2] Byzantine title, commonly given to bishops.

[3] Elpidius, a deacon at whose hands Basil received the present letter from Eusebius of Samosata, and by whom Basil sent a letter of consolation to the Egyptian bishops in exile for the faith in Palestine (Letter CCLXV).

δαπανηθείς, ὃς ἀπορίᾳ τῆς τρεφούσης αὐτὸν
ὕλης, τῇ ξηρᾷ ταύτῃ σαρκὶ οἷον θρυαλλίδι
κεκαυμένῃ περιειλούμενος, μαρασμὸν [1] καὶ χρονίαν
ἐπήγαγεν ἀρρωστίαν· τὰ δὲ ἐφεξῆς, ἡ ἀρχαία
πληγή μου, τὸ ἧπαρ τοῦτο διαδεξάμενον, ἀπέ-
κλεισε μέν με [2] τῶν σιτίων, ἀπεδίωξε δὲ τῶν
ὀμμάτων τὸν ὕπνον, ἐν μεθορίοις δὲ κατέσχε
ζωῆς καὶ θανάτου, τοσοῦτον ζῆν ἐπίτρεπον, [3]
ὅσον τῶν ἀπ' αὐτοῦ δυσχερῶν ἐπαισθάνεσθαι.
ὥστε καὶ ὕδασιν ἐχρησάμην αὐτοφυῶς θερμοῖς
καί τινας παρ' ἰατρῶν ἐπιμελείας κατεδεξάμην.
ἄπαντα δὲ ἤλεγξε τὸ νεανικὸν τοῦτο κακόν· ὅ, τοῦ
μὲν ἔθους παρόντος, κἂν ἄλλος ἐνέγκοι, ἀμελε-
τήτως δὲ προσπεσόντος οὐδεὶς οὕτως ἀδαμάντινος
ὥστε ἀντισχεῖν.

Ὑφ' οὗ πολὺν ὀχληθεὶς χρόνον, οὐδέποτε οὕτως
ἠνιάθην ὅσον νῦν, ἐμποδισθεὶς παρ' αὐτοῦ πρὸς
τὴν συντυχίαν τῆς ἀληθινῆς ἀγάπης σου. οἵας
γὰρ ἀπεστερήθημεν [4] θυμηδίας οἶδα καὶ αὐτός, εἰ
καὶ ἄκρῳ δακτύλῳ τοῦ γλυκυτάτου μέλιτος τῆς
παρ' ὑμῖν ἐκκλησίας ἀπεγευσάμην πέρυσιν.

Ἐγὼ δὲ καὶ ἄλλων ἀναγκαίων ἕνεκεν πραγμάτων ἐδεόμην εἰς ταὐτὸν [5] γενέσθαι τῇ θεοσεβείᾳ σου
καὶ περὶ πολλῶν μὲν ἀνακοινώσασθαι, πολλὰ δὲ
μαθεῖν. καὶ γὰρ οὐδέ ἐστιν ἐνταῦθα οὐδὲ ἀγάπης
ἀληθινῆς ἐπιτυχεῖν. ὅταν δὲ καὶ πάνυ τις ἀγα-
πῶντα εὕροι, [6] οὐκ ἔστιν ὁ δυνάμενος παραπλησίως
τῇ τελείᾳ σου φρονήσει καὶ τῇ ἐμπειρίᾳ, ἣν ἐκ

---

[1] μαρασμώδη E, Harl., Med., editi antiqi.
[2] με om. E.   [3] ἐπιτρέπων editi antiqi.
[4] ἀπεστερήθην editi antiqi.   [5] εἰς ταὐτό Harl.

I had spent in this illness; I was greatly wasted by
the fever which, through lack of fuel to nourish it,
enfolded this withered flesh of mine as though it
were a burnt wick and brought on languor and prolonged weakness; and then next this liver of mine
(my ancient scourge), following the fever, barred me
from foods, drove sleep from my eyes, and kept me
on the verge of life and death, allowing me only so
much of life as to keep me sensible of its discomforts.   Therefore I resorted to the use of naturally
hot waters and received some attention from
physicians.   But all these things were put to shame
by this lusty malady, which, if one were accustomed
to it, anybody might endure, but when it attacks
without warning, no one is so hardy as to withstand.
    Though I have been troubled by this disease for
a long time, never have I been so distressed as now,
since I have been prevented by it from meeting with
your true Charity.[1]   Of what gladness of heart we
have been deprived I myself also know, even though
it was with but my finger-tip that I tasted last year
of the very sweet honey of your church.
    Because of other pressing matters as well I wanted
to meet with your Holiness and both to consult with
you about many things and to learn many things
from you.   For here it is not possible to meet with
even genuine charity.   But though one may at times
find a person who shows even very great charity,
there exists no one who is able, in a manner comparable with your perfect wisdom and the experience

[1] Byzantine title.

---

6 εὕρῃ editi antiqi.

321

πολλῶν τῶν περὶ τὰς ἐκκλησίας συνελέξω καμάτων, δοῦναι γνώμην ἡμῖν περὶ τῶν προκειμένων.

Τὰ μὲν οὖν ἄλλα οὐκ ἐνῆν γράφειν· ἃ δ' οὖν
καὶ ἐξενεγκεῖν ἀσφαλὲς ταῦτά ἐστιν. ὁ πρεσβύτερος Εὐάγριος, ὁ υἱὸς Πομπηϊανοῦ τοῦ Ἀντιο-
χέως, ὁ συναπάρας ποτὲ ἐπὶ τὴν δύσιν τῷ
μακαρίῳ Εὐσεβίῳ ἐπανῆκε νῦν ἐκ τῆς Ῥώμης,
ἀπαιτῶν ἡμᾶς ἐπιστολὴν αὐτὰ τὰ παρ' ἐκείνων
γεγραμμένα ἔχουσαν αὐτολεξεὶ (ἀνεκόμισε δὲ
ἡμῖν εἰς τοὐπίσω τὰ παρ' ἡμῶν, ὡς οὐκ ἀρέσαντα
τοῖς ἀκριβεστέροις τῶν ἐκεῖ), καὶ πρεσβείαν τινὰ
δι' ἀνδρῶν ἀξιολόγων ἤδη κατεπείγεσθαι, ὑπὲρ
τοῦ εὐπρόσωπον ἔχειν ἀφορμὴν τοὺς ἄνδρας τῆς
ἐπισκέψεως ἡμῶν.

Οἱ κατὰ Σεβάστειαν τὰ ἡμέτερα φρονοῦντες,
Εὐσταθίου τὸ ὕπουλον τῆς κακοδοξίας ἕλκος
ἀπογυμνώσαντες, ἀπαιτοῦσί τινα παρ' ἡμῶν ἐκκλησιαστικὴν [1] ἐπιμέλειαν.

---

[1] αὐτῶν add. E.

---

[1] Evagrius, known as of Antioch, the dates of whose birth
and death are uncertain. He was consecrated bishop over
one of the parties at Antioch in 388–389. He went to Italy
with Eusebius, Bishop of Vercelli, and at the death of that
prelate returned to Antioch in company with St. Jerome.
He was probably the ascetic who trained St. John Chrysostom
in monastic discipline. He belonged to the Eustathian
division of the orthodox church at Antioch. He also aided
Pope Damasus in getting the better of his rival Ursinus.
After nine or ten years he returned to the East, stopping
en route at Caesarea to visit Basil (373). Later, from
Antioch, Evagrius wrote Basil a harsh letter, accusing him
of love of strife and controversy. Basil's reply is a model
of courteous sarcasm. Later Evagrius became the instrument for prolonging the schism. Cf. Theodoret, *Ecc. Hist.*
5, 23 ; and St. Basil, Letter CLVI.

which you have gathered from your many labours for the churches, to offer advice on the matters which lie before us.

Now there are some things which I cannot put in writing; the things which I can set forth with safety are these: The presbyter Evagrius,[1] son of Pompeianus [2] of Antioch, who formerly went to the West in company with Eusebius [3] of blessed memory, has now returned from Rome, demanding from us a letter containing the very things written by them word for word (and our own letter he has brought back to us again on the ground that it was not pleasing to the more strict of the people there), and he also asks that a sort of embassy of influential men be sent in haste, that the men may have a reasonable occasion for visiting us.

Those at Sebaste who feel as we do, having laid bare the festering ulcer of Eustathius' [4] evil doctrine, demand from us some ecclesiastical attention.

[2] Pompeianus of Antioch, the father of Evagrius, was, according to St. Jerome, a descendant of the officer of that name who accompanied Aurelian against Zenobia of Palmyra (273).

[3] St. Eusebius, Bishop of Vercelli, 283–371. According to St. Ambrose, he was the first bishop of the West to unite the monastic with the clerical life; cf. Ambrose, Letter LXIII, *Ad Vercellenses*. Entirely orthodox, at the synod of Milan (355), he refused to sign the document condemning St. Athanasius. In 363, on his return to Vercelli from exile, he became one of the chief opponents of the Arian bishop Amentius of Milan. The Church honours him as a martyr on December 16.

[4] Eustathius of Sebaste (*circ.* 300–377), one of the chief founders of monasticism in Asia Minor and for a time the intimate friend of St. Basil. He hesitated all his life between the various forms of Arianism, and finally became the leader of the Pneumatomachians condemned by the First Council of Constantinople.

323

Ἰκόνιον πόλις ἐστὶ τῆς Πισιδίας, τὸ μὲν παλαιὸν
μετὰ τὴν μεγίστην ἡ πρώτη, νῦν δὲ καὶ αὐτὴ
προκάθηται[1] μέρους, ὅ, ἐκ διαφόρων τμημάτων
συναχθέν, ἐπαρχίας ἰδίας οἰκονομίαν ἐδέξατο.
αὕτη καλεῖ[2] καὶ ἡμᾶς εἰς ἐπίσκεψιν,[3] ὥστε αὐτῇ
δοῦναι ἐπίσκοπον. τετελευτήκει γὰρ ὁ Φαυστῖνος.

Εἰ οὖν δεῖ μὴ κατοκνεῖν τὰς ὑπερορίους χειροτο-
νίας, καὶ ποίαν τινὰ χρὴ δοῦναι τοῖς Σεβαστηνοῖς
ἀπόκρισιν, καὶ πῶς πρὸς τὰς τοῦ Εὐαγρίου διατε-
θῆναι γνώμας, ἐδεόμην διδαχθῆναι αὐτὸς δι' ἐμαυτοῦ συντυχὼν τῇ τιμιότητί σου, ὧν[4] πάντων ἀπεστερήθην διὰ τὴν παροῦσαν ἀσθένειαν. ἐὰν μὲν
οὖν ᾖ τινος ἐπιτυχεῖν ταχέως πρὸς ἡμᾶς ἀφικνου-
μένου, καταξίωσον περὶ πάντων ἀποστεῖλαί μοι
τὰς ἀποκρίσεις· εἰ δὲ μή, εὖξαι ἐλθεῖν ἐπὶ νοῦν
μοι, ὅπερ εὐάρεστον ᾖ τῷ Κυρίῳ. ἐν δὲ τῇ
συνόδῳ μνήμην ἡμῶν κέλευσον γενέσθαι, καὶ
αὐτὸς δὲ πρόσευξαι ὑπὲρ ἡμῶν, καὶ τὸν λαὸν
συμπαράλαβε, ἵνα τὰς λειπομένας ἡμέρας ἢ ὥρας
τῆς παροικίας ἡμῶν καταξιωθῶμεν δουλεῦσαι, ὡς
ἔστιν εὐάρεστον τῷ Κυρίῳ.

CXXXIX

Τοῖς Ἀλεξανδρεῦσιν

Ἡμᾶς μὲν ἡ ἀκοὴ τῶν γεγενημένων κατά τε τὴν
Ἀλεξάνδρειαν καὶ τὴν λοιπὴν Αἴγυπτον διωγμῶν

---

[1] προκάθηται] πρώτη κάθηται tres MSS. [2] καλεῖ om. E.
[3] κεκλήκει add. E. [4] ὡς Harl., Med.

---

[1] i.e. Antioch.
[2] For Faustinus cf. Letter CLXI. He was succeeded by John I, who in turn was succeeded by Amphilochius.

LETTER CXXXIX

Iconium is a city of Pisidia, in olden times the first after the greatest,[1] and now also it is the capital of that territory which, made up of different sections, has received the management of its own government. This city urges me to make it a visit, that we may give it a bishop. For Faustinus[2] has died.

Whether, therefore, I should not decline these ordinations beyond our borders, and what sort of an answer I should give to the Sebastines, and how I should be disposed toward the propositions of Evagrius, on all these matters I need to be instructed by a personal meeting with your Honour, but I have been deprived of all this by my present ill-health. If, then, it is possible to find anyone who is coming to us soon, deign to send me your answers on all these questions; but if not, pray that there may come to my mind that thing which is most pleasing to the Lord. And order that remembrance of us be made in the synod, and do you yourself pray for us, and join the people with you in prayer, that we may be thought worthy to serve during the remaining days or hours of our sojourn as is acceptable to the Lord.

LETTER CXXXIX

To the Alexandrians[3]

Long since has the rumour reached us of the persecutions that have taken place throughout Alexandria and the rest of Egypt, and it has rent

[3] Written in 373 to the Alexandrians to console them and to encourage them to great constancy, harassed as they were by a terrible persecution. The persecution referred to is the one caused by Valens, who tortured the Eastern Catholics from 369 to the end of his reign.

πάλαι κατέλαβε, καὶ διέθηκε τὰς ψυχάς, ὡς εἰκὸς
ἦν. ἐλογισάμεθα γὰρ τὸ ἔντεχνον τοῦ διαβολικοῦ
πολέμου· ὃς [1] ἐπειδὴ εἶδεν ἐν τοῖς παρὰ τῶν
ἐχθρῶν διωγμοῖς πληθυνομένην τὴν Ἐκκλησίαν
καὶ μᾶλλον θάλλουσαν, μετέστρεψεν ἑαυτοῦ
τὴν βουλήν,[2] καὶ οὐκέτι ἐκ τοῦ προφανοῦς πολεμεῖ,
ἀλλὰ κεκρυμμένα ἡμῖν τὰ ἔνεδρα [3] τίθησι, καλύπ-
των αὐτοῦ τὴν ἐπιβουλὴν διὰ τοῦ ὀνόματος ὃ
περιφέρουσιν, ἵνα καὶ πάθωμεν τὰ αὐτὰ τοῖς
πατράσιν ἡμῶν, καὶ μὴ δόξωμεν πάσχειν ὑπὲρ
Χριστοῦ, διὰ τὸ Χριστιανῶν ὄνομα ἔχειν καὶ τοὺς
διώκοντας. ταῦτα λογιζόμενοι πολὺν χρόνον
ἐκαθέσθημεν ἐπὶ τῇ ἀγγελίᾳ τῶν γεγενημένων [4]
ἐκπεπληγμένοι. καὶ γὰρ τῷ ὄντι ἤχησαν [5] ἡμῶν
ἀμφότερα τὰ ὦτα μαθόντα τὴν ἀναιδῆ καὶ μισάν-
θρωπον αἵρεσιν τῶν διωξάντων ὑμᾶς, ὅτι οὐχ
ἡλικίαν ᾐδέσθησαν, οὐ τοὺς ἐν τῇ πολιτείᾳ [6]
καμάτους, οὐ λαῶν ἀγάπην· ἀλλὰ καὶ ᾐκίσαντο
τὰ σώματα, καὶ ἠτίμωσαν, καὶ ἐξορίαις παρέδωκαν,
καὶ διήρπασαν τὰς ὑπάρξεις ὧν εὑρεῖν ἠδυνήθη-
σαν, οὔτε τὴν παρὰ ἀνθρώπων κατάγνωσιν [7]
ἐντρεπόμενοι, οὔτε τὴν φοβερὰν τοῦ δικαίου κριτοῦ
ἀνταπόδοσιν προορώμενοι. ταῦτα ἡμᾶς ἐξέπληξε
καὶ μικροῦ ἔξω ἐποίησε τῶν λογισμῶν. συνεισῆλθε
δὲ τούτοις τοῖς διαλογισμοῖς κἀκείνη ἡ ἔννοια·
ἆρα μὴ ἐγκατέλιπεν ἑαυτοῦ τὰς ἐκκλησίας παντελῶς ὁ Κύριος ; ἆρα μὴ ἐσχάτη ὥρα ἐστί, καὶ ἡ
ἀποστασία διὰ τούτων λαμβάνει τὴν εἴσοδον, ἵνα
λοιπὸν ἀποκαλυφθῇ ὁ ἄνομος, ὁ υἱὸς τῆς ἀπωλείας,

our hearts, as was natural. For we took thought of
the ingenuity of the devil's warfare,—how the devil,
when he saw the Church multiplying and flourishing
still more amid the persecutions of its enemies,
changed his plan, and no longer fights openly, but
places hidden snares for us, concealing his plot by
means of the name which his followers bear, that we
may suffer as our fathers did and yet not seem to
suffer for Christ, because of the fact that our persecutors also bear the name of Christians. Considering these things we sat for a long time amazed at the
report of what had happened. For in truth both
our ears rang on learning of the shameless and cruel
heresy of your persecutors, in that they showed no
respect for age, nor for the labours of a life well
spent, nor for charity toward the people ; nay, they
even tortured their bodies, and dishonoured them,
and gave them over to exile, and plundered the
property of whomsoever they could find, neither
giving heed to the condemnation of men nor looking
forward to the fearful requital of the just Judge.
These things have stricken us and have almost put
us out of our senses. And along with these reflections there comes into our mind this thought also :
Has not the Lord abandoned His churches utterly ?
Is not this the last hour, when apostasy uses these
means to gain entrance, "so that at length the man
of sin may be revealed, the son of perdition, who

---

¹ πῶς editi antiqi.
² ἑαυτοῦ τὴν βουλήν] αὐτοῦ τὴν ἐπιβουλήν editi antiqi.
³ κεκρυμμένα ἡμῖν τὰ ἔνεδρα] κεκρυμμένας ἡμῖν τὰς ἔνεδρας E.
⁴ γενομένων Coisl. secundus, tres Regii.
⁵ ἤγησεν E.   ⁶ πολιᾷ editi antiqi.
⁷ κατάκρισιν E, Med.

ὁ ἀντικείμενος, καὶ ὑπεραιρόμενος ἐπὶ πάντα λεγόμενον Θεὸν ἢ σέβασμα ;

Πλὴν εἴτε πρόσκαιρός ἐστιν ὁ πειρασμός, βαστάσατε αὐτόν, οἱ καλοὶ τοῦ Χριστοῦ ἀγωνισταί· εἴτε καὶ τῇ παντελεῖ φθορᾷ τὰ πράγματα παραδίδοται,[1] μὴ ἀκηδιάσωμεν πρὸς τὰ παρόντα, ἀλλ' ἀναμείνωμεν τὴν ἐξ οὐρανῶν ἀποκάλυψιν καὶ ἐπιφάνειαν τοῦ μεγάλου Θεοῦ καὶ Σωτῆρος ἡμῶν Ἰησοῦ Χριστοῦ. εἰ γὰρ πᾶσα ἡ κτίσις λυθήσεται καὶ μεταποιηθήσεται τὸ σχῆμα τοῦ κόσμου τούτου, τί θαυμαστὸν καὶ ἡμᾶς, μέρος ὄντας τῆς κτίσεως, παθεῖν τὰ κοινὰ πάθη καὶ παραδοθῆναι θλίψεσιν, ἃς κατὰ τὸ μέτρον τῆς δυνάμεως ἡμῶν ἐπάγει ἡμῖν ὁ δίκαιος κριτής, οὐκ ἐῶν ἡμᾶς πειρασθῆναι ὑπὲρ ὃ δυνάμεθα, ἀλλὰ διδοὺς σὺν τῷ πειρασμῷ καὶ τὴν ἔκβασιν, τοῦ δυνηθῆναι[2] ὑπενεγκεῖν ;

Ἀναμένουσιν ὑμᾶς, ἀδελφοί, οἱ τῶν μαρτύρων στέφανοι· ἕτοιμοί εἰσιν οἱ χοροὶ τῶν ὁμολογητῶν προτεῖναι ὑμῖν τὰς χεῖρας καὶ ὑποδέξασθαι ὑμᾶς εἰς τὸν ἴδιον ἀριθμόν. μνήσθητε τῶν πάλαι ἁγίων, ὅτι οὐδεὶς τρυφῶν οὐδὲ[3] κολακευόμενος τῶν στεφάνων τῆς ὑπομονῆς ἠξιώθη, ἀλλὰ πάντες, διὰ μεγάλων θλίψεων πυρωθέντες, τὸ δοκίμιον ἐπεδείξαντο.[4] οἱ μὲν γὰρ ἐμπαιγμῶν καὶ μαστίγων πεῖραν ἔλαβον, ἄλλοι δὲ ἐπρίσθησαν, οἱ

---

[1] παραδίδονται editi antiqi.   [2] ἡμᾶς add. E.
[3] οὐ editi antiqi.   [4] ὑπεδείξαντο E.

opposeth and is lifted up above all that is called
God or that is worshipped "? [1]

Yet if the trial be momentary, bear it, brave
champions of Christ; or even if all has been given
over to utter destruction, let us not grow listless in
the face of present circumstances, but let us await
the revelation from heaven and the epiphany of our
great God and Saviour, Jesus Christ. For if all
creation shall be dissolved and the scheme of this
world be transformed, what wonder is it that we also,
being a part of creation, should suffer the common
doom and be given over to afflictions, which the
just Judge brings upon us according to the measure
of our strength, "not permitting us to be tempted
above that which we are able, but granting also with
temptation issue, that we may be able to bear it "? [2]

There await you, brothers, the martyrs' crowns;
the choirs of the confessors are ready to extend to
you their hands and to receive you among their own
number. Remember the saints of old, that no one
of them who indulged himself or yielded to flattery
was thought worthy of the crown of patient endur-
ance, but that they all, having through great afflictions
been tried by fire, proved their metal. For some
" had trial of mockeries and stripes," while others
" were cut asunder," and still others " were put to

---

[1] 2 Thess. 2. 4.
[2] Cf. 1 Cor. 10. 13: πειρασμὸς ὑμᾶς οὐκ εἴληφεν εἰ μὴ ἀνθρώπινος·
πιστὸς δὲ ὁ Θεός, ὃς οὐκ ἐάσει ὑμᾶς πειρασθῆναι ὑπὲρ ὃ δύνασθε,
ἀλλὰ ποιήσει σὺν τῷ πειρασμῷ καὶ τὴν ἔκβασιν τοῦ δύνασθαι ὑμᾶς
ὑπενεγκεῖν. " Let no temptation take hold on you, but such
as is human. And God is faithful, who will not suffer you to
be tempted above that which you are able; but will make
also with temptation issue, that you may be able to bear
it."

δὲ[1] ἐν φόνῳ μαχαίρας ἀπέθανον. ταῦτά ἐστι
τὰ σεμνολογήματα τῶν ἁγίων. μακάριος ὁ
καταξιωθεὶς τῶν ὑπὲρ Χριστοῦ παθημάτων.
μακαριώτερος δὲ ὁ πλεονάσας ἐν τοῖς παθήμασι·
διότι οὐκ ἄξια τὰ παθήματα τοῦ νῦν καιροῦ πρὸς
τὴν μέλλουσαν δόξαν ἀποκαλυφθῆναι[2] εἰς
ἡμᾶς.

Εἰ μὲν οὖν ἦν δυνατὸν αὐτόν με παραγενέσθαι,
οὐδὲν ἂν προετίμησα τῆς συντυχίας ὑμῶν, ὥστε
καὶ ἰδεῖν τοὺς ἀθλητὰς τοῦ Χριστοῦ, καὶ περιπτύξασθαι, καὶ κοινωνῆσαι τῶν προσευχῶν καὶ
τῶν πνευματικῶν ἐν ὑμῖν χαρισμάτων. ἐπειδὴ δὲ
τὸ σῶμά μοι λοιπὸν ὑπὸ χρονίας νόσου καταινά-
λωται, ὡς μηδὲ ἀπὸ τῆς κλίνης δύνασθαί με
καταβαίνειν, καὶ οἱ ἐφεδρεύοντες ἡμῖν πολλοί, ὡς
λύκοι ἅρπαγες, ἐπιτηροῦντες καιρὸν, πότε δυνηθῶσι διαρπάσαι τὰ πρόβατα τοῦ Χριστοῦ,
ἀναγκαίως ἐπὶ τὴν διὰ τοῦ γράμματος ἐπίσκεψιν
ἦλθον, παρακαλῶν προηγουμένως μὲν ἐκτενεῖς
τὰς ὑπὲρ ἐμοῦ ποιεῖσθαι ὑμᾶς δεήσεις, ἵνα
καταξιωθῶ τὰς γοῦν λειπομένας ἡμέρας ἢ ὥρας
δουλεῦσαι τῷ Κυρίῳ κατὰ τὸ εὐαγγέλιον τῆς
βασιλείας, ἔπειτα καὶ συγγνώμην ἔχειν μου τῇ
ἀπολείψει καὶ τῇ βραδυτῆτι ταύτῃ τῶν γραμμάτων. μόλις γὰρ ηὐπορήσαμεν ἀνθρώπου τοῦ
δυναμένου ἐξυπηρετήσασθαι ἡμῶν τῇ ἐπιθυμίᾳ·
λέγομεν δὲ τὸν υἱὸν ἡμῶν Εὐγένιον τὸν μονά-
ζοντα, δι᾽ οὗ παρακαλῶ εὔξασθαι ὑπὲρ ἡμῶν καὶ
τῆς Ἐκκλησίας πάσης, καὶ ἀντιγράψαι ἡμῖν τὰ
περὶ ὑμῶν, ἵνα γνόντες εὐθυμότερον διατεθῶμεν.

[1] ἐπρίσθησα:, οἱ δὲ] ἐπειράσθησαν· ἐπρίσθησαν E.
[2] ἀποκαλύπτεσθαι E.

death by the sword." [1] These are the proud boasts of the saints. Blessed is he who is deemed worthy of suffering for Christ! And more blessed is he who abounds in sufferings; for "the sufferings of this time are not worthy to be compared with the glory to come that shall be revealed in us." [2]

Now if it had been possible for me to be with you in person, I should have preferred nothing to such meeting with you, that I might see the athletes of Christ, and embrace you, and to share in your prayers and in your spiritual acts of grace. But since my body has been wasted by a long sickness, so that I am not even able to leave my bed, and since they are many who lie in wait for us, like rapacious wolves, watching for an opportunity when they may be able to seize the sheep of Christ, of necessity have I been reduced to visit you by letter, urging you above all to make earnest supplications for me, that I may be thought worthy to spend at least the remaining days or hours in serving the Lord according to the Gospel of His kingdom, and, in the second place, asking you to grant me pardon for my absence and for the tardiness of this letter. For with difficulty have we found a man who is able to carry out our desire ; we mean our son Eugenius, the monk, through whom I ask you to pray for us and for the entire Church, and to write us in answer about your affairs, that on being informed we may be of better cheer.

---

[1] Cf. Heb. 11. 36–37 : ἕτεροι δὲ ἐμπαιγμῶν καὶ μαστίγων πεῖραν ἔλαβον ἔτι δὲ δεσμῶν καὶ φυλακῆς· ἐλιθάσθησαν, ἐπρίσθησαν, ἐπειράσθησαν, ἐν φόνῳ μαχαίρας ἀπέθανον. " And others had trial of mockeries and stripes, moreover also of bonds and prisons. They were stoned, they were cut asunder, they were tempted, they were put to death by the sword."

[2] Rom. 8. 18.

CXL

Τῇ Ἀντιοχέων Ἐκκλησίᾳ [1]

Τίς δώσει μοι πτέρυγας, ὡσεὶ περιστερᾶς ; καὶ πετασθήσομαι [2] πρὸς ὑμᾶς καὶ καταπαύσω τὸν πόθον ὃν ἔχω ἐπὶ τῇ συντυχίᾳ τῆς ὑμετέρας ἀγάπης. νυνὶ δὲ οὐχὶ πτερύγων ἐνδεῶς ἔχω μόνον, ἀλλὰ καὶ αὐτοῦ τοῦ σώματος, πάλαι μέν μοι ὑπὸ μακρᾶς τῆς [3] ἀρρωστίας πεπονηκότος, νῦν δὲ ὑπὸ τῶν συνεχῶν θλίψεων παντελῶς συντετριμμένου. τίς γὰρ οὕτως ἀδαμάντινος τὴν ψυχήν, τίς οὕτω παντελῶς ἀσυμπαθὴς καὶ ἀνήμερος, ὡς [4] ἀκούων τοῦ πανταχόθεν ἡμᾶς [5] προσβάλλοντος στεναγμοῦ, οἷον ἀπό τινος χοροῦ κατηφοῦς κοινόν τινα θρῆνον καὶ σύμφωνον προσηχοῦντος, μὴ οὐχὶ παθεῖν τὴν ψυχήν, καὶ κατακαμφθῆναι εἰς γῆν, καὶ ταῖς ἀμηχάνοις ταύταις μερίμναις παντελῶς ἐκτακῆναι ; ἀλλὰ δυνατὸς ὁ ἅγιος Θεὸς δοῦναί τινα λύσιν τῶν ἀμηχάνων καὶ χαρίσασθαι ἡμῖν τινὰ τῶν μακρῶν πόνων ἀναπνοήν. ὥστε καὶ ὑμᾶς τὴν αὐτὴν ἔχειν ἀξιῶ παράκλησιν καὶ τῇ ἐλπίδι τῆς παρακλήσεως χαίροντας ὑμᾶς τὸ παρὸν ἀλγεινὸν τῶν θλίψεων ὑπομένειν. εἴτε γὰρ ἁμαρτημάτων ἀποτίννυμεν δίκας, ἱκαναὶ αἱ μάστιγες πρὸς παραίτησιν [6] λοιπὸν τῆς ἐφ᾽ ἡμῖν ὀργῆς τοῦ Θεοῦ· εἴτε εἰς τοὺς ὑπὲρ τῆς εὐσεβείας ἀγῶνας διὰ τῶν πειρασμῶν τούτων κεκλήμεθα, [7] δίκαιος ὁ ἀθλοθέτης μὴ ἐᾶσαι ἡμᾶς πειρασθῆναι

---

[1] τῇ ἐκκλησίᾳ Ἀντιοχείας παραμυθητικὴ E.
[2] πετανθήσομαι Regius.   [3] τῆς om. E.   [4] ὥς E.
[5] ἡμῖν Reg. secundus, Coisl. secundus.

LETTER CXL

To the Church of Antioch[1]

"Who will give me wings like a dove, and I will fly"[2] to you and end the longing which I have for converse with your Charity? But as it is I lack, not only wings, but my very body also, for it has suffered for a long time from my chronic illness and is now quite crushed by its continuous afflictions. For who is so hard of heart, who so wholly without sympathy and kindness, that, when he hears the lamentations which assail us from all sides, issuing as it were from a doleful choir intoning in unison a kind of universal dirge, does not suffer at heart, and is not bowed down to earth, and is not utterly wasted away by their present desperate anxieties? But the holy God has power to grant relief from our desperate straits and to bless us with a respite from our prolonged labours. So I feel that you also may well possess the same consolation, and, rejoicing in the hope of that consolation, endure the present pain of your afflictions. For if we are paying a penalty for sins, our scourging will suffice to appease henceforth God's wrath towards us, or if through these trials we have been called into the contest on behalf of the true religion, the arbiter of the contest is just and

---

[1] Written in 373.
[2] Cf. Psal. 54. 7 : καὶ εἶπα Τίς δώσει μοι πτέρυγας ὡσεὶ περιστερᾶς, καὶ πετασθήσομαι καὶ καταπαύσω; "And I said : Who will give me wings like a dove, and I will fly and be at rest ?"

---

[6] παρέκτισιν editi antiqi.   [7] βεβαιούμεθα editi antiqi.

ὑπὲρ ὃ δυνάμεθα ὑπενεγκεῖν, ἀλλ' ἐπὶ τοῖς προ-
πεπονημένοις ἀποδοῦναι ἡμῖν τὸν τῆς ὑπομονῆς
καὶ τῆς εἰς αὐτὸν ἐλπίδος στέφανον. μὴ οὖν
ἀποκάμωμεν ἐναθλοῦντες εἰς τοὺς ὑπὲρ τῆς εὐσεβείας ἀγῶνας, μηδὲ δι' ἀνελπιστίας τὰ πονηθέντα
ἡμῖν προώμεθα. οὐ γὰρ μία πρᾶξις ἀνδρείας οὐδὲ
βραχὺς πόνος τὸ τῆς ψυχῆς καρτερὸν διαδείκνυ-
σιν, ἀλλ' ὁ δοκιμάζων ἡμῶν τὰς καρδίας διὰ μακρᾶς καὶ παρατεταμένης τῆς δοκιμασίας βούλεται
ἡμᾶς τῆς δικαιοσύνης στεφανίτας ἀποδειχθῆναι.[1]

Μόνον ἀνένδοτον φυλασσέσθω τὸ φρόνημα
ἡμῶν, ἄσειστον τὸ στερέωμα τῆς εἰς Χριστὸν
πίστεως διατηρείσθω, καὶ ἥξει ἐν τάχει ὁ ἀντι-
ληψόμενος ἡμῶν· ἥξει καὶ οὐ χρονιεῖ. προσδέχου
γὰρ θλῖψιν ἐπὶ θλῖψει, ἐλπίδα ἐπ' ἐλπίδι, ἔτι
μικρόν, ἔτι μικρόν. οὕτως οἶδε ψυχαγωγεῖν τῇ
ἐπαγγελίᾳ τοῦ μέλλοντος τοὺς ἑαυτοῦ τροφίμους
τὸ Πνεῦμα τὸ ἅγιον. μετὰ γὰρ τὰς θλίψεις ἡ
ἐλπίς, ἐκ τοῦ σύνεγγυς δὲ πάρεστι τὰ ἐλπιζό-
μενα. κἂν γὰρ ὅλον τις εἴποι τὸν ἀνθρώπινον
βίον, σμικρότατόν ἐστι διάστημα παντελῶς,
συγκρίσει ἐκείνου τοῦ ἀπεράντου αἰῶνος τοῦ ἐν
ταῖς ἐλπίσιν ἀποκειμένου.

Πίστιν δὲ ἡμεῖς οὔτε παρ' ἄλλων γραφομένην
ἡμῖν νεωτέραν παραδεχόμεθα, οὔτε αὐτοὶ τὰ τῆς
ἡμετέρας διανοίας γεννήματα παραδιδόναι τολμῶ-
μεν, ἵνα μὴ ἀνθρώπινα ποιήσωμεν[2] τὰ τῆς εὐσεβείας ῥήματα· ἀλλ' ἅπερ παρὰ τῶν ἁγίων πατέρων
δεδιδάγμεθα, ταῦτα τοῖς ἐρωτῶσιν ἡμᾶς διαγγέλλο-
μεν. ἔστι τοίνυν ἐκ πατέρων ἐμπολιτευομένη τῇ

---

[1] ἀναδειχθῆναι editi antiqi.

will not permit us to be tried beyond what we can endure,[1] nay, for what we have already endured He will give us the crown of patience and of our hope in Him. So let us not weary of the contest in the struggle for the true religion, and let us not in despair give up the fruits of our labours. For it is not a single act of courage nor yet a labour for a brief space that proves the soul's strength, but He who makes trial of our hearts wishes by means of a long and protracted trial that we may be appointed winners of the crown of righteousness.

Only let our spirits be kept unyielding, the steadfastness of our faith in Christ maintained unshaken, and presently He will come who will take our part ; He will come and not delay. For you must look forward to affliction upon affliction, hope upon hope, for yet a little while, yet a little while. Thus does the Holy Spirit know how to beguile his nurslings by the promise of the future. For beyond the afflictions is hope, and near at hand are the objects of our hope. For even if one should speak of the whole of human life, it is indeed a very short span altogether as compared with that endless eternity which lies yonder in our hopes.

As to creed, we accept no newer creed written for us by others, nor do we ourselves make bold to give out the product of our own intelligence, lest we make the words of our religion the words of man ; but rather that which we have been taught by the holy Fathers do we make known to those who question us. We have, then, enfranchised in our church

---

[1] Cf. 1 Cor. 10. 13. See previous letter, p. 329, note 2.

---

[2] λογίζωνται editi antiqi.

ἐκκλησίᾳ ἡμῶν ἡ γραφεῖσα παρὰ τῶν ἁγίων
πατέρων πίστις τῶν κατὰ τὴν Νίκαιαν συνελθόν-
των·[1] ἣν ἡγούμεθα μὲν διὰ στόματος εἶναι καὶ
παρ' ὑμῖν, οὐ παραιτούμεθα δέ, ἵνα μὴ ὄκνου
ἔγκλημα ἀπενεγκώμεθα, καὶ αὐτὰ τὰ ῥήματα
ἐνσημᾶναι τῷ γράμματι. ἔστι δὲ ταῦτα. πιστεύομεν εἰς ἕνα Θεὸν Πατέρα παντοκράτορα,
ὁρατῶν τε πάντων καὶ ἀοράτων ποιητήν. καὶ εἰς
ἕνα Κύριον Ἰησοῦν Χριστὸν τὸν Υἱὸν τοῦ Θεοῦ,
γεννηθέντα ἐκ τοῦ Πατρὸς μονογενῆ· τουτέστιν,
ἐκ τῆς οὐσίας τοῦ Πατρός· φῶς ἐκ φωτός, Θεὸν
ἀληθινὸν ἐκ Θεοῦ ἀληθινοῦ· γεννηθέντα οὐ ποιη-
θέντα, ὁμοούσιον τῷ Πατρί, δι' οὗ τὰ πάντα
ἐγένετο, τά τε ἐν τῷ οὐρανῷ καὶ τὰ ἐν τῇ γῇ. τὸν
δι' ἡμᾶς τοὺς ἀνθρώπους καὶ διὰ τὴν ἡμετέραν
σωτηρίαν κατελθόντα·[2] σαρκωθέντα, ἐνανθρωπήσαντα, παθόντα, καὶ ἀναστάντα τῇ τρίτῃ ἡμέρα·
ἀνελθόντα εἰς οὐρανούς, ἐρχόμενον κρῖναι ζῶντας
καὶ νεκρούς. καὶ εἰς τὸ ἅγιον Πνεῦμα. τοὺς δὲ
λέγοντας, ἦν ποτέ, ὅτε οὐκ ἦν· καί, πρὶν γεννηθῆναι οὐκ ἦν· καί, ὅτι ἐξ οὐκ ὄντων ἐγένετο· ἢ
ἐξ ἑτέρας ὑποστάσεως ἢ οὐσίας φάσκοντας εἶναι,
ἢ τρεπτόν, ἢ ἀλλοιωτὸν τὸν Υἱὸν τοῦ Θεοῦ, τούτους
ἀναθεματίζει ἡ καθολικὴ καὶ ἀποστολικὴ Ἐκκλησία.

Πιστεύομεν τούτοις. ἐπειδὴ δὲ ἀδιόριστός

---

[1] ἡμῖν add. E.

from the time of the Fathers the creed which was written by the holy Fathers convened at Nicaea; and this we believe is repeated among you also, but, in order that we may not incur the charge of reluctance, we do not refuse to put into writing the very words themselves. They are as follows: "We believe in one God, the Father Almighty, Maker of all things visible and invisible. And in one Lord, Jesus Christ, the Son of God, born of the Father, the only begotten, that is, the substance of the Father. Light of light, true God of true God; begotten, not made, consubstantial with the Father, by whom all things were made both in heaven and on earth. Who for us men and for our salvation came down; and was incarnate and was made man; suffered and rose again on the third day. He ascended into heaven, and shall come to judge the living and the dead. And (we believe) in the Holy Ghost. But as for those who say 'There was when He was not,' and 'Before He was begotten He was not,' or that 'He came into existence from what was not,' or who profess that the Son of God is of a different person or substance, or that the Son of God is changeable or variable, these the Catholic and Apostolic Church anathematizes." [1]

This do we believe. But since the doctrine of the

---

[1] The Benedictine editors point out that Saint Leontius brought the Nicene Creed to Caesarea, and that Hermogenes, the successor of Leontius, bravely defended it, according to Letter LXXXI. Hermogenes' successor, Dianius, however, signed several Arian formulae, but the Nicene Creed continued to be maintained. Furthermore, in Letter LI Dianius is described as supporting it.

---

[2] ἐκ τῶν οὐρανῶν add. editi antiqi.

ἐστιν ὁ περὶ τοῦ ἁγίου Πνεύματος λόγος, οὔπω
τότε τῶν πνευματομάχων ἀναφανέντων, τὸ χρῆναι ἀναθεματίζεσθαι τοὺς λέγοντας τῆς κτιστῆς
εἶναι καὶ δουλικῆς φύσεως τὸ Πνεῦμα τὸ ἅγιον
ἐσίγησαν. οὐδὲν γὰρ ὅλως τῆς θείας καὶ μακαρίας
Τριάδος κτιστόν.

CXLI

Εὐσεβίῳ, ἐπισκόπῳ Σαμοσάτων

Ἐδεξάμην ἤδη δύο ἐπιστολὰς παρὰ τῆς ἐνθέου
καὶ τελειοτάτης φρονήσεώς σου, ὧν ἡ μὲν ὑπέγρα-
φεν ἡμῖν ἐναργῶς, ὅπως μὲν προσεδοκήθημεν ὑπὸ
τοῦ λαοῦ τοῦ ὑπὸ τὴν χεῖρα τῆς ὁσιότητός σου,
ὅσον δὲ ἐλυπήσαμεν ἀπολειφθέντες τῆς ἁγιωτάτης
συνόδου. ἡ δὲ ἑτέρα, ἡ παλαιοτέρα μέν, ὡς
εἰκάζω τῷ γράμματι, ὕστερον δὲ ἡμῖν ἀποδοθεῖσα,
διδασκαλίαν περιεῖχε πρέπουσάν σοι καὶ ἡμῖν
ἀναγκαίαν, μὴ καταρραθυμεῖν τῶν ἐκκλησιῶν τοῦ
Θεοῦ, μηδὲ κατὰ μικρὸν προΐεσθαι τοῖς ὑπεναν-
τίοις τὰ πράγματα, ἀφ' ὧν τὰ μὲν ἐκείνων αὐξήσει,

---

[1] They flourished in the countries adjacent to the Helles-
pont. They denied the divinity of the Holy Ghost, hence
the name Pneumatomachi or Combators against the Spirit.
Macedonius, their founder, was intruded into the see of
Constantinople by Arians (A.D. 342) and enthroned by
Constantius, who had for a second time expelled Paul, the
Catholic bishop. They are sometimes called Macedonians,
after the name of their founder.

[2] *i.e.* the Fathers of Nicaea.

[3] Written in 373. In this letter Basil answers two complaints of Eusebius : that Basil had not come to him, and
that Basil should take up more energetically the defence of
orthodoxy.

LETTER CXLI

Holy Spirit had not yet been defined, for no Pneumatomachi [1] had as yet arisen at that time, they [2] were silent about the need of anathematizing those who say that the Holy Spirit is of a created and servile nature. For nothing at all in the divine and blessed Trinity is created.

LETTER CXLI

To Eusebius, Bishop of Samosata [3]

I HAVE already received two letters from your divine and consummate Wisdom, [4] and one of these vividly described to us how we had been expected by the people under the episcopal sway of your Holiness, and how much disappointment we occasioned by being absent from the most holy synod. The other letter, of an earlier date, as I judge by the writing, but delivered to us after the first-mentioned, contained an admonition which does credit to yourself and is necessary for us—not to neglect the churches of God nor little by little to surrender the control of affairs to our adversaries, with the result that their interests will increase and ours will be

---

St. Eusebius, Bishop of Samosata (Commagene), died in 379. His feast is celebrated on June 22 by the Greeks and June 21 by the Latins. His life reflects more than any other the unrest and troubles of the Eastern Church between 361 and 379. Eusebius was a moderate partisan of the Creed of Nicaea. He was threatened by Constantius, and, under Valens, could only traverse his diocese in disguise in order to sustain the faith of his people. A decree of 373 banished him to Thrace. Finally, when after the death of Valens (376) he returned to Commagene, an Arian woman killed him by hitting him with a stone. Cf. Tillemont, note 64.

[4] A title in Byzantine times.

τὰ δὲ ἡμέτερα μειωθήσεται. καὶ οἶμαι πρὸς
ἑκατέραν ἀποκεκρίσθαι· πλὴν ἀλλὰ καὶ νῦν,
ἐπειδὴ ἄδηλον εἰ οἱ πιστευθέντες τὴν διακονίαν
διέσωσαν ἡμῶν τὰς ἀποκρίσεις, περὶ τῶν αὐτῶν
ἀπολογοῦμαι· πρὸς μὲν τὴν ἀπόλειψιν ἀληθεσ-
τάτην πρόφασιν γράφων, ἧς οἶμαι τὴν ἀκοὴν
καὶ μέχρι τῆς σῆς ὁσιότητος διαβεβηκέναι, ὅτι
ὑπὸ ἀρρωστίας κατεσχέθην τῆς μέχρις αὐτῶν με
τῶν πυλῶν τοῦ θανάτου καταγαγούσης. καὶ ἔτι
καὶ νῦν, ἡνίκα ἀπέστελλον περὶ τούτων, λείψανα
φέρων τῆς ἀρρωστίας ἔγραφον. ταῦτα δέ ἐστι
τοιαῦτα, ὥστε ἐξαρκεῖν ἑτέρῳ νοσήματα[1] εἶναι
δύσφορα.

Πρὸς δὲ τό, ὅτι οὐ ῥᾳθυμίᾳ ἡμετέρᾳ τὰ τῶν
ἐκκλησιῶν τοῖς ἐναντίοις προδέδοται, εἰδέναι
βούλομαι τὴν θεοσέβειάν σου, ὅτι οἱ κοινωνικοὶ
δῆθεν ἡμῖν τῶν ἐπισκόπων, ἢ ὄκνῳ, ἢ τῷ πρὸς
ἡμᾶς ὑπόπτως ἔχειν ἔτι καὶ μὴ καθαρῶς, ἢ τῇ
παρὰ τοῦ διαβόλου ἐγγινομένῃ πρὸς τὰς ἀγαθὰς
πράξεις ἐναντιώσει, συνάρασθαι[2] ἡμῖν οὐκ ἀνέχον-
ται. ἀλλὰ σχήματι μὲν δῆθεν οἱ πλείους ἐσμὲν
μετ᾽ ἀλλήλων, προστεθέντος ἡμῖν καὶ τοῦ χρηστοῦ Βοσπορίου, ἀληθείᾳ δὲ πρὸς οὐδὲν ἡμῖν τῶν
ἀναγκαιοτάτων συναίρονται· ὥστε με καὶ ὑπὸ τῆς
ἀθυμίας ταύτης τὸ πλεῖστον μέρος πρὸς τὴν
ἀνάληψιν ἐμποδίζεσθαι, συνεχῶς μοι τῶν ἀρ-

[1] ἑτέρων νοσήματα E ; ἑτέρῳ νοσήματα Harl., Med. ; ἑτέρων
νοσήματι editi antiqi.

340

diminished. I think I have answered both letters; but since it is not clear whether those entrusted with the mission succeeded in delivering our replies, I shall now defend myself once more as regards these same matters. As regards my absence, I am writing a most truthful excuse, the report of which, I think, has travelled even to your Holiness —that I was detained by an illness which brought me down to the very gates of death. And again even now, as I tell you about these things, I am writing while still suffering the after-effects of my illness. And these are of such a character that for another man they would pass for maladies not easy to endure.

As to the other matter, to explain that it is through no negligence on our part that the interests of the churches have been surrendered to our adversaries, I wish your Reverence to know that the bishops who pretend to be in communion with us, either because of reluctance, or again on account of being suspicious of us and not frank and open towards us, or finally on account of the opposition to good works which is fomented by the devil, do not permit themselves to assist us. But while ostensibly the majority of us are united with one another, the excellent Bosporius [1] also having been added to our number, yet in reality they render us no assistance in the most urgent matters; consequently my recovery is being hindered for the most part by my discouragement, since all

---

[1] Bosporius, an intimate friend of Basil, was Bishop of Colonia in Cappadocia Secunda. Cf. Letter LI.

---

[2] συναιρεσθαι editi antiqi.

ρωστημάτων ἐκ τῆς σφοδρᾶς λύπης ἀποστρεφόντων.[1]

Τί δ᾽ ἂν ποιήσαιμι μόνος, τῶν κανόνων, ὡς καὶ
αὐτὸς οἶδας, ἐνὶ τὰς τοιαύτας οἰκονομίας μὴ συγ-
χωρούντων ; καίτοι τίνα θεραπείαν οὐκ ἐθερά-
πευσα ; ποίου κρίματος αὐτοὺς οὐκ ἀνέμνησα τὰ
μὲν διὰ γραμμάτων, τὰ δὲ καὶ διὰ τῆς συντυχίας ; ἦλθον γὰρ καὶ μέχρι τῆς[2] πόλεως κατὰ
ἀκοὴν τοῦ ἐμοῦ θανάτου. ἐπεὶ δὲ ἔδοξε τῷ Θεῷ
ζῶντας ἡμᾶς παρ᾽ αὐτῶν καταληφθῆναι, διελέχθημεν αὐτοῖς τὰ εἰκότα. καὶ παρόντα μὲν αἰδοῦνται,
καὶ ὑπισχνοῦνται τὰ εἰκότα πάντα, ἀπολειφθέντες
δὲ πάλιν πρὸς τὴν ἑαυτῶν ἀνατρέχουσι γνώμην.
ταῦτα καὶ ἡμεῖς τῆς κοινῆς καταστάσεως τῶν
πραγμάτων ἀπολαύομεν, προδήλως τοῦ Κυρίου
ἐγκαταλιπόντος ἡμᾶς, τοὺς διὰ τὸ πληθυνθῆναι
τὴν ἀνομίαν ψύξαντας τὴν ἀγάπην. ἀλλὰ
πρὸς πάντα ἡμῖν ἀρκεσάτω ἡ μεγάλη σου καὶ
δυνατωτάτη πρὸς Θεὸν ἱκεσία. τάχα γὰρ ἂν
ἢ γενοίμεθά τι τοῖς πράγμασι χρήσιμοι, ἢ
διαμαρτόντες[3] τῶν σπουδαζομένων, φύγοιμεν τὴν
κατάκρισιν.

[1] ἀποστρεφόντων E.
[2] τῆς om. E.

the symptoms of my disease continually recur as the result of my exceeding grief.

But what can I do single-handed, when the Canons,[1] as you yourself well know, do not grant to one man the appropriate administrative powers? And yet what remedy is there that I have not applied? What decision have I failed to bring to their attention, partly by letters, and partly by personal interviews? For they even came to the city at a report of my death. But since it was pleasing to God that they should find us still alive, we addressed them in language proper to such an occasion. They are reverent in my presence, and promise all that they should, but on leaving me they once more return to their own opinion. In all this we, as well as others, are but feeling the effect of the general condition of affairs, for the Lord has clearly abandoned us, seeing that we have grown cold in our love on account of the widespread increase of lawlessness. But to combat all this let your great and most powerful supplication to God assist us. For perhaps we may be of some use in the situation, or, if we fail in what we desire, may escape condemnation.

[1] These canons, which were falsely ascribed to the apostles, are sometimes cited by Basil among the canonical epistles. He seems here to refer to the 27th, where it is ordained that in each province the bishops should not initiate anything of an important character without the opinion or consent of him who is first in rank among them, and that each one should be content with those things which belong to his own district; but he should not do anything without the good-will of all. Basil was very scrupulous in observing this canon. Cf. the note of the Benedictine editors.

---

³ διαμαρτάνοντες editi antiqi.

CXLII

Νουμεραρίῳ ἐπάρχων[1]

Συνήγαγον μὲν[2] πάντας ἐν τῇ συνόδῳ τοῦ
μακαρίου μάρτυρος Εὐψυχίου τοὺς ἀδελφοὺς
ἡμῶν τοὺς χωρεπισκόπους, ὥστε γνωρίμους
ποιῆσαι τῇ τιμιότητί σου. ἐπεὶ δὲ ἀπελείφθης,
διὰ γραμμάτων αὐτοὺς ἀναγκαῖόν ἐστι προσαχ-
θῆναί σου τῇ τελειότητι. γνώριζε τοίνυν τὸν
ἀδελφὸν τόνδε ἄξιον ὄντα τοῦ πιστεύεσθαι παρὰ
τῆς σῆς φρονήσεως διὰ τὸν φόβον τοῦ Κυρίου.
καὶ ἅπερ ἂν τῶν πτωχῶν ἕνεκεν ἀναφέρῃ σου τῇ
ἀγαθῇ προαιρέσει, καταξίωσον ὡς ἀληθεύοντι
πείθεσθαι καὶ τὴν δυνατὴν ἐπικουρίαν παρέχεσθαι
τοῖς καταπονουμένοις. καταξιώσεις δὲ δηλονότι
καὶ πτωχοτροφίαν τῆς συμμορίας τῆς ὑπ᾽ αὐτὸν
ἐπισκέψασθαι καὶ πάντη ἀνεῖναι τῆς συντελείας.
τοῦτο γὰρ ἤδη καὶ τῷ ἑταίρῳ σου συνήρεσε τὴν
μικρὰν κτῆσιν τῶν πενήτων ἀλειτούργητον καταστῆσαι.

---

[1] ἐπαρχιῶν Reg. secundus, Coisl. secundus.
[2] συνήγαγον μὲν] συνηγάγομεν E, Reg. secundus.

---

[1] Written in 373. Νουμεραρίῳ is merely the transcription
of a Latin title. There were two Numerarii in every province. The Benedictine editors remark that Valens had
decreed in 365 that the Numerarii of the Consulares and
Praesides should henceforth be called *tabellarii*. But
perhaps that law was little observed, or, as has happened in
many other letters of Basil, the heading has been added
since Basil's time by the scribes.

LETTER CXLII

To the Prefects' Accountant[1]

I convened all our brethren, the Chorepiscopi,[2] at the synod of the blessed martyr Eupsychius,[3] in order to introduce them to your Honour. But since you were absent, it is now necessary that they be introduced to your Perfection by letter. Know, then, that this present brother is worthy of being trusted by your Wisdom through his fear of the Lord. Moreover, whatever matters he may refer to your goodwill as regards the welfare of the poor, deign to believe him as a man who speaks the truth and to offer to the afflicted the greatest assistance possible. In particular, you will have the kindness to inspect the home for the poor in the district under his care, and to exempt it entirely from taxation. For it has already pleased your colleague also to make the small property of the poor immune from assessment.

---

[2] Cf. Letter LIII and note.

[3] Eupsychius appears in the Roman calendar, and his martyrdom is celebrated on April 9. During the reign of Julian he assisted in the demolition of a temple of Fortune in the city of Caesarea in Cappadocia. All who took part in this affair were condemned either to death or banishment (cf. Sozomen, *H. E.* 5, 11). Eupsychius was beheaded, but the temple of Fortune was never rebuilt. In its place a church in memory of Eupsychius was erected. To the festival of the dedication of this church Basil summoned all the bishops of Pontus by a letter which is still extant (Letter CCLII). Furthermore, we find Basil eagerly entreating Eusebius of Samosata to be present at the festival of Eupsychius on Sept. 7, 372 (cf. Basil, Letter C; also Greg. Naz., Letters XXVI and XXVII).

CXLIII

Ἑτέρῳ νουμεραρίῳ

Εἰ μὲν αὐτῷ μοι δυνατὸν ἦν συμπαρεῖναι τῇ τιμιότητί σου, δι' ἐμαυτοῦ ἂν πάντως ἀνήνεγκα περὶ ὧν ἐβουλόμην καὶ προέστην τῶν καταπονουμένων. ἐπεὶ δέ με ἀρρωστία σώματος καὶ ἀσχολίαι πραγμάτων ἀφέλκουσιν,[1] ἀντ' ἐμαυτοῦ σοι τὸν ἀδελφὸν τόνδε τὸν χωρεπίσκοπον συνίστημι, ὥστε σε αὐτῷ γνησίως προσχόντα χρήσασθαι συμβούλῳ, ὡς φιλαλήθως καὶ ἐμφρόνως δυναμένῳ συμβουλεῦσαι περὶ τῶν πραγμάτων. τὸ γὰρ πτωχοτροφεῖον τὸ παρ' αὐτοῦ οἰκονομούμενον ἐπειδὰν καταξιώσῃς θεάσασθαι (ὄψει γάρ, εὖ οἶδα, καὶ οὐ παραδραμῇ, ἐπειδὴ οὐδὲ ἄπειρος[2] εἶ τοῦ ἔργου, ἀλλ', ὡς ὁ δεῖνά μοι ἀνήνεγκεν, ἐν τῶν ἐν τῇ Ἀμασείᾳ ἐξ ὧν ἔδωκέ σοι ὁ Κύριος διατρέφεις), ἐπειδὰν οὖν ἴδῃς καὶ τοῦτο, πάντα αὐτῷ παρέξῃ[3] τὰ ἐπιζητούμενα. ἤδη γάρ μοι καὶ ἑταῖρός σου κατεπηγγείλατο φιλανθρωπίαν τινὰ περὶ τὰ πτωχοτροφεῖα. τοῦτο δὲ λέγω, οὐχ ἵνα ἄλλον αὐτὸς μιμήσῃ (σὲ γὰρ εἰκὸς ἑτέροις εἶναι

---

[1] ἀνθέλκουσιν editi antiqi.   [2] ἄπορος E, Reg. secundus.
[3] παρέξεις editi antiqi.

---

[1] Written in 373. Cf. previous letter, note 1.
[2] Cf. Letter LIII and note.
[3] A city in the Pontus, situated on the Iris.
[4] By the word "colleague" here is not meant the other accountant to whom the previous letter is addressed, because in that letter also Basil remarks that he has been promised

LETTER CXLIII

To the Other Accountant [1]

IF it had been possible for me to call upon your
Honour, I should certainly have brought to your
attention in person the matters about which I wished
to consult you, and I should have championed the
cause of the afflicted. Since, however, illness of
body and the pressure of affairs detain me, I am
now recommending to you in my place this brother,
the chorepiscopus,[2] that you, paying him sincere
attention, may treat him as your counsellor, since he
is able truthfully and prudently to advise you concerning our affairs. For instance, when you are
kind enough to look at the home for the poor that
is administered by him (for you will see it, I am
sure, and will not pass it by, since you are not
unfamiliar with the work, but, as a certain person
has informed me, you are supporting one of the
homes at Amasea [3] with the means which the Lord
has bestowed upon you)—when, therefore, you see
this home also, you will furnish him with whatever
he requests. For already your colleague [4] has also
promised me some beneficence for the homes for
the poor. But I am saying this, not to induce you
to imitate another (for there is every reason why

help for the poor by the addressee's colleague. Since there
were but two accountants, this probably refers to another
officer who had very similar duties. The Benedictine editors
conjecture him to be the prefects' officer ($\tau\rho\alpha\kappa\tau\epsilon\nu\tau\grave{\eta}s$ $\tau\hat{\omega}\nu$
$\dot{\epsilon}\pi\acute{\alpha}\rho\chi\omega\nu$), to whom the next letter is addressed, and who is
asked to fulfil certain promises he has made. However, it
may be that Basil, to gain his end, is craftily telling each of
the two what the other has promised.

τῶν καλῶν ἡγεμόνα), ἀλλ᾽ ἵνα γνῷς ὅτι δὴ περὶ αὐτῶν τούτων καὶ ἄλλοι ἡμᾶς ἐδυσωπήθησαν.[1]

CXLIV

Τρακτευτῇ τῶν ἐπάρχων

Γνωρίζεις πάντως τόνδε ἐκ τῆς κατὰ τὴν πόλιν συντυχίας, ὅμως δέ σοι αὐτὸν καὶ διὰ τῆς ἐπιστολῆς προσάγομεν συνιστῶντες, ὅτι εἰς πολλά σοι τῶν σπουδαζομένων χρήσιμος ἔσται, διὰ τὸ καὶ συνετῶς καὶ εὐλαβῶς δύνασθαι ὑποτίθεσθαι τὰ πρακτέα. ἃ δὲ ἐμοὶ εἰς τὸ οὖς διελέχθης, ταῦτα νῦν ἐστὶ καιρὸς ἐπιδείξασθαι, ἐπειδάν σοι ὁ προειρημένος ἀδελφὸς τὰ τῶν πτωχῶν ὑποδείξῃ.

CXLV

Εὐσεβίῳ, ἐπισκόπῳ Σαμοσάτων

Οἶδα τοὺς μυρίους πόνους[2] σου, οὓς ἀνέτλης ὑπὲρ τῶν ἐκκλησιῶν τοῦ Θεοῦ, καὶ τῶν ἀσχολιῶν τὸ πλῆθος οὐκ ἀγνοῶ, ἃς ἔχεις, τὴν οἰκονομίαν οὐ παρέργως ἀλλὰ κατὰ τὸ θέλημα τοῦ Κυρίου διατιθέμενος. καὶ τὸν ἐκ γειτόνων ὑμῖν ἐπικαθήμενον ἐννοῶ,[3] ᾧ ἀνάγκη ὑμᾶς, ὥσπερ ὄρνιθας

---

[1] ἐδυσώπησαν E, editi antiqi.
[2] κόπους quattuor MSS.　　　[3] ἐννοῶ om. E.

---

[1] Written in 373 and on the same occasion.

LETTER CXLV

you should be the leader of the rest in noble deeds),
but in order that you may know that others also
regarding these very matters have shown us a
reverent respect.

LETTER CXLIV

To the Prefects' Officer [1]

You are surely acquainted with this man through
your interview with him in the city, but nevertheless we are introducing and commending him to
you also by letter, because he will be useful to you
in many matters which now engage your attention,
as he is a man capable of advising you intelligently
and piously as to what must be done.   And now
you will have the opportunity of giving proof of the
things you once whispered into my ear, when the
brother whom we have mentioned shall have laid
before you the condition of the poor.

LETTER CXLV

To Eusebius, Bishop of Samosata [2]

I know the innumerable tasks which you have
taken upon yourself in defence of the churches
of God, and I am not unaware of the multitude of
activities which occupy you, since you conduct your
administration in no cursory manner but in accordance with the will of the Lord.   And I bear in mind
him [3] who besieges you from close at hand, to avoid
whom each one of you must, like birds cowering before

[2] Written in 373.   For this Eusebius, cf. Letter CXLI,
p. 339, note 3.
[3] i.e. Valens.

ἀετῷ ὑποπτήσσοντας, μὴ πόρρω τῆς σκέπης
ἕκαστον ἀποτρέχειν. τούτων με οὐδὲν λέληθεν.
ἀλλ' ὁ πόθος πρᾶγμα βίαιον, καὶ ἐλπίσαι τὰ μὴ
ἐνδεχόμενα καὶ ἐγχειρῆσαι τοῖς ἀδυνάτοις·[1] μᾶλλον
δὲ ἡ ἐπὶ Κύριον ἐλπὶς ἰσχυρότατον πάντων. οὐ
γὰρ ἀλόγῳ ἐπιθυμίᾳ, ἀλλ' ἰσχύϊ πίστεως προσδοκῶ καὶ πόρον ἐν ἀμηχάνοις φανήσεσθαι καὶ
πάντων ῥᾳδίως σε[2] τῶν κωλυμάτων περιγε-
νήσεσθαι, πρὸς τὸ ἰδεῖν σε τὴν φιλτάτην τῶν
ἐκκλησιῶν, καὶ μέντοι καὶ[3] ὀφθῆναι παρ' αὐτῆς·
ὃ πάντων αὐτῇ τῶν ἀγαθῶν προτιμότατον, τῷ σῷ
προσβλέψαι προσώπῳ καὶ τῆς σῆς ἀκοῦσαι
φωνῆς. μὴ τοίνυν αὐτῇ τὰς ἐλπίδας ἀτελεῖς
καταστήσῃς. καὶ γὰρ πέρυσιν ἀπὸ τῆς Συρίας
ἐπανελθών, ἣν ἐδεξάμην ἐπαγγελίαν, ταύτην
διακομίσας, πῶς οἴει μετέωρον αὐτὴν κατέστησα
ταῖς ἐλπίσι; μὴ οὖν εἰς ἄλλον καιρὸν ὑπέρθῃ τὴν
ἐπίσκεψιν αὐτῆς,[4] ὦ θαυμάσιε. καὶ γὰρ ἐὰν ᾖ
δυνατὸν ἰδεῖν αὐτήν ποτε, ἀλλ' οὐχὶ καὶ μεθ'
ἡμῶν, οὓς ἐπείγει ἡ νόσος ἀπᾶραι λοιπὸν τοῦ
ὀδυνηροῦ τούτου βίου.

CXLVI

Ἀντιόχῳ[5]

Οὐκ ἔχω μέμψασθαί σοι[6] ἀργίαν οὐδὲ ῥαθυ-
μίαν, ὅτι καιροῦ παραπεσόντος[7] γραμμάτων ἀπε-

---

[1] ποιεῖ add. editi antiqi.
[2] ῥᾳδίως σε] περιγενέσθαι editi antiqi.
[3] καὶ] κἄν E.
[4] αὐτῶν Harl.
[5] τῷ αὐτῷ ἐπισκόπῳ E.
[6] σου E.
[7] παρεμπεσόντος editi antiqi.

an eagle, never stray far from your place of shelter.
None of these facts has escaped me. However,
desire is a powerful thing, forcing one both to hope
for that which is unattainable and to undertake that
which is impossible; nay, rather, our hope in the
Lord is the strongest of all.[1] For not by means
of unreasoning desire but through the strength of
faith I expect that a way will appear in desperate
straits and that you will easily surmount all obstacles,
so that you may see your most beloved church, and,
moreover, may also be seen by her; and this she
holds in esteem above all blessings—to gaze upon
your countenance, and to listen to your voice.
Therefore do not cause her hopes to be unfulfilled.
For when, returning from Syria last year, I brought
with me the promise which I had received, to what
pitch of hopeful expectation do you think I raised
her? Accordingly, do not defer to another occasion
your visit to her, admirable sir. For even if it is
possible to see her some day, it may not, however,
be possible to see her and also us, since our sickness
is urging us soon to depart from this painful life.

LETTER CXLVI

To Antiochus [2]

I CANNOT blame you for laziness or indifference,
because when an opportunity for writing was at

---

[1] Cf. St. Augustine *in Ps.* 3: "Vita vere mortalis spes
est vitae immortalis"; and St. Greg., *Moral.*: "Spes in
aeternitatem animum erigit, et idcirco nulla mala sentit."
Cf. also Ovid, *Pont.* 1, 7.

[2] Written in 373 to Antiochus, the nephew of Eusebius,
Bishop of Samosata. Letters CLVII, CLVIII, and CLXVIII
are also addressed to him.

σιώπησας. ἦν γὰρ διὰ τῆς τιμίας ἐμοὶ χειρὸς
διεπέμψω προσηγορίαν πολλῶν ἐπιστολῶν τιμιω-
τέραν ποιοῦμαι. ἀντὶ οὖν ταύτης προσαγορεύω
σε, καὶ παρακαλῶ σπουδαίως ἀντέχεσθαι τῆς
κατὰ ψυχὴν σωτηρίας, πάντα τὰ πάθη τῆς
σαρκὸς παιδαγωγοῦντα τῷ λόγῳ, καὶ διηνεκῶς
τὴν περὶ Θεοῦ ἔννοιαν, οἷον ἐν ναῷ τινι ἁγιωτάτῳ,
τῇ σαυτοῦ ψυχῇ ἐνιδρυμένην ἔχοντα· ἐπὶ πάσης
δὲ πράξεως καὶ παντὸς λόγου πρὸ ὀφθαλμῶν
λαμβάνειν τὸ τοῦ Χριστοῦ [1] δικαστήριον, ὥστε
σοι τὰς κατὰ μέρος ἐνεργείας συναχθείσας ἐπὶ
τῆς ἀκριβοῦς ἐκείνης καὶ φοβερᾶς ἐξετάσεως
δόξαν ἐν τῇ ἡμέρᾳ τῆς ἀνταποδόσεως ἐνεγκεῖν,
ἐπὶ πάσης τῆς κτίσεως τῶν ἐπαίνων ἀξιουμένῳ.
εἰ δὲ καταδέχοιτο τὴν μέχρις ἡμῶν ὁδὸν ὁ μέγας,
οὐ μικρὸν κέρδος ἰδεῖν σε μετ᾽ αὐτοῦ ἐπὶ τῆς
ἡμετέρας.

CXLVII

Ἀβουργίῳ

Μῦθον ἐνόμιζον τέως τὰ τοῦ Ὁμήρου, ὅτε
ἐπῄειν αὐτοῦ τὸ ἕτερον μέρος τῆς ποιήσεως, ἐν ᾧ
τὰ τοῦ Ὀδυσσέως πάθη μεταδιδάσκει. ἀλλ᾽
ἐκεῖνα τὰ μυθικὰ τέως καὶ ἄπιστα πάνυ ἡμᾶς
πιθανὰ νομίζειν ἐδίδαξεν ἡ περὶ τὸν πάντα ἄριστον
Μάξιμον περιπέτεια. καὶ γὰρ καὶ [2] οὗτος ἄρχων

---

[1] Κυρίου editi antiqi.   [2] καί om. E.

---

[1] i.e. Eusebius of Samosata.

[2] Written in 373. Basil asks his friend Aburgius to use
his influence in behalf of Maximus, former governor of
Cappadocia, who has been unjustly accused of embezzlement,

hand you kept your silence. For the greeting which you sent me in your honoured hand I hold in greater esteem than many letters. I therefore in turn send my greetings to you, and I exhort you to cleave zealously to the salvation of your soul, moderating all the affections of the flesh by reason, and constantly keeping the thought of God firmly established in your soul, as in a most holy temple ; and in every word and in every deed hold before your eyes the judgment of Christ, so that, when all your several activities have been brought before that strict and terrible scrutiny, they may bring you glory on the day of reward, when you are accounted worthy of praise in the presence of every creature. And if that great man [1] should take upon himself a journey to us, it would be no small gain to see you with him in our country.

LETTER CXLVII

To Aburgius [2]

I used to think the works of Homer fable, whenever I read the second part of his poem in which he gives his strange version of the sufferings of Odysseus. But what formerly seemed to me fabulous and incredible the calamity which has befallen our most excellent Maximus has taught me to consider as altogether probable. For Maximus was a ruler over

stripped of his office and property, and forced to flee to Caesarea. Aburgius was a wealthy layman, to whom Basil often appealed in behalf of his unfortunate acquaintances and friends. Other letters to Aburgius are XXXIII, LXXV, CXCVI, CLXXVIII, and CCCIV. On Maximus, cf. Letter XCVIII.

ἐγένετο ἔθνους οὐ φαυλοτάτου, ὥσπερ ἐκεῖνος ὁ
στρατηγὸς τῶν Κεφαλλήνων. καὶ πολλὰ χρήματα
ἄγων ἐκεῖνος γυμνὸς ἐπανῆλθε, καὶ τοῦτον οὕτως
ἡ συμφορὰ διέθηκεν, ὡς κινδυνεῦσαι ἐν ἀλλοτρίοις
ῥάκεσιν ὀφθῆναι τοῖς οἴκοι.[1] καὶ ταῦτα πέπονθε,
Λαιστρυγόνας τάχα που ἐφ᾽ ἑαυτὸν παροξύνας,
καὶ Σκύλλῃ περιπεσὼν ἐν γυναικείᾳ μορφῇ
κυνείαν ἐχούσῃ ἀπανθρωπίαν καὶ ἀγριότητα.
ἐπεὶ οὖν μόλις αὐτῷ ὑπῆρξε τὸν ἄφυκτον
τοῦτον διανήξασθαι κλύδωνα, σὲ δι᾽ ἡμῶν ἱκετεύει,
ἀξιῶν αἰδεσθῆναι τὴν κοινὴν φύσιν καὶ ἐπὶ ταῖς
παρ᾽ ἀξίαν αὐτοῦ συμφοραῖς ἀλγήσαντα, μὴ
σιωπῇ κρύψαι τὰ κατ᾽ αὐτόν, ἀλλὰ διαγγεῖλαι
τοῖς ἐν δυνάμει, ὥστε μάλιστα μὲν καὶ γενέσθαι
τινὰ αὐτῷ βοήθειαν πρὸς τὴν σκευωρηθεῖσαν[2]
ἐπήρειαν· εἰ δὲ μή, δημοσιευθῆναι γοῦν τὴν
προαίρεσιν τοῦ εἰς αὐτὸν ἐμπαροινήσαντος.
ἀρκοῦσα γὰρ τῷ ἠδικημένῳ παραμυθία ἡ τῶν
ἐπιβουλευσάντων αὐτῷ τῆς πονηρίας φανέρωσις.

CXLVIII

Τραϊανῷ

Πολλὴν φέρει τοῖς καταπονουμένοις παραμυθίαν καὶ τὸ ἔχειν ἀποδύρασθαι τὰς ἑαυτῶν
συμφοράς, καὶ μάλιστα ὅταν ἀνδρῶν ἐπιτύχωσι
δυναμένων ἐκ τῆς τοῦ τρόπου καλοκἀγαθίας

---

[1] οἰκείοις editi antiqi. [2] σκαιωρηθεῖσαν Harl., Clarom.

[1] Written in 373. Another appeal in behalf of Maximus ;
cf. preceding letter. The Trajan addressed here may be the

no mean people, just as Odysseus was the war-chief
of the Cephallenians. Odysseus took with him
great riches, but on his return was empty-handed,
and Maximus has been reduced by his misfortune to
such a plight that he is very likely to appear to his
people at home in borrowed rags. And all this he
has suffered, perhaps because he has aroused some
Laestrygones against himself, or has fallen in with a
Scylla, woman in shape but dog in savagery and
fierceness. Since, then, he has barely been able to
swim out of this present engulfing sea of trouble, he
supplicates you through us, asking you to respect our
common kind and out of compassion for his unmerited
sufferings not to hide his affairs in silence, but bring
them to the notice of those in authority, in order, if
possible, that he may have some assistance to
combat the malice that has been worked up against
him, or, if this is not possible, that at least the
intention of the man who has dealt outrageously
with him may be made known to the public. For it
is satisfying comfort to a man who has suffered from
injustice to have the wickedness of his persecutors
brought to light.

LETTER CXLVIII

To Trajan [1]

It brings great comfort to men in trouble to be
able to lament their misfortunes, especially when
they meet with those who by reason of the nobility
of their character are able to sympathize with suffer-

commander-in-chief of the army under Valens ; but this is
by no means certain.

συμπαθῆσαι τοῖς ἀλγεινοῖς. ὅθεν καὶ ὁ αἰδεσιμώτατος ἀδελφὸς Μάξιμος, ὁ τῆς πατρίδος ἡμῶν
ἡγησάμενος, παθὼν οἷα οὐδέπω ¹ τις ἀνθρώπων
ἕτερος, καὶ πάντων μὲν γυμνωθεὶς τῶν προσόντων,
ὅσα τε ἦν αὐτῷ πατρῷα καὶ ὅσα ἐκ προτέρων
πόνων ὑπῆρχε ² συνειλεγμένα, κακοπαθήσας δὲ τῷ
σώματι μυρία ταῖς ἄνω καὶ κάτω πλάναις, καὶ
οὐδὲ αὐτὴν τὴν ἐπιτιμίαν ἀνεπηρέαστον διασώσας,
ἧς ἕνεκα πάντα πονεῖν τοῖς ἐλευθέροις σύνηθες,
πολλὰ μὲν πρὸς ἡμᾶς ³ περὶ τῶν συμβάντων
αὐτῷ ἀπωλοφύρατο, ἠξίωσε δὲ δι' ἡμῶν ὡς ἐν
κεφαλαίῳ φανερὰν γενέσθαι σοι τὴν περιστᾶσαν
αὐτῷ τῶν κακῶν Ἰλιάδα. κἀγώ, ἐπειδὴ ἄλλως
οὐδὲν ἀφελεῖν αὐτοῦ τῶν δεινῶν ἠδυνήθην, ἑτοίμως
ταύτην ἔδωκα τὴν χάριν· τὸ ὀλίγα ἐκ πολλῶν ὧν
ἤκουσα παρ' αὐτοῦ διαγγεῖλαι τῇ κοσμιότητί σου,
ἐπειδὴ αὐτὸς ἐρυθριᾶν μοι ἐδόκει τὰς ἑαυτοῦ
συμφορὰς ἐναργῶς διηγήσασθαι.

Εἰ γὰρ καὶ οὐ ⁴ πονηρὸν τὸν ἠδικηκότα συνίστησι τὰ γενόμενα,⁵ ἀλλ' οὖν γε τὸν πεπονθότα
τῆς ἐλεεινοτάτης ὄντα μερίδος δείκνυσιν, ἐπειδὴ
αὐτὸ τὸ περιπεσεῖν τοῖς θεηλάτοις κακοῖς ἀπόδει-
ξίν πως ἔχειν δοκεῖ τοῦ παραδεδόσθαι τοῖς πάθεσιν. ἀλλ' ἀρκεῖ αὐτῷ πρὸς παραμυθίαν τῶν
συμβάντων τὸ εὐμενεῖ αὐτὸν προσβλέψαι τῷ
ὄμματί σε καὶ τὴν πολυαρκῆ χάριν, ἧς πάντες
ἀπολαύοντες δαπανᾶν οὐ δύνανται, τὴν τῆς σῆς
ἡμερότητος λέγω, καὶ ἐπ' αὐτὸν ἀφεθῆναι. ὅτι
δὲ καὶ ἐν δικαστηρίοις μεγάλη αὐτῷ ἀφορμὴ
πρὸς τὴν νίκην ἡ παρὰ σοῦ ῥοπή, πάντες ἀκριβῶς

---

¹ οὔπω E, editi antiqi.   ² ὑπῆρχε om. E.
³ ὑμᾶς E.

ing. For this reason our most honourable brother Maximus, the late governor of our country, after experiencing such misfortunes as no other man ever did, having been stripped of all his possessions, both those which he had inherited and those that had been amassed by his former labours, and having endured a thousand bodily sufferings because of his wanderings from place to place, and having been unable to keep unassailed by malice even his civil rights, in defence of which freemen are wont to endure everything—after all this he has bewailed to us at length what has happened to him, and has asked that through us there be made known to you in summary the Iliad of woes which envelops him. And as I was unable to relieve him of his distress in any other way, I readily granted this favour—to report to your Decorum an account of a few of the many things I have heard from him, inasmuch as he seemed to me to be too modest to give you a plain account of his troubles himself.

For even if the facts of the case do not prove the author of the injustice to be a wicked man, yet they at least show the victim's lot to be the most pitiful of all, since the very fact of his having fallen into divinely inflicted distress seems somehow to be proof of his having been delivered over to his sufferings. But it suffices to console him for what has befallen if you but look upon him with a kindly eye and extend to him that abundant grace which all men draw upon but cannot exhaust—I mean the grace of your leniency. And that the weight of your influence in the tribunal will be a great step towards victory we are

---

a οὐ add. Capps.   *b* γεγονότα editi antiqi.

πεπείσμεθα. δικαιότατος δὲ πάντων καὶ αὐτὸς
οὗτος, ὁ τὴν ἐπιστολὴν ἡμῶν, ὥς τι ὄφελος αὐτῷ
ἐσομένην, ἐπιζητήσας· ὃν μετὰ τῶν ἄλλων
ἴδοιμεν τῇ κατὰ δύναμιν αὐτοῦ[1] φωνῇ τὴν σὴν
εὐφημοῦντα σεμνότητα.

CXLIX

Τραϊανῷ

Καὶ αὐτὸς ὑπέβαλες ὀφθαλμῷ τὴν κακοπάθειαν
τοῦ πρότερον μὲν εὐδοκίμου, νῦν δὲ ἐλεεινοτάτου
πάντων Μαξίμου, τοῦ ἄρξαντος τῆς πατρίδος
ἡμῶν, ὡς οὐκ ὤφελεν![2] οἶμαι γὰρ ἂν πολλοῖς
ἀπευκτὴν ἔσεσθαι τὴν τῶν ἐθνῶν ἀρχήν, εἰ πρὸς
τοιοῦτον[3] πέρας μέλλουσι καταστρέφειν αἱ προ-
στασίαι. ὥστε τί δεῖ ἡμᾶς τὰ καθ' ἕκαστον
ἀπαγγέλλειν, ὧν τε εἴδομεν, ὧν τε ἠκούσαμεν,
ἀνδρὶ διὰ πολλὴν τῆς διανοίας ὀξύτητα ἱκανῷ ἐξ
ὀλίγων τῶν πραχθέντων στοχάσασθαι τὰ λειπόμενα ; πλὴν ἐκεῖνό γε εἰπών, ἴσως οὐ περιττός
σοι φανήσομαι, ὅτι πολλῶν ὄντων καὶ δεινῶν τῶν
εἰς αὐτὸν τολμηθέντων πρὸ τῆς σῆς παρουσίας,
τοιαῦτα γέγονε τὰ μετὰ ταῦτα, ὡς φιλανθρωπίαν
ποιῆσαι νομισθῆναι τὰ φθάσαντα. τοσαύτην
εἶχεν ὑπερβολὴν ὕβρεως καὶ ζημίας καὶ τῆς
εἰς αὐτὸ τὸ σῶμα κακοπαθείας, τὰ δὴ ὕστερον
αὐτῷ παρὰ τοῦ κρατοῦντος ἐξευρεθέντα. καὶ νῦν

---

[1] αὐτοῦ om. E.   [2] ὤφειλεν editi antiqi.
[3] τοιοῦτο E.

---

[1] Written in 373. Another appeal for Maximus. The

358

all convinced with certainty. And this man who has asked the present letter of us, in the hope that it would be of some help to him, is himself also the most upright of men; and may we see him among the rest voicing with all his might the praises of your August Reverence.

LETTER CXLIX

To Trajan [1]

You yourself have seen with your own eyes the distress of Maximus, once held in high repute, but now the most pitiful of all mortals, the late Prefect of our country—would that he had never been such! For I think that the governorship of peoples would be avoided by many if their high position were likely to come to such an end. So what need is there of our relating in detail what we have seen and heard to a man who by great keenness of mind is able to conjecture from a few events all that is left untold? But in saying the following perhaps I shall not seem to you to be going too far— that although many and terrible were the outrages perpetrated upon him before your arrival, those which followed were of such a character that the earlier must be reckoned as acts of kindness. Such was the excess of abuse and loss of property and even bodily injury in the measures lately devised against him by the ruler. And now he has come

MSS. give this letter as to the same Trajan; cf. previous letters. If this Trajan is the one suggested in note 1 of the previous letter, he could have had no personal knowledge of the troubles of Maximus. However, the identity of this Trajan is by no means certain.

ἔμφρουρος ἥκει τὰ λείψανα τῶν ὧδε κακῶν αὐτοῦ
ἀποπληρώσων, ἐὰν μὴ σὺ τὴν μεγάλην σαυτοῦ
χεῖρα ὑπερσχεῖν ἐθελήσῃς τῷ καταπονουμένῳ.
περιττὸν μὲν οὖν οἶδα ποιῶν, τὴν σὴν χρηστότητα
εἰς φιλανθρωπίαν παρακαλῶν. πλὴν ἀλλ' ἐπειδὴ
βούλομαι γενέσθαι χρήσιμος τῷ ἀνδρί, ἱκετεύω
σου τὴν σεμνοπρέπειαν προσθεῖναί τι τῇ ἐκ
φύσεως περὶ τὸ καλὸν σπουδῇ δι' ἡμᾶς, ὥστε
ἐναργὲς τῷ ἀνδρὶ γενέσθαι τῆς ὑπὲρ αὐτοῦ παρακλήσεως ἡμῶν τὸ ὄφελος.

CL

Ἀμφιλοχίῳ, ὡς παρὰ Ἡρακλείδου

Ἐγὼ καὶ τῶν ὁμιληθέντων ἡμῖν πρὸς ἀλλήλους
ποτὲ μέμνημαι, καὶ ὧν τε αὐτὸς εἶπον, ὧν τε
ἤκουσα παρὰ τῆς εὐγενείας σου, οὐκ ἐπιλέλησμαι.
καὶ νῦν βίος μέν με δημόσιος οὐ κατέχει. εἰ γὰρ
καὶ τῇ καρδίᾳ ὁ αὐτός εἰμι καὶ οὔπω τὸν παλαιὸν
ἀπεδυσάμην ἄνθρωπον, πλὴν τῷ γε σχήματι, καὶ
τῷ μακρὰν ἐμαυτὸν ποιῆσαι τῶν τοῦ βίου πραγμάτων, ἔδοξα λοιπὸν οἷον ἐπιβεβηκέναι τῆς ὁδοῦ
τῆς κατὰ Χριστὸν πολιτείας. καθέζομαι δὲ ἐπ'
ἐμαυτοῦ, ὥσπερ οἱ εἰς πέλαγος ἀφιέναι μέλλοντες
ἀποσκοπεύων[1] τὸ μέλλον. οἱ μὲν γὰρ πλέοντες

---

[1] σκοπεύων E.

---

[1] Written in 373. Amphilochius, later consecrated Bishop
of Iconium, had abandoned his practice of the law and was
living in retirement at Ozizala, not far from Nazianzus, the
see of his uncle Gregory. The following letters of St. Basil
addressed to Amphilochius have been preserved : CLXI,
CLXXVI, CXC, CXCI, CC, CCI, CCII, CCXVIII, CCXXXI,

under guard to finish off the remnants of the evils suffered here, unless you are willing to stretch out your mighty hand to protect the victim of misfortune. I know that I am doing a superfluous thing when I exhort your Excellency to do an act of kindness. But as I desire to be of some service to the man, I beg your Grace to add something to your natural zeal for the good, and this on our account, that the man may know clearly the benefit derived from our intercession in his behalf

LETTER CL

To Amphilochius, as if from Heracleidas[1]

I REMEMBER the matter which we once discussed together, and I have not forgotten both what I myself said and what I heard from your Nobility. And now public life does not hold me back. For although I am the same at heart and have not yet put off the old man—except at least ostensibly, that is, by having removed myself far from the affairs of life—I seem to have entered, as it were, upon the way that is in accordance with Christ's polity. And I sit by myself, scanning the future as do those who are about to put out to sea. For those who sail

CCXXXII, CCXXXIII, CCXXXIV, CCXXXV, CCXXXVI, and CCXLVIII, besides those dealing with the canons.

Heracleidas, a young friend of Amphilochius and also a retired lawyer, was living at St. Basil's famous hospital at the time this letter was written. This letter was written to Amphilochius in the name of Heracleidas to explain why Heracleidas had not joined him in his retirement, to describe what Heracleidas was doing at Caesarea, and to urge Amphilochius to get in touch with St. Basil, if possible, so that he might learn from him many needed lessons.

ἀνέμων χρήζουσι πρὸς τὴν εὔπλοιαν, ἡμεῖς δὲ
τοῦ χειραγωγήσοντος ἡμᾶς καὶ ἀσφαλῶς διὰ τῶν
ἁλμυρῶν κυμάτων τοῦ βίου παραπέμψοντος.
χρῄζειν γὰρ ἐμαυτὸν λογίζομαι πρῶτον μὲν
χαλινοῦ πρὸς τὴν νεότητα, ἔπειτα κέντρων πρὸς
τὸν δρόμον τῆς εὐσεβείας. τούτων δὲ πρόξενος
λόγος [1] δηλονότι, νῦν μὲν παιδαγωγῶν ἡμῶν τὸ
ἄτακτον, νῦν δὲ τὸ νωθρὸν τῆς ψυχῆς διεγείρων.
πάλιν μοι χρεία φαρμάκων ἑτέρων, ὥστε τὸν ἐκ
τῆς συνηθείας ἀποπλύνασθαι ῥύπον. οἶδας γὰρ
ὅτι ἡμεῖς, οἱ πολὺν χρόνον ἐνεθισθέντες τῇ ἀγορᾷ,
ἀφειδῶς μὲν ἔχομεν τῶν ῥημάτων, ἀφυλάκτως δὲ
πρὸς τὰς ἐν τῇ διανοίᾳ συνισταμένας ἐκ τοῦ
πονηροῦ [2] φαντασίας. ἡττήμεθα δὲ καὶ τιμῆς
καὶ τὸ ἐφ' ἑαυτοῖς τι φρονεῖν οὐ ῥᾳδίως ἀποτιθέ-
μεθα. πρὸς ταῦτα μεγάλου μοι δεῖν καὶ ἐμπείρου
λογίζομαι διδασκάλου. ἔπειτα μέντοι καὶ τὸν
ὀφθαλμὸν τῆς ψυχῆς ἀποκαθαρθῆναι, ὥστε πᾶσαν
τὴν ἀπὸ τῆς ἀγνοίας ἐπισκότησιν, οἱονεί τινα
λήμην, ἀφαιρεθέντα, δύνασθαι ἐνατενίζειν τῷ
κάλλει τῆς δόξης τοῦ Θεοῦ, οὐ μικροῦ ἔργον
κρίνω, οὐδ' ἐπ' ὀλίγον τὴν ὠφέλειαν φέρειν.

Ἃ καὶ τὴν σὴν λογιότητα συνορᾶν, καὶ ἐπιθυ-
μεῖν ὑπάρξαι τινὰ εἰς ταύτην τὴν βοήθειαν
ἀκριβῶς ἐπίσταμαι· [3] καὶ ἐάν ποτε δῷ ὁ Θεὸς
εἰς ταὐτὸν ἀφικέσθαι τῇ κοσμιότητί σου, δηλονότι
πλείονα μαθήσομαι ὑπὲρ ὧν φροντίζειν με χρή.
νῦν γὰρ ὑπὸ πολλῆς ἀμαθίας οὐδὲ ὅσων [4] ἐνδεής
εἰμι γνωρίζειν δύναμαι· πλήν γε ὅτι οὐδὲν μετε-
μέλησέ μοι τῆς πρώτης ὁρμῆς, οὔτε ὀκλάζει μου

---

[1] τις add. E.
[2] τοῦ πονηροῦ] τῆς πονηρίας quinque MSS.

require winds for a fine voyage, while we require someone to lead us by the hand and escort us safely over the briny billows of life. For I consider that I myself require, first of all a bridle to restrain my youth, then spurs for the race of piety. And that which provides these two things is manifestly·reason, at one time schooling our insubordination, at another rousing up the sluggishness of our souls. Again, I have need of other remedies to wash away the stains contracted from habit. For you know that we who have been for a long time accustomed to public life are unsparing of speech and are not on our guard against the images which are stirred up in our minds by the evil one. And we are easy victims to preferment and cannot easily lay aside some degree of pride in ourselves. In guard against these things I think that I have need also of a great and experienced teacher. Then, moreover, the task of cleansing the eye of the soul, so that, when once freed, as from a kind of rheum, from all the darkness of ignorance, it may be able to look steadily upon the beauty of the glory of God, calls, I judge, for no small labour and brings no small benefit.

I know full well that your Eloquence perceives all this, and that you desire that someone shall be at hand to render such aid ; that if ever God grants that I have a meeting with your Decorum, I shall certainly learn more regarding those matters about which I must needs be concerned. For now, on account of my great ignorance, I cannot even know how many things I lack ; and yet I by no means regret this first attempt, nor does my soul sink at the

---

³ πέπεισμαι E, Med.   ⁴ ὅσον E.

ἡ ψυχὴ πρὸς τὸν σκοπὸν τοῦ κατὰ Θεὸν βίου,
ὅπερ ἠγωνίασας ἐπ' ἐμοί, καλῶς καὶ προσηκόντως
ἑαυτῷ ποιῶν, μήποτε στραφεὶς εἰς τὰ ὀπίσω
στήλη γένωμαι ἁλός, ὅπερ γυνή τις ἔπαθεν,
ὥσπερ[1] ἀκούω. ἀλλ' ἔτι μέν με[2] καὶ αἱ ἔξωθεν
ἀρχαὶ συστέλλουσιν, ὥσπερ λειποτάκτην τινὰ
τῶν ἀρχόντων ἀναζητούντων.[3] ἐπέχει δέ με
μάλιστα ἡ ἐμοῦ αὐτοῦ καρδία, ἐκεῖνα μαρτυροῦσα
ἑαυτῇ ἅπερ εἴρηκα.

Ἐπειδὴ δὲ συνθηκῶν ἐμνήσθης, καὶ κατηγο-
ρεῖν ἐπηγγείλω, γελάσαι με ἐποίησας ἐν ταύτῃ
τῇ κατηφείᾳ μου, ὅτι ἔτι ῥήτωρ εἶ καὶ τῆς
δεινότητος οὐκ ἀφίστασαι. ἐγὼ γὰρ οὕτω[4]
νομίζω, εἰ μὴ πάντῃ ὡς ἀμαθὴς διαμαρτάνω τῆς
ἀληθείας, μίαν εἶναι ὁδὸν τὴν πρὸς Κύριον
ἄγουσαν, καὶ πάντας τοὺς πρὸς αὐτὸν πορευο-
μένους συνοδεύειν ἀλλήλοις καὶ κατὰ μίαν συνθή-
κην τοῦ βίου πορεύεσθαι. ὥστε ποῦ ἀπελθὼν
χωρισθῆναί σου δύναμαι καὶ μὴ μετὰ σοῦ ζῆν
καὶ μετὰ σοῦ δουλεύειν Θεῷ, ᾧ κοινῇ προσε-
φύγομεν; τὰ μὲν γὰρ σώματα ἡμῶν τόποις
διασταθήσεται, ὁ δὲ τοῦ Θεοῦ ὀφθαλμὸς κοινῇ
ἀμφοτέρους ἐφορᾷ[5] δηλονότι, εἴπερ οὖν ἄξιος
καὶ ὁ ἐμὸς βίος ὑπὸ τῶν ὀφθαλμῶν τοῦ Θεοῦ
ἐποπτεύεσθαι· ἀνέγνων γάρ που ἐν Ψαλμοῖς, ὅτι

---

[1] ὥς E. [2] με om. E.
[3] ἀνεπιζητούντων editi antiqi. [4] οὕτως E.
[5] ὁρᾷ E.

---

[1] Cf. Gen. 19. 26 : καὶ ἐπέβλεψεν ἡ γυνὴ αὐτοῦ εἰς τὰ ὀπίσω,
καὶ ἐγένετο στήλη ἁλός. " And his wife, looking behind her,
was turned into a statue of salt."

prospect of the life that is in accordance with God—the matter which caused you, rightly and in a manner befitting yourself, to be anxious about me, lest turning back I might become a " statue of salt," as I hear happened to a certain woman.[1] And yet it is true that powers from without still hamper me, like officers who seek to bring back a deserter ; but most of all it is my own heart which restrains me, bearing witness to itself to the very things that I have mentioned.

But when you mentioned agreements, and announced that you would be the accuser, you made me laugh in spite of my present dejection, because you still play the rôle of a public man and have not given up cleverness.[2] As for me, this is my opinion —that, unless in my ignorance I have altogether missed the truth, there is only one way leading to the Lord, and all who travel toward Him are companions of one another and travel according to one agreement as to life. Consequently, where can I go and yet be separated from you, and not live with you and with you serve God, to whom we have both together fled ? For though our bodies will be separated in space, yet the eye of God is assuredly gazing upon us both in common—if indeed my life is worthy to be looked upon by the eyes of God ; for I have read somewhere in the Psalms that " the eyes of

---

[2] Apparently Amphilochius and Heracleidas had made an agreement with each other to abstain from public life. Heracleidas having broken this agreement, Amphilochius threatened to bring action against him. The parallel in Attic law is in cases of ἀτιμία (loss of civil rights), when a public man is debarred from δημοσία (public service) ; and ἀγγέλλειν is the technical term for the denunciation.

Ὀφθαλμοὶ Κυρίου ἐπὶ δικαίους. ἐγὼ μὲν γὰρ
εὔχομαι καὶ σοὶ καὶ παντὶ τῷ παραπλησίως[1]
σοι προαιρουμένῳ καὶ τῷ σώματι συνεῖναι, καὶ
πᾶσαν νύκτα καὶ ἡμέραν μετὰ σοῦ κλίνειν τὰ
γόνατα πρὸς τὸν Πατέρα ἡμῶν τὸν ἐν τοῖς
οὐρανοῖς, καὶ εἴ τις ἄλλος ἀξίως ἐπικαλούμενος
τὸν Θεόν. οἶδα γὰρ τὴν ἐν ταῖς προσευχαῖς
κοινωνίαν πολὺ τὸ κέρδος φέρουσαν.[2] ἐὰν δέ,
ὁσάκις ὑπάρξῃ μοι ἐν διαφόρῳ γωνιδίῳ[3] παρερ-
ριμμένῳ[4] στενάζειν, ἀκολουθήσει μοι πάντως τὸ
ψεύδεσθαι, μάχεσθαι μὲν[5] πρὸς τὸν λόγον οὐκ
ἔχω, ἤδη δὲ ὡς ψεύστου[6] ἐμαυτὸν κατακρίνω,
εἴ τι τοιοῦτον κατὰ τὴν παλαιὰν ἀδιαφορίαν
ἐφθεγξάμην, ὅ[7] με τῷ κρίματι τοῦ ψεύδους
ὑπόδικον καθιστᾷ.

Γενόμενος δὲ πλησίον Καισαρείας, ὥστε γνωρίσαι τὰ πράγματα, καὶ αὐτῇ παραβαλεῖν τῇ πόλει
μὴ ἀνασχόμενος, τῷ πλησίον προσέφυγον πτωχο-
τροφείῳ, ὥστε ἐκεῖ μαθεῖν περὶ ὧν ἐβουλόμην.
εἶτα κατὰ συνήθειαν ἐπιδημήσαντι τῷ θεοφιλεστάτῳ ἐπισκόπῳ ἀνήνεγκα περὶ ὧν ἐπέταξεν
ἡμῖν ἡ λογιότης σου. καὶ ἃ μὲν ἀπεκρίνατο,
οὔτε τῇ μνήμῃ φυλαχθῆναι παρ' ἡμῶν δυνατὸν
ἦν, καὶ ἐπιστολῆς ὑπερέβαινε μέτρον· ὡς ἐν
κεφαλαίῳ δὲ περὶ τῆς ἀκτημοσύνης ἐκεῖνο ἔφη
τὸ μέτρον εἶναι, ὥστε εἰς τὸν ἔσχατον χιτῶνα
ἕκαστον ἑαυτῷ περιστάναι[8] τὴν κτῆσιν. καὶ
παρείχετο ἡμῖν ἐκ τοῦ Εὐαγγελίου τὰς ἀποδείξεις·
μίαν μέν, ὡς Ἰωάννου τοῦ βαπτιστοῦ εἰπόντος·

---

[1] παραπλήσιον editi antiqi.   [2] ἔχουσαν tres MSS. recent.
[3] γονιδίῳ editi antiqi.   [4] παρε͵ριμένως E.
[5] μέν add. E, editi antiqi.   [6] ψεύστης E.

the Lord are upon the just." [1] For I do indeed pray
to be with you in the body also, as well as with everyone who makes a choice similar to yours, and every
night and day to bend my knees with you before
our Father who is in heaven, as well as with anyone
else who worthily calls upon God. For I know that
association in prayer brings great gain. But if,
whenever I happen to utter a complaint as I lie cast
aside in a corner different from yours, the charge of
falsehood is certain to follow me, I cannot fight
against the accusation, but forthwith condemn
myself as a liar, if I ever during my earlier period of
indifference said anything which makes me liable to
the charge of falsehood. [2]

But when I came near enough to Caesarea to
observe the situation, refraining, however, from visiting the city itself, I took refuge in the neighbouring
poor-house, that I might gain there the information I
wished. Then I laid before the most God-beloved
bishop, who had come to visit the place according to
custom, the matters as to which your Eloquence had
instructed us. And though it was impossible for us to
keep in memory what he said in reply, and it passed
beyond the limits of a letter, yet in general on the
subject of poverty he said that this was the measure,
—that each should limit his possession to the last
tunic. And he furnished us with proofs from the
Gospel—one from John the Baptist, who said : " He

---

[1] Cf. Psal. 33. 16 : ὅτι ὀφθαλμοὶ Κυρίου ἐπὶ δικαίους, καὶ ὦτα
αὐτοῦ εἰς δέησιν αὐτῶν. " The eyes of the Lord are upon the
just : and His ears unto their prayers."

[2] Amphilochius had apparently found fault with Heracleidas
in consequence of a complaint, and had accused him of
repenting having entered upon the ascetic life.

COLLECTED LETTERS OF SAINT BASIL

Ὁ ἔχων δύο χιτῶνας μεταδότω τῷ μὴ ἔχοντι·
ἑτέραν δέ, ὡς τοῦ Κυρίου τοῖς μαθηταῖς ἀπαγο-
ρεύσαντος μὴ¹ ἔχειν δύο χιτῶνας. προσετίθει δὲ²
τούτοις καὶ³ τό· Εἰ θέλεις τέλειος εἶναι, ὕπαγε,
πώλησόν σου τὰ ὑπάρχοντα, καὶ δὸς πτωχοῖς.
ἔλεγε δὲ καὶ τὴν τοῦ μαργαρίτου παραβολὴν
εἰς τοῦτο φέρειν· ὅτι ὁ ἔμπορος ὁ εὑρὼν τὸν
πολύτιμον μαργαρίτην ἀπελθὼν ἐπώλησεν ἑαυτοῦ
πάντα τὰ ὑπάρχοντα καὶ ἠγόρασεν ἐκεῖνον. προσετίθει δὲ τούτοις, ὅτι οὐδὲ ἑαυτῷ τινὰ ἐπιτρέπειν
χρὴ τὴν τῶν χρημάτων διανομήν, ἀλλὰ τῷ τὰ τῶν
πτωχῶν οἰκονομεῖν πεπιστευμένῳ.⁴ καὶ τοῦτο
ἀπὸ τῶν Πράξεων ἐπιστοῦτο· ὅτι πωλοῦντες τὰ
προσόντα αὐτοῖς, φέροντες ἐτίθουν παρὰ τοὺς
πόδας τῶν ἀποστόλων, καὶ παρ' ἐκείνων διεδίδοτο
ἑκάστῳ, καθότι ἄν τις χρείαν εἶχεν. ἔλεγε γὰρ
ἐμπειρίας χρῄζειν τὴν διάγνωσιν τοῦ ἀληθῶς δεομένου καὶ τοῦ κατὰ πλεονεξίαν αἰτοῦντος. καὶ ὁ
μὲν τῷ θλιβομένῳ διδοὺς τῷ Κυρίῳ ἔδωκε, καὶ
παρ' αὐτοῦ λήψεται τὸν μισθόν· ὁ δὲ τῷ περιερ-
χομένῳ παρασχόμενος παντὶ προσέρριψε κυνί,
φορτικῷ μὲν διὰ τὴν ἀναίδειαν, οὐκ ἐλεεινῷ δὲ
διὰ τὴν ἔνδειαν.

Περὶ δὲ τοῦ πῶς χρὴ βιοῦν ἡμᾶς καθ' ἡμέραν,

¹ μή om. E. ² καί add. E.
³ καί om. E. ⁴ ἐμπεπισιευμένῳ editi antiqi.

---

¹ Luke 3. 11.
² Cf. Matt. 10. 9 and 10: μὴ κτήσησθε χρυσόν, μηδὲ
ἄργυρον, μηδὲ χαλκὸν εἰς τὰς ζώνας ὑμῶν, μὴ πήραν εἰς ὁδόν, μηδὲ
δύο χιτῶνας, μηδὲ ὑποδήματα μηδὲ ῥάβδαν. "Do not possess
gold, nor silver, nor money in your purses: nor scrip for
your journey, nor two coats, nor shoes, nor a staff."
³ Matt. 19. 21.

that hath two coats, let him give to him that hath none " ; [1] and another from our Lord, who warns His disciples not to have two tunics.[2] He added to these this also : " If thou wilt be perfect, go sell what thou hast and give it to the poor." [3] And he said too that the parable of the pearl referred to this—that the merchant who found the precious pearl went away, sold all his possessions and bought it. And he added to these words that it was not necessary for anyone to take upon himself the distribution of his goods, but only to commit this task to him to whom the management of the alms of the poor had been entrusted. And he proved this from the Acts,[4] to wit : " Selling their goods they took and laid the price of the things before the feet of the Apostles, and distribution was made by them to everyone according as he had need." For he said that experience was necessary for distinguishing between the man who is truly in need and the man who begs through avarice. And while he who gives to the afflicted has given to the Lord, and will receive his reward from Him, yet he who gives to every wanderer casts it to a dog, that is troublesome on account of his shamelessness, but not pitiable because of his need.

And as to how we should live day by day, he had

---

[4] Cf. Acts 4. 34 and 35 : οὐδὲ γὰρ ἐνδεής τις ὑπῆρχεν ἐν αὐτοῖς· ὅσοι γὰρ κτήτορες χωρίων ἢ οἰκιῶν ὑπῆρχον, πωλοῦντες ἔφερον τὰς τιμὰς τῶν πιπρασκομένων, καὶ ἐτίθουν παρὰ τοὺς πόδας τῶν ἀποστόλων· διεδίδοτο δὲ ἑκάστῳ καθότι ἄν τις χρείαν εἶχεν. " For neither was there anyone needy among them. For as many as were owners of lands or houses, sold them, and brought the price of the things they sold, and laid it down before the feet of the apostles. And distribution was made to everyone, according as he had need." It is to be noted that Basil's " by them " does not appear in the Acts.

ὀλίγα μὲν ἔφθη εἰρηκὼς ὡς πρὸς τὸ τῆς ὑποθέσεως
μέγεθος· πλὴν ἀλλ᾽ ἐβουλόμην παρ᾽ αὐτοῦ ἐκείνου
σε μαθεῖν. ἐμὲ γὰρ ἀφανίζειν τὴν ἀκρίβειαν τῶν
διδαγμάτων οὐκ εὔλογον. ηὐχόμην δὲ μετὰ σοῦ
ποτὲ καταλαβεῖν αὐτόν, ἵνα καὶ τῇ μνήμῃ ἀκριβῶς
φυλάξας τὰ λεχθέντα, καὶ τῇ σεαυτοῦ συνέσει
προσεξεύρῃς τὰ λείποντα. ἐκεῖνο γὰρ μέμνημαι
ἐκ τῶν πολλῶν ὧν ἤκουσα, ὅτι ἡ περὶ τοῦ πῶς
χρὴ ζῆν τὸν Χριστιανὸν διδασκαλία οὐ τοσοῦτον
δεῖται λόγου ὅσον τοῦ καθημερινοῦ ὑποδείγματος.
καὶ οἶδα ὅτι, εἰ μή σε κατεῖχεν ὁ δεσμὸς τῆς
γηροκομίας τοῦ πατρός, οὐκ ἂν οὔτε αὐτὸς ἄλλο
τι προετίμησας τῆς συντυχίας τοῦ ἐπισκόπου, οὔτ᾽
ἂν ἐμοὶ συνεβούλευσας καταλιπόντι τοῦτον εἰς
ἐρημίας πλανᾶσθαι. τὰ μὲν γὰρ σπήλαια καὶ
αἱ πέτραι ἀναμένουσιν ἡμᾶς, αἱ δὲ παρὰ τῶν
ἀνδρῶν ὠφέλειαι οὐκ ἀεὶ ἡμῖν παραμένουσιν.
ὥστε, εἰ ἀνέχῃ μου συμβουλεύοντος, τυπώσεις
τὸν πατέρα μικρὸν ἐπιτρέπειν σοι ἀναχωρεῖν
αὐτοῦ καὶ περιτυγχάνειν[1] ἀνδρὶ πολλὰ καὶ ἐκ
τῆς ἑτέρων πείρας καὶ ἐκ τῆς οἰκείας συνέσεως
καὶ εἰδότι καὶ παρέχειν τοῖς προσιοῦσιν[2] αὐτῷ
δυναμένῳ.

CLI

Εὐσταθίῳ ἀρχιάτρῳ[3]

Εἴ τι ὄφελος ἡμετέρων[4] γραμμάτων, μηδένα
χρόνον διαλίπῃς ἐπιστέλλων ἡμῖν καὶ διεγείρων[5]
ἡμᾶς πρὸς τὸ γράφειν. αὐτοὶ μὲν γὰρ προδήλως

---

[1] συντυγχάνειν Med. [2] προσοῦσιν E.
[3] ἀρχιητρῷ Harl., E. [4] ὑμετέρων E, Vat. [5] ἐγείρων E.

time enough to say only a little considering the
importance of the subject; but I should prefer you
to have learnt about this from the man himself. For
it is not fitting that I should spoil the precision of
his instructions. But I prayed that I might some
time visit him in company with you, in order that
you, guarding his words carefully in your memory,
might by the application of your own intelligence
find out in addition whatever he left unsaid. For of
the many things that I heard, I remember this—
that teaching a Christian how he ought to live does
not call so much for words as for daily example.
And I know that, if you were not chained by the
obligation of caring for your aged father, you yourself would have preferred nothing to a talk with the
bishop, nor would you have counselled me to leave
this person and go wandering in the desert. For
while the caves and the rocks will wait for us, yet
the aid which true men can give will not always
abide with us. Wherefore, if you will permit me to
advise you, you will press upon your father to permit
you to leave him for a little while and to betake
yourself to a man who both knows much from the
experience of others, as well as from his own wisdom,
and can impart it to those who come to him.

LETTER CLI

To Eustathius, a Physician [1]

If there is any profit in our letters, at no time
cease writing to us and urging us to write. For we

[1] Written in 373. Cf. also Letter CLXXXIX, which is
addressed to the same Eustathius but may well belong to
Gregory of Nyssa.

ἡδίους γινόμεθα ἐντυγχάνοντες ἐπιστολαῖς συνε-
τῶν ἀνδρῶν ἀγαπώντων τὸν Κύριον· εἰ δὲ καὶ
αὐτοί τι ἄξιον σπουδῆς εὑρίσκετε[1] παρ' ἡμῖν,
ὑμέτερον εἰδέναι τῶν ἐντυγχανόντων. εἰ μὲν οὖν
μὴ ὑπὸ τοῦ πλήθους τῶν ἀσχολιῶν ἀπηγόμεθα,
οὐκ ἂν τῆς ἐκ τοῦ γράφειν συνεχῶς εὐφροσύνης
ἀπειχόμεθα. ὑμεῖς δέ, οἷς ἐλάττους αἱ φροντίδες,
ὁσάκις ἂν οἷόν τε ᾖ κατακηλεῖτε ἡμᾶς τοῖς γράμμασι. καὶ γὰρ τὰ φρέατά φασιν ἀντλούμενα
βελτίω γίνεσθαι. ἐοίκασι δέ σου[2] αἱ ἐξ ἰατρικῆς
παραινέσεις εἰς πάρεργον χωρεῖν, οὐχ ἡμῶν ἐπα-
γόντων τὸν σίδηρον, ἀλλ' ἑαυτοῖς ἐκπιπτόντων
τῶν ἀπαχρειουμένων.

Ὁ μὲν οὖν τοῦ Στωϊκοῦ λόγος· ἐπειδή, φησί,
μὴ γίνεται τὰ πράγματα ὡς βουλόμεθα, ὡς γίνεται
βουλόμεθα.[3] ἐγὼ δὲ τοῖς μὲν πράγμασι τὴν
γνώμην συγκατατίθεσθαι[4] οὐ καταδέχομαι, τὸ
δὲ ἀβουλήτως τινὰς ποιεῖν τι τῶν ἀναγκαίων οὐκ
ἀποδοκιμάζω. οὔτε γὰρ ὑμῖν τοῖς ἰατροῖς τὸ
καίειν τὸν ἄρρωστον ἢ ἄλλως ποιεῖν ἀλγεῖν
βουλητόν· ἀλλ' οὖν καταδέχεσθε πολλάκις τῇ
δυσχερείᾳ τοῦ πάθους ἑπόμενοι· οὔτε[5] οἱ πλέοντες
ἑκουσίως ἐκβάλλουσι τὰ ἀγώγιμα, ἀλλ' ὥστε
διαφυγεῖν τὰ ναυάγια ὑφίστανται τὴν ἐκβολήν,
τὸν ἐν πενίᾳ βίον τοῦ ἀποθανεῖν προτιμῶντες.
ὥστε καὶ ἡμᾶς οἴου ἀλγεινῶς μὲν καὶ μετὰ μυρίων
ὀδυρμῶν φέρειν τὸν χωρισμὸν τῶν ἀφισταμένων,
φέρειν δ' οὖν ὅμως· ἐπειδὴ τοῦ Θεοῦ καὶ τῆς

---

[1] εὑρήσετε editi antiqi. [2] σοι E.
[3] βουλώμεθα editi antiqi.
[4] συμμετατίθεσθαι Harl., Reg. primus, et Vat.
[5] οὔτε] οἵ τε E.

on our part are certainly made more happy by reading letters from wise men who love the Lord, and if you on your part find anything worth while in ours, it is for you who read them to know. If, then, we were not distracted by our manifold duties, we should not refrain from the pleasure of writing constantly; but do you, whose cares are less, console us as often as is possible by writing. For, as they say, "Wells become better for being used." And your advice drawn from the art of medicine seems to go for naught, since it is not we who are applying the knife, but those who resort to its use are being driven out by each other.[1]

Now a Stoic saying goes: "Since things do not happen as we wish, we wish them as they happen." But as for me, though I cannot accommodate my mind to things as they are, yet I do not object to men in certain situations doing unwillingly a thing that is inevitable. For neither is it the wish of you physicians to cauterize the sick or cause them pain in any other way (although you do often consent to it in recognition of the seriousness of the malady), nor do navigators willingly throw overboard their cargo,[2] but with a view to escaping shipwreck they submit to this throwing overboard, preferring life in poverty to death. So pray believe that we also, while enduring with sorrow and countless lamentations the separation from those who leave our ranks, yet endure it nevertheless; because to the lovers of

[1] Eustathius, the bishop, and his followers are using the knife upon each other.

[2] According to the Benedictine editors the cargo thrown overboard represents the loss of unity suffered by the Sebastenes when they left the communion of Eustathius. Cf. Letter CCXXXVII.

ἐπ᾽ αὐτὸν[1] ἐλπίδος οὐδὲν τοῖς τῆς ἀληθείας
ἐρασταῖς προτιμότερον.

CLII

Οὐΐκτορι στρατηλάτῃ

Ἄλλῳ μέν τινι μὴ ἐπιστέλλων, τάχα ἂν
δεξαίμην δικαίως ἔγκλημα ῥαθυμίας ἢ λήθης.
σοῦ δὲ πῶς ἔστιν ἐπιλαθέσθαι, οὗ παρὰ πᾶσιν
ἀνθρώποις λαλεῖται τὸ ὄνομα ; πῶς δὲ καταρραθυμῆσαι,[2] ὃς πάντων σχεδὸν τῶν κατὰ τὴν οἰκουμένην τῷ ὕψει τῶν ἀξιωμάτων ὑπερανέστηκας ;
ἀλλὰ δήλη ἡμῶν ἡ αἰτία τῆς σιωπῆς· ὀκνοῦμεν
δι᾽ ὄχλου γίνεσθαι[3] ἀνδρὶ τοσούτῳ. εἰ δὲ πρὸς
τῇ λοιπῇ σου ἀρετῇ καὶ τοῦτο κατεδέξω, οὐ μόνον
πεμπόμενα παρ᾽ ἡμῶν δέχεσθαι γράμματα, ἀλλὰ
καὶ ἐλλειφθέντα ἐπιζητεῖν, ἰδοὺ καὶ γράφομεν
νῦν τεθαρρηκότως[4] καὶ γράψομέν γε εἰς[5] τὸ
ἐφεξῆς, εὐχόμενοι τῷ ἁγίῳ Θεῷ δοθῆναί σοι τὴν
ἀμοιβὴν τῆς περὶ ἡμᾶς τιμῆς. ὑπὲρ δὲ τῆς
Ἐκκλησίας προέλαβες ἡμῶν τὰς παρακλήσεις,
πάντα ποιήσας ὅσα ἂν ἡμεῖς ἐπεζητήσαμεν. ποιεῖς
δὲ οὐκ ἀνθρώποις χαριζόμενος, ἀλλὰ Θεῷ τῷ
τιμήσαντί σε, ὃς τὰ μὲν ἔδωκεν ἐν τῇ νῦν ζωῇ
ἀγαθά, τὰ δὲ δώσει ἐν τῷ μέλλοντι αἰῶνι, ἀνθ᾽
ὧν μετὰ ἀληθείας ἐπορεύθης τὴν ὁδὸν αὐτοῦ,
ἀκλινῆ τὴν καρδίαν ἐν τῇ ὀρθότητι τῆς πίστεως
ἀπ᾽ ἀρχῆς εἰς τέλος διασωσάμενος.

---

[1] ἐπ᾽ αὐτὸν] ἑαυτῶν E.
[2] οὗ παρὰ . . . καταρραθυμῆσαι om. E.
[3] γενέσθαι multi MSS.
[4] τεθαρρηκότες editi antiqi.   [5] πρός editi antiqi.

truth " nothing is to be preferred to God and to our hope in Him."

LETTER CLII

To Victor, the General [1]

Were I to neglect writing to any other man, I should perhaps justly incur the charge of carelessness or forgetfulness. But in your case how is it possible to forget one whose name is on the lips of everyone, or to become careless about one who surpasses in the loftiness of his honours almost all who dwell on earth? But the reason for our silence is clear: we hesitate to disturb so great a man. But if in addition to your other virtues you possess this one also,—that you not only accept such letters as we do send but also miss those which we have failed to send, behold! we write now with confidence and in the future too shall write, praying to the holy God that recompense be given you for the honour you show us. Moreover, you have anticipated our appeals on behalf of the Church, having done all that we could have asked. And in what you do you seek to win favour, not with men, but with God who has honoured you, who has given you some blessings in this present life and will give you others in the world to come, in recompense for your travelling His way with truth, keeping your heart unswervingly in the orthodox faith from the beginning to the end.

[1] Written in 373. Victor was a distinguished general under Valens, a man of high character, consul in 369, and an orthodox Christian. Cf. Gregory Nazianzene, Letters CXXXIII and CXXXIV. In 378 he united with Trajanus, Arintheus, and other generals in remonstrating with Valens on his Arianism. Cf. Theod., *H. E.*, 4, 30; and Amm. Marc. 31, 7.

CLIII

Βίκτορι ἀπὸ ὑπάτων

Ὁσάκις ἂν ἡμῖν ὑπάρξῃ γράμμασιν ἐντυχεῖν
τῆς κοσμιότητός σου, τοσαυτάκις χάριν ὁμολογοῦμεν τῷ Θεῷ, ὅτι διαμένεις καὶ μεμνημένος ἡμῶν
καὶ ὑπ' οὐδεμιᾶς διαβολῆς τὴν ἀγάπην ἐλαττῶν,
ἣν ἅπαξ κρίσει τῇ ὀρθοτάτῃ ἢ συνηθείᾳ χρηστῇ
ἀναλαβεῖν κατεδέξω. εὐχόμεθα οὖν τῷ ἁγίῳ
Θεῷ καὶ σὲ διαμεῖναι ἐν τῇ ὁμοίᾳ πρὸς ἡμᾶς
διαθέσει, καὶ ἡμᾶς ἀξίους εἶναι τῆς παρὰ σοῦ
τιμῆς, ἣν τιμᾷς ἡμᾶς διὰ τοῦ γράμματος.

CLIV

Ἀσχολίῳ, ἐπισκόπῳ Θεσσαλονίκης [1]

Καλῶς ἐποίησας, καὶ κατὰ τὸν τῆς πνευματικῆς
ἀγάπης νόμον, κατάρξας τῶν πρὸς ἡμᾶς γραμμάτων καὶ τῷ ἀγαθῷ ὑποδείγματι πρὸς τὸν
ὅμοιον ζῆλον ἡμᾶς ἐκκαλεσάμενος. καὶ γὰρ ἡ μὲν
τοῦ κόσμου φιλία ὀφθαλμῶν δεῖται καὶ συντυχίας,
ὥστε ἐκεῖθεν ἀρχὴν τῆς συνηθείας γενέσθαι, οἱ δὲ
πνευματικῶς ἀγαπᾶν εἰδότες οὐ τῇ σαρκὶ προξένῳ
κέχρηνται τῆς φιλίας, ἀλλὰ τῇ τῆς πίστεως

---

[1] Ἀσχολίῳ μονάζοντι καὶ πρεσβυτέρῳ Coisl. secundus, Reg.
secundus, Vat. et Paris. Ἀσχολίῳ μονάζοντι Reg. primus,
Bigot.

---

[1] Written in 373, and in all probability to the same Victor
as is addressed in the previous letter.

LETTER CLIII

To Victor, the Ex-Consul [1]

As often as it falls to our lot to read a letter from
your Decorum, so often do we acknowledge our
thanks to God, that you both continue to be mindful
of us and that you maintain undiminished by any
slander the love which once for all through sound
judgment or through excellent habit you deigned
to assume for us.   We therefore pray to the holy
God that you may persist in the same disposition
towards us, and that we on our part may be worthy
of the honour which you show us by writing to us.

LETTER CLIV

To Ascholius, Bishop of Thessalonica [2]

You have acted rightly, and according to the law
of spiritual charity, in writing to us first and in
challenging us by your good example to the like
zeal.   For while worldly love needs the eyes and
personal contact that there may arise thence a beginning of intimacy, yet those who know how to
love in the spiritual way do not depend upon the
flesh to promote their love, but through the fellow-

[2] Written in 373.   St. Ambrose (Letter XV, 12) says of
Ascholius : Ad summum sacerdotium a Macedonicis obsecratus
populis, electus a sacerdotibus.   Letter XV of St. Ambrose
was written to the church at Thessalonica on the occasion of
Ascholius' death.   Ascholius baptized Theodosius at Thessa-
lonica in 380, before his Gothic war, and was present at the
Council of Constantinople in 381.   Cf. Letters CLXIV and
CLXV, also Socrates, *Ecc. Hist.* V, 6 and 8.

κοινωνίᾳ πρὸς τὴν πνευματικὴν συνάφειαν ἄγονται.
χάρις οὖν τῷ Κυρίῳ τῷ παρακαλέσαντι ἡμῶν
τὰς καρδίας ἐν τῷ δεῖξαι [1] ὅτι οὐκ ἐν πᾶσι κατέ-
ψυκται ἡ ἀγάπη, ἀλλ' εἰσί που τῆς οἰκουμένης οἱ
τῆς Χριστοῦ μαθητείας τὸν χαρακτῆρα δεικνύντες.
καὶ τοίνυν ἔδοξέ μοι τὸ καθ' ὑμᾶς ἐοικέναι πρᾶγμα
ἄστροις ἐν νυκτερινῇ συναφείᾳ· [2] ἄλλοις κατ'
ἄλλα μέρη τοῦ οὐρανοῦ διαλάμπουσιν, ὧν
χαρίεσσα μὲν ἡ λαμπρότης, χαριέστερον δὲ δήπου
τὸ ἀπροσδόκητον. τοιοῦτοι δὲ καὶ ὑμεῖς οἱ τῶν
ἐκκλησιῶν φωστῆρες, ὀλίγοι παντελῶς καὶ
εὐαρίθμητοι ἐν τῇ σκυθρωπῇ ταύτῃ καταστάσει,
οἷον ἐν σκοτομήνῃ διαφαινόμενοι, πρὸς τῷ ἐκ τῆς
ἀρετῆς χαρίεντι, ἔτι καὶ τῷ σπανίῳ τῆς εὑρέσεως
τὸ περιπόθητον ἔχοντες.

Ἐγνώρισε δέ σου τὴν διάθεσιν ἡμῖν τὸ γράμμα
αὐτάρκως. εἰ γὰρ καὶ μικρὸν ἦν τῷ πλήθει τῶν
συλλαβῶν, ἀλλὰ τῇ γε ὀρθότητι τῆς διανοίας
ἀρκοῦσαν ἡμῖν τῆς προαιρέσεως τὴν ἀπόδειξιν
ἔδωκε. τὸ γὰρ περὶ τὸν μακαριώτατον Ἀθανά-
σιον ἐσπουδακέναι δεῖγμα ἐναργέστατον τοῦ
ὑγιῶς [3] ἔχειν περὶ τὰ μέγιστα. ἀντὶ οὖν τῆς ἐπὶ
τοῖς γράμμασιν εὐφροσύνης πολλὴν οἴδαμεν
χάριν τῷ τιμιωτάτῳ υἱῷ ἡμῶν Εὐφημίῳ· ᾧ
καὶ αὐτὸς εὔχομαι πᾶσαν ὑπάρχειν βοήθειαν
ἐξ ἁγίου· καὶ σὲ συνεύχεσθαι ἡμῖν παρακαλῶ, ὅπως ἂν ἀπολάβοιμεν αὐτὸν ἐν τάχει
μετὰ τῆς κοσμιωτάτης ὁμόζυγος [4] αὐτοῦ, θυγα-
τρὸς δὲ ἡμῶν ἐν Κυρίῳ. παρακλήθητι δὲ
καὶ αὐτὸς μὴ ἐν προοιμίοις ἡμῖν στῆσαι τὴν

---

[1] ἐκ τοῦ δεῖξαι editi antiqi.   [2] συννεφείᾳ E.
[3] ἁγίως editi antiqi.

ship of the faith are brought to the union of the
spirit. So thanks be to the Lord who has consoled
our hearts by showing that charity has grown cold
in all men, but that there exist somewhere in the
world men who display the mark of Christ's teaching! And indeed your function has seemed to me
like that of the stars in nightly concurrence : they
illuminate one portion of the heavens after another,
and while their brightness is delightful, more delightful still, methinks, is the suddenness of their
coming. Such are you who are lights of the churches,
very few and easily numbered in this present gloomy
state of affairs, shining as in a moonless night, not
only giving delight through your virtue, but also
arousing, by the rarity with which you are found,
our deep affection.

Your letter made known sufficiently your disposition towards us. For even if it was brief in
the number of its syllables, yet in the integrity of
its sentiments it gave us an adequate proof of your
purpose. For the zeal you have shown for the most
blessed Athanasius gives the clearest possible evidence of your soundness in the matters of greatest
importance. In return, then, for the joy received
from your letter we express our great thanks to our
most honoured son Euphemius,[1] for whom I also pray
that all assistance may be at hand from the Holy
One. I urge you also to join us in our prayer, that
we may soon receive him back accompanied by his
most discreet wife, our daughter in the Lord. And
as for yourself, we beg you not to stop our happiness

---

[1] The bearer of the letter from Ascholius to Basil.

---

4 συζύγου editi antiqi.

εὐφροσύνην, ἀλλὰ διὰ τῆς ἀεὶ παραπιπτούσης
προφάσεως ἐπιστέλλειν καὶ τὴν πρὸς ἡμᾶς διάθεσιν τῷ πυκνῷ τῆς ὁμιλίας αὔξειν, καὶ τὰ περὶ
τῶν αὐτοῦ[1] ἐκκλησιῶν, ὅπως ἔχει κατὰ τὴν
συμφωνίαν, σημαίνειν· περὶ δὲ[2] τῶν ἐνταῦθα
προσεύχεσθαι, ὥστε γενέσθαι καὶ παρ' ἡμῖν
γαλήνην μεγάλην, ἐπιτιμήσαντος τοῦ Κυρίου
ἡμῶν τῷ ἀνέμῳ καὶ τῇ θαλάσσῃ.

CLV

Ἀνεπίγραφος ἐπὶ ἀλείπτῃ

Πρὸς πολλὰς τὰς διὰ τῆς ἐπιστολῆς ἣν πρώτην
καὶ μόνην κατηξίωσεν ἡμῖν ἡ εὐγένειά σου δια-
πέμψασθαι ἐγγεγραμμένας κατηγορίας ἀπορῶ[3]
ἀπολογήσασθαι, οὐ διὰ τὴν τοῦ δικαίου ἔνδειαν,
ἀλλὰ διὰ τὸ ἐν πλήθει τῶν ἐπιφερομένων δύσκολον εἶναι τῶν καιριωτέρων τὴν προτίμησιν, καὶ
ὅθεν δεῖ πρῶτον ἡμᾶς ἄρξασθαι τῆς θεραπείας.
ἢ τάχα δεῖ αὐτῇ[4] τῇ τάξει τῶν γεγραμμένων
χρησαμένους ὁδῷ πρὸς ἕκαστον ἀπαντᾶν.

Τοὺς ἐπὶ Σκυθίαν ἀπαίροντας ἐντεῦθεν μέχρι
σήμερον οὐκ ἐγνωρίσαμεν· ἀλλ' οὐδὲ τῶν ἐκ τῆς
οἰκίας[5] ὑπέμνησαν ἡμᾶς, ὥστε προσειπεῖν σε[6]

[1] σαυτοῦ editi antiqi.   [2] τε E.   [3] ἀπορῶν E.
[4] δεῖ αὐτῇ] δι' αὐτήν E.   [5] οἰκείας editi antiqi.
[6] σε om. E.

---

[1] Written in 373. According to the Benedictine edition
the person addressed is Julius Soranus, a relative of Basil
and a duke of Scythia. The sub-title may have been added
by a copyist. It applies to Soranus, inasmuch as he was "a

at its beginning, but on every pretext that arises to write and thus enhance your disposition towards us by frequent communication, and to keep us informed about the condition of your churches as regards harmony; and as for our own affairs, we beg you to pray that a great calm may come about among us also, after our Lord has rebuked the wind and the sea.

LETTER CLV

WITHOUT ADDRESS, ON THE CASE OF A TRAINER [1]

As regards the many accusations which are contained in the first and only letter which your Nobility has deigned to send us, I am at a loss how to defend myself, not through lack of a just cause, but through the fact that in the multitude of the charges brought it is difficult to make a choice of the more apposite and to know at what point we should first begin our healing treatment of the matter. Or perhaps we should employ the very order of the written items and methodically meet them one by one.

Until to-day we had no knowledge of those who are departing hence for Scythia; in fact, no member even of your household suggested to us that we

---

trainer" ($\dot{\alpha}\lambda\epsilon\dot{\iota}\pi\tau\eta s$) and encourager of martyrs. In Letter CLXIV Basil calls Ascholius "trainer" of the martyr Sabas. On the present letter and Letters CLV, CLXIV, and CLXV, which have to do with transferring the remains of the Gothic martyr Sabas (died April 372) to Caesarea in Cappadocia, cf. G. Pfeilschefter, *Ein neues Werk des Wulfila, Veröffentlichungen aus dem Kirchenhistor*, Seminar, München, 1907, pp. 192–224. This letter is one of the earliest references to the preservation of the relics of martyrs.

δι' αὐτῶν, καίτοι πάνυ διὰ σπουδῆς τιθεμένους ἐπὶ
πάσης προφάσεως προσφθέγγεσθαί σου τὴν τιμιότητα. ἐπιλαθέσθαι δέ σου ἐν προσευχαῖς ἀδύνατον,
εἰ μὴ πρότερον τοῦ ἔργου ἡμῶν ἐπιλαθώμεθα, εἰς ὃ
ἔταξεν ἡμᾶς ὁ Κύριος. μέμνησαι γὰρ πάντως τῶν
κηρυγμάτων τῶν ἐκκλησιαστικῶν, πιστὸς ὢν τῇ
τοῦ Θεοῦ χάριτι, ὅτι καὶ ὑπὲρ τῶν ἐν ἀποδημίαις
ἀδελφῶν δεόμεθα, καὶ ὑπὲρ τῶν ἐν ταῖς[1] στρατείαις
ἐξεταζομένων, καὶ ὑπὲρ παρρησιαζομένων διὰ τὸ
ὄνομα Κυρίου, καὶ ὑπὲρ τῶν τοὺς πνευματικοὺς
καρποὺς ἐπιδεικνυμένων, ἐν τῇ ἁγίᾳ Ἐκκλησίᾳ
τὰς εὐχὰς ποιούμεθα· ὧν πάντως ἐν τοῖς πλείοσιν[2]
ἢ καὶ ἐν τοῖς πᾶσι νομίζομεν καὶ τὴν σὴν ἐμπερι-
λαμβάνεσθαι τιμιότητα. ἰδίᾳ δέ σου ἡμεῖς πῶς
ἂν ἐπιλαθώμεθα, τοσαῦτα ἔχοντες τὰ κινοῦντα
ἡμᾶς πρὸς μνήμην, ἀδελφὴν τοιαύτην, ἀδελφιδοὺς[3]
τοιούτους, συγγένειαν οὕτω χρηστήν, οὕτως
ἀγαπῶσαν ἡμᾶς, οἶκον, οἰκέτας, φίλους, ἐξ ὧν, κἂν
μὴ βουλώμεθα, ἀναγκαίως ὑπομιμνησκόμεθά σου
τῆς ἀγαθῆς προαιρέσεως ;

Περὶ δὲ τοῦδε ὁ ἀδελφὸς ὁ δεῖνα οὐδὲν ἡμῖν
ἤνεγκεν ἐπαχθές, οὐδὲ παρ' ἡμῶν βλάπτουσα
αὐτόν τις κρίσις ἐξενήνεκται οὐδεμία. τρέψον οὖν
τὴν λύπην ἐπὶ τοὺς τὰ ψευδῆ διηγησαμένους,
ἀπολύσας πάσης μέμψεως καὶ τὸν χωρεπίσκοπον
καὶ ἐμέ. εἰ δέ τινα δίκην γυμνάζει ὁ σχολαστικὸς
ὁ δεῖνα, ἔχει δικαστήρια δημόσια καὶ νόμους.
ἀξιῶ οὖν ὑμᾶς ἐπὶ τούτοις μηδεμίαν ἔχειν
μέμψιν.

---

[1] ταῖς om. E.   [2] χρόνοις E, editi antiqi.
[3] ἀδελφικήν E.

should salute you through them, although we are
eagerly disposed to salute your Honour on every
occasion. And we cannot forget you in our prayers,
unless we first forget the labours to which the Lord
has appointed us. For you surely remember, since
by the grace of God you are faithful, the invocations [1]
of the Church—that we both make supplication for
our brethren who are sojourning abroad, and offer
prayers in the Holy Church for those who are
enrolled in military service, and for those who speak
out boldly for the sake of the name of the Lord,
and for those who show the fruits of the Spirit; and
certainly in the greater number of these prayers, or
even in all of them, we consider that your Honour
also is included. And in private how can we forget
you when we have so many things to prompt us to
remember you—such a sister, such nephews, a kins-
folk so good, so affectionate towards us, house, household, and friends, on account of whom, even if we
do not wish it, we are constrained to remember
your goodwill?

But in regard to this present matter a certain
brother has brought us no unpleasant news, nor has
any decision whatever been given out by us which
might cause injury to him. Therefore turn your
indignation against those who have made the false
statements, absolving the chorepiscopus and myself
from all blame. And if this certain learned fellow is
making ready any legal action, he has public courts
and laws. Therefore I request you to put no blame
on us in these matters.

---

[1] κηρύγματα here seems to denote an appointed liturgy.
For a similar meaning of the word, cf. Cyprian, Letter
LXXV, from Firmilianus.

Αὐτὸς δὲ ὅσα ποιεῖς ἀγαθά, σεαυτῷ θησαυρίζεις·
καὶ ἣν παρέχῃ ἀνάπαυσιν τοῖς διὰ τὸ ὄνομα τοῦ
Κυρίου διωκομένοις, ταύτην σεαυτῷ ἐν ἡμέρᾳ τῆς
μισθαποδοσίας προετοιμάζεις. καλῶς δὲ ποιήσεις,
ἐὰν καὶ λείψανα μαρτύρων τῇ πατρίδι ἐκπέμψῃς,[1]
εἴπερ, ὡς ἐπέστειλας ἡμῖν, ὁ ἐκεῖ διωγμὸς ποιεῖ
καὶ νῦν μάρτυρας τῷ Κυρίῳ.

CLVI

Εὐαγρίῳ πρεσβυτέρῳ

Τοσοῦτον ἀπέσχον τοῦ δυσχερᾶναι πρὸς τὸ
μῆκος τῶν γραμμάτων, ὥστε καὶ μικρά μοι ἔδοξεν
εἶναι ἡ ἐπιστολὴ ὑπὸ τῆς κατὰ τὴν ἀνάγνωσιν
ἡδονῆς. τί γὰρ ἥδιον ἄκουσμα τοῦ τῆς εἰρήνης
ὀνόματος; ἢ[2] τί τοῦ ὑπὲρ τῶν τοιούτων βουλεύεσ-
θαι ἱεροπρεπέστερον καὶ μᾶλλον τῷ Κυρίῳ
κεχαρισμένον; σοὶ μὲν οὖν παράσχοι ὁ Κύριος
τὸν μισθὸν τῆς εἰρηνοποιίας, οὕτω καλῶς προαιρουμένῳ καὶ σπουδαίως ἐγκειμένῳ πράγματι
μακαριστῷ. ἡμᾶς δὲ νόμιζε, τιμία κεφαλή,
ἕνεκα[3] μὲν τοῦ προῃρῆσθαι καὶ εὔχεσθαι ἰδεῖν
ποτὲ τὴν ἡμέραν ἐν ᾗ πάντες τὸν αὐτὸν πληρώ-
σουσι σύλλογον, οἱ ταῖς διανοίαις ἀλλήλων μὴ
ἀπεσχισμένοι, μηδενὶ παραχωρεῖν τῶν εἰς τὴν
σπουδὴν τούτων πρωτείων. καὶ γὰρ ἂν εἴημεν

---

[1] ἐκπέμψῃ E.   [2] ἢ om. Harl., Med.
[3] ἕνεκεν E.

---

[1] Written in the late autumn of 373 ; cf. Loofs 31, note 3.
Evagrius, commonly known as of Antioch to distinguish him

As for yourself, whatever good deeds you perform, you are laying them up as a treasure for yourself; and whatever alleviation you render to those who are being persecuted for the sake of the name of the Lord, this you are preparing for yourself on the day of reward. And you will do well, if you send the relics of martyrs to your native land, since, as you have written us, the persecution which is taking place there is even now making martyrs to the Lord.

LETTER CLVI

To Evagrius, the Presbyter[1]

So far was I from being displeased at the length of your letter, that it seemed even short to me because of the pleasure I got from reading it. For what is sweeter to the ears than the name of peace? Or what is more befitting the sacred office and more pleasing to the Lord than to deliberate on matters such as these? Therefore may the Lord render to you the reward of peace-making, you who so nobly undertake and so zealously pursue a most blessed work. But know, honoured sir, that—on account of the choice we have made and the prayers we offer that we may yet see the day when all those who are not divided from one another in mind shall fill the same assembly—of those foremost in zeal for this end we yield to none. For we would truly be the

from others of the same name, especially Evagrius the historian. The dates of his birth and his death are uncertain, but he is known to have been consecrated by the dying Paulinus in 388 (an act which prolonged the Meletian schism at Antioch), and seems to have lived until at least 392; cf. Letter CXXXVIII.

ὡς ἀληθῶς πάντων ἀνθρώπων ἀτοπώτατοι, σχισ-
μασι καὶ κατατομαῖς ἐκκλησιῶν ἐφηδόμενοι,[1]
καὶ μὴ τὴν συνάφειαν τῶν μελῶν τοῦ σώματος
τοῦ Χριστοῦ τὸ μέγιστον τῶν ἀγαθῶν τιθέμενοι.
ὅσον μέντοι τῆς ἐπιθυμίας ἡμῖν περίεστι, τοσοῦτον
γίνωσκε τῆς δυνάμεως ἐνδεῖν. οὐ γὰρ ἀγνοεῖ σου
ἡ τελεία φρόνησις, ὅτι τὰ χρόνῳ κρατυνθέντα
πάθη πρῶτον μὲν χρόνου δεῖται πρὸς τὴν διόρθωσιν, ἔπειτα ἰσχυρᾶς καὶ εὐτονωτέρας ἀγωγῆς,[2] εἰ
μέλλοι[3] τις τοῦ βάθους αὐτοῦ καθικνεῖσθαι, ὥστε
πρόρριζα ἐξελεῖν τῶν καμνόντων τὰ ἀρρωστήματα. οἶδας δὲ ὃ λέγω, καὶ εἰ δεῖ τρανότερον
εἰπεῖν, οὐδεὶς ὁ φόβος.

Τὴν φιλαυτίαν ἔθει μακρῷ ταῖς ψυχαῖς ἐρριζω-
θεῖσαν εἰς ἀνὴρ ἀνελεῖν οὐχ οἷός τε, οὐδ᾽ ἐπιστολὴ
μία, οὐδὲ χρόνος βραχύς. τὰς γὰρ ὑπονοίας καὶ
τὰς ἐξ ἀντιλογιῶν παρατριβὰς παντελῶς ἀναιρεθῆ-
ναι, μὴ ἀξιοπίστου τινὸς μεσιτεύοντος τῇ εἰρήνῃ,
ἀμήχανον. καὶ εἰ μὲν ἐπέρρει ἡμῖν τὰ παρὰ τῆς
χάριτος καὶ ἦμεν δυνατοὶ λόγῳ καὶ ἔργῳ καὶ τοῖς
πνευματικοῖς χαρίσμασι δυσωπῆσαι τοὺς ἀντι-
διατιθεμένους, ἔδει κατατολμῆσαι τοῦ τοσούτου
πράγματος. τάχα δὲ οὐδ᾽ ἂν τότε συνεβούλευσας
ἡμῖν μόνοις ἐλθεῖν ἐπὶ τὴν ἐπανόρθωσιν, ὄντος τοῦ
ἐπισκόπου τῇ τοῦ Θεοῦ χάριτι, ᾧ ἡ φροντὶς ἀνῆκε[4]
προηγουμένως τῆς ἐκκλησίας· ὃν οὔτε αὐτὸν ἐλθεῖν πρὸς ἡμᾶς οἷόν τε, καὶ ἡμῖν ἀποδημήσειν[5]
τέως ὑπὸ τοῦ χειμῶνος οὐ ῥᾴδιον, μᾶλλον δὲ
παντελῶς ἀδύνατον, οὐ μόνον καθότι τὸ σῶμά

---

[1] ἐνηδόμενοι Harl., Reg. secundus.
[2] διαγωγῆς editi antiqi.   [3] μέλοι E.
[4] ἀνήκει editi antiqi.   [5] ἀποδημεῖν editi antiqi.

386

most unnatural of all men, if we rejoiced in the schisms and divisions of the churches, and did not consider the union of the members of the body of Christ to be the greatest of all blessings. However, you should know that our power is as deficient as our desire is abundant. For your perfect wisdom is not unaware of the fact that evils which have been strengthened by time need time first of all for their correction, then a strong and vigorous method of treatment, if one is to get at the very bottom of them, so as to tear out by the roots the complaints of the ailing. But you know what I mean, and if it is necessary to speak more clearly, there is no cause for fear.

Self-love, when rooted in the mind by long habit, no one man can eradicate, no one letter, no short time. For the complete elimination of suspicions and of the clashes arising from controversies is impossible, unless there be some trustworthy man to act as a mediator in the interest of peace. And if all the strength of divine grace should flow upon us, and if we were able by word and deed and the gifts of the Spirit to move our opponents, then it would be necessary for me to undertake so great a task. Yet perhaps even in that case you would not have advised us to set about the work of correction all alone, since he[1] who by the grace of God is the bishop is the man upon whom the care of his church falls chiefly ; and it is not possible for him to come to us in person, and because of the winter it is not easy for us in the meantime to go abroad, or rather it is altogether impossible, not

---

[1] Meletius of Antioch.

μοι[1] ὑπὸ μακρᾶς ἀρρωστίας ἀπείρηκεν, ἀλλ' ὅτι
καὶ αἱ τῶν Ἀρμενιακῶν ὀρῶν αἱ[2] ὑπερβάσεις
μικρὸν ὕστερον ἄβατοι[3] γίνονται καὶ τοῖς πάνυ
καθ' ἡλικίαν σφριγῶσι. γράμματι δὲ αὐτῷ
σημᾶναι[4] ταῦτα οὐ παραιτήσομαι. οὐ μέντοι
προσδοκῶ τι ἐκ τῶν γραμμάτων ἀξιόλογον ἀπο-
βήσεσθαι, τῆς τε τοῦ ἀνδρὸς ἀκριβείας στοχαζό-
μενος καὶ αὐτῆς τῆς φύσεως τῶν γραμμάτων· ὅτι
οὐ πέφυκεν ἐναργῶς δύνασθαι δυσωπεῖν ὁ διαπεμ-
πόμενος λόγος. πολλὰ γὰρ δεῖ εἰπεῖν, πολλὰ καὶ
ἀντακοῦσαι, καὶ λῦσαι τὰ ὑποπίπτοντα, καὶ
ἀνθυπενεγκεῖν[5] τὰ ὑφορμοῦντα, ὧν οὐδὲν δύναται
ὁ ἐν τοῖς γράμμασι λόγος, ἀργὸς καὶ ἄψυχος ἐν
τῷ χάρτῃ διερριμμένος.

Πλὴν ἀλλ', ὅπερ ἔφην, οὐκ[6] ἀποκνήσω γράψαι.
γίνωσκε μέντοι, ὡς ἀληθῶς εὐλαβέστατε καὶ
πολυπόθητε ἡμῖν[7] ἀδελφέ, ὅτι οὐδεμία μοι πρὸς
οὐδένα τῇ τοῦ Θεοῦ χάριτι ἰδιάζουσά ἐστι
φιλονεικία. οὐδὲ γὰρ πολυπραγμονήσας οἶδα τὰ
ἐγκλήματα, οἷς ἕκαστος ὑπεύθυνος ἢ ἔστιν ἢ
ὀνομάζεται. ὥστε οὕτως ὑμᾶς προσέχειν τῇ
ἡμετέρᾳ διανοίᾳ προσήκει, ὡς μηδὲν ἡμῶν δυναμένων ποιῆσαι κατὰ πρόσκλισιν,[8] μηδὲ προειλημ-
μένων εἰς τὴν κατά τινων διαβολήν. μόνον εἰ
εὐδοκία γένοιτο[9] τοῦ Κυρίου ἐκκλησιαστικῶς
πάντα καὶ ἀκολούθως πραχθῆναι.

Ἐλύπησε δὲ ἡμᾶς ὁ ποθεινότατος υἱὸς Δωρόθεος[10]
ὁ συνδιάκονος, ἀπαγγείλας περὶ τῆς εὐλαβείας
σου, ὅτι ὤκνησας μετασχεῖν αὐτῷ τῆς συνάξεως.

---

[1] μου E, Med. [2] αἱ om. E. [3] ἀδύνατοι E.
[4] σημῆναι tres MSS. [5] ἀντεπενεγκεῖν E.

only because my body is worn out by long illness, but also because the passes over the Armenian mountains become a little later impassable even to those who are in the very vigour of youth. And I shall not hesitate to point this out to him in writing. However, I do not look for anything worth while to result from letters, judging from the man's strictness and the very nature of anything written; for the transmitted word is obviously by nature incapable of moving men. For there are many things to be said, many things to be heard from the other side, objections to be solved, one's own reasons to be advanced, none of which can be accomplished by the written word, inert and lifeless as it is, spread out upon the sheet of paper.

However, as I have said, I shall not refrain from writing. Be assured, however, in truth our most pious and beloved brother, that by God's grace I have no private quarrel with anyone at all. For I have not even had the curiosity to find out their charges to which the accused either are severally liable or are said to be liable. Consequently it is fitting that you should pay heed to our opinion, knowing that we are incapable of acting from bias and have not been prejudiced by the slander directed against any of the parties. Would only that the approval of the Lord might be granted, that everything be done in the Church's manner and in the proper form.

Our most beloved son Dorotheus, our deacon, caused us sorrow when he informed me about your Piety, that you refused to take part with him in

---

6 οὐδ' editi antiqi. 7 ἡμῶν E.
8 πρόσκλησιν editi antiqi. 9 γίγνοιτο editi antiqi.
10 Θεόδωρος unus ex Regiis.

καίτοι οὐ τοιαῦτα ἡμῖν ἦν τὰ ὡμιλημένα,[1] εἴ τι ἐγὼ
μέμνημαι. ἀποστεῖλαι μέντοι πρὸς τὴν δύσιν
ἐμοὶ μὲν παντελῶς ἐστιν ἀδύνατον, οὐδένα ἔχοντι
τῶν εἰς τὴν διακονίαν ταύτην ἐπιτηδείων. τῶν
δὲ αὐτόθεν ἀδελφῶν, ἐάν τις αἱρῆται τὸν ὑπὲρ τῶν
ἐκκλησιῶν κόπον ἀναδέξασθαι, οἶδε δηλονότι καὶ
πρὸς τίνας ὁρμήσει, καὶ ἐπὶ ποίῳ σκοπῷ, καὶ παρὰ
τίνων ἐφοδιασθῇ τοῖς γράμμασι, καὶ ποταποῖς
τούτοις. ἐγὼ μὲν γὰρ ἐν κύκλῳ περισκεψάμενος
ὁρῶ μεθ᾽ ἑαυτοῦ οὐδένα. καὶ εὔχομαι μὲν τοῖς
ἑπτακισχιλίοις ἐναριθμηθῆναι τοῖς μὴ κάμψασι
γόνυ τῇ[2] Βάαλ. πλὴν ὅτι ζητοῦσι καὶ ἡμῶν τὴν
ψυχὴν οἱ πᾶσι τὰς ἑαυτῶν ἐπιβάλλοντες χεῖρας.
οὐ μέντοι τούτου γε ἕνεκεν ἐλλείψομέν τι τῆς
ὀφειλομένης σπουδῆς ταῖς τοῦ Θεοῦ ἐκκλησίαις.

CLVII

Ἀντιόχῳ

Πῶς οἴει βαρέως ἤνεγκα διαμαρτὼν σου τῆς
συντυχίας κατὰ τὸ θέρος ; καίτοι οὐδὲ ἡ τῶν[3]
ἄλλων τοιαύτη γέγονεν, ὥστε μέχρι κόρου ἡμῖν
προελθεῖν· ἀλλ᾽ οὖν καὶ ὄναρ ἰδεῖν τὰ ποθούμενα
φέρει τινὰ τοῖς ἀγαπῶσι παραμυθίαν. σὺ δὲ
οὐδὲ ἐπιστέλλεις, οὕτως ἀργὸς εἶ, ὥστε μηδὲ τὴν

---

[1] ὡμολογημένα editi antiqi.   [2] τῷ editi antiqi.
[3] ἡ τῶν] ἐτῶν E.

---

[1] Written in 373. Other letters to Antiochus, nephew
of Eusebius, are CXLVI, CLVIII, and CLXVIII. Letter
CCXXXIX makes reference to Antiochus. Since the present

his religious service. And yet such were not the matters which were discussed by you and me, if I recollect at all. To send a representative to the West, however, is absolutely impossible for us, since I have no one suitable for this mission. But if any one of the brothers with you chooses to take upon himself this task in behalf of the churches, he knows, doubtless, to what person he shall proceed, for what purpose, and by whom he shall be furnished with letters, and by what sort of letters. For when I look about me, I see in my own followers no one at all. And I pray to be numbered amongst the seven thousand who have not bent the knee to Baal. I will only add that those who are laying their hands on all are seeking our soul also. But not on this account shall we be at all remiss in the zeal that is due to the churches of God.

LETTER CLVII

To Antiochus [1]

You can imagine how disappointed I was at failing to meet you during the summer! And yet our meeting in other years was also not of such a character as to reach the point of satiating us. However, to see even in dreams the objects of one's desire brings some little comfort to those who love. But you do not even write, so slothful are you; con-

and the following letters are both couched in similar terms, the Benedictine editors are inclined to believe that they are really addressed to different people. Furthermore, the slothfulness of which Basil complains would befit Eusebius much better than Antiochus, who could not travel without his uncle's permission.

ὑπόλειψιν[1] ἄλλῃ τινὶ αἰτίᾳ μᾶλλον ἢ τῷ ἀργῶς
ἔχειν πρὸς τὰς ὑπὲρ τῆς ἀγάπης ἀποδημίας λογίζεσθαι. ἀλλὰ τοῦτο μὲν πεπαύσθω ἡμῖν. εὔχου
δὲ ὑπὲρ ἡμῶν καὶ παρακάλει τὸν Κύριον μὴ
ἐγκαταλιπεῖν ἡμᾶς, ἀλλ᾽ ὡς ἐκ τῶν ἐπελθόντων
παρήγαγεν ἡμᾶς πειρασμῶν, οὕτω καὶ ἐκ τῶν
προσδοκωμένων ῥύσασθαι εἰς δόξαν τοῦ ὀνόματος
αὐτοῦ, ἐφ᾽ ᾧ ἠλπίσαμεν.

CLVIII

Ἀντιόχῳ

Ἐπειδὴ ἀντέστησάν μοι αἱ ἁμαρτίαι μου πρὸς
τὸ μὴ δυνηθῆναί με ἣν πάλαι εἶχον ἐπιθυμίαν
τῆς ὑμετέρας συντυχίας ἀγαγεῖν εἰς πέρας,
γράμμασι γοῦν παραμυθοῦμαι τὴν ἀπόλειψιν·
καὶ παρακαλοῦμεν[2] μὴ διαλιπεῖν[3] μεμνημένους
ἡμῶν ἐν ταῖς προσευχαῖς, ἵνα, ἐὰν ζῶμεν, καταξιωθῶμεν ὑμῶν ἀπολαῦσαι, εἰ δὲ μή, διὰ τῆς
βοηθείας τῶν προσευχῶν ὑμῶν μετὰ ἀγαθῆς
ἐλπίδος μεταναστεύσωμεν[4] ἀπὸ τοῦ κόσμου
τούτου. τὸν δὲ ἀδελφὸν τὸν ἐπὶ ταῖς καμήλοις[5]
παρατιθέμεθα ὑμῖν.

CLIX

Εὐπατερίῳ,[6] καὶ τῇ θυγατρί

Ὅσην εὐφροσύνην παρέσχε μοι τὸ γράμμα τῆς
κοσμιότητός σου εἰκάζεις πάντως αὐτοῖς[7] τοῖς

---

[1] ἀπόλειψιν E. [2] ὑμᾶς add. editi antiqi.
[3] διαλείπειν editi antiqi. [4] μεταναστῶμεν editi antiqi.
[5] ταῖς καμήλοις] τὰς καμήλους editi antiqi.
[6] Εὐπατρίῳ E, Med. [7] αὐτός editi antiqi.

sequently your failure to visit me is likewise to be attributed to no other reason than that you are slothful about undertaking journeys to gratify your affection. However, let us say no more about this. But pray for us and beg the Lord not to desert us, but just as He has led us out of past trials, so to deliver us also from those which are imminent, unto the glory of His name wherein we have placed our hope.

LETTER CLVIII

To Antiochus [1]

Since my sins have risen up against me, rendering it impossible for me to realize the desire which I have long had of visiting you, by letter at least I can palliate my failure to appear; and we exhort you not to leave off making mention of us in your prayers, so that, if we live, we may be deemed worthy of enjoying you, and if not, that by the aid of your prayers we may pass on from this world with good hope. And we put in your care the brother who is in charge of the camels.

LETTER CLIX

To Eupaterius and his Daughter [2]

How much pleasure the letter of your Decorum afforded me you certainly can infer from the very

---

[1] Written in 373. Cf. the previous letter with note.
[2] Written about 373, on the Nicene Creed and the Holy Ghost. Eupaterius and his daughter are otherwise unknown.

ἐπεσταλμένοις. τί γὰρ ἂν ἥδιον γένοιτο ἀνθρώπῳ εὐχὴν ποιουμένῳ φοβουμένοις Θεὸν ἀεὶ προσομιλεῖν καὶ τοῦ παρ' αὐτῶν κέρδους μεταλαμβάνειν, γραμμάτων τοιούτων, δι' ὧν ἡ Θεοῦ γνῶσις ἐπιζητεῖται; εἰ γὰρ τὸ ζῆν ἡμῖν Χριστός, ἀκολούθως καὶ ὁ λόγος ἡμῶν περὶ Χριστοῦ ὀφείλει εἶναι, καὶ ἡ ἔννοια καὶ πᾶσα πρᾶξις τῶν ἐντολῶν αὐτοῦ ἠρτῆσθαι, καὶ ἡ ψυχὴ ἡμῶν κατ' αὐτὸν μεμορφῶσθαι. χαίρω τοίνυν περὶ τοιούτων ἐρωτώμενος καὶ συγχαίρω τοῖς ἐρωτῶσιν. ἡμῖν τοίνυν ἑνὶ μὲν λόγῳ ἡ τῶν ἐν Νικαίᾳ συνελθόντων πατέρων πίστις πασῶν τῶν ὕστερον ἐφευρεθεισῶν¹ προτετίμηται· ἐν ᾗ ὁμοούσιος ὁμολογεῖται ὁ Υἱὸς τῷ Πατρί, καὶ τῆς αὐτῆς ὑπάρχων φύσεως ἧς ὁ γεννήσας. φῶς γὰρ ἐκ φωτός, καὶ Θεὸν ἐκ Θεοῦ, καὶ ἀγαθὸν ἐξ ἀγαθοῦ, καὶ τὰ τοιαῦτα πάντα, ὑπό τε τῶν ἁγίων ἐκείνων ὡμολογήθη· καὶ ὑφ' ἡμῶν νῦν, τῶν εὐχομένων κατ' ἴχνη βαίνειν ἐκείνοις, προσμαρτυρεῖται.

Ἐπειδὴ δὲ τὸ νῦν ἀνακύψαν παρὰ τῶν ἀεὶ² καινοτομεῖν ἐπιχειρούντων ζήτημα, παρασιωπηθὲν τοῖς πάλαι διὰ τὸ ἀναντίρρητον, ἀδιάρθρωτον κατελείφθη (λέγω δὴ τὸ περὶ τοῦ ἁγίου Πνεύματος). προστίθεμεν τὸν περὶ τούτου λόγον ἀκολούθως τῇ τῆς Γραφῆς ἐννοίᾳ· ὅτι ὡς βαπτιζόμεθα, οὕτω καὶ πιστεύομεν· ὡς πιστεύομεν, οὕτω καὶ δοξολογοῦμεν. ἐπειδὴ οὖν βάπτισμα ἡμῖν δέδοται παρὰ τοῦ Σωτῆρος εἰς ὄνομα Πατρὸς καὶ Υἱοῦ καὶ

---

¹ εὑρεθεισῶν E.   ² τι add. editi antiqi.

¹ Cf. Phil. 1. 21 : ἐμοὶ γὰρ τὸ ζῆν, Χριστός· καὶ τὸ ἀποθανεῖν κέρδος.   "For me, to live is Christ : to die is gain."

tenor of your letter. For what could be sweeter to a man who prays that he may ever associate with God-fearing men and derive some of the profit such association yields than such letters as help us in our search for the knowledge of God? For if "to us, to live is Christ," [1] accordingly also our speech ought to be about Christ, and our thoughts and all our actions should depend upon His commands, and our souls should be moulded according to Him. I therefore rejoice when I am questioned about such matters and congratulate those who put the questions. As for us, then, to state it in a word, the creed of the Fathers who assembled at Nicaea has been honoured by us before all those formulated later, and in this the Son is confessed to be consubstantial with the Father, and to be of the same nature as the One who begot Him. For Light of Light, and God of God, and Good of Good (and all descriptions of this kind) has He been confessed to be by those holy men; and by us now, who pray that we may walk in their footsteps, witness to this is also borne.

But since the question which has now been brought up by those who are always attempting to make innovations, and which was passed over in silence by the men of former times because there was no dispute about it, has remained unexplained (I mean the question concerning the Holy Ghost), we are adding the explanation of this according to the sense of the Scriptures : namely, that as we are baptized, so also do we believe ; as we believe, so also do we recite the doxology. Since, then, baptism has been given to us by our Saviour in the name of the Father and of the Son and of the Holy Spirit,

ἁγίου Πνεύματος, ἀκόλουθον τῷ βαπτίσματι τὴν
ὁμολογίαν τῆς πίστεως παρεχόμεθα, ἀκόλουθον
δὲ καὶ τὴν δοξολογίαν τῇ πίστει, συνδοξάζοντες
Πατρὶ καὶ Υἱῷ τὸ ἅγιον Πνεῦμα, τῷ πεπεῖσθαι
μὴ ἀλλότριον εἶναι τῆς θείας φύσεως. οὐ γὰρ ἂν
τῶν αὐτῶν μετέσχε τιμῶν τὸ ἀπεξενωμένον κατὰ
τὴν φύσιν. τοὺς δὲ κτίσμα λέγοντας τὸ Πνεῦμα
τὸ ἅγιον ἐλεοῦμεν, ὡς εἰς τὸ ἀσυγχώρητον πτῶμα [1]
τῆς εἰς αὐτὸ βλασφημίας διὰ τῆς τοιαύτης φωνῆς
καταπίπτοντας. ὅτι γὰρ διώρισται κτίσις θεότητος οὐδενὸς λόγου προσδεῖ τοῖς κατὰ μικρὸν [2] ταῖς
Γραφαῖς ἐγγεγυμνασμένοις. ἡ μὲν γὰρ κτίσις
δουλεύει, τὸ δὲ Πνεῦμα ἐλευθεροῖ· ἡ κτίσις ζωῆς
προσδεής ἐστι, τὸ Πνεῦμά ἐστι τὸ ζωοποιοῦν· ἡ
κτίσις διδασκαλίας προσδεῖται, τὸ Πνεῦμά ἐστι
τὸ δίδασκον· ἡ κτίσις ἁγιάζεται, τὸ Πνεῦμά ἐστι
τὸ ἁγιάζον. κἂν ἀγγέλους εἴπῃς, κἂν ἀρχαγ-
γέλους, κἂν πάσας τὰς ὑπερκοσμίους [3] δυνάμεις,
διὰ τοῦ Πνεύματος τὴν ἁγιωσύνην λαμβάνουσιν.
αὐτὸ δὲ τὸ Πνεῦμα φυσικὴν ἔχει τὴν ἁγιότητα,
οὐ κατὰ χάριν λαβόν, ἀλλὰ συνουσιωμένην αὐτῷ·
ὅθεν καὶ τῆς προσηγορίας τῆς τοῦ ἁγίου ἐξαιρέτως
τετύχηκεν. ὃ τοίνυν φύσει ἅγιον, ὡς φύσει ἅγιος

----

[1] πταῖσμα duo MSS.
[2] κατὰ μικρὸν] κἂν μικρὸν editi antiqi.
[3] ὑπερκοσμίας editi antiqi.

----

[1] Cf. Rom. 8. 2 : ὁ γὰρ νόμος τοῦ πνεύματος τῆς ζωῆς ἐν
Χριστῷ Ἰησοῦ ἠλευθέρωσέ με ἀπὸ τοῦ νόμου τῆς ἁμαρτίας καὶ τοῦ
θανάτου. "For the law of the spirit of life, in Christ Jesus,
hath delivered me from the law of sin and death."
[2] John 6. 64.

we offer the confession of our faith in accordance
with our baptism, and in accordance with our faith
we also recite the doxology, glorifying the Holy
Spirit along with the Father and the Son, because
we are convinced that He is not foreign to the
divine nature. For that which had been alienated by
its nature could not have shared in the same honours.
And we pity those who call the Spirit a creature,
because they fall into the unpardonable error of
blasphemy against Him by the use of such language.
For the fact that any creature is distinct and
separate from the Godhead needs no argument for
those who are even a little versed in the Scriptures.
For the creature is a slave, but the Spirit sets free ; [1]
the creature is in need of life, and " it is the Spirit
that quickeneth " ; [2] the creature needs teaching,
and it is the Spirit that teaches ; [3] the creature is
sanctified, and it is the Spirit that sanctifies. [4] And
if you name angels, and archangels, and all the
heavenly powers, it is through the Holy Spirit that
they receive their holiness. But the Spirit of Himself has natural sanctity, not receiving it by grace,
but by being joined substantially to Him ; whence
also He has received the distinctive title of " holy."
And He therefore is holy by nature, as the Father

[3] Cf. John 14. 26 : ὁ δὲ Παράκλητος, τὸ Πνεῦμα τὸ Ἅγιον,
ὃ πέμψει ὁ Πατὴρ ἐν τῷ ὀνόματί μου, ἐκεῖνος ὑμᾶς διδάξει πάντα,
καὶ ὑπομνήσει ὑμᾶς πάντα ἃ εἶπον ὑμῖν. "But the Paraclete,
the Holy Ghost, whom the Father will send in My name, he
will teach you all things, and bring all things to your mind,
whatsoever I shall have said to you."

[4] Cf. Rom. 15. 16 : ἵνα γένηται ἡ προσφορὰ τῶν ἐθνῶν
εὐπρόσδεκτος, ἡγιασμένη ἐν Πνεύματι Ἁγίῳ, "that the oblation
of the Gentiles may be made acceptable and sanctified in the
Holy Ghost."

ὁ Πατήρ, καὶ φύσει ἅγιος ὁ Υἱός, οὔτε αὐτοὶ τῆς θείας καὶ μακαρίας Τριάδος χωρίσαι καὶ διατεμεῖν ἀνεχόμεθα, οὔτε τοὺς εὐκόλως τῇ κτίσει συναριθμοῦντας ἀποδεχόμεθα.

Ταῦτα, ὥσπερ ἐν κεφαλαίῳ, ἀρκούντως τῇ εὐλαβείᾳ ὑμῶν εἰρήσθω. ἀπὸ γὰρ μικρῶν σπερμάτων γεωργήσετε τὸ πλεῖον τῆς εὐσεβείας, συνεργοῦντος ὑμῖν [1] τοῦ ἁγίου Πνεύματος. δίδου γὰρ σοφῷ ἀφορμήν, καὶ σοφώτερος ἔσται. τὴν δὲ τελειοτέραν διδασκαλίαν εἰς τὴν κατ᾽ ὀφθαλμοὺς συντυχίαν ὑπερθησόμεθα, δι᾽ ἧς καὶ τὰ ἀντικείμενα ἐπιλύσασθαι, καὶ πλατυτέρας τὰς ἐκ τῶν Γραφῶν παρασχέσθαι μαρτυρίας, καὶ πάντα τύπον τὸν ὑγιῆ τῆς πίστεως βεβαιώσασθαι δυνατόν. τὸ δὲ νῦν ἔχον συγγνώμην νείματε τῇ βραχύτητι. καὶ γὰρ οὐδ᾽ ἂν ἐπέστειλα τὴν ἀρχήν, εἰ μὴ μείζονα ἡγούμην τὴν βλάβην ἀρνήσασθαι τὴν αἴτησιν παντελῶς, ἢ ἐλλιπῶς παρασχέσθαι.

CLX

Διοδώρῳ

Ἀφίκετο ἡμῖν γράμματα τὴν ἐπιγραφὴν ἔχοντα Διοδώρου, τὰ δὲ ἐφεξῆς ἄλλου τινὸς πρέποντα εἶναι μᾶλλον ἢ Διοδώρου. δοκεῖ γάρ μοί τις τῶν τεχνικῶν,[2] τὸ σὸν πρόσωπον ὑποδύς, οὕτως ἑαυτὸν ἀξιόπιστον ἐθελῆσαι ποιῆσαι τοῖς ἀκρωμένοις. ὅς γε, ἐρωτηθεὶς ὑπό τινος, εἰ θεμιτὸν

---

[1] ἡμῖν Harl.

[2] τις τῶν τεχνικῶν] τάχα τις τῶν βαναύσων τεχνιτῶν Harl.

is holy by nature, and the Son is holy by nature; and neither do we, for ourselves, tolerate the separation and severance of any member from the divine and blessed Trinity, nor do we receive those who are ready to reckon any member as a part of creation.

Let these statements, as a summary, be sufficient for your Piety. For from small seeds you will produce by cultivation the greater part of piety, the Holy Spirit co-operating in you. For "give an occasion to a wise man, and wisdom shall be added to him."[1] But we shall postpone a fuller explanation until we shall have a meeting face to face, which will enable us to resolve objections, and to furnish fuller testimony from the Scriptures, and to confirm every sound article of faith. But for the present grant pardon to my brevity. For I should not have written in the beginning, had I not thought it a greater harm to refuse the request altogether than to comply with it imperfectly.

LETTER CLX

To Diodorus [2]

A letter has come to us bearing the superscription of Diodorus, but all that follows is more appropriately to be ascribed to anyone rather than to Diodorus. For it seems to me that some cunning fellow, having put on the mask of your personality, wished in this way to make himself seem trustworthy to his hearers. This person, when asked by someone whether it was

---

[1] Prov. 9. 9.
[2] Written in 373 or 374, on marriage with a deceased wife's sister. Cf. Letter CXXXV and note.

αὐτῷ[1] πρὸς γάμον ἀγαγέσθαι τῆς γυναικὸς τελευτησάσης τὴν ἀδελφήν, οὐκ ἔφριξε τὴν ἐρώτησιν,
ἀλλὰ καὶ πράως ἤνεγκε τὴν ἀκοήν, καὶ τὸ ἀσελγὲς
ἐπιθύμημα πάνυ γενναίως[2] καὶ ἀγωνιστικῶς
συγκατέπραξεν. εἰ μὲν οὖν παρῆν μοι τὸ γράμμα,
αὐτὸ ἂν ἀπέστειλα καὶ ἐξήρκεις[3] σαυτῷ τε
ἀμῦναι καὶ τῇ ἀληθείᾳ. ἐπεὶ δὲ ὁ δείξας πάλιν
ἀφείλετο καὶ ὥσπερ τι τρόπαιον καθ᾽ ἡμῶν
περιέφερε, κεκωλυκότων τὸ ἐξ ἀρχῆς, ἔγγραφον
ἔχειν λέγων τὴν ἐξουσίαν, ἐπέστειλα νῦν σοι,
ὥστε διπλῇ τῇ χειρὶ ἡμᾶς ἐλθεῖν ἐπὶ τὸν νόθον
ἐκεῖνον λόγον καὶ μηδεμίαν αὐτῷ ἰσχὺν κατα-
λιπεῖν, ἵνα μὴ ἔχῃ βλάπτειν ῥᾳδίως τοὺς ἐντυγ-
χάνοντας.

Πρῶτον μὲν οὖν, ὃ μέγιστον ἐπὶ τῶν τοιούτων
ἐστί, τὸ παρ᾽ ἡμῖν ἔθος, ὃ ἔχομεν προβάλλειν,
νόμου δύναμιν ἔχον, διὰ τὸ ὑφ᾽ ἁγίων ἀνδρῶν τοὺς
θεσμοὺς ἡμῖν παραδοθῆναι. τοῦτο δὲ τοιοῦτόν
ἐστιν· ἐάν τις πάθει ἀκαθαρσίας ποτὲ κρατηθεὶς
ἐκπέσῃ πρὸς δυεῖν ἀδελφῶν ἄθεσμον κοινωνίαν,
μήτε γάμον ἡγεῖσθαι τοῦτον,[4] μηθ᾽ ὅλως εἰς
ἐκκλησίας πλήρωμα παραδέχεσθαι πρότερον ἢ
διαλῦσαι αὐτοὺς ἀπ᾽ ἀλλήλων. ὥστε, εἰ καὶ
μηδὲν ἕτερον εἰπεῖν ἦν, ἐξήρκει τὸ ἔθος πρὸς τὴν
τοῦ καλοῦ[5] φυλακήν. ἐπειδὴ δὲ ὁ τὴν ἐπιστολὴν
γράψας ἐπιχειρήματι κιβδήλῳ κακὸν τοσοῦτον
ἐπειράθη τῷ βίῳ ἐπαγαγεῖν, ἀνάγκη μηδὲ ἡμᾶς
τῆς ἐκ τῶν λογισμῶν βοηθείας ὑφέσθαι· καίτοι γε

---

[1] αὐτόν editi antiqi.   [2] αὐτῷ add. editi antiqi.
[3] ἐξήρκει editi antiqi.   [4] τοῦτο editi antiqi.
[5] κακοῦ E.

lawful for him to take in marriage the sister of his deceased wife, did not shudder in horror at the question, but, on the contrary, he even listened to it calmly, and quite gallantly and boldly gave his support to the licentious desire! Now, if the letter were actually at hand, I should have forwarded it to you, and you would be quite competent to defend both yourself and the truth. But since the person who showed me the letter took it away with him again and carried it about as a sort of trophy won from us who had forbidden this practice from the beginning, saying that he had a written permission, I am now writing to you that we may attack that spurious document with our combined strength and that we may leave it no validity, lest it should be the means of harming, as it easily might, those who chance to read it.

In the first place, then—a consideration that is very important in such matters—there is the custom observed among us, which we can cite in defence of our position, a custom having the force of a law, because our ordinances have been handed down to us by holy men. And this custom is as follows: If any man, overcome by a passion of impurity, shall fall into unlawful intercourse with two sisters, we do not consider this a marriage, nor do we receive them into the membership of the Church at all until they separate from one another. Therefore, even if nothing further were to be said, the custom is sufficient to safeguard what is right. But since the writer of the letter has attempted by his deceitful argumentation to introduce such an abomination into our lives, we on our part must not omit any argument that may be of assistance to us, although in

ἐπὶ τῶν σφόδρα ἐναργῶν μείζων ἐστὶ τοῦ λόγου ἡ
παρ' ἑκάστου πρόληψις.

Γέγραπται,[1] φησίν, ἐν τῷ Λευιτικῷ· Γυναῖκα ἐπ'
ἀδελφῇ αὐτῆς οὐ λήψῃ ἀντίζηλον, ἀποκαλύψαι
τὴν ἀσχημοσύνην αὐτῆς ἐπ' αὐτῇ, ἔτι ζώσης αὐτῆς.
δῆλον δὴ οὖν ἐκ τούτου εἶναί φησιν ὅτι συγ-
χωρεῖται λαμβάνειν τελευτησάσης. πρὸς δὴ
τοῦτο πρῶτον μὲν ἐκεῖνο ἐρῶ· ὅτι, ὅσα ὁ νόμος
λέγει, τοῖς ἐν τῷ νόμῳ λαλεῖ· ἐπεὶ οὕτω γε καὶ
περιτομῇ, καὶ Σαββάτῳ, καὶ ἀποχῇ βρωμάτων
ὑποκεισόμεθα. οὐ γὰρ δή, ἐὰν μέν τι εὕρωμεν
συντρέχον ἡμῶν ταῖς ἡδοναῖς, τῷ ζυγῷ τῆς
δουλείας τοῦ νόμου ἑαυτοὺς ὑποθήσομεν, ἐὰν δέ τι
φανῇ βαρὺ τῶν νομίμων, τότε πρὸς τὴν ἐν Χριστῷ ἐλευθερίαν ἀποδραμούμεθα. ἠρωτήθημεν εἰ
γέγραπται λαμβάνειν γυναῖκα ἐπ' ἀδελφῇ. εἴπο-
μεν, ὅπερ ἀσφαλὲς ἡμῖν καὶ ἀληθές, ὅτι οὐ
γέγραπται. τὸ δ' ἐκ τῆς τοῦ ἀκολούθου ἐπιφορᾶς
τὸ σιωπηθὲν συλλογίζεσθαι νομοθετοῦντός ἐστιν,
οὐ τὰ τοῦ νόμου λέγοντος· ἐπεὶ οὕτω γε ἐξέσται
τῷ βουλομένῳ κατατολμῆσαι καὶ ἔτι ζώσης τῆς
γυναικὸς λαμβάνειν τὴν ἀδελφήν. τὸ γὰρ αὐτὸ
τοῦτο σόφισμα καὶ ἐπ' ἐκείνου ἁρμόζει. γέγραπται γάρ, φησίν· οὐ λήψῃ ἀντίζηλον, ὡς [2] τήν γε
ἔξω τοῦ ζήλου λαβεῖν οὐκ ἐκώλυσεν. ὁ δὴ συνη-
γορῶν τῷ πάθει ἀζηλότυπον εἶναι διοριεῖται τὸ

---

[1] γάρ add. E.   [2] ὥστε E.

---

[1] Lev 18. 18.
[2] i.e. the Levitical law does not apply to Christians; if it
did, they would have to practise circumcision, etc.

matters which are perfectly obvious the instinctive sentiment of the individual is of greater weight than formal reasoning.

It is written, he says, in Leviticus:[1] "Thou shalt not take thy wife's sister for a harlot, to rival her, neither shalt thou discover her nakedness while the wife is yet living." He therefore insists that it is evident from this passage that it is lawful to take her when the wife is deceased. In reply I have this to say in the first place : that whatever the law says, it says to those who are within the law;[2] since, if the law is interpreted in this way, we shall be subject to circumcision also, to the observance of the Sabbath, and to abstinence from meats. For surely it cannot be that, if we find anything in the law which fits in with our pleasures, we can subject ourselves to the yoke of servility to the law, but if any of the provisions of the law appears harsh, we can have recourse to the freedom which is in Christ! We were asked whether it is written that a man may take a woman as a wife after her sister. We said what in our opinion is incontestable and true—that it is not so written. But to reason out by the application of logical inference a point which has been passed over in silence in the law is a matter for the lawgiver and not for him who recites the provisions of the law; for in the latter event it will be possible for anyone who so wishes to presume to take the sister even while the wife is still living. For he applies this same sophism in the following argument also. For it is written, he says, "Thou shalt not take thy wife's sister for a harlot to rival her," so that the law did not prohibit taking the woman who is outside of rivalry. So the man who pleads for his passion will take the position

ἦθος τῶν ἀδελφῶν. ἀνηρημένης οὖν τῆς αἰτίας,
δι᾽ ἣν ἀπηγόρευσε τὴν ἀμφοτέρων συνοίκησιν, τί
τὸ κωλῦον ἔσται ¹ λαμβάνειν τὰς ἀδελφάς ; ἀλλ᾽
οὐ γέγραπται ταῦτα, φήσομεν. ἀλλ᾽ οὐδὲ ἐκεῖνα
ὥρισται. ἡ δὲ ἔννοια τοῦ ἀκολούθου ὁμοίως
ἀμφοτέραις ² τὴν ἄδειαν δίδωσιν. ἔδει δέ, καὶ
μικρὸν ἐπὶ τὰ κατόπιν τῆς νομοθεσίας ἐπαναδρα-
μόντα, ἀπηλλάχθαι πραγμάτων.

Ἔοικε γὰρ οὐ πᾶν εἶδος ἁμαρτημάτων περι-
λαμβάνειν ὁ νομοθέτης, ἀλλ᾽ ἰδίως ἀπαγορεύειν
τὰ τῶν Αἰγυπτίων, ὅθεν ἀπῆρεν ὁ Ἰσραήλ, καὶ
τὰ τῶν Χαναναίων, πρὸς οὓς μεθίσταται. ἔχει
γὰρ οὕτως ἡ λέξις. κατὰ τὰ ἐπιτηδεύματα γῆς
Αἰγύπτου, ἐν ᾗ παρῳκήσατε ἐπ᾽ αὐτῆς, οὐ
ποιήσετε· καὶ κατὰ τὰ ἐπιτηδεύματα γῆς Χαναάν,
εἰς ἣν ἐγὼ εἰσάξω ὑμᾶς ἐκεῖ, οὐ ποιήσετε, καὶ ἐν
τοῖς νομίμοις αὐτῶν οὐ πορεύσεσθε. ὥστε τοῦτο
εἰκός ³ που τὸ εἶδος τῆς ἁμαρτίας μὴ ἐμπολι-
τεύεσθαι τότε παρὰ τοῖς ἔθνεσι· διὸ μηδὲ τῆς ἐπ᾽
αὐτῷ φυλακῆς προσδεηθῆναι τὸν νομοθέτην, ἀλλ᾽
ἀρκεσθῆναι τῷ ἀδιδάκτῳ ἔθει πρὸς τὴν τοῦ μύσους
διαβολήν. πῶς οὖν, τὸ μεῖζον ἀπαγορεύσας, τὸ
ἔλαττον ἐσιώπησεν ; ὅτι ἐδόκει πολλοὺς ⁴ τῶν
φιλοσάρκων, πρὸς τὸ ἔτι ζώσαις ἀδελφαῖς συνοικεῖν, τὸ ὑπόδειγμα βλάπτειν τοῦ πατριάρχου.

Ἡμᾶς δὲ τί χρὴ ποιεῖν ; τὰ γεγραμμένα λέγειν,
ἢ τὰ σιωπηθέντα προσεξεργάζεσθαι ; αὐτίκα τὸ

---

¹ ἐστί editi antiqi. ² ἀμφοτέροις editi antiqi.
³ εἰκός] εἰ καί editi antiqi. ⁴ πολλοῖς editi antiqi.

---

¹ Lev. 18. 3. ² Probably Jacob ; cf. Gen. 29 ff.

that the disposition of sisters precludes jealousy between them. Therefore, he will argue, if the cause is removed which led the law to forbid cohabitation with two women, what will there be to prohibit a man's taking the sisters? But we shall say, this is not what is written. But the former matter likewise is not defined. The logical inference, however, gives the permission to both sisters alike. But what we ought to do in order to get rid of the difficulty is to go back a little to the state of affairs preceding the promulgation of the law.

For the lawgiver does not seem to be covering all sorts of sin, but to be forbidding particularly the sins of the Egyptians, from whom Israel had gone forth, and those of the Canaanites, to whom Israel was migrating. The words read as follows: "You shall not do according to the custom of the land of Egypt, in which you dwelt: neither shall you act according to the manner of the country of Canaan, into which I will bring you, nor shall you walk in their ordinances.'[1] Therefore it is likely that the form of sin here referred to was not at that time being practised among the Gentiles; and that, for this reason, it was not incumbent upon the lawgiver to provide against it, but that he was satisfied with the custom, which came from no instruction, for discrediting the abomination. How was it, then, that while forbidding the greater, he kept silent about the less? It was because the example of the patriarch[2] seemed to harm many of those who were given over to the flesh, inducing them to cohabit with sisters still living.

But as for us, what ought we to do? To say what is written or to work out for ourselves such questions as are passed over in silence? For instance, it is not

μὴ δεῖν μιᾷ ἑταίρᾳ κεχρῆσθαι πατέρα καὶ υἱὸν ἐν
μὲν τοῖς νόμοις τούτοις οὐ γέγραπται, παρὰ δὲ τῷ
προφήτῃ μεγίστης κατηγορίας ἠξίωται. Υἱὸς
γάρ, φησί, καὶ πατὴρ πρὸς τὴν αὐτὴν παιδίσκην
εἰσεπορεύοντο. πόσα δὲ εἴδη ἄλλα τῶν ἀκα-
θάρτων παθῶν τὸ μὲν τῶν δαιμόνων διδασκαλεῖον
ἐξεῦρεν, ἡ δὲ θεία Γραφὴ ἀπεσιώπησε, τὸ σεμνὸν
ἑαυτῆς ταῖς τῶν αἰσχρῶν ὀνομασίαις καταρρυ-
παίνειν οὐχ αἱρουμένη, ἀλλὰ γενικοῖς ὀνόμασι τὰς
ἀκαθαρσίας διέβαλεν[1] ὡς καὶ ἀπόστολος Παῦλός
φησι· Πορνεία δὲ καὶ ἀκαθαρσία πᾶσα μηδὲ
ὀνομαζέσθω ἐν ὑμῖν, καθὼς πρέπει ἁγίοις, τῷ τῆς
ἀκαθαρσίας ὀνόματι τάς τε τῶν ἀρρένων ἀρρητο-
ποιίας καὶ τὰς τῶν θηλειῶν περιλαμβάνων. ὥστε
οὐ πάντως ἡ σιωπὴ ἄδειαν φέρει τοῖς φιληδόνοις.

Ἐγὼ δὲ οὐδὲ σεσιωπῆσθαι τὸ μέρος τοῦτό
φημι, ἀλλὰ καὶ πάνυ σφοδρῶς ἀπηγορευκέναι τὸν
νομοθέτην. τὸ γάρ, Οὐκ εἰσελεύσῃ πρὸς πάντα
οἰκεῖον σαρκός σου, ἀποκαλύψαι ἀσχημοσύνην
αὐτῶν, ἐμπεριεκτικόν ἐστι καὶ τούτου τοῦ εἴδους
τῆς οἰκειότητος. τί γὰρ ἂν γένοιτο οἰκειότερον
ἀνδρὶ τῆς ἑαυτοῦ γυναικός, μᾶλλον δὲ τῆς ἑαυτοῦ
σαρκός; οὐ γὰρ ἔτι εἰσὶ δύο, ἀλλὰ σὰρξ μία.
ὥστε διὰ τῆς γυναικὸς ἡ ἀδελφὴ πρὸς τὴν τοῦ
ἀνδρὸς οἰκειότητα μεταβαίνει. ὡς γὰρ μητέρα
γυναικὸς οὐ λήψεται, οὐδὲ θυγατέρα τῆς γυναικός,
διότι μηδὲ τὴν ἑαυτοῦ μητέρα, μηδὲ τὴν ἑαυτοῦ
θυγατέρα, οὕτως οὐδ' ἀδελφὴν γυναικός, διότι

---

[1] Amos 2. 7.
[2] Eph. 5. 3. Basil omits, after ἀκαθαρσία, ἢ πλεονεξία, "or
covetousness."
[3] Lev. 18. 6.

written, in these laws, that father and son may not live with the same concubine, but in the prophet[1] such a case is thought worthy of explicit mention. "For the son and his father," he says, "have gone to the same young woman." And how many other forms of impure passions has the instruction of the demons discovered, though the divine Scripture has passed them over in silence, not choosing to sully its dignity with the naming of shameful things, but, instead, has censured impurities in general terms! As the Apostle Paul[2] says : "But fornication and all uncleanness, let it not so much as be named among you, as becometh saints," thus comprehending under the term "uncleanness" all abominable actions of both males and females. Therefore silence does not at all give licence to lovers of pleasure.

I assert, however, that this class of actions has not been passed over in silence, but that the lawgiver has forbidden them in very strong terms. That passage :[3] "No man shall approach to her that is near of kin to him, to uncover her nakedness," also includes this form of relationship. For what could be more closely related to a man than his wife, or rather than his own flesh? For "they are not two, but one flesh."[4] Therefore, through the wife the sister passes into relationship with the husband. For just as he will not take to himself his wife's mother, nor his wife's daughter, because he does not take his own mother nor his own daughter, so he will not take his wife's sister, because he does not take his

---

[4] Cf. Matt. 19. 5 and 6: καὶ προσκολληθήσεται τῇ γυναικὶ αὐτοῦ, καὶ ἔσονται οἱ δύο εἰς σάρκα μίαν· ὥστε οὐκέτι εἰσὶ δύο, ἀλλὰ σὰρξ μία. "And shall cleave to his wife, and they two shall be in one flesh. Therefore now they are not two, but one flesh."

μηδὲ ἀδελφὴν ἑαυτοῦ. καὶ τὸ ἀνάπαλιν, οὐδὲ τῇ
γυναικὶ ἐξέσται τοῖς οἰκείοις τοῦ ἀνδρὸς συνοικεῖν.
κοινὰ γὰρ ἐπ᾽ ἀμφοτέρων τῆς συγγενείας τὰ
δίκαια. ἐγὼ δὲ παντὶ τῷ περὶ γάμου βου-
λευομένῳ διαμαρτύρομαι, ὅτι παράγει τὸ σχῆμα
τοῦ κόσμου τούτου, καὶ ὁ καιρὸς συνεσταλμένος
ἐστίν, Ἵνα καὶ οἱ ἔχοντες γυναῖκας ὡς μὴ ἔχοντες
ὦσιν. ἐὰν δέ μοι παραναγινώσκῃ τὸ Αὐξάνεσθε
καὶ πληθύνεσθε, καταγελῶ τοῦ τῶν νομοθεσιῶν
τοὺς καιροὺς μὴ διακρίνοντος. πορνείας παραμυθία ὁ δεύτερος γάμος, οὐκ ἐφόδιον εἰς ἀσέλγειαν.
εἰ οὐκ ἐγκαρτερεύονται, γαμησάτωσαν, φησίν,
οὐχὶ δὲ [1] καὶ γαμήσαντες παρανομείτωσαν.

Οἱ δὲ οὐδὲ πρὸς τὴν φύσιν ἀποβλέπουσιν οἱ
τὴν ψυχὴν λημῶντες τῷ πάθει τῆς ἀτιμίας, πάλαι
διακρίνασαν τὰς τοῦ γένους προσηγορίας. ἐκ
ποίας γὰρ συγγενείας τοὺς γεννηθέντας προσαγο-
ρεύσουσιν ; [2] ἀδελφοὺς αὐτοὺς ἀλλήλων ἢ ἀνεψιοὺς
προσεροῦσιν ; ἀμφότερα γὰρ αὐτοῖς προσαρμόσει
διὰ τὴν σύγχυσιν. μὴ ποιήσῃς, ὦ ἄνθρωπε, τὴν
θείαν μητρυιὰν τῶν νηπίων· μηδὲ τὴν ἐν μητρὸς
τάξει θάλπειν ὀφείλουσαν, ταύτην ἐφοπλίσῃς ταῖς
ἀμειλίκτοις ζηλοτυπίαις. μόνον γὰρ τὸ γένος [3]
τῶν μητρυιῶν καὶ μετὰ θάνατον ἐλαύνει τὴν
ἔχθραν. μᾶλλον δὲ οἱ μὲν ἄλλως πολέμιοι τοῖς

---

[1] δέ om. E.   [2] προσαγορεύουσιν E.
[3] μῖσος editi antiqi.

---

[1] 1 Cor. 7. 31.

own sister. And, conversely, it will not be permitted
to the wife to cohabit with the relatives of her
husband. For the laws governing relationship are of
common application to both. But I earnestly declare
to everyone who is concerning himself about marriage, that "the fashion of this world passeth away" [1]
and that "the time is short"; and "that they also
who have wives, be as if they had none." [2] And if
he reads this passage to me: [3] "Increase and
multiply," I laugh at him, because he does not
distinguish the times of the promulgations of the
law. Second marriage is a relief from fornication,
not a means to lasciviousness. "But if they do not
contain themselves, let them marry," [4] he says, but
not "even though they are married let them break
the law."

But those whose souls are blinded by their infamous passion do not look even at nature, which
long ago distinguished the several titles of kinship.
Under what heading of relationship will those who
marry sisters name their sons? Will they call them
brothers or cousins of one another? For both names
will be appropriate to them on account of the confusion. Do not, sir, make the aunt the stepmother of
your little ones; do not arm with implacable jealousy
her who ought to cherish them in the place of their
mother. For it is the race of stepmothers alone
which carries its hatred even after death; or rather,
those who are in any other manner hostile to the

---

[2] Cf. 1 Cor. 7. 29 : τοῦτο δέ φημι, ἀδελφοί, ὁ καιρὸς συνεσταλ-
μένος· τὸ λοιπόν ἐστιν ἵνα καὶ οἱ ἔχοντες γυναῖκας, ὡς μὴ ἔχοντες
ὦσι. "This therefore I say, brethren, the time is short; it
remaineth, that they also who have wives, be as if they had
none."

[3] Gen. 1. 28.   [4] 1 Cor. 7. 9.

τεθνηκόσι σπένδονται, αἱ δὲ μητρυιαὶ τοῦ μίσους μετὰ τὸν θάνατον ἄρχονται.

Κεφάλαιον δὲ τῶν εἰρημένων, εἰ μὲν νόμῳ τις ὁρμᾶται πρὸς τὸν γάμον, ἤνοικται πᾶσα ἡ οἰκουμένη· εἰ δὲ ἐμπαθὴς αὐτῷ ἡ σπουδή, διὰ τοῦτο καὶ πλέον ἀποκλεισθήτω, Ἵνα μάθῃ τὸ ἑαυτοῦ σκεῦος κτᾶσθαι ἐν ἁγιασμῷ καὶ τιμῇ, μὴ ἐν πάθει ἐπιθυμίας. πλείονά με[1] λέγειν ὡρμημένον τὸ μέτρον ἐπέχει[2] τῆς ἐπιστολῆς· εὔχομαι δὲ ἢ τὴν παραίνεσιν ἡμῶν ἰσχυροτέραν τοῦ πάθους ἀποδειχθῆναι, ἢ μὴ ἐπιδημῆσαι τῇ ἡμετέρᾳ τὸ ἄγος τοῦτο, ἀλλ᾽ ἐν οἷς ἂν ἐτολμήθη τόποις ἐναπομεῖναι.

CLXI

Ἀμφιλοχίῳ, χειροτονηθέντι ἐπισκόπῳ

Εὐλογητὸς ὁ Θεός, ὁ τοὺς καθ᾽ ἑκάστην γενεὰν εὐαρεστοῦντας αὐτῷ ἐκλεγόμενος, καὶ γνωρίζων τὰ σκεύη τῆς ἐκλογῆς, καὶ κεχρημένος αὐτοῖς πρὸς τὴν λειτουργίαν τῶν ἁγίων· ὁ καὶ νῦν σε φεύγοντα, ὡς αὐτὸς φῄς, οὐχ ἡμᾶς, ἀλλὰ τὴν δι᾽ ἡμῶν προσδοκωμένην κλῆσιν, τοῖς ἀφύκτοις δικτύοις τῆς χάριτος σαγηνεύσας, καὶ ἀγαγὼν εἰς τὰ μέσα τῆς Πισιδίας, ὥστε ἀνθρώπους

---

[1] μοι E. [2] ἐπέσχε editi antiqi.

---

[1] Cf. Herodotus 4, 154, and Euripides, *Alcestis* 309, where stepmothers are said to be as dangerous to their predecessor's children as vipers. In antiquity the unkindness of stepmothers was proverbial.

dead make their peace with them, but stepmothers begin their hatred after death.[1]

The summing up of what has been said is this: If anyone is bent upon lawful marriage, the whole world is opened to him; but if his haste is due to passion, let him be restrained all the more, "that every one of you should know how to possess his vessel in sanctification and honour, not in the passion of lust."[2] The limits of the letter forbid me, though eager, from speaking further. But I pray that either our exhortation may be proved stronger than passion, or that this abomination may not visit our district, but that it may be confined to the places where it has been ventured!

LETTER CLXI

To Amphilochius, on his Consecration as Bishop [3]

Blessed is God, who selects those in each generation who are pleasing to Him and makes known the vessels of His election,[4] and uses them for the ministry of the saints; He who even now has ensnared you with the inescapable nets of His grace, when, as you yourself admit, you are trying to escape, not us, but the expected call through us, and who has brought you into the midst of Pisidia, so that

---

[2] 1 Thess. 4. 4 and 5.

[3] Written in 374. Cf. Loofs, 46, note 5. For Amphilochius, cf. Letter CL and note.

[4] Cf. Acts 9. 15: εἶπε δὲ πρὸς αὐτὸν ὁ Κύριος, Πορεύου, ὅτι σκεῦος ἐκλογῆς μοί ἐστιν οὗτος, etc. "And the Lord said to him: Go thy way: for this man is to me a vessel of election," etc.

ζωγρεῖν τῷ Κυρίῳ καὶ ἕλκειν ἀπὸ τοῦ βυθοῦ
εἰς τὸ φῶς τοὺς ἐζωγρημένους ὑπὸ τοῦ διαβόλου
εἰς τὸ ἐκείνου θέλημα. λέγε οὖν καὶ σὺ τὰ τοῦ[1]
μακαρίου Δαβίδ· Ποῦ πορευθῶ ἀπὸ τοῦ πνεύματός σου; καὶ ἀπὸ τοῦ προσώπου σου, ποῦ
φύγω; τοιαῦτα γὰρ θαυματουργεῖ ὁ φιλάνθρωπος ἡμῶν Δεσπότης. ὄνοι[2] ἀπόλλυνται, ἵνα
βασιλεὺς Ἰσραὴλ γένηται. ἀλλ' ἐκεῖνος μὲν
Ἰσραηλίτης ὢν τῷ Ἰσραὴλ ἐδόθη· σὲ δὲ ἡ
θρεψαμένη καὶ πρὸς τοσοῦτον ἀναβιβάσασα τῆς
ἀρετῆς ὕψος οὐκ ἔχει, ἀλλὰ τὴν γείτονα ὁρᾷ τῷ
ἰδίῳ κόσμῳ σεμνυνομένην. ἐπειδὴ δὲ εἷς λαὸς
πάντες οἱ εἰς Χριστὸν ἠλπικότες καὶ μία Ἐκκλησία νῦν οἱ Χριστοῦ, κἂν ἐκ διαφόρων τόπων
προσαγορεύηται, χαίρει καὶ ἡ πατρὶς καὶ εὐφραί-
νεται ταῖς τοῦ Κυρίου οἰκονομίαις, καὶ οὐχ ἡγεῖται
ἕνα ἄνδρα ἐζημιῶσθαι, ἀλλὰ δι' ἑνὸς ἐκκλησίας
ὅλας προσειληφέναι. μόνον παράσχοι ὁ Κύριος
καὶ παρόντας ὁρᾶν ἡμᾶς[3] καὶ ἀπόντας ἀκούειν
τὴν προκοπήν σου τὴν ἐν τῷ εὐαγγελίῳ καὶ τὴν
εὐταξίαν τῶν ἐκκλησιῶν.

Ἀνδρίζου τοίνυν καὶ ἴσχυε, καὶ προπορεύου
τοῦ λαοῦ, ὃν ἐπίστευσε τῇ δεξιᾷ σου ὁ Ὕψιστος.
καὶ ὡς νοήμων κυβέρνησιν ποιησάμενος, πάσης
ζάλης ἀπὸ τῶν αἱρετικῶν πνευμάτων ἐγειρομένης

---

[1] τοῦ om. E.   [2] ἐχθροί editi antiqi.
[3] ὑμᾶς editi antiqi.

---

[1] Psal. 138. 7.
[2] Cf. 1 Kings 9. 3: καὶ ἀπώλοντο αἱ ὄνοι Κεὶς πατρὸς Σαοὺλ·
καὶ εἶπεν Κεὶς πρὸς Σαοὺλ τὸν υἱὸν αὐτοῦ Λάβε μετὰ σεαυτοῦ ἓν
τῶν παιδαρίων, καὶ ἀνάστητε καὶ πορεύθητε καὶ ζητήσατε τὰς

you may take men captive for the Lord and bring those who had already been taken captive by the devil from the depths into the light according to His will. Therefore you also may speak the words of the blessed David: " Whither shall I go from the spirit? or whither shall I flee from thy face?"[1] For such wonders does our kind-hearted Master work. " Asses are lost"[2] in order that a king may be given to Israel. But that man, being an Israelite, was given to Israel; yet the country which nurtured you and brought you up to such a height of virtue does not possess you, but beholds her neighbour priding herself upon her own ornament. But since all who have placed their hopes in Christ are one people and the followers of Christ are now one Church, even though He is called upon from divers places, your fatherland both rejoices and is made happy by the dispensations of the Lord, and she does not believe that she has lost one man, but that through one man she has acquired whole churches. May the Lord only grant that we being present may see, and also being absent may hear of, your progress in the Gospel and of the good discipline of your churches.

Play the man, then, and be strong, and go before the people whom the Most High has entrusted to your right hand. And like a wise helmsman who has assumed the command of a ship, rise superior in your resolution to every blast that is stirred up by

ὄνους. " And the asses of Cis, Saul's father, were lost: And Cis said to his son Saul: Take one of the servants with thee, and arise, go, and seek the asses." Basil may mean that the predecessors of Amphilochius in the see of Iconium, i.e. Faustinus and John, were not very wise bishops. Cf. Letter CXXXVIII.

ὑψηλότερος γενόμενος τῇ γνώμῃ, ἀβάπτιστον
τοῖς ἁλμυροῖς καὶ πικροῖς τῆς κακοδοξίας κύμασι
διαφύλασσε[1] τὴν ὁλκάδα, ἀναμένων τὴν γαλήνην,
ἣν ποιήσει ὁ Κύριος, ἐπειδὰν εὑρεθῇ φωνὴ ἀξία
τοῦ διαναστῆσαι αὐτὸν πρὸς τὴν ἐπιτίμησιν τῶν
πνευμάτων καὶ τῆς θαλάσσης. εἰ δὲ βούλει
ἡμᾶς λοιπὸν ὑπὸ τῆς μακρᾶς ἀρρωστίας ἐπειγο-
μένους[2] πρὸς τὴν ἀναγκαίαν ἔξοδον ἐπισκέψασθαι,
μήτε καιρὸν ἀναμείνῃς, μήτε τὸ παρ' ἡμῶν
σύνθημα, εἰδὼς ὅτι πατρικοῖς σπλάγχνοις πᾶσα
εὐκαιρία ἐστὶ περιπτύσσεσθαι τέκνον ἀγαπητὸν
καὶ λόγου παντὸς κρείττων ἡ κατὰ ψυχὴν
διάθεσις.

Βάρος δὲ ὑπερβαῖνον τὴν δύναμιν μὴ ὀδύρου.
εἰ μὲν γὰρ αὐτὸς ἦς ὁ μέλλων φέρειν τὸ βάσταγμα
τοῦτο, οὐδὲ οὕτως ἂν ἦν βαρύ, ἀλλ' ἀφορητὸν
παντελῶς. εἰ δὲ Κύριος ὁ συνδιαφέρων, Ἐπίρριψον ἐπὶ Κύριον τὴν μέριμνάν σου, καὶ αὐτὸς
ποιήσει. μόνον ἐκεῖνο παραφυλάσσειν ἐν πᾶσι
παρακλήθητι, μὴ αὐτὸς τοῖς μοχθηροῖς ἔθεσι
συμπεριφέρεσθαι, ἀλλὰ τὰ κακῶς προειλημμένα
διὰ τῆς δεδομένης σοι παρὰ Θεοῦ σοφίας μετα-
τιθέναι πρὸς τὸ χρήσιμον. καὶ γὰρ ἀπέστειλέ
σε Χριστὸς οὐχ ἑτέροις κατακολουθεῖν, ἀλλ'
αὐτὸν[3] καθηγεῖσθαι τῶν σωζομένων. καὶ παρακαλοῦμεν προσεύχεσθαι ὑπὲρ ἡμῶν, ἵνα, ἐὰν μὲν
ἔτι ὦμεν ἐπὶ τῆς ζωῆς ταύτης, ἰδεῖν σε μετὰ τῆς
ἐκκλησίας καταξιωθῶμεν· ἐὰν δὲ ἀπελθεῖν λοιπὸν
προσταχθῶμεν, ἐκεῖ ὑμᾶς ἴδωμεν παρὰ τῷ Κυρίῳ,

---

[1] διαφύλαξαι editi antiqi.   [2] ἀπαγομένους E.

[3] αὐτῶν E.

the winds of heresy, and preserve your ship unsubmerged by the briny and bitter waves of error, awaiting the calm which the Lord will cause as soon as a voice is found worthy of rousing Him to rebuke the winds and the sea. And if you wish to visit us soon, driven on as we are by our long sickness towards the inevitable departure, do not await a suitable occasion nor the summons from us, knowing that to a father's heart every occasion is good for the embracing of a well-beloved child and that his soul's affection is a better summons than any spoken word.

Do not lament that the weight is beyond your strength. For if it were you alone that were to bear this burden, it would not be merely heavy but utterly unendurable. But if it is the Lord who helps you bear it, "cast thy care upon the Lord," [1] and He himself shall do it. Only, I beg you, be on your guard on every occasion against this—against being yourself carried away by wicked customs, but, through the wisdom granted you by God, transforming the evil customs which have hitherto had sway into something good. For Christ sent you forth, not to follow others, but yourself to guide those who are on the way to salvation. And we urge you to pray for us, in order that, if we are still in this life, we may be thought worthy of beholding you and your church ; but if we are ordered soon to go hence, may we behold all of you there with the Lord, your church

---

[1] Cf. Psal. 55. 23 : ἐπίρριψον ἐπὶ Κύριον τὴν μέριμνάν σου, καὶ αὐτός σε διαθρέψει· οὐ δώσει εἰς τὸν αἰῶνα σάλον τῷ δικαίῳ. "Cast thy care upon the Lord, and he shall sustain thee : he shall not suffer the just to waver for ever." Also 1 Peter 5. 7 : πᾶσαν τὴν μέριμναν ὑμῶν ἐπιρρίψαντες ἐπ' αὐτόν, ὅτι αὐτῷ μέλει περὶ ὑμῶν. "Casting all your care upon him, for he hath care of you."

τὴν μὲν ὡς ἄμπελον εὐθηνοῦσαν ἐπ᾽ ἀγαθοῖς
ἔργοις, σὲ δέ, ὡς σοφὸν γεωργὸν καὶ ἀγαθὸν
δοῦλον ἐν καιρῷ διδόντα τοῖς ὁμοδούλοις τὸ
σιτομέτριον, πιστοῦ καὶ φρονίμου οἰκονόμου τὸν
μισθὸν κομιζόμενον.

Οἱ σὺν ἡμῖν πάντες ἀσπάζονταί σου τὴν
εὐλάβειαν. ἐρρωμένος καὶ εὔθυμος ἐν Κυρίῳ
εἴης· εὐδοκιμῶν ἐπὶ χαρίσμασι Πνεύματος καὶ
σοφίας φυλαχθείης.

CLXII

Εὐσεβίῳ, ἐπισκόπῳ Σαμοσάτων

Ἔοικέ μοι τοῦτο καὶ ὄκνον ἐμποιεῖν πρὸς τὸ
γράφειν καὶ ἀναγκαῖον αὐτὸ πάλιν ὑποδεικνύναι.
ὅταν μὲν γὰρ πρὸς τὸ τῆς ἐπιδημίας τῆς ἐμαυτοῦ
ἀπίδω[1] χρέος καὶ τὸ τῆς συντυχίας ὑπολογίσω-
μαι ὄφελος, πάνυ μοι[2] τῶν ἐπιστολῶν ὑπερορᾶν
ἔπεισιν ὡς οὐδὲ σκιᾶς λόγον ἐκπληροῦν δυναμένων
πρὸς τὴν ἀλήθειαν· ὅταν δὲ πάλιν λογίσωμαι,
ὅτι μόνη παραμυθία ἐστὶ τῶν μεγίστων καὶ
πρώτων διαμαρτόντα προσειπεῖν ἄνδρα τοσοῦτον,
καὶ ἱκετεῦσαι συνήθως[3] ὥστε μὴ ἐπιλανθάνεσθαι
ἡμῶν ἐπὶ τῶν προσευχῶν, οὐ μικρόν τί μοι κρίνειν
τὸ τῶν ἐπιστολῶν ἔπεισι. τὴν μὲν οὖν ἐλπίδα
τῆς παρουσίας οὔτε αὐτὸς ῥίψαι τῆς ψυχῆς
βούλομαι, οὔτε τὴν σὴν θεοσέβειαν ἀπογνῶναι.
αἰσχύνομαι γὰρ εἰ μὴ ταῖς σαῖς εὐχαῖς τοσοῦτον

---

[1] ἐπίδω editi antiqi.   [2] με editi antiqi.
[3] τὰ συνήθη editi antiqi.

flourishing like a vine in good works, and you yourself, like a wise husbandman and a good servant who gives meat in due season to your fellow-servants, procuring the reward of a faithful and wise overseer.

All those who are with us send greetings to your Piety. May you be strong and cheerful in the Lord, and enjoying good repute for the blessings of the Spirit and of wisdom, may you be preserved.

LETTER CLXII

To Eusebius, Bishop of Samosata [1]

THE following consideration, it seems to me, both induces hesitation as to writing and again indicates that writing is necessary. Whenever, that is, I contemplate my obligation to remain at home and then consider the advantage of a personal meeting, I am inclined to despise letters utterly as being incapable of amounting to even a shadow's worth as regards the truth; but when, on the other hand, I consider that the only consolation for one who is deprived of the greatest and the foremost men is to address so great a man, and regularly to beg him not to forget us in his prayers, I am inclined to judge correspondence by letter to be of no small importance. I do not wish, however, either to banish from my mind all hope of a visit, or to give up my acquaintance with your Holiness. For I am ashamed of not seeming to be encouraged by your

[1] Written after Easter of 374. Cf. Loofs, 46, note 5. Basil is still hopeful of being able to visit Eusebius.

φανείην θαρσῶν, ὡς καὶ νέος ἐκ γέροντος ἔσεσθαι, εἰ τούτου γένοιτο χρεία,[1] οὐχ ὅπως ἐρρωμενέσ τερος μικρὸν ἐξ ἀσθενοῦς καὶ ἐξιτήλου παντάπασιν, ὁποῖος δὴ νῦν εἰμί.

Τοῦ δὲ μὴ ἤδη παρεῖναι τὰ αἴτια λόγῳ μὲν εἰπεῖν οὐ ῥάδιον, οὐ μόνον ὑπὸ τῆς παρούσης ἀσθενείας ἐξειργομένῳ, ἀλλ' οὐδὲ σχόντι[2] ποτὲ τοσαύτην τοῦ λόγου δύναμιν, ὥστε παντοδαπὴν καὶ ποικίλην νόσον ἐναργῶς ἐξαγγεῖλαι. πλὴν ὅτι ἀπὸ τῆς ἡμέρας τοῦ Πάσχα μέχρι[3] νῦν πυρετοὶ καὶ διάρροιαι, καὶ σπλάγχνων ἐπανα- στάσεις, ὥσπερ κύματά με[4] ἐπιβαπτίζοντα ὑπερσχεῖν οὐκ ἐᾷ. τὰ δὲ παρόντα οἷα καὶ τίνα ἦν, εἴποι ἂν καὶ ὁ ἀδελφὸς Βάραχος,[5] εἰ καὶ μὴ τῆς ἀληθείας ἀξίως, ἀλλ' ὅσον μαρτυρῆσαι τῇ αἰτίᾳ τῆς ὑπερθέσεως. πάνυ δὲ πέπεισμαι, εἰ γνησίως ἡμῖν συνεύξαιο, πάνθ' ἡμῖν λυθήσεσθαι[6] ῥᾳδίως τὰ δυσχερῆ.

CLXIII

Ἰοβίνῳ κόμητι

Εἶδόν σου τὴν ψυχὴν ἐν τοῖς γράμμασι. καὶ γὰρ τῷ ὄντι οὐδεὶς γραφεὺς χαρακτῆρα σώματος οὕτως ἀκριβῶς ἐκλαβεῖν δύναται ὡς λόγος ἐξεικονίσαι τῆς ψυχῆς τὰ ἀπόρρητα. τότε γὰρ τὸ[7] τοῦ ἤθους εὐσταθές, καὶ τὸ τῆς τιμῆς

---

[1] τούτου γένοιτο χρεία] καὶ τοῦτο γένοιτο χρεῖος editi antiqi.
[2] οὐδὲ σχόντι] οὐδ' ἔχοντι E.   [3] τοῦ add. E.
[4] τε E.   [5] Βάρουχος editi antiqi.
[6] λυθήσεται editi antiqi.   [7] τό om. E.

prayers to such an extent as even to expect to become young instead of old, if there should be need of that—to say nothing of becoming a little bit stronger instead of the weak and altogether powerless creature that I now am.

The reason why I am not already present with you is not easy to explain in words, not only because I am hampered by my present infirmity, but also because I never gained a command of language sufficient to enable me to describe clearly my varied and complex sickness.   But the truth is that, from the day of Easter until now, fevers, dysenteries, and rebellions of my bowels, drenching me like recurring waves, have not permitted me to emerge.   As for my present condition, our brother Barachus can tell you what it is in detail, if not adequately to the truth, at least sufficiently to attest the reason for my delay. But I am entirely convinced that, if you should really join your prayers to ours, we should easily be freed from all our troubles.

LETTER CLXIII

To Count Jovinus[1]

I saw your soul in your letter.   For truly no painter can grasp so accurately the characteristics of the body as words can portray the secrets of the soul.   For when I read your letter, its words adequately delineated to us the soundness of your

---

[1] Written after Easter of 374.   Cf. Loofs, 46, note 5. Jovinus, a count of the Empire, appears from this letter to have been on intimate terms with Basil.   Nothing more is known of him.

ἀληθινόν,[1] καὶ τὸ τῆς γνώμης ἐν πᾶσιν ἀκέραιον [2]
ἱκανῶς ἡμῖν ὁ ἐν τοῖς γράμμασι λόγος ἐχα-
ρακτήρισεν· ὅθεν καὶ μεγάλην ἡμῖν παραμυθίαν
τῆς ἀπολείψεώς σου παρέσχετο. μὴ τοίνυν
διαλίπῃς τῇ ἀεὶ παραπιπτούσῃ προφάσει χρώ-
μενος πρὸς τὸ ἐπιστέλλειν καὶ τὴν διὰ μακροῦ
ταύτην ὁμιλίαν χαρίζεσθαι· ἐπειδὴ τῆς κατ᾽
ὀφθαλμοὺς συντυχίας [3] ἀπόγνωσιν ἡμῖν λοιπὸν
ἡ ἀσθένεια τοῦ σώματος ἐμποιεῖ. ἣν ὁπόση
ἐστὶν ἐρεῖ σοι ὁ θεοφιλέστατος ἐπίσκοπος Ἀμφι-
λόχιος, ὁ καὶ γνωρίσας τῷ ἐπὶ πλεῖον συγγε-
γενῆσθαι ἡμῖν καὶ δυνατὸς ὢν λόγῳ παραστῆσαι
τὰ θεαθέντα. γνωρίζεσθαι δὲ βούλομαι τὰ
ἐμαυτοῦ δυσχερῆ οὐκ ἄλλου τινὸς ἕνεκεν ἢ τῆς
πρὸς τὸ ἐφεξῆς συγγνώμης, ὡς μὴ ῥαθυμίας ἔχειν
κατάγνωσιν ἐὰν ἄρα ἐλλίπωμεν [4] τὴν ἐπίσκεψιν
ὑμῶν. καίτοιγε οὐκ ἀπολογίας μᾶλλον ἢ παραμυθίας δεῖ πρὸς τὴν ζημίαν ταύτην. εἰ γὰρ ἦν
μοι δυνατὸν συνεῖναί σου τῇ σεμνότητι, πολλῷ
ἂν ἐγὼ τῶν παρ᾽ ἄλλοις σπουδαζομένων ταύτην
ἐμαυτῷ προτιμοτέραν ἐθέμην.

CLXIV

Ἀσχολίῳ, ἐπισκόπῳ Θεσσαλονίκης

Ὅσης ἡμᾶς εὐφροσύνης ἐνέπλησε τὰ γράμματα
τῆς ὁσιότητός σου ἡμεῖς μὲν οὐκ ἂν ῥᾳδίως

---

[1] ἀληθές editi antiqi.   [2] καίριον E, editi antiqi.
[3] ὁμιλίας editi antiqi.   [4] ἐλλείπωμεν E.

---

[1] The visit of Amphilochius in 374 was probably the first
of a series of frequent visits. Basil was his spiritual father.
Amphilochius preferred to make his visits to Basil in the

character, the genuineness of your worth, and the integrity of your mind in everything ; and so it brought to us great consolation for your absence. Therefore do not leave off availing yourself of any excuse that arises from time to time for writing me and for conferring on me the boon of this too long interrupted conversation ; for our bodily weakness causes us now to despair of a personal interview. How serious an illness it is will be explained to you by our most God-beloved bishop Amphilochius,[1] who possesses both the knowledge by reason of having been much with us, and the ability to set forth in speech whatever he has seen. And I wish my difficulties to be known for no other object than your pardon in the future, that we may not be condemned for indifference if we do fail to pay you the visit. And yet there is not so much need of a defence as of some consolation to me for my loss therein. For if it had been possible for me to be with your August Reverence, I should have considered this as worth far more to me than the objects for which others earnestly strive.

LETTER CLXIV

To Ascholius, Bishop of Thessalonica[2]

How great was the joy with which the letter of your Holiness filled us we cannot easily describe,

autumn, because the anniversary of Basil's hospital was celebrated at that time. This hospital had a special interest for him, because it was here that he and Heracleidas had passed a solemn crisis in their lives. Cf. Letter CL.

[2] Written in 374. For this Ascholius, cf. Letter CLIV. The following letter is also addressed to him.

ἐνδείξασθαι δυνηθείημεν, ἀσθενοῦντος τοῦ λόγου
πρὸς τὴν ἐνάργειαν·[1] αὐτὸς δὲ καὶ παρὰ σεαυτῷ[2]
εἰκάζειν ὀφείλεις, τεκμαιρόμενος τῷ κάλλει τῶν
ἐπεσταλμένων. τί γὰρ οὐκ εἶχε τὰ γράμματα;
οὐ τὴν πρὸς Κύριον ἀγάπην; οὐ τὸ περὶ τοὺς
μάρτυρας θαῦμα, οὕτως ἐναργῶς τὸν τρόπον
τῆς ἀθλήσεως ὑπογράφοντα, ὥστε ὑπ᾽ ὄψιν
ἡμῖν[3] ἀγαγεῖν τὰ πράγματα; οὐ τὴν περὶ
ἡμᾶς αὐτοὺς τιμήν τε καὶ διάθεσιν; οὐχ ὅ τι ἂν
εἴποι τις τῶν καλλίστων; ὥστε, ὅτε εἰς χεῖρας
τὴν ἐπιστολὴν ἐδεξάμεθα, καὶ ἀνέγνωμεν αὐτὴν
πολλάκις, καὶ τὴν βρύουσαν ἐν αὐτῇ χάριν τοῦ
Πνεύματος κατεμάθομεν, νομίσαι ἡμᾶς ἐπὶ τῶν
ἀρχαίων καιρῶν γεγενῆσθαι, ἡνίκα ἤνθουν αἱ
ἐκκλησίαι τοῦ Θεοῦ, ἐρριζωμέναι τῇ πίστει,
ἡνωμέναι τῇ ἀγάπῃ, ὥσπερ ἐν ἑνὶ σώματι μιᾶς
συμπνοίας διαφόρων μελῶν ὑπαρχούσης· ὅτε
φανεροὶ μὲν οἱ διώκοντες, φανεροὶ δὲ οἱ διωκόμενοι·
πολεμούμενοι δὲ οἱ λαοὶ πλείους ἐγίνοντο, καὶ τὸ
αἷμα τῶν μαρτύρων ἄρδον τὰς ἐκκλησίας πολυ-
πλασίονας τοὺς ἀγωνιστὰς τῆς εὐσεβείας ἐξέτρεφε,
τῷ ζήλῳ τῶν προλαβόντων ἐπαποδυομένων τῶν
ἐφεξῆς. τότε Χριστιανοὶ μὲν πρὸς ἀλλήλους
εἰρήνην ἤγομεν,[4] εἰρήνην ἐκείνην, ἣν ὁ Κύριος
ἡμῖν κατέλιπεν, ἧς νῦν οὐδ᾽ ἴχνος ἡμῖν λοιπὸν
ὑπολέλειπται, οὕτως αὐτὴν ἀπηνῶς ἀπ᾽ ἀλλήλων
ἀπεδιώξαμεν. πλὴν ἀλλ᾽ ὅτι αἱ ψυχαὶ ἡμῶν
πρὸς τὴν παλαιὰν ἐκείνην μακαριότητα ἐπανῆλθον,
ἐπειδὴ γράμματα μὲν ἦλθεν ἐκ τῆς[5] μακρόθεν,
ἀνθοῦντα τῷ τῆς ἀγάπης κάλλει, μάρτυς δὲ ἡμῖν

---

[1] ἐνέργειαν E.   [2] σεαυτοῦ Harl.

words being too weak to set it clearly forth, but
you ought to be able to guess it by yourself,
deducing it from the beauty of what you wrote.
For what did the letter not contain? Did it not
contain love for the Lord? And admiration for the
martyrs, describing so clearly the manner of their
struggle that you brought the incidents before our
eyes? And respect and love for ourselves? Did it
not contain whatever one might mention of the most
noble attributes? Consequently, when we took the
letter in our hands, and read it again and again,
and perceived the grace of the Spirit that abounded
therein, we thought that we were back in the olden
times, when the churches of God flourished, taking
root in the faith, united by charity, there being,
as in a single body, a single harmony of the various
members; when the persecutors indeed were in
the open, but in the open were also the persecuted;
when the laity, though harassed, became more
numerous, and the blood of the martyrs watering
the churches nurtured many times as many champions of religion, later generations stripping themselves for combat in emulation of their predecessors.
Then we Christians had peace among ourselves,
that peace which the Lord left to us, of which
now not even a trace any longer remains to us, so
ruthlessly have we driven it away from one another.
But the fact is that our souls had already returned
to that old-time happiness when a letter came
from far away, blossoming with the beauty of
charity, and a witness had arrived among us from

---

³ ἡμῶν editi antiqi.   ⁴ εἴχομεν editi antiqi.
⁵ γῆς E, Harl., Med., Reg. primus, Vat., Bigot. alter.

ἐπεδήμησεν ἐκ τῶν ἐπέκεινα Ἴστρου βαρβάρων,
δι' ἑαυτοῦ κηρύσσων τῆς ἐκεῖ πολιτευομένης
πίστεως τὴν ἀκρίβειαν. τίς ἂν τὴν ἐπὶ τούτοις
εὐφροσύνην τῶν ψυχῶν ἡμῶν διηγήσαιτο ;[1] τίς
ἂν ἐπινοηθείη δύναμις λόγου ἐναργῶς ἐξαγγεῖλαι
τὴν ἐν τῷ κρυπτῷ τῆς καρδίας ἡμῶν διάθεσιν
δυναμένη ; ὅτε μέντοι εἴδομεν τὸν ἀθλητήν,
ἐμακαρίσαμεν αὐτοῦ τὸν ἀλείπτην, ὃς παρὰ τῷ
δικαίῳ κριτῇ τὸν τῆς δικαιοσύνης στέφανον καὶ
αὐτὸς ἀπολήψεται, πολλοὺς εἰς τὸν ὑπὲρ τῆς
εὐσεβείας ἐπιρρώσας ἀγῶνα.

Ἐπεὶ δὲ καὶ τοῦ μακαρίου ἀνδρὸς Εὐτυχοῦς
εἰς μνήμην ἡμᾶς ἤγαγες, καὶ ἐσέμνυνας ἡμῶν τὴν
πατρίδα ὡς αὐτὴν παρασχομένην τῆς εὐσεβείας
τὰ σπέρματα, εὔφρανας μὲν ἡμᾶς τῇ ὑπομνήσει
τῶν παλαιῶν, ἐλύπησας δὲ τῷ ἐλέγχῳ τῶν
ὁρωμένων. οὐδεὶς γὰρ ἡμῶν Εὐτυχεῖ τὴν ἀρετὴν
παραπλήσιος, οἵ γε τοσοῦτον ἀπέχομεν βαρβά-
ρους ἐξημερῶσαι τῇ δυνάμει τοῦ Πνεύματος καὶ
τῇ ἐνεργείᾳ τῶν παρ' αὐτοῦ χαρισμάτων, ὥστε
καὶ τοὺς ἡμέρως ἔχοντας τῇ ὑπερβολῇ τῶν
ἁμαρτιῶν ἡμῶν ἐξηγριῶσθαι. ἑαυτοῖς γὰρ λογι-
ζόμεθα καὶ ταῖς ἡμετέραις ἁμαρτίαις τὴν αἰτίαν
τοῦ ἐπὶ τοσοῦτον χυθῆναι τὴν τῶν αἱρετικῶν
δυναστείαν. σχεδὸν γὰρ οὐδὲν μέρος[2] τῆς οἰκουμένης διαπέφευγε τὸν ἐκ τῆς αἱρέσεως ἐμπρησμόν.

---

[1] διηγήσηται E.   [2] ἔτι add. editi antiqi.

the barbarians beyond the Danube,[1] proclaiming in person the strictness of the faith which is practised in that region. Who could describe the joy our souls felt at this? What power of speech could be devised that would be capable of announcing in clear terms the emotion hidden in our hearts? When, however, we saw the athlete, we blessed his trainer,[2] who will likewise receive at the hands of the just Judge the crown of righteousness, since he has strengthened many for the struggle in defence of our religion.

But since you have recalled to our minds the blessed man Eutyches,[3] and have exalted our fatherland for having by itself furnished the seeds of our religion, you cheered us indeed by calling up the past, but distressed us by exposing the conditions which we see to-day. For no one of us is comparable to Eutyches in virtue, since we are so far from having tamed the barbarians by the power of the Spirit and by the operation of His graces, that we have even by the enormity of our sins made savage those who were gentle. For we must impute to ourselves and to our sins the blame that the domination of the heretics has become so widespread. For almost no part of the world has escaped the conflagration of

---

[1] Basil regularly calls the Danube by the name Ister; cf. Letter XL.

[2] Ascholius is here called the trainer of the martyr Sabas; cf. the title of Letter CLV.

[3] A Christian of Cappadocia who was taken prisoner by the Goths in 260, and with some of his fellow-captives became a martyr for the faith, but only after he had already sown the seeds of the gospel in the land of his captivity. Cf Philost. *H.E.* 2, 5.

τὰ δὲ σὰ διηγήματα, ἐνστάσεις ἀθλητικαί,[1] σώματα ὑπὲρ τῆς εὐσεβείας καταξαινόμενα, θυμὸς
βαρβαρικὸς ὑπὸ τῶν ἀκαταπλήκτων[2] τὴν καρδίαν
καταφρονούμενος, αἱ ποικίλαι βάσανοι τῶν διωκόντων, αἱ διὰ πάντων ἐνστάσεις τῶν ἀγωνιζομένων,
τὸ ξύλον, τὸ ὕδωρ, τὰ τελειωτικὰ τῶν μαρτύρων.
τὰ δὲ ἡμέτερα οἷα ; ἀπέψυκται[3] ἡ ἀγάπη· πορθεῖ-
ται ἡ τῶν πατέρων διδασκαλία· ναυάγια περὶ τὴν
πίστιν πυκνά· σιγᾷ τῶν εὐσεβούντων τὰ στό-
ματα· λαοὶ τῶν εὐκτηρίων οἴκων ἐξελαθέντες ἐν
τῷ ὑπαίθρῳ πρὸς τὸν ἐν οὐρανοῖς Δεσπότην τὰς
χεῖρας αἴρουσι. καὶ αἱ μὲν θλίψεις βαρεῖαι,
μαρτύριον δὲ οὐδαμοῦ, διὰ τὸ τοὺς κακοῦντας
ἡμᾶς τὴν αὐτὴν ἡμῖν ἔχειν προσηγορίαν. ὑπὲρ
τούτων αὐτός τε δεήθητι τοῦ Κυρίου, καὶ πάντας
τοὺς γενναίους ἀθλητὰς τοῦ Χριστοῦ εἰς τὴν
ὑπὲρ τῶν ἐκκλησιῶν[4] προσευχὴν συμπαράλαβε,
ἵνα εἴπερ ἔτι χρόνοι τινὲς ὑπολείπονται τῇ
συστάσει τοῦ κόσμου, καὶ μὴ πρὸς τὴν ἐναντίαν
φορὰν συνελαύνεται τὰ πάντα, διαλλαγεὶς ὁ
Θεὸς ταῖς ἑαυτοῦ ἐκκλησίαις ἐπαναγάγῃ αὐτὰς
πρὸς τὴν ἀρχαίαν εἰρήνην.

----

[1] ἐνστάσεις ἀθλητικαί] ἔντασις ἀθλητική editi antiqi.
[2] ἀπλήκτων E.   [3] ἔψυκται E.
[4] τῶν ἐκκλησιῶν] τῆς Ἐκκλησίας E.

----

[1] *i.e.* the gladiatorial contests in which Christians were
made to fight.
[2] The following words from the Benedictine note, which
illustrate this mode of martyrdom, are from a letter of the
Gothic Church which was supposed to have been sent to the
Church of Caesarea along with the body of the martyr

heresy. But your story—contestants confronting
each other,[1] bodies torn to pieces for religion's sake,
barbarian rage treated with contempt by men
undaunted of heart, the various tortures applied by
the persecutors, the firm resistance of the contestants throughout, the beam, the water,[2]—these
are the instruments for the perfecting of martyrs!
But of what sort are ours? Charity has grown cold.
The teaching of the Fathers is being destroyed;
shipwrecks in the faith are frequent; the mouths
of the pious are silent; the laity driven from the
houses of prayer raise in the open their hands to the
Master in heaven. And though grievous are our
afflictions, yet nowhere is martyrdom, because those
who harm us have the same appellation as ourselves.
On behalf of these do you yourself beseech our
Lord, and unite all the noble athletes of Christ in
prayer on behalf of the churches, in order that, if
there is still some time left for the existence of the
world, and the universe is not being driven in the
opposite direction,[3] God may become reconciled
with His churches and lead them back to their
ancient peace.

Sabas: τότε κατάγουσιν αὐτὸν εἰς τὸ ὕδωρ εὐχαριστοῦντα καὶ
δοξάζοντα τὸν Θεόν . . . καὶ ῥίψαντες αὐτόν, καὶ ἐπιθέντες αὐτῷ
ξύλον κατὰ τοῦ τραχήλου, ἐπίεζον εἰς τὸ βάθος. καὶ οὕτω τε-
λεωθεὶς διὰ ξύλου καὶ ὕδατος, ἄχραντον ἐφύλαξεν τῆς σωτηρίας τὸ
σύμβολον, ὢν ἐτῶν τριάκοντα ὀκτώ. "Then they bring him
down to the water, as he gives thanks and glorifies God,
. . . and having thrown him down, and placed a beam of
wood upon his neck, they cast him into the deep. And so
having met his end *by beam and water*, he kept the symbol
of salvation undefiled, at the age of thirty-eight years." St.
Sabas suffered martyrdom under Athanaricus, king of the
Goths, towards the end of the fourth century.

[3] *i.e.* to destruction.

CLXV

Ἀσχολίῳ, ἐπισκόπῳ Θεσσαλονίκης

Παλαιὰν ἡμῖν εὐχὴν ὁ ἅγιος Θεὸς ἐξεπλήρωσε, καταξιώσας ἡμᾶς γράμμασι τῆς ἀληθινῆς σου θεοσεβείας ἐντυχεῖν. τὸ μὲν γὰρ μέγιστον καὶ τῆς μεγίστης σπουδῆς ἄξιον αὐτόν σε ἰδεῖν καὶ ὀφθῆναί σοι, καὶ τῶν ἐν σοὶ τοῦ Πνεύματος χαρισμάτων δι' ἑαυτῶν ἀπολαῦσαι· ἐπειδὴ δὲ τοῦτο ἥ τε τοῦ τόπου διάστασις ἀφαιρεῖται, καὶ αἱ ἰδίᾳ ἑκάτερον ἡμῶν κατέχουσαι περιστάσεις, δευτέρας εὐχῆς ἄξιον γράμμασι συνεχέσι τῆς ἐν Χριστῷ σου [1] ἀγάπης τρέφεσθαι τὴν ψυχήν. ὃ καὶ νῦν ἡμῖν ὑπῆρξεν, ὅτε ἐλάβομεν εἰς χεῖρας τὴν ἐπιστολὴν τῆς συνέσεώς σου· πλέον γὰρ ἢ διπλασίους ἐγενόμεθα τῇ ἀπολαύσει τῶν ἐπεσταλμένων. καὶ γὰρ ἦν τῷ ὄντι καὶ αὐτήν σου καθορᾶν τὴν ψυχήν, οἷον δι' ἐσόπτρου τινὸς τῶν λόγων διαφαινομένην. πολυπλασίονα δὲ ἡμῖν τὴν εὐφροσύνην ἐποίει οὐ μόνον τὸ τοιοῦτον εἶναί σε ὁποῖον ἡ πάντων μαρτυρία παρίστησιν, ἀλλ' ὅτι τὰ ἐν σοὶ καλὰ τῆς πατρίδος ἡμῶν ἐστι σεμνολογήματα. οἷον γὰρ εὐθαλής τις κλάδος ῥίζης γενναίας ἀφορμηθεὶς τῶν πνευματικῶν καρπῶν τὴν ὑπερορίαν ἐνέπλησας. ὥστε εἰκότως ἡ πατρὶς ἡμῶν τοῖς οἰκείοις βλαστήμασιν ἐπαγάλλεται. καὶ ἡνίκα τοὺς ὑπὲρ τῆς πίστεως ἀγῶνας διῆλθες,[2] ἐδόξαζε τὸν Θεόν,

---

[1] σου om. E. [2] διῆλθες editi antiqi.

---

[1] Written in 374. Cf. Letters CLIV and CLV with notes. According to the Benedictine edition this letter is

LETTER CLXV

LETTER CLXV

To Ascholius, Bishop of Thessalonica [1]

The holy God has fulfilled for us a prayer of long standing, having deemed us worthy to receive a letter from your true Holiness. For although the most important thing and worthy of our greatest zeal is to see you yourself and to be seen by you, and to enjoy at first hand the graces of the Spirit that are in you; yet since both distance in space and the preoccupations which detain each of us severally deprive us of this, it is worthy of a secondary prayer that our spirits may be nourished by frequent letters of your charity in Christ. And this is what has happened to us now, when we have taken into our hands the letter of your Sagacity; for our spirits have increased to more than double through the enjoyment of your communication. For it was possible actually to observe even your very soul reflected by your words as by a mirror. And our joy was increased many fold, not only by the fact that you are such a man as the testimony of all asserts, but also because the noble qualities in you are a source of pride to our own country. For like a vigorous branch sprung from a noble root you have filled with spiritual fruits the country beyond our own borders. Rightly, therefore, does our country glory in her own offshoot. And when you were struggling in the contests for the faith, she glorified

undoubtedly not addressed to Ascholius, but to Soranus, duke of Scythia. In Letter CLV Basil requested his relative Julius Soranus to send him relics of the Gothic martyrs. The present letter is an answer to Soranus for his prompt compliance in sending the relics of Saint Sabas.

ἀκούουσα τὴν τῶν πατέρων ἀγαθὴν κληρονομίαν
διαφυλαττομένην ἔν σοι.

Οἷα δέ σου [1] καὶ τὰ παρόντα ; μάρτυρι, νέον [2]
ἀθλήσαντι [3] ἐπὶ τῆς γείτονος ὑμῖν βαρβάρου, τὴν
ἐνεγκοῦσαν ἐτίμησας, οἷόν τις εὐγνώμων γεωργὸς
τοῖς παρασχομένοις τὰ σπέρματα τὰς ἀπαρχὰς
τῶν καρπῶν ἀποπέμπων. ὄντως [4] πρέποντα
ἀθλητῇ Χριστοῦ τὰ δῶρα· μάρτυς τῆς ἀληθείας
ἄρτι τὸν τῆς δικαιοσύνης ἀναδησάμενος στέφανον·
ὃν καὶ ὑπεδεξάμεθα χαίροντες, καὶ ἐδοξάσαμεν
τὸν Θεὸν τὸν ἐν πᾶσι τοῖς ἔθνεσι πληρώσαντα
λοιπὸν τὸ εὐαγγέλιον τοῦ Χριστοῦ αὐτοῦ. παρακέκλησο δὲ καὶ ἡμῶν τῶν ἀγαπώντων σε μεμνῆσθαι ἐν ταῖς προσευχαῖς, καὶ σπουδαίως ὑπὲρ τῶν
ψυχῶν ἡμῶν προσεύχεσθαι τῷ Κυρίῳ, ἵνα
καταξιωθῶμέν ποτε ἄρξασθαι καὶ αὐτοὶ δουλεύειν
τῷ Θεῷ [5] κατὰ τὴν ὁδὸν τῶν ἐντολῶν αὐτοῦ, ἃς
ἔδωκεν ἡμῖν εἰς σωτηρίαν. [6]

CLXVI

Εὐσεβίῳ, ἐπισκόπῳ Σαμοσάτων [7]

Τὰ πάντα τίμιος ὢν ἡμῖν καὶ τῶν φίλων ἐν
τοῖς γνησίοις ὁ αἰδεσιμώτατος ἀδελφὸς ἡμῶν

[1] σοι Med.
[2] μάρτυρι νέον] μαρτυρεῖ νέῳ editi antiqi.
[3] ἀνθήσαντι E.   [4] γάρ add. editi antiqi.
[5] Κυρίῳ E.   [6] αὐτοῦ add. E.
[7] πρεσβύτερος ὤν add. E, editi antiqi.

---

[1] Written in the late summer of 374. Cf. Loofs 46, note
5. For Eusebius, cf. previous letters addressed to him in
this volume. The present letter seems to be correctly
assigned to Gregory of Nazianzus by the Benedictine edition.
The style is quite unlike Basil's epistolary style, but very

God, having heard that the goodly heritage of the Fathers was being preserved in you.

But of what nature also are your present deeds! With a martyr, who but lately finished his struggle in the barbarian land neighbouring your own, you have honoured the land which bore you, sending, like a grateful husbandman, the first fruits back to those who supplied the seed. Truly worthy of Christ's athlete are the gifts; a martyr of the truth who has just been wreathed with the crown of righteousness; and we not only received him with joy, but also glorified the God who among all the Gentiles has already fulfilled the gospel of His Christ. But let me beg you to remember in your prayers us who love you, and for our souls' sake earnestly to pray to the Lord that we also may be thought worthy one day to begin to serve God according to the way of the commandments which He has given us unto salvation.

LETTER CLXVI

To Eusebius, Bishop of Samosata [1]

Though our most reverend brother Eupraxius [2] has been held in honour by us in every respect and counted among our true friends, he has been looked

similar to that of Gregory. Moreover, Eusebius had written to Gregory at the time assigned to this letter, and since Eupraxius was passing through Cappadocia on his way to Eusebius, it gave Gregory an opportunity to send his answer. Furthermore, the present letter is found in only four MSS. of Basil, Coislinianus 237, Vaticani 713 and 435, and Marcianus 79. This is a small proportion of the many extant MSS. of Basil, and no one of these four is included in the most ancient group.

[2] A disciple and intimate friend of Eusebius of Samosata.

431

Εὐπράξιος τιμιώτερος ὤφθη καὶ γνησιώτερος ἐκ
τῆς περὶ σὲ διαθέσεως· ὅς γε καὶ νῦν οὕτως
ὥρμησε πρὸς τὴν σὴν θεοσέβειαν (ἵν᾽ εἴπω τὸ τοῦ
Δαβίδ), ὡς ἔλαφος πολὺ δίψος καὶ οὐ φορητὸν
ποτίμῳ καὶ καθαρᾷ πηγῇ καταψύχουσα. καὶ
μακάριος ὅ σοι πλησιάζειν ἠξιωμένος.[1] καὶ
μακαριώτερος δὲ ὁ ὑπὲρ Χριστοῦ παθήμασι καὶ
τοῖς ὑπὲρ ἀληθείας ἱδρῶσι τοιαύτην ἐπιθεὶς
κορωνίδα, ἧς ὀλίγοι τῶν φοβουμένων τὸν Θεὸν
τετυχήκασιν. οὐ γὰρ ἀβασάνιστον ἐπεδείξω τὴν
ἀρετήν, οὐδὲ ἐν εὐδίας καιρῷ μόνον ὀρθῶς ἔπλευσας
καὶ τὰς τῶν ἄλλων ψυχὰς ἐκυβέρνησας, ἀλλ᾽ ἐν
ταῖς δυσχερείαις τῶν πειρασμῶν διεφάνης,[2] καὶ
τῶν διωκόντων γέγονας ὑψηλότερος τῷ γενναίως
μεταστῆναι τῆς ἐνεγκούσης.

Καὶ ἄλλοι μὲν τὸ πατρῷον ἔδαφος ἔχουσιν,
ἡμεῖς δὲ τὴν ἄνω πόλιν·[3] ἄλλοι τὸν ἡμέτερον ἴσως
θρόνον, ἡμεῖς δὲ Χριστόν. ὦ τῆς πραγματείας!
οἵων ὑπεριδόντες, οἷα κεκομίσμεθα· διήλθομεν
διὰ πυρὸς καὶ ὕδατος· πιστεύω δὲ ὅτι καὶ ἐξελευ-
σόμεθα εἰς ἀναψυχήν. οὐ γὰρ[4] ἐγκαταλείψει
ἡμᾶς ὁ Θεὸς εἰς τέλος, οὐδὲ περιόψεται τὸν ὀρθὸν
λόγον δεδιωγμένον· ἀλλὰ κατὰ τὸ πλῆθος τῶν
ὀδυνῶν ἡμῶν αἱ παρακλήσεις αὐτοῦ εὐφρανοῦσιν
ἡμᾶς. τοῦτο μὲν οὖν καὶ πιστεύομεν καὶ εὐχόμεθα. σὺ δέ, παρακαλῶ, ὑπερεύχου τῆς ταπεινώ-

---

[1] καὶ μακάριος . . . ἠξιωμένος] om. E.

upon as more honoured and truer as the result of his affection for you; for he has now also hastened to your Holiness in like manner, to use the words of David,[1] as a hart which quenches a great and unendurable thirst at a sweet and a pure fountain. And blessed is he who has been thought worthy to associate with you. But even more blessed is he who has crowned his sufferings for Christ's sake and his labours for truth's sake with such a crown as few of those who fear God have obtained. For the virtue you have shown has not been untested, nor in a time of calm only have you correctly sailed your course and guided the souls of the others, but amid the difficulties of your trials you have shone forth, and you have risen superior to your persecutors by nobly departing from the land which bore you.

And others indeed possess the land of their fathers, but we the heavenly city; others perhaps have our throne, but we have Christ! Oh, profitable exchange! For disdaining what things, what things have we gained! We have gone through fire and water; but I trust that we shall also come out into a place of refreshment. For God will not forsake us for ever, nor will He suffer the orthodox doctrine to be persecuted; nay, according to the multitude of our pains His comforts shall gladden us. This at any rate we both believe and pray. But do you, I beseech you, pray for our humility, and as often as

---

[1] Cf. Psal. 41. 2: ὃν τρόπον ἐπιποθεῖ ἡ ἔλαφος ἐπὶ τὰς πηγὰς τῶν ὑδάτων, οὕτως ἐπιποθεῖ ἡ ψυχή μου πρὸς σέ, ὁ θεός. "As the hart panteth after the fountains of water; so my soul panteth after thee, O God."

---

[2] ἀνεφάνης E.   [3] καί add. E.   [4] εἰς τέλος add. E.

σεως ἡμῶν, καὶ ὁσάκις ἂν ἐμπίπτῃ καιρός, εὐλογεῖν
ἡμᾶς διὰ γραμμάτων μὴ κατόκνει, καὶ εὐθυμοτέρους
ποιεῖν τὰ κατὰ σεαυτὸν δηλῶν, ὃ ποιῆσαι νῦν
κατηξίωσας.

CLXVII

Εὐσεβίῳ, ἐπισκόπῳ Σαμοσάτων

Καὶ γράφων καὶ μεμνημένος εὐφραίνεις ἡμᾶς,
καὶ τὸ τούτου μεῖζον, εὐλογῶν ἡμᾶς ἐν τοῖς γράμμασιν. ἡμεῖς δέ, εἰ μὲν [1] ἄξιοι τῶν σῶν παθημάτων καὶ τῆς ὑπὲρ Χριστοῦ ἀθλήσεως, κατηξιώθημεν ἂν καὶ μέχρι σου [2] γενόμενοι περιπτύξασθαί σου τὴν [3] θεοσέβειαν καὶ τύπον λαβεῖν
τῆς ἐν τοῖς παθήμασι καρτερίας. ἐπειδὴ δὲ
ἀνάξιοι τούτου τυγχάνομεν, πολλαῖς θλίψεσι καὶ
ἀσχολίαις ἐνεχόμενοι, ὃ δεύτερόν ἐστι ποιοῦμεν·
προσαγορεύομεν τὴν σὴν τελειότητα, καὶ ἀξιοῦμεν
μὴ κάμνειν σε μεμνημένον ἡμῶν. οὐ γὰρ ὠφέ-
λεια μόνον ἡμῖν τῶν σῶν καταξιοῦσθαι γραμμάτων, ἀλλὰ καὶ καύχημα πρὸς τοὺς πολλοὺς καὶ
καλλώπισμα, ὅτι λόγος ἡμῶν ἐστι παρὰ ἀνδρὶ
τοσούτῳ τὴν ἀρετὴν καὶ τοσαύτην ἔχοντι πρὸς
Θεὸν οἰκειότητα, ὥστε καὶ ἄλλους οἰκειοῦν
δύνασθαι καὶ λόγῳ καὶ ὑποδείγματι.

[1] εἰ μὲν] ἐσμέν editi antiqi.
[2] κατηξιώθημεν . . . σου] εὐχόμεθα ἰδεῖν Ε.
[3] σήν Ε.

---

[1] Written in the late summer of 374.   Cf. Loofs 46, note
5.   On Eusebius of Samosata see previous letters.   The
Benedictine edition rightly assigns this letter to Gregory of

an occasion shall present itself, do not hesitate to bless us by letter and to make us more joyful by informing us of your own affairs, as you have just now deigned to do.

LETTER CLXVII

To Eusebius, Bishop of Samosata [1]

By writing and by being mindful of us you cause us pleasure, and, even more important than this, by blessing us in your letters. As for us, if we had been worthy of your sufferings and of your struggle for Christ's sake, we should have been permitted, coming to visit you, to embrace your Piety and to take you as a model of patience in sufferings. But since we are doubtless unworthy of this, being subject to many afflictions and cares, we are doing what is next best: we salute your Perfection, and we beg you not to become weary of remembering us. For not only is it a benefit to us to be thought worthy of your letters, but it is also a boast in the eyes of people at large and an ornament that some account is taken of us by a man so eminent in virtue, and who enjoys such intimacy with God that he is able to win others also over to Him by both word and example.

Nazianzus. Tillemont's objection that "afflictions and cares" fit Basil better than Gregory does not seem worthy. Gregory also had much to occupy him at this time. Furthermore, the fact that this letter is found regularly among the MSS. of Gregory, and in only Coislinianus 237, Vaticanus 713, Marcianus 79, and Mediceus IV. 14 of the MSS. of Basil, would in itself seem sufficient reason for assigning the letter to Gregory.

435

CLXVIII

Ἀντιόχῳ πρεσβυτέρῳ, ἀδελφιδῷ συνόντι ἐν τῇ
ἐξορίᾳ

Ὅσον ὀδύρομαι τὴν ἐκκλησίαν τὴν στερηθεῖσαν
τῆς τοῦ τοιούτου ποιμένος ἐπιστασίας, τοσοῦτον
μακαρίζω ὑμᾶς καταξιωθέντας ἐν τοιούτῳ καιρῷ
συνεῖναι ἀνδρὶ τὸν μέγαν ὑπὲρ τῆς εὐσεβείας [1]
διαθλοῦντι ἀγῶνα. πέπεισμαι γὰρ ὅτι ὁ Κύριος
καὶ ὑμᾶς τῆς αὐτῆς μερίδος καταξιώσει τοὺς
καλῶς ἀλείφοντας καὶ ἐπεγείροντας αὐτοῦ τὴν
προθυμίαν. ἡλίκον δὲ κέρδος ἐν ἡσυχίᾳ βαθείᾳ
ἀπολαύειν ἀνδρὸς τοσαῦτα μὲν ἐκ τῆς μαθήσεως
τοσαῦτα δὲ ἐκ τῆς πείρας τῶν πραγμάτων συνειλη-
χότος! ὥστε πέπεισμαι ὑμᾶς νῦν ἐγνωκέναι
τὸν ἄνδρα, ἡλίκος ἐστὶ τὴν σύνεσιν· διότι ἐν τῷ
παρελθόν τι χρόνῳ καὶ αὐτὸς τὴν διάνοιαν εἶχεν
εἰς πολλὰ σχιζομένην καὶ ὑμεῖς οὐκ ἤγετε σχολὴν
ἀπὸ τῶν τοῦ βίου πραγμάτων, ὥστε ὅλοι προσ-
κεῖσθαι τῷ πνευματικῷ νάματι τῷ ἀπὸ καθαρᾶς
καρδίας τοῦ ἀνδρὸς προχεομένῳ. ἀλλὰ παράσχοι
ὁ Κύριος ὑμᾶς καὶ αὐτῷ παράκλησιν εἶναι καὶ
αὐτοὺς μὴ δεῖσθαι τῆς ἑτέρων παρηγορίας· ὅπερ
οὖν καὶ πέπεισμαι περὶ τῶν καρδιῶν ὑμῶν, τεκμαιρόμενος τῇ τε ἐμαυτοῦ πείρᾳ, ἣν πρὸς ὀλίγον
ὑμῶν ἐπειράθην, καὶ τῇ μεγάλῃ διδασκαλίᾳ τοῦ
καλοῦ καθηγητοῦ, οὗ μιᾶς ἡμέρας συνουσία αὐταρ-
κές ἐστιν ἐφόδιον πρὸς σωτηρίαν.

---

[1] ἐκκλησίας tres MSS. recentiores.

---

[1] Written in the late summer of 374. Cf. Loofs 46, note 5.

LETTER CLXVIII

LETTER CLXVIII

To the Presbyter Antiochus, Eusebius' Nephew,
who was with him in Exile [1]

Much as I lament the Church's having been
deprived of the care of such a shepherd,[2] equally do
I congratulate you for having been accounted worthy
at such a crisis to be present with a man who is
fighting in the great contest in defence of our
religion. For I am convinced that the Lord will
account you also, who anoint him for the contest and
stimulate his zeal, worthy of the same lot. But what
an advantage it is to enjoy now in profound peace a
man who has accumulated both so much from his
learning and so much from his experience in affairs!
I am therefore persuaded that you have now come
to know the man, how great he is in wisdom;
because in the past he on his own part kept his
mind distracted on many things, and you on yours
lacked the leisure from the affairs of life which would
enable you to devote yourself wholly to the spiritual
stream which flows from the pure heart of the man.
But may the Lord grant that you may be a comfort
to him in turn and may not yourself require consolation from others. And indeed I am convinced that
this will be the case so far as the hearts of you both
are concerned, judging not only from my experience,
wherein I made trial of you both for a short time,
but also by the great instruction of the Good
Teacher, whose company for a single day is a
sufficient viaticum for salvation.

Theodoret, IV. 12 and 13, describes the scene of Eusebius'
forced departure into exile at the command of Valens.

  [2] *i.e.* Eusebius.

CLXIX

Γρηγορίῳ Βασίλειος

Πρᾶγμα μὲν ὑπέστης ἐπιεικὲς καὶ [1] ἥμερον καὶ φιλάνθρωπον τὴν τοῦ καταφρονητοῦ Γλυκερίου (τέως γὰρ οὕτω γράφομεν) αἰχμαλωσίαν συναγαγών, καὶ τὴν κοινὴν ἀσχημοσύνην ἡμῶν, ὡς οἷόν τε ἦν, συγκαλύψας. δεῖ δὲ [2] ὅμως τὴν σὴν εὐλάβειαν μαθοῦσαν τὰ κατ᾽ αὐτὸν οὕτω λῦσαι τὴν ἀτιμίαν.

Οὗτος ὁ νῦν σοβαρὸς καὶ σεμνὸς ὑμῖν Γλυκέριος ἐχειροτονήθη μὲν παρ᾽ ἡμῶν τῆς κατὰ Οὐήνεσαν [3] ἐκκλησίας διάκονος, ὡς καὶ τῷ πρεσβυτέρῳ διακονήσων καὶ τοῦ ἔργου τῆς ἐκκλησίας ἐπιμελησόμενος. καὶ γάρ ἐστιν, εἰ καὶ τὰ ἄλλα δύστροπος ὁ ἀνήρ, ἀλλὰ τὰ ἐπίχειρα οὐκ ἀφυής. ἐπεὶ δὲ κατέστη, τοῦ μὲν ἔργου ἠμέλησε τοσοῦτον ὅσον οὐδὲ τὴν ἀρχὴν γεγονότος· παρθένους δὲ ἀθλίας συναγαγὼν κατ᾽ ἰδίαν ἐξουσίαν καὶ αὐθεντίαν, τὰς μὲν ἑκούσας προσδραμούσας αὐτῷ (οἶσθα δὲ τὸ τῶν νέων περὶ τὰ τοιαῦτα πρόχειρον), τὰς δὲ ἀκούσας ἀγελαρχεῖν ἐπεχείρησε, καὶ πατριαρχίας ὄνομα ἑαυτῷ καὶ σχῆμα περιθείς, ἐξαίφνης ἐσοβαρεύσατο, οὐκ ἔκ τινος ἀκολουθίας [4] καὶ εὐσεβείας ἐπὶ τοῦτο ἐλθών, ἀλλ᾽ ἀφορμὴν βίου

---

[1] ἐπιεικὲς καὶ] ἐπιεικῶς Harl.
[2] συγκαλύψας. δεῖ δέ om. E.
[3] Σύννασαν Harl.   [4] δικαίας add. editi antiqi.

---

[1] Written about 374. Letters CLXIX, CLXX, and CLXXI treat of the strange doings of the deacon Glycerius. Cf. W. M. Ramsay, *The Church in the Roman Empire before A.D. 170*, 2nd ed., London, 1893, pp. 443-464.

LETTER CLXIX

Basil to Gregory [1]

You have, it is true, undertaken a kind, clement, and humane work in collecting the captive band of the contemptible Glycerius (for at the present time we must use this term) and in hiding our common shame as far as possible: but your Reverence ought, nevertheless, first to learn the facts about him and then to wipe out this dishonour.

This Glycerius, who is at present looked upon by you as merely an impetuous and swaggering fellow, was ordained by us as deacon of the church of Venesa,[2] with the idea that he should both serve the presbyter and look after the work of the church. For, however intractable the man is in other respects, yet he is not without natural talent as regards odd errands. But after he was appointed, he neglected his work as if it had not existed at all, but collecting some unfortunate virgins on his own authority and responsibility, some running to him willingly (and you know the tendency of young people in such matters) and others against their will, he undertook to be the leader of the company, and having invested himself with the name and apparel of a patriarch, he suddenly began to give himself airs, adopting this course, not from any motive of obedience or of piety, but because he preferred this source of livelihood,

The Gregory addressed is either of Nyssa or Nazianzus. Manuscript evidence favours Gregory of Nazianzus, but there are arguments in favour of Gregory of Nyssa. Cf. *Vita Basilii*, XXXI, 4.

[2] Other spellings are Veësa, Venata, and Synnasa.

ταύτην ὥσπερ ἄλλος τινὰ προστησάμενος· καὶ
μικροῦ τὴν ἐκκλησίαν πᾶσαν ἀνάστατον πεποίηκε,
περιφρονῶν μὲν τὸν ἑαυτοῦ πρεσβύτερον, ἄνδρα
καὶ πολιτείᾳ καὶ ἡλικίᾳ αἰδέσιμον, περιφρονῶν δὲ
τὸν χωρεπίσκοπον [1] καὶ ἡμᾶς ὡς οὐδενὸς ἀξίους,
θορύβων δὲ ἀεὶ καὶ ταραχῶν πληρῶν τὴν πόλιν
καὶ σύμπαν τὸ ἱερατεῖον.

Καὶ τέλος, ἵνα τι μὴ [2] λόγῳ ἐπιτιμηθῇ μικρὸν
παρ' ἡμῶν καὶ τοῦ χωρεπισκόπου πρὸς τὸ μὴ
καταφρονεῖν αὐτὸν (καὶ γὰρ καὶ τοὺς νέους
ἐγύμναζεν εἰς τὴν αὐτὴν ἀπόνοιαν), πρᾶγμα
διανοεῖται λίαν τολμηρὸν καὶ ἀπάνθρωπον.
συλήσας νῶν παρθένων ὅσας ἠδύνατο, καὶ νύκτα
τηρήσας, δραπέτης γίνεται. πάνυ σοι δεινὰ ταῦτα
φανεῖται.[3] σκόπει καὶ τὸν καιρόν. ἤγετο μὲν ἡ
ἐκεῖσε σύνοδος καὶ πολὺ πανταχόθεν, ὡς εἰκός,
ἐπέρρει τὸ πλῆθος. ὁ δὲ ἀντεξῆγε τὸν ἑαυτοῦ χορὸν
νέοις ἑπόμενον καὶ περιχορεύοντα, καὶ πολλὴν
μὲν κατήφειαν κινοῦντα τοῖς εὐλαβέσι, πολὺν δὲ
γέλωτα τοῖς ἀκρατέσι καὶ τὴν γλῶσσαν ἑτοιμο-
τέροις. καὶ οὐκ ἀρκεῖ ταῦτα, καίπερ τηλικαῦτα
ὄντα τὸ μέγεθος· ἀλλ' ἔτι καὶ τοὺς γονεῖς, ὡς
πυνθάνομαι, τῶν παρθένων τὴν ἀτεκνίαν οὐ
φέροντας, καὶ τὴν διασπορὰν ἐπαναγαγεῖν
βουλομένους, καὶ μετ' ὀδυρμῶν προσπίπτοντας,
ὡς εἰκός, ταῖς ἑαυτῶν θυγατράσι, περιυβρίζει καὶ
ἀτιμοῖ [4] ὁ θαυμαστὸς νεανίσκος μετὰ τοῦ ληστρι-
κοῦ συντάγματος.

Ταῦτα μὴ ἀνεκτὰ φανήτω τῇ σῇ εὐλαβείᾳ· καὶ

---

[1] ἐπίσκοπον E, Med.
[2] μή Combefisius, who would thus replace τι.
[3] φαίνεται Harl.

just as another man would choose one or another occupation ; and he has all but overturned the whole Church, scorning his own presbyter, a man who is venerated for both his conduct and his age, and scorning his chorepiscopus and ourselves as if deserving no consideration at all, and continually filling the city and the whole sanctuary with tumults and disturbances.

And at last, in order to avoid receiving some slight verbal rebuke from us and from his chorepiscopus so that he should cease treating us with contempt (for he proceeded to train the young men also to the same folly), he is now planning an exceedingly daring and abominable thing. Having stolen from us two as many of the virgins as he could, and having watched for a night, he has become a fugitive. These things will seem quite dreadful to you. Consider also the occasion he chose. The local festival was being held, and a great crowd from all sides, as was natural, was gathering. And he led out his own troop in turn, following young men and dancing about them, and causing great shame to the pious, but much laughter to the boisterous and the more glib-tongued. And these acts are not enough, although they are such in enormity, but he goes still further, as I hear, when the parents of the virgins, finding the loss of their children intolerable, wish to bring home the scattered company and throw themselves with tears, as is natural, at their daughters' feet, this admirable young fellow and his predatory band even insult and flout them.

Let not these things appear tolerable to your

---

⁴ ἀτιμάζει Harl.

γὰρ κοινὸς [1] πάντων ἡμῶν ὁ γέλως· ἀλλὰ μάλιστα
μὲν αὐτὸν κέλευσον μετὰ τῶν παρθένων ἐπανελ-
θεῖν· τύχοι γὰρ ἄν τινος φιλανθρωπίας εἰ μετὰ
σῶν ἐπανήκοι γραμμάτων· εἰ δὲ μή, τάς γε
παρθένους ἀπόπεμψον τῇ μητρὶ αὐτῶν τῇ ἐκκλησίᾳ. εἰ δὲ μή,[2] τάς γε βουλομένας τυραννεῖσθαι
μὴ συγχωρήσῃς, ἀλλ᾽ ἐπανελθεῖν τύπωσον πρὸς
ἡμᾶς. ἢ μαρτυρόμεθά σοι[3] ὡς καὶ Θεῷ καὶ
ἀνθρώποις, ὅτι μὴ καλῶς ταῦτα γίνεται μηδὲ
θεσμοῖς ἐκκλησίας. Γλυκέριος δὲ εἰ μὲν ἐπανέλ-
θοι μετ᾽ ἐπιστήμης καὶ τῆς πρεπούσης [4] εὐσταθείας, τοῦτο ἄριστον, εἰ δὲ μή, ἔστω πεπαυμένος
τῆς ὑπηρεσίας.

CLXX

Γλυκερίῳ

Μέχρι τίνος ἀπονοῇ, καὶ κακῶς μὲν [5] βουλεύῃ
περὶ σεαυτοῦ, κινεῖς δὲ [6] ἡμᾶς, αἰσχύνεις δὲ τὸ
κοινὸν τάγμα τῶν μοναστῶν; ἐπάνελθε οὖν τῷ
Θεῷ θαρρῶν καὶ ἡμῖν, οὓ τὴν φιλανθρωπίαν
μιμούμεθα. εἰ γὰρ καὶ πατρικῶς ἐπετιμήσαμεν,
ἀλλὰ καὶ συγγνωσόμεθα πατρικῶς.[7] ταῦτά σοι
παρ᾽ ἡμῶν, ἐπειδὴ πολλοί τε ἱκετεύουσιν ἄλλοι,
καὶ πρὸ τῶν ἄλλων ὁ σὸς πρεσβύτερος, οὗ τὴν
πολιὰν αἰδούμεθα καὶ τὴν εὐσπλαγχνίαν. εἰ δὲ
μακρύνεις [8] ἀφ᾽ ἡμῶν, τοῦ βαθμοῦ μὲν πάντως [9]

---

[1] κοινόν editi antiqi.   [2] τοῦτο add. editi antiqi.
[3] σοι] Θεὸν καὶ ἀνθρώπους Harl. ; σε E.
[4] παρούσης E, editi antiqi.   [5] μέν om. E.
[6] δὲ] μέν E, editi antiqi.
[7] πνευματικῶς apud Gregorium.

Reverence; for the ridicule affects us all in common; but if possible command him to return with the virgins; for he would meet with some consideration if he should come back with a letter from you; but if this cannot be, at least send back the virgins to their mother the Church. And if this is impossible, do not allow those at least who wish to return to be tyrannized over, but order them to come back to us. Otherwise we protest to you and also to God and men that these things are not done rightly nor in accord with the laws of the Church. Yet if Glycerius should return with understanding and with the becoming steadiness of mind, this would be best, but if not, let him be deposed from his ministry.

LETTER CLXX

To Glycerius[1]

How far will you go in your folly, and while acting unwisely concerning your own self, stir us to anger and put to shame the whole order of monks? Return, therefore, putting your confidence in God and in us who imitate His benevolence. For even though we have rebuked like a father, yet we shall also grant pardon like a father. This is the treatment you will receive at our hands, since many others are making pleas on your behalf and above the rest your own presbyter, whose grey hairs and kindness of heart we revere. But if you continue to hold aloof from us, then you have fallen

---

[1] For the date and content see the preceding letter.

---

[8] μακρύνοις Harl.   [9] παντός Reg. secundus.

ἐκπέπτωκας, ἐκπεσῇ δὲ καὶ τοῦ Θεοῦ μετὰ τῶν
μελῶν σου καὶ τῆς στολῆς, οἷς ἄγεις τὰς νέας,
οὐ πρὸς Θεόν, ἀλλ᾽ εἰς βάραθρον.

CLXXI

Γρηγορίῳ [1]

Ἐπέσταλκά σοι καὶ πρώην περὶ Γλυκερίου καὶ
τῶν παρθένων. οἱ δὲ οὐδέπω καὶ τήμερον ἐπανή-
κασιν, ἀλλ᾽ ἔτι μέλλουσιν, οὐκ οἶδα ὅθεν καὶ
ὅπως. οὐ γὰρ ἂν ἐκεῖνό σου καταγνοίην, ὡς ἐφ᾽
ἡμετέρᾳ διαβολῇ τοῦτο ποιεῖς, ἢ αὐτὸς πάσχων
τι πρὸς ἡμᾶς, ἢ ἄλλοις χαριζόμενος. ἡκέτωσαν
οὖν μηδὲν δεδοικότες· σὺ γενοῦ τούτου [2] ἐγγυητής.
καὶ γὰρ ἀλγοῦμεν τεμνομένων [3] τῶν μελῶν, εἰ καὶ
καλῶς [4] ἐτμήθησαν. εἰ δὲ ἀντιτείνοιεν, ἐπ᾽ ἄλλους
τὸ βάρος, ἡμεῖς δὲ ἀπυπλυνόμεθα.

CLXXII

Σωφρονίῳ ἐπισκόπῳ

Ὅπως ηὔφρανας ἡμᾶς τοῖς [5] γράμμασιν οὐδὲν
δεόμεθα γράφειν. εἰκάζεις γὰρ πάντως αὐτοῖς

---

[1] ἑταίρῳ add. E.
[2] σὺ γενοῦ τούτου] συγγένου τούτων editi antiqi. τούτων
apud Gregorium.
[3] τεμνομένων] τεμνόμενοι τῶν μελῶν apud Gregorium.
[4] κακῶς E, editi antiqi.   [5] τοῖς om. E.

---

[1] Cf. Tim. 3. 13 : οἱ γὰρ καλῶς διακονήσαντες, βαθμὸν ἑαυτοῖς
καλὸν περιποιοῦνται, καὶ πολλὴν παρρησίαν ἐν πίστει τῇ ἐν

entirely from your grade,[1] and you will also fall
from God with your songs and your finery, by which
you are leading the young women, not to God, but
to the pit.

LETTER CLXXI

To Gregory[2]

I HAVE written to you recently about Glycerius
and his virgins. And they have not yet to this
day returned, but are still delaying; why and how
I know not. For I could not lay the blame for this
matter against you and say that you are doing this
to discredit us, either because you have some
grievance against us yourself, or are doing it as a
favour for others. Therefore let them come, fearing
nothing; do you become surety for this. For we
are pained when our members are cut off, even if
they have been justly cut off. But if they resist, the
burden will rest upon others, and we are absolved.

LETTER CLXXII

To Sophronius, Bishop[3]

How you have pleased us by your letter we need
not write. For you can certainly surmise it from

Χριστῷ 'Ιησοῦ. "For they that have ministered well shall
purchase to themselves a good degree, and much confidence
in the faith which is in Christ Jesus." The "degree" mentioned by Basil here is the diaconate.

[2] For date and content cf. Letter CLXIX and note.

[3] Written in 374. This Sophronius is distinguished by the
Benedictine edition from the Sophronius, *magister officiorum*,
to whom Letters XXXII, LXXVI, XCVI and others are
addressed. The present Sophronius is otherwise unknown.

οἷς ἐπέστειλας τοιούτοις οὖσι.¹ τὸν γὰρ πρῶτον καρπὸν τοῦ Πνεύματος, τὴν ἀγάπην, ἔδειξας ἡμῖν διὰ τοῦ γράμματος. τούτου δὲ τί ἂν γένοιτο τιμιώτερον ἡμῖν ἐν τῇ παρούσῃ τῶν καιρῶν καταστάσει, ἡνίκα διὰ τὸ πληθυνθῆναι τὴν ἀνομίαν, ἐψύγη τῶν πολλῶν ἡ ἀγάπη; οὐδὲν γὰρ οὕτω σπάνιον νῦν ὡς ἀδελφοῦ συντυχία πνευματικοῦ, καὶ ῥῆμα εἰρηνικόν, καὶ πνευματικὴ κοινωνία, ἣν εὑρόντες ἐν τῇ σῇ τελειότητι ὑπερευχαριστήσαμεν τῷ Κυρίῳ, δεόμενοι καὶ τῆς τελείας ἐπὶ σοὶ μετασχεῖν εὐφροσύνης. εἰ γὰρ ἐπιστολαὶ τοιαῦται, ὁποία ἡ συντυχία; καὶ εἰ πόρρωθεν οὕτως αἱρεῖς, πόσου ἄξιος ἔσῃ ἐγγύθεν ἡμῖν ἐπιφανείς; εὖ δὲ ἴσθι,² εἰ μὴ μυρίων ἀσχολιῶν περιεῖχε πλῆθος³ καὶ αἱ ἀπαραίτητοι αὗται ἀνάγκαι αἷς ἐνδεδέμεθα, αὐτόν με ἐπειχθῆναι πρὸς τὴν σὴν τελειότητα. καίτοιγε⁴ μέγα μοι ἐμπόδιόν ἐστι πρὸς τὰς κινήσεις ἡ παλαιὰ αὕτη τοῦ σώματος ἀρρωστία, ἀλλ' ὅμως οὐκ ἂν ὑπελογισάμην τοῦτο ἐμπόδιον τῆς προσδοκωμένης ἕνεκεν ὠφελείας. τὸ γὰρ ἀνδρὶ τὰ αὐτὰ φρονοῦντι καὶ τὴν τῶν πατέρων πρεσβεύοντι πίστιν, ὡς ὁ τῶν τιμίων ἀδελφῶν καὶ συμπρεσβυτέρων λόγος,⁵ καταξιωθῆναι περιτυχεῖν, ὄντως ἐστὶν εἰς τὴν ἀρχαίαν μακαριότητα τῶν ἐκκλησιῶν ἐπανελθεῖν, ὅτε ὀλίγοι μὲν ἦσαν οἱ νοσοῦντες περὶ ζητήσεις, ἐν ἡσυχίᾳ δὲ ἦσαν πάντες, ἐργάται ὄντες τῶν ἐντολῶν⁶ ἀνεπαίσ-

---

¹ τοιούτοις οὖσι om. E.
² εὖ δὲ ἴσθι] ὥστε με E; ὥστε μοι Med.
³ ἡμᾶς add. editi antiqi.   ⁴ καίτοι E.
⁵ περὶ σοῦ add. editi antiqi.
⁶ τοῦ Θεοῦ add. editi antiqi.

the very nature of the things you said in your letter.
For you have shown us the first fruit of the Spirit,
charity, through your letter. And what could be
more precious to us than this in the present condition of the times, when, "because iniquity hath
abounded, the charity of many hath grown cold"?[1]
For nothing is so rare now as a meeting with a
spiritual brother, and peaceful discourse, and spiritual
communion; and since we have found this communion in your Perfection, we have rendered exceeding thanks to the Lord, beseeching also that
we may share in the perfect joy that is in you. For
if your letters are such, what would a meeting be!
And if you can move me so from a distance, how
estimable will you be when you appear to us from
near at hand! But be assured that if we were not
encompassed about by a multitude of countless preoccupations and by the present inexorable necessities
by which we are constrained, I should have hastened
to your Perfection in person. And yet a great
obstacle to my moving about is this old infirmity
of my body; but nevertheless I should have paid
no heed to this obstacle for the sake of the anticipated profit. For to be thought worthy of meeting
a man who holds the same opinions as myself and
who reverences the faith of the Fathers, according
to the account of our honoured brethren and fellow-
presbyters, is in truth to return to the old-time
blessedness of the churches, when those were few
who suffered from the malady of inquiry, and all
were in peace, being workmen fulfilling the com-

---

[1] Cf. Matt. 24. 12: καὶ διὰ τὸ πληθυνθῆναι τὴν ἀνομίαν,
ψυγήσεται ἡ ἀγάπη τῶν πολλῶν. "And because iniquity hath
abounded, the charity of many shall grow cold."

χυντοι, διὰ τῆς ἁπλῆς καὶ ἀπεριέργου ὁμολογίας
λατρεύοντες τῷ Κυρίῳ, καὶ[1] ἄσυλον τὴν πίστιν
καὶ ἀπερίεργον τὴν εἰς Πατέρα καὶ Υἱὸν καὶ
ἅγιον Πνεῦμα διαφυλάσσοντες.

CLXXIII

Πρὸς Θεοδώραν κανονικήν[2]

Ὀκνηροὺς ἡμᾶς ποιεῖ πρὸς τὸ γράφειν τὸ μὴ
πεπεῖσθαι τὰς ἐπιστολὰς ἡμῶν πάντως[3] ἐγχειρί-
ζεσθαι τῇ σῇ ἀγάπῃ ἀλλὰ κακίᾳ τῶν διακονούντων
μυρίους προεντυγχάνειν ἑτέρους· καὶ μάλιστα νῦν
οὕτω τεταραγμένων[4] τῶν κατὰ τὴν οἰκουμένην
πραγμάτων. διόπερ ἀναμέτω[5] τρόπον τινὰ μεμφ-
θῆναι[6] καὶ[7] ἀπαιτηθῆναι βιαίως τὰς ἐπιστολάς,
ὥστε αὐτῷ τούτῳ τεκμηρίῳ χρήσασθαι τῆς ἀπο-
δόσεως. καὶ γράφοντες μὲν οὖν καὶ σιωπῶντες
ἓν ἔργον ἔχομεν ἐν ταῖς καρδίαις ἡμῶν, φυλάσσειν
τὴν μνήμην τῆς κοσμιότητός σου, καὶ προσεύχεσθαι τῷ Κυρίῳ δοῦναί σοι τελέσαι τὸν δρόμον
τῆς ἀγαθῆς πολιτείας καθὰ προείλου. τῷ ὄντι

---

[1] λατρεύοντες τῷ Κυρίῳ, καί om. E, Med.
[2] Θεοδώρᾳ κανονικῇ editi antiqi. ; περὶ βίου κανονικοῦ add. Harl.
[3] πάντας editi antiqi. [4] τεταγμένων editi antiqi.
[5] ἀναμένομεν editi antiqi. [6] πεμφθῆναι E.
[7] καί om. E.

---

[1] Cf. 2 Tim. 2. 15 : σπούδασον σεαυτὸν δόκιμον παραστῆσαι
τῷ Θεῷ, ἐργάτην ἀνεπαίσχυντον ὀρθοτομοῦντα τὸν λόγον τῆς
ἀληθείας. "Carefully study to present thyself approved

mandments and needing not to be ashamed,[1] serving
the Lord through a simple and not too elaborate
confession, and preserving inviolate and not too
elaborate their faith in the Father, Son, and Holy
Ghost.

LETTER CLXXIII

To Theodora, a Canoness [2]

We are rendered hesitant about writing by the
fact that we are not entirely assured that our letters
are placed in the hands of your Charity, but instead,
through the baseness of our messengers, innumerable
others read them first; and especially now when
throughout the world things are so disturbed.
Therefore I am waiting to be found fault with in
a measure and to have my letters forcefully demanded, so that I may treat this as itself a proof
of their delivery. However, both when writing and
when silent we keep in our hearts one duty—to
guard the memory of your Decorum and to pray
the Lord to grant that you may complete the course
of good conduct of life even as you have chosen.

---

[1] unto God, a workman that needeth not to be ashamed, rightly
handling the word of truth."

[2] Written about the year 374. Canonicae were women
who devoted themselves to education, district visiting,
funerals, and various charitable works, and living in community apart from men. Cf. Socrates 1. 17 ; Sozomen 8. 23.
Rules were laid down for their guidance, as Basil here sets
forth, but St. Augustine in 423 drew up the first general
rules for such communities of women. They were distinguished from nuns in not being bound by vows, and from
deaconesses as not so distinctly discharging ministerial
duties.

449

γὰρ οὐ μικρὸς ἀγὼν ὁμολογοῦντι¹ τῆς ἐπαγγελίας
τὰ ἐφεξῆς ἐπάγειν. τὸ μὲν γὰρ προελέσθαι τὴν
κατὰ τὸ εὐαγγέλιον πολιτείαν παντός, τὸ δὲ καὶ
μέχρι τῶν μικροτάτων ἄγειν τὴν παρατήρησιν,
καὶ μηδὲν τῶν ἐκεῖ γεγραμμένων παρορᾶν, τοῦτο
πάνυ ὀλίγοις τῶν εἰς ἡμετέραν γνῶσιν ἡκόντων
κατώρθωται· ὥστε καὶ γλώσσῃ πεπεδημένῃ κε-
χρῆσθαι² καὶ ὀφθαλμῷ πεπαιδαγωγημένῳ κατὰ
τὸ βούλημα τοῦ εὐαγγελίου, καὶ χερσὶν ἐνεργεῖν
κατὰ τὸν σκοπὸν τῆς εὐαρεστήσεως τοῦ Θεοῦ,
καὶ πόδας κινεῖν καὶ ἑκάστῳ τῶν μελῶν οὕτω
κεχρῆσθαι ὡς ἐξ ἀρχῆς ὁ Δημιουργὸς ἡμῶν
ᾠκονόμησε· τὸ ἐν τῇ καταστολῇ κόσμιον, τὸ ἐν
ταῖς συντυχίαις τῶν ἀνδρῶν πεφυλαγμένον, τὸ
ἐν βρώμασιν αὔταρκες, τὸ ἐν τῇ κτήσει³ τῶν
ἀναγκαίων ἀπέριττον. ταῦτα πάντα μικρὰ μὲν
ἁπλῶς οὕτω λεγόμενα, μεγάλου δὲ ἀγῶνος εἰς τὸ
κατορθωθῆναι χρῄζοντα, ὡς ἐπ' αὐτῆς⁴ τῆς ἀληθείας εὕρομεν. καὶ μὲν καὶ τὸ ἐν τῇ ταπεινο-
φροσύνῃ τέλειον, ὡς μήτε προγόνων περιφανείας
μεμνῆσθαι, μήτε, εἴ τι ὑπάρχει⁵ ἡμῖν ἐκ⁶ φύσεως
πλεονέκτημα ἢ κατὰ σῶμα ἢ κατὰ ψυχήν, τούτῳ
ἐπαίρεσθαι, μήτε τὰς ἔξωθεν περὶ ἡμῶν ὑπολήψεις
ἀφορμὴν ἐπάρσεώς τε καὶ φυσιώσεως ποιεῖσθαι,
ταῦτα τοῦ εὐαγγελικοῦ ἔχεται βίου. τὸ ἐν
ἐγκρατείᾳ εὔτονον, τὸ ἐν προσευχαῖς φιλόπονον,
τὸ ἐν φιλαδελφίᾳ συμπαθές, τὸ πρὸς τοὺς δεομένους κοινωνικόν,⁷ τὸ τοῦ φρονήματος κατα-
βεβλημένον, ὁ συντριμμὸς τῆς καρδίας,⁸ τὸ τῆς
πίστεως ὑγιές, τὸ ἐν σκυθρωπότητι ὁμαλόν, μηδέ-

---

¹ ὁμολογοῦντά τι editi antiqi.   ² χρῆσθαι editi antiqi.

For truly it is no slight struggle for one who makes a profession to carry out the consequences of his promise. For choosing the evangelical life is in the power of anyone, but carrying out its observance even to the smallest details, and overlooking none of the written rules—this has been accomplished successfully by very few who have come to our knowledge; as, for example, to keep the tongue fettered and the eye disciplined according to the intent of the Gospel, and to work with the hands with a view to pleasing God, and to move the feet and so to use each of the limbs as our Creator ordained from the beginning; modesty in dress, circumspection in the society of men, moderation in food, simplicity in the acquisition of necessities. All these things are small when thus simply mentioned, but require a great struggle to be observed successfully, as in very truth we have discovered. And, furthermore, perfection in humility, so that we shall neither remember any distinction of ancestry, nor, if we possess by nature any advantage whether of body or of mind, be elated by this, nor to make others' opinions of ourselves an occasion of exaltation and pride—these things belong to the evangelical life. Also constancy in self-control, assiduity in prayer, sympathy in fraternal charity, generosity toward the needy, subjection of pride, contrition of heart, soundness of faith, equability in despond-

---

3 κτήσει E ; κυήσει editi.

4 ὡς ἐπ' αὐτῆς] εὑρήκαμεν editi antiqi.

5 ἐνυπάρχει editi antiqi.   6 ἐκ om. E.

7 τὸ πρὸς τοὺς δεομένους κοινωνικόν om. E.

8 τὸ πρὸς τοὺς δεομένους κοινωνικόν add. E.

ποτε τῆς ἐννοίας ἡμῶν λειπούσης τοῦ φοβεροῦ
καὶ ἀπαραιτήτου δικαστηρίου τὴν μνήμην πρὸς ὃ
ἐπειγόμεθα μὲν ἅπαντες, μέμνηνται δὲ αὐτοῦ καὶ
τὴν ἀπ᾿ αὐτοῦ ἔκβασιν ἀγωνιῶσιν ἐλάχιστοι.

CLXXIV

Πρὸς ἐλευθέραν

Ἐγώ, καὶ πάνυ βουλόμενος συνεχῶς ἐπιστέλλειν τῇ εὐγενείᾳ ὑμῶν, ἐπέσχον[1] ἐμαυτὸν ἀεί,
μήπως δόξω τινὰς ὑμῖν πειρασμοὺς ἐπεγείρειν
διὰ τοὺς φιλέχθρως[2] πρὸς ἡμᾶς διακειμένους καί,
ὡς ἀκούω, μέχρι καὶ τούτων τὴν ἔχθραν ἐλαύ-
νοντας, ὥστε πολυπραγμονεῖν[3] εἴ πού τις καὶ
γράμμα ἡμέτερον δέχοιτο. ἐπειδὴ δὲ αὐτή, καλῶς
ποιοῦσα, κατῆρξας τοῦ γράμματος καὶ ἐπέστειλας
ἡμῖν ἃ[4] ἐχρῆν περὶ τῶν κατὰ τὴν[5] ψυχήν σου
πραγμάτων ἀνακοινουμένη, προετράπην εἰς τὸ
ἀντεπιστεῖλαι, ὁμοῦ μὲν τὰ ἐν τῷ παρελθόντι[6]
χρόνῳ ἐλλειφθέντα ἐπανορθούμενος, ὁμοῦ δὲ καὶ
πρὸς τὰ ἐπεσταλμένα παρὰ τῆς σῆς εὐγενείας
ἀποκρινόμενος.

Ὅτι μακαρία ἐστὶ[7] ψυχὴ ἡ νυκτὸς καὶ ἡμέρας
μηδεμίαν ἄλλην μέριμναν στρέφουσα ἢ πῶς ἐπὶ
τῆς μεγάλης ἡμέρας, καθ᾿ ἣν πᾶσα ἡ κτίσις
περιστήσεται τὸν κριτὴν τὰς εὐθύνας τῶν πεπραγμένων ἀποδιδοῦσα, καὶ αὐτὴ δυνηθῇ κούφως ἀπο-

---

[1] ἀπέσχον editi antiqi.   [2] φιλεχθῶς editi antiqi.
[3] φιλοπραγμονεῖν E, Harl.

ency, never letting pass from our minds the remembrance of the awful and inexorable tribunal, towards which we all indeed are hastening, though very few are mindful of it or solicitous about what the issue therefrom shall be.

LETTER CLXXIV

To a Widow [1]

I, ALTHOUGH wishing very much to write regularly to your Nobility, have always checked myself, that I may not seem to occasion you any trials on account of those who are ill-disposed toward us, and, as I hear, push their hatred so far that they make much ado if anyone perchance receives even a letter from us. But since you yourself, quite properly, have taken the initiative in writing and in your letter have communicated what you should as regards the affairs of your soul, I have been moved to reply, at one and the same time both rectifying my omissions in the past, and replying to the present communications of your Nobility.

Take note that the soul is blessed which by night and day revolves no other anxiety than how on the great day, on which all creation shall stand about the Judge and give an account of its deeds, it also shall be able easily to discharge the reckoning of

[1] Written in 374.

4 ὡς E.
6 παρόντι E.

5 τήν om. E.
7 ή add. E.

θέσθαι τὸν λόγον τῶν βεβιωμένων. ὁ γὰρ ἐκείνην
τὴν ἡμέραν καὶ τὴν ὥραν πρὸ ὀφθαλμῶν τιθέμενος,
καὶ ἀεὶ μελετῶν τὴν ἐπὶ τοῦ ἀπαραλογίστου[1]
κριτηρίου ἀπολογίαν, ὁ τοιοῦτος ἢ οὐδὲν παντελῶς
ἢ ἐλάχιστα ἁμαρτήσεται, διότι[2] τὸ ἁμαρτάνειν
ἡμῖν κατὰ ἀπουσίαν τοῦ φόβου τοῦ Θεοῦ[3] γίνεται.
οἷς δ' ἂν ἐναργὴς παρῇ τῶν ἀπειλουμένων ἡ
προσδοκία, οὐδένα καιρὸν δώσει τοῖς τοιούτοις
ὁ σύνοικος φόβος εἰς ἀβουλήτους πράξεις ἢ
ἐνθυμήσεις ἐκπεσεῖν.

Καὶ μέμνησο τοίνυν τοῦ Θεοῦ, καὶ ἔχε τὸν
αὐτοῦ φόβον ἐν τῇ καρδίᾳ, καὶ πάντας εἰς τὴν
κοινωνίαν τῶν εὐχῶν παραλάμβανε. μεγάλη γὰρ
καὶ ἡ τῶν δυναμένων δυσωπεῖν τὸν Θεὸν βοήθεια.
καὶ μὴ διαλίπῃς ταῦτα ποιοῦσα. καὶ γὰρ καὶ
ζῶσιν ἡμῖν τὴν ἐν σαρκὶ ταύτῃ[4] ζωὴν ἀγαθὴ
ἔσται βοηθὸς ἡ προσευχή, καὶ ἀπερχομένοις
ἐντεῦθεν ἐφόδιον διαρκὲς πρὸς τὸν αἰῶνα τὸν
μέλλοντα. ὥσπερ δὲ ἡ φροντὶς πρᾶγμά ἐστιν
ἀγαθόν, οὕτω πάλιν ἡ ἀθυμία καὶ ἡ ἀπόγνωσις
καὶ τὸ δυσελπίστως ἔχειν πρὸς σωτηρίαν τῶν
βλαπτόντων ἐστὶ τὴν ψυχήν. ἐπέλπιζε τοίνυν
τῇ ἀγαθότητι τοῦ Θεοῦ, καὶ ἐκδέχου αὐτοῦ τὴν
ἀντίληψιν, γινώσκουσα ὅτι, ἐὰν καλῶς καὶ γνησίως
πρὸς αὐτὸν ἐπιστραφῶμεν, οὐ μόνον οὐκ ἀπορ-
ρίψει ἡμᾶς εἰς τὸ παντελές, ἀλλ' ἔτι λαλούντων
ἡμῶν τὰ ῥήματα τῆς προσευχῆς ἐρεῖ· Ἰδοὺ
πάρειμι.

---

[1] ἀπαραλογήτου editi antiqi.   [2] διόπερ E.

the life it has lived. For he who sets that day and
hour before his eyes and ever meditates upon his
defence before the tribunal which cannot be deceived, such a man will sin either not at all or very
little, because sinning comes to pass in us through
absence of the fear of God. But to whomsoever
there is present the vivid expectation of the threatened
punishments, the fear which dwells in such will give
them no opportunity of falling into ill-considered
actions or thoughts.

Be mindful, then, of God, and keep the fear of
Him in your heart, and invite all to communion in
your prayers. For great is also the aid of those who
are able to importune God. And do all these things
without ceasing. For both while we live this life in
the flesh will prayer be to us a goodly helper, and
when we depart hence it will be a sufficient viaticum
for the world to come. But just as anxious thought
is a good thing, so again despondency, despair, and
the attitude of misgiving as regards salvation are
things that harm the soul. Hope, then, in the
goodness of God, and expect His help, knowing that,
if we turn to Him rightly and sincerely, not only
will He not cast us off utterly, but will say even as
we are uttering the words of our prayer : " Behold, I
am with you."

---

[3] Κυρίου editi antiqi.　　　　[4] ταύτην E.

CLXXV

Μαγνηνιανῷ[1] κόμητι

Πρώην ἐπέστελλέ μοι ἡ σεμνότης σου ἄλλα τινὰ καὶ περὶ πίστεως γράψαι ἡμᾶς ἐναργῶς προστάσσουσα. ἀλλ᾽ ἐγὼ τὴν μὲν σὴν περὶ τὸ πρᾶγμα ἄγαμαι σπουδήν,[2] καὶ εὔχομαι τῷ Θεῷ ἀνενδότως σοι τῶν ἀγαθῶν τὴν αἵρεσιν ἐνυπάρχειν καὶ ἀεί σε προκόπτοντα καὶ γνώσει καὶ ἔργοις ἀγαθοῖς τελειοῦσθαι· διὰ δὲ τὸ μὴ βούλεσθαι περὶ πίστεως σύνταγμα καταλιμπάνειν μηδὲ γράφειν διαφόρους πίστεις, παρετηρησάμην μὴ[3] ἀποστεῖλαι ἃ ἐπεξητήσατε.

Πλὴν δοκεῖτέ μοι περιηχεῖσθαι παρὰ τῶν αὐτόθι, τῶν μηδὲν ἐργαζομένων, οἳ[4] ἐπὶ διαβολῇ ἡμετέρᾳ λέγουσί τινα, ὡς ἐκ τούτου ἑαυτοὺς συστήσοντες,[5] ἐὰν ἡμῶν τὰ αἴσχιστα καταψεύσωνται. ἐκείνους μὲν γὰρ φανεροῖ ὁ παρελθὼν χρόνος, καὶ προϊοῦσα ἡ πεῖρα φανερωτέρους ποιήσει. ἡμεῖς δὲ παρακαλοῦμεν τοὺς ἠλπικότας εἰς Χριστὸν μηδὲν παρὰ τὴν ἀρχαίαν περιεργά-ζεσθαι πίστιν, ἀλλ᾽ ὡς πιστεύομεν, οὕτω καὶ βαπτίζεσθαι, ὡς δὲ βαπτιζόμεθα, οὕτω καὶ δοξο-λογεῖν. ὀνόματα δὲ ἡμῖν ἀρκεῖ[6] ἐκεῖνα ὁμολογεῖν,

---

[1] Μαγνινιανῷ Med.   Μαγνημιανῷ editi antiqi.
[2] σπουδήν om. E.   [3] μή add. Capps.
[4] ὁ editi antiqi.   [5] συστήσαντες editi antiqi.
[6] ἀρκεῖν Med.

---

[1] Written about 374. This Magnenianus may be the one mentioned in Letter CCCXXV, but he is otherwise unknown. Another MS. reading is Magninianus.

LETTER CLXXV

JUST recently your Dignity wrote to me about certain other matters and explicitly commanding that we should write you concerning the faith. But while I admire your zeal regarding the matter, and pray God that you may adhere unswervingly to your choice of the good and that, always advancing in both knowledge and good works, you may become perfect; yet because I do not wish to leave behind me any work on the faith or to compose sundry creeds, I have kept to my resolution not to send what you have sought.[2]

However, you seem to me to be compassed by the din of men of that place,[3] who do no deed but say things in order to slander us, thinking to get credit for themselves from this, if they utter the most shameful lies about us. For the past reveals their characters and subsequent experience will reveal them even more clearly. But we exhort those who have put their hope in Christ not to concern themselves too much about any faith except the old, but, just as we believe, so also to be baptized, and just as we are baptized, so also to repeat the doxology.[4] And it is sufficient for us to confess those names which we

---

[2] A short time later Basil did this very thing for Amphilochius of Iconium, and wrote the treatise *De Spiritu Sancto*.

[3] The Benedictine edition (*Vita Basilii* XXX) thinks that the allusion is to Atarbius of Neocaesarea and some of his presbyters.

[4] Cf. Basil, *De Spiritu Sancto* 26.

ἃ παρελάβομεν παρὰ τῆς ἁγίας Γραφῆς καὶ τὴν
ἐπὶ τούτοις καινοτομίαν διαφεύγειν. οὐ γὰρ ἐν
τῇ ἐφευρέσει τῶν προσηγοριῶν ἡ σωτηρία ἡμῶν,
ἀλλ' ἐν τῇ ὑγιεῖ περὶ τῆς θεότητος εἰς ἣν πεπιστεύκαμεν ὁμολογίᾳ.

CLXXVI

Ἀμφιλοχίῳ, ἐπισκόπῳ Ἰκονίου

Παράσχοι ὁ ἅγιος Θεὸς ἐρρωμένῳ σοι τὸ σῶμα,
καὶ ἀπὸ πάσης ἀσχολίας ἀνειμένῳ, καὶ πάντα
πράττοντι κατὰ νοῦν, τὴν ἐπιστολὴν ἡμῶν ταύτην
εἰς χεῖρας ἐλθεῖν, ἵνα μὴ ἄπρακτος ἡμῶν ἡ
παράκλησις[1] γένηται, ἣν παρακαλοῦμεν νῦν
ἐπιφανῆναί σε ἡμῶν τῇ πόλει, ἐπὶ τῷ σεμνοτέραν
γενέσθαι τὴν πανήγυριν, ἣν δι' ἔτους ἄγειν ἐπὶ
τοῖς μάρτυσιν ἔθος ἐστὶν ἡμῶν τῇ ἐκκλησίᾳ.
πέπεισο γάρ, τιμιώτατέ μοι καὶ ποθεινότατε ὡς
ἀληθῶς, ὅτι πολλῶν εἰς πεῖραν ἐλθὼν ὁ παρ'
ἡμῖν[2] λαὸς τῆς οὐδενὸς οὕτως ἀντέχεται ἐπιτυχίας,
ὡς τῆς σῆς παρουσίας· τοιοῦτον κέντρον ἀγάπης
ἐκ τῆς μικρᾶς ἐκείνης συντυχίας ἐναφῆκας. ἵνα
οὖν καὶ ὁ Κύριος δοξασθῇ, καὶ λαοὶ εὐφρανθῶσι,
καὶ τιμηθῶσι μάρτυρες, καὶ ἡμεῖς οἱ γέροντες τῆς
ὀφειλομένης ἡμῖν παρὰ τέκνου γνησίου τύχωμεν
θεραπείας, καταξίωσον ἀόκνως μέχρις ἡμῶν
διαβῆναι, καὶ προλαβεῖν τὰς ἡμέρας τῆς συνόδου,
ὥστε ἐπὶ σχολῆς ἡμᾶς ἀλλήλοις συγγενέσθαι
καὶ[3] συμπαρακληθῆναι διὰ τῆς κοινωνίας τῶν

---

[1] παράκλησιν E.   [2] ἡμᾶν editi antiqi.
[3] καί om. E.

have received from the Holy Scripture and to shun innovation in addition to them. For not in the invention of appellations lies our salvation, but in the sound confession of the Divinity in which we have declared our faith.

LETTER CLXXVI

To Amphilochius, Bishop of Iconium [1]

May the holy God grant that this letter of ours come into your hands, finding you strong in body, free from all occupation, and faring in all respects according to your wish, in order that our invitation may not be in vain, which we now extend to you to visit our city, for the purpose of rendering more impressive the festival which it is the custom of our church to celebrate annually in honour of the martyrs.[2] For be assured, my most honoured and truly cherished brother, that although our people have had experience of many visitors, they insist upon the visit of no one so urgently as they do upon your coming; so potent was the barb of love which you implanted in them on the occasion of the former brief visit. In order, therefore, that the Lord may be glorified, the people made happy, the martyrs honoured, and we old men receive the deference due to us from a true son, deign to come to us without hesitation, and to anticipate the days of the synod, so that we may converse at leisure with each other and be mutually

---

[1] Written in 374. Basil invites Amphilochius to a festival in honour of St. Eupsychius, and asks that he come three days before the feast.

[2] *i.e.* Damas and Eupsychius. For Eupsychius, *cf.* Letters, C, CLII, and CCLII.

πνευματικῶν χαρισμάτων. ἔστι δὲ ἡ ἡμέρα τῇ
πέμπτῃ τοῦ Σεπτεμβρίου. διὸ παρακαλοῦμεν
πρὸ τριῶν ἡμερῶν ἐπιστῆναι, ἵνα καὶ τοῦ
πτωχοτροφείου τὴν μνήμην μεγάλην ποιήσῃς τῇ
παρουσίᾳ. ἐρρωμένος καὶ εὔθυμος ἐν Κυρίῳ
ὑπερευχόμενός μου διαφυλαχθείης μοι καὶ τῇ τοῦ
Θεοῦ [1] ἐκκλησίᾳ χάριτι τοῦ Κυρίου.

CLXXVII

Σωφρονίῳ μαγίστρῳ

Καταλέγειν μὲν πάντας τοὺς δι' ἡμᾶς εὐερ-
γετηθέντας παρὰ τῆς σῆς μεγαλονοίας οὐ ῥάδιον·
οὕτω πολλοὺς μὲν [2] σύνισμεν ἑαυτοῖς εὐπεποιη-
κόσι διὰ τῆς μεγάλης σου χειρός, ἣν ὁ Κύριος
ἡμῖν σύμμαχον ἐπὶ τῶν μεγίστων καιρῶν ἐχαρίσατο. δικαιότατος δὲ πάντων καὶ ὁ νῦν προσαγόμενος διὰ τοῦ γράμματος ἡμῶν τυγχάνει,[3] ὁ
αἰδεσιμώτατος [4] ἀδελφὸς Εὐσέβιος, παραλόγῳ
συκοφαντίᾳ περιπεσών, ἣν ἀποσκεδάσαι μόνης
ἐστὶ τῆς σῆς ὀρθότητος. διὸ παρακαλοῦμεν, καὶ
τῷ δικαίῳ χαριζόμενον, καὶ πρὸς τὸ ἀνθρώπινον

---

[1] Χριστοῦ Ε.   [2] μέν om. E.
[3] τυγχάνειν editi antiqi.   [4] ἡμῶν add. editi antiqi.

---

[1] This date seems to be a mistake for the seventh, the day
of St. Eupsychius in the Greek calendar.

[2] By μνήμη the Benedictine edition understands the "mem-
orial" church or chapel erected by Basil in his hospital at
Caesarea, i.e. the church in the sense of a memorial. Cf.
Letter XCIV. For the use of μνήμη in this sense Du Cange

consoled through the communion of spiritual gifts. The day is the fifth of September.[1] Accordingly we urge you to arrive three days beforehand, in order that you may also make great by your presence the memorial chapel[2] of the house of the poor. In good health and joyful in the Lord, praying for me, may you be preserved to me and to the Church of God by the grace of the Lord.

LETTER CLXXVII

To Sophronius, Master[3]

To enumerate all those who for our sake have been benefited by your Magnanimity is not easy ; to so many are we conscious of having done good through your mighty hand, which the Lord has graciously given to us as an ally in most critical times. But most worthy of all happens to be the one now being introduced to you through our letter, our most reverend brother Eusebius,[4] who has fallen under an absurd calumny, which it is in the power of your uprightness alone to repel. Therefore we urge you, favouring what is right, considering the

cites *Act. Conc. Chalced.* 1,144. He explains it as being equivalent to Latin *memoria*, i.e. *aedes sacra in qua extat sancti alicuius sepulcrum.* For such a use of *memoria*, cf. Augustine, *De Civ. Dei*, 22, 10 : *Nos autem martyribus nostris non templa sicut diis sed memorias sicut hominibus mortuis fabricamus.*

[3] Written in 374. Sophronius, *magister officiorum*, was a fellow-student of Basil at Athens, and a friend of Gregory of Nazianzus. Other letters to this Sophronius are LXXVI, XCVI, CLXXVII, CLXXX, CXCII, and CCLXXII.

[4] Eusebius of Samosata. Cf. letters addressed to him.

461

COLLECTED LETTERS OF SAINT BASIL

ἀφορῶντα, καὶ ἡμῖν τὰς συνήθεις παρεχόμενον
χάριτας, ἀντὶ πάντων γενέσθαι τῷ ἀνδρί, καὶ
προστῆναι αὐτοῦ μετὰ τῆς [1] ἀληθείας. ἔχει γὰρ
οὐ μικρὰν συμμαχίαν τὴν ἀπὸ τοῦ δικαίου· ἣν
εἰ μὴ ὁ παρὼν καιρὸς καταβλάψειε, πάνυ ῥάδιον
σαφῶς καὶ ἀναντιρρήτως ἐπιδειχθήσεσθαι.[2]

CLXXVIII

Ἀβουργίῳ

Πολλοὺς οἶδα πολλάκις συστήσας τῇ τιμιότητί
σου καὶ γενόμενος ἐπὶ μεγίστων καιρῶν χρήσιμος
ἱκανῶς τοῖς καταπονουμένοις. οὐ μὴν τιμιώτερόν
γε ἐμοὶ οὐδ' ὑπὲρ μειζόνων ἀγωνιζόμενον οἶδα
πρότερον παραπέμψας τῇ κοσμιότητί σου τοῦ
ποθεινοτάτου υἱοῦ Εὐσεβίου, τοῦ νῦν τὴν ἐπιστολὴν ταύτην ἐγχειρίζοντός σοι παρ' ἡμῶν. ὃς
ποταπῷ μὲν συμπέπλεκται πράγματι αὐτός, ἂν
τύχοι τινὸς καιροῦ, διηγήσεταί σου τῇ σεμνότητι.
ἃ δὲ παρ' ἡμῶν λεχθῆναι προσῆκε ταῦτά ἐστι·
μὴ παρασυρῆναι τὸν ἄνδρα, μηδὲ τῷ πολλοὺς
πεφηνέναι τοὺς ἐπὶ ταῖς χαλεπωτάταις πράξεσιν
ἑαλωκότας καὶ αὐτόν τι τῆς τῶν πολλῶν ὑπονοίας
παραπολαῦσαι· ἀλλὰ τυχεῖν δικαστηρίου, καὶ
εἰς ἐξέτασιν αὐτοῦ τὸν βίον ἀχθῆναι. ῥᾷστα
γὰρ οὕτω καὶ ἡ συκοφαντία φανερὰ γενήσεται,

[1] τῆς om. E.   [2] ἐπιδε.χθῆναι editi antiqi.

lot of man, and conferring your customary favours upon us, to do your utmost for the man, and in company with the truth to defend him. For he has no mean alliance in having justice on his side, and unless the present crisis should interfere with this, it will be quite easy to give clear and irrefutable proof.

LETTER CLXXVIII

To Aburgius [1]

I know that I have often recommended many men to your Honour and that in the greatest crises I have proved sufficiently useful to those in affliction. But no man more honoured in my eyes or fighting for more important things have I ever before, I know, sent to your Decorum than our most beloved son Eusebius, who now places in your hands this letter from us. And in what sort of a difficulty he is involved he himself, if he should find an opportunity, will relate to your Dignity. But what is fitting that we ourselves should say is this: that the man should not be swept aside nor, because there are many who have clearly been caught in the most grievous acts, should he also in any degree incidentally derive disadvantage from the suspicion existing against the many; on the contrary, he should obtain a trial, and his life should be subjected to examination. For in this way both will the calumny very easily become manifest, and this man, having

[1] Written in 374, on the same subject as the preceding. Previous letters addressed to Aburgius are XXXIII, LXXV, and CXLVII.

καὶ ὁ ἀνὴρ τυχὼν τῆς δικαιοτάτης προστασίας
κῆρυξ ἔσται διηνεκὴς τῶν ὑπηργμένων αὐτῷ
παρὰ τῆς σῆς ἡμερότητος.

CLXXIX

Ἀρινθαίῳ

Καὶ φιλελεύθερόν σε εἶναι καὶ φιλάνθρωπον τό
τε τῆς φύσεως εὐγενὲς καὶ τὸ πρὸς πάντας
κοινωνικὸν ἱκανῶς ἡμᾶς ἐκδιδάσκει. διὸ θαρροῦντως[1] πρεσβεύομεν ὑπὲρ ἀνδρὸς λαμπροῦ μὲν
ἄνωθεν καὶ ἐκ προγόνων, πλείονος δὲ δι᾽ ἑαυτὸν
τιμῆς καὶ αἰδοῦς ἀξίου διὰ τὴν ἐνυπάρχουσαν
αὐτῷ τῶν τρόπων ἡμερότητα· ὥστε σε παρακληθέντα ὑφ᾽ ἡμῶν παραστῆναι αὐτῷ ἀγωνιζομένῳ
δίκην, τῆς μὲν ἀληθείας ἕνεκεν[2] εὐκαταφρόνητον,
ἐναγώνιον δὲ ἄλλως διὰ τὸ τῆς συκοφαντίας βαρύ.
μεγάλη γὰρ ἂν γένοιτο αὐτῷ ῥοπὴ πρὸς σωτηρίαν,
εἰ καταξιώσειάς τι ῥῆμα φιλάνθρωπον ὑπὲρ
αὐτοῦ προέσθαι,[3] προηγουμένως μὲν τῷ δικαίῳ
χαριζόμενος, ἔπειτα καὶ ἡμῖν τοῖς ἐξαιρέτοις
σου τὴν συνήθη τιμὴν καὶ χάριν καὶ ἐν τούτῳ
χαριζόμενος.

---

[1] θαρροῦντες tres recent. MSS. [2] ἕνεκα editi antiqi.
[3] προτέσθαι editi antiqi.

---

[1] According to the Benedictine edition, the circumstances
referred to are Valens' cruelties upon those who were accused
of inquiring by divination as to who were to succeed him on
the throne. Cf. Amm. Marcell. 29, 1, 2.

received your most just protection, will be a perpetual herald of the benefits conferred upon him by your Clemency.[1]

LETTER CLXXIX

To Arinthaeus[2]

That you are a lover both of freedom and of mankind the nobility of your nature and your accessibility to all sufficiently informs us. Therefore with confidence do we address you in behalf of a man who is indeed distinguished through long lineage and through his ancestors, but worthy through his own merit of greater honour and respect because of the inherent gentleness of his character; so that at our exhortation you may assist him in his fight against a charge which, so far as the truth is concerned, deserves nothing but contempt, but for the rest is dangerous on account of the seriousness of the calumny. For it would be of great influence towards his safety if you would deign to say a kind word on his behalf, since in the first place you would be assisting justice, and secondly to us your chosen friends you would be showing in this instance also your accustomed honour and favour.

[2] Written in 374. Arinthaeus was an able general under Valens. He was a friend of Basil and a staunch protector of the Church, although, as was usual in that age, he deferred baptism till his death-bed. Cf. Letter CCLXIX. He was consul in 372, and must have died before Basil (379). If we are to believe Theodoret (*Eccl. Hist.* 4, 30), he seconded the general Trajan's rebuke of Valens in 378; so he must have died but a few months before Basil. Cf. Tillemont, *Empereurs*, 5, 100.

CLXXX

Σωφρονίῳ μαγίστρῳ, Εὐμαθίου ἕνεκεν

Ἀνδρὶ ἀξιολόγῳ περιτυχὼν περιστάσει οὐκ ἀνεκτῇ κεχρημένῳ ἔπαθον τὴν ψυχήν. τί γὰρ οὐκ ἔμελλον, ἄνθρωπος ὤν, ἀνθρώπῳ ἐλευθέρῳ παρ' ἀξίαν ἐμπεπλεγμένῳ πράγμασι συναλγεῖν; καὶ βουλευσάμενος[1] πῶς ἂν γενοίμην αὐτῷ χρήσιμος, μίαν εὗρον λύσιν τῆς κατεχούσης αὐτὸν δυσχερείας, εἰ τῇ σῇ κοσμιότητι ποιήσαιμι γνώριμον. σὸν οὖν τὸ ἐφεξῆς, τὴν σαυτοῦ σπουδήν, ἣν εἰς πολλοὺς ἐφ'[2] ἡμῖν μάρτυσιν[3] ἐπιδέδειξαι, καὶ αὐτῷ παρασχέσθαι.

Τὸ δὲ πρᾶγμα γνωρίσει ἡ ἐπιδοθεῖσα παρ' αὐτοῦ δέησις τοῖς βασιλεῦσιν, ἣν καὶ λαβεῖν εἰς χεῖρας καὶ συμπρᾶξαι τῷ ἀνδρὶ τὰ δυνατὰ παρακλήθητι. καὶ γὰρ Χριστιανῷ χαρίζῃ,[4] καὶ εὐγενεῖ, καὶ ἀπὸ λόγου πολλοῦ τὸ αἰδέσιμον ἐπαγομένῳ. ἐὰν δὲ προσθῶμεν, ὅτι καὶ ἡμεῖς μεγάλην διὰ τῆς εἰς αὐτὸν εὐποιίας ὑποδεχόμεθα[5] χάριν, πάντως, κἂν μικρὸν ᾖ ἄλλως τὸ ἡμέτερον, ἀλλὰ τῆς σῆς σεμνότητος ἀεὶ ἐν λόγῳ ποιεῖσθαι τὰ καθ' ἡμᾶς ἀνεχομένης, οὐ μικρὸν φανεῖται τὸ χαρισθὲν ἡμῖν.

---

[1] οὖν add. editi antiqi. [2] ὑφ' editi antiqi.
[3] μάρτυρας E. [4] χαρίζει editi antiqi.
[5] ἀποδεχόμεθα E ; ἀποδεξόμεθα editi antiqi.

---

[1] Written in 374. Nothing is known about this Eumathius, except for the present letter.

LETTER CLXXX

To Sophronius, the Master, in behalf of
Eumathius.[1]

On meeting an estimable man who found himself
in an unbearable situation I suffered in my soul.
For why, since I am man,[2] was I not to sympathize
with a free man involved in troubles beyond his
deserts? And in deliberating how I could be
helpful to him, I found but one solution of the
difficulty that besets him—if I should make him
known to your Decorum. The rest, therefore,
depends upon you—to place at his disposal also that
zeal of yours which on our testimony you have
shown to many.

The petition presented by him to the emperors
will inform you of the facts; and pray be kind
enough to take this into your hands and do all in
your power for the man. For you are doing a
favour to a Christian, to a man of noble birth, and to
one who wins respect through his great learning.
And if we add that we also shall receive a great
kindness through your good offices to him, assuredly,
even though our concerns are in general of small
importance to you, yet, since your August Reverence
always deigns to give consideration to our affairs, the
favour granted to us will not appear small.

---

[2] Cf. Menander, *Frag.* 602 K : οὐδείς ἐστί, μοι ἀλλότριος, ἂν
ᾖ χρηστός· ἡ φύσις μία πάντων, τὸ δ' οἰκεῖον συνίστησιν
τρόπος. "For me none is a foreigner if so be he is good.
One nature is in all and it is character that makes the tie of
kin." Cf. also Terence, *Heaut. Tim.* 77.

CLXXXI

Ὀτρηίῳ Μελητινῆς

Οἶδα ὅτι καὶ τῆς σῆς εὐλαβείας τοσοῦτον
ἅπτεται ὁ χωρισμὸς τοῦ θεοφιλεστάτου ἐπισκόπου Εὐσεβίου ὅσον καὶ ἡμῶν αὐτῶν. ἐπεὶ οὖν
ἀμφότεροι χρήζομεν παρακλήσεως, ἀλλήλοις
γενώμεθα παραμυθία. καὶ σύ τε ἡμῖν ἐπίστελλε
τὰ ἐκ Σαμοσάτων, ἡμεῖς τε ἅπερ ἂν μάθωμεν
ἀπὸ τῆς Θρᾴκης ἀπαγγελοῦμεν. φέρει γὰρ ἐμοὶ
μὲν τὸ γινώσκειν τοῦ λαοῦ τὴν ἔνστασιν οὐ
μικρὰν ῥᾳστώνην ἐκ τῶν παρόντων λυπηρῶν, τῇ
δὲ σῇ χρηστότητι τὸ διδάσκεσθαι ἐν οἷς ἐστὶν ὁ
κοινὸς ἡμῶν πατήρ. ἀμέλει καὶ νῦν οὐ γράμμασι
σημαίνειν ἔχομεν· ἀλλ’ αὐτὸν παρεστήσαμέν σοι
τὸν ἀκριβῶς εἰδότα [1] καὶ ἀπαγγέλλοντα [2] ἐν οἷς
αὐτὸν κατέλιπε, καὶ ὅπως καὶ φέροντα τὰ συμπίπτοντα. εὔχου τοίνυν καὶ ὑπὲρ αὐτοῦ καὶ
ὑπὲρ ἡμῶν, ἵνα ὁ Κύριος ταχεῖαν ἀπαγάγῃ τῶν
δεινῶν τούτων τὴν λύσιν.

CLXXXII

Τοῖς πρεσβυτέροις Σαμοσάτων [3]

Ὅσον λυπούμεθα ἐνθυμούμενοι τὴν ἐρημίαν τῆς
ἐκκλησίας, τοσοῦτον μακαρίζομεν ὑμᾶς εἰς τοῦτο

---

[1] ἰδόντα E.

[2] ἀπαγγελοῦντα Coisl. secundus et Reg. secundus.

[3] Παυλίνῳ πρεσβυτέρῳ ἐν ἐξορίᾳ ὄντι Claromontanus. Παυλίνῳ
πρεσβύτῃ editi antiqi.

LETTER CLXXXI

To Otreius of Meletine [1]

I know that the removal of the most God-beloved bishop Eusebius touches your Reverence as much as it does even ourselves. Since, then, we both need consolation, let us be a solace to each other. And do you write to us the news from Samosata, and we shall report what we learn from Thrace.[2] For to me the knowledge of the steadfastness of your people brings no small alleviation of our present miseries, as does to your Uprightness information regarding the condition of our common father. To be sure, even now we cannot inform you by letter; but we have commended to you one who accurately knows and reports in what state he left him and how, moreover, he is bearing his afflictions. Pray, therefore, both for him and for us, that the Lord may bring a quick release from these troubles.

LETTER CLXXXII

To the Presbyters of Samosata [3]

As much as we grieve in considering the desolation[4] of the Church, equally do we felicitate you on

---

[1] Written in 374. Otreius, one of the leading orthodox prelates of the fourth century, was at Tyana in 367, and at Constantinople in 381. Meletine, now Malatia, in Armenia Minor.

[2] Eusebius was in exile there at this time.

[3] Written in 374.

[4] The reference is chiefly to the exile of Eusebius.

φθάσαντας τὸ μέτρον τῆς ἀθλήσεως, ὃ παράσχοι
ὑμῖν[1] ὁ Κύριος μακροθύμως παρελθεῖν, ἵνα καὶ
τῆς πιστῆς οἰκονομίας καὶ τῆς γενναίας ἐνστάσεως,
ἣν ὑπὲρ τοῦ ὀνόματος τοῦ Χριστοῦ ἐπεδείξασθε,
τὸν μέγαν μισθὸν ὑποδέξησθε.

CLXXXIII

Πολιτευομένοις Σαμοσάτων[2]

Ὅταν ἀπίδω ὅτι ὁ μὲν πειρασμὸς κατὰ πάσης
ἤδη κέχυται τῆς οἰκουμένης, καὶ αἱ μέγισται τῶν
ἐπὶ Συρίας πόλεων τῶν ἴσων ὑμῖν[3] πεπείρανται
παθημάτων, οὐ πανταχοῦ δὲ οὕτω δόκιμον καὶ
διαπρεπὲς ἐπ' ἀγαθοῖς ἔργοις τὸ βουλευτήριον, ὡς
τὸ ὑμέτερον νῦν ἐπὶ τῇ σπουδῇ τῶν ἀγαθῶν
ἔργων διαβεβόηται, ἐγγύς εἰμι καὶ χάριν ἔχειν[4]
τοῖς οἰκονομηθεῖσιν. εἰ γὰρ μὴ ἐγεγόνει ἡ θλίψις
αὕτη, οὐκ ἂν ὑμῶν διεφάνη τὸ δόκιμον. ὥστε
ἔοικεν, ὅπερ ἐστὶ κάμινος χρυσῷ, τοῦτο εἶναι ἡ
ὑπὲρ τῆς εἰς Θεὸν ἐλπίδος θλίψις τοῖς ἀντι-
ποιουμένοις τινὸς ἀρετῆς.

Ἄγε οὖν, ὦ θαυμάσιοι, ὅπως τοῖς προπεπονη-
μένοις ἄξια ἐπαγάγητε τὰ ἑπόμενα, καὶ φανῆτε
μεγάλῃ κρηπῖδι ἀξιολογωτέραν ἐπιτιθέντες τὴν

---

[1] ἡμῖν Ε, Med.
[2] ἀγαπητικὴ προσφώνησις add. Reg. secundus, Coisl. secundus.
[3] ἡμῖν editi antiqi.
[4] ἐπί add. Ε.

---

[1] Written in 374, on Eusebius' exile.

your having already arrived at this limit of your struggle, through which may the Lord grant that you may pass patiently, in order that both for the faithful stewardship and for the noble steadfastness which you have shown for Christ's name, you may receive the great reward.

LETTER CLXXXIII

To the Senate of Samosata [1]

Whenever I observe that our trial has now become spread over the whole earth, and that the greatest cities of Syria have experienced sufferings the equal of your own, but that nowhere has the Senate shown itself so tested and distinguished in good works as yours has now been proclaimed because of its zeal for good works, I am almost even thankful for what has been ordained. For if this affliction had not come, neither would your probity have been made manifest. So it seems that what a furnace is to gold,[2] such is this affliction, endured on behalf of our hope in God, to those who lay claim to some degree of virtue.

Come then, O admirable men, see that to your labours already accomplished you add others to follow that are worthy of them, and that on the great foundation you are seen to place a capstone

---

[2] Cf. Prov. 17. 3 : ὥσπερ δοκιμάζεται ἐν καμίνῳ ἄργυρος καὶ χρυσός, οὕτως ἐκλεκταὶ καρδίαι παρὰ Κυρίῳ. "As silver is tried by fire, and gold in the furnace : so the Lord trieth the hearts." Cf. also Prov. 27. 21 : δοκίμιον ἀργύρῳ καὶ χρυσῷ πύρωσις, ἀνὴρ δὲ δοκιμάζεται δ.ὰ στόματος ἐγκωμιαζόντων αὐτόν. "As silver is tried in the fining-pot and gold in the furnace : so a man is tried by the mouth of him that praiseth."

κορυφήν,¹ καὶ περίστητε μὲν τὸν ποιμένα τῆς
ἐκκλησίας, ὅταν δῷ ὁ Κύριος αὐτὸν ἐπὶ τῶν ἰδίων ²
φανῆναι θρόνων,³ ἄλλος ἄλλο τι τῶν ὑπὲρ τῆς
Ἐκκλησίας τοῦ Θεοῦ πεπολιτευμένων ἡμῖν ⁴
διηγούμενοι, ἐν δὲ τῇ μεγάλῃ τοῦ Κυρίου ἡμέρᾳ
ἕκαστος κατὰ τὴν ἀναλογίαν τῶν πεπονημένων
παρὰ τοῦ μεγαλοδώρου Θεοῦ δεχόμενοι τὴν ἀντίδοσιν. ἡμῶν δὲ μεμνημένοι καὶ ἐπιστέλλοντες
ὁσάκις ἂν ᾖ δυνατόν, δίκαιά τε ποιήσετε τοῖς
ἴσοις ἡμᾶς ἀμειβόμενοι, καὶ ἅμα οὐ μικρῶς ⁵ ἡμᾶς
εὐφρανεῖτε, τῆς ἡδίστης ἡμῖν φωνῆς ὑμῶν ἐναργῆ
σύμβολα διὰ τῶν γραμμάτων διαπεμπόμενοι.

CLXXXIV

Εὐσταθίῳ, ἐπισκόπῳ Ἱμμερίας ⁶

Οἶδα ὅτι στυγνοποιὸν πρᾶγμα ἡ ὀρφανία καὶ
πολυάσχολον, διὰ τὸ ἐρημίαν ἐπάγειν τῶν
προεστώτων. ὅθεν λογίζομαι καὶ τὴν σὴν εὐλάβειαν ἐπιστυγνάζουσαν τοῖς συμβεβηκόσι μὴ
ἐπιστέλλειν ἡμῖν, καὶ ὁμοῦ ἐν πλείονι εἶναι νῦν
ἀσχολίᾳ, περιτρέχειν ⁷ τὰ τοῦ Χριστοῦ ποίμνια
διὰ τὴν πανταχόθεν τῶν ἐχθρῶν ἐπανάστασιν.
ἀλλ' ἐπειδὴ πάσης λύπης παρηγορία ἡ πρὸς
τοὺς ὁμοψύχους ἐστὶν ὁμιλία, καταξίου ὁσάκις
ἂν δυνατόν σοι ἐπιστέλλειν ἡμῖν, καὶ αὐτός τε

¹ κορωνίδες Reg. secundus, Coisl. secundus, Paris.
² τῶν ἰδίων] τὸν ἰδίον E. ³ θρόνον E.
⁴ ὑμῖν E. ⁵ σμικρᾶς E.
⁶ Ἐμμέρως Coisl. secundus, Reg. secundus.
⁷ περιέπειν E, Med.

more distinguished still, and that you may stand about the shepherd [1] of the Church, whenever the Lord grants him to appear on his proper throne, each one relating to us some different act performed on behalf of the Church of God, and on the great day of the Lord each one receiving from the bountiful God a reward proportionate to his labours. But if you are mindful of us and write as often as is possible, you will do what is just by requiting us with like for like, and at the same time you will gladden us not a little by sending us through your letters vivid symbols of your voice which we find most sweet.

LETTER CLXXXIV

To Eustathius, Bishop of Himmeria [2]

I know that orphanhood brings sadness and causes much concern, because it occasions a loss of those who are placed over us. Wherefore I consider that your Piety also, because he is saddened by what has come to pass, fails to write to us, and at the same time that he is at this moment still more preoccupied, in having to visit [3] the flocks of Christ because of the uprising of the enemy on every side. But since discourse between those of like minds is a consolation for every grief, deign as often as you can

---

[1] Eusebius, in exile at this time. Cf the preceding letters.

[2] Written in 374. Himmeria was in Osrhoene. This Eustathius is otherwise unknown.

[3] The Benedictine edition suggests the reading περιτρέχειν τε, "and is visiting."

ἀναπαύεσθαι ἐν τῷ φθέγγεσθαι πρὸς ἡμᾶς, καὶ
ἡμᾶς παρηγορεῖν ἐν τῷ μεταδιδόναι ἡμῖν τῶν
σεαυτοῦ ῥημάτων. τοῦτο δὲ καὶ ἡμεῖς σπου-
δάσομεν ποιῆσαι ὁσάκις ἂν ἡμῖν ἐνδιδῷ τὰ πράγματα. εὔχου δὲ καὶ αὐτὸς καὶ πᾶσαν τὴν
ἀδελφότητα παρακάλεσον σπουδαίως δυσωπεῖν
τὸν Κύριον, ἵνα δείξῃ ποτὲ ἡμῖν λύσιν τῆς περιε-
χούσης ἡμᾶς κατηφείας.

CLXXXV

Θεοδότῳ, ἐπισκόπῳ Βεροίας

Οἶδα ὅτι, εἰ καὶ μὴ ἐπιστέλλεις ἡμῖν, ἀλλ᾽ ἐν
τῇ καρδίᾳ σου ὑπάρχει ἡ μνήμη ἡμῶν. καὶ τοῦτο
τεκμαίρομαι, οὐχ ὅτι αὐτὸς ἄξιός εἰμι μνήμης
τινὸς δεξιᾶς, ἀλλ᾽ ὅτι ἡ σὴ ψυχὴ πλουτεῖ ἐν τῇ
τῆς ἀγάπης περιουσίᾳ. πλὴν ἀλλ᾽ ὅσον δυνατόν
σοι ταῖς παρεμπιπτούσαις προφάσεσι κέχρησο
εἰς τὸ ἐπιστέλλειν ἡμῖν, ἵνα καὶ ἡμεῖς μᾶλλον
εὐψυχῶμεν μανθάνοντες τὰ περὶ ὑμῶν, καὶ
ἀφορμὴν λαμβάνωμεν εἰς τὸ καὶ αὐτοὶ σημαίνειν
ὑμῖν τὰ ἡμέτερα. οὗτος γάρ ἐστιν ὁ τρόπος τῆς
ὁμιλίας τοῖς τοσοῦτον διεζευγμένοις [1] τῷ σώματι,
ὁ δι᾽ ἐπιστολῶν, οὗ μὴ ἀποστερῶμεν ἀλλήλους,
καθόσον ἂν ἐνδιδῷ τὰ πράγματα. παράσχοι δὲ
ὁ Κύριος καὶ τὴν κατ᾽ ὀφθαλμοὺς ἡμῖν συντυχίαν,
ἵνα καὶ τὴν ἀγάπην αὐξήσωμεν καὶ τὴν εἰς τὸν
Δεσπότην ἡμῶν εὐχαριστίαν πλεονάσωμεν ἐπὶ
μείζοσι ταῖς παρ᾽ αὐτοῦ δωρεαῖς.

---

[1] διαζευγνυμένοις editi antiqi.

to write to us, and thus both to gain strength for yourself by speaking to us, and to console us by making us sharers of your words. And this too we also shall endeavour to do as often as circumstances permit us. And do you yourself pray, and exhort the whole brotherhood earnestly to importune the Lord, that He may one day show us release from the sorrow that surrounds us.

LETTER CLXXXV

To Theodotus, Bishop of Berrhoea [1]

I know that, even though you do not write to us, yet in your heart there exists the memory of us. And I judge this, not because I myself am worthy of any assurance of remembrance, but because your soul is rich in the abundance of charity. But nevertheless, in so far as it is possible for you, do make use of the opportunities that offer themselves to write to us, in order that we may be of better courage on learning of your affairs, and that we too may ourselves receive an opportunity of making ours known to you. For this is the means of conversation for those who are so widely separated in person, I mean correspondence by letter, and of this let us not deprive each other, in so far as circumstances may permit. And may the Lord grant us also a meeting face to face, in order that we may both increase our charity and multiply our thanksgiving to our Master for His still greater gifts.

[1] Written in 374. Theodotus was orthodox Bishop of Berrhoea in Syria under Valens. Nothing more is known about him.

INDEX OF PROPER NAMES

477

INDEX OF PROPER NAMES

INDEX OF PROPER NAMES

INDEX OF PROPER NAMES